Dena's stories reflect the magic she writes about. She first draws you in by awakening your curiosity. Then she fascinates you with the lyricism of the story and opens the door to liminal spaces within you. In *To Dance with Dakinis*, you travel to medieval Tibet and India, during extraordinary times. You meet ordinary people dealing with human suffering and you visit magical lakes and mountains. As the story unfolds across three lifetimes, you get a glimpse of the time between lives through the eyes of Usha, who is working through her karmic residues, and her inexhaustible love for Satya. You also meet the great Mother, Dalha and through her dakinis, teachers and the great Guru Rinpoche! As Dena unravels the threads that links together these three lives, she also shares with you the spiritual history of Tibet and India and the deep interconnection of these two great civilizations. She helps to awaken your awe and love for the Mother, and reclaim the healing power of the feminine energy that has been violated for millennia and continues to be suppressed. You are very likely to experience spiritual courage, great compassion, and deep healing but also to be held by profound depths of reverence and quietude by the time you finish this fascinating book.

Raghu Ananthanarayanan, Ritambhara āchārya sangha

This book will quench your spiritual thirst with its springs of timeless wisdom. You'll meet adepts, gurus, gods, goddesses, dakinis, and simply some loving souls who guide us life after life, without admitting their spiritual stature.

Dena, who was once Padma, Claire, and Devaki among other incarnations, recounts her deeply touching tales that are a potpourri of her experiences and learning amidst the cultural settings of the times she lived in. Call it Life's sense of brilliant humor or justice, that the person you resented the very sight of, becomes a dear relative in the next; an illiterate low-caste woman in one life is reborn as a queen; the unfulfilled love of one life comes to ultimate fruition in another one; and so much more. It may suddenly strike you that all our feelings of resentment, anger or pride are ultimately futile—and what a liberating realization that is! Life doesn't forget anything—neither your good deeds and vows, nor your wrong deeds or thoughts that you tried to hide from all. Let the messages contained in this book be your Guru; may you too loosen the strings that hold you down and initiate the search for your Self.

Apexa Shah

To Dance with Dakinis

In Search of Self

Dena Merriam

The profits from this book will be donated to the Global Peace Initiative of Women (GPIW.org) to empower people everywhere in their quest to make this a more peaceful world.

The Global Peace Initiative of Women • 100 United Nations Plaza • Suite 28A • New York, NY • 10017

FIRST EDITION

ISBN 979-8-9868061-1-2

Cover Painting: Kali Levitov

Book Design: Deb Tremper, Six Penny Graphics

Editing: Parvati Markus

Proofing: Toni Briegel

Cover Design and Art Direction: Kesang Marstrand & Six Penny Graphics

Literary Agent & Consultants: Yorwerth Associates, LLC

Distributed by SCB Distributors

I dedicate this book to my Tibetan son of past days.
May he continue to flourish and provide benefit to the world.

I also dedicate this book to the people of Tibet, to all those past and present who have passed through that land.

May Guru Rinpoche, Yeshe Tsogyal, and the Bon gods and goddesses continue to protect and bless this sacred homeland.

May the Dharma guide us individually
and as a human community.

Contents

Part 11
Late Thirteenth Century, Bharat (India)

Chapters

Introduction

Friends often ask me about the process of recalling memories of people and events of long ago. They pose questions to which I have no answer. All I can say is that what I write is from my personal experiences. I do, however, call upon what is known as poetic license to bring my experiences to life, to add richness and detail in the hope that my reader will be able to enter the time periods and realms about which I write. If some of my writings seem fantastical, I can only say that life itself is fantastical. We see only the surface of things, and there is far more to what we encounter than appears to the human mind. Most of us can't perceive our history with our family and acquaintances or know the cause of events, but we can be certain that there are hidden back stories, layers upon layers of interwoven events as I have tried to portray in all my books. I have also hoped to show that linear time has no true relevance. At a certain point, past, present, and future converge in an eternal now, and whether or not we are aware of it, we live in all time periods and all dimensions at once. My focus has long been the complex and mysterious workings of cause and effect, karmic unfolding, and the neutralizing of the mental imprints known as samskara in the hope that whatever understanding is gained will help us to become more aware in our daily lives, more conscious of the big picture, of the vastness that is condensed for our convenience into a tiny frame.

The story I now write about begins in the year 2006. I had been invited by a great Buddhist teacher, the Venerable Master Sheng Yen, to help organize an interfaith gathering for the opening of his Chan Retreat Center in Taiwan, which was a grand event taking place over several days. My organization, The Global Peace Initiative of Women (GPIW), had brought a delegation of spiritual teachers representing different faiths from around the world to take part in the opening ceremonies. We were all seated in the beautiful Chan Meditation Hall when suddenly I saw a clear image, a vision of a young man around seventeen. For some reason I immediately knew him to be my future grandson.

Neither of my two sons was married, although they were both dating women. Over the next few days of celebratory events, the presence of this young man remained with me. I began to wonder to which of my two sons this soul would be born. As I looked closely, I saw that his eyes were Asian. My older son was dating an Asian woman, and when I returned home, I learned they had become engaged. Seven months later they married. Upon my return to the US, I lost sight of this young man who had remained with me during my trip to Taiwan, but I clearly felt a connection had been made. This soul, whoever he was, had reached out and found me.

Six months after my older son's marriage, Master Sheng Yen was coming to his retreat center in upstate New York and invited me to join a retreat he was leading. Since my path is Kriya Yoga, not Buddhism, I hesitated, but the idea of spending ten days in silent meditation was too appealing to refuse. I greatly admired Master Sheng Yen, who was an early supporter of GPIW and, after some reflection, I decided to join the retreat. There, once again, this grandson appeared to me, not as a young man but as a toddler, and throughout the ten days I felt his presence. When I returned home, my eldest son informed me that his wife was pregnant with my first grandchild.

When I saw the babe an hour or so after his birth, he turned to look at me and smiled. We had our first conversation. As he grew older, he shared memories of his past with me, which were at first quite vivid.

Initially, he spoke of India, and then later Tibet. As a young child he acted out the stories of Hanuman and was devoted to both Krishna and Shiva. A few years later, it was Tibet that tugged at his heart. I spent much time with him during his early years and came to realize how deep his connection was with those two lands and how old our relationship was. Throughout his early years, he showed a remarkable knowledge and understanding of historical events and religious matters, things that I didn't know about. His intellectual curiosity and acumen amazed me, as well as his familiarity with Tibetan Buddhism. It was this young grandson, no more than six or seven years old, who introduced me to the Tibetan deity Palden Lhamo. I took him to meet Tibetan teachers and he spoke to them about Tibet's military strategy during the 1950s. So much of the past was still alive in that young mind. Our relationship was the spark that lit the fire which was to draw me back into my own past.

In raising my own two sons, I saw in their early years remnants of their previous births. If one observes closely and listens to a child before they become fully acclimated to their current surroundings, one can perceive many hints of their past, which can be helpful in guiding their future direction. So, it was with this first grandchild of mine. His brother, my second grandson, who is still quite young, feels a deep connection to both Japan and Korea, and I am watching to see whether he reveals his history to me.

My eldest grandson was not the only Tibetan influence in my life. A dear friend of mine, Hanne Strong, who has strong links to both Bon and Tibetan Buddhism, was one of the inspirations behind the founding of The Global Peace Initiative of Women. Around the time of its founding in 2002, her sister Marianne, also a practitioner of Tibetan Buddhism, began to work with me, and Hanne's daughter Kris, another western Tibetan Buddhist, became a key part of our team.

I was surrounded by Tibetan Buddhists and found an easy convergence between that tradition and my yogic background and practice, deeply rooted in the ancient knowledge of the Vedic *rishis* (sages), but I didn't truly understand the connection between these two great paths. Then one day my own memories of old Tibet returned, but the story that emerged was not one I would have envisioned. I hadn't known of my association with Bon, the ancient indigenous religion of Tibet, which previously I knew little about and which came as quite a surprise.

I never know how to describe the unlocking of memories, so I refrain from attempting. The story that I now tell is one of love, search, and the struggle to understand the deeper truths. Some lives are turning points when important steps are taken in one's spiritual awakening. The life in Tibet that I describe in this book was such a one. The focus of my journey began to turn inward, and the question of my true nature began to emerge for the first time. It was a lifetime when love had to be supplemented by discernment, when lessons were given so missteps would not be repeated, when trust in higher beings had to be cemented in the mind.

I recount in detail three successive lives and the time between those visits to earth. We all need to become comfortable with the fact that we live in many dimensions, and our time here is only a temporary stay. In the first part of this book, I refer to Tibet by its old name of Böd, and I refer to India by the name the Tibetans called it, Gyagar. I also refer to a place called Zhang Zhung, the western part of the Tibetan plateau, which is where Tibetan civilization may be said to have begun and which also saw the beginnings of Bon. The spiritual center of Zhang Zhung was Mt. Kailash, or Mt. Tise, as it is known to the Tibetans.

I have tried to convey something of the ancient culture of Böd. Although sometimes portrayed as primitive, old Tibet was a highly sophisticated culture, at one time among the most expansive and significant empires in the world, with much trading and wealth. Like all empires, it eventually broke apart and the focus of its people shifted to spiritual rather than worldly attainment, due to an influx of extraordinary beings. The spiritual history of Tibet goes far back in time to the days of the ancient rishis of India when there was much cross-fertilization between these lands—before even the thought of boundaries arose.

Many people misunderstand the ancient Bon tradition, associating it with superstition, thinking it nothing more than shamans and spells.

This narrative is the story of a Bonpo woman, a follower of Bon, who gradually comes to integrate the wisdom of Buddhism with the older Bon ways—an integration that was to become a key characteristic of Tibet. It is a story of the effort to preserve the indigenous wisdom that had been revealed in a higher age, but that suffered what may be called "spiritual contamination" due to a decline in understanding. The second part of the book deals with a rebirth in India, known in older times as Bharat, during a time of enormous destruction of its indigenous past. Fortunately, for India, renewal was on the horizon, as it will be one day for Tibet.

It is perhaps not necessary, but it can be helpful to peer into the past to understand better the intricate interweaving that connects one life to another. In my first book, *My Journey Through Time*, I trace back to a series of lives dating from the fifteenth century onward. In a successive book, *When the Bright Moon Rises*, I describe a life in eighth century China, as well as an earlier life during the collapse of the Han Empire, also in China, when some of the events told in this current book were initiated – setting in motion the chain of cause and effect. *To Dance with Dakinis* fills in the missing centuries between those time frames and then goes back even further. These writings are part of my ongoing meditation on the universal law of cause and effect, which propels the cycle of rebirth. The more deeply we understand this process, the more we can consciously shape our future.

Some of the stories in this book refer to accounts in other books I have written. There are references to that life in Han China told in *When the Bright Moon Rises* and to an incident described in *Rukmini and the Turning of Time*, but it is not necessary to have read those books to follow the narrative. It took many centuries for certain samskaras from the lifetimes described in those books to come to the fore and be resolved.

Those who have read my earlier books will also be familiar with a being I call Satya. He appears again in this narrative as he is a constant presence for me in the place I abide between earthly births. It is difficult to separate lives and to view them piecemeal because they are all interconnected, one continuous flow of learning, despite the changing of names and faces. Seeing this interconnection reveals a beauty to the whole process of birth, death, and rebirth; we realize that we meet friends again and again and make peace with those with whom we have had difficulties.

My dear readers, I am no different than you. I have undergone great hardships and loss and have had to climb up from the chasm so I could catch a glimpse of the light, of the wonders that lie ahead if only we persist. I have had many guides and helpers along the way, as we all have. I am still nowhere near the end of the journey, if there is an end of which we can speak, but I have learned a few things along the way that may be helpful to others, which is the reason I share so many intimate details of my long excursion.

When we think there is no hope left, that is when we must awaken the will to persist, for the Divine always sends a lifeline. It is for us to see it. Our journey is full of twists and turns, but if we remain steady and unshakable, we will reach that plane of truth and indescribable joy.

PART 1

Twelfth-Century Tibet

A land ancient in wisdom, for the *lha* (Gods) walked here, leaving their imprints in the mountains and rivers and in the dust for us to discover.

CHAPTER 1

Childhood in Böd

I was born in the Year of the Horse, in Lhasa, the city of light, where the sun shines most days of the year and the sky paints a deeper, more clarified hue of blue than anywhere else on earth. It was a bustling town with a thriving community of merchants and traders, to which my family belonged. I was the fourth of five children, the oldest girl. My eldest brother, Sonam Jigme, was fourteen years my senior and took charge of much of the family in my early years when my father was traveling to and from the Song Empire in the east (present-day China), trading musk, salt, fur, and medicines for the much-valued Han tea, jade, and silk. For centuries, there had been a prosperous trading relationship between the two regions, and our family became relatively wealthy as a result. Two other brothers followed the birth of Sonam Jigme—Kipu Nyima and Jampa Norbu. Then I came along, and two years later my younger sister, Pumo Zangmo.

We lived a few streets away from the main market in a two-story stone house that was relatively spacious for our town, with two large rooms on the first floor, three smaller rooms on the second, and an area for cooking on the roof when weather permitted. A small area of healing medicinal plants, tenderly cared for by my mother, shared space on the roof, where my mother also conducted her Bon ceremonies.

The constant clatter of mule and pony hooves on the dirt roads was the background hum to our daily activities, even penetrating our sleep at night. Often, I fell asleep and awoke in the morning to the sound of traders carting their wares to and from the market stalls. My extended family of uncles and cousins had several shops in the main market, selling the goods other family members brought from the Great Song and from Gyagar (India). We were very much a part of the age-old trading community that has trod so often over rough but familiar routes; our people knew each and every mountain pass and welcomed the trek through valleys, with their lush vegetation and more welcoming climate.

Our city was surrounded by mountains, littered with rocks of all sizes, with sparse brush and a few trees to adorn them. The outskirts of the city hosted poplars, while fruit-bearing trees dotted the landscape, and beyond grew fields of barley, hemmed in by a scattering of small pine forests.

Much of my childhood was defined by the existence of two seemingly separate worlds—one of ancient Bon, and the other the realm of the Buddhas—living side by side but presenting what appeared to me to be contradictions. This was even reflected in my naming. My father, the devoted Buddhist, named me Padma, meaning "lotus," for his most revered Guru Rinpoche, also known as Padmasambhava; my mother named me Tshomo, meaning "lake woman," for the goddess of the sacred lake Nam Tsho, where she had spent much of her childhood and which was the center of her spiritual life. Thus, I was known as Padma Tshomo; my father and siblings called me Padma, and my mother and her family called me Tshomo. Living between two traditions, I often struggled to know where I belonged. This was reflected in so many aspects of my life, and my lifelong challenge was to integrate these two worlds. Unlike other family members who shifted easily between their Bon and Buddhist identities, I often felt the two worlds colliding, creating what I later learned was a false opposition.

My parents could not have been more different from one another. My mother claimed lineage from both Zhang Zhung and Sumpa, Bon strongholds to the north and west. A stout, somewhat stocky woman, she could brave the rugged landscapes of the rural dry lands and weather the biting cold of the northern terrain. She was somewhat of an untamed woman, firm in her convictions, who liked to draw upon her tribal ancestry in speaking her mind. Her midnight eyes were protectively fierce, but rarely did she show this side of her nature to her family. Strangers of questionable character might encounter her jarring looks and demeanor, but to my sister and me she offered a blanket of security. I often felt that if a bandit or wild yak were to come across her on some remote desert path, they would turn and flee in fear—such was the power of her stance and presence.

With a deep bronze complexion, her hair dressed in two long braids that framed her face and swung around her waist, she was outgoing and full of nature wisdom; she knew and conversed with the plants, the stones, mountains, and waterways, claiming she received messages from them. She knew medicine and was admired in the community, which sought her secret concoctions and healing powers. She believed in spirits and omens, oracles, shamans, and magic, and kept us entranced with her stories, of which there was no end. In fact, my mother lived in the world of spirits, who seemed to be her intimate companions.

My father was the opposite—a reserved man of slight frame and lighter complexion, manicured, neatly dressed and adorned, with braided hair fashioned into a bun on the top of his head. He was partly from an aristocratic background and had refined features and soft speech. Generations of his family had lived in Lhasa. Generous and knowledgeable about all things, he lived in the realm of the mind and sought every opportunity to turn inward. While my mother performed her rituals and ceremonies on the rooftop, often scented with burning juniper, he could be found sitting quietly in the small meditation corner in the room where they slept. While she told stories of flying adepts, he read us lines from sacred texts and spoke of the transformative inner work of Guru Rinpoche. All her knowledge came from the elements of nature; his came from texts and meditational insight. How was I to choose between them? Despite their differences, they shared an undeniable bond of love and respect.

There was one area of our life in which my father predominated—our education. At his insistence, not only his sons but also his daughters were to be educated, a rarity in our time, and this was to be one of his great gifts to Pumo and me.

Since my father often led the trading caravans, I was left mostly in my mother's care, and she filled my ears with tales of ancient Zhang Zhung, the birthplace of the civilization we knew as Böd. Her father's family hailed from that sacred region, descending from the ancient Mu tribe, or so she often said. The Mu tribe was known for their learnedness and role in spreading the teachings of Bon, and she took great pride in this association. It was the Mu people who had settled this plateau long ago, she once declared to Pumo and me.

When I asked my father about this ancient ancestry, he smiled and replied, "The Mu tribe has its origins far back in time, so how can we know? But that is what your mother believes and, of course, I believe your mother." There was something in the tone of his voice, or perhaps an element of wryness in his smile, that made me wonder what he really thought. When out of my father's hearing, my mother would transport Pumo and me, the only children truly interested in her tales, into an ancient world full of magic and mystery; we loved those imaginative journeys with her, but I never knew how much to believe.

"The sacred land of Zhang Zhung was first ruled by nonhumans," she once explained. "The *lha* (divine beings) appeared out of the sky wielding magical powers. They could fly from mountaintop to mountaintop, turn themselves into wild tigers and leopards, and speak with the animals, maintaining the balance among them. They could run across the water, pass through mountains and control the weather through their sacred language. These first rulers helped to organize the creatures living here. Benevolent and kind-hearted, they took care of the humans and made sure their needs were met. They were beautiful beings," my mother mused, her eyes misting over as if longing for those days. "It was a time when humans lived in close association with the celestial lha and the terrestrial spirits who live in the water and forests. Over time, sadly, our worlds separated. I believe this was the work of the demons who ruled after the lha."

"Demons lived here?" I asked in alarm.

My mother nodded. "When it was time for the lha to depart their bodies, they simply disappeared into the sky, leaving a rainbow but no corpse behind. Then one day, the last of the lha to rule died as we mortals do, leaving behind his remains, and so that era ended. Perhaps it was because they had begun to intermarry with humans," she reflected.

"Is that really true?" I asked, as Pumo, seated beside me, drank in every word my mother spoke, seemingly carried away as much as my mother was. "Did nonhumans really rule this land?"

Again, she nodded. "It is true. Every history states this, but that was very long ago, even before the time of the great Tonpa Shenrab (founder of Bon), who, as you know, lived some sixteen thousand years ago, around the time when the great melting took place, which formed so many of our sacred lakes. I believe the creation of the lakes was the work of the lha, providing water and preparing this land for human habitation."

"Tell us the story of Tonpa Shenrab," I eagerly requested, as Pumo and I sat on the rooftop one warm afternoon watching my mother prepare a special medicine. As on most days, the sun hung like a brilliant fireball in the sky; the air was clear and dry, not yet touched by summer rains. Although I had heard this story many times, each telling was slightly different, and I never knew what new element she would add. Putting aside her medicine pot, she came to sit on the floor beside us. When my mother narrated her tales, she used her whole body to express herself—her eyes opening wide, her facial expressions changing from one moment to the next, and her hands moving about as if they were an essential part of the storytelling.

She smiled. "I never tire of speaking of that wondrous man. It was after the time when the Iha ruled. The *nagas* (ancient serpent-like spirits) came to rule after them and then a race of demons called the *dud*, who fought viciously with one another; then came the *srin*, who were also violent. Finally, humans came to rule and they named the land Böd. I may have gotten the order mixed up; I am not sure. Anyhow, among the humans, there were some who were more refined, like the lha; they may have been descendants of the intermarriages. And there were some who were more physical, more brute-like. The ones who were like the lha could still commune with the gods and spirits. In order to ensure that their descendants could do the same, they developed rituals to help them maintain a relationship of mutual love and exchange with the nature spirits and with the lha. But there were also demonic forces that sought to disrupt these relationships, just as we have today." Turning to Pumo, she said, "There have always been forces of light and darkness. That is part of this world."

"But *Apa-la* (father) would say that demons are in our own mind," mused Pumo, who was leaning more and more toward Buddhism.

"What lies within also lies without. The outer world is a mirror of the inner. Your father would agree with that," *Ama-la* (mother) responded, before continuing with her story. "Tonpa Shenrab was born into a royal lineage in a peaceful region, a place to the west called Olmo Lungring. He married and had a family. Then one day a powerful demon named Khyab-pa kidnapped his daughter and stole seven beautiful horses from him, taking them to Khangpo, a region in Zhang Zhung. This demon was looking for a fight, and Tonpa Shenrab was ready to face him. Flying on his great Garuda (the king of the birds, a great eagle), Shenrab set out to rescue his daughter. Even when going into battle, his appearance was most noble and refined. He was dressed in a golden silk robe, and part of his hair was wrapped in a knot on top of his head, while the rest fell in long plaits along his shoulders and chest.

"A fierce battle ensued at the headwaters of the four great rivers that arise near Mt. Tise (Mt. Kailash). Thunderbolts blasted the sky, and lightning strikes shook the earth as the demon unleashed his vast power. But with graceful bearing and calm demeanor, Shenrab was able to tame his fury. He countered not with anger, but with love, knowing that love is the most powerful force in the universe.

"As the demon wielded his weapons, Shenrab saw the inner cause of the demon's anger and sought to dissolve it by cracking open his heart, which had long been frozen shut. First, he captured Khyab-pa's father, and that demon who had shown love to no one suddenly became vulnerable when he saw that his father was willing to sacrifice himself for the sake of his son. Khyab-pa had never felt his father's love before, but when he saw his father captured, his heart opened. Seeing this, Shenrab released the demon's father and spoke gently to Khyab-pa, subduing and transforming his anger. The demon surrendered to him and eventually became one of Shenrab's leading disciples. After this battle, those who had gathered there saw Shenrab seated on a crystal lotus, descending from the sky onto the peak of Mt. Tise; rainbows spread across the sky and flowers rained down. This is what happens when love conquers anger."

Pumo and I looked at one another with a bit of skepticism. I believed in Shenrab's power to conquer demons, but the part about the crystal lotus and the flowers was a bit too much to accept. Our mother was not finished and continued her story.

"Some say Shenrab returned to Olmo Lungring after the battle, where he eventually gave up royal life and became a wandering ascetic. But others say that he established himself at Mt. Tise, which is what I believe. Adepts from around the world began to gather there. He taught them how to transform anger into love and how to protect life by taming unruly spirits and emotions. Mount Tise became the capital and spiritual center of Zhang Zhung, where one could commune with the deities who live there. Since that time, it has been home to many, many adepts, who have gained mystical powers by engaging in difficult spiritual practices in the caves that surround the sacred mountain.

"There are many sacred mountains in our land, where the gods live, but Mt. Tise is the most sacred because it contains the presence of Gekkho (the main Bon deity) and his consort, the great goddess Drablai Gyalmo, who abides nearby in Tsho Ma-pham (Lake Manasarovar). They say that she is mighty to behold, emanating a radiance far greater than countless suns; she wears ornaments in her hair that illuminate her endless strands like stars lighting vast pockets of space. Indeed, she encompasses the whole universe. In her gentle form, she is the white goddess mounted on a peaceful lioness, blessing all with the arrow of life held in her hand; in her fierce form, she becomes a multiarmed goddess wielding every conceivable weapon. No force can oppose her. She is our protector, keeping demons at bay and removing obstacles in our life. When you encounter any difficulty, you must pray to the great Drablai Gyalmo, with full belief in her power and compassion," my mother concluded. This was not the first time we heard such counsel, but I could not help but wonder if I would ever feel ready to beckon such a fearsome goddess.

Some days later, Pumo and I again found Ama-la on the rooftop preparing medicine. Seating ourselves on the floor nearby, we watched her grinding dried plants into a fine powder-like substance. Neither of us had a particular interest in learning about plant medicine, but we watched patiently, hoping that she would be inspired to share one of her tales. It was always to hear her stories that we sought out time alone with her, while our brothers were either tending to our family's shops in the market or accompanying our father on the trading caravans.

"After Tonpa Shenrab, were there any masters who had similar powers?" asked Pumo curiously, now ten years old and almost as inquisitive as I.

Ama-la smiled and nodded as she put aside her work and turned toward our eager faces. "Zhang Zhung had many great sages who had gained mystical powers, and even today they live among us but remain mostly hidden. Powers are given for the purpose of protecting life, but, sadly, in our time they are misused, so the true masters who have such powers rarely display them.

"During the height of Zhang Zhung, there was a royal sage who would bounce thunderbolts as if they were balls, but he did that only to scare the demons away and to maintain the peace. There was another sage who lived on Mount Tise who traveled by flying on clouds when he needed to go from one place to another, but, again, he would do so discreetly so as not to frighten the people. And there were several who were known to fly on their drums." She chuckled and added, "What a quick way to get around. And stories are told of a sage who rode the moon as if it were a horse, traveling far beyond our earth. As you see, the adepts have found many ways to transcend physical limitations and move from place to place in this world of ours.

"I have heard that another adept used to recite his mantras on a string of beads made of lightning. I think that also must have been to keep the demons at bay. And in times of great drought, there are those even today who call the clouds and command them to release the rain. There are many stories of such adepts, and they were all masters of Bon. In earlier times, they could display their powers openly. Today it is not common to do so." Pumo's face broke into an amused smile, but I looked up at the sky, wondering how anyone could ride the moon or pray on a string of lightning.

How we loved her stories, which stirred our imagination. And how we cherished this time with our mother, when she spoke openly about her love for the land she considered her true home, that ancient place once known as Zhang Zhung. I had to admit, it was the magic that appealed to me, and a desire quietly stirred within me to one day witness magic like that which my mother described.

Months after one of these conversations, our father returned from his travels, having traversed long, winding trade routes through mountain passes and low-lying valleys, through barren landscapes and alpine forests—bearing the much-awaited tea, jade, and beautiful silk and brocade material. A few days after his return, Pumo and I were watching as he unpacked the crates of goods he had brought to sell in the market, when she suddenly related to him the story of Tonpa Shenrab rescuing his daughter and turning the demon into a most loyal disciple.

Sitting down and pulling Pumo close, encircling her with his arm, he replied, "But you know who the great conqueror of demons is, don't you?"

She nodded. "Guru Rinpoche, of course."

I listened as our father once again recounted the feats of that great master who had enshrined Buddhism in our land. "Tonpa Shenrab lived long, long ago, further back, really, than our memory can recall, but I will tell you the story of a man who lived not so long ago, a mere few hundred years before our time. That man is the *tsampo* (king) Trisong Detsen, who unified our country and created a great empire. He turned our land into one of the strongest empires in the world, safe from invasions from the north and east; we were in control of essential trading routes, which helped us to prosper. To protect what he had built, he sought to establish Buddhism firmly in our country, and to do so he embarked on a great enterprise—the building of temples and monasteries in all corners of the land.

"He encountered many problems. Floods and lightning strikes would destroy whatever part of the temple building was being constructed, causing many in the court to worry that he had disturbed the ancestral deities with his desire to spread Buddhism. They took these troubles as an inauspicious sign and cautioned him to end his building initiative and to halt the spread of Buddhism. Trisong Detsen was very wise, and he knew that the teachings of the Buddha were destined to take firm root in this land, that the future of our people depended on deepening our commitment to Buddhism. The obstacles had to be overcome, and this meant pacifying the unruly spirits.

"The tsampo had heard of a great yogi living in the western land of Oddiyana (a region of medieval India) who had full mastery over the demons and forces of nature, so he asked another great Buddhist master, Santaraksita, to bring this yogi to Böd. As soon as he arrived in this land, Guru Rinpoche saw what the trouble was. Calling out each spirit by name, he challenged them to reveal themselves; then he went on to tame and transform them into guardian spirits to protect the temples and monasteries that were being constructed. Do you know how he tamed them?" he asked, looking at me and Pumo. We knew the answer but shook our heads, wanting to hear again from him a story we had heard many times. "They felt the tremendous love emanating from Guru Rinpoche, as light radiates from the sun. Wherever he went, he awakened the hearts of people and changed them by his love; he taught that the way to conquer mischievous spirits is through love. That is why the people didn't want to let him leave our land. He stayed a long time but finally had to return home. When he did, he trusted his disciples to continue spreading the love and wisdom that are the true strength of our people."

"He sounds a lot like Tonpa Shenrab," I murmured, wondering what the difference was between those two.

"But could he fly on clouds and ride the moon like a horse?" asked wide-eyed Pumo. I watched as Apa-la smiled and replied, "Of course. There is nothing he can't do. Guru Rinpoche is a master of the three realms, but he uses his powers discreetly and only when needed, as is wise to do. But the greatest miracle of all is the inner transformation that he engenders. Much more difficult than flying through the sky is transforming the negative emotions in oneself and in others. The greatest challenge is to change our behavior and our thoughts."

Suddenly I felt confused. "But," I hesitated, and then began again. "But Apa-la, Trisong Detsen was not such a good man."

My father turned his calm eyes to face me and asked gently, curiously, "Why do you say so?"

"Because he conquered Zhang Zhung and did many bad things. He suppressed the language of Zhang Zhung and he tried to eliminate the teachings of Bon, didn't he?" My voice grew quiet, knowing I was speaking disrespectfully of a man whom my father so greatly admired.

He smiled. "Your mother has been telling you stories of Zhang Zhung, hasn't she? What you say is true, but he did all of that for good reason. Trisong Detsen was a manifestation of Avalokiteshvara, the deity of infinite compassion, and he would not have acted without a compassionate cause—perhaps, in the end, to save many lives. Perhaps the actions he took were necessary to unify Böd and build a single, strong empire that could withstand invasions from the north and east. To unify this land, we had to have a common language and a single tsampo as ruler.

"In addition, over time many followers forgot the deeper teachings of Bon. Some say there was spiritual contamination and that the teachings had become impure. I believe Tonpa Shenrab was a Buddha, but he lived a very long time ago. Eventually, the teachings became rigid and overly ritualistic, and superstition crept in. Trisong respected the ancestral Bon teachings, but he felt they could best be understood and practiced through an integration with Buddhism. Their principles concur; they are not in opposition, Padma. It was the court officials at that time who didn't understand this, and that is why divisions arose among the nobles, with some clinging to the ancient ways for their own purposes and others wanting an integration with Buddhism. Over time, those divisions eased, and today there is no competition between these two teachings. In truth, they are one and the same, although articulated differently, having come to us during very different eras.

"Your mother has told you stories of her beloved goddess of Nam Tsho, whom you were named after, hasn't she?" I nodded. He smiled and continued, "Perhaps she doesn't know that the goddess's consort, the mountain deity Nyenchen Tanglha, was ordained by Guru Rinpoche himself and was also a protector of Trisong Detsen. You see this integration. A Bon deity protected the one who spread Buddhism throughout this land. And the sacred Nam Tsho is very much revered by Buddhist pilgrims and ascetics, who inhabit the caves around her waters and engage in deep meditation practice."

I nodded, but in my heart, I didn't feel this integration. I felt only confusion. Leaving Pumo to assist my father, I sought refuge in the street, reflecting on what was the true cause of my conflict. My mother spoke of the nature spirits and how they can help or thwart us. She often took me to an alpine forest outside of Lhasa and asked me to feel the spirits there—spirits that inhabited the trees, lived in rocks, and even abided deep in the earth. She was intimately connected to these spirits and could often predict future events based on what they conveyed to her. My father and three brothers, all practicing Buddhists, only spoke of the mind and practices that helped them realize the true nature of being. They had no use for the nature spirits and spent no time speaking to them. Which path was I to choose?

Pumo found me walking alone down a neighboring lane and, seeing a most serious expression on my face, asked what was wrong. Of all the people in the family, she was the one with whom I could speak most freely. Turning to her, I replied in a serious tone, "I don't know whether I am a Bonpo (a follower of Bon), like Ama-la, or a Buddhist, like the rest of our family."

"Why do you have to choose?" she asked innocently. When I didn't answer, she affirmed. "I am both. Some days, when I am with Ama-la, I am a Bonpo and speak to the spirits who live all around. On other days, I think more like a Buddhist. Padma, we are lucky to have the protection of both Tonpa Shenrab and Guru Rinpoche." I nodded and didn't speak further about my doubts.

Several weeks after this incident, my mother asked me to accompany her to the forest to collect some special plants. It was a ride of about thirty minutes by horseback. After we had alighted and collected the plants, my mother guided our horses to a small body of water so we could rest before heading home. There was nothing she liked more than sitting by a river, a lake, or even a shallow stream. After we had seated ourselves on a large rock by the water, my mother asked, "Did I ever tell you about the great lake goddess?"

"Many times—but tell it again. I never tire of your stories." I knew that this time she would alter the story, as she would want to convey a slightly different message, and so I was eager to hear it. Ama-la's mother was from Sumpa, a sister kingdom to Zhang Zhung, situated to the east of that land and also a center of Bon. Her mother grew up not far from Nam Tsho, which is the largest body of salt water in the whole region and home to the powerful goddess she loved. In fact, all the lakes were ruled by goddesses, consorts of the mountain gods, who most often protectively encircled them.

"Nam Tsho Chukmo is the consort of the mountain god Nyenchen Thanglha," began my mother. She is a great matriarch who cares for the well-being of all living creatures. Once, when my grandmother was very young, this goddess cured her of an illness, and so my family has great reverence for her. Some years later, after she was cured, my grandmother went to the beautiful sacred lake, which is as clear and radiant as a blue crystal, to make an offering to the goddess, as she was preparing for marriage. She described to me what she saw. I was young when she told me, but I have never forgotten. She said that as she was standing by the side of the lake and expressing her gratitude, she saw a beautiful white form emerge from the water and smile at her. Then the goddess tossed a handful of pink flowers in her direction. It was not the season for flowers, and my grandmother was greatly surprised. One flower landed by my grandmother's feet, and she picked it up and saved it carefully, treasuring it until her death at an old age."

I had never heard the part about the flowers before and asked in amazement, "The goddess really gave her a flower?" She nodded. "And did you ever see this flower?" Again, she nodded and continued.

"I have told you that my mother moved to Lhasa when she married. For many years, she was sickly, and so I spent much time during my childhood with that grandmother, who lived not far from Nam Tsho. My grandmother would go to the lake quite often, and on occasion when I was there, she would bring me along. I was very moved by her devotion to the goddess and will never forget the stories she told me about her. That is why your father takes me there every few years, and I will also take you there before your marriage so you can meet her." My mother's voice was reminiscent and dreamy, as it always was when she shared her stories.

"Did you ever see her, the goddess, I mean?" I asked curiously, thinking that if my mother had actually seen her, then I would believe.

"In a dream once," she said. "But I will tell you that story another day."

I was fourteen and had no thought of marriage, but I was very curious about the goddess. "Do you think if we go to the lake, she will show herself to me?" I asked.

My mother was thoughtful. "Except for that one dream, I have not seen her myself, but Opame has, and perhaps she can intervene." Opame was a Bon shamaness whom my mother visited from time to time. She lived not far from Nam Tsho but would come to Lhasa every year to visit her daughter. My mother had great faith in her predictions and always returned from visiting her feeling very much uplifted. Once or twice, my mother had taken me along with her, and I watched in amazement as the shamaness arranged her mirror, flat bell and drum, and began invoking the spirits. Burning juniper filled the air with a most fragrant scent, supposedly to attract the spirits. I was a bit fearful of Opame, not confident that the spirits she conjured would always be the benevolent ones.

"I might be afraid to meet the goddess," I murmured as I stared into the rambling stream of water before us, wondering if there were spirits in the water watching us at that moment.

"Why would you be afraid, Tshomo? You were born after I had prayed to the goddess, and it was she who named you. Surely, she takes an interest in your life."

"You mean she spoke through Opame?" I asked, knowing that it was the shamaness who had given me the name Tshomo.

She nodded. "Opame is the means through which she speaks to me, and I to her. You mustn't be afraid of Nam Tsho Chukmo. She is most benevolent." In this regard, I was not like my mother. I knew that spirits and deities spoke through shamans, but I didn't want any such arrangement. If the goddess were to speak to me, I wanted to hear from her directly, not through someone whom I was not sure I could trust.

The following year, my mother arranged for the two of us to travel to Nam Tsho by horse. The journey there was to take only two days. My mother seemed very anxious as we embarked on the trip, and when I questioned her she replied that she had an urgent matter to discuss with the shamaness. I didn't press her further.

I didn't know what to expect from the journey but was eager for the opportunity to travel outside of Lhasa, a rare event for me. It was the warmer months and the best time of year to travel; the rains had not yet begun, and even the nights were balmy enough to sit outside. The journey itself was exciting; seeing new landscapes and encountering nomadic communities along the way opened my horizons in ways I had not imagined. Upon seeing the sacred lake Nam Tsho, I naturally entered a reverential state, for which I was not prepared, and it took me a few minutes to find my voice. When I did speak, I conveyed my awe to my mother. Never had I imagined that such a beautiful, ethereal scene existed in our world.

"No wonder the goddess would choose to live here!" I exclaimed. The vast turquoise sea before me seemed endless and reflected the brilliant radiance of the sun. Surrounded by snow-capped mountains—the manifestation of her consort, Nyenchen Tanglha—the waters were calm and placid, gently draping the shoreline and signifying her benevolence. They emitted a soothing whisper, and I could imagine the goddess speaking through the lulling lapping of water.

After fully prostrating herself, my mother rose and stood silently for a few moments, clearly moved by the sight of the lake, and I couldn't deny that my feelings were the same. I heard her quietly ask for blessings for the family and the people of our land, and then she sat down and closed her eyes as I seated myself beside her, not daring to speak, not wanting to break the quietude. When I saw her emerge from her interior state a short time later, I couldn't help but murmur, "How beautiful." The colors seemed to change with the movement of the sun, deepening as the sun journeyed across the sky. I had never imagined there was such a place as this on earth.

Finally, my mother spoke: "For so long I have wanted to bring you here to meet her, the radiant one who protects all who call upon her. Eons ago, those two great gods, Nam Tsho Chukmo and Nyenchen Tanglha, came together and married in this very spot, vowing to bless all those who came here, people and animals alike. Together they subdued the demons who were seeking to take over the area, and even the elemental spirits who were vying for control. It was they who brought harmony and prosperity to this region. The barren land that we see today was once their pastures, rich with grasses and plants that fed the animals and humans. It was they who gave us these nourishing waters."

After a brief pause, she continued with a half-smile, "There is a legend that says the goddess once had an affair with a lesser god named Boji, and that Nyenchen Tanglha grew jealous and cut off his legs." Pointing to a lower mountain, she said, "That is Mt. Boji over there, the lower one. The legend also states that the wounds he suffered transformed over time into valleys and mountain passes, and those became the trade route to Shigatse, which has served the traders for so long. It is said that to compensate for his anger, Nyenchen Tanglha created hundreds of sacred springs in this area with pure water to nourish travelers, and he established many sacred places for pilgrims to nurture their spirit." She was quiet for a few moments as I stared out at the lake, wondering what the legend could mean.

"Do gods and goddess have love affairs?" I finally inquired.

"There is always some truth to legends. The challenge is to uncover the meaning, the kernel of truth. Perhaps the goddess knew that an exchange of love with Boji would lead to the creation of those mountain passes, which would make travel possible. Or perhaps she didn't have an affair at all, and it was only a way to explain how the passes came to be, but I believe it was their intervention that made travel possible through this difficult terrain."

"If this land was once fertile and rich, then why did they allow it to become barren?" I asked curiously.

"What would your father say? Impermanence. That is also a Bon teaching. Everything is changing all the time. Rich land becomes barren through overuse and misuse, and then it can rest and regenerate and become rich again. These are the cycles of nature, which the spirits and the deities oversee. But change takes place over hundreds and sometimes thousands of years. Once, in the most ancient of times, this land of Böd was tropical, lying further to the south, replete with tropical forests. But over hundreds of millennia, perhaps thousands, the land shifted north and grew to the great heights that we have today. Who knows what it will be millennia from now."

"You sound like Apa-la when you speak of impermanence."

"Truth is one, Tshomo. Followers of Bon and Buddhism reach the same goal. Some people prefer one path over the other, but you don't have to choose. You can be a Bonpo and a Buddhist at the same time. That is what living with your father has taught me, and I believe he would say the same about living with me. This lake is sacred to the Buddhists as well. The islands in the lake are home to many Buddhist ascetics, who flock here because they feel the presence of the goddess and benefit from the powerful spiritual energy she generates."

I nodded but was still not convinced. There was nobody except Pumo with whom I could share my conflicted feelings. I spent several hours that day with my mother by the lake. It was only as evening threatened to darken our path back to the tent community where we were staying, the home of the Drokpa (nomads), the people of the solitudes, that my mother could tear herself away. The next day she went to visit Opame alone, leaving me with the Drokpa family who was hosting us. They lived not far from the lake in a small community of only a few dozen people. The tent they offered to those on sacred journeys was small, the accommodation barely adequate, but my mother seemed not to notice. Her grandmother had lived sparsely in a similar fashion, and I suspected that the living arrangement reminded her of that woman whom she so treasured. I spent the morning watching the family go about their daily business—the son taking a small herd of goats to find some meager grass to feed on, and the daughters helping their mother prepare the afternoon meal of *tsampa* (meal made from roasted barley flour) with the barley we had brought them. In the morning, we had been served only *po cha* (butter tea); we had also gifted them the tea, which had been carried all the way from the Song Empire and distributed even to remote corners of Böd.

As I was drinking the tea, I realized that the sacrifices my father had made through his arduous and dangerous journeys, which brought our family prosperity, also served so many others by providing them with goods they would not otherwise have had. I had often resented his absences, which sometimes stretched to more than a year, but seeing how much this family depended on and enjoyed their tea, I gained a new appreciation for my father's efforts.

When she returned, my mother did not speak of what the shamaness had told her, but her manner was subdued and quiet. As she busied herself with helping the matron of the household prepare the afternoon meal, I had no time alone with her. I suspected she had asked Opame about my marriage, but I didn't ask any questions, afraid of what the answer might be. I knew that marriage was approaching, but I had not been told of any candidates and wondered if I was to have any say in the matter.

Every day we would take our po cha with the Drokpa family and then ride to the lake, remaining there for several hours. As soon as we would arrive, Ama-la would prostrate herself fully and then sit silently with closed eyes as I sat beside her quietly, trying not to show my impatience or boredom. When she would emerge from silence, she would tell me stories of the goddesses of Sumpa. Although it was her maternal home, she always said her origins were Zhang Zhung and that Sumpa was spiritually part of that kingdom.

"A part of me is truly from Sumpa," she said to me one day as we gazed out into the lap of the endlessly flowing lake. "In the past, many Sumpa communities were ruled by women, and perhaps it was because the goddess Nam Tsho Chukmo was a formidable warrior. Women were considered to be guardians of the family's well-being. I saw that strength in my grandmother and mother, and I hope that you also will have that same strength of will and determination, Tshomo, for you also are a Sumpa woman."

I nodded, thinking that my mother was the same. In so many ways, she was the foundation of our family, providing the strength for all of us. Treasuring this time alone with her, I asked for a story, one I hadn't heard before. After gazing thoughtfully at the water for a few moments, she began.

"For many millennia, the mountain gods and lake goddesses came to watch over the world, but as they desired to remain hidden, they often appeared in the form of an animal, sometimes that of a wild yak. It was at such a time that they taught the adepts how to work with the bears, wolves, and other wild animals, who sometimes became servants to the sages. There was a couple named Shebu Rakhuk and Odenma who were masters of wild animals. They manifested as tigers or leopards and dissolved obstructions, then turned into vultures and flew off. This was their way of protecting people from adverse situations, but some said it was also for their enjoyment, to experience the carefree life of the animals. Stories about them abounded, and people didn't know when they encountered a wild animal whether it was, in fact, a dangerous creature or one of the adepts or goddesses in disguise. The lesson is that when one encounters any animal, see that animal as possibly being a sage." My mother smiled as she recounted this tale. After a few minutes of silence, she began again with another story.

"I don't think I have ever told you about the great master of Zhang Zhung named Dami Theke, who alone could defeat a vast army. People were baffled by such rumors about him and wondered what his secret was. One day a powerful army approached the area where he lived. The villagers were terrified because they had no army of their own. No one was coming to their defense except the lone sage Dami Theke. In great fear, the villagers huddled around and peeked out from behind bushes and small structures to watch as this solitary man entered the field to face the army alone. When the army saw a lone man, unaccompanied by other warriors, they laughed and shouted words of scorn, so sure were they of victory. He watched quietly and patiently as they had their fun, pointing their weapons at him threateningly. Then, to everyone's surprise, instead of taking up a weapon, he simply threw his hat into the sky. Everyone thought he was crazy, a madman. Didn't he realize the danger he was in, or did he not care about his own life? But to the shock of all who were present, his hat turned into a gigantic eagle that began violently attacking all the soldiers, who, in a fit of fear, fled the scene. In other words, he had full command over the material realm through the power of his mind.

"There were many rumors about him; one was that when troublesome spirits came around, he simply threw books at them, which turned into loudly braying donkeys that chased the spirits away. He lived to be quite old, and when it was his time to leave this world, his body transformed into a beautiful dragon that rose into the sky and disappeared into rainbows of light. That is surely a good way to depart!" Ama-la exclaimed with a smile. I couldn't tell if she was serious or not, so I simply looked at her in disbelief, wondering how a hat could turn into a bird and books into braying donkeys. If I saw it, I would believe it, I said to myself, and if such a person exists today, I would surely like to see something of that nature.

When she saw the questioning expression on my face, she assured me, "It is true. It is all true. Tshomo, both the Bon and Buddhist masters have such powers. But powers are not to be sought; they come naturally when one attains a high level of realization. It is the realization that one must seek, not magic. One can be attracted by magic, but it doesn't lead one to the truth." Looking out over the lake, she was quiet for a while. Neither of us spoke. Although I never quite knew what to make of her tales, I had to admit they captivated me, and I loved hearing her tell them.

She broke the silence. "This will be my last visit here," she said softly. "I am glad I was able to bring you before your marriage, and if I am not able to bring Pumo, you must promise me that you will bring her before her marriage to get the blessing of the goddess."

"Why won't you bring her, Ama-la?" I asked innocently. "I am sure she will want to come with you."

"Just promise me."

"Ama-la, you will bring her, just as you have brought me."

"Promise me," she requested more urgently, taking my hand and looking into my eyes. Reluctantly, I did so. Then she added, "When I am no longer here, do not mourn, for the goddess will protect you. I have been assured of that."

"What do you mean, Ama-la?" I asked nervously, wondering which goddess she was referring to. Unlike her, I was fearful of the warrior goddess and had no intention to seek her.

"I am not speaking of Drablai Gyalmo. I don't believe she is your goddess, although she has a very peaceful side as well as a fierce one. I am sure the goddess who will come to you will be gentle and will soothe you with her love, as that will be the best way to reach you."

A week had passed since our arrival when the Drokpa family informed us that they were hosting another family in a few days, and my mother took that as a sign for us to return home. The next morning, we arose early and rode to the lake for one last visit. Sitting beside the water, which was ruffled by a gently sweeping wind, I asked in a low voice, not wanting to disturb the quiet ambience that hugged the lake, "Ama-la, have you seen Nam Tsho Chukmo yet?"

Nodding, she replied in a loving tone, "She came to me once again in a dream last night and confirmed what Opame had told me. After seeing her, I am now ready to leave here. The goal of my life has been fulfilled."

I was both pleased and shaken by her response. What did she mean that her goal had been fulfilled? Something about her tone introduced a shadow into our midst. For the first time, the thought of her death intruded into my mind. How could my mother die? If that was the purpose of our trip to Nam Tsho, then I didn't want any part of it. I didn't want to be here. I didn't want the goddess to confirm anything. I didn't want to hear anything that would change my life. I wanted my life to stay just the way it was.

Sensing my uneasiness, my mother looked at me and said, "There is nothing to worry about, Tshomo. Everything will be fine, just as it should be." Wanting to chase away any worried thoughts, I asked what the goddess looked like. "How can I describe her?" she replied. "Her face, beautifully formed, is white. Her form emanates a radiance brighter than the sun, so bright that I could hardly look at her until she shaded herself. Then I could gaze upon her. Abundant jewels of many colors dotted her dark hair, which flowed down to the ground. She was seated on a serpent, in the middle of the great sea lake—the one we are sitting beside now. Smiling, she blessed me and told me some things about the future, which I cannot share.

"It was the same image she revealed to me years ago in a dream after my grandmother died. I was very sad at that time because my *amrgas* (grandmother) was my connection to the lake and the goddess. Nam Tsho Chukmo appeared in a dream and asked, "Why are you sad now that she has come to me? You should rejoice in her joy. After that, my sadness left me and I realized that I had my own connection to the goddess, a bond that had always been there but that I hadn't realized. It took my grandmother's death for me to know this."

"Will you tell Apa-la about your dream?" I asked hesitantly.

She shook her head. "There is no need. He has his own path to follow."

Why would she not share with him such a powerful experience? I wondered. Did she think he would doubt her? Did he doubt the existence of the goddess? I decided not to ask anything further.

We had awakened at dawn so that we could visit the lake before departing. My mother had wanted to see the sun's first light flicker across the vast expanse of water. It had truly been a magical sight and worth riding through the cool morning air to see. Now the sun was well on its journey across the morning sky and sunlight flooded the sea. Noticing the passage of time, my mother prostrated and indicated that we had to return to the Drokpa family, bid them farewell, pack up our horses, and begin the journey back to Lhasa.

That visit left a deep imprint on my mind, one that stayed with me for years after. Shortly after we returned home, my mother took sick. She said it was exhaustion from the journey, but I grew anxious, as she remained weak and ill for several weeks. My father was about to embark on the last of his trips, one that would take him away for many months. He was hesitant to leave my mother in her ailing condition, but, gathering her strength, she assured him that she would be fine. This last trip was necessary to secure the funds for their future and to enable my eldest brother, Sonam Jigme, to take over fully. He had been traveling with my father for many years, while Kipu and Jampa helped my uncles with our shops in the main market.

"When I return," he told my mother, "we will retire to Yarlung Valley, and you and I will finally have some days together of rest and peace." My mother nodded, but I was confused because she had always said she wanted to spend her last days by Nam Tsho. Now they would go to Yarlung Valley, near Samye Monastery. My father had long been a major benefactor of the monastery, and I knew he wanted to spend more time in meditation under the direction of the senior monks. I also knew of the significance of that place to Guru Rinpoche. It was there, in his meditation cave, that he had subdued the demons and rebellious spirits so that Buddhism could take root. He had helped to design and begin the building of the monastery, and my father would naturally be drawn there. But what about my mother? Would her dreams then not be fulfilled? I didn't dare question my father but assured him that Pumo and I would see to our mother's recovery while he was away.

In fact, she did recover soon after my father's departure, but her return to health was not to last long. One day, as she, Pumo, and I were seated on the rooftop, she looked at us and in a serious tone said, "Never forget your Bon heritage. We are women of Zhang Zhung and Sumpa. When Böd loses its link to its past, that is when it will become weak and susceptible to outside invasions and influences."

A few days later, on a walk home from the market, she again said to Pumo and me, in a somber tone, "You are Sumpa women. The blood of that land runs through you."

"What does that mean, Ama-la?" asked Pumo, a bit timidly. "What is a Sumpa woman?"

My mother stopped walking, and we did as well. Gazing at her two daughters, turning her eyes from Pumo to me and then back to Pumo, she replied slowly, emphasizing her words, "We keep our face to the fiercest of winds and don't turn away. We endure whatever comes in our path. Internally, we are as free as a wild yak, as strong as a mountain, as clear as a lake, and as steady as earth herself. That is what it means to be a Sumpa woman. Never forget that."

Later that day, Pumo took me aside and asked what Ama-la had meant. "Why is she telling us this now?" she asked.

I didn't want to reveal to her my fears, my sense that she was preparing us for her departure, so I replied, "We both will soon marry, Pumo, most likely to Buddhists, and she doesn't want us to forget our Bon heritage. That is all."

Only months later, after my father arrived back in Lhasa, she took sick again. It was as if she had been waiting for his return before leaving this world.

I was nearly sixteen when my mother died. She never told me what the goddess had said in her dream when we visited the sacred lake, but I suspected she had informed my mother of her impending death. A most peaceful glow shone on my mother's face in those last days, and I hoped that this was a sign of Nam Tsho Chukmo's blessing.

CHAPTER 2

Strange Encounters

"Impermanence," repeated my father softly for a second time, as he gazed compassionately into the grieving faces of Pumo and me. Even though three months had passed since my mother's death, we had a hard time returning to our daily routine. We mourned her greatly. As a result of many years of meditation practice, my father was handling this change in our family circumstances much better than we were, displaying little emotion. My three brothers, all having married years earlier, were engaged with work and their respective families and seemed too busy for prolonged mourning. It was Pumo and I who were closest to our mother and who tried to keep her alive by continually referring to the stories she had told us.

Her death had the effect of creating in me an ironclad determination to become a true Bonpo, to follow all that she believed and shared with me, but in truth I had little understanding of how to do this or what it meant. But despite my lack of knowledge, I was determined to follow the Bon ways.

One morning, my father informed me in a serious tone that after the mourning period passed, I would be married. "Before your mother's death, she arranged for your marriage, Padma."

"She did?" I looked at him in surprise, hearing this for the first time. "She never mentioned it to me."

"She has arranged for you to marry Yeshe Dorje. She was waiting for my return so that we could tell you together, but then she became too ill and left it in my hands. I hope you are happy about this. He is one of the finest men around. I have gotten to know him well on our long journeys together."

Yeshe was a close acquaintance of our family, the dearest friend of my eldest brother, Sonam, and he was someone to whom I felt deeply attracted, although I was far too shy to admit it. Born into an aristocratic and devoutly Buddhist family, he was trained from early childhood to become a monk. But during his adolescent years, he rebelled against these plans and decided instead to go out on his own to see the world, much to his family's dismay. Despite their disapproval, he embarked on a long trip west to the Pala Empire (in northeastern India) and further south through much of Gyagar, a place for which he had developed great fondness. He was away for many years, and after returning he became acquainted with Sonam and decided to accompany him and my father to Chang'an to the east (in China). Yeshe's family had large agricultural tracts, and his cousins bred some of the finest horses in our region. He knew that these cousins were not pleased with the middlemen who brought their horses to the Song Empire for trading, where there was much demand; several times these traders had cheated them out of their due profits. Eager for travel and wanting to help his family, Yeshe formed a partnership with my father and brothers, who began adding horses to the goods we traded. This turned out to be very lucrative for everyone, and a warm bond was formed between our families.

I knew the match was a good one for our family, far better than we could have expected. His family was well above ours in status, but that didn't matter to me. Over the past year, I had sensed that Yeshe was attracted to me, for whenever he visited our home, which was frequently, I often found him gazing at me in a way that made me look aside, confused about my own feelings. Although I found him physically attractive and had to prevent myself from staring at him when he wasn't looking at me, what drew me the most was his manner and knowledge, and his somewhat rebellious nature. In many ways he was a balance of my mother's qualities and those of my father—somewhat austere in his personal habits and reserved at times, but also resistant to outer controls and determined to find his own way in life, regardless of societal expectations, and I had to admit that this combination appealed to me.

At the mention of marriage, I nodded to my father and went off to be alone so that I could sort out my feelings. Did I want to marry Yeshe Dorje? His image came before me: a slender man of medium height and build, with nicely formed facial features and neatly braided hair tied in a bun on top of his head. He was well educated and knew much about the world from his extensive travels. There was an inner strength about him that I found comforting. He was a man upon whom one could rely. I envied the close friendship he had with Sonam and often wanted to join in their banter together, but was far too shy before my brother's friend, who, like my brother, was fourteen years my senior.

I had great love and regard for my brother Sonam, and I knew of his respect for his dear friend Yeshe. He would make no important decisions about life without first consulting him. When it had been time for his own marriage, it was Yeshe whom Sonam turned to for counsel. I had heard them discussing marriage, and after listening to Yeshe speak about the qualities to seek in a wife, my respect for him had increased. Not long ago, I asked Sonam why Yeshe had not yet married, and Sonam replied teasingly, "He is waiting for you, my dear sister." I hadn't taken him seriously then, but now I saw it was true.

What were my feelings? I recalled that on numerous occasions I had drawn close to listen quietly as Yeshe narrated to Sonam stories of his travels, filled with tales of extraordinary beings. The only other person who could tell such stories was Ama-la, I thought at the time. As I reflected on my possible marriage to Yeshe Dorje, I thought about his calm manner and austere nature. I had heard my brother tease him about his plain woolen clothing, and I heard Yeshe's laugh and response: he had no interest in the fine silks and furs that others desired, for he had seen too much during his travels through Gyagar to care about such things. My mother had felt the same and instilled this sentiment in Pumo and me. All the embellished robes that my father brought back for her from the Song she had put away for the wives of my brothers when they married, saying she much preferred a simpler dress. I had to admit that I greatly admired Yeshe Dorje. There was only one catch—his commitment to Buddhism. I had just determined to follow the way of Bon, so how could I marry a devoted Buddhist?

As I was unwinding my thoughts about this marriage, my father sought me out to know what my feelings were. "You are at the age for marriage," he said quietly. "Yeshe Dorje has admired you for some time but waited until you were old enough before approaching us."

"How do you know that his family will consent?" I asked my father, wondering if they would truly agree to marriage with a family that was not of their status.

My father chuckled. "Don't you know Yeshe Dorje? He follows his heart and does not abide by convention. I believe they were so happy when he returned to them after years of travel that they would agree to whatever he desired, and they have already given their consent." He looked at me, expecting a smile, but when one didn't appear, he asked in a concerned tone, "Why aren't you happy? Don't you like him?"

"Wouldn't Ama-la want me to marry a Bonpo?" I stammered.

He chuckled. "When your mother and I discussed this, she told me that he would help you understand Bon. One of the reasons she took you to Nam Tsho was to consult with the shamaness, who confirmed her feelings. This is a most auspicious marriage, Padma, one that seems to have been planned in the distant past, according to the shamaness. Now I only have to worry about finding a good marriage for Pumo, and your mother is not here to help me with that."

Noticing my still-hesitant expression, he continued. "Padma, I am afraid you have misunderstood your mother all these years. She herself had a very happy marriage with a Buddhist, so why wouldn't you? You have created a false separation in your mind, something your mother never did. She had her ways and I had mine, but they were never in conflict. We respected each other's path. One's spiritual journey is a private matter, and each person has their own individual path to follow. But you will be surprised at how much the Bonpos and Buddhists have in common." He smiled and added, "After all, who are the ones who have kept the sacredness of Nam Tsho all these years, who meditate, pray, and enter deep states of communion on her islands and in the caves that surround her? Who could love her more than the Buddhist monks? She is sacred not only to the followers of Bon but also to the Buddhists. As I have told you many times, you can be both, and your husband-to-be, Yeshe Dorje, would fully agree. Of that I am certain. You can rest assured and know that he has great respect for our ancient ways and our ancestral deities, as have I. Buddhism was never meant to supplant Bon but to supplement it, to provide new avenues for reaching the supreme realization."

"Why do I feel conflicted then?" I asked tentatively.

"Your doubts are a creation of your mind. If you learn to subdue the mind, you will overcome those doubts. You must learn to tame the restless, doubting mind. Therein lie the demons that Guru Rinpoche and others were able to conquer. Demons are not only external to us; they are internal as well. They come in the form of anger, doubt, and fear. You must conquer them and free yourself of their hold. This can only come about through meditation. How many times have I told you this? I am hoping Yeshe can help you learn meditation."

I could not help but notice that his words about inner demons were almost the same as those Ama-la spoke when we sat by Nam Tsho. Were the spiritual paths of my parents really more alike than different? Were Bon and Buddhism merely two different roads to the same goal? Had I really created an artificial separation? But then why at the end of her life had Ama-la instructed me to adhere to the way of Bon? I had never discussed spiritual matters with Yeshe, and I could only hope that he would accept the Bon practices I was now set on mastering.

"Apa-la, if this marriage is the wish of you and Ama-la, then I can only consent."

He smiled. "I know how much you trust your mother and the goddess, and I hope you have that same trust in me. I nodded and granted him the smile for which he had been waiting.

When Pumo heard about my impending marriage, she took me aside. "Padma, are you happy about this? It is all so sudden."

Hugging her, I confessed, "I am not ready to leave you, Pumo, but it is not so sudden after all. Ama-la finalized it when we returned from Nam Tsho. It was for this reason that we made the journey, to confirm what had already been initiated. She wanted to see me married before she died but could not. I can only follow her wishes. Besides, I have great admiration for Yeshe Dorje and believe I will grow to love him. There is nobody else I would want to marry. I am drawn to his somewhat rebellious nature; the fact that he left his family and went his own way; and, even now, that he delayed marriage for so long when his family had attempted to secure a marriage for him many times. It's just that I finally decided I am a Bonpo, and now I am marrying a Buddhist, a serious one at that. I don't want to be dissuaded. I don't want to be influenced by a husband."

"Then don't be," she replied firmly, in a proud voice. "We are Sumpa women, Padma. Isn't that what Ama-la told us. We keep our face to the fiercest of winds and don't turn away. Surely you will achieve your goal. I have faith in you."

Gazing fondly at my younger sister, I wondered who between us was truly the elder one. My mother's death had changed her and given her a certain perspective that comes with the passing of childhood and entry into adult life.

I married Yeshe Dorje and found him to have the same steady, endearing presence that my father possessed and a wisdom in both practical and spiritual matters. He and Sonam took charge of the trading caravans and embarked on long, arduous journeys, full of danger from difficult mountain passes and ever-present bandits. I was able to remain with Pumo and my father in our family home during the first two years of marriage.

Then came time for my father to arrange for Pumo's marriage. As a longtime benefactor of Samye monastery, Apa-la had befriended one of the artists there named Tashi Chodruk, a painter of temple murals. He admired the depth of this young man's concentration and skills and thought he would make a good husband for Pumo, who had a strong creative interest. Generations ago, Tashi's family came from the kingdom of Kashmir, along with numerous other artists, to decorate the temples being built.

Pumo was pleased with this arrangement, so she and I set out for Nam Tsho to receive the blessing of the goddess, as I had promised my mother. I feared that the journey would fill me with sadness and that I would acutely feel my mother's absence, but, surprisingly, it didn't turn out that way. As soon as I saw that great sea lake stretching out to the horizon, I rushed to greet her, filled with joy; and I could not help but feel our mother beside us, smiling at her two daughters as we stood before the grand expanse of water.

"Isn't the lake so beautiful, Pumo?" I asked effusively. "Ama-la spent much of her childhood near here and she loved this place. I feel her presence, as if she is standing here right beside us. Perhaps she now abides here with the goddess. Perhaps that is why she didn't seem sad to die."

"It is indeed beautiful," she murmured. "It is Ama-la's blessing that we could come here together. She made you promise to bring me, knowing you would fulfill that promise."

We sat down by the side of the lake and stared out at the water, taking in the scene before us, and I remembered my mother's words of a few years earlier. "Ama-la told me that Sumpa women once led the clans. There was a time when they held dominant social and political positions, and the royal succession was matrilineal. Pumo, you and I are Sumpa women, in addition to everything else."

She smiled. "She told me the same thing when the two of you returned from the lake that year. She told me never to forget our Sumpa heritage. It is strange, because when we were young she only spoke of Zhang Zhung, and then in her last year she began speaking of her Sumpa ancestry. I wonder why?"

"She didn't distinguish between the two sister kingdoms. I think she knew she was going to die young, and she wanted us to draw upon that warrior heritage to be able to withstand her departure and continue on with our lives," I replied reflectively.

"Do you think any of our ancestors were women warriors?" she asked curiously.

"Most likely."

When Pumo was young, she loved to hear stories of the miracles performed by the Bon masters, but more recently she wanted to hear about the warrior goddesses, something I knew too little about. "Padma, you and I are still very young and don't yet know our own strength, but we will discover it. In our family, only you and I feel keenly that connection to our Bon heritage, and we will always support one another. We will make sure that we become the powerful Sumpa women that Ama-la would want us to be."

"Pumo, when I came here with her, she told me the story of Atak Lumo, a great female warrior of this region who magically manifested in the middle of this lake as a beautiful maiden dressed in rainbows. Initially, she had been a shepherdess of the demon king Dud Lutsen, but one day she encountered the hero Ling Gesar, who was traveling through the land, and that encounter changed her. At first, she attacked him with her bow and arrows for entering the kingdom of Dud Lutsen without permission, and he fought back. They were an even match. During the battle he recognized her competence in warfare and her potential as a ruler, and he thought to free her from the demon king so that she could come into her own power. She must have sensed this, because at a certain point in the battle she came to see Ling Gesar for the hero that he was, and she stopped resisting him. At that moment, he won her friendship and made her the ruler of the eastern Changthang (Upper Tibet). Her true nature was benevolent, and Ling Gesar had seen that. Eventually, she became mother to all the creatures in her kingdom."

Pumo smiled. "Only Ama-la could tell such stories, and I suspect that she fully believed them."

"I always thought that you did. I am the skeptical one."

"I half believe," she replied pensively. "I think there is truth in everything she told us, but the challenge is to find that truth. What I understand from that story is that there were many famous women warriors who defended our land, our customs, and beliefs. And perhaps this most magnificent body of water, which is our sea, really, gave those women strength and purpose, and perhaps there are beings here whom we can't see. I feel the uplifting, almost magical atmosphere of this place, and I believe there is a goddess who abides here, as Ama-la so often said."

Pumo and I stayed at Nam Tsho for only two days, but this time together bonded us in a new way. We connected to our Sumpa roots and to the goddess, and our mourning over Ama-la's death transformed into gratitude for how much she had given us. Instead of the sorrow of absence, it was the joy of her presence that we found at the lake.

Yeshe and Sonam returned from their journey, Pumo was married, and my father retired to the monastery. Sonam, with his wife and two children, were now living in our family home. Yeshe's family lived away from Lhasa, and so he found a modest home for us in the city, not far from where Pumo was living with her husband's family. Yeshe knew that the years ahead would involve much travel for him, and I was grateful that he made sure I would be within easy walking distance of my sister.

Soon after we had settled into our new home, Yeshe surprised me one evening by asking whether I was interested in finding a Bon master to teach me. I had never discussed with him my inner conflict or my newfound commitment to follow the way of Bon, but somehow he knew.

"Yeshe, that is my greatest desire, but I don't even know where to look, how to begin," I responded gratefully. So Apa-la was right, I thought. Yeshe didn't object at all to my interest in Bon and, in fact, was supporting it.

"When I return from Amdo, I will help you." Yeshe had to travel to his family's horse- breeding farms about a family matter, but the journey would not be a long one, so I didn't mind waiting. However, I didn't need to wait or have his help. Shortly after he left, I learned that my mother's shamaness, Opame, was in Lhasa visiting her daughter, and I urged Pumo to accompany me on a visit to her.

"I am not seeking any messages from spirits," I assured her. "I only need help in finding a Bon teacher." Reluctantly, she agreed. As a child, Pumo was once adversely affected by Opame when the shamaness entered a trance, and after that my mother refrained from bringing her on any further visits. I also had a slight fear of her, but I had hidden it well and my mother never knew. Now I was going for a different matter, not for predictions or messages, and so I felt no timidity. Besides, there was no one else I could ask for help in finding a teacher.

When we arrived at the home of Opame's daughter, she graciously received us and offered us po cha and snacks. Pumo and I waited patiently for the shamaness to receive us while her daughter chatted away about one thing or another. After an hour, I began to get restless. As I made a sign to Pumo that perhaps we should leave, the woman appeared, having come from a trance session.

After apologizing for keeping us waiting, she sat down on a low seat across from us and studied us both intensely. Pumo looked away, but I returned her gaze. Opame was a large, odd-looking woman, and if not for her dress, you wouldn't be able to tell if she was a man or woman at all. Her thin plaited hair was wrapped tightly in rings on top of her head. A prominent nose dominated her face, and small piercing eyes peered out from above her high cheekbones. I hadn't seen Opame in a number of years and she looked older than I remembered. Facial hair now dotted her chin and the sides of her mouth, unusual for a woman, and I had to prevent myself from staring at it. Her gaze was such that I felt if one got on her wrong side, she might strike you down, but when she spoke, there was a gentleness about her that revealed her benign nature. My mother had totally trusted and adored this woman, and she was no stranger to us. Before I could begin to explain my reason for coming, she began to speak.

"You are looking for a Bon teacher. There are many such teachers, but those of true knowledge are rare—rare indeed." I nodded, not daring to respond. "I assume it is for you, Tshomo?" Again, I nodded. "What is it you want to learn? Rituals? Magic?"

At the mention of magic, my eyes lit up, but I replied, "Rituals," thinking this a more appropriate answer.

She was thoughtful, then said, "I could teach you that myself, but my visits here are rare and becoming less frequent as age catches up with me." She laughed quietly. The shamaness was quite a bit older than my mother, perhaps in her seventh or eighth decade of life. I couldn't quite tell. She continued: "There is a woman I have heard much about. She is called Dalha (moon goddess), and some say that she is associated with a goddess of one of our sacred lakes. I had some interaction with her many years ago, and then one day she disappeared from here. I heard that she went wandering through what was once the land of Zhang Zhung and that she returned a year or so ago and is now living outside of Lhasa, an easy trip by horse. I can tell you where to find her and you can use my name as an introduction. I don't know whether she takes students, but what I do know is that she is one of the rare true masters, who will teach you far more than rituals." She was quiet and then I heard her murmur, "How I would love to see her once more, but time is not something I have much of any longer."

Pumo looked at me anxiously, wondering what my reaction would be. I expressed my gratitude for pointing me in a direction, giving me a place from which to start. Our visit with Opame was a brief one, as we were not looking to her for further information about our lives. We left shortly after this conversation. On the way home, Pumo asked me if I was serious about trying to find that woman Dalha.

I nodded and said that since I had finally decided what I am, I wanted to pursue my path. I would be lucky to find such a teacher here in Lhasa and not have to travel anywhere.

"Then wait for Yeshe to return, or take one of our brothers with you," Pumo insisted.

"The two of us can manage on our own," I replied, with conviction.

"The two of us? When did I agree to accompany you?" she asked, with a look of alarm.

"I know you won't let me go alone," I commented. It took some coaxing, but several weeks later Pumo rode with me, following the directions that Opame had provided. Just outside of Lhasa, beyond the markets and larger homes, past the area where the poorer families lived, we rode through a small alpine forest. Coming out of the gathering of trees, I caught sight of a very small cottage down a dirt path. Tying our horses to a nearby tree, we hesitantly walked up the path and knocked on the door. There was no answer. After knocking again and waiting several minutes, Pumo suggested we leave. We started to retreat down the pathway, when the door cracked open, barely wide enough for a young woman about my age to poke her head through.

"I am sorry, but Dalha cannot see you today," the young woman called.

"We will come back another time," Pumo hurried to say, eager to get away.

"When is a good time to visit her?" I asked. She shrugged her shoulders and closed the door.

"How strange," I murmured, as I paused and stood staring at the closed door. And how rude, I thought. We had taken the initiative to make the trip, and she wouldn't even greet us.

"Let's get out of here. I feel uneasy," urged Pumo, tugging at my sleeve.

A few days later, I decided to return on my own, without telling Pumo. I knew she would discourage me. When I arrived the second time, it was the same as the first. I was told by the young woman that the one known as Dalha couldn't see me.

"Is she ill?" I asked. The woman shook her head. "When can I meet her?" She shrugged and closed the door.

I went a third time and received the same reception. On this attempt, I pleaded with the woman who came to the door. "Please, tell Dalha that Opame has sent me. My name is Padma Tshomo and I very much want to meet her, to learn from her." Shaking her head, she closed the door, leaving me baffled and dejected. Why wouldn't she at least meet me? Was I so unqualified to be her student? Over the next few weeks, I made several more attempts, with no success. Finally, I went back to see Opame's daughter. Opame had left Lhasa weeks earlier, but her daughter kindly invited me in for tea. Before I could explain that the woman called Dalha would not meet me, she smiled and told me of her own strange encounter with the woman.

"I was curious about my mother's description of Dalha and couldn't get her out of my mind, so I rode out to her cottage to meet her a few days ago."

"Were you able to see her then? Did that young woman let you in?"

"She did. When I arrived, the shamaness wasn't home, but I waited. She returned about an hour later with a large grey bird perched on her shoulder. It was a very strange sight. I discovered that she is a rather enigmatic woman, who speaks in riddles. Many people think my mother has a strange appearance, but it is nothing compared to Dalha," she laughed.

"What do you mean?" I asked curiously.

"I can't explain it, and I can't even describe her. When I was seated before her, in a certain light and from a certain angle she looked more ancient than anyone I have ever seen, but from another angle she looked young and beautiful. I can't even tell you if her hair was black or white, or perhaps it changed from one color to another. All I remember clearly is her laughter. When she laughed, which she did numerous times during our brief meeting, her whole body shook with joy.

"When she greeted me, her first words were, 'I went to get your mother. She had to see me one more time.' Not comprehending, I rose from my seat for a moment, in surprise, and then sat back down again on the low seat in the small entry room, where I had been enjoying the po cha served by the young woman who I presumed was her granddaughter. Dalha seated herself across from me, and as soon as she did, the bird flew off her shoulder onto the floor and nestled itself beside her as if it wanted to listen to teachings. But there were no teachings. She spoke a few sentences about my mother, which I didn't understand. Honestly, I can't recall much of what she said, because I was so entranced by that bird.

"After she spoke to me, she turned to the bird, seated beside her, and said gently, almost lovingly, 'It is time now to spread your wings.' As she spoke those words, the bird spread out its wings, which were quite large, and as the bird took a few steps toward me, I drew back in fear; its wingspan took up much of the room. 'Now cut the strings,' said Dalha in a loud, stern voice. The bird hesitated for a moment, lifted its piercing dark eyes to mine and began to make loud noises, and then it jumped onto the ledge of an open window and flew off. Dalha laughed and disappeared through a door into a back room, muttering, 'Now you are free. Now you are free.' That meeting left me with a very uneasy feeling. I had never looked into the eyes of a bird before or been up close to one of that size. As it made those noises, it seemed as if it was trying to communicate with me. I have been thinking about this for the last two days, unable to sleep or to concentrate on anything. I cannot understand the meaning."

"How very strange," I muttered, thinking that perhaps it was best that I hadn't met the woman after all. "Maybe it was an omen," I murmured.

"I have thought of that and sent a messenger to my mother, hoping she could interpret the incident for me. I am waiting for her response."

Not knowing what else to say, I thanked her and left, but as much as I tried to get the strange story out of my mind, I couldn't.

A week later, Pumo came to visit. I had discovered that I was pregnant but hadn't told her the news and was eager to do so. As we were sitting together, I told her that I was expecting a child.

"It's a shame we won't be able to ask Opame anything about the child," she mused.

"Why not? I will bring the baby to her for a blessing after he is born."

"Are you so sure the baby is a he?" she asked teasingly.

"I know Yeshe very much wants a son, so I am hoping, for his sake.

Often he speaks about all the things he plans for our son, as if he is already a reality."

"Well, we won't be able to bring your son to meet Opame, because she died a little while ago." It had only been a few months since we had visited her at her daughter's home.

"She died?" Pumo nodded. "So suddenly? How do you know?"

"A few days ago, I was in the market and ran into a servant from her daughter's house, and she told me."

"I must visit her daughter and pay my respects," I hurried to say.

"It's not possible, at least not now," she replied, shaking her head. "The servant told me that as soon as Opame's daughter heard this, she left for Nam Tsho, and they don't know when she will return. I could see from our last visit how attached she was to her mother, but we will certainly visit her when she returns."

After hearing of Opame's death, the story of Dalha and the bird became even more perplexing, but I didn't want to dwell on it because it awakened a fear in me that I hadn't even known was there. Yeshe had returned from Amdo, and I wanted to focus on our relationship and the family that we would soon become. After learning of the pregnancy, he said he wouldn't travel again until after the birth of the child, and I was glad at the prospect of spending time with my husband, who had become very dear to me.

Yeshe's calming manner soon chased away the unspoken fear that had sprouted in me. He loved to tell stories of the Buddhist masters, stories that had a different focus from the ones my mother used to tell. "I will tell you a story of a great master from Zhang Zhung," he began one evening.

"You know stories of Zhang Zhung?" I asked curiously. He nodded, and I added, "My mother's father came from there. She said he was a descendent from one of the ancient tribes."

"Sonam has told me, and I know of your affinity with that ancient kingdom. I also was very drawn to it when I was younger and traveled to many sacred places there on my way home from Kashmir. The story

I will tell you is not a legend. It is a true account, and when I first heard it, I developed a longing to travel to Gyagar.

"Two hundred years ago, an unusual child was born into a non-Buddhist family. I assume they were followers of Bon. He was known as Rinchen Zangpo. Have you heard of him?" I shook my head. "By the age of two, he was tracing Sanskrit letters in the dirt and would sit quietly with folded palms. Throughout his childhood, his parents would find him deeply absorbed in meditation, even though he had no teacher. At the age of thirteen, he announced that he was leaving them to travel to Gyagar. His parents realized that he was a most unusual child and that they would not be able to prevent him from leaving, and so they agreed to let him go, as long as he found someone to accompany him. He found a companion and, at his young age, embarked on this difficult journey of crossing high mountain passes and enduring days of bitter cold. I know firsthand how challenging it is in those places to find food and to shield oneself from the weather. First, he traveled to Kashmir, where he met an old brahmin named Shraddakaravarman, and this man became his guru. Under his guru's guidance, he perfected his knowledge of Sanskrit and studied many philosophical and tantric texts in the original Sanskrit. Then he traveled throughout Gyagar, meeting many adepts and sages, and after thirteen years he finally returned to Böd.

"Since he was young when he had left Böd, he didn't realize the degree to which tantric practices had already come here, but in Gyagar, he learned the true tantra—the esoteric practices reserved for those of deep wisdom and compassion who had overcome their egoic traits. When he returned to Böd, he heard that a number of supposed masters were now teaching tantra here. There was one charismatic teacher called Buddha Star, who had a large devoted following due to his display of mystical powers, such as lecturing his students while suspended in the air in a state of levitation. Rinchen heard these stories, but he wasn't impressed. After all, in Gyagar he had met true masters who understood the deeper secrets of tantra, and he wasn't interested in the mere display of outer powers. However, after hearing so much about this man, Rinchen decided to meet him. Before doing so, however, he spent many weeks in meditation.

"Then he went to find this Buddha Star. When he arrived at the place where the man was teaching, he found him giving his talk while levitating high in the air. Hundreds of students had gathered around to witness the strange sight. Immediately, Rinchen saw that the man had acquired certain powers but lacked true realization. Walking up to him, in front of all who were seated there, Rinchen pointed his finger at Buddha Star, like this." Yeshe paused, extended his arm and pointed his finger in the air, with a stern look on his face. "As soon as Rinchen did this, the man spun head over heels and plunged to the ground. When he realized what Rinchen had done, the man picked himself up and ran away. Humiliated for having been exposed, he was not heard from again.

"Rinchen saw that the teaching of the sacred tantra had degenerated and was now being used to attain powers. Self-appointed masters were popping up everywhere. People were singing the sacred texts in the streets as a way of entertainment. Approaching the *tsenpo* (king), he offered to bring some of the true masters from Gyagar to Tibet to help rectify the situation and address this degeneration. The tsenpo at that time was Yeshi O. He agreed and asked Rinchen to return to Kashmir and invite to Böd those who could help revive the true tantric teachings, which had first been brought to our land by Guru Rinpoche. Upon returning to his much-loved Kashmir, Rinchen sought out the best teachers and artists and brought them back to Böd. Those artists and their descendants are the ones who have decorated our temples with such beautiful Buddhist murals."

"The great-great-grandfather of Pumo's husbandTashi, was one of those artists," I added.

He nodded. "But Rinchen's greatest contribution was in translation. As a child, he could write in Sanskrit; he must have known that sacred language in his previous birth. That made it possible for him to work with other able men to translate the great Buddhist texts into our own language, and this made Buddhism far more accessible to a greater number of our people. Yeshi O, who was a devout Buddhist, recognized the spiritual stature of Rinchen and sought guidance from him. Retreating to the monastery in his last years, the tsenpo spent much time in meditation under the direction of Rinchen and the masters he had brought back to Böd.

"Padma, although spiritual masters may attain many powers, it is not magical feats that reveal the true spiritual stature of a person," he said, in way of ending. "If they do display such powers, it must be for a purpose, to teach a particular lesson, not to impress and attract large numbers of followers. This is true in Bon as well as in Buddhism."

"Then what is the way to know a true teacher?" I asked.

"One who is selfless, with no ego identity, who is in control of the mind and emotions, who is pure and serves the well-being of all, who is filled with love and service and joy—such a one is a true teacher. I will help you find a Bon teacher if that is what you desire."

"I would rather wait," I replied hesitantly, "until after I give birth."

"That is fine. In the meantime, I have a surprise for you. I have arranged for us to travel to Nam Tsho. I have never been to the lake, and I know how much that place means to you. We will ask for a blessing for the child growing in your womb."

My eyes lit up. Though I had been to the lake with Ama-la and Pumo, it would be a totally different experience to go there with Yeshe. He arranged for us to stay with the family of the head of the Drokpa community in that area, and the accommodations, although hardly lavish, were more comfortable than when I had visited the two previous times.

The day of our arrival in the region was busy, offering gifts and exchanging pleasantries with the host family, but on the second day we made our way to the lake. As I stood there, Yeshe fully prostrated himself, something I had seen my mother do but which I had not done myself, and this struck me. Did he have more devotion to the goddess than I had?

We sat for a while in silence as he meditated, and I lay down to rest by the side of the lake, tired from our journey. I was now in the fourth month of pregnancy and was still feeling occasional nausea and fatigue. A cold wind blew over the water, brushing against my face, and I pulled my woolen jacket tightly around my neck. After some time, I fell asleep, and when I awoke I found Yeshe standing up, packing up the few things we had taken with us. Several hours had passed.

I quickly rose as Yeshe mused, "Hermits have long lived on the islands of this lake and in the caves tucked away in mountain recesses. I am sure there must be an adept or two on one of those islands, but it is impossible to cross over to meet them, except in winter when the water freezes." I looked out over the lake, wondering if those hermits had seen the goddess just as my mother had.

The second and third days were spent walking along the shore of the lake, viewing it from different angles, and riding to caves that dotted the surrounding mountains. I had not done so on the previous visits, and it was thrilling to find ancient artifacts and meet the few ascetics whom we encountered along the way. On the last day, we climbed to one of the caves. The walk was difficult for me, and I found a place to sit on a large, low rock. We had finished the water in our traveling jug, and Yeshe asked me to rest while he went to find a spring to refill the jug. In the distance was the grand lake, and from the height of the mountain ridge, I watched as light shimmered across the water in a mesmerizing dance, making it seem almost translucent. That is a sign of the goddess, I thought. One could almost see forms dancing there, and I imagined that the goddess and my mother were present in that light, aware of me as I was aware of them. This feeling brought a smile to my face. So absorbed was I in the scene that I was not aware of the presence of a woman standing beside me until she spoke.

"It is time; it is time now," she said in a low, gravelly voice. I turned to look at who had spoken. A rather stout, elderly woman stood before me, dressed like a Drokpa herder in simple woolen clothing, with a red woolen hat covering her head and long ear flaps that reached nearly to her chin. A thin band of fur lined the sides of her cap. "Time to go," she called more loudly as she took off her hat and, with a great thrust, flung it into the air. Then I watched as the hat turned into a great eagle and flew away, high into the sky. In astonishment, I turned my eyes from the bird to her. She was no longer facing me, and from the angle that I now saw her, she looked to be quite young, around the age my mother would have been. Turning to look at me once more, she spoke in loud, raspy voice, "When you fulfill the three promises you made, then I will send for you." With those words, she took off with great speed and disappeared into the nearby cave.

I sat there, too stunned to move. A few minutes later, Yeshe found me this way.

"What's wrong," he asked when he saw the shocked expression on my face. "Are you not feeling well?"

"Yeshe, go into that cave and see if you can find the woman who just entered there." After handing me the jug of water, he entered the cave but returned a few minutes later.

"There is nobody there, Padma. It is a shallow cave and there is nowhere to go. Did you see someone?"

"It is nothing. Perhaps I imagined the whole thing. I am not feeling well, Yeshe. We should head back."

The rest of the day and night, I was overcome with nausea, and so Yeshe decided that we should return home. The long ride back, spread over two days, did not help me, and it was a most difficult journey. By the time we reached Lhasa, I had to take to my bed. For two days I struggled with abdominal pain, and on the third day I miscarried. My precious child was gone.

"She took him from me," I whispered when it was over. "That woman, whoever she is, took my child. But why? Why, on that sacred spot, on a sacred pilgrimage, did she take him from me?"

CHAPTER 3

A Shaken Faith

I was devastated by the loss of the child, but Yeshe was able to handle it far better than I, telling me that I was young, and promising that we would have many more children. The most disturbing part to me was that it shook my faith in Nam Tsho Chukmo, the goddess my mother so adored. It had been after my first visit to Nam Tsho that my mother was taken away from me; and now, after another visit, I lost my child. What was I to think? What was I to believe? Had I not been a good enough Bonpo?

The strange episode with that enigmatic woman also left me shaken. Had she really turned her hat into an eagle, or had I imagined it? I remembered the story my mother had told me about the Bon sage who did such a thing, but I didn't really believe it then. Now I had seen it with my own eyes, or at least I thought I had. Again and again, I reviewed in my mind the experience but finally concluded that due to thirst and exhaustion, I had created an experience that was not real. Yeshe could not find that woman who had entered the cave, and so there hadn't been anybody. That realization rattled my confidence in myself, but I didn't share my thoughts with anyone.

To cheer me up, Yeshe found me a Bon teacher, a woman who came to our home regularly and told me stories of the various lake goddesses and mountain gods and taught me rituals to chase away unwanted spirits and protect against negative spells. All of that was well and good, but it wasn't enough. She couldn't ease my doubts and concerns or help establish my faith in the goddess. When, on occasion, she spoke of magic, I turned my eyes away so she wouldn't see the fear that arose. Whereas once I had been intrigued by my mother's stories of magical events, now I sought to evade any reference to such things.

One morning as I was waking from sleep, I heard an internal voice say, "You had wanted to see magic and now that you have, you are afraid. What is it that you want?" The words disturbed me, and, after hearing them, I recalled the story Yeshe had told me about Buddha Star, the adept who was able to levitate but was not a teacher in the true sense of the word. I remembered my mother saying so often that it was not powers we should seek but realization. Had I been too intrigued by the allure of magic? I wondered. As I sat trying to identify the voice I had heard in sleep, I thought it had the same rasping sound of the woman I had imagined by the cave near Nam Tsho, the one who had turned her hat into an eagle. Was she real or not?

I still could not bring myself to share that experience with anyone, because whenever I thought to speak of it with Pumo or Yeshe, it sounded absurd. I dared not admit that I had seen for myself a woman turn a hat into an eagle. I was sure they would think the same thing that I thought on many days, that in my faint and weak condition, I had imagined the whole experience. But after hearing that woman's voice upon awakening, the sense that it might have been real returned to me, and I remembered that she had said something about three promises. Don't focus on the hat, I told myself; focus on what she told you. Again and again, I searched my mind, unwinding my memories back to the earliest days of my youth, but I could not recall any promises I had made, except the one to bring Pumo to Nam Tsho, and that promise had been fulfilled. If that woman was real, then what could she have meant? I was torn between wanting to know the truth and wanting to push the whole episode out of my mind.

Months passed and I was meeting regularly with my Bon teacher. Yeshe was pleased because her visits served to distract me from my loss. He began traveling again, embarking, with Sonam, on trade expeditions to the Song Empire, which took him away for many months at a time. Pumo was now pregnant and often spent time watching her painter husband as he worked on murals at a temple in Lhasa. I could see that she was becoming increasingly engrossed in the Buddhist world, but I was not surprised, because she had always been inclined that way. She never asked about my Bon teacher, and I never offered any details. We both were busy with our lives. We saw each other less frequently and I was beginning to miss our closeness.

Whenever I visited Pumo's new home, I was captivated by the many beautiful objects from Kashmir. Tashi's grandfather had visited their ancestral homeland, bringing back exquisite Buddhist art as well as depictions of deities from the religion of the Kashmiri Brahmins. According to Tashi, there was a natural integration of multiple religious streams in Kashmir, and the people sincerely respected and appreciated each other's religion. Just like here, he had said. But I had my doubts about here. If we, the people of Böd, integrated the old and new, then why did I feel in me the colliding of two worlds? Why did I feel the need to choose either Buddhism or Bon and reject the other?

After many months of studying with my Bon teacher, I decided to visit Pumo, whom I hadn't seen in several weeks. When I arrived, I was surprised to find her engrossed in painting a scroll. I didn't know that she had taken up that work herself. Looking at the half-finished painting, I remarked on the detail and delicacy of the work. The fine lines of the face and gracefulness of the figure revealed a skill I didn't know she had.

"Who is it of?" I asked.

"Tara," she replied softly, with a smile.

"Tara? The Buddhist goddess?"

"Why do you call her a Buddhist goddess? She is the great Goddess, who is called by many names. We can also call her Drablai Gyalmo if you prefer."

"You think they are one and the same?"

"Different manifestations," she replied, gazing down at the image before us.

"I think of Drablai Gyalmo as being fierce. This goddess is gentle," I remarked reflectively.

She smiled. "Oh, Tara has a fierce form as well, just as Drablai Gyalmo has a most gentle form. They manifest to us as needed to suit the situation."

I was quiet, burdened by the thought that Pumo was drifting away from me. Her husband was a wonderful man and perfectly suited to her, but she was moving more and more into his world, spending much time at Buddhist monasteries, while I still didn't know where I belonged. I didn't stay long at Pumo's home that day.

Yeshe returned from his travels, and I soon became pregnant again. This time he pampered me, hardly ever leaving my side. Nine months later I gave birth to a girl, and we named her Samaya, meaning "sacred promise," because Yeshe had promised that we would have many children. It was easy for me to forget my spiritual confusion as I busied myself with this new addition to our family.

During this time, my father died. His last years had been spent in quiet retreat, with infrequent visits to the family, but I felt keenly his loss. While the family conducted Buddhist rituals, I led a Bon ceremony for him, very much aware that among my siblings, it was only I who attempted to keep alive that part of our heritage. Some months later, I asked my Bon teacher not to come anymore. Noticing this, Yeshe asked why.

"I don't feel that I can learn anything more from her," I replied simply. "Besides, I am busy with Samaya."

"Busyness is no excuse. You mustn't ignore your spiritual needs."

"Yeshe, what I am seeking is more than rituals and ceremonies. I am not satisfied with that alone. The right teacher will come to me in time."

"So true," he replied, with a nod. "Then I leave it to you."

A year later, I was pregnant again and another daughter, Dolma, was born. Two years later a third daughter, Yara, came to us. We had three small girls, each two years apart. With each birth, Yeshe had expressed great joy, and yet I knew how much he wanted a son. He never stopped talking about the training he would give that son, the exposure to the world that he would provide. But no more children came.

I had three young ones, and I was satisfied. A year or so after Yara was born, I was in the market purchasing some food items when a woman about my age approached me.

"She is calling you to come visit her now," she said mysteriously, without even introducing herself. I looked at the stranger addressing me, assuming she had mistaken me for someone else. She was a slight petite woman with a pleasant appearance, a youthful round face and smiling eyes. Two tightly woven braids draped over her shoulders and chest. She was dressed in a plain blue *chuba* (Tibetan dress) with no decoration, and she wore no jewelry. There was nothing extraordinary about her and I tried to recall where I might have seen her.

"Have we met before?" I asked in surprise.

She nodded. "Come tomorrow and she will meet you." As she described the place where she lived, I remembered that it was the cottage of the woman called Dalha, the one that the shamaness Opame had suggested I visit, the one who had refused to see me time after time. As I recalled the rejections of years earlier, an old hurt emerged.

"I no longer need to see her," I replied coldly.

"You do." With those words, she turned and walked away. I stood there debating what to do, wondering how that woman had found me. Should I ignore the request or venture out to try to meet her once again? Perhaps she would refuse me, as she had so many times in the past. More than eight years had gone by since I had ridden to the cottage, and yet the feelings of rejection and disappointment that I experienced then were still very vivid. Besides, I felt that she was somehow connected to the death of Opame, and this disturbed me. Yeshe was traveling and I couldn't consult him. I didn't want to ask Pumo to accompany me, as I knew she would try to dissuade me from going.

After debating with myself throughout the night, I realized that I would not be able to resist trying to meet Dalha once more. Perhaps there was no connection between her and Opame's death. Perhaps that was my imagination, just as the hat turning into an eagle could have been a trick of the mind. Early the next morning, my horse and I embarked on the path that I remembered all too well, despite the passing of years. When I arrived, I stood for several minutes on the pathway before approaching the door, fully expecting that there would be no answer to my knock. But before I could even reach the door, it opened, and the young woman welcomed me in. After I had entered a small room, she invited me to sit and make myself comfortable while she made po cha.

"Is Dalha here?" I asked. She nodded. "Will she meet me today?"

Again, she nodded and replied, "She has been waiting for you."

I sat there while she boiled water and made the tea. I watched as she carefully took out a few sweets from a small box and set them on the low table before me. About an hour passed without either of us speaking a word. After a while, a woman entered from another room. She was standing in the shadows, and I couldn't see her clearly, but I heard her say in a rasping voice, "You have fulfilled your three promises and so I have sent for you, as I said I would." As she stepped out of the shadows and into the morning light that was streaming through the window, I immediately recognized her as the woman whom I had met at the cave years earlier when I visited Nam Tsho with Yeshe. I slowly rose and stared at her, as fear gripped my heart. She was the one who had taken my child, who had caused the miscarriage.

Half frozen, I stood there for several moments; then I turned and fled without a word. Exiting the cottage, I hurried down the pathway, quickly untied and mounted my horse, and rode away as fast as I could. When I arrived home, I gathered my three children into my arms, fearful that Dalha might seek to take them from me. Who was she? What were her powers and what did she want with me? And what were those promises she spoke of? I couldn't understand anything, and it was all so disturbing.

The next day, I went to see Pumo. I knew not to say a word to her about my visit to Dalha. I just wanted to sit and watch her work on the beautiful image of Tara, a peaceful goddess I now wanted to know.

"Why are you so quiet today?" she asked, as I watched her paint. "You seem distracted."

"Do I? Tell me stories of Tara."

"What is there to tell? I don't know much about her, but I love to sit before her image. She is very calming and protective."

"I need her protection now," I ventured to say quietly.

"Why? What is wrong?"

"I need her protection for Samaya, Dolma, and Yara."

She smiled. "What are you worried about, Padma? You have given birth to three healthy daughters. Perhaps it's the memory of the miscarriage that makes you worry."

"Perhaps," I replied fearfully. "Can I take one of the scrolls home with me so I can come to know this goddess?"

Putting aside her brush, she looked at me. "Of course. But I can also paint you an image of Drablai Gyalmo if you like, or of Nam Tsho Chukmo. I know how you have wanted to know those goddesses." I shook my head and insisted that she bring me the image of Tara when she had finished.

Several nights later, I had a terrible dream. I saw myself as a young child holding the hand of a woman who seemed to be my mother. We were standing in a square of a small village, and before us was a woman about my mother's age being burnt alive. Her face was contorted with pain as the flames engulfed her. She was too weak to even cry out, but I heard her deep, agonizing moans. The scene was horrific, and I turned my head away so as not to see it, but my mother forced me to look back at her, holding my face in the direction of the burning woman. And I heard her say, "This is what will happen to you if you become like her."

I woke up in a terrible sweat, breathing heavily. Getting out of bed, I went to look at the children, sleeping together in the next room. How peaceful they looked. Pumo was right. I had nothing to fear. My children were fine. It was only a nightmare, I told myself. Perhaps the visit to Dalha had awakened a fear in me and that had caused the dream.

Several months later, I had the same nightmare, and then it came a third time. The dreams were so sensory and vivid, as if they were real experiences, and each time I awoke with a searing pain in my heart.

During this period, I was so distressed that I hardly left the house; I ate and slept little. I was quite shaken and didn't know how to pull myself out of this disturbed state. The image I had seen haunted me and followed me everywhere. I dreaded lying down at night and busied myself with whatever I could find to do to avoid sleeping. My inability to function normally was affecting the household, and the young woman who helped me with daily chores was growing concerned. One day she disappeared for a few hours, and when she returned, she brought Pumo back with her. She had gone to tell my sister of my condition. All my sister had to do was take one look at me to know that something was terribly wrong, and finally I had to reveal to her what I was going through.

"Why are you letting this dream disturb you? It is just a dream," she said, trying to calm me after I described the scene I had witnessed.

"No, Pumo. It was not just a dream. I know that young girl was me, even though she looked very different. She was being forced to watch a woman being burnt alive. Where could that have been, and who would do such a thing? Pumo, my faith in everything that I once believed in has been shaken, and I don't know where to turn."

A look of concern crossed her face. She was thoughtful for a few minutes, as if trying to recall something, and then replied, "if you are so sure it was you, then it might be a memory from a past birth."

"Or a vision of the future," I said fearfully.

"Do you really want to pursue this? Sometimes it is better to let such things go, not to pay them much mind. I am sure the dreams will pass."

"Whatever it is that I experienced, I don't think I can ignore it," I said quietly. "It is not letting me. The image is too strong, too powerful, and too painful."

"I remember that Ama-la once told us about the sacred lake Lhamo La-tso, which is endowed with magical powers," she mused. "A powerful goddess lives in the lake, known to both the Bon followers and Buddhists. The Buddhists call her Palden Lhamo, but she has other names. She is also called Tsho Lhamo and Jemo Maksoma. Do you remember that Ama-la told us that if you stare into that lake, sometimes you can see scenes from your past incarnations or future events? It is not far from Lhasa. If you insist on pursuing this, I will take you there."

"I don't know what to do."

"Sometimes seeing too much makes things worse, but, on the other hand, it could help you understand what you are experiencing."

"Pumo, let's go to that lake. I have tried rituals, invocations to the goddess, even sitting before the painting of Tara you gave me, but nothing I have done has been able to shake that scene from my mind. I remember Ama-la saying that she had wanted to visit that lake goddess, but three days of fasting is required and it is a very difficult climb to reach the lake. Do you think we can manage?"

"I think we can manage the climb but not if we fast, and so we will have to forego that and ask the goddess to forgive us."

Several days later, we were on our way. I had taken my three children to stay with my second brother, Jampa, and his wife, telling them that Pumo and I were going on a pilgrimage to one of the sacred lakes and would be back in a week's time.

It took two days of travel to reach Lhamo La-tso, which was southeast of Lhasa. Along the way, we found families to stay with. We arrived very early on the morning of the third day and immediately began the climb, thinking we would only spend an hour or so at the lake and then turn back to Lhasa. The ascent was extremely difficult, more challenging than anything I had ever attempted, but when we surmounted one of the surrounding mountains, the sight of her waters was magical, making the journey well worth the effort. She lay like a turquoise gem nestled between barren peaks. She was not an endless expanse of water like Nam Tsho, but rather a self-contained and enclosed jewel, not vast but deep. The warmer weather had arrived but the rains had not yet come, and a sprinkling of snow still teased the mountaintops.

The climb had exhausted me, and I didn't think my legs could make it down the mountain to reach the shore. For a few moments, I stood there watching the sunlight glitter on the still water and then sank onto the ground.

"Come, Padma," said Pumo, reaching down to help me up. "We have traveled this far; we must go all the way."

"Pumo, suppose nothing happens. Suppose I stare into the water and don't see anything. Then we will have come all this way for nothing."

"Why did we travel to Nam Tsho? Not for visions, but to meet the goddess. We have come here to meet this goddess, and if she shows you nothing, then that is the blessing you will receive."

"My faith has been so badly shaken," I murmured.

"Then I hope she will restore that faith. Come, let us go down to meet her." Still, I hesitated. "Are you afraid of what you might see?" she asked.

"Let me rest a little and gather my strength," I sighed.

She would not have it, saying firmly, "We are Sumpa women warriors. We don't rest, Padma, and we are not afraid." I allowed her to help me to my feet again and slowly followed as she descended the sloping mountain. It took some time, but finally we reached the lake's edge. The water was crystal clear, a most beautiful blue, reflecting the sky and every cloud that passed over. You could see it all in her slightly undulating surface. To view the sky, one had only to stare into the mirror of the lake, and so I did. Looking down, I watched the reflection of a few clouds drifting by, leaving in their wake only the radiance of the sun glaring back from the water. We spent quite some time sitting by the lake, and as the hour passed, my fear eased. No image appeared to me, and I thought that perhaps the goddess would bless me by ensuring that I would have no more nightmares. That was all I was asking.

"I don't see anything, Pumo. Do you?"

"I see monasteries when I look into the lake. Am I seeing the past or future? I don't know. But how could it be my future? I am a married woman with children, and what place do monasteries hold in my future?"

"Perhaps you will paint their walls," I replied without thinking.

She laughed. "Me, a woman? What do you see, Padma?"

"Nothing, and I am glad."

We got up to leave, and I stared for a last time into the cool, still surface. As I was about to turn my eyes away, an image formed out of the stillness, the same one I had seen in my dream—a young girl clutching her mother's hand as her mother forced her to watch the burning of a woman. Enormous pain swept through me as I saw the body incinerate, and with a contorted face, I turned my gaze from the water to Pumo, who was taking in my every expression.

"What is it?" she asked nervously, her hand on my arm. "What do you see?"

"The same image that has haunted me in dreams. But now I don't know—am I the child or the burning woman? Is it an image from the past or future?" Sinking onto the ground with my body shaking, I looked at her pleadingly. "Pumo, there must be someone who can help erase this image from my mind."

"Calm yourself, Padma. Let us leave from here. I am sure that once we are home, some clarity, some blessing will be given. The goddess will not leave you without an answer."

Rising and subduing my emotions, I murmured, "My only wish and prayer is to drive that image from my mind. If it is a memory from the past, I want to forget it. If it is of the future, I don't want to see it. That is my prayer to the goddess."

"I have no doubt she will respond," she replied, firmly gripping my hand. Together we began to climb the sloping mountain. I wanted to take a last look at the lake, so as we reached the top, I turned to catch a glimpse of the sunlight playfully dancing over the water's surface before beginning the climb down the other side. Several hours had passed since we first arrived, and the sun was making its slow descent, casting a different glow over the lake, highlighting new shades of color.

We had encountered no one else during our time at the lake, but once we descended the mountain, my eyes caught sight of a lone woman seated on the ground not far from where we were walking.

I didn't think to approach her until Pumo said, "Let's see if that elderly woman is in need. She is alone, and it is getting late. I nodded and followed. As we came closer to the woman, my feet stopped in their tracks and I stood still, hardly breathing. Turning to me, Pumo asked what was wrong. Why had I stopped? Our horses were just ahead.

"That woman is Dalha!" I exclaimed in a whispered voice. "I don't want to meet her. We must turn around and go another way."

"Dalha, the woman we tried to visit so long ago?" I nodded. "Then let's definitely go speak with her. Opame had recommended her. Don't you remember? You were so disappointed that we couldn't meet her then."

We stood a short distance away, close enough for me to recognize the woman, but far enough that she wouldn't hear us speaking. But somehow her speech reached my ears, although her words seemed to be coming from inside of me. It was an internal voice I heard, the same raspy voice I had heard months ago upon awakening. "There is no need to be afraid of me, Tshomo. I didn't cause Opame's death. She knew she was dying and wanted to meet me once more, but she had little time and so flew to me in the form of a bird. She asked me to help break her last attachment to this world, her attachment to her daughter, and so I called that daughter to my home so she could meet her one last time. And I didn't cause your miscarriage. That was destined to be. That son of yours was going to die in childbirth, but I spared both him and you that suffering, only hastening his departure and finding a new birth for him, one which he would survive."

I knew that Pumo was not hearing those words, and she continued to stare at me, perplexed at my reaction. After hearing Dalha, I slowly began to walk in her direction, and when I reached where she was seated, I sat down on the ground in front of her as Pumo did the same.

"Lhamo La-tso has responded to you and called me here," Dalha said quietly in a voice that was no longer rasping but lulling and gentle. "That painful memory from the past, so deeply engraved in your mind, will not serve you now. I will suppress it until the time is right." I heard her words and then I didn't, as my tired mind, weakened from the difficult climb and inner struggle, entered a light sleeping state. I only came out of that state when I heard her ask, "What blessing do you seek from the goddess? What is your heart's desire?"

Without thinking, I heard myself say, "To give my husband a son."

"That has already been determined," she replied quietly. "And a special son he will be." Then turning to Pumo, she asked what blessing she sought.

Pumo also replied immediately, "To bring the goddess alive through painting."

Dalha chuckled and said, "That has also already been determined. What you saw in the lake was the future. You will paint beautiful images in many monasteries, which will long be admired. Palden Lhamo is a powerful goddess, but it does not matter what name you call her. It is only important that you learn to live in the company of the goddess. Talk with her, walk with her, visualize her by your side, and then she will become real to you. Now, is there anything else either of you want to ask of me?"

"Dalha, what did you mean by three promises?"

She smiled. "Those three promises from the past became your three daughters, and you have fulfilled those promises as you once said you would, taking responsibility for those souls. But I can't reveal any more to you now. It is not the right time."

"Dalha, how strange for us to meet you here. We have not met you before and so how do you know us?" asked Pumo.

"Your mother was very dear to me," she responded in a loving tone.

"You knew her?" I asked in surprise. My mother had never mentioned to us the name of Dalha.

She smiled. "I knew her long ago when she lived in Zhang Zhung, in an earlier incarnation. Then, she did not know me by the name Dalha, because I was not known by that name." Without another word, she rose and began to walk away.

Seeing that she had no means of travel, Pumo called out, "Dalha, take one of our horses. It has food supplies and can take you back to Lhasa."

Turning to face us, she grinned and replied with amusement, "Why would I need a horse when I can ride more swiftly on the crescent moon?" Then, turning again, she walked away at great speed.

That night, the crescent moon shone brightly in the clear dark sea of the sky.

CHAPTER 4

The Story of Dalha

No nightmares of a burning woman dared to visit me again. No longer was I haunted by a vision I couldn't understand. Since the visit to Lhamo La-tso, a peacefulness had descended over me, and I was enormously grateful for that, attributing it both to the goddess of the lake and to Dalha. I was also embarrassed that I had misunderstood her so dramatically, and I wanted to make up for it in some way. It took me months to gather the courage to ride out to Dalha's cottage alone. Once there, I felt too timid to knock on the door, so I found a place to sit quietly, with closed eyes, among the trees outside her cottage and internally asked her to forgive me for misjudging her, for doubting and being fearful of her.

Over a period of a few months, I did this several times, never knocking. When the moment was right, I thought, I would meet her again. On the fourth visit, I heard the cottage door open, footsteps tapping against the dirt path and then a gentle voice inviting me inside.

Opening my eyes, I saw in front of me the young woman who I presumed lived in the cottage with Dalha. "I didn't mean to disturb you," I murmured.

"You are not disturbing me at all," she replied, with a smile. "I have seen you coming here but didn't want to interfere with your meditation."

Getting up from my seat on the ground, I followed her down the narrow, overgrown path and into the small cottage. Once inside, she began preparing po cha and some light food, just as she had done when I previously visited. I hurried to say that I could not stay long and didn't want to inconvenience her, but she went about fixing the refreshments and replied, "You are here to learn about Dalha, aren't you? That will take some time."

That had not been the reason for my trips to her cottage, but the young woman understood that this was my underlying desire. I wanted to know who this woman called Dalha was. Had I been fortunate enough to come across a true adept, a Bonpo, a rare master? She told me that Dalha was not there, and I was surprised to find myself somewhat relieved. As she served me tea and snacks, her warm and friendly manner helped me to overcome my reserve. During my last visit, we had sat in silence as I waited for Dalha to appear, and then I ran out of the cottage without giving an explanation or even saying goodbye. Now I felt the need to apologize.

With an awkward smile, I began. "I am sorry for the way I behaved on my last visit, but I was so surprised when I saw Dalha and a bit scared because I had seen her once before in very bizarre circumstances. I recently met her again and she explained everything. But you and I haven't introduced ourselves. I am Padma Tshomo."

"I am Bhasundara. Dalha settled me in this cottage, which was abandoned when we found it. She doesn't really live here; she stays with me whenever she comes to Lhasa, but I have no way of knowing when that will be."

"Where does she live, then?" I asked curiously.

"Everywhere and nowhere," she replied enigmatically.

"Is she a nomad?" I asked curiously.

A faint smile crossed Bhasundara's lips as she replied, "There are no words to truly describe what she is, and I stopped trying long ago."

"Are you her daughter?" She shook her head. "Her granddaughter?" Again, she shook her head. "Related in any way?"

"Yes and no."

"Bhasundara, you are almost as mysterious as she is," I commented, with a slight laugh. After a pause, I asked, "Can a person really turn a hat into an eagle?"

"No, a person can't," she affirmed, but seeing the confused look on my face, she added, "but Dalha can."

"She can do magic, then? Is she a Bon master?"

"I can't answer that question, and I wouldn't call what she does magic. I know she would never claim that. There are those few who have mastered the laws of the physical world and can change matter, transcending the natural laws through the power of their mind. Let me explain how I came to know Dalha.

"I was born in a small nomadic community in a remote area of what used to be called Zhang Zhung. We lived in tents and moved around from place to place. We were poor, in the material sense, but very rich spiritually. The elders of my community came together at night, studied the skies, and made many predictions. They could foretell when drought would come, when storms would arise, when outside forces would invade our area. My father was quite a bit older than my mother and was one of those elders with great wisdom. I had no siblings. My father died when I was young, and my mother conducted rituals according to what the elders told her. She was especially adept at warding off troublesome spirits. Even now, so many years later, I remember the power of her rituals."

"She was a Bonpo, then?" I asked eagerly.

"You can call her whatever you like. To me, she was simply a very wise woman who knew how to work with the spirits. When I was around ten years old, a disease spread through our community and she died, along with many others. Our leaders had foreseen this but could not prevent it from happening. This disrupted our lives, as the disease had divided us. Some blamed the elders, saying that they had lost the ability to commune with the natural forces and that our rituals had lost their power. Others said it was because we had lost faith in the elders and had angered the spirits. The community split up and each family went its own way. It was very sad because we had stayed together for such a long time despite the many challenges of life in that harsh environment.

"The tents were taken down, the goods packed on the backs of mules and ponies, and people began to depart for other regions in Böd, but I had nowhere to go. My mother had only recently died. Her younger sister said she would take me into her family, but as we began to travel, I somehow became separated from them and found myself alone in the wild. All day, I sat on the ground waiting for my mother's sister to return for me, to somehow find me. Darkness set in, and the sound of animals reached my ears, but I was not afraid. I remembered the words of my father, to look above and follow the stars. He had taught me a little about how to figure out the various directions from the placement of the stars in the sky, and so I began to walk. I walked through the night and slept during the day.

"By the second day, I was weak from hunger, but I kept walking. Finally, I encountered Dalha, but I will tell the story of that meeting another time. She seemed to know my plight. She knew the community and what had happened; she knew that people had lost faith in the elders and the rituals. She didn't explain much but simply said to me, 'It's time to move on.' As you will discover, she is a woman of few words. She told me that I could accompany her, but she warned that the path would not be easy and that I would have to endure many hardships. But I was already used to that. Some years later, I asked her why she had taken responsibility for me, and she replied, 'Even at that young age, your resolve was firm. I tested you and you were not deterred, so how could I not take you on.'

"For many years, I traveled with her to all parts of Böd and witnessed the most extraordinary happenings, but then she brought me here. We found an old, abandoned hut and transformed it into this lovely little cottage, and she taught me how to heal illnesses through the plant medicines and with stones."

"Stones?" I asked in amazement.

She nodded. "Some of them also have healing properties."

"My mother loved the stones as well and always collected them," I murmured. "But she never spoke of their healing properties."

"Not many people know of that," she responded.

"And where is Dalha now?" I asked. She shrugged her shoulders. "Bhasundara, have you not wanted to marry and have a family?"

"That life is not for me," she replied quietly. "I have no desire, but even if I wanted that, it would not be given."

"Why do you say that?"

"Dalha has shown me some things about my future."

I was pensive for a few moments, wondering how much I could ask. Then I thought to befriend this woman and be honest with her. "In addition to that one time I met Dalha here, I met her two other times—once at Nam Tsho outside a cave. After speaking with me for a few minutes, she disappeared into the cave, but when my husband went to look, nobody was there. It was a shallow cave, and she could not have come out without me seeing her. She simply disappeared. Afterwards I thought that I had imagined the whole incident, that she was not real. That was why I was frightened when I came here and saw her. The second time I met her was only months ago at Lhamo La-tso. Again, she was there alone, with no horse or animal for travel. How does she move about?"

Bhasundara's eyes lit up with amusement and drawing close to me, she replied, "You will have to ask her that yourself."

"Have you never been afraid of the things you have seen, like hats turning into birds?"

"I am only afraid when Dalha seems far away," she replied gently. "When I don't feel her presence, that is when I am afraid."

"Do you know anything about her past, where she came from?"

"Tshomo, you are so full of questions. I know nothing about Dalha, and everything I need to know."

"You speak in riddles," I muttered. "Well, I guess all I need to know is that she is an accomplished Bonpo," I said firmly, "and I am looking for a Bonpo teacher." Bhasundara smiled without answering, and I continued, "When she returns, can you let me know so that I can come and ask her to be my teacher?"

"It is not that way, Tshomo," she replied quietly. "You cannot go to her. She must come to you. But I am here, and you can come see me any time. I have a feeling that you and I will quickly become friends."

I left Bhasundara more than a little perplexed, but I decided to visit again before too long. A few weeks later, I found myself sitting at her table. I had brought her tea that Yeshe had carried back from the Song Empire, and I watched as she heated the water and made po cha.

"Last time I was here, you said you would describe your first meeting with Dalha. I am eager for that story." Since my last visit, I had not been able to get Dalha or Bhasundara out of my mind. What touched me the most was Dalha's care for this child whom she found wandering alone. I imagined that the meeting was not a mere coincidence and that Dalha had specifically gone to find her.

"Do you really want to know?" she asked mischievously. I nodded. "It will make the turning of a hat into an eagle seem quite tame. As I told you, I was a young girl, lost and alone, trying to find the family of my mother's sister, hoping that they were also looking for me. As I was walking, I came across a baby yak lying on the ground, seemingly wounded. I approached it to see what was wrong, but as I drew closer, I heard loud grunting sounds from behind. Turning around, I saw a large wild yak snorting threateningly. My mother had tried to teach me how to communicate with animals, and remembering her words, I looked into the face of the yak as it approached and silently said that I meant no harm to the little one, but the yak didn't seem to understand. It continued to come nearer, grunting with displeasure. Actually, wild yaks are not dangerous, but, like all animals, they defend their young.

"Quickly realizing that my communication efforts were not working, I began to back away, but the yak came closer and closer, and I became quite afraid. Suddenly, from out of a low-lying bush, a growling tiger leapt to my side, causing the yak to flee. Even the baby yak got up and ran. It had only fallen and was not badly hurt. The tiger had appeared so suddenly, but for some reason I was not afraid. I felt a peaceful aura around it. My mother had once told me that sometimes the lha and great sages take the form of animals. She said you can tell by their eyes. At that moment, her words came back to me, and when I looked into the tiger's luminous green eyes, I realized it was not a tiger at all."

"What was it?" I asked in astonishment.

"Just then, I heard a woman calling my name from behind, and I turned to see if it was my aunt, although it wasn't her voice. No one was there. When I turned my eyes back to the tiger, the animal was gone and Dalha stood before me."

"Bhasundara, is that true?" She nodded. "I would hardly believe that story if I had not heard it from you personally."

"You see, Tshomo, I grew up in a place where such things happen. The elders told us many stories like this, mostly about the sages of our region, but for the first time, I saw it with my own eyes and realized that this woman was one of those sages."

"My mother also told me similar stories, but they were always of very ancient times," I reflected and then asked, "What happened next?"

"I told you the rest. She knew my name and what had happened to my parents and the community. She didn't say it, but I believe that she had come to find me. I have an old connection with her, as many of us do, and she finds us. She will find you again, Tshomo. She tries to teach us patience, and she waits to see whether we follow her counsel. She gave you some counsel when you met last, didn't she?" I tried to recall but couldn't quite remember. "Didn't she tell you to live in the presence of the goddess, to keep her with you always?"

"I think that she did, but how did you know?"

Bhasundara didn't answer my question, but rather advised me, "Don't expect to meet her again until you have sincerely tried to do what she has asked."

I was intrigued by Bhasundara and couldn't stay away. I knew that she was busy tending to ill people in the city and I didn't want to disturb her, but I found myself unable to resist going back to visit her a few weeks later. As much as I protested, she insisted on making me po cha and offering snacks. I found myself opening up to Bhasundara in a way that I had not confided in anyone except Pumo. Feeling quite comfortable with her, I told her the reason I had gone to the sacred Lhamo La-tso, about the terrible nightmares and how they had gone away. A year had now passed without any disturbing dreams.

"I went with Dalha to that lake once quite a number of years ago," she revealed. "It was when we were traveling through much of Zhang Zhung," she said as she served me the tea. As if recalling that time, a shadow passed over her usually cheerful countenance.

"Did you see any visions of your past?" I asked curiously.

She shook her head and then replied, "When people look into that lake, some see the past and some see the future. Of course, there are many of us who see nothing at all but shimmering turquoise water. We had been traveling for many months and were quite a distance from the lake when Dalha suddenly changed direction and told me that we had to immediately go to Lhamo La-tso. I didn't ask any questions but struggled to keep up with her great speed. Dalha's horse at that time could practically fly and never seemed to tire. It was often quite an effort to keep up with them.

"We arrived at the lake at dawn, and she asked me to wait for her in a place below the mountain that stood between us and the lake. I was worried because I knew that the climb would be difficult, but she assured me that she would have no problem. So I sat down to wait, expecting it would be a few hours before she returned. The day passed, and as I watched the sun travel well beyond the midpoint in the sky, I grew concerned and decided to follow her footsteps. It took me some time, but when I finally descended the slope of the mountain toward the lake, I found her sitting by the side of the water, gently weeping and speaking out loud, addressing someone who wasn't visible. I was taken aback, as I had never seen her cry and didn't know whether to approach her.

"Over the years, we had witnessed many deplorable sights and much suffering. We had just come from an area where there had been an epidemic and many, many people had died, leaving behind grieving family members. I knew that she felt their pain as her own. At such times, her eyes always shone with such kindness and compassion, and on occasion I could see small droplets of water welling up in the corners of her eyes, but I had never seen her cry. I assumed that she must have experienced a disturbing vision in the lake, and I waited anxiously for a sign that I should approach her. Surely, she would notice me and ask me to come to her. As I stood there waiting, my spiritual sight opened and I saw a female light form—so beautiful, emitting an array of brilliant colors—seated beside her and cradling her in her arms. I stood there transfixed and watched as the goddess used her garment to wipe away Dalha's tears, and I understood that she was experiencing the combined sorrow of all those whose suffering we had witnessed. They were the tears of so many people flowing through her eyes, and the goddess was comforting them through her. Dalha was the vehicle through which the goddess could reach them. The vision lasted for several minutes and then disappeared as Dalha caught sight of me and smiled. She again became her usual cheerful, buoyant self and then instructed me to sit in meditation to receive the blessing of Palden Lhamo.

"I cannot claim to have truly understood what I witnessed. I never asked Dalha about it or mentioned it, and she never offered any explanation. I have spoken of it to no one and don't even know why I am sharing this with you. But that day, I came to see Dalha in a totally different light. To me, she became the visible form of the invisible goddess, the one witnessing all our struggles and trials, enduring it with us as our most intimate companion, the one upon whose shoulder we can cry and who wipes away our tears. You once asked me who Dalha is. That is who she is."

She was quiet for a few moments and then said thoughtfully, "I know that you want to ask me about her relationship with your mother, so I will tell you. Your mother nearly died when she was a child, and it was Dalha who brought her back to life. Even though she was not meant to live a long life, Dahla was able to give her an extension."

I looked at her in surprise and said, "My mother never told me."

"Your mother never knew, but she might have remembered that when she was about five or six, she was staying with her grandmother, the one who lived by Nam Tsho, and she became very sick. This grandmother loved your mother dearly and was beside herself at the thought that she would lose her. She called Opame's mother, who was a much respected shamaness. This woman conducted many rituals but finally said there was nothing more she could do for the child; it was her time to die. Your mother's grandmother was very devoted to the goddess of the lake, Nam Tsho Chukmo, and prayed ardently to her, refusing to accept the loss of this child. Every day, she would go to the lake and beseech her to save her granddaughter. Mysteriously, one day Dalha showed up, and after spending some time alone with your mother, she recovered. Then Dalha disappeared and the family never saw her again.

"Dalha never forgets people she has known in this life and in the past. That is how it is with her. I am sure your meeting with her is not a casual matter. There is a longer-term significance, which only you can know. But I have already told you, Tshomo, that she will not appear to you if you do not take to heart what she has told you. If you want her to teach you, you must show her that you are willing to be taught."

"But I am willing to be taught, eager, in fact," I protested.

Bhasundara smiled and replied quietly. "Words alone will not do, Tshomo. You must open your heart to the goddess and call her into your life."

CHAPTER 5

Dalha and Guru Rinpoche

Bhasundara's words stayed with me for a long time, and I continued to reflect on what I had heard about the mysterious one known as Dalha. I was eager to meet her again but didn't know how to abide by her counsel to me. How was I to befriend the goddess, one I didn't even know how to address? And which goddess? The only comfort I had was in my new friendship with Bhasundara, and I decided to develop that relationship as much as I could. Maybe through my association with her I would learn how to approach the goddess.

My three young daughters kept me very busy, and Yeshe was traveling a great deal, which left me occupied with many household affairs. I didn't have much spare time to visit with friends, but every few weeks I managed to find a few hours to ride out to Bhasundara's cottage in the hope that she would be there, and with an even more distant hope that Dalha would show up. Sometimes Bhasundara was home, but quite often she was not, so I would sit outside for a while waiting for her return. On many days, I left disappointed.

It had been several months since I had been able to see Bhasundara. She had not been home on my last few excursions there, but I went again, determined to wait until she arrived. As soon as I descended from my horse, I heard her call me and, turning, caught sight of her delicate frame popping through the doorway, cheerfully beckoning me to come in for po cha. She seemed as eager to see me as I was to meet her.

As soon as I was seated in the small entry room, I asked, as I always did, if Dalha had come since my last visit. As usual, she shook her head. Sensing my disappointment, she said that she would share a story about Dalha and Guru Rinpoche.

"Guru Rinpoche?" I inquired in a surprised tone, not expecting to hear anything about that Buddhist master from a Bonpo, which is what I assumed both Bhasundara and Dalha were. What has Dalha to do with him? I shouldn't have been taken aback, because he was known to everyone in Böd and even the Bonpos respected him. But I had some reservations, believing him to be at least partly responsible for suppressing Bon.

"You know that Guru Rinpoche's father was a great Bon master, don't you?" I shook my head. "It is true. You shouldn't think of him only as a Buddhist. He is one of those universal masters who serve all nations, not only the people of Böd, and who serve all the worlds, not only this one." I was quiet and she continued. "Our history says that our tsenpo Trisong Detsen called him to Böd, but Dalha told me that he came at the behest of the goddess, despite what people say."

"That is a different story from the one I have heard," I remarked. "I learned that Trisong Detsen called him here to suppress the Bon spirits who were disturbing the building of Buddhist monasteries and temples."

"He came to transform, not suppress, the spirits. But what is a Bon spirit anyway? A spirit is a spirit; it's we humans who assign to them a religion or nationality. There is no such thing in the spirit world. The great Guru sought to enlighten Bon, not eradicate it; to remind people of its true meaning and purpose, and to free them of superstition, which had so firmly taken hold."

"Did Dalha actually meet him, then? He has been dead for so many centuries."

"Dead," she chuckled, and was quiet for a few moments before beginning her story. "For about ten years, before I came to live in

Lhasa, I traveled with Dalha through many parts of Böd. While we were traveling, we had many experiences with Guru Rinpoche. I didn't understand them, but I came to realize that behind all happenings is a hidden story, which most often is not revealed. I will tell of one encounter with the great Guru.

"We were traveling through a remote area of the western part of what was once Zhang Zhung, when Dalha suddenly stopped, leaped off her horse and sat down in the middle of the path, as if waiting for someone. I didn't question her but rather sat down beside her. After some time, a traveling monk came to us and, looking intensely at Dalha for a few moments, asked, 'Where can I find Guru Rinpoche?' Smiling at him, she replied mysteriously, 'He travels on the whipping tail of the wind and speaks through the song of the full, radiant moon. You can find him there but be mindful or you will miss him.'

"'Should I travel east or west?' he mused, more to himself than to us.

"'A fierce wind is brewing in the west, and it is the night of the full moon,' she replied in an eerie voice.

"'Then I will travel east so I don't encounter the storm,' the monk said hurriedly and, bowing, continued on his way. Shaking her head, Dalha muttered, 'Foolish man. He didn't hear a word I said.'

"She continued to sit where we were, and after some time another man approached from the opposite direction. This man asked, 'Where is the great Guru now?' and she replied, 'His radiant tears will soon wash the earth, satisfying its long thirst.' The man also asked which way to travel, and she replied, 'There is drought in the west.'

"'Drought!' he exclaimed. 'Then there will be no food.'

"'Be mindful of what I say, or you will miss him,' she advised, looking intently at the man. Thanking her for warning him of the drought, the man said that he would travel east. Turning around, he hurried away in that direction. After he left, Dalha again shook her head and muttered, 'Foolish man. No one listens to my words.' I was silent all this time, completely perplexed by the situation. A few more people passed by, asking Dalha which way to travel, and each time she answered mysteriously.

When they left in a hurry, she would shake her head and mutter that nobody would listen to her.

"Several hours later, another man came along the path, and this one asked where he could find the consort of Guru Rinpoche, the one known as Yeshe Tsogyal. Smiling at him, Dalha replied serenely, 'She sits in the center of the storm, abiding in his spaceless presence. Those two, they can never be unbound.'

"'Where is the storm?' he asked.

"'In a place known as the mind,' she replied. As soon as she spoke those words, the man thanked her, sat down, and entered meditation. After a few minutes, she got up and said to me, 'Finally, I meet a man who hears. He is the one I have waited for. He will find them, and now it is time for us to move on.'

"'Dalha, what was this all about and where are we going?'

"'We are going west. A great storm will soon be brewing there.'

"'Then why are we going in that direction?'

"She looked at me for several long moments and then said quietly, with deep compassion, 'My dear, there is great drought. People are without food. How can we not go to them? Where I go, he will follow, and where he goes, the rains come.'

"'Dalha, I don't understand,' I protested as she climbed onto her horse.

"'Why must you understand?' she asked as she began to ride away.

"Quickly, I climbed onto my horse and followed her. We rode for many hours that day. The air was calm and as still as a sleeping lake, and the thought entered my mind that perhaps she was mistaken. There was no sign of wind or storm. Everything was very dry; clearly, we had entered a region long deprived of rain. Along the way, we passed small groups of very thin-looking nomads, all heading away from the drought-stricken area. Several times, Dalha stopped and told them that the rains would come that night and that there was no need to leave, but nobody listened to her.

"Just before nightfall, she got off her horse and said that we would spend the night there. It was a very remote, deserted area, with no inhabitants to be seen. I was a little uneasy, but I didn't question her.

Together we set up the tent and took out the food we had. The night was still calm when it was time for sleep, but Dalha showed no indication that she wanted to rest. I didn't want to leave her sitting alone outside, although my body was very fatigued, so I stayed with her for a while. It was the night of a full moon, and with no humidity, the sky was as clear as could be. The moon predominated, far outshining the lesser lights. It was one of those nights when the moon seemed closer than usual, as if one could almost reach out and touch it.

"We sat in silence, and I watched as Dalha gazed up at the moon for a long time. Slowly my eyes became drowsy, and I told her that I was going into the tent to sleep. She nodded without responding. Her eyes seemed to be locked in the embrace of the moon, as if she was communicating with it, but I was too tired to think much about anything. Once inside, I fell asleep immediately.

"Sometime later in the night, I was awakened by the sound of a howling wind ripping through the rushing air. Opening my eyes, I looked to the other side of the tent, which was flapping and shaking, and saw that Dalha was not inside. I quickly got up and tried to open the tent to bring her in, but the wind was far too strong. I called out to her many times but there was no response. Feeling that I had to somehow get out, I continued trying to pry open the tent flap. When I finally managed to get out and glance around, I saw that she was nowhere in sight. A pounding rain blurred my vision, but I still ran here and there calling out to her as loudly as I could. Dalha had been wearing only a light woolen jacket, so I was terribly anxious—fearful, really. Several times the wind almost pushed me over, but I refused to go back into the tent and continued shouting for her.

"Then I heard her response, telling me not to make such a fuss, to go inside and be quiet. 'Don't disturb the whole world with your fears,' she admonished me. I heard her, but looking all around, I couldn't see her anywhere. With much difficulty, I managed to make my way back into the haven of the tent, and I sat there praying that she would be all right, that no harm would come to her. There was no possibility of my going back to sleep that night.

"After a short while, the wind stopped beating and the rain slowed into a gentle patter, and the sound of deep laughter reached my ears, but it was not Dalha's voice. It was a man's laugh. Peeking outside, I saw Dalha not far away, seated alone with a beautiful light encircling her. Not wanting to disturb her, I remained in the tent, waiting for her to come inside. It was nearly dawn when she did, and to my surprise her clothing was not wet at all. Anyone else would have been shivering, drenched by the rains, but not her. That is the mystery of Dalha.

"Her first words to me were, 'Two things block one's vision: a restless mind and a perturbed heart. It is anger and fear that disturb the heart. You must not keep company with either.'

"'I couldn't help worrying about you, Dalha,' I protested in a humbled voice.

"'Find the cause of your worry,' she advised gently.

"'Dalha, what happened last night?' I asked.

"'A storm came.'

"'Why did you remain outside in the storm and worry me so?' I rarely questioned her, but I had truly been frightened.

"'How could I miss it?' she replied with a smile. 'I love to ride the whipping winds and sing to the tune of the full moon.'

"'Was there nothing more?'

"'What more are you looking for?'

"'I heard a man's laughter. Was it Guru Rinpoche?'

"'If you heard him, then he was there. You should only believe what you see and hear,' she replied enigmatically and then added, 'A good rain came, and there will be more. The drought is now over.'

"Later that day, I asked her to explain what she had said to those people we had met along the way. She replied that only one with a clear, calm mind could understand the meaning behind the words. Those who couldn't understand must wander a bit longer.

"This was all she would say about that experience, and for quite some days I tried to make sense of it. She had told me to trust what I heard, and I had clearly heard a man's laughter that night in the storm. She had said that the great Guru could be found on the whipping tail of the wind, and during the night of the storm she had stayed outside to see that. My conclusion was that it was Guru Rinpoche who had brought the rains and that Dalha was somehow involved with that. I began to suspect there was a relationship between those two."

I had been so caught up in her story that I was nearly breathless and didn't respond right away. "Bhasundara, I think I would have been so frightened by the storm that I wouldn't have known what to do," I finally managed to say.

"You would have done nothing differently because there was nothing else to do. I have often found myself in such situations with Dalha, where I have had to wait to see what would happen, because she rarely explains herself. I will tell you one more story, which took place about a year later when we were traveling to Mt. Tise and Mapham Tsho.

"I had long wanted to go to Mt. Tise, because it is where Tonpa Sherab called together the adepts so many millennia ago. It was the ancient spiritual center of Zhang Zhung, and I knew it was still a very powerful place. When Dalha announced that we had to travel there, I was full of anticipation. I expected to have profound sacred experiences meditating at that holy mountain, where, it is said, the high deities still live. But something quite different was in store for us. Dalha had said that there was an adept who lived in a cave near that mountain whom she had to meet, and so we rode to his place. She seemed to know exactly where this cave was situated, and I naturally thought she had been there before and was acquainted with this adept. Because the conditions are so harsh in that region, most of the hermits living there are quite advanced in their practices, and I was really looking forward to meeting this man whom we were traveling so far and over such difficult terrain to reach.

"To my shock, when we arrived, this adept treated us rather rudely, asking why we had come to disturb him and then demanding that we leave him alone so that he could continue his meditations. Dalha was completely unperturbed and answered him mysteriously, as always. She said we had been sent by the one he was seeking and that she had been asked to spend the night there, but that we would leave the next morning. He looked at her as if she was a crazy woman." Bhasundara paused and laughed lightly, adding, "Some people do see her that way.

"When the man saw that we weren't going to leave and that he would have to share the rather small cave with us for the day and night, he grunted and then went off into a corner to be by himself. Throughout the day, he appeared to be in meditation, but Dalha whispered that his mind remained very much on us, getting angrier and angrier at our intrusion as the hours passed. I whispered to her that we should leave because the tension in the cave was so unpleasant. This was not what I had expected or desired from my first and perhaps only trip to the most sacred Mt. Tise. But she replied that we would leave in the morning, as planned. Toward evening, the man came out of meditation and prepared some food for himself. He did not offer us anything—not a cup of tea, water, or a morsel of food—and he hadn't spoken a word to us after our initial exchange. That night he wrapped himself in several blankets and slept by the fire, again without acknowledging our presence.

"Dalha didn't seem to mind, but this man's blatant disrespect made me angry, so angry, in fact, that I had to struggle to prevent myself from harshly reprimanding him. The night was bitter cold and I thought to creep closer to the fire, but the man was huddled up there, and Dalha rested her hand on my arm and shook her head, indicating that I should not approach him. She offered me her jacket, but I refused, telling her that I was not cold, although I was shivering so fiercely that you could almost hear my teeth clattering. It was then that I felt a warm blanket of air embrace me. Soothed by that warmth, I soon fell asleep sitting up, next to Dalha, with my back against the wall of the cave.

"I awoke at dawn to find Dalha crouching outside before a fire she had made, cooking some food. The man was still asleep inside. I saw that she was heating up millet and vegetables in the pot we always carried with us. It was impossible to get vegetables in that region at that time of year, so I asked her how she had gotten the food.

"Instead of answering directly, she said quietly, 'We had a visitor last night. I had to prepare food for him, and this is what is left. I will offer it to this man and then we will leave. But first, you must eat.' She spooned some food into a small wooden bowl, and I ate what she had made, which was most delicious. Dalha has a way of spicing up food to give it a deep, rich taste. She does this with few ingredients, and I always wonder at her cooking ability.

"'What about you, Dalha? Aren't you going to eat?' I asked. She told me that she had already eaten in the night with the guest and that they had had many good laughs together. As she said that, I remembered hearing laughter while I was sleeping and recognized it as the same deep laugh of the man that I had heard a year earlier during the storm.

"I was reflecting on this when our host began to stir. He woke up and saw us but didn't greet us or speak. Dalha handed him a bowl of warm millet and vegetables and said that we must now be on our way. He nodded and took the food without thanking us, and Dalha left him with these parting words, 'What you see is not always what is. Don't mistake appearance for reality.' He was so busy eating that I doubt he paid much mind to what she said.

"She also had words for me. Before climbing onto our horses, she turned to me and said, in a voice that was sterner than usual, 'Expectations bring disappointment. Better to live without them.' Then she added, 'Blessings can come in the most unusual ways. Don't let anger interfere.'

"'Why did that man act so rudely?' I asked, wondering why she had not said anything to him about his behavior.

"'What is it that blocks one's vision?' she asked me in response to my question.

"'A restless mind and a perturbed heart,' I replied faintly, remembering her words to me.

"'And what perturbs the heart?' she asked, looking at me patiently.

"'Anger and fear,' I replied quietly. She nodded.

"'Your anger at the man prevented you from seeing the great one who came last night. It is not that hermit I am concerned about, but you. You fell into the pit of anger. Be mindful of all such traps.' Getting onto her horse, she began to ride away, and I had no choice but to follow. Tshomo, the story does not end here. There is more."

I had been following Bhasundara's narrative eagerly, hanging on her every word, hoping it was not the end. As she spoke of Dalha, her presence became real to me, and it was almost as good as having her there in the flesh.

After a slight pause, she continued: "I asked Dalha where we were going, and she replied, 'To a yogini who lives not far from here. We will be received much more warmly there.' Dalha seemed to know exactly where she wanted to go. About thirty minutes later, after picking our way slowly along rocky mountain trails, we arrived at a small hut that was hardly a hut at all, but rather an enclosure composed of piled stones built onto the side of a hill. Pushing open the rickety wooden door, which was hardly a door, we entered a small, dark room where a woman about Dalha's age was seated by a stove, the only noticeable object in the room.

"She seemed to know Dalha, because she rose immediately and greeted her warmly, saying, 'You have come after all this time.' I glanced around while they exchanged greetings. The hut was composed of that single small room, the dirt floor covered by worn mats. In one corner was a pile of old blankets. In another were a few tattered cushions for seating. Near the stove were a few pots, cups, and bowls. That was all.

"The yogini offered us po cha to warm ourselves and set out some food that had been heating on the stove, treating us as honored guests—a great contrast to the place we had just left. It was a relief to be so graciously received. This woman called Dalha by a different name, but I was used to that because people have various names for her. I was the one who first began calling her Dalha, but that is another story, which I will tell you at another time.

"'You must spend several days with me,' the woman insisted. Dalha nodded, and I spoke up to recount the story of the rude man in the cave, the one who would not even acknowledge us.

"'He doesn't think much of women,' she explained with a small laugh, 'and so I am not surprised that he treated you that way.'

"'I didn't mind for myself, but for Dalha.'

"'It is of no matter,' said Dalha, brushing off the subject.

"'I have experienced worse treatment from him,' the woman expressed. I looked at her inquisitively. She turned to face Dalha, who nodded her approval, and the yogini proceeded to tell me her story. 'Several years ago, that man called together the ascetics from throughout this area. I heard about this gathering from another one of the hermits and traveled by foot all the way to that man's cave, where I found about a dozen male hermits seated in meditation. Sitting down near the others, I felt the powerful energy and quickly entered a deep interior state. Soon, though, I was abruptly brought back to outer consciousness by that man, who stood before me and sternly instructed me to leave the gathering, saying that my presence was disturbing the sacred vibration. He told me that the hermits had come together to combine their spiritual efforts to combat a rising negative force and that I would only distract them. I responded by saying that I saw no reason to leave and would like to join their meditation. In response, he began hurling insults at me in front of the others until, unable to bear the humiliation, I was forced to depart. Along the walk back to my hut, I encountered many mishaps and almost lost my life.

"'The Compassionate One, Guru Rinpoche, saved me,' she explained quietly. 'My emotions had been aroused, my mind disturbed, and because I was not attentive, while climbing one of the steep inclines I tripped over a large rock and nearly fell into a very deep hole. At that very moment, a man, looking like a simple nomad, happened to be passing by. He reached out and prevented me from falling and helped to steady my steps. Then, looking at me intently, he said, 'When the heart and mind are disturbed, danger comes. Do not be affected by the confusion in the minds of others and be grateful for the gifts you receive.' As he walked away, I realized that he was the great Guru himself. I could tell by his gaze. Those were no ordinary eyes. That night I had a powerful experience in meditation, one that confirmed for me that indeed the man who had saved me was the great Guru. I realized that had I not been insulted and forced to leave the gathering, perhaps I never would have met that beneficent one. This is how he works, in such mysterious ways. My humiliation turned out to be a great blessing, because had he not come to me, I might have missed that important teaching.'

"I was struck by her story but didn't understand how humiliation could be a teaching," continued Bhasundara. "Observing my confusion, Dalha leaned over and whispered to me, 'Humiliation awakens one from the illusion of pride. It hammers the ego, which needs a good hammering every now and then.'" Bhasundara smiled as she recalled those words of Dalha. Then she paused and reminded me to drink the tea she had served. I had been so engrossed in her words that I had not taken a sip or tasted the food she had set before me. As I lifted the cup to my mouth, she continued, "When I heard the yogini's story, I thought it very strange that Dalha had insisted on going to the cave where that nasty man was living. Clearly, she was aware of our host's experience, so why did she want to meet the man who had insulted her friend? In answer to my unasked question, Dalha responded quietly, 'I wanted to give him one more chance, to see whether he had changed in these few years. Sadly, he has not and will now have to pay the price.'

"I wondered what she meant by that, but our discussion ended there. We had long since finished our food and were sitting around the stove talking. The conversation now ebbed away, leaving a soothing silence in its place. Only then did I realize how tired my body was. Sensing this, our host rose and went to the corner of the room where mats and blankets were piled and made a bed for me, indicating that I should come and take my rest. I did and fell asleep instantly but awoke sometime in the middle of the night. The woman, deep in meditation, was still seated on the floor by the stove, which was continuing to radiate heat, but Dalha was not in the hut. I didn't get up right away to go look for her because I was quite chilled, despite the blankets. So I lay there, curled up, until my ears caught the metallic sound of clashing swords coming from outside, as if we were being attacked. In a panic, I jumped up and pushed open the door of the hut, where I found the spritely body of Dalha engaged in a most elaborate sword dance. Oddly, though, there was nobody else there. I had clearly heard the hard-hitting sound of sword against sword, but there was only Dalha, who was wielding a long sword in her right hand and waving it as she leapt from side to side with great speed, as if fighting a combatant. I watched for a few moments and then a bitter wind blew, forcing me back inside. I crept back under the blankets but didn't fall asleep again until I heard her enter the hut.

"By morning, I had only the vaguest memory of the incident and wondered if I had dreamed it. The next night I stayed awake, and as I drew the blankets tightly around me, I heard Dalha quietly leave the hut and engage once again in her sword battle. I wondered where she had gotten the sword, as we had never possessed one, and I hadn't noticed a sword in the hut. Some time passed before she finally came inside, and after that I fell asleep. When I awoke, I knew that what I had heard had not been a dream, but I dared not say anything in front of our host.

"On the third day, as nightfall was approaching, we heard footsteps along the path to the hut. Peering outside, to my surprise, I saw the rude ascetic hurrying toward us, the one who had treated us so badly. I waited in anticipation of what would follow, thinking to myself that whatever was to happen had been planned by Dalha. I quickly informed her and our host of his arrival. Exchanging glances, they simply nodded, not at all perturbed, as I was, by his uninvited appearance.

"As soon as the man entered the hut and his eyes fell upon Dalha, who was calmly seated by the stove, a look of shock crossed his face and he exclaimed, 'So it is you!' At that moment, Dalha's eyes became fierce, something I had never seen before, but she didn't speak. She only glared at him. Falling to the ground, he prostrated himself and spoke in a much-humbled tone, saying, 'Last night while I was asleep, my cave shook and then collapsed. I escaped just in time; it was a miracle that I survived. In the night, before the collapse, I had a dream in which a voice told me to travel to this hut, where a woman wearing a red hat was staying, and there I would find my guru. Is that you?' he asked hesitantly, looking up into the face of Dalha. As you may have observed, Dalha always wears that red hat no matter where she is, inside a dwelling or out.

"Dalha shook her head and spoke in the low, gravelly voice that she sometimes assumes, replying, 'No. Guru Rinpoche has sent you to this great woman yogini, whom you once insulted. She is the one who must accept you.'" Bhasundara laughed, as a look of surprise crossed my face. "Tshomo, you should have seen that man's expression when Dalha spoke those words; it was worth all the difficulties we had endured. Had I not witnessed that scene, I never would have believed that someone could change so rapidly. It was surely a miracle.

"The man didn't respond, and Dalha's eyes looked as if they would burn right through him, while our host sat there silently. I wondered what would come next. After a few moments, the man began to plead with our host to accept him as a disciple. Finally, she replied, 'How can you seek teachings from one whom you felt was unworthy?'

"'After I forced you to leave, one by one, the others left, claiming that I was the unworthy one,' he replied humbly. 'I regret the way I spoke to you.' Then, turning to Dalha, he murmured apologetically, 'I didn't recognize you when you appeared at my cave. I didn't know that it was he who sent you.'

"'There is no need to recognize me,' she replied sternly. 'Everyone who approaches you should be treated as the great Guru himself. This you have failed to do again and again. How will you rectify yourself?'

"'I will start at the beginning,' he murmured. Turning to face our host, he said in a pleading tone, 'I will fix up this hut for you and build another one for myself nearby, fetch wood and water for you, and perform any chore you need, if only you will accept me.'

"The yogini didn't respond right away but then replied calmly, 'What need have I of your service when the great One himself takes care of me?'

"Prostrating himself fully, the ascetic spoke softly: 'It is he who has sent me to you. Will you turn me away?'

"Letting out a playful laugh, she replied, 'That is another matter. How can I turn away a request from the great One?'

"'So be it,' announced Dalha firmly, as she rose and made ready to leave. 'I am glad to see this matter come to conclusion.' Then I heard her whisper to our host, 'You will turn him into a good student, I have no doubt, and spare him from much future suffering.'

"'Are we leaving now, Dalha?' I asked nervously as I watched her movements. It was already dark.

"'Our work here is done. There is no need to stay.' With a quick goodbye, we left the hut, climbed onto our horses, and rode away. That night as we sat in our tent, Dalha told me that Guru Rinpoche had been in the hut with us and that the man had seen him. That was how she knew for certain he was sincere. He could not have seen the guru had his heart not changed, and that was why her friend accepted him as a student. 'If his cave had not fallen in and he had not had the dream and come to our yogini friend, he would have had to endure much suffering in a future life. Now he has the chance to be spared,' she said, 'and all due to the compassion of the great Guru. In addition,' Dalha added quietly, 'I was worried about my aging friend, who has nobody to look after her. The great Guru saw this and responded, as he always does. Now this once irritable man, who had disdain for women, will care for her. So many needs have now been met,' she said with a slight laugh.

"I couldn't sleep that night, as I was so disturbed by the fact that this unruly man had seen Guru Rinpoche and I had not, despite my years of devotion. In the middle of the night, Dalha, knowing that I was awake, scolded me, saying, 'After all that, you are still holding on to your anger. That is why you couldn't see the one who was right in front of you. That man let it go, but you could not. As soon as the cave collapsed, he woke up from his delusion of anger. Do I need to collapse this tent to awaken you?'

"At that moment, I released the tears I had been holding back. In a gentler voice, Dalha comforted me, saying, 'Anger arises, but you must learn not to hold on to it. Let it go. Just as the waves in a lake come and go, so you must let these negative emotions pass through you, without giving them any credence. Don't cling to them, Bhasundara. Don't cling to anything.'

"That experience was a great teaching. I have had many opportunities after that to learn not to hold on to anger. Dalha is a relentless teacher.

She sees one's weak spots and brings experience after experience to help uproot the traits that are obstacles to one's progress. For me, it was anger at injustice, but one can't hold on even to that. For you, Tshomo, it will be your fear. I see it lurking there in your mind, and I am sure you will have ample opportunities to overcome it."

A shudder shot through me as she spoke those words. To change the subject, I asked, "Is that the end of the story, then?"

Bhasundara nodded. "The next day as we packed up our tent, I asked Dalha about what I had witnessed during the night, the sword dance and the ferocity I had seen in her eyes. She replied to me thoughtfully, saying, 'Anger is born of thwarted desire and unmet expectation, but there is also the appearance of anger that is born of compassion and is not really anger at all, but rather a fierce determination; only that can bring a beneficial result. Fire is needed to burn away dross, but in the burning of that dross, there is joy—great joy—at the prospect of the freedom that will come.' Her words sank deep into my mind, and I reflected on them for years after. Even now, they return to me. I came to understand why all the goddesses have both gentle and fierce demeanors. That fierceness is needed every bit as much as the gentler side. It was after that experience at Mt. Tise that I also came to understand how the two of them, Guru Rinpoche and Dalha, work hand in hand. No longer do I make any distinction between them, and neither should you."

A slight smile broke across Bhasundara's lips as she saw the look of amazement on my face. I knew that I would have been terribly afraid had I seen that fierce side of Dalha, as I had been frightened when I first met her. I was glad that this was not a side that she showed to me. I also knew that Bhasundara was sharing so much for a reason. Perhaps she was becoming the vehicle through which Dalha could reach me, but what was the message for me? That I couldn't quite grasp. I knew that I wasn't ready for the kind of training Bhasundara had received, and I was glad to take only the smallest steps toward Dalha. The thought occurred to me that it was enough for me now to experience her from a distance.

I was hesitant to leave Bhasundara, but I knew that I had to return home to my children. I had stayed far longer than planned. Thanking my friend and telling her that I would come again soon to visit, I left her cottage. On the ride back to Lhasa, I began to feel more strongly that it was Dalha speaking to me through the voice of Bhasundara, that, in fact, she had already accepted me into her care.

Struck by this realization, I pulled the reins of the horse and came to a sudden halt. Staring out at the path ahead, I realized that without my knowing it, she had fulfilled one of my greatest desires, to find someone to teach me. I didn't have to go anywhere. I didn't even need to be in her presence. She was giving me the teachings I needed, and all I had to do was to listen and try to understand the message behind the words.

I had been struggling with how to abide by her counsel to live with the goddess, so often wondering what that meant—a goddess who seemed distant and abstract, unknowable. But, bit by bit, listening to Bhasundara's stories, I was coming to know Dalha in a very intimate way, and it became clear to me that she was the one whose presence I had to keep close, not any faraway goddess. I would focus my mind on her and try to absorb the teachings she was giving me through Bhasundara.

Is this the way she works, I wondered in amazement? All this time I had thought of Bhasundara's stories as entertaining tales about a mysterious woman. But no longer. When I reflected on the stories I had heard that day, I realized that Dalha's actions did not seem quite so unfathomable. I now saw them as acts of compassion, as Bhasundara had indicated, and knew that I was only beginning to understand her.

CHAPTER 6

A Long-Awaited Gift

Although it was late, I didn't return home right away. Rather than riding through the alpine forest that separated Dalha's hut from Lhasa, I descended from my horse and walked slowly alongside him, deeply immersed in thought. Before leaving the forested area, I found a place to sit. How I wished now that I could speak with my father, who had passed away a few years earlier. He had been an ardent devotee of Guru Rinpoche, but I had never paid much attention when he would tell us stories about him, and now I couldn't remember any of them. I had always thought of Guru Rinpoche as belonging solely to the Buddhists and so shut him out of my mind, but now I wanted to find out everything I could about him.

After leaving family life for the monastery, my father had visited his children infrequently, only once or twice a year. He had always been a quiet, inward-looking man, the opposite of my outward-going mother, and in his later years he had become even more so, and I hadn't sought him out. Although I knew him to be a person of great knowledge, I had been too absorbed in my own internal conflict to inquire about Guru Rinpoche or the other great Buddhist masters. I now understood that this was out of a false sense of loyalty to my mother. Clinging to the Bon path had been my way of feeling connected to her; it had helped me overcome, to some degree, the separation caused by her early death.

But that was no longer needed. Dalha was teaching me to integrate the two traditions. I didn't have to choose.

Although several years had passed since I had seen Dalha at Lhamo La-tso, as I sat in the forest, I became very much aware of her presence. It was she, I knew, who had inspired Bhasundara to speak that day of Guru Rinpoche, and I understood that the purpose was to help me resolve the conflict that had troubled me since childhood. For the first time, I berated myself for not having taken more seriously the Buddhist stories that my father had shared with me during my growing up years. "But now I have Yeshe!" I suddenly exclaimed out loud, rising from my seat on the ground. In many ways he was like my father, wise and inward looking, well read on all matters relating to Buddhism, and most disciplined in his meditation practice, but he was also far more accessible, expressive, humorous, and eager to share with me. My relationship with my husband had far surpassed any expectations of a loving, intimate relationship. As I stood there in the forest, I realized that since our marriage, I had done the same with him that I had with my father, preventing myself from benefiting from his extensive knowledge. I decided that this would no longer be the case, and suddenly I was overcome with the desire to see my husband. Yeshe had been traveling for several months but was due to return home any day. Perhaps he had already arrived. The very thought sent me leaping onto my horse's back and galloping homeward, with new appreciation for my husband.

Another week was to pass before Yeshe's return. For the first few days after his arrival, he was busy with the children, as he always was when returning from a long journey, to make up for all the time away, so we had no opportunity to speak privately. Finally, we had an evening alone. I had never told him the details of my few meetings with Dalha, but he knew about her and understood that she was someone I respected a great deal. He was pleased because he had always wanted me to find a Bon teacher. At the very beginning of our marriage, he had told me, "The spiritual path is a very private one. Only share with me what you feel comfortable sharing." Not wanting to pry, he rarely questioned me about my spiritual life, and rarely did I volunteer any information.

He was aware of my budding friendship with Bhasundara, and this pleased him. Having friends to support and help you along your spiritual journey is important, he had told me. But somehow, I had excluded Yeshe from this category. I hadn't thought of him as a spiritual companion, in part because I viewed us as pursuing two different spiritual paths. When he would begin to speak of his Buddhist practice or tell a story of a Buddhist teacher, something in me would shut down, perhaps because I thought it might threaten my long-held convictions. I had never considered that in drawing a curtain between us, I was closing him out of my spiritual life and refusing to enter his. Over time, I think he came to understand that I had drawn clear boundary lines between Bon and Buddhism. Now I wanted to tell him that those boundaries were being erased, only I didn't quite know where to begin.

"What do you know about Guru Rinpoche?" I asked one evening when we were alone, chatting in the room where we slept. Still tired from his long journey, he was resting on the bed. It was the first night since his return that he managed to stay awake after the children had gone to sleep.

He smiled at my question. "I have spoken to you about him many times."

"You may have spoken, but perhaps I haven't heard. Now I want to hear," I replied softly.

"Why this sudden interest?"

"I learned from Bhasundara how deeply he is loved by Dalha, and I was surprised."

He chuckled. "Why should this surprise you?"

"Did you know that he travels on the wind?" I asked, opening my eyes wide, thinking this would shock him.

"And on the rays of the sun," he added, amused by my newborn interest. "It is said that on the tenth day of the waxing moon, he appears in the rays of the sun and blesses all sentient beings. Special ceremonies are conducted on those days. There are many, many stories of that great Guru and his *dakini* consort (a female embodiment of enlightened energy), which I will share with you another day," he said in a weary voice. "He sees far into the future and has trained many disciples to continue his work centuries and millennia from now. Among them are twenty-five who are well advanced in spiritual realization and who have vowed to be reborn, wherever and whenever he directs them, to help alleviate the suffering of humankind. It is also said that he has hidden many secret teachings for these reborn disciples to discover in the future, teachings appropriate for the different ages. I don't think there will ever be an end to those discoveries. Even after a thousand years, his reborn disciples will come with new readings of ancient teachings to help us remember. Some of these teachings are hidden away in Samye Monastery, which is where our son will go for training."

"Our son, Yeshe?" I looked at him despairingly. He never stopped talking about this son who had not yet arrived. Our youngest daughter was now eight years old, and in those eight years I had not gotten pregnant again. I would have given up on the thought of having another child if not for Yeshe's strong desire for a son, but despite his desire, this baby refused to appear. I had not forgotten Dalha's words to me about having a son when Pumo and I had seen her last at Lhamo La-tso, but it didn't seem that her prediction was coming to fruition. Yeshe was now in his mid-forties, and his many years of long voyages were wearing him out. Why did he still long for a son when we had three wonderful daughters to celebrate, I wondered? I was more than content with what had been given.

Yeshe closed his eyes. I could see how tired he was, so I didn't press him further. I simply whispered, "Let me know the next tenth day of the waxing moon, and I will look for that great Guru in the sunlight. Perhaps he will bless us with the son for whom you yearn."

Another year passed. Pumo was getting ready to leave Lhasa with Tashi and her three children. He had been commissioned to paint murals for a new temple under construction several hours away, and she was going with him. Increasingly, Pumo was working alongside Tashi at the monasteries. When I asked how they allowed her to do so, she replied with a slight laugh, "The monks don't know that I am a woman."

"How can they not know?" I asked in astonishment.

She explained: "I wear Tashi's clothing, tie up my hair and look down at the ground when I am in their presence, so they don't get a clear view of my face. Tashi introduces me as his assistant, and I don't think they ever imagine that he would bring along a woman."

"That is brave of him," I remarked. "He must regard your work highly." I was proud of my sister. In her youth, she had always admired paintings, but never in her wildest dreams had she thought that one day she would be painting Buddhist murals at some of the most prominent monasteries. I knew that she viewed this as a blessing from Dalha, who had told her as much during our visit to lake Lhamo La-tso. Dalha's prediction for Pumo had come true, but what of mine—what of that son she had foretold?

"Initially, I was only painting the borders, the floral designs," Pumo explained. "But Tashi has been pleased with my work, and now has me painting all sections of the murals. Padma, we may be gone for two years or more, as the monastery is extensive and there is much work. I want to go back to the lake before we leave. I had hoped to visit it on the fifteenth anniversary of Ama-la's death, but it wasn't possible then."

I was thoughtful for a few moments, remembering that the last time I had visited the lake was with Yeshe, just before my miscarriage. That visit had left me fearful, but that fear was long gone. It was time to return.

We decided to stay with the same Drokpa family who had hosted us on our first visit many years earlier. Pumo had painted a small image of the goddess Nam Tsho Chukmo to give to the family, and I brought gifts of tea that Yeshe had carried back on his last journey to the Song as well as other food items. Pumo made all the arrangements and the two of us set out alone, leaving our children with their fathers and the family helpers. I had forgotten how arduous the trip was—a journey that included riding and climbing up and through mountain passes—but I also understood that such challenges are a necessary part of any pilgrimage.

Many years had passed, and I had also not remembered the trip's spectacular beauty, which encompassed so many different terrains and landscapes. It was the warmer months, and flowering bushes and edible plants clothed the meadows, providing much food for the wandering yaks and goats and the occasional Drokpa family. It was only as we ascended past the tree line that the colors became sparser, the air thinner, and the brilliant sunlight more startling. I remembered from my previous visits how filled with awe I had been each time I glimpsed the great sapphire lake in the distance, as seen from one of the mountain peaks. This time, as we approached, it was like entering an ethereal realm. The brilliance of the sun shining on her waters enhanced her natural color, which was clearer than any blue gem I had ever seen.

Tired from the arduous journey, we rested in our tent the first day, taking our meal with the host family. On the second day, we went to the lake and sat quietly by her side. After an hour of silence, Pumo began to unpack some items from the bag she was carrying, taking out three small jugs filled with water, two small metal bowls, and her prayer beads. At several points along the journey, she had stopped to ask directions to fresh-water springs. She would taste the water, and if it was sweet, she filled one of the small jugs, but she said that this water was not for drinking. We had other jugs to quench our thirst and that of our horses. I wondered what she was doing, but didn't inquire, thinking perhaps she wanted to save the water in case we ran low.

As we sat by the sacred lake, she arranged everything on the ground before us and asked, "Do you remember Ama-la speaking to us about the spirits in the natural world?" I nodded. "Do you remember what she called them? I have forgotten."

"I remember very well, because so many times I heard Ama-la calling them by name when she would do the rituals." I was thoughtful for a few moments as I tried to imagine my mother speaking with the nature spirits, and then I began. "The spirits that live in the earth are called

Sadak, and Ama-la said they help or hinder the growth of plants. It is important to be on good terms with them and to treat them respectfully. If we harm the soil, they will respond by withholding their energies, and poor crops or even famine will follow. They can also cause earthquakes.

"The spirits that reside in rocks and trees are called the *Nyen*. They can also be beneficial or troublesome, depending on how we treat them. If we don't tend to our forests properly, the Nyen will withdraw their protective energy and fire will consume the trees. They can also cause landslides. Ama-la often spoke with the Nyen who live in the stones. It seemed she was on intimate terms with them, and that is why she always kept small stones with her."

"You are right, Padma. I had forgotten about that. Wherever we went, Ama-la took great care to look at the stones and consciously select certain ones to keep with her."

I nodded. "She once told me that some stones are protective, housing beneficial powers and spirits, but negative spirits can also hide themselves in stones, so one had to learn to discern. Pumo, I never understood how spirits can live in stones, because stones are not alive like trees and the earth."

"How do we know that, Padma, and what does it mean to be alive? Consciousness is everywhere, in everything."

"I suppose you are right," I replied thoughtfully. "The spirits that reside in the air are called the *Tsen*. They keep the air clean and pure, and in this way the Tsen nourish life. They carry seeds and bring cooling breezes to diminish the heat. But if we contaminate the air, they will become angry and carry diseases to us through it. They can also cause storms and bring much destruction if not treated with respect.

"The ones that live in water are the *Lu*. As long as we keep the rivers and lakes clean and pure, they will nourish all living beings and bring adequate rain. But if we disregard the lakes and dirty them, disrupting their flow, droughts and floods can come. When I came here with Ama-la, she said that by looking into a lake, river, or stream you can tell if the Lu are happy or not. If the waters are clear and freely moving, that is a good sign."

"The Lu in this lake are happy," Pumo murmured, as she looked out over the moving fields of water that inched up to the shoreline in a rhythmic pulse.

"No one would dare dirty the waters of this sacred lake," I replied firmly. "When Ama-la used to take me to the forest, we would sit by the stream and she would show me how to express gratitude to the Lu spirits, but I can't say that I do that now, even though I know such rituals help keep the balance in nature. Whenever she did her rituals, no matter where she was, she would always acknowledge the Sadak, the Nyen, the Tsen, and the Lu because they were all related, she said, and if she left out one, the others would feel it. The earth, the trees, the stones, the mountains, the rivers and lakes, and the air were all part of one family, she often told me."

"I never learned any of the rituals," replied Pumo, with a note of regret, "and I have forgotten much of what Ama-la told us. But I feel we need to make an offering, Padma, to the water spirits. The last time you came with Yeshe, you didn't make an offering and you had the miscarriage. I have been thinking about why that happened. Perhaps you did something to offend the water spirits. When you came the first time with Ama-la, she made an offering, didn't she?"

I nodded. "She did a ritual by the side of the lake, but I didn't pay much attention. I have to admit, Pumo, that after Ama-la died, I lost my sense of connection to the spirits and hardly give them much thought. Even though I am a Bonpo and want to be like her, I doubt that I can ever be, that I can ever fully believe what she believed." I had never expressed my doubts to her, or to anyone, for that matter, as my feelings were not something I wanted to readily admit, even to myself. For years I conducted the rituals I had learned but cannot say that I saw or felt any results from them. They didn't make me feel any closer to the spirits.

"Do you remember what Apa-la used to say?" she asked, looking at me in surprise. Nodding, I replied with a smile. "He would often repeat these words: 'That is what your mother believes, and I believe your mother, and so I also believe.'"

"Let us pretend that Ama-la is watching us and let us do a ceremony, as she would want us to do, to acknowledge and offer respect to the spirits here. Before leaving Lhasa, I asked around to find out what type of offering would be appropriate," explained Pumo. "The waters of Nam Tsho are salty, and I was told that these water spirits like to taste sweet fresh water. That is why I gathered the water from the freshwater springs along our journey." Handing me a metal bowl, she poured water from each of the three jugs into one of the two bowls she had brought and asked me to do the same. Then, standing up and taking her prayer beads in her hand, she looked at me apologetically and said, "I only know Buddhist chants."

"I know the Bon prayers. I will chant first and then you chant."

"After we do this, Padma, you must ask the goddess for a blessing, and I will do the same."

I sighed. "What can I ask for, Pumo, except a son for Yeshe, and I have asked for that so many times already."

"Ask again," she whispered as she closed her eyes. "Perhaps this time, here at this sacred place, the goddess will respond." Standing beside her, I began to recite the words that I had heard Ama-la say, invoking the Sadak, the Nyen, the Tsen, and the Lu.

After I finished, Pumo began to chant a Buddhist mantra I had never heard before. I didn't even know that she knew the chants, but it was not surprising, considering that she had been spending much time at Buddhist temples and monasteries. I listened to the rhythmic droning until her voice receded, merging into the lapping waves. We were each holding a bowl filled with clear spring water. After a few moments of silence, I opened my eyes and saw her toss the water into the lake as she called out to the Lu spirits to receive the offering, expressing gratitude to them for keeping the water pure and clear. As I did the same, I made an additional prayer to the Lu to help me bear a son for my husband.

When we were finished, we sat back down, and I thanked Pumo. "It is good that we have honored the spirits here. Even people who don't believe in them should do so because it must bring some benefit. What did you pray for, Pumo?"

She looked at me tenderly. “I prayed that your wish for a son be fulfilled. I prayed both to Tara and Nam Tsho Chukmo.”

I was touched by her words, realizing that she had brought me here for this purpose. “And I prayed to Dalha,” I said quietly. “She is the one I pray to these days. Bhasundara has told me that I can’t go find Dalha. She has to find me, but I do yearn to see her again.”

“It has been many years now since we met her at Lhamo La-tso. Do you think you would recognize her?” she asked.

“Of course. How could I not?”

We stayed three days at the lake and then began the journey home. Along the way, we stopped again at the freshwater springs to fill our jugs, but this time the water was for our consumption and for our horses. On one of our rest stops, Pumo tripped over a rock and sprained her ankle, and so on our third stop for water, I told her to rest by the horses. I took two of the water jugs and went to find the spring, which was only a short walk away.

When I arrived, I found an older woman standing at the spot where water was abundantly spouting from the ground and flowing down through a pile of rocks. I watched as she filled her cup with water and took a drink. “It is very sweet, isn’t it,” I commented, without paying much attention to her. She nodded and, holding out her cup to me, said, “I see you are thirsty, child. Take a drink from my cup.” Graciously declining, I bent down to the spring, without looking at her closely, as my mind was on filling the jugs and getting back to Pumo as quickly as possible. We still had a long ride ahead of us. Strangely, as I placed one of my jugs before the running water, the water stopped flowing from the earth.

She chuckled. “The Lu are playing with you. The world does not turn on belief. Believe in them or not, they do what they are meant to do.” Still holding out her cup for me, she gently urged again, “Drink from my cup, child, and see behind appearances. It is your own desire from the past and the desire of your husband that will bring this son to you. Do not waver in your faith.”

Still reluctant to take the cup she was holding out to me, I stood up and, for the first time, took a good look at her. I didn't think she was someone I had met before, but then how did she know that I had been doubting the spirits, and how did she know of my desire for a son? When I still didn't take the cup from her hand, she shook her head and, putting down her half-filled cup, began to walk away, muttering, "You must learn to see what is right before your eyes."

It was not until she had nearly disappeared behind some bushes that I saw the red hat through the maze of bramble and brush. When she had been by the spring, she had not worn that hat and she had not looked like Dalha, but now I hurried after the woman whom I suspected was her. Again and again, I called out, looking in all directions, but she was nowhere to be found. For several moments, I stood there in a daze, trying to make sense of what had happened and berating myself for not having recognized her. Then it occurred to me that Dalha wanted me to drink from her cup.

Walking back to the spring, I lifted the cup and drank all the water that was left, still upset that I had not seen through her disguise. As soon as I finished drinking, the water from the spring began to flow again, and I filled our two jugs, my emotions too roiled for me to pay much heed to her words. I had been longing to see her and she had come to me, but I had not recognized her.

"The red hat—she wasn't wearing it at first"—I muttered, as I walked back to Pumo in a distracted state. That distinctive red woolen hat, draped over her ears and the back of her neck and lined with a small band of fur around the edges, was clearly a sign that it was her. Did she not want me to recognize her, or had she been testing me? On the ride back to Lhasa, her words returned to me, and I wondered if she was reaffirming the blessing of a son. She had also said that the spirits were real. They were conscious in the water, the earth, the trees, stones, and air. Although I hadn't fully believed my mother, I had to believe her. I didn't say anything to Pumo, but as we drew closer to Lhasa, I became convinced that Dalha, by her very appearance to me, had bestowed a blessing. After all, it was she to whom I had prayed at the lake.

Yeshe had been waiting anxiously for my return and received me with greater affection and desire than ever before. We had been apart for much of our marriage, but this brief separation seemed to have increased his ardor for me. The night of my return we came together in a powerful union of love. Nine months later, our son Tenzin Sangye was born.

Yeshe had not been surprised when I told him of my pregnancy. When I mentioned the rituals Pumo and I had conducted at the lake, the Buddhist chanting and the Bon prayers, he smiled and replied, "The day that you returned from the lake was the tenth day of the waxing moon." He viewed Tenzin as a gift from Guru Rinpoche, and I viewed him as a gift from the one I knew as Dalha, whose cup I had shared.

CHAPTER 7

The Training of a Monk

I hadn't seen Bhasundara during the whole time of my pregnancy, which had been a difficult one and had kept me close to home. Shortly after the baby was born, she surprised me with a visit. I didn't know how she knew about the birth, because I hadn't even been able to confide in her that I was pregnant, but somehow, she was aware. Previously, all our interactions had been at her cottage. I had preferred it that way, thinking it best to keep a separation between my family and spiritual life. Now she was meeting my family for the first time. Yeshe was at home, and he was the first to greet her. I watched the respectful interaction between the two of them before introducing her to my daughters and newborn son. In the years that I had known her, Bhasundara had not lost her childlike ways or looks. Although we were close in age, she could have been mistaken for a young maiden, not only because of her small stature and slender, sprightly form, but also her sparkly eyes and playful nature. After some light conversation with the children, I was able to draw her outside for some time alone in our sparse garden, carrying with me my newborn son.

"I've come to perform a blessing ritual for him," she explained, laying out on a small table the items she had brought—a *shang* (round ritual bell), a *melong* (round metal mirror), a flat drum, a brass bowl, and some juniper for burning. We sat in silence for several minutes and then she began ringing the bell, burning the juniper, and invoking the spirits as she beat the drum. Calling upon both Dalha and Guru Rinpoche, she asked them to bless the child. This surprised me, as I had never heard her call upon Guru Rinpoche when conducting a Bon ritual, but I was pleased. When she finished the ritual, I asked her what had inspired her to invoke them both.

"He is your child, but also Yeshe's," she replied in a serious tone. "You must let him find his own path. Besides, I hope you understand by now that wherever one of those two great masters is, the other is present as well."

I smiled as I replied, "Yes, you have tried hard to make me understand that." After a pause, I asked, somewhat hesitantly, "Bhasundara, do you think this child will show an interest in spiritual matters? Yeshe is so sure of it. Tenzin has barely arrived in the world and my husband already has great plans for him." My three daughters had expressed little interest in spiritual affairs, and I never pressed them in any way. I suspected that this son would be different.

"You will have to wait and see what is in store for him," she replied noncommittally.

"It was Dalha who first told me, many years ago, that I would have a son. I so wish she could be here to bless him," I murmured as Bhasundara rose from her seat, packed up her ritual items and prepared to leave. I rose as well, making a motion to see her out.

"She already has blessed him," she replied in a matter-of-fact tone. I looked at her questioningly. "At the spring that day when you were returning from Nam Tsho. Don't you remember?"

"How did you know about that?" I had not told Bhasundara of that meeting, ashamed as I was of not having recognized Dalha.

"I know that you didn't recognize her at first, Tshomo, but don't blame yourself. There is a lesson in that. A similar thing happened to me recently. I will tell you that story." We both sat down again and I waited expectantly.

She didn't speak right away. Her eyes glazed over, as if hesitating to share the experience, but after a few moments she began. "These past weeks, I have been tending to a very sick young boy who wasn't responding to the plant remedies I prepared for him. I was baffled and distracted, struggling to understand what was wrong with the formula. I had combined three plants known to treat his ailment, but the medicine wasn't having any effect. One day when I was in the market, a young woman approached me and handed me a packet of dried herbs, telling me that this was the missing ingredient needed to help treat the boy. That was all she said. I hesitated to take it, but she pressed the package into my hand and disappeared into the stream of people passing by.

"I was a little annoyed and assumed that she had mistaken me for someone else. After all, how could she possibly know who I was treating and what his ailment was? And why did she think she knew the plants better than I, who have studied under Dalha for many years. I was about to toss the packet away, when I thought I heard laughter and the words, 'You think you know all there is to know!' Sometimes the mind can play tricks, and I assumed it was my imagination. Even so, I didn't throw it away. When I got home, I opened the packet and recognized the herb, but it was not one used for treating the boy's ailment and I thought the herb might even make the boy sicker, so I put it aside.

"Over the next few days, my distress increased as I saw the boy's condition worsening, but I stubbornly decided to stick with my formula. I made another attempt, slightly changing the proportions of the three plants I was using, but, again, the medicine produced no good effect and I was really beside myself, unsure of what to do.

"I hadn't seen Dalha in a long time, and she had also been absent from my thoughts. I had been so disturbed by my failed medicinal treatment that I had not even thought to call upon her. Then she appeared in my dream and scolded me, saying, 'How stubborn you are. Accept what I give you. It will heal both the boy and you.'

"This time I heard her. I awoke from the dream and began to create a new formula, combining the three plants I had used previously and adding the herb the woman in the market had given me. To my surprise, the boy recovered quite quickly. Clearly, the special herb had strengthened the formula, making it more potent and stimulating the healing process.

"I wondered about the meaning of this whole experience. Why had I been so resistant? Why had I not seen Dalha's hand behind that woman? Why did I not heed her voice the first time she spoke within me? Many days had passed between the time I received the herb and when I used it, and during that time the poor boy could have died because of my stubbornness and pride. It was a very humbling experience for me. After living with Dalha for so many years, I still don't always recognize when she comes in disguise or sends a messenger, when she speaks to me through the voice of someone else. One must develop discernment to know what is real and what is not, and that is not easy. We are continually growing and learning how to attune ourselves to that inner guidance, which is often subtle and so easy to dismiss.

"Had you walked away from the spring that day and not taken the water Dalha had offered you, you would have missed the blessing. But you did recognize her in the end."

"It was the red hat," I murmured. "Without that, I would not have known her. But, Bhasundara, was it the water that helped me to conceive?"

She laughed. "Not at all. That is the point. It was Dalha's blessing, which came when the conditions were right. With the young boy I was treating, it was also not really the medicine that healed him, but Dalha's blessing. She never likes to take credit for things and so she used that plant medicine as a vehicle to test my faith and to bring me back into attunement with her. As long as I was not feeling that direct connection with her, she could not extend her healing power through me to the boy. My attunement was necessary, but I had been too distracted and sure of myself. It was my pride that blocked her guidance. I have learned a great lesson."

"Was she, then, that young woman in the market?"

"Perhaps and perhaps not. Most likely, Dalha was working through the woman, but I won't even ask her when I see her next, because it doesn't matter. It was her voice I heard internally bringing a message, and I didn't listen. I was too hardheaded." Bhasundara knocked her fist against her head gently and laughed.

"How do we develop discernment, Bhasundara?"

"That is a question to which there is no easy answer. But I do know that attunement helps to develop discernment. One must keep the mind unperturbed and unruffled. Your experience at the spring was similar, only it was Dalha herself who appeared to you then, but your mind was elsewhere. She was testing you to see whether you could recognize her. You must know, Tshomo, that she does not always appear in the beloved form that we know best. She can come in any form. Remember that she first appeared to me in the body of a tiger. When you returned home from the lake, you conceived so quickly; it wasn't the water that made you conceive, but the blessing flowing from Dalha."

"It was also the tenth night of the waxing moon," I murmured, wondering if Bhasundara even knew that story about Guru Rinpoche and the beneficent deeds he performs on that day.

"Have you not understood, Tshomo? There is no difference between them—her blessing, his blessing. Why do you distinguish between the two? Her appearance that day was no accident. Weren't you delayed by a day in returning home?"

I nodded. "We had a few mishaps on the first day of our journey back and had to travel more slowly."

"That was also Dalha," she smiled. "She wanted to meet you at the spring and have you return home at the right moment. So much depends on timing," she said quietly. "After all, the stars also have to be in the right alignment."

"Bhasundara, when will Dalha return? I am truly yearning to see her, to thank her. This time I will be sure to recognize her."

She laughed. "Don't be so sure of that. Do you remember when you first wanted to meet Dalha and she said she would see you only after you had fulfilled three promises you had made?" I nodded. "Some time ago, in your past birth, you made a promise to the ones who were born as your daughters, and it was only after you gave birth to them that she would meet you. Dalha can see into the past and future; she clears the way of obstacles and allows things to come to fruition at the right time. That is her magic. As to when or if she will return to Lhasa, I never know. It is rare for me to meet her these days, and she has told me that one day she simply won't return in her physical form. When that time comes, we will have to find her on the wings of the wind and in the long strands of sunlight. But we should do that now, Tshomo, and not wait to see her in the flesh. That is the consciousness she wants us to attain. With or without physical form, she speaks to us through our mind, and it is we who must learn to hear her."

From the start, my relationship with my son was different from that with my other children. My three daughters were all quite independent minded and, even in childhood, not particularly attached to me. None of them took an interest in spiritual matters, although they considered themselves Buddhist. The two oldest had a strong fondness for horses, and Yeshe was already considering marrying our first daughter, Samaya, to the son of a cousin who raised horses in Amdo. This pleased her greatly. The second daughter expressed a similar desire and wanted to be near her older sister. She was still too young for marriage, but Yeshe was already thinking of prospects. The youngest girl, Yara, was eleven and she showed the greatest interest in her young brother.

Due to the way in which Tenzin Sangye had been conceived, I felt a spiritual bond with him immediately, and this bond grew and deepened over time. When I would look at him, I would think of Dalha; I knew that for Yeshe, it was Guru Rinpoche who had facilitated his birth. This child held the dual blessings of our two traditions. However, this never caused Yeshe any conflict as it had for me.

The integration in my own mind of Bon and Buddhism had already begun, so I was fully at ease when Yeshe began to impart Buddhist teachings to him from his earliest days. When Tenzin was as young as four, Yeshe described how the great Guru Rinpoche came to our land to lay the foundation for Buddhism. "Our great tsenpo Trisong Detsen had built an extensive and mighty empire," Yeshe explained, "even occupying Chang'an, the capital of the Tang Empire. But Guru Rinpoche turned Trisong's interest from outer conquest to the inner conquest of the mind, and this changed the course of our history. He awakened compassion in our tsenpo so that he would not continue his expeditions of conquest to expand our territory. It is the mind's territory that must be expanded, he instructed, not geographical boundaries. Do you understand why, Tenzin?"

Our young son nodded, but then asked question upon question about that time when our empire was one of the largest and most powerful in the world. I was quiet, not wanting to bring up my own questions about Trisong Detsen and the suppression of Bon.

At other times Yeshe would speak of the princess Yeshe Tsogyal, who became the consort of Guru Rinpoche. I would draw closer to listen because I knew nothing of that great yogini. As I learned, she was born a princess but, rejecting all suitors, abandoned royal life to live in the charnel grounds of Samye Monastery, where she engaged in twelve years of the most austere and intense meditation practice. I also learned that during this time, she flew to Oddiyana in visions to see the great Guru. Among all her compassionate acts was her entry into the hell realms to liberate her greatest adversary. It was the latter deed that intrigued me the most, because after coming to know Dalha, I was beginning to understand that the greatest magic is the inner transformation that a master facilitates, not any outward feat.

That night when we were alone, I asked Yeshe what it meant to go into the hell realms. He was thoughtful for a moment and then replied, "For Yeshe Tsogyal to undertake that, she had to experience everything her adversary was experiencing. It was not simply a journey through those mind realms. To reach him, she had to undergo the experiences herself, and only the most compassionate and stable mind could withstand that. It is not something that most meditators can do, even those who are advanced in their practice. All the demons that the mind creates are encountered; all the negative forces in the universe that impede awakening. To reach her adversary, she had to know the darkness that clouded his mind and transform it into light. One can understand how one might undertake this for a loved one, but to undertake it for an adversary means that she had overcome all self-identification. She didn't see him as her adversary because she recognized no 'other.' She had transcended the identity of the princess and even of the yogini Yeshe Tsogyal."

Her story was one that was repeated many times as Tenzin Sangye was growing up. I knew that Yeshe wanted him to realize that both men and women can become buddhas, that both can submit themselves to the most severe austerities for the sake of awakening to their true nature.

Yeshe also taught him the history of our land, how it was first settled by nonhumans with magical abilities, much in the same way that my mother had related that history to me. He told Tenzin that after the lha left, the nagas came and then the demonic race of the dud, and so on.

"When I was traveling through Gyagar, I heard another story, which was confirmed by some scholars here," claimed Yeshe one evening. Tenzin, now eight years old, loved history more than anything else and he listened attentively to any story of our past, especially when it included battles. "Several thousand years ago, before the time of Shakyamuni Buddha, there was a great war that encompassed nearly all the kingdoms in the area we now call Gyagar. The battle was fierce, as some of the warriors had knowledge of powerful mantra weapons. A great deity had taken birth at that time; he was known as Shri Krishna and was advising the side of righteousness. One of the famous warriors in that war, Rupati Maharaj, is said to have fled from the scene of the battle and led his army through the mountains, coming to the land of Zhang Zhung, where he became the king and helped to organize the tribes living here. Some say he fled from the war because of the horrors he witnessed. But others say that this maharaja came to Böd after the war and that he was the grandson of Janamejaya Maharaj, who was the great-grandson of the greatest warrior of the time, Arjuna. When and why he came, we don't know, but there is a historical record of this raja arriving in Böd and helping to organize and govern the tribes. The Sakyas are said to be his descendants."

"Is that true?" I asked curiously, always amazed at the vast store of Yeshe's knowledge.

"True?" he smiled. "How can we know? What we do know is that there is an ancient relationship between our land and the land of Gyagar. Your very own Tonpa Shenrab came from that region, and his teachings are not different from those of the ancient Vedic rishis. That is why we will send our son to Gyagar, to Nalanda Mahavihara (a monastic university), when he gets older so he can learn something of that tradition."

"To Nalanda," I whispered unhappily. "So far away." I knew little of that great place of learning except that it was far from Lhasa.

"Our son will travel far, Padma. You must accept that."

A year after this conversation, I entered the room where Yeshe was teaching Tenzin about another towering Buddhist figure and sat down to listen. "About two hundred years ago, there was a teacher named Atisa from Vikramshila, another great mahavihara in the Pala Empire (in India). He was famous not only for his philosophical insight and great humility, but also for his knowledge of advanced tantric practices and his devotion to the goddess Tara, the same goddess your Aunt Pumo reveres."

"The goddess in her paintings?" Tenzin asked.

Yeshe nodded and continued. "Atisa was born into a royal family. His father was Raja Kalyanachandra, and his grandfather was Raja Srichandra of the Chandra Dynasty. At the age of twenty-eight, he was ordained by Abbot Silaraksita. In addition to studying all the Buddhist texts, he studied Sanskrit, Vaishnavism, and Shaivism and became a master of tantric practices." Seeing Tenzin's confused expression, he added, "I know you don't know what those are, but you will learn when you go to Nalanda. He also studied art, music, and logic. He had a brilliant mind and was a master of so many fields. He excelled at debating and was able to deftly correct misunderstandings of complex religious concepts. Eventually he was appointed the abbot of Vikramshila. Word of Atisa's accomplishments reached our tsenpo, and he sent scholars to Vikramshila to listen to his teachings. One of them was so impressed that he pleaded with Atisa to come to Böd to teach here.

"Atisa intended to stay for only three years, but he never left our land. He remained here throughout his life and had a great impact. During that time, our society was in turmoil, with constant skirmishes between competing warlords. Monasteries, dependent on patronage from the local nobility, got involved in these conflicts and they trained tantric adepts in sacred mantras that were used both to create and destroy. Spiritually, there was much degradation during this time. Secret tantric mantras were being chanted in the marketplace alongside the buying and selling of goods. Atisa saw that the misuse of the teachings was dictated by the thirst for power, and he worked hard to change this damaging trend, to return the teachings to the sacred purpose for which they had been given."

Tenzin was listening attentively, but I was becoming uneasy with the tenor of the conversation. "Isn't he too young for all of this, Yeshe?" I asked quietly, but I was interrupted by Tenzin, who eagerly asked about the secret tantric teachings that had the power to create and destroy.

Smiling, Yeshe responded that only a guru could teach him that. "I am not your guru, Tenzin; I am only your father. But I want to prepare you for the day when you will meet that one. Atisa's disciple Dromton built a small monastery north of Lhasa for serious meditators and tantra practitioners. I will take you there one day, but you will study at Samye Monastery, which was built under the guidance of the great Guru Rinpoche."

My heart froze when I heard those words. Was I to have no say in my son's future? Was he to have no say? Was it all predecided? Was he destined to become a monk with no opportunity to choose his path? Would I have no chance to teach him about my Bon heritage, about the goddess of the lake? A battle that I thought had long ago been settled began to arise anew within me. But it was not this conflict that troubled me most, as there was another matter brewing. As Tenzin approached his tenth birthday, Yeshe announced that the two of them would join the caravan traveling to the Song Empire. Since the birth of Tenzin,

Yeshe had not ventured far. My brothers' sons had taken over most of the trading and traveling, but suddenly he wanted to return to the Song and take Tenzin with him. I protested loudly, but to no avail.

"I want him to learn the Han language," insisted Yeshe gently. "It will be very useful in the future."

"He can learn it here," I replied, in way of rebuke. We had been tensely discussing Yeshe's decision for days.

"It is not the same. We will travel through the Song Empire, and I will take him to meet Buddhist and Daoist teachers at different places. Before he enters the monastery, I want him to have that experience. Padma, you must trust me on this matter. He will be safe, I promise you."

"He is so young," I retorted tearfully.

Putting his arm around me, he replied tenderly, "He will always be young to you, but he will soon be a man. Padma, he is our most precious gift. I would sacrifice all I have to give him every opportunity to contribute as he is able. Please trust me."

It was true that Yeshe's whole life since the birth of Tenzin had been devoted to his education. There was a quiet urgency in his voice that I could not ignore. Suddenly it occurred to me that Yeshe was aging and that he wanted to share this experience with his son before he was too old to make such a long and arduous journey. Up until Tenzin's birth, my husband had welcomed every trip, always eager to see foreign places and meet new people. He had a zeal for new experiences, and I suspected he wanted to foster the same in his son. Looking at him sorrowfully, I no longer objected. Nodding my head, I laid it against his chest and whispered, "I do trust you. It is simply that I will miss you both so much." My life had been totally wrapped up with Tenzin since his birth, as had Yeshe's, and I could not imagine what would fill my days without him by my side.

I assented, but my heart was not at rest. Pumo was living far from Lhasa, and I could not turn to my brothers, as they would have no sympathy for my position. They had taken their sons along on the trading caravans when they were not much older than Tenzin. So, with nowhere else to turn, I went to find Bhasundara.

CHAPTER 8

A Lesson on Love

When I reached Bhasundara's cottage, she was mounted on her horse, about to depart from home. As soon as she saw the concerned expression on my face, she jumped down and led me inside. I had not seen Bhasundara very frequently since the birth of Tenzin, only an occasional visit every few months or so. Most often when I rode out to her cottage, she was not there, but sometimes I would be surprised to find her sitting at the table with a cup of po cha, as if she was expecting me. I rarely asked about Dalha anymore because she seemed to always be away from Lhasa.

As I sat by Bhasundara's side in the entry room, I released the pent-up emotions through my tears, telling her that Yeshe was again joining the trading caravan and this time taking Tenzin with him. They would be gone for over a year, at the very least. She listened quietly and then asked why I was so upset. Both my husband and son were in good health. They would have guards along the way to protect them from bandits. Yeshe knew the route well and was highly adept at traveling through the terrain. Tenzin would gain a great deal of life experience and valuable knowledge, which would serve him well in the years ahead. What was there to fret about?

"I can't imagine my life without him by my side," I explained, drying my tears. "Since his birth we have not been separated even for a day. It will be hard for me to be without him. He is still so young. It is my love for him…"

"That is not love," she interrupted brusquely. I looked at her questioningly. "Tshomo, you are mixing up love with attachment. Your love for him should allow you to think beyond yourself and to consider what he will gain by traveling with his father. Yeshe's time is limited; you know that as well as I. Let him give your son all he can give while he is still here."

"What do you mean 'his time is limited'?" I asked, furrowing my brow. Although Yeshe was many years older than me, I had never given much thought to our age difference and, strangely, had not considered that he might die before me.

"Never mind that. We are talking about Tenzin. In the future, your son will travel far, and you might as well begin letting go of your clinging. Yeshe is very wise to take him away now, and when he returns, be prepared for him to enter the monastery. That is his future."

"I am not prepared for that," I replied in a low tone.

"Then get prepared." Her voice was a bit harsh, and I looked at her mournfully. She went on in a gentler tone. "You only have to let go of your clinging. You can begin by allowing him to leave without making such a fuss, without causing him or his father to feel bad. Let the boy be excited for this trip with his father. For the first ten years of living with Dalha, I was with her every minute. When she started leaving me alone, traveling for weeks and months on end, I would get frightened, unused to her absence. I would plead with her to take me with her, to let me continue accompanying her. When she saw this attachment, this clinging, she quickly cut the strings." Bhasundara paused and smiled as if remembering, then continued. "I quickly learned not to ask. The more I wanted to be with her, the more she would remove herself, staying away longer. And then there were times that I would face a very difficult trial whenever she left, and I was forced to seek her inside. But it took me a long time to learn this.

"Once, when she had been gone for many months, I began to miss her intensely, so I called out to her internally. After a few days of beseeching as earnestly as I knew how, she appeared to me in a dream. Even though it was years ago, I still remember it clearly. She was standing by the side of a wide, beautiful lake, which I recognized as Nam Tsho. In the dream, she didn't speak, but she radiated immense joy. I woke up and was determined to find her. However, I had misread the dream, thinking that her purpose in coming to me was to give me a clue as to where she was. The image I saw of the lake looked exactly like an area she had once taken me to, and I left immediately for that place. I rode my poor horse very hard, without stopping for rest. I was so eager to see her and proud that I had understood the dream, or so I thought. In my mind, she was clearly calling me there. When I arrived at the lake, I searched everywhere, but she was nowhere to be found. I spent days there trying to find her and finally had to return home, dejected. On the way back, I heard an inner voice say, 'Clinging is not love. It blocks love.'

"When I heard those words, I realized my mistake. I had been missing her physical form; in the dream she showed me her transcendent form, but I hadn't understood. I was ashamed that I had been so rash as to set out immediately for Nam Tsho, instead of feeling gratitude for what she had given me—a vision of herself in a most beatific state.

"That experience was a turning point for me. Since then, I have not allowed myself to cling to anybody or anything, not even my own body! When Dalha showed up at the cottage several weeks later, she let me know that she was aware I had gone to Nam Tsho in search of her. She sat me down and exclaimed, 'Foolish girl, to cling to this frail physical form! You must distinguish between attachment and love. Attachment grows out of self-interest, one's own desires and needs, not the well-being of the other. Love is not an emotion. It is a state of being. Don't be caught in narrow emotions. You must become love itself.'

"When I heard those words, something lit up inside of me and I understood her meaning. How can you miss someone, Tshomo, when you realize they are never really apart from you? Even though Dalha had been far away, in terms of physical distance, she had been aware of my mental state and had come to me in a dream. If I had truly understood her omnipresence, I would not have suffered. How can you feel apart from someone who is not separate from you?" Bhasundara paused again and her eyes assumed a faraway look. After a few moments, she added, "It took me many years to realize that clinging is much deeper than only our attachment to people and places. We cling to our outlooks, our beliefs, viewpoints and identities. We must release all of these to find out who we truly are. Only then do we become love itself. This I have learned from Dalha."

As I listened to Bhasundara, my despair drifted away. This was the effect she always had on me, calming my emotions and lifting me into a more settled, peaceful state. I sat there for several minutes without speaking and then said, "You have had the benefit of being trained by Dalha. I can only try to learn from your experiences, but I am not at that stage, Bhasundara. I still have these very human emotions and desires."

She smiled and replied gently, "As we all do."

"Every time you speak of Dalha, I feel a yearning to see her again. But I know there is no point in asking where she is or when she will return."

"Did you not hear the story I just told you, Tshomo?" she asked, with eyes open wide. 'Have you heard nothing of what I said? She is everywhere and nowhere at the same time. Find her inside of yourself."

"There you go, speaking again in riddles." Then I mumbled, "Perhaps if I call out to her, she will come to me in a dream."

"You can search the whole universe, Tshomo, and not find her, or go nowhere and be in her presence. Have patience, and one day the very idea of separation will not exist in your mind. When that happens, clinging will dissolve like a speck of dust dispersing in the air." Sighing, she added, "Perhaps it will give you some comfort to know that I am quite confident you will see her again, Tshomo, and very soon."

Remembering that Bhasundara was on her way to bring medicines to the city, I didn't stay much longer. As I was leaving, she called out to me, "Tshomo, when Yeshe leaves with Tenzin, have him take you to stay with your daughters in Amdo while they are away. That will bring you some relief."

Nodding, I thanked her. She was right. My two oldest daughters had young children, whom I hardly saw. This could be a time to get to know them. But neither they nor anybody else could take the place of Tenzin, and I knew his departure would leave me with an emptiness that would not easily be filled.

When I returned home, Yeshe readily agreed that I should spend my time in Amdo, dividing the days between the households of our two eldest daughters and their families. Sensing my still-troubled heart, he put his arm around me and spoke deliberately, "I have seen Tenzin's mental capability. He has much to offer the world, and we must give him every opportunity to reach his potential. Neither your desires nor mine can interfere with that. We must sacrifice all that we need to for this son of ours." I nodded, very much hoping that I might come to feel as he did.

Although I felt much better after seeing Bhasundara, I couldn't understand her words. My attachment to Tenzin was because of my love for him. Wasn't it natural for a mother to feel this way? Why would I want to give up my attachment to him?

A few weeks later, Yeshe, Tenzin, and I embarked for Amdo. After leaving me with my eldest daughter, Samaya, they continued on to catch up with the caravan, which was traveling south through Kham on the way to Chengdu. Their departure left a gaping hole in my heart that no amount of distraction could heal. The passing days did not see any improvement in my condition. For weeks I tried to busy myself with household duties, putting on a cheerful face in front of my daughter and her children, but once alone, I felt only absence. I couldn't understand why I had fallen into such a deep dejection. Samaya was sensitive to my moods and tried to engage me by asking questions about Bon beliefs, taking me to sit by lakes and streams and for walks along the grassy plains near her village home. I greatly appreciated her efforts, but nothing seemed to pull me out of my sorrowful state.

After staying three months with Samaya, I went to stay with my second daughter Dolma and her family, who lived only a few hours away. Several months later, I returned to Samaya's home. I was beginning to feel that I was a burden, as they had busy lives and I didn't feel I could contribute much, especially as each daughter lived with her husband's family. But Samaya would not let me return home until her father had come to retrieve me, and so I stayed on, struggling with an emptiness that threatened to engulf me. Nine months into my visit, Samaya and her husband asked me to accompany them to a nearby horse market, where they were looking to sell several ponies they had raised. I agreed, not wanting to hurt their feelings, knowing that they were doing their best to cheer me up. Before he left, Yeshe told Samaya that my favorite horse, which I'd had for a number of years, had recently died, and he asked her to find a new one to my liking that I could ride back to Lhasa. I hadn't thought of this much during my stay, but Samaya reminded me of it now. Nodding, I told her that any of the ponies she bred would do, but she insisted that I look at the different breeds at the market before choosing.

The ride to the market was slow, as we had numerous horses tied to the cart in which we rode. I knew little about horses but could see that the special breed they raised was a strong and hardy one, well suited to the mountain paths; they had great endurance and would fetch a good price. Soon after we arrived, Samaya and her husband were besieged by prospective buyers. Not terribly interested in the dealings, I wandered off on my own.

After walking around for a while and watching the many activities taking place in the market, my attention was drawn to an older Drokpa woman standing by a large, handsome white horse. She seemed to be in the process of purchasing it. The horse had a most unusual and striking stance, and I drew closer to get a better look. As I did, I heard the seller describe the rare, almost magical, qualities of the animal—how it could run faster than any other horse he had ever seen, that it didn't need much food, water, or rest—and I could see her nodding. How gullible of her, I thought, smiling to myself. Why would an old woman need such a fast horse anyhow? The woman was alone, and the thought entered my mind that somebody should warn her not to be so easily convinced. She wasn't facing me, and I could only see her back, but the one thing that struck me was her red hat, which strikingly resembled the one that Dalha always wore. All the more reason I should come to her rescue, I thought. Inching closer, I heard the man quote an exorbitant price. Although the horse was quite stunning, the amount was much too high. Even I knew that. Instead of negotiating, as one always does, she immediately agreed to what he asked.

What a naïve woman, I thought. She doesn't realize that he is taking advantage of her. For a moment I thought to intervene and bring her to Samaya, who had smaller ponies, much better suited to her small stature. At least I had to warn her that his price was too high. But before I could protest, I saw her take out a pouch and hand him the money, completing the deal.

Her tattered grey woolen skirt and jacket presented the appearance of poverty, and I wondered how she had come up with such a large sum. I couldn't see the expression on her face since she was turned away from me, but the man's face was beaming. I couldn't help but wonder if she had any inkling that the man was robbing her. After debating internally for a moment, I decided to see if she needed help. Perhaps she was a foreigner and was not aware of the cost of horses, or perhaps she had difficulty with the dialect. Why would she purchase such an expensive animal, and what was an elderly woman doing alone at a horse market? I felt impelled to intervene.

"*Amrgas* (grandmother)," I called as I stood a few steps behind her. "Can I help you?"

"Help me!" she exclaimed in a strong voice, as she slowly turned around. "It is I who have come to help you."

"Dalha!" I could not believe my eyes. The worn, bent form that I had seen from behind, the woman whom I had pitied for being misled, was none other than Dalha.

She smiled. "Come, Tshomo. I don't have much time. Let us sit somewhere." Leading the newly purchased horse, she guided me to the edge of the market, where we could sit undisturbed.

"What are you doing here in Amdo?" I asked after we settled ourselves on the ground, the horse by our side. She gazed at me steadily for a few moments and then spoke in a gentle voice.

"To find you, of course, to pull you out of this dejected state. You have allowed yourself to flounder about for too long. It is enough already."

I didn't answer, but my eyes began to tear as my emotional turmoil again arose. She seemed to know my thoughts and addressed them in a firm tone. "Your state of mind has nothing to do with your son," she said. "Your dejection is not due to his absence. Rather, it is you who have made yourself absent, losing yourself in a maze of useless thoughts, keeping the goddess at a distance. You have shut her out. You came into this life searching for her, but you have wandered away. Come back, my child. You know well that all problems come from within, not from anything external. It is the misperceived absence of the goddess, the distance you have created in your mind, that is causing your suffering, not your son."

As she spoke those words, it dawned on me how long it had been since I had given any thought to the goddess. Even Dalha had been mostly absent from my mind since the birth of Tenzin. "I don't even know where to begin looking, Dalha," I murmured.

"Where does she abide, Tshomo? In Nam Tsho? In the forest? The mountains? Where can you find her?" I looked at her without responding, not knowing the answer. "In here. This is her home," she replied to her own question, pointing to my heart. "Right here. Find out who you are, Tshomo, and you will find the goddess. Look within the mind for the answer—not the thinking, logical mind, which is ever restless, but the still, luminous mind, which shines like the sacred Nam Tsho, and out of which everything emerges."

I looked down at the ground, ashamed of my confusion. Gazing up at the sky, she broke into a joyful laugh. Then, turning back to me, she became more serious and said, "When you surmount one problem, another will always pop up. That is the nature of the world. For so long you desired a son, and yet that did not make you happy. You want to hold on to him, but even if you could, it wouldn't bring you happiness, because this is not really about your son. He is not the reason for your dejection."

Although I heard her words, I did not really understand them, as it seemed so clear to me that my state of mind was a result of my separation from Tenzin. His absence had left an empty hole in my life. Instead of addressing this, she began again to speak of the goddess. "You have turned the goddess into a concept, an ideal, an external being bound by form and name, rather than an ever-living presence that exists in everything and everywhere. In this stone," she said as she picked up a nearby small rock, "and in this soil." She dug her hand into the ground beneath us. "And in you. Don't create a false separation between you and her. Don't think of her as separate. She is the very life within you. You must talk with that inner being constantly, and your true needs will be answered.

"It is the nature of the lower mind to limit and confine and to see reality only in the external world, but if you keep focusing the mind within, you will find the jewel that you are seeking. The mind can be a friend or a foe, but through training, the mind can more assuredly become your ally. That is the purpose of all spiritual endeavors, even the rituals that you conduct—to align the inner and outer spiritual forces."

Dalha's words sounded more Buddhist than Bon, more like Yeshe than what I remembered from my mother's Bon teachings, and so again I looked at her perplexed. Reading my mind, she chuckled and answered this thought. "Tshomo, whoever said I was a Bonpo? Or a Buddhist? It is you who have sought to define me. I am both and neither, as I hope you will be one day. The luminous mind, the nature of pure being, is beyond definition. Don't place limitations on yourself."

As she was speaking, I remembered my confusion some years earlier over which goddess to worship, over what name to call her. The Bon goddesses whom my mother had worshipped did not feel familiar to me. I felt no real connection to Drablai Gaylmo or Nam Tsho Chukmo. I had begun to feel more drawn to the benevolent form of Tara, but even she was not one I would naturally call upon.

Sensing my lack of clarity, Dalha said, "I will tell you a story about an incident that happened long ago." I had heard many stories about Dalha from Bhasundara, but she had never spoken to me about her life. Looking at her with a pleased expression, I pushed aside my questioning mind as she began.

"Many, many years ago, I was traveling around Zhang Zhung to many of the sacred lakes, listening to the hermits tell tales of the gods and goddesses who protect the mountains and lakes. There are thousands of them, so many that I became confused. I didn't know which one to make my special companion. I was sitting there thinking of all the different goddesses when a hermit approached me and asked my name. At that moment, my mind went completely blank, and I forgot what name I was called." She chuckled. "Dalha is the name that Bhasundara gave to me, but this incident took place long before I had met her, and nobody called me by that name then. When I didn't answer, this hermit again asked my name. Suddenly, my many names from numerous journeys to earth and beyond came to me and I began recounting all of them. I must have recited at least a hundred, when the hermit stopped me and asked, 'So many names. Which one should I call you?'

"'You can call me any of those names,' I murmured, 'or no name at all.'"

"'But I want to call you something,' he insisted.

"'Then pick whichever name you like,' I replied immediately. 'I have been all of them.'"

"The hermit smiled and mentioned a name. When he spoke it, I remembered that this was what people were calling me at that time in Zhang Zhung. In my long list, I had not mentioned that one because I had forgotten it; I had forgotten the name of this body. So how did that hermit know?"

I shook my head and asked, "How did he know?"

Dalha smiled in amusement. "The hermit turned to leave, and as he walked away, his form turned into the beautiful goddess that I had seen before in visions, one whose name I didn't know. I then understood the purpose of her disguised visit. Tshomo, you and I have had many births in many places, many names and many faces. In your life now, some people call you Tshomo and some call you Padma, and some call you Padma Tshomo, but you are the same no matter what they call you. The goddess is like that. She is one and she is many. There is no contradiction in that. She has more names and forms than you can count, but in the ultimate sense, she is one. Whichever form appeals to you, keep that form close."

I looked across at Dalha, her thin white braids cascading down her shoulders and chest, framing a delicately lined, deeply bronzed face, which appeared most beautiful to me. As I gazed into her joy-lit eyes, so full of love and wisdom, a great yearning awoke in me, causing me to murmur, "Dalha, the form that appeals to me the most is yours." In that moment, I thought nobody could be more attractive, more wondrous than her.

A hearty laugh escaped her lips and she said, "Then that will do. Keep me close as your constant companion. I continually speak to you, Tshomo, but you have not been listening. You must learn to hear when I speak.

"Tshomo, most people mistake attachment for love. Attachment comes from wanting to hold on to something for oneself, but love is beyond the limitations of self. In this love, there is no separation and thus no suffering. There is no grasping, no holding on. I will tell a story about such a love. You know about the life of Yeshe Tsogyal, the consort of Guru Rinpoche?" I nodded. "You know she was born the daughter of a tsenpo and that as a young girl, she refused all marriage proposals and fled to the charnel grounds of Samye Monastery, the monastery that Guru Rinpoche had envisioned and helped to create. She spent twelve years there engaging with all the negative forces that sought to overcome her. During that time, her love and compassion expanded to such an extent that it even reached beings in distant universes. Her purpose in taking birth was to manifest this love in the human body.

"Toward the end of her time of deep meditation practice, she saw that her main oppressor had been cast into the darkest of realms, and her immediate thought was to save him from the dire suffering that awaited him. But this would mean passing through the densest of realms, where many demonic forms lived. Most who entered those realms remained trapped there for eons. But she had attained a state of consciousness that allowed her to see all beings as held within the one being of her beloved consort, who had achieved union with the supreme reality. Without a moment's thought for her own welfare, she embarked on this inner journey, passing through hell realm after hell realm, until she reached the place where that opponent was now trapped and undergoing great torment, and she was able to rescue and transform that being. This story is well known, and you may have heard it before, but it is not the end of the tale.

"Guru Rinpoche had left Böd much earlier to return to the kingdom of his birth, where his advanced disciples were waiting. Yet he was very much aware of the activities of his consort, living far away in Böd. He recognized that her love was such that everywhere she looked and everything she saw was to her another form, another appearance of her consort, and he wanted her to teach this to his students. To do so, he devised a plan. He disappeared and traveled to a distant part of the universe and allowed a fierce demon to terrorize his disciples. In great fear, they gathered together and called upon the gods and goddesses for protection, but these deities realized that this was Guru Rinpoche's test and did not appear. Then they called upon their great Guru, but he also did not come to save them; the one who responded was his consort, the yogini Yeshe Tsogyal. Quicker than the blink of an eye, she flew from her distant place in Böd to where the disciples were cowering in fear before this mighty demon.

"After twelve years of intense austerities, she was quite a sight to see, dressed in torn clothing, so thin and worn that it hardly covered her body. She appeared to them ragged and disheveled, her hair straggly and unkempt, her body thin and frail, her face marked with dirt and ash. Nobody knew who she was, and so the disciples tried to turn her away, dismissing her as an unruly woman. Unfazed by their rudeness, she would not depart. She wouldn't budge, no matter what they said to her. At first, she stood there staring intently at the horrific demon before her; then she began walking toward the demon, who had a wide assortment of deadly weapons in his many hands. Of course, she had none. As she came closer to him, he let out a shattering cry that made mountains erupt, emitting poisons and ash into the air. Still, her eyes remained steady and calm, and her face wore a most tender expression, because all she saw before her was her beloved consort. She recognized no other being. She came closer and closer. The disciples were sure that the demon would consume her, but nobody came to her defense.

"Finally, she stood right before that frightening creature, and in a burst of love, with a gentle smile on her face, she reached out to touch him. At her loving touch, his body transformed into that of Guru Rinpoche himself. This was the moment of their union. Because she recognized no other being, she became one with him. Her form disappeared into his, and she found herself back in Böd at the charnel grounds of Samye Monastery. The disciples learned a great lesson that day and discovered that the one who had saved them was none other than the great Guru's consort, who was one with the great Guru himself.

"Why do I tell you this story, Tshomo?" She looked at me expectantly, but I didn't answer. Finally, she responded. "The only thing that matters is where the mind is. Her mind was fully engrossed in Guru Rinpoche, and so she saw him in all creatures, in the light and in the darkness. Her love was such that there was not even the slightest thought of self. That is the way to overcome fear and attachment. Hold on to nothing; cling to nothing. When you give up everything, then everything comes to you freely. Do you understand what I am saying?"

"I am trying to understand," I murmured.

"That is enough for today," she said. She rose to leave and I also got up from the ground. "Remember the love between Yeshe Tsogyal and Guru Rinpoche, and remember what she had to endure to achieve that union. Nothing of value can be gained without sacrifice, and what is to be gained is worth every sacrifice. You are only giving up the lesser for the greater. What we think of as a sacrifice is in fact no sacrifice at all. Yeshe Tsogyal gave up food and sleep, and even care for her own body, but what she gained was the love of the universe—a love so great that few can contain it." Gently caressing the back of the stately white horse, she added, "He is my gift to you. I wanted you to have the fastest horse I could find in all of Böd to speed you toward your goal."

"For me!" I exclaimed. "But why?"

"Your old horse recently died, didn't he? You need a new one, don't you?"

I looked at her in amazement, wondering how she knew that. Despite knowing Dalha for so many years, her words never ceased to confound me. Then I couldn't help saying, "But Dalha, you paid way too much."

Looking at me tenderly, she replied, "I paid just the right amount. That poor man has a sick child. The amount I gave him will cover the needs of his family for some time. As long as I was here, I thought to make myself useful." She smiled. "It was I who put that price into his head, knowing how much he would need."

"But, Dalha, don't you need a horse to go where you are going?"

"When have I ever needed a horse to travel?" With those words and a joyous chuckle, she gently patted me on the shoulder. As she stood there, I looked into her eyes, which were gazing at me intently. For a moment, I thought I saw the form of a youthful, beautiful woman, a body composed of light superimposed upon the body of Dalha, as if floating within it. The impression lasted but a second, and then it was gone.

"Do not think the great Guru is unaware of you. It was he who shot an arrow at my heart, showing me your pain. It was that arrow that bought me to you," came her words from inside of me. In amazement, I took a step forward as Dalha turned and hurried away. I was not ready to let her leave me, but she was gone, disappearing into the groups of people moving from one stall of animals to the next. A moment later, a high-pitched whistling call caused me to look up into the sky, where I caught sight of a large eagle flying away, its expansive wings gliding freely on a wisp of wind.

"Goodbye, Dalha," I whispered. Despite the noise of the market, crowded with horses, mules, and yaks, and a wide variety of people of all ages and types, I heard her reply: "There is no goodbye, for I will keep coming to remind you to look inside to find what you are seeking."

Those words were to drift down through the many layers of my still-muddled mind, buried until circumstances caused them to arise. Again, I was left with the question of who she was. Who was this woman who appeared under the most mysterious of circumstances and spoke the most mysterious of words?

CHAPTER 9

Departing Gifts

"Where did you get such a striking horse?" asked Samaya in amazement, when she saw me returning to her and her husband, leading the animal along.

"It was a gift," I replied simply, hoping she wouldn't press me further.

"A gift? Such an expensive one. Ama-la, who gave you this exquisite stallion?" As she ran her hand along the mane and back of the horse admiringly, she commented, "He is a rare beauty."

"Dalha," I replied simply.

"Your teacher, Dalha?" I nodded. "She is here?" Again, I nodded. "Why did she give you such a gift?" she asked, frowning. My children had never met Dalha, but they knew Bhasundara, and were aware that I regarded Dalha as my Bon teacher. My daughters were especially suspect of anything magical or out-of-the-ordinary, and so I kept much from them.

"It is a long story, Samaya. She knew my horse had died, and she knew that this gift would make me happy. And it has. She really cheered me up."

"If it makes you happy, Ama-la, that is enough. And you have needed a new horse."

The visit from Dalha did indeed lift my spirits and this joyous feeling was to last for weeks. Every time I saw the horse, I thought of her and her kindness, and it brought a smile to my face. That day at the horse market was the first time that I had had an extensive conversation with Dalha. In the past she had showed up at the most unexpected times, and there were those occasions when I hadn't recognized her until she was gone, but this time I did recognize her, and she had sat and talked with me. More than the gift, her presence is what brought joy to my heart. I didn't know what it was about her that had this effect but, whatever it was, I felt uplifted.

I didn't understand her words about the goddess living inside of me, but I tried my best to keep my mind on her as she had advised me to do. I had heard part of the story of Yeshe Tsogyal from my husband, but Dalha's telling was slightly different, and I found myself returning to that story again and again. Many days, I would walk alongside my new horse, speaking to him as I would to a friend, and slowly, almost without my notice, I found that days would go by without missing Tenzin.

Another nine months were to pass before Yeshe and Tenzin arrived in Amdo to take me home. Tenzin had left as a boy but returned as a young man, taller than I and with a maturity far advanced for his age. When I saw the relationship that had flourished between my son and husband, I could not help but think how foolish I had been to try to hold him back, a shortsightedness that would have remained had Dalha not come to expand my vision.

Tenzin returned fluent in the Han language, an ability he could not have gained had he stayed home with me, and one which would prove invaluable in the years ahead. For weeks I was to hear much about their travel through the Song Empire, the vast number of people living in the cities, the navy the emperor had established, the wealth and large number of scholars, who held a prominent place in society.

"Are you planning for Tenzin to enter government?" I asked Yeshe one day after I realized the extent of their travels.

He shook his head. "Monks should not enter the fray of government, but he should be aware of all that is happening around him, in our kingdom and neighboring ones." As I was soon to learn, my son's knowledge of history and his debating skills were now his father's pride.

"How did the Tibetan empire decline?" asked Yeshe of Tenzin one evening after we had finished our evening meal, not long after we had arrived back in Lhasa.

Tenzin smiled. "There were many factors," he began. "But mostly it was Guru Rinpoche who turned our tsenpo Trisong Detson's attention from conquering the outer world to mastering the inner one."

"Go on," his father prodded.

"Trisong Detson abdicated to devote the rest of his life to meditation and his eldest son became the tsenpo, but that son died soon after. The second son took the throne, but he was ill prepared and so Trisong had to return to power. When Trisong died a few years later, a third son challenged the second son and was killed. The second son remained the tsenpo and continued to spread Buddhism, but the fighting among the sons had left a stain. Am I right, Apa-la?" Yeshe nodded and asked him to continue. "The next tsenpo was Ralpachen, and he spent a lot of money on building monasteries and on Buddhist projects, which caused resentment and polarized the court. He was killed and his brother Darma the Ox became tsenpo. All this infighting greatly weakened the empire. Darma the Ox had the support of the anti-Buddhist ministers and he cut the spending on Buddhist projects, shut down colleges, ended support for the monasteries, and purged the court of Buddhists." Tenzin finished speaking and I was left speechless, not aware until that moment that he knew more about our history than I did.

"How did you learn all of this, Tenzin?" I asked in amazement. He and Yeshe exchanged glances and they both smiled. But they were not finished discussing the matter.

"And what happened to Darma the Ox?" asked Yeshe.

"Due to his anti-Buddhist activity, he was killed by a Buddhist monk named Lhalung Palgyi Detsen, the ninth abbot of Samye Monastery." Tenzin's tone turned serious and was laced with disapproval.

He stopped speaking but Yeshe challenged him. "The monk killed the tsenpo because of his profligate ways and because he was harming the dharma. Wasn't that a just cause?"

Tenzin didn't answer right away and Yeshe urged him to respond. "Wasn't he saving lives by killing Darma the Ox? Wasn't he justified?"

"Ap-la, he was not," began Tenzin tenuously. "Even though he was the abbot of Samye Monastery, and even though he was defending Buddhism, that does not justify taking a life. Of what use are the teachings then? His emotions overcame his discrimination and no good came of that act. It hastened the end of the empire. Darma the Ox had no heirs and so after he was killed, his queen adopted a boy and made him the tsenpo. But that boy had no qualifications. The empire was already overstretched and was losing much of its wealth; people went without food and the cities in the east began to fall to the Tang Empire. Disorder spread; Buddhist temples and royal tombs were robbed, and monks were turned out of monasteries to fend for themselves. Nobody had the power to hold the empire together. Perhaps it was the result of this deed. You have taught me that when a person of knowledge commits a wrong deed, the outcome is much worse than if an ignorant person commits the same act."

"That is true," replied Yeshe, pleased at our son's response. "You are saying that killing is not sanctioned even if it is done in defense of Buddhism?"

Tenzin nodded, gazing earnestly at his father for approval. Yeshe smiled, and Tenzin continued. "You have taught me that in life, there are difficult situations where in the moment one might justify an action that goes against dharma. As much as that abbot opposed the anti-Buddhist activities of the tsenpo, in my mind he was not justified in killing him. Perhaps the tsenpo would have died of natural causes a few years later, or perhaps people would have risen up against him on their own. In the end, Darma the Ox, despite his anti-Buddhist activities, did not harm the dharma because many new lineages sprang up at that time. The monks who were forced from their monasteries in central Tibet took refuge in

Amdo and continued to spread the teachings there. The lesson is to look beyond short-term goals to see the longer-term effects. If the abbot of Samye of that time truly had faith in Guru Rinpoche, he would not have killed the tsenpo. He must have realized his error because he fled after committing the deed and was not heard from again."

I had been listening quietly, greatly impressed with the dialogue between my husband and son, but now ventured to ask a question of my own. "Tenzin, I see that you can reason things through clearly. Trisong Detsen is greatly revered by the Buddhists, but was he justified in suppressing Bon in order to spread Buddhism?"

Yeshe turned to me and smiled, whispering, "The same old question."

Tenzin was thoughtful for a moment and then asked with a slight smile, "Do I have to be the mediator between my parents' beliefs?"

"Answer her," encouraged Yeshe. "You and I have not spoken of this. I am also eager to hear your thoughts."

Tenzin was quiet for a few moments and then hesitantly began. "Bon is very ancient and is part of the beliefs of every one of us who live in this land. But over time, in all traditions, a certain purity is lost and a renewal is needed. It happened with Bon, and I am sure it will happen with Buddhism. In fact, it already has. Apa-la has told me of those Buddhist teachers who use their mystical powers for impure purposes. I believe that Trisong Detsen wanted to suppress superstition and the misuse of occult powers, not the ancient Bon wisdom, and perhaps he wanted to shift the focus from outer worship to the inner work of awakening the pure mind. I don't believe he would have suppressed the deeper Bon knowledge, which is not dissimilar from Buddhism. Am I right, Ama-la?" I nodded and smiled. "And I believe the great master Guru Rinpoche is above all religions. He is a universal teacher for us all, for the Buddhists and the Bonpos and everyone else in the world. It's just that the Buddhists have claimed him, but he belongs to all. Am I right, Ama-la?"

"If I did not hear your words myself, I would not believe that such wisdom could come from a child," I replied proudly. "You are correct. My Bonpo teacher Dalha has great love for Guru Rinpoche." As I spoke those words, I remembered my conversation with Dalha a year earlier when she said that it was I who had proclaimed her to be a Bonpo. She had never indicated that she considered herself as that.

"A child! What child? I don't see any child here," replied Yeshe emphatically. "I see only a monk and a very wise one at that."

Later that evening when Yeshe and I were alone, he said to me, "One should not fault a teacher for the misunderstanding of the students. The true Buddhists know the wisdom of Bon, but there are many who believe that to practice one religion, you must reject the others. This could not be further from the truth."

This was a teaching that Yeshe had repeated to me over the years, but now I finally was coming to understand it. I asked him if he was still set on Tenzin becoming a monk. "Are you not trying to make him fulfill your own desires instead of asking what he wants?" I could not help but suggest.

"It is not a matter of what I want, Padma. It is what he wants and was born for. I knew early on that my life was not for the monastery, but Tenzin has such a thirst for knowledge, for learning, and he can only get that in the monastery. He can always leave after he gains what he needs."

I sighed. Seeing the bond that had developed between those two, I knew that no matter what I said, it would have no effect. "When would he need to enter the monastery?" I asked, assuming I would have a few more years with my son.

"Now," he replied.

"He is only twelve!" I protested, but as I did, Dalha's face came before me, calming my rising emotions. What had she told me about the difference between love and attachment? Had I still not let go of my clinging? Was I thinking of my own needs or of what was best for Tenzin?

Putting his arm around me, Yeshe pulled me toward him and spoke in a comforting tone. "He is at the right age. If you could see how he absorbs everything that is said to him and integrates it with all his other knowledge. Trust me, Padma, I know what is best for our son. I have already spoken with him, and he is eager. If he were not, I would not encourage it. This is coming more from him than from me. And besides, it is time for the two of us to have some years together alone."

How could I resist Yeshe's soothing tone and warm embrace, and I could not help but yield.

Several months later Yeshe took Tenzin to Samye Monastery in the Chimpu Valley, south of Lhasa, to begin his training as a monk. Yeshe's family members had long been benefactors of the monastery and Yeshe also had given generously over the years.

The day they left, I climbed up onto my beautiful white horse and rode out to see Bhasundara, whom I hadn't visited since returning from Amdo. Fortunately, she was home, and as was often the case, she seemed to be expecting me. Po cha and some snacks were set out when I entered the small entry room. She was seated at the table and got up to greet me when I arrived, telling me to sit and warm myself with the hot tea. After some casual conversation, I told her that I had seen Dalha.

"In Amdo?" she asked.

I nodded. "It was you who suggested I go there. Did you know she would be in Amdo?"

"Tshomo, she would have found you wherever you were. When was it that you met her?"

"Nearly a year ago. Have you seen her since then?" I asked.

Looking at me with clear, steady eyes, she replied, "She left her body soon after that." As she spoke those words a wave of distress and disbelief passed through me. Seeing my emotional reaction, she added, "She is not gone, only her physical form is. But I hardly think of that body as her anymore."

"Dalha has died?" I asked in a whisper as I struggled to accept the truth of her words.

"If you think of her as the body, then yes. As Dalha would say, everything in this world is impermanent. Nothing remains forever. Her body was quite aged, and I think she was eager to be free of it. She came back shortly before you saw her in Amdo. She stayed with me for about a week, which was most unusual, and nothing else seemed out of the ordinary. But when I look back to that time, I understand now that she was preparing me. She took great care to oversee the medicinal plants I was growing, and she showed me new places not far from here where I could find rare healing plants. She wanted to set everything in order and then she left without telling me that she would not return. I said goodbye as I always did, expecting I would see her again at some point in the future.

"Several weeks after she left here, I was walking in the woods one day when a shiny object on the ground caught my eye. It was not one, but several shiny stones partially embedded in the soil. The sunlight filtering through the branches had fallen on them, and the stones sparkled with great luminosity. I bent down and dug them out; they were shimmering like the bluest blue crystal lake, like Nam Tsho herself. I had never seen such stones and had no idea what they were. That afternoon it rained and after the rain had cleared a most beautiful full rainbow appeared from one side of the sky to the other. An eerie feeling came over me and the thought then entered my mind that Dalha had left her physical form.

"I decided to find out about the property of the stones, thinking they might have healing qualities, so I took them into the city to show them to a gem dealer. When he saw the stones, he asked excitedly where I had gotten those precious gems. I wouldn't tell him and replied that I just wanted to know what they were. He told me that they were a rare gem, not native to our area, and he mentioned the name, which I can't remember. He saw that I didn't understand their value and was very eager to purchase them. At first, he offered a low price but when I refused, he kept raising the price, finally offering me much gold for the stones. I wasn't interested in selling them. I just wanted to learn their healing properties, but he didn't know anything about that. He kept pressing me to acquire them, but I wouldn't part with them because to me, they were a gift from Dalha. It is said that when a great soul leaves this world, he or she bestows gifts. I put it all together, the rare gems and the rainbow, and I knew it was her way of telling me that she was going. But she is hardly gone, Tshomo. I hear her speaking to me more consistently that I did before. It seems that she is closer to me now. Our Dalha is now free, free of all bodily limitations. How can we not be happy for her, Tshomo?"

My heart's rapid beat slowed as I listened to Bhasundara's words. So Dalha had come to give me a gift as well, a gift that would be a constant reminder of her presence. Bhasundara got up and went into the other room. When she returned, she brought with her a box and opened it so that I could see for myself the sparkling blue gems she had described.

"These must be very precious!" I exclaimed. Never had I seen such clear and shining blue stones. Lifting up one of the gems, she placed it in my hands and asked me to feel the energy.

"It is a powerful stone, isn't it?" she asked.

I nodded, "No wonder it is so valuable."

"Dalha always wanted me to be able to take care of myself. I know that. That is why she taught me about the plants so I could be useful to the community and be self-sufficient. I know these stones are very precious, but I hope I never need to sell them, as they are her gift to me. If I do ever find myself in a desperate situation, these stones will see me through."

"I also hope you never need to sell them," I murmured, placing the gem carefully back in the box.

"There are numerous other people in Lhasa who were close to Dalha. When I realized that she had left her body, I went to visit a few of them. Each one had been given a sign, or left a gift, and for each it was something very personal suited to their individual need."

"She gave me a horse, Bhasundara, who is right outside. When I met her in Amdo, it was soon after the horse I had had for many years died, and I had been reluctant to replace him. The horse she gave me is very special and I go nowhere without him. The strange thing is, I never have to tie him up. He never wanders off. He seems to understand me and listens to my every command. Most important, he is a constant reminder of Dalha. One thing saddens me though. Few people will ever know about Dalha. Many of our Buddhist monks are well known and greatly revered. They have the respect of the whole community, but who knows of her? There are no paintings, no statues, no books about her. How will she be remembered?"

Bhasundara smiled. "Does any of that matter, Tshomo? Dalha is like the wind, swift and unseen doing her work, but she leaves her mark, and no one who encounters her is left untouched. That is the sign of her greatness, just like the breezes leave a fragrance in their wake."

Bhasundara was thoughtful for a few moments and then continued. "I have not told you this story. When Dalha first found me as a child, that night I asked her name, but she didn't respond. I asked a few times, but she continued to remain quiet. The air was cold and dry. It was the night of the red full moon, which seemed larger and closer to us than usual, casting a subtle light on the landscape. It was bright enough so that we could see each other quite clearly. We had finished our meal. She had fed me so well, better than I had ever eaten before, and yet I found that strange because there was no place around us to get any food. She had taken it all out of the small bag she was carrying. As the night progressed, the air became bitter cold, but a warm current embraced me, and I was not uncomfortable. She had given me her jacket and sat beside me with only a light woolen top and skirt, and yet heat emanated from her body as if it were a stove.

"My parents were Bonpos and often spoke of the lha and their magic. Even though I was so young, I could see that she was truly extraordinary and had a magic of her own. I had to know what to call her and so after we had eaten, I asked again for her name. She was still silent, and then I looked up at the moon, and I said to her, 'I know who you are. You saved me and now there is a full moon, shining more brightly than I have ever seen, and so I think you have come from there. You are the Goddess of the Moon, Dalha.'

"She laughed joyfully, and replied, 'Then you may call me that.' This is how she got that name. During our years of travel together, I have heard people call her by different names, but to me she will always be Dalha. The name caught on and most people in Lhasa came to know her as that.

"Many years later, Dalha told me that I had once lived among the Han people toward the end of the Han Dynasty (3rd century China) and that I had been a Daoist and worshipped the Goddess of the Moon, whom the Han people call Chang'e. She said that I had lived in the forest and had spent my life serving my Daoist master. It was because of my devotion and service to him that she found me and has taken care of me. The reason she didn't tell me her name was that she wanted to see if my devotion to the Goddess of the Moon was still strong within me. Without my even knowing it, that feeling came up when I met her. I don't remember anything of the past, Tshomo, but it makes sense to me, and if Dalha said it, then it must be true. As a child when I was living with my parents, I remember how drawn I was to sit outside and watch the moon at night. I still do that. It must be because of my past devotion to that goddess."

"Do you think then that Dalha is her?" I asked in astonishment.

She shrugged her shoulders, but her tone grew more serious. "It doesn't matter to me who she is. All I know is the love she has shown me and the love I have returned. We shouldn't be sad, Tshomo. She has only gone home. She did not come into our world for fame or acknowledgement, for any recognition, or to gather a large following, but only to help her children find their way home, step by step."

I was at a loss for words and a period of silence followed. Finally, Bhasundara interrupted the quietude and asked in a lighter tone, "Will you introduce me to your new horse? I would like to meet this gift from Dalha."

I led her to where the horse was waiting. Seeing the beautiful white stallion, Bhasundara greeted him as she would a person. Then she stroked his mane and patted him on the back. "What is your name?" she asked, looking into the eyes of the horse.

"I call him Anpu (love)," I replied, answering for him.

"Anpu?" I nodded. A strange name for a horse.

"When Dalha came to me in Amdo, she spoke mostly of a higher love, not the limited emotion we think of as love; she said that love is a state of being that we must aspire for. I feel that was her message to me, and to be reminded of it every day, I call this horse, this gift from her, Anpu."

"Tshomo, there is a way to communicate with this horse."

"I know. He seems to understand me."

"You can transfer images to him. For example, if you want him to bring you here, picture my cottage in your mind and try to send that image to him. Animals think in terms of images not words. If you want him to bring you to Samye Monastery, picture it in your mind, look directly into his eyes, and send the image to him. Once he has taken a route, he will remember it. Dalha taught me this. It is a way to communicate with animals, especially those ready to take the next step in their spiritual journey. It is important that we treat them not as ignorant beings but as fellow travelers on the path. Dalha has given you a special gift, but as with all her gifts, the most important part is left to be uncovered. She has told me many times that when something is taken, something more precious is given. Now we must wait and see what she has in store for us."

"Whatever it is, Bhasundara, at least we have each other. In the past Dalha had often taught me through you, and I have no doubt that she will continue to speak to me through your voice."

CHAPTER 10

Knowing Yeshe

It had been four years since Tenzin entered Samye Monastery and he was home for a visit. Seeing how he had grown into such a thoughtful young man, I could not contest Yeshe's wisdom in sending him to the monastery. He was home but a few days when he took me aside and told me that the Abbot Tashi Dorje was sending a delegation of monks to Nalanda Mahavihara, the university in the Sena Empire (India) to study, and he had been chosen to go. Again, he was leaving, and this time he'd be further away; disapproval arose in me. I started to protest that he was too young to travel so far, when Yeshe entered the room.

"I will not go without your permission and blessing, Ama-la," he said decidedly, hoping to win me over. With a glance and nod of his head, Yeshe indicated to Tenzin that he should leave the room.

"This is your doing, isn't it," I proclaimed. Yeshe didn't answer. "He is only sixteen. Why would they send such a young monk? You must have arranged this." Yeshe looked at me tenderly without responding. "Why is it, Yeshe, that the only thing we ever argue about is Tenzin? I want to keep him close, but you are always sending him away, farther and farther from me. Going to the monastery was bad enough, but now you are allowing him to embark on such a dangerous journey." I knew that travel through the Himalayas to Gyagar was no minor matter.

"Come, sit with me." He took my hand and led me out into our small garden. "Whatever he has received at Samye Monastery cannot compare to what he will gain by going to Nalanda. Monks from many faraway kingdoms come to study there. Here he can learn Buddhist philosophy, but there he can learn Sanskrit, the Vedas, and the many streams of Vedic philosophy, logic, and advanced mathematics. There is no comparison. He will be taught not only by Buddhist monks but also by Kashmiri scholars and Brahmin pundits. It is the oldest and most esteemed place of learning in the world. How can we not celebrate that he has been chosen to go as part of this very selective delegation? It is only because of his great potential that the Abbot has chosen him."

"Did Abbot Tashi Dorje really choose him?" I asked meekly, aware that my wanting to hold on to my son was in many ways selfish.

Yeshe smiled as he looked at me with glowing eyes. "You do not realize, my dear, that our son is one of the most outstanding young monks in the monastery, with a great ability to comprehend subtle philosophical truths. I told you long ago that we must make any and every sacrifice to give him the opportunity to fulfil his potential."

"Is Nalanda then so special?" I asked, beginning to yield. It was always hard for me to counter Yeshe's arguments.

"The library is said to have several million books and manuscripts. Without doubt it is the largest library in the world. When the Chinese monk Xuanzang traveled to Gyagar, he spent two years studying at Nalanda and returned home with nearly 700 Buddhist texts. Our monks have been studying there and bringing back texts as well. The exposure they have received is greatly influencing and shaping the Buddhism of Böd. You know that I have always wanted Tenzin to understand other religions as well as his own. When he traveled with me through the Song Empire, I made sure that we met Daoist masters, and at Nalanda he will meet and study with famed Brahmin teachers. This is what I want for our son."

"I just want him to have a happy life and to be safe," I murmured.

Tenzin stood before us. He had come to say goodbye. I had made peace with his leaving and, although teary-eyed, I did not cling to him, but rather told him to learn all he could so that he could bring back his knowledge and enlighten the people of Böd. Ironically, it was now Yeshe who held on to him, hugging him tightly, and for the first time, I saw tears in the eyes of my usually composed husband. An uneasy feeling swept through me to see him like that. Yeshe was reaching his sixtieth year and was beginning to have bouts of poor health. Was he thinking he might not see his son again? I quickly brushed this thought from my mind.

Releasing his hold and looking intently into Tenzin's eyes, Yeshe instructed him on how to make the best use of his time at Nalanda. "Seek out those of wisdom and gain knowledge from the brahmins," was his counsel. "Learn the intricacies of the Sanskrit language. Apply yourself to the fullest. Make good use of the vast library. The years will pass and before you know it, it will be time to come home." There had been no time limit set to the journey of the monks from Samye Monastery. They were leaving with no set date of return, but we knew it would be a few years before we would see our son again.

After Tenzin's departure, Yeshe and I settled back into the quiet life we had established for ourselves after our son had left for Samye Monastery, with Yeshe spending the early morning hours in meditation and the afternoons devoted to our time together. In many respects, these were the happiest years of my married life. Yeshe had traveled so often while I was raising our daughters that I had not truly gotten to know him, and even after he had stopped joining the trade caravans, he was tied up with various business dealings in Lhasa and matters related to his family's lands and horse farms. All of that had now been handed over to the next generation.

I had always seen my husband as a wise and gentle man, but now I came to know the extent of his wisdom, and I found that although he was a professed Buddhist, he was in reality a man of many faiths. One day as we were walking through an alpine forest outside of Lhasa, he began speaking with reverence of a Daoist hermit he had met while traveling through the Song Empire with Tenzin.

"You sound almost like a Daoist yourself," I exclaimed in amusement.

"I am," he smiled. "And a Bonpo and a Shaivite. When I was only a few years older than Tenzin, traveling through the Sena Empire, I met a Kashmiri Brahmin, a devotee of the god Shiva, and I nearly became a follower. No, I did become a follower." He chuckled.

We stopped walking and sat down on a large boulder. I was carrying a small basket of food items and laid them out for Yeshe to eat. He handed me the water jug he had been holding and I took a long drink before passing it back to him.

"Yeshe, is it good to follow so many paths? Isn't it better to stick to one?" I asked in a serious tone.

"I do stick to one, you know that, but never do I allow my mind to think it superior to the others. I have met enlightened men and women from a number of different paths. I followed this Kashmiri Brahmin back to Kashmir and met his female teacher, a very powerful tantrika, who had the same ability to transform objects, the same magic that you seek in the Bonpo adepts. I stayed with him for several months and that is how I came to understand that his teachings were the same as what I had learned from Buddhism, although expressed differently."

"After seeing all that Dalha could do, magic no longer impresses me," I replied firmly. "It is true that in my younger days I was intrigued by it, from stories my mother used to tell us, but after coming to know Dalha...," I didn't finish the sentence. The very mention of Dalha brought her image to my mind and a surge of devotion welled up within me.

He finished my thought, "You then understood that the greatest magic is the inner transformation." I nodded. "We all have shadows that live within us, Padma, shadows from the past that we prefer not to see, and so we push them away. The adept knows how to transform those shadows into light and free us from past inclinations, habits, and ways of thinking. I never told you of my experience when I met the woman master in Kashmir, did I?" I shook my head. "It was she, a Kashmiri tantric, a Hindu, who introduced me to Guru Rinpoche and turned me into a Buddhist. When I left my family, I also turned away from all they tried to impose on me. Because they had tried to force me to become a monk, I rejected Buddhism. It was that Kashmiri Brahmin who gave me back my religion."

"You never told me about her."

"When have we ever had so much time alone to speak like this? It was a very personal experience, which I haven't shared with anyone. You know that I was not much older than Tenzin, only eighteen, when I left home, much to my family's dismay. They had made all the arrangements for me to enter Samye Monastery, but I resisted. My father pressed me so strongly that I decided to go as far away as I could. I wanted to see the world and, after a heated discussion with my father, I announced that I would travel to Gyagar and not return until I had found my place in the world."

"Weren't you frightened to travel that difficult route alone?" I asked, trying to imagine my respectful husband arguing with his father, with whom he had had such a loving relationship during the years that I had known him. At least Tenzin was not traveling alone but going as part of a delegation led by seasoned travelers.

Yeshe smiled. "I was an arrogant and restless youth then. It was my years of traveling through Gyagar that tamed me. I had rejected all that I had been brought up with; I wanted to experience the world for myself and decide on my own which path to follow. I was open to all. After a number of years of traveling from one place to another, visiting temples, working at menial labor, I met the Kashmiri brahmin I told you about. Along the way I encountered a number of hermits and sages, but he was the first who truly impressed me. He was modest and humble, a married man who had come to the Sena Empire on some business matters. I was on my way to visit Nalanda Mahavihara, which I had heard so much about, when I met him. Because of that meeting, I never made it to Nalanda. There was something about the intensity of this man's gaze, as if he could peer deep into one's soul, that struck me, and without any hesitation I followed him back to Kashmir. He invited me to stay with him and his wife, and I did odd jobs for him around his home. After a few weeks, he told me about his teacher, who was a master of tantra, and I asked to meet her.

"He delayed and delayed but finally after several months he took me to meet her. She was a very ordinary looking woman, stout, middle-aged, dressed in a colorful wool *pheran* (Kashmiri robe) and a floral head covering that wrapped around the back of her ears, resting on her back, in the style of people in that region." Yeshe looked thoughtful as he described her. "My first impression was that there was nothing special about this woman. She served us tea and chatted with us about mundane matters. Then as my friend indicated that it was time to leave, she told him to wait in another room, saying that she wanted to spend some time with me alone. I wondered if she was going to reveal a great teaching, some hidden mystery of the universe and I waited eagerly, but she just sat there without speaking, staring at me.

"After quite some time of silence, I began to wonder what this was all about and I started to relax, slouching a bit on my cushion on the floor as I waited for her to begin teaching. Suddenly in a firm voice, she told me to sit up straight and close my eyes. I did as she commanded, and then, I don't know what happened, but a huge force like a lightning bolt shot up my spine and I was gone—somewhere out in space. I had separated from this form of Yeshe and felt the whole universe was my body; my consciousness was everywhere. All of space, the planets and star systems, existed within me. I was the all-encompassing love and bliss that sustains the universe. It was most ecstatic and liberating. There are no words to describe that state of awareness. I have never experienced anything quite like that again, although I have had glimpses and the memory remains with me." Yeshe closed his eyes and became quiet for a few moments, as if trying to recall the experience. "When I returned to normal consciousness, I couldn't speak for some time. When I gained my voice again, I asked her what I had experienced, and she replied with one word: 'Shiva.'

"After some time, she helped me get up and led me into the room where my friend was waiting. As we were preparing to depart, she said to me, this time in a gentle tone, 'Go home and find Guru Rinpoche. He will give you what you need.' I didn't know much about Guru Rinpoche at that time, only that he had helped to spread Buddhism throughout our land of Böd.

"After we left the master's home, my friend told me that I had been alone with his teacher for nearly four hours. I was astounded because it felt like no more than a few minutes. When I tried to describe my experience to him, he replied, 'I believe that the state you tasted, you Buddhists would call *sunyata*. We call that Shiva. What you call emptiness, we call completeness. One must empty oneself of all that is unreal, of all illusion and sense of separateness, of all conceptual thought and qualifications, in order to come to that state of completeness, of wholeness, of unity. That luminous awareness contains all things and all places, all time and space, but is beyond them, and is as it was before they came into existence.'

"I became a different person after this. That one experience permanently altered me. A few days later I headed home. On the journey, I realized there was no outer way to meet the great Guru, who had left his bodily form so many centuries earlier, but I could meet him internally, and that is what I set out to do. Once I arrived back here, I began applying myself to the study of Buddhism, focusing my meditations on Guru Rinpoche. I debated whether to become a monk, but then I met your brother and he asked for my help with the caravan. He knew of my travel experience, and there was something inside of me that still resisted monkhood. I think it was because I was meant to meet you." Yeshe smiled. "My family had long ago given up on the idea of trying to make a monk out of me, and they were simply glad to have me back. They saw how I had changed and had become a dutiful son, eager to help manage our family's business matters. That Kashmiri man who brought me to his guru became my model. He was married with a family and ran a business, and yet he had a profound understanding of spiritual matters. Kashmir is a very special place where Buddhists,

Hindus, and Sufis gather, not only to discuss and exchange ideas but also to experience the sublime together."

Full of questions, after a few moments I asked, "Yeshe, you are so devoted to meditation, have you never had that experience again?"

His tone was thoughtful as he replied, "I could not have reached that state on my own. I believe it would have taken me many lifetimes. It was the blessing and gift of that woman tantric, whose name I don't even remember. We are taught not to yearn for anything, not even that. But through Guru Rinpoche's blessings, there have been times when I have experienced a taste, a momentary expansion into that awareness. I believe that when all my desires and ambitions have worked themselves out, then it will come again. I am on the path, which is all that matters."

"The state of Shiva," I whispered. "I cannot imagine what that is like."

"You will one day, Padma. After this life is over, our journey continues and continues until we reach that realization."

"Pumo has always wanted to go to Kashmir, and you have stirred this desire now in me. If I went, do you think I would meet such a tantric?"

He chuckled. "You don't have to go anywhere, Padma, except inside."

"You sound just like Dalha," I mused, remembering her last words to me. Deep inside, I knew that Yeshe was right. I didn't have to go to Kashmir. I had an amazing spiritual teacher, Dalha, who had come to me. We sat for a few moments in silence and then I asked, "If you were so set against becoming a monk, why then were you so certain it was the right path for Tenzin? Did you not do to him what your father had tried to do to you?"

"After Tenzin was born, I had a dream in which he was still a small boy but wearing the clothing of a monk, so I went to see an astrologer. He confirmed for me that this was a strong possibility, a desire from his past life during which he didn't have access to learning. Tenzin is driven by a thirst for knowledge. I saw this clearly when we were traveling through the Song Empire. Although he was still young, he was not shy when speaking with elders and could engage in mature conversations with them. Many people commented to me about this. I had an overbearing father and so resisted authority, but Tenzin has no such problem." Yeshe smiled. "Now that I have given him the best there is, he can do as he pleases. He will have had the most advanced education possible, and when he returns from Nalanda, if he decides to leave the monastery and marry, I will fully support him. For my family, they wanted the prestige of having one of their sons at Samye, and I was the youngest and only possible candidate. I have no interest in such prestige. I only want what is best for Tenzin. I have told you many times, we must make any sacrifice for his sake."

Hearing about Yeshe's past gave me insight into a part of him I hadn't known before. We had been married for many years, and yet so much of our time had been taken up with the details of daily life that I had not inquired as much as perhaps I should have about his early life. He was a man who kept much to himself, reserved and inward looking. In many ways he had the qualities of a monk, disciplined and almost austere in his personal habits.

I had greatly respected Yeshe when I married him and even had been somewhat awed by the extent of his knowledge, but I didn't call my sentiments for him at that time love. It took me some years to realize how my feelings had evolved. Now, during this time alone together, I saw how deep that love had grown, but I knew it was not the type of love of which Dalha had spoken. My love for Yeshe was still one of attachment and clinging. The thought of our parting brought intense pangs to my heart. He was my strength and my comfort, the one who kept turning my mind continually to spiritual matters. He was my everything, and I could not imagine what life would be like without him.

We sat there silently in the forest as the day's light began to wane. Neither of us seemed to want to move or speak. As I looked around at the surrounding trees, my eyes fell on a small, hardly noticeable stream of water flowing nearby, barely making a gurgling sound, and it reminded me of my mother. Never would she come to the forest without first acknowledging the spirits who inhabited the water and trees, but I didn't think to do that anymore. That had been such an important part of my childhood with her, even of my early adult years, and yet I had put aside that habit. I wondered if I had wronged her by neglecting something she had tried to instill in me.

"My mother often brought me here to this very forest," I said quietly. "She knew how to commune with the elemental spirits. Whenever we would come, she greeted them and made offerings. She taught me to do the same, but I don't do that anymore. Yeshe, I think that over time I have drifted away from my Bon practices."

"You shouldn't think of those rituals as Bon practices only. I saw many people in Gyagar do the same, and the Buddhist shamans and masters are also in communion with those spirits. But it is not the nature spirits that should preoccupy us. It is true that they maintain the balance in the natural world, and we must respect them by acknowledging their presence. The teachings and goals of Bon are the same as Buddhism, and the same as that of my Kashmiri friends—understanding the true nature of the mind, awakening compassion, expanding our consciousness, and becoming one with the deities. That, I believe, is what Bon teaches." After a pause, he added, "Didn't Tonpa Shenrab teach that underlying all existence is the primordial consciousness, which is our true nature, the foundation of the mind, the source of all? It is ignorance that shrouds this awareness."

"You know more about the deeper teachings of Bon than I do," I replied with a slight laugh. "Whatever little I know is from Bhasundara and Dalha, but most of what they told me, I didn't understand."

"What don't you understand, Padma?"

"When I last saw Dalha, she told me that the goddess is within me, not anything external. I still find it hard to grasp her meaning."

"Within and without, it is the same. The external world is but a projection, a dream of the dreamer. One can only understand this by going within to know oneself as the dreamer, with no true separate identity. The preoccupied human mind can't grasp this reality, and so we must empty the mind of its false preoccupations to see clearly. No words can describe the experience I had while sitting with that Kashmiri tantric, but I know what I experienced, and it forever changed me. From then on, I saw the world differently. I know that I am not separate from the dreamer creating all of this, no different from the deities themselves. Of course, that consciousness is not with me most of the time, but once had, that awareness never fully leaves."

"So the goddess is truly within me," I murmured.

"You are her projection," he replied in a voice as soft as a summer breeze. "And she is trying to wake up this projection so that you will remember you are none other than her. Who else could we be but her creations?" It was now almost fully dark, and I became aware that if we didn't immediately retrace our steps, we would have a hard time finding our way back.

"Well, this projection thinks we must leave this peaceful forest now, so we don't get lost," I replied in an amused tone as I rose from my seat on the boulder.

Two years passed and I could see that Yeshe's energy was declining: he was resting more during the day and engaging in far less physical work around the house. He caught me by surprise one morning when he told me that he was planning to visit Lhamo La-tso, the residing place of the deity Palden Lhamo, a journey he had long wanted to make, where one could peer into the lake and sometimes see one's past or future.

"It is a difficult journey, Yeshe," I commented, trying to dissuade him. "I went there once with Pumo when I was much younger, and it was challenging even then. At your age it will be even more strenuous."

"What pilgrimage is not difficult," he replied with a slight smile. "I will take my faithful walking stick."

"Then I will accompany you," I answered reluctantly. I had no desire to return to the lake, but I was more reluctant to let Yeshe travel alone. In truth it was not the difficulty of the journey that made me hesitant but the fear of what I might see when looking into the still waters of the lake. The last time I went I had been having horrible nightmares of a child witnessing the burning of a woman. I had long put aside those dreams, which had ceased to trouble me, but at the mention of the lake and the prospect of another visit, the memory of what I had experienced put me on edge.

A few weeks later the warmer weather arrived and we were enroute. I was comforted by the fact that I had my beloved horse Anpu with me. With him along, I felt Dalha's protection. I had met Dalha unexpectedly on my first visit to Lhamo La-tso and I half-expected to meet her again, although my mind told me this was impossible as she was long gone from this world.

Yeshe had made inquiries before leaving for our journey and was able to find a path through the mountains that was far easier to cross, making it possible for us to ride our horses almost to the edge of the lake, something that Pumo and I had not been able to do. For some reason, she and I had taken a more difficult route. Yeshe, far more accustomed to mountain travel, seemed to have a way of making the mountains bend to his will, revealing unnoticed pathways through the higher peaks.

A few pilgrims were seated by the lake when we arrived. We found a secluded spot and Yeshe sat down to meditate. I did the same, but meditation was not my strength. After a brief period of unsuccessfully trying to quiet my mind, I got up and began to walk around. Standing by the edge of the lake, I peered into her turquoise still waters, and was relieved to find no image staring back at me. I saw nothing of the past or future and was glad for that. I had brought with me a small brass bowl and bell, and taking them out of the pouch I carried, I conducted a brief ritual, one I had seen my mother and Bhasundara both do numerous times. Filling the bowl with water I had gathered from a nearby spring, I gently poured it into the lake and called upon the spirits of the water to receive my offering. Then I recited prayers of gratitude and prayers of protection for Tenzin and for the health and wellbeing of my family.

After I finished, I sat down and took in the beautiful scene before me. The clear pure waters were protected on all sides by bald mountaintops, greened on their lower slopes by recent summer rains. How I loved the lakes of our region, more stunning I imagined than anywhere in the world. Where else on earth were the lakes so close to the sky with such pure rarified air? The sky and water were like loving companions, reflecting one another. It had been so long since I had visited one of our sacred lakes, and I was grateful that Yeshe had insisted on making the journey. I never took these pilgrimages for granted, knowing full well that I might not have the opportunity again. I could not delve into what was called the interior worlds, as Yeshe did, but sitting by the water, feeling at one with the natural landscape, that was my meditation, and it led me into a very peaceful and joyous frame of mind.

The image of Dalha arose in my mind and I relived the scene of meeting her after Pumo and I had descended one of the mountains surrounding the lake. But as much as I tried, I couldn't remember her words, only that she told me I would have a son. As I sat there thinking of her, a smile crossed my face. Her body was gone, but her presence was real. I could feel her beside me, and I silently addressed her. "I know you are here, Dalha, watching me, as you always do." Glancing over to where Yeshe was seated, I saw that he was still deep in meditation and, after sitting for some more minutes, I decided to walk a bit further before returning to him. We had arrived at the lake early in the morning and the sun had now passed its noon zenith. Many hours had passed without him moving, but by the time I returned to Yeshe's side, he was beginning to stir and slowly open his eyes. From the look on his face, I could see that he had traveled far into the interior landscape, and I wondered if he had gone to the place where the Kashmiri tantric had taken him. But I never asked about his meditations or inner experiences and didn't do so now.

When he saw me, Yeshe smiled and rose from his seat on the ground. "We can leave now," he said simply. In silence we walked to where our horses were waiting and rode back through the mountains to where we had stayed the night before, a tent owned by a nearby Drokpa family.

After taking a meal with the family, we retired to our tent. Yeshe fell into a deep sleep rather quickly, but I lay awake for what seemed like hours. Finally, when I did drift off, I had the same dream that had haunted me in the past, which had disappeared for so many years only to re-emerge now. I saw myself as a young girl covering my face with my hands as my mother tried to force me to watch a woman who had been set on fire. It was a frightening scene, and I awoke with a start. Why had that dream returned after so many years? I wondered if it was the effect of the goddess Palden Lhamo, who was said to have a fierce nature. As I lay there, I heard Anpu making loud noises, as if he had also been frightened by something. Wrapping my blanket tightly around me, I went outside to see if he was alright. When he saw me approach, he began to shake his head so vigorously that his mane flew about in the windy air. Hugging him, I assured him that I was fine. It was cold outside, but I didn't want to go back inside the tent. I dared not shut my eyes again. Seating myself on the cold ground and gazing up into the star bejeweled sky, I tried to empty my mind, to erase the image that had so frightened me.

It was then that I heard Dalha's words from long ago when she had met me at this very lake, words I had forgotten. She had told me that she would suppress the nightmare for a time. Since it had come again, I suspected this meant there was something I had to resolve. I began to question whether I was revisiting a memory from the past or seeing something of the future. Was I that child or was I the woman on fire? At these thoughts, my body began to tremble.

I was so preoccupied that I didn't hear Yeshe step outside the tent, and his voice startled me. "Why are you out here in the middle of the night? You are trembling from cold."

"I couldn't sleep, and I wanted to enjoy the beauty of the night sky," I replied, attempting to hide my disquietude. "At home, we don't see quite so many stars."

"It is a clear night with no cloud cover or humidity and so the stars appear brighter and nearer to earth," he said quietly, sitting down beside me. "It is a rare opportunity for us to be here together, so let us enjoy the night sky." I extended the blanket to cover him as well, and as he put his arm around me, I rested my head against his shoulder. Yeshe's presence helped to ease the fright caused by the dream. I felt content to sit there beside him, feeling the warmth of his body, so very contented.

"I don't want this moment to pass," I murmured.

"It will pass, Padma, and we mustn't cling to it. But the memory will always be there. Memories recede, but they don't disappear. They stay with us from life to life."

"Did you have a good meditation by the lake, Yeshe?" I saw him nod but he said nothing, and I didn't press him. "While you were meditating, I made an offering to the water spirits and the goddess Palden Lhamo."

"Did you?" he asked. I nodded. "Then be prepared, my dear. She always responds, but not always in the way we think or desire. She is known to clear out *samskaras* (the imprints from past lives). She will free you from something."

"Is she a goddess who lives in the outside world or within us?" I asked in a drowsy voice.

He chuckled. "Both. Her power is within you, but her power can also take an external form."

"How is that possible, Yeshe?"

"It is all the mind, dear, the unfathomable luminous mind, the creator of all."

As we sat under the shimmering sky, for the first time I shared with Yeshe the nightmare that had pursued me since early adulthood, which had been suppressed but which had now returned.

"It is a memory from the past," he replied quietly. "Don't let it frighten you. Whatever needs to be worked out, will be. Palden Lhamo is the perfect one to call upon. She will guide you through this process. Hugging me more tightly as he spoke those words, he added, "Remember, love is the antidote to all suffering. Fill your heart with love; that is the only guidance you need."

"But how, Yeshe?" I asked internally. "But how?"

We returned home to our daily routine, but Yeshe's attention seemed to be elsewhere. Displaying greater reserve and quietude than usual, he spent more time in his morning meditation. Despite his apparent preoccupation, however, he also began paying more attention to every detail of the household affairs. I had never paid much mind to financial matters, but Yeshe now wanted me to know where all the valuables were, to understand the finances of the stores where we sold the teas, jade and silks carried back by our caravans from the Song Empire. One day he assured me that I would get income from the stores after he was gone.

"Why must you talk like that?" I responded with a frown. "That is years away."

"You forget that I am quite a bit older than you."

"Age doesn't matter. You are in good health." He didn't reply.

Many months passed and then one day Yeshe announced that he had to make a trip to Amdo to see his nephew about a matter relating to the trade caravan, and while there he would visit our daughters. "I haven't seen Samaya and Dolma in a long time," he told me.

"Then I should accompany you," I suggested.

He shook his head. "The last trip to the lake tired you out. You should stay here and rest." Hesitantly, he added, "I won't be gone long." Something in his tone alarmed me and I found myself protesting, saying that I didn't want him to travel alone.

He smiled, "I have traveled quite far on my own, but if it makes you feel better, I will take two guards with me."

"Take Anpu with you. He is our fastest horse." I didn't say it, but I also felt that Anpu had a protective quality about him, carrying something of Dalha in his spirit. He nodded.

Still, I had an uneasy feeling. Yeshe was no longer young and the journey to Amdo was a long one over difficult terrain. In the end, as I always did with Yeshe, I relented. The day that he was to leave, anxiety got the better of me and I clung to him as I had rarely done.

"What if you don't come home, Yeshe? What if I lose you?" I asked tearfully.

Pulling me away from his chest, with both hands holding my shoulders firmly, he looked into my eyes and spoke calmly and soothingly, "If, for some reason, I don't return, then I promise I will find you again. That is my promise, Padma, and I have never broken a promise. We have more than this one life, you know, much more."

"But I want to keep you with me in this life," I replied emotionally.

"We mustn't fear death or shrink from it," he reflected. With a smile, he added, "I am only going to visit our daughters, not far away at all. No matter what happens, I will always be with you. Don't think that I won't."

"Four months, Yeshe. That is all I give you. You must return to me within four months' time."

One evening four months later, almost to the day, my two daughters, Samaya and Dolma, appeared at my door. As soon as I saw them, I knew why they had come. Our beloved Yeshe had died.

CHAPTER 11

The Burning of Knowledge

There are no words, no tears, no way to express deep grief, which churns one's insides until one feels hollowed out, as if there is nothing left of oneself. The mind knows that death is part of life, but the heart doesn't easily accept what the mind knows. My churning went on and on while my family tried in every way to ease my sorrow, but nothing could bring back my beloved husband. Had he been ill and at home, I would have been able to say a proper goodbye, to express the depth of my love, but I knew that this was not what he wanted. It would have been too painful for him to watch my clinging, my agony at the thought of his departure, and perhaps that was why he chose to leave while away from me, so I would not attempt to hold him back.

My family members had all gathered around me—all except for Tenzin, who was still away at Nalanda. My three brothers, my daughters Samaya and Dolma, and my youngest daughter Yara each pressed me to come live with them. Only Pumo was silent. Three weeks had passed since Yeshe had died and I was as if in a stupor, unable to make any decisions, unable to envision a life without my husband.

In my mind I kept revisiting what Dolma had told me about his last days. After spending some time with Samaya and her family, my eldest daughter had gone with him to stay with Dolma. He had been in a very happy mood, entertaining the family with stories of his travels. His relationship with our second daughter, who doted on him, was very special. Growing up, she had been the one most affectionate with him, and on this last visit, he spent much time with her alone, asking about the details of her life and giving her much counsel regarding her children. No one seemed to notice or understand the gravity of his failing health.

One morning, a few weeks after he and Samaya had arrived at Dolma's, Yeshe rose early and rode out on my horse Anpu, without telling anyone. He loved to ride through the grasslands, the endless plains that seemed as expansive as the sky, and so they assumed he had only gone for an outing. When he didn't return by late day, Dolma sent two of the guards out to search for him. They found Anpu, who led them to Yeshe in the nearby mountains, which he had never had the opportunity to climb. It was there that they found his body, still as stone, seated in meditation. Dolma was distraught, blaming herself for not taking better care of him, and I had all I could do to comfort her after she arrived in Lhasa, leaving me little time to attend to my own grief.

With my family around, I had few opportunities to be alone. But even in their midst, I would go over in my mind my last conversation with Yeshe as he was getting ready to depart for the journey. Silently now, I peppered him with questions: when you left me, did you know you were not coming home? Did you want to die alone so that I would not hold you back? Why could you not have shared with me what you were facing? Why did you not prepare me? Questions with no answers.

"Then it is settled, Padma, we will close up the house and you will come live with me," insisted my eldest brother, Sonam. He was the same age as Yeshe and also not in good health; his eldest son and his family lived with Sonam and his wife. As much as I adored him, to live with my brother and his family was not what I wanted. Touched by his plea, I looked at him helplessly, unable to voice my opposition. This brother, who had assumed the role of the head of the family after our father had died, determined all the major decisions in our extended family. Yeshe had been his closest friend, and I knew that he felt it was his responsibility to care for me, his sister and his dear friend's wife. How could I refuse him? Fortunately, Pumo stepped in.

"Sonam, don't press her now," interjected my sister as she put her arm around me. "Can't you see that she is in no condition to make any decisions. We must wait until Tenzin returns. He will know what to do. Padma needs time to get adjusted. Everyone should now go home. I will stay with her until Tenzin returns."

I looked at her gratefully. How I wanted to be alone with her now so that I could deal with my own grief. I wanted nothing more than to keep my mind on Yeshe, remembering our life together. I didn't want to think of the future. I wanted to remain in the past.

"Are you sure?" Sonam asked with a frown, gazing at me. "I don't feel comfortable leaving you alone."

"I am not alone," I replied quietly. "Pumo will be here with me. But she is right. You should all return to your lives, and I will call for you if I need anything. Right now, it is best for me to wait for Tenzin." Reluctantly, he and my other brothers gave up pressing me to live with them. Instead of spending hours with me every day, they would check up on me once or twice a week, always bringing food from their household, and I had to admit that I was comforted by their care. After a few days, at Pumo's insistence, Samaya and Dolma returned to Amdo, and my youngest daughter Yara returned her attention to the demands of her life. Only Pumo was left with me. I was relieved because she knew how to live in silence; she allowed me to dwell in the past and encouraged me to speak when I needed to of my life with Yeshe.

A week later, she asked when Tenzin would be returning. "He is not coming home yet," I replied.

"Not coming home. Hasn't the abbot sent word to him about his father's death?"

I shook my head. "When the abbot heard about Yeshe, he came to see me, saying that he would immediately send a message for Tenzin to return, but I asked him not to, not to let him know about his father. He needs to finish his studies there. That is what Yeshe would have wanted and that is what I want, Pumo. As much as I need my son now, I can't interfere with his studies. He will return soon enough, I am sure."

She sighed. "I don't want to press you to come live with me, because I know that all your memories are tucked away in this house you shared with Yeshe, so I will stay with you until Tenzin returns, however long that is." I looked at her gratefully. Pumo and her husband were now living several hours away from Lhasa, working on murals for a new monastery. Her children were grown, and I knew that her husband Tashi wanted her to stay with me, but as much as I appreciated her comfort, I knew it was not right to keep her indefinitely from her painting of Buddhist images.

Taking her hands in mine, I looked into the loving face of my sister and gently insisted that it was time for her to return to her husband. "Pumo, you've stayed with me for many weeks and helped me get through the most difficult time, but I have to get used to my life alone. And it's time for you to get back to painting, to helping Tashi. Tenzin has been gone for almost four years, and I am sure he will return soon, any week now perhaps." I managed a smile, hoping to convince her. There was no need to further disrupt her life. After several days I managed to assure her that I would be fine, fully able to cope on my own. "After all, we are Sumpa women," I reminded her with a feigned smile. A week later she left.

For the first time since Yeshe's death, I was alone. In all those weeks, I had seen Bhasundara only once. She had come to me as soon as she heard of Yeshe's death, but my family was around me then and we were not able to speak privately. She had asked me to visit her after everyone had gone home. Now I was able to do that.

Riding on Anpu, who knew the path quite well, I sped to her cottage, which over time had been enlarged and made more comfortable. Bhasundara never liked to accept payment for caring for people who were ill. She always said it was the plant medicine that did the healing, and the plants had no need for payment. But in return, many people tended to her needs. One family had enlarged and reconstructed her broken down cottage so that she now had a proper place to live, modest though it was. At first, she had resisted this change because it had been she and Dalha who had fixed up the old cottage that had been in a state of great disrepair, but not wanting to offend the man, whose daughter she had healed, she finally had consented.

Bhasundara was home when I arrived, and in front of her I released the avalanche of tears that I had tried so hard to restrain in front of my family, but if I had expected sympathy and coddling, this was not what I received. When between sobs I cried out that I had lost my dearest friend, she responded in a somewhat detached tone, "Who lost him and what has been lost?" I was in no mood for her riddles and allowed the tears to flow freely. Finally, she spoke to me in a more sympathetic tone.

"Days before he left for Amdo, Yeshe came to see me."

"Yeshe came here?" I asked in a tearful voice as she handed me a cloth to wipe my eyes. Yeshe had never been to Bhasundara's cottage, so I wondered how he knew where she lived. "How did he find you?"

A fleeting smile crossed her lips as she replied. "It was Anpu who brought him." When she told me this, I remembered that right before Yeshe had left for Amdo, he asked to borrow Anpu. She continued. "He told me that when the two of you had gone to the sacred lake, Lhamo La-tso, in meditation he saw that his time of departure was near. He wasn't sorry, Tshomo. He was ready, but he told me that he hadn't been able to spend much time with his two daughters in Amdo over the past many years, and he wanted to see them once more. He also thought it would be easier to depart this world if you were not together. That is why he left for the trip without you, but he wanted to take something of you with him. I know you gave him your precious Anpu for the journey." Bhasundara was quiet for a few moments and then continued. "He knew how dependent you had become on him, and he said that you must find your own strength, come into your own spiritual power, and it is time for you to do that, Tshomo. He had great confidence in you, as do I.

"When he was here, he asked me to perform a Bon ritual, which I did. When I finished, I turned to him and saw his eyes wide open, staring ahead intensely as if he were looking through me. With the slightest smile, he gently closed his eyes, shifted into meditation, and stayed that way for a long time, at least two hours. I could feel a powerful spiritual energy around us and didn't want to leave him, so I entered meditation myself, experiencing a deeply peaceful and joyful state. After some time, I opened my eyes and waited as he gradually returned to the external world.

"We didn't speak at first because his attention was still withdrawn, but after a while I asked him what he had experienced. He told me that while I was performing the ritual, he saw standing behind me the form of a tantric master he had once met when he was in Kashmir. She had come to show him how to leave his body consciously when the time came. We spoke only briefly and then he told me he had to get back to you, that he was spending as much time with you now as possible. I walked him to where Anpu was waiting and before mounting, he said, 'This will be a difficult time for Padma. Stay by her side as much as possible. She receives tremendous upliftment through your friendship and teaching.' He spoke with strong feelings and, of course, I promised to do so. Then he told me that on your trip to Lhamo La-tso together, you had that nightmare again and he feared some old samskara would soon emerge. He was concerned about this, but I assured him that Dalha would be there to guide you through it. It was only after I had given him this assurance that he smiled, thanked me, and departed."

My eyes moistened again as I murmured, "He was facing death and still thinking of me."

"You know your husband, Tshomo. Isn't that the way he was? I had only met him a few times, but I could tell how deeply he cared for you and how responsible he was. He knew it would be difficult for you to be without him. I am sure he thought that I could help you, because I have lived alone all these years and have found it to be exactly what is needed for spiritual effort. That is what you must focus on now, Tshomo, your spiritual life. Many of your married years were spent apart from Yeshe. This will be no different."

"But he won't be coming home anymore. I was always waiting for him to return, but now... now there is no more waiting."

"We all meet again and again," she replied in an even tone. "We disappear and then appear again. You should be grateful for what you did have." Her words brought me little comfort, but there was something else on my mind that I had to ask her about.

"Yeshe was a devoted Buddhist. He asked you to perform a Bon ritual and, when you did, a Kashmiri Shaivite master appeared to him. It doesn't make sense."

She cracked a faint smile and answered with a question, "Have you still not settled this issue?" I looked at her inquisitively. "How many times have I explained that Buddhism and Bon exist in harmony? One does not exclude the other. How many times has Dalha told you this?" She poked me almost teasingly. "I think your husband had a deep understanding of Bon, and also of the Kashmiri teachings, which are no different."

I was quiet for a few moments and then reflected, "Truthfully, over the years of living with Yeshe, hearing so much about Guru Rinpoche and Yeshe Tsogyal, I naturally have gravitated toward Buddhism and my connection to Bon has weakened. I want to recapture that."

"Why?" she asked.

I was surprised by her response and asked, "What do you mean 'why'? I am a Bonpo."

"What does it mean to you to be a Bonpo?"

Her voice was challenging, and her question caught me off guard. At first, I didn't know how to answer. After a few moments I replied, "To conduct the rituals, of course, and to acknowledge and speak to the nature spirits, and . . ."

Shaking her head, she cut me off. "It is not enough to speak to the spirits, Tshomo. You must learn to listen to them, for they can provide the answers to all your problems, great and small. A Bonpo knows how to listen and learn from nature, which holds much wisdom. Nature knows how to harmonize opposing forces and can help foster harmony and balance in your mind. You need to learn to listen."

"How can I hear that which doesn't speak?" I mumbled more to myself than to her.

"Tshomo, where is the mind?" she asked me abruptly. I pointed to my head, wondering how that was relevant, but again she shook her head. "The mind is everywhere, in the water, in the trees, in the grasses. That all-knowing mind can speak to you through any means. The nature spirits are part of that great universal mind. The more one is in harmony and communion with them, the more one opens to that vast awareness of which we and they are a part."

"You have become a Buddhist, Bhasundara," I replied in a somewhat challenging tone.

"Tshomo, why do you keep needing to define everyone? In my time with Dalha she spoke more to me about Guru Rinpoche than anyone else. I used to wonder why, then I realized that she gives everyone exactly what they need. Although I was born into a Bon family and community and perform Bon rituals, I believe my future will lie more in the Buddhist realm and she wanted to align me with that great guru. I have spoken with other people in Lhasa who have told me that she only told them stories of Tonpa Shenrab. She deals with each of us differently. There is no one set of rules for Dalha."

"Yeshe was able to integrate it all so easily," I replied with a small sigh. "Although I am trying, I am not yet able to do that. Now that I am alone and must face life on my own, I need to find myself again, find my identity apart from Yeshe. Dalha always urged me to keep my mind on the goddess, but I have not been able to do that. She is the only one who is real to me, because I think of her as my teacher and friend, someone who knows and understands me, someone I can talk with…"

Bhasundara laughed lightly and muttered, "As if the goddess isn't." Then turning my mind to Dalha, she said, "There are many reasons why she gave Anpu to you; it was not only for your sake, Tshomo. Great adepts also help animals evolve, and Anpu is at the stage when a certain leap is possible, a jump to a human birth. Her blessing bestowed on him a special intelligence and the gift of memory. That is why he easily recalls routes and people and seems to understand when you speak to him. His next birth, I believe, will be a human one."

"Really?" She nodded. "That doesn't surprise me. He is smarter than any other horse I have known."

"Dalha had great sympathy for animals. She once told me that she remembered well taking birth as an animal, and still liked to take an animal form every now and then so as not to forget their abilities and limitations. She especially loved the birds and the freedom they had to fly, and that was why she sometimes assumed their form."

"She continues to amaze me, and hearing about her never fails to uplift me," I replied in wonderment, feeling much better than when I first arrived. After reflecting for a few moments, I added, "If only I could follow Dalha's guidance and find the goddess. I believe only she can heal this deep hurt in my heart." Bhasundara smiled but didn't answer. "Why are you smiling like that, Bhasundara?"

"Why do you keep distinguishing between Dalha and the goddess? Have you not realized that they are one and the same? And where did she tell you to look to find the goddess?" Bhasundara pointed to my heart, as Dalha had done in Amdo when I had seen her last. She was quiet for a few moments and then began again. "To cheer you up, I will tell you a story about something that happened to me a few years ago. Do you remember when I told you about the precious stones that I found in the forest after Dalha had left her body?"

I nodded. "You still have them, don't you?"

She shook her head. "After I found them, I realized that Dalha must have manifested them for me, and so I treasured them. Of course, I didn't understand their value and that was not what was important to me. It was the fact that I saw them as Dalha's parting gift to me, like Anpu was to you. You know that I have never had a lock on my door, but I got a lock after that. I purchased a small box and hid them away, buried under a blanket, but every night before my meditation, I would take out the box, hold one of the gems and think of Dalha. They became my most precious possession, the only possession I really cared about, but they were also becoming a burden because I was growing so attached to them. First it was subtle, and then not so subtle; those stones began to control me. They were always in the back of my mind. I mistakenly confused them with Dalha, but Dalha is not anything material.

"Then one day I was called to tend to a man who was gravely ill. He had once held a prestigious position in the government and had enjoyed wealth, but for some reason had lost everything. He had many children to care for and his wife was desperate at the thought of losing him. I couldn't save the man, and as he lay dying, I saw how distraught he was knowing that his wife and children would have no means of support. The thought entered my mind to bring him the stones, and so I did, telling him that I had found them in the forest, probably lost by a traveling merchant, and that I had no need of them. I offered them to him. Initially he refused, but I was insistent, and in the end, he accepted the gift and died soon after. I helped the wife sell those gems and that is what spared his family from a dire future."

As Bhasundara was speaking, my eyes opened wide in disbelief. But she wasn't finished. "As soon as those gems were out of my hands, I felt such a relief, a sense of freedom," she continued with a smile. "Then a few nights later I was awakened by the sound of Dalha laughing. You have heard her laughter, Tshomo. It is so distinctive. There was no mistaking it. And then I heard the words internally, 'that man was a great devotee of Guru Rinpoche. Due to an old samskara he had been deprived of his position and lost his wealth, but despite all his difficulties he never lost his faith or devotion to the great Guru, and that Guru has now taken care of his family. That is the love of the guru for the students. It is a mutual love.' Tshomo, don't you see? Guru Rinpoche didn't spare that man from going through trials because he had to learn certain lessons and reap the result of past actions, but he eased his mind of his greatest worry. Internally, the man had fully surrendered to him and accepted his fate."

"I don't understand, Bhasundara, what you are saying? It was Dalha who left you those gems. How is Guru Rinpoche involved in this at all?" I asked in a somewhat annoyed tone. Increasingly, my friend was associating Dalha with Guru Rinpoche, and I was not able to understand why.

"The great masters work in concert," she replied quietly. "They are one mind. Remember the one universal mind we just spoke about, of which we are all expressions?" She paused while I looked at her blankly. "Perhaps it is not easy to comprehend, but I have seen it work in such a way again and again, and I have told you many stories like this. Sometimes you pray to a particular deity or form and another form responds, showing you there is only One. But Tshomo, the whole experience held a most important lesson for me."

"What lesson? It seems to me that you lost your security for the future."

She leaned forward and her voice dropped to an almost inaudible pitch as she replied, "Surrender. Total and complete submission to the guru, or the goddess, or the dharma, however you want to think of that one higher truth. It is all the same. By surrender, I don't mean to a personality, an individual, but to the higher Self, of which the awakened ones are but expressions, manifestations, as we are. It is the surrender of the narrow, limited ego to that higher all-knowing Self. That is why Dalha kept telling you to look within for the one you seek." Bhasundara paused, sensing that I wasn't following her and so returned to the story of the stones.

"I knew that it was Dalha who had put into my mind the idea of giving those precious stones to the dying man. Their purpose with me had been served, and I was to gain greater freedom in passing them along than in hoarding them. The stones were not my security. Dalha is. My love for her is the only security I have. As I thought about it more deeply, I wondered if Dalha was not helping me repay an old debt. The fact that I responded so quickly without any hesitation made me think that perhaps I had owed that man something from a previous birth, and Dalha was helping me to repay it. Perhaps that was the reason why she had me find those gems in the first place, and had I clung to them I would not have been able to satisfy that old samskara."

Turning my eyes away from hers, I murmured, "That all seems very complicated. I don't understand how Dalha could have arranged all of that."

"If you think of her as a personality, as merely a Bonpo woman who knows a bit of magic, then it doesn't make sense. But if you see her as one with the universal mind, it makes perfect sense. Karma is complex, far more than the thinking logical mind can fathom. That is why only one of great realization can help us work through the many samskaras that lie hidden within the folds of our being."

Then she added, "But there was another teaching for me. I knew that Dalha wanted me to give up even my attachment to her. I had begun to associate the gems so strongly with her, and she was helping to break this illusion. She took care of me in another way, and this was most touching. Soon after I had given the gems away, a family, whose daughter I had tended to, insisted on helping me repair and expand my cottage. Other things came my way as well, and I understood that an important principle of the universe is to let the energy flow through you, not to block it, not to hold on to anything. By clinging, you are preventing the flow of energy, like a dam bottling up the life force. Don't cling, Tshomo, even to Yeshe. Let him go and you will feel even greater love. After I learned of Yeshe's passing, I went into meditation and felt his joy, the expansion of his consciousness. Try to be aware of that. He accumulated much merit in this life and that merit will carry him forward.

"Remember that when something is taken, something else is given. Love will flow to you from another direction, of that I am sure. It is a law of the universe. The universe will provide for you, Tshomo, and I don't mean in terms of wealth. You will have everything you need for the next step in your journey, since everything you need is within you. If you want to find the goddess, look within. If you want to find Dalha, look inside, for that is where she resides."

"If she is not a Bonpo adept capable of magic, then who is she?" I asked, opening my eyes wide as I turned to fully face Bhasundara.

"That is not the right question to ask, Tshomo. The right question, the only question, is 'who are you,'" she replied with a caring look. "When you have found the answer to that, you will know who Dalha is."

Bhasundara's words brought some relief to my sorrowing mind, but they also left me with a sense of my own lack. I had come to her for sympathy, but I had received something else. It was as if she wanted to jolt me out of my depressed state and turn my attention in another direction. In the process, I became increasingly aware of what I considered to be my spiritual incompetency. I so admired her clarity of mind. Bhasundara was incredibly receptive to Dalha's guidance; instinctively she knew to give the gems away and didn't hesitate. I knew that I would not have been able to do that. My faith was not so strong, and I had no concept of surrender. Surrender to what, to whom? Where or who was this higher Self of which she spoke? As much as I was awed and comforted by Dalha, I did not regard her as someone to whom I would surrender my every wish, my every desire, my very being, the way Bhasundara had.

How was I then to gain such receptivity and clarity? The only way I could think of was to devote myself more to my Bon practices and this is what I attempted to do. As often as I could, I would ride Anpu to the forest, bringing my ritual items, and I would address the nature spirts and perform the rituals I had learned. I thought often of Bhasundara's words that a true Bonpo was one who not only spoke to the nature spirits, but also listened to them. I had no idea how to do that. All I knew was that the rituals I performed did not have the impact I desired. Why had Yeshe been so affected by the Bon ritual that Bhasundara had performed, and I, a confirmed Bonpo, could not feel the spiritual power of the rituals? What was I lacking? This question haunted me, enhancing my sense of inadequacy. I questioned my spiritual commitment, which I had not done when Yeshe was alive. I even began to wonder why Yeshe had married me, when in my mind he was so much further advanced in spiritual practice and knowledge. I watched myself sink deeper and deeper into the pit of self-doubt. The visit to Bhasundara, while offering a temporary balm, did not prevent the downward spiral that now took over me.

It was at this time that I received a visit from the abbot of Samye Monastery. Nearly six months had passed since Yeshe's death and I assumed he was coming to check up on me, to see how I was getting along. I was expecting to hear praise of Tenzin, as was usually the case. After serving him tea and food, I asked about my son, waiting to hear how he was excelling at Nalanda, winning the admiration of the monks there. Instead, he responded with silence.

"Is Tenzin well? Is anything wrong??" I asked with a slight tremble in my voice as an ever-present underlying anxiety about my son came to the surface.

"Tenzin is fine," he assured me. "He and most of the other monks will soon begin their journey home. They should be back in a few months."

"Has he finished his studies then?" I asked, relieved. He didn't answer right away. "I want him to stay there until he has completed his studies," I insisted. "This is what his father would want."

"That is no longer possible," he replied quietly.

"Why?" I inquired.

"Nalanda has been destroyed." His voice was barely audible but in it I could hear his pain.

I didn't understand him and asked in a quiet voice, "What do you mean, destroyed?"

A bitter expression settled on his face. "I mean destroyed, burned down by the Turkic General Muhammad bin Bakhtiyar Khalji. He is known to be a brutal man and is on a rampage massacring Hindus and Buddhists and burning all places of learning." He shook his head and continued, "This is the third attack on Nalanda and now nothing is left. The library burned for three days. Millions of books and manuscripts are gone. It is a sad day, a very sad day for the seekers of knowledge. Two of our monks were killed. Tenzin and some of the others had gone to see the remains of Vikramshila Mahavihara (destroyed by Khalji in 1193) when it happened, and so fortunately they were spared the sight of the destruction. Vikramshila is gone and now also Nalanda, as well as some of the other places of learning. One of the monks who was killed was an older man, Norbu Dorje, a man of high spiritual realization and a mentor for the younger monks. You may have heard Tenzin speak of him. His death is a great loss for us."

"Norbu Dorje was killed," I repeated quietly in disbelief, trying to absorb what he was telling me. He nodded. "Tenzin has spoken of him often," I murmured. "He helped Tenzin a great deal when he first entered the monastery and was almost like a father figure. For Tenzin to lose both his father and this mentor at the same time…" my voice fell off.

"As soon as the monks return, I will send Tenzin to you without delay. A few of our monks are staying behind to try to salvage whatever they can from the library, but I have sent a messenger to ask that Tenzin return with the rest of the group. Our monks are fortunate, they can return here, but the monks who must stay will suffer under Khalji's rule."

I was in too much of a daze to respond, relieved that my son was safe but deeply pained by the tragedy, especially knowing how it would affect Tenzin. After the Abbot left, I tried to understand what had happened. Who would destroy a place of learning? For what purpose? It was beyond my comprehension. From that moment on, the thought of what had happened to Nalanda occupied my mind, and I had to put aside my lingering sorrow over Yeshe's death and feelings of my own spiritual shortcomings. What did my personal challenges matter in the face of such a colossal tragedy? I could only imagine what my son and so many thousands of monks and spiritual seekers were experiencing.

For several months I waited anxiously for my son's return. When I saw Tenzin for the first time after four years, I was at a loss for words. He was a man now, towering over me. His demeanor was quiet and inward looking, like his father. Tenzin had always had a cheerful and thoughtful disposition, but in addition he now displayed a maturity that was most comforting at a time when uncertainty gripped both my personal life and the life of our society. When he first arrived back at the monastery, after weeks of travel, one of the monks there had offered condolences over the death of his father, and so by the time he reached me, he already knew about Yeshe's passing. It was a blow, I could see by the pained look in his eyes when he met me, but he was restrained in showing his grief. When he pressed me for details about his father's last days, I shared with him that we had gone to the sacred Lhamo La-tso, and in meditation Yeshe had had a premonition of his impending death. I told him what little I knew of his last days in Amdo, how he had gone off alone and left his body while in meditation in the mountains. He pressed me for specific dates and times. Then he told me that he had had a most uplifting dream of his father around that time. His father had been in a very joyous state and spoke only a few words.

"He told me how proud he was of me and that I should continue my studies," said Tenzin quietly. "But Ama-la, I can continue my studies here at home. I don't have to be in the monastery for that."

Tenzin was clear that he should leave the monkhood and come live with me. He said that he would spend the mornings studying and the afternoons working in one of our family's shops. Instead of objecting, I nodded my approval. So relieved was I to have him back that I thought this was the best course, at least for me. At that moment I wasn't thinking of what was best for Tenzin.

Every day he would rise early, sit for a while in his father's meditation seat and then before going to the shop, spend some time translating manuscripts that had been rescued. At first, he didn't want to speak of the fire or what had happened to Nalanda. But over time he began to open up, and I learned that he had lost friends and teachers in the tragedy. "When I left to return home, Ama-la, the vast university was still burning. Even after weeks, the fires didn't stop. The destruction was on such a scale that it was hard to comprehend."

"What kind of people would do this?" I asked in dismay.

"The Ghurid Empire is collapsing. It has been weakening for years, and their Turkic Mamluk fighters have gained control."

"The Mamluks, I have not heard of them," I murmured. "Your father had never mentioned them." Yeshe had spoken of the Ghurid invaders from Gandhar (Afghanistan) who continually invaded Gyagar, seeking the wealth of kingdoms to its south. During Yeshe's travels he had learned that the Ghurids had been converted from Buddhism to Islam when Mohammed of Ghazni had conquered them. But who was this new tribe, the Mamlucks?

"The Mamluks are the Turkic slaves of the Ghurids," Tenzin explained. "They originate from the Khalaj tribe that migrated and settled in Gandhar about two hundred years ago. They are uneducated and uncultured. The Ghurids used the Mamluks to fight their wars against the Sena Empire. As the Ghurid Dynasty weakened, the Mamluks grew in power. They seek to eradicate Buddhism and attacked Nalanda twice before, but this time, so much has been destroyed that it is unlikely it can be restored.

"Before I left, I heard a rumor. The story is that their leader, Bakhtiyar Khalji, became sick and none of the doctors in his court could cure him. He was advised to seek help from Rahul Sri Bhadra, the head of Nalanda, who is an expert in Ayurveda, the Vedic medical system. At first, he refused to call in a non-Muslim, but as he became sicker, he had no choice but to relent. When Rahul Sri Bhadra arrived, Khalji placed a restriction on him. He didn't want to take Ayurveda treatments, so Bhadra had to cure him without the use of any medicine. Bhadra knows the power of mantra and prayer and asked Khalji to repeat continually for several days a passage from the Koran, the holy book of the Muslims. Because Khalji had a firm faith in those verses and kept his mind focused, he was cured. Instead of being grateful, he was furious that this scholar knew more than the physicians in his court, and he decided to destroy the Hindu and Buddhist learning centers, the scholars, teachers, and students. It is just a story, Ama-la, and it is unlikely to have happened in the way the rumor states, but it says something about the mindset of those people. They are seekers of power, not of knowledge, and cannot tolerate the wisdom of traditions other than their own. They are driven by ignorance and their means are brutal. It is tragic that they have conquered the northern parts of Gyagar, but we should be grateful they have not come here. Böd will be a place of refuge for Buddhists and all seekers of knowledge. I believe many of the monks from Nalanda will now flee here."

As I listened to Tenzin's sober description of events, for the first time I became seriously concerned about what was taking place outside of our neatly contained world of Lhasa. Earlier in my life I had shown no interest in politics or history, but since Tenzin's return with his father from the Song Empire years earlier, my curiosity had developed. Tenzin was like a history book himself, retaining all knowledge he gained from manuscripts and discussions with scholars. Previously, I had listened to his discussions with Yeshe, but I was now taking on a new role, eager for understanding myself, knowing that Böd was not truly safe from outside invasions. The Mongols of the northern steppes had for years been infiltrating Amdo, and Yeshe had once said that it was only a matter of time before they were strong enough to take the region by force. Was Böd's future to be the same as the fate of Gyagar, to be occupied and taken over by an external power? I hoped that the merit accumulated by our Buddhist and Bon adepts would prevent this.

Day after day, I watched Tenzin completely engrossed in his studies and in translating into our language manuscripts that he and some of the others had brought back from the remains of Vikramshila. When Tenzin had left Nalanda, since the fires were still burning, they had not been able to get into the library to see what remained, but they were fortunate to bring back some texts from that other great university. As I observed him, the counsel of Bhasundara about letting go came to me. A few weeks later, I went alone to the forest, to the place where Yeshe and I had frequently gone in those last months together, and after sitting quietly for some time, I performed my usual ritual.

"How I miss having you here to guide me, Yeshe," I murmured to the sedate, unruffled air while my heart throbbed with the pain of his absence. I had not visited this place since we had been there together, but I felt that if I came to the spot where we had so often sat in quiet reflection, I would receive some guidance on what to do about our son. As I silently called out to Yeshe, the unmoving air gave way to a slight breeze, which brushed across my face, and I took that as a sign from the spirits; they were acknowledging my presence and my offering, and I thanked them. I realized I was not alone; they were there with me, as perhaps he was.

"Help me, Yeshe, make the right decision." I whispered again and again. Sitting there, wondering how to guide my son, the calming forest air brought a clarity to my mind and awakened the memory of what Yeshe had repeatedly said to me over the years. "We must make any and every sacrifice for the sake of our son. He has much to offer the world."

"You were right then, Yeshe, and are right now. I must not think of myself. I must do what is best for Tenzin." As I stood up, Bhasundara's words about listening to nature's guidance returned to me and for the first time I thought to myself, so this is how it is. This is how the nature spirits speak to one, through one's own mind. A communion had clearly taken place. I had come to the forest confused, not knowing what to do about my son, but I was leaving with a clear mind. Whether it was the spirits of the trees, of the wind, or the stones that lined the forest floor, I didn't know, but those spirits were now guiding me at a time when I needed it most, and I prostrated myself in gratitude.

Returning home, I told Tenzin that it was time to begin thinking about his return to the monastery. Three months had passed since he arrived home from Nalanda.

Seated at his writing desk, he looked up at me inquiringly. Smiling, I replied to his unasked question. "Your destiny is not to work in a tea shop or to be a tea trader, but to be a teacher. I am quite clear about that."

"But you will need me, Ama-la, and it is my responsibility," he replied firmly.

"You will always be here for me, as your father is. But it is time for me to find my own way in life. Nobody can help me. It is a path that I must walk alone."

After a few days of discussion, Tenzin relented. When I saw the eagerness in his eyes, I knew I had made the right decision. My son returned to the monastery, and I began to contemplate what that next step in my journey would be.

CHAPTER 12

A Storm Brews

I was waiting, waiting for something, but I didn't know what. I was no longer waiting for my husband to return to me, but rather for something else to manifest, perhaps related to that nightmare that had come to me again after Yeshe's passing. Before his death, Yeshe had made provisions for all my future needs and so I suffered no want. I continued my life, learning to be more solitary, struggling with loneliness and the feeling of my own spiritual limitation. Three years had gone by since Tenzin's return to Samye Monastery when I received a message from the Abbot urging me to visit. I had never quite overcome my underlying anxiety over Tenzin's wellbeing, so I hurried on Anpu to the monastery.

Normally, Yeshe would take several days to reach Samye, allowing plenty of rest stops for his horse, but I knew that if I left at the first light of dawn, Anpu could reach there in a day if we paused for only brief stops. I had ridden to Samye with Yeshe numerous times after Tenzin had first entered the monastery, but that was years ago, and I had never made the trip without him. The path was straight forward, following the Lhasa River as it wound its way south and east to join with the Yarlung Tsangpo (Brahmaputra River). In the past, we would always travel leisurely to Samye, stopping frequently to relish the river's beauty. On occasion, when I was moved to do so, I would conduct a ritual by the river's edge while Yeshe sat in meditation. Once we had even taken time to climb the sand dunes that lined the northern bank. I was a woman who loved the lakes of our land, encased in the earth like shimmering jewels surrounded by the mountain gods who protected them, but Yeshe loved this river more than any other body of water. Our walks and reflections by the rushing cobalt-blue waters were an added treat to the joy of visiting the monastery and seeing our son. Now the ride brought up many precious memories, but I didn't allow myself time to dwell on them, as my mind anxiously rehearsed all the possible ills that could have befallen my son.

I reached the monastery as the sun was setting, and after taking Anpu to the Samye stables, I went to find the Abbot. Before meeting me, he insisted that I be served an evening meal, so I ate and drank while I waited eagerly for his arrival. When he finally came into the reception room to greet me, he seemed cheerful enough. I was relieved but wondered why his message had a sense of urgency to it. I would not have ridden Anpu so fast if it were just a normal visit. My first question was about Tenzin, and my voice must have revealed my anxiety, because he immediately assured me that there was nothing to worry about, and I sighed in relief.

"But he has had some minor mishaps," he began in a halting voice, "and that is why I called you here."

"What kind of mishaps?" I asked with a tightening throat.

"Nothing serious, I assure you. This is not really about Tenzin, but about you. Let me explain." He was quiet for a few moments while I looked at him questioningly. Then he continued, "About a three-hour ride from here, closer to Lhasa, a new monastery has been built. I knew the abbot that oversaw the construction and organization of the monastery. He was a good monk but rather weak, and he allowed others to control him, to put into his mind ideas of grandeur. One of the monks there quickly rose through the ranks and became the top advisor to the abbot. This monk was very ambitious and competitive with our monastery. He began spreading word that Samye was old and outdated, too restricted by tradition and lacking people of spiritual stature." The Abott paused and chuckled, then added, "How can spiritual knowledge be outdated!

We have the history, respected elders of great wisdom, and the best of the young, and perhaps that is what caused his envy.

"Eventually this monk did attract some attention, significant donations, and he began to draw many aspirants. Over the past few years our young monks have held a number of debates with the monks of that monastery, and our young men have always far surpassed theirs. Your son, Tenzin Sangye, led some of those debates; there was nobody there of his intellectual level and so this monastery began to notice him.

"Several months ago, the abbot mysteriously died, and his ambitious advisor became the new abbot, calling himself Zerdan Rinpoche. That was not his name previously, but this is how he is now known. A rumor spread that the previous abbot had been murdered. Since I knew him quite well and was somewhat fond of the man, I decided to investigate; sadly, I came to the conclusion that his death was not by natural means, but I had no proof and so could not make any claim.

"To elevate himself, this Zerdan began to spread the word that he is the reincarnation of the great tantric master Atisa, who is known for his ability to transmute negative forces, demonic energies, much like Guru Rinpoche." The Abbot laughed scornfully but then turned serious, "To make such a claim is no laughing matter. Since I have the highest regard for Atisa, I decided to expose this man, and I went to meet Atisa's disciples at Radrang Monastery, just north of Lhasa. Some of them knew of Zerdan's claim but laughingly dismissed him. One of the monks, who took Zerdan more seriously, told me that the man had studied with a tantric adept and had gained certain occult powers, but he had taken the left-handed path and become a sorcerer. He felt that the man could be dangerous because of his ability to manipulate people and gain a following. After hearing this, I could not let the matter be. If he had caused the death of the abbot, this had to be exposed.

"Around the time that I was investigating this matter, your son began to have some minor mishaps, one after another in quick succession—a fall that badly twisted his ankle, then a sprained wrist that prevented him from writing when he was working on an important text, and after that a bad cold that caused him to lose his voice before an important debate. Then there was a fire in his room, which he immediately put out, and other such things. I took notice, and at first I thought Zerdan was targeting him because your son excels in debate. After some thought, I decided to go meet this man and confront him. A few of the senior monks here at Samye were very concerned and cautioned me not to incite him. If this man has indeed gained certain powers, he could be quite destructive, and they didn't want to attract his wrath to our monastery.

"I went to meet him but tempered my speech and didn't say anything about the death of the previous abbot. He asked many questions about Tenzin Sangye's family and background, which I carefully avoided answering, but as I was sitting there, I became convinced that it isn't your son at all whom he is targeting, but you. Your son is only the means for reaching you."

"Me!" I exclaimed in astonishment. "Why would he be after me? I have never met the man and don't know anything about him. I have never heard of him until now."

"I don't know the answer to that. Only you would know. I wanted to warn you about him because he may come soliciting donations, saying that it is for the protection of your son. Don't believe that and don't get involved with him. He is a man who has acquired more than a few mental tricks, and I don't underestimate the damage he can cause. Let us monks handle him." He chuckled and added, "Some of our monks also have such capabilities, but they use their gifts only for the protection of dharma, not for personal gain. This man uses his powers to gratify his ego and to control people. That is dangerous to himself and to others. The generosity of Yeshe Dorje and his family toward Samye Monastery is widely known. Perhaps that is the reason why he has shown an interest in you. I believe all these incidents with your son is only to gain your attention, but your son is well protected." Although he emphasized those last words, they were not the words that sunk in. I only understood that this man was causing trouble for Tenzin.

"If he approaches you, you might want to get your eldest brother

Sonam Jigme to respond on your behalf," continued the Abbot. "He is a man of sound judgement and will know how to deal with this situation."

Nodding, I thanked him for informing me and told him that I would certainly be on guard. I then asked to see my son. The Abbot immediately called for him, and then excused himself so that we could have some time alone.

As soon as Tenzin arrived, I could not help but embrace my emotionally restrained son, and then expressed in an anxious tone my concern over the mishaps, but Tenzin dismissed them as minor distractions. From our discussion, it was clear to me that he was not aware of anything the Abbot had told me. His only concern was about me; how I was managing and why I had come. Once I convinced him that I was fine and had only come to inquire about his health, Tenzin seemed relieved. After spending an hour or so together, he withdrew for the night, saying that the monks had to retire early, and I retreated to the guest house.

The next morning, I again met briefly with Tenzin and then retrieved Anpu and began to ride home, thinking I would travel more leisurely, perhaps even spending the night in one of the tent communities along the way. I hadn't gone far when I decided to stop by the river, which was racing at an unusually rapid pace that day, surging up in white crested waves, revealing a wildness I hadn't seen before. It created an unsettling feeling within me. As I sat there reflecting on the Abbot's words of caution, a memory was re-kindled; the nightmare of the woman being burned alive, and as soon as I saw that vivid, life-like image and heard the woman's cries, instinctively I shuddered and placed my hands over my eyes, just as the child in the dream did. Why did this image keep haunting me, awakening such fear in me?

I decided to perform a ritual to chase away the vision. I was unprepared, as I hadn't brought any ritual items, but I remembered that Bhasundara had once told me that all one needed was a leaf or a drop of water and a sincere heart. The greatest offering is your thoughts, she had once told me. Gathering some leaves and sticks and setting them into a sacred formation, I sat down on the river's edge and began to chant in a barely audible voice. Then cupping my hands into the rushing river, I sprinkled some water over my offering. I closed my eyes, addressed the deity of the river, and asked for a protection blessing for Tenzin. In my heart, I was also asking to eradicate forever that painful scene from my mind. After I had finished, I placed the sticks and leaves into the river and watched the restless waters carry them away, as I whispered, "Please, Lu spirits, accept my offering to you and protect my son."

Rising, I climbed onto Anpu and was about to get back onto the path leading to Lhasa when I decided to change course and go to the monastery of that man Zerdan. I knew where it was by the Abbot's description. I didn't know exactly why I felt compelled to go there, but somehow recalling the nightmare made me think that perhaps that horrible image had something to do with that man. The Abbot clearly felt that Zerdan was seeking to draw me to him. If he was trying to reach me, it was far better for me to go to him, I reasoned, as perhaps then he would leave Tenzin alone. I didn't want to involve Sonam in this matter because he was battling ill heath, and I didn't want to alarm any other family member. All the Abbot's warnings fled from my mind, carried away by the rushing waters, as did his assurance that Tenzin was protected. All I could think about was the need for me to safeguard my son.

It was nearly noon when I arrived at Zerdan Rinpoche's monastery, but I stood outside for close to an hour, gathering the courage to enter. Then I had a long wait, as I was told that the master was terribly busy and never saw people without appointments. I had given my name and said that I was interested in making a donation. Several hours passed before his assistant, who introduced himself as Lobsang Rinpoche, finally came to usher me into the room where Zerdan received guests. There was something about Lobsang's appearance that made me recoil as soon as I saw him. The most outspoken feature on his thin face, hollowed by aging cheeks, were his dark beady eyes that emitted a piercing gaze, designed to unsettle one. An inner voice told me to turn around and leave, but I didn't listen. Instead, I followed Lobsang Rinpoche through the long, dimly lit corridor leading into the room where Zerdan was waiting.

I had no expectations, and when I entered room, I was startled by the power of Zerdan's presence. He was an attractive man of medium height and build, about my age, with thick eyebrows crowning a pair of dark, magnetic eyes. His features were nicely formed, his complexion on the lighter side. His expression was one of extreme confidence, almost arrogance. He wore an elaborate gold-colored robe and gold hat on his head. I stood there at the entrance of the room, intimidated by his commanding voice, as he instructed me to come sit across from him. At first, I didn't move, but at his second command, I slowly walked over and sat in the waiting seat.

"So, you are Padma Tshomo, the mother of the famous Tenzin Sangye." It was not a question but rather a statement. I nodded, disturbed that he referred to my son in this way. Was he mocking me, I wondered? "I have heard your son debate. He has quite an intellect, but his abilities have not yet been developed. He would do well to study under me. Samye cannot give him what he needs, and I am looking for students of his potential." I didn't respond, uneasy that he was focusing on my son.

He continued. "I have come to revive the teachings of the great Atisa, to bring tantra to our monks. This is what is needed now to safeguard our land and repel the forces seeking to invade us." Again, I didn't respond. I thought of what the Samye Abbot had told me of Ranpang, the monastery established by Atisa's students; that was where the deeper teachings of tantra were being practiced, but I didn't dare contradict him. I knew the danger to which he was referring; all of Lhasa was on edge because of it. The Turkic General Bhaktiyar Khalji, the one who had destroyed Nalanda, was organizing a campaign to invade Böd. The threat of an invasion was real, but could the monks really prevent this through their tantric practices? I had never heard of such a thing.

He continued to speak about his ability to awaken the innate powers in his followers, while gazing steadily at me. His voice, which at first had been strong and imposing, suddenly became gentle and soothing, and I listened as he described the importance of awakening the inner powers of his monks. After a while, his words became a background drone and

I could no longer follow as a wave of fatigue overtook me, and my eyes grew unbearably heavy. I struggled to stay alert, knowing that I had to resist the tremendous temptation to close my eyes and sleep, but the fog coming over my mind was too strong, and I fell into a somnolent state. Then words reached me, jolting me out of the stupor, words naming the amount he needed for a new building to accommodate the growing number of monks who were coming to help him ward off the invaders, and I found myself nodding in agreement. I heard him laugh and say, "We are grateful, Padma Tshomo, for your generous donation. Your association with our monastery will be a boon to both you and your son, you will see. This will provide much protection for that gifted son of yours, whether or not he comes to study in our monastery. I will send Lobsang Rinpoche to your home to receive the funds in a week's time."

I was now able to open my eyes fully, not quite sure of what had happened. I heard the amount he had mentioned, and I knew I had somehow agreed, but I was confused, still in a daze and didn't have the presence of mind to object or to question him. Zerdan rose and beckoned his assistant, who came and led me out of the room, down the long hallway and outside. Although he pressed me to stay the night as it would soon be dark, I refused, eager to get away. Before leaving me, he named the day that he would come to collect the donation.

After he left me, I looked back at the building and wondered what had just happened. Had I really offered to make such a large donation? Had I been so tired from the long journey of the day before that I had fallen asleep? Had I been alert, I never would have offered such a donation, which would deplete much of my resources, but now it was too late to turn back. I took in a few breaths and said to myself that what was done had been done. If the funds would ensure the protection of Tenzin, it was worth it. Hadn't Yeshe told me to make any sacrifice for his sake? I will stay away from that man in the future, I thought, even though I hadn't found out what I had come for—whether or not he had any connection to the frightening dream.

"I am sorry, Anpu, we have to ride fast to get back to Lhasa before it is too late," I whispered to my horse before climbing onto him. As we entered the path, a foreboding feeling came over me. That man has a dark aura, I said to myself as we sped through the night. I didn't quite know what an aura was, but I had heard of such things and felt a darkness around him, an overwhelming heaviness, an absence of any love or care. When sitting before the Samye Abbot, with his gentle, caring expressions, I always felt uplifted. But in the presence of this man, I felt fearful and powerless. It was as if I lost my voice, unable to protest or defend myself when in his company. This had to be a sign to stay away.

I had never ridden alone so late under the night sky, but fortunately the moon lit the way for me. Nevertheless, I was more than a little timid, knowing there could be bandits lurking in the shadows; every sound, even that of the quietly whistling wind, kept me on edge, making me ride even faster, hoping that Anpu's protective presence would keep me safe. It was well past midnight when we arrived home.

A week later Lobsang Rinpoche came with a younger monk to receive the donation. The younger monk spoke effusively about his teacher, telling stories of his miraculous powers, while I listened, uncomfortable with the tenor of the conversation. Before leaving, Lobsang took me aside and said quietly, "Rinpoche knows you have had troubling dreams. He can explain them and free you so that you will never have such dreams again." Then he stated the day and time that he would be available to see me.

I simply nodded but was noncommittal, aware of a quiet inner voice telling me not to go. As I stood in the doorway watching the two of them walk toward their horses, I heard Lobsang say to the younger monk, "Rinpoche assured me that she would return. He said there is a strong karmic link between them and that she cannot help but do his bidding."

Those last words troubled me and for days my mind was a muddle of conflicting thoughts—to go or not to go back to the monastery. I had not shared with anyone in my family the repeating nightmare I had had in my earlier years, and so would not be able to explain why I felt compelled to visit Zerdan, a man of such questionable reputation. To ease my mind, I decided to visit my eldest brother Sonam, who had some of the same qualities as my father—integrity, strong convictions, a protective impulse, and complete devotion to the Buddhist path. Sonam's wife had passed away a year earlier, and after that his health had begun to decline. He had developed a strident and persistent cough that wouldn't go away, despite the best efforts of numerous doctors. I had even brought Bhasundara to see him, but her medicines also did not fully eradicate the cough. When I arrived, I saw immediately that my brother was not well and decided not to mention Zerdan to him, but he seemed to know already that I had visited his monastery.

"You have been to see that disreputable man and even made a large donation. Why, Padma? What has come over you? Did he threaten you?" he asked in a stern but questioning tone, disapproval sketched across his face. I didn't answer because I was at a loss for words. How could I explain that I had made a donation without even knowing that I had. But he wouldn't accept my silence and after pressing me, I finally said quietly, "He is praying for the protection of Böd. Isn't that a good cause, Sonam?"

"Padma, all the monks are praying for the safeguarding of Böd. That man is dangerous, and you must stay away from him. If you want to make a donation, it should be to Samye Monastery, where Tenzin is in training. You know that." This was the first time in my memory that Sonam had spoken so harshly to me, and his displeasure pained me. He knew the exact amount of my donation, and when I asked him who else knew, he said all of our relatives and many people in Lhasa. Zerdan had announced it publicly. At the thought of the embarrassment this would cause my family, who were known supporters of Samye, I shrunk back in shame. "You are giving him credibility," he continued. "That is what he wants, but I will not allow him to use our family, and you, the wife of Yeshe Dorje, to his benefit." In a gentler tone he added, "I should have insisted that you come live with me after Yeshe's death. Many times, he had asked me to assure him that if he died before me, I would take care you. I have not fulfilled my promise to my dearest friend."

"You have, Sonam. You have looked after me. Nobody could have done better," I replied in a cracking voice.

"I am of a mind to go see that man myself and to tell him to stay away from my family."

"Don't do that, Sonam," I pleaded. "Not in your condition."

"Then promise me, you will have nothing more to do with him. He is a fraud." I nodded, determined that I would do as he asked. Sonam's irritation further unsettled me. I wasn't able to explain to him what had happened, and I knew that my mistake was going to see Zerdan in the first place. Sonam's anger exacerbated his condition, and he began to cough incessantly, at which point his daughter entered and asked that I leave so he could rest.

Over the next few days, I received visits from my two other brothers, each of whom reinforced Sonam's message, and this increased my humiliation. Never had I given them cause to scold me before. But the words of Lobsang Rinpoche lingered in my mind. What kind of karmic connection did I have with Zerdan? How could he have known about the recurring nightmare? The more I thought about it, the more convinced I became that he was somehow connected to the dream, and my mind would not rest until I found out what that horrible nightmare was all about.

After a few more days of great unease, I rode back to Zerdan's monastery, not realizing that it was the very day that he had requested I return. When I arrived, Lobsang explained that his master was not meeting anyone, as he was spending all his time in meditation and prayer for the protection of Böd, but that he had made time especially for me. I expressed my gratitude and after ushering me into the reception room, he left me alone with Zerdan.

"The demonic forces are attacking us, and it is taking all of my energy to protect this land," he said solemnly.

"The military situation is very tense, I know," I replied quietly.

"But we will succeed in repelling the invaders. Of that, I am sure." His voice was not only one of conviction but also arrogance. How could he be so sure, I wondered, when we all knew the danger posed by Khalji's army? "Now describe to me the dream that has been haunting you."

Instead of answering, I asked, "How do you know about that?"

Smiling, he replied, "I know many things about you, Padma Tshomo. If you want me to help you, you must describe it to me."

"I see myself as a child witnessing the burning of a woman. It is a frightening image, a most horrendous sight, and it awakens great pain in me," I replied in a shaky voice.

"You are not the child. You are the woman burning. It is a premonition of the future, a demonic possession. That is why it frightens you. I can help you, but you must come here regularly."

"A demonic possession?" I exclaimed in disbelief. "Why would that be?"

"I will help you if you allow me. I am well trained in battling demons," he replied in the same authoritative tone he had used when I first met him. He began to speak about how he subdued demons and as I listened to him a wave of fatigue came over me and my eyelids grew heavy. Seeing this, he instructed me to relax, to close my eyes and listen to his chanting, which he said was to entice the demons to come out of hiding. I did as he commanded and allowed myself to drift as his seductive tones soothed my mind, calming me. I rested in a semi-sleep state, until I heard him clap his hands, thrusting me back into normal waking consciousness. As I opened my eyes, I heard him say that the generous donation I had offered would serve to free me of the demons.

I was too confused to say much, but I requested that he keep my visit secret and the donation anonymous. "If my family finds out, I will have to cut all ties with you," I managed to say. He nodded, saying I should come back in a month for another session to repel the negative forces that were seeking to inhabit me, saying that I needed much protection at this time, as did my son. He didn't fail to mention Tenzin's name and that served to further unnerve me. Lobsang Rinpoche appeared in the doorway and led me out. As we walked through the long hallway, he told me that there was no one in all of Böd more capable of battling the demonic energies and that he would succeed in repelling the forces attacking Böd as well as the forces threatening me.

This time I knew it was not the journey that had brought about such strong fatigue. It was not the ride that had clouded my mind and caused such disorientation. He had done something to me. But what was done was done, and now to fulfill my obligation I would have to sell most of my precious items, treasures that Yeshe had brought back from his travels, and the thought of doing so caused me great pain. But it wasn't this that disturbed me the most. It was his interpretation of the dream. As soon as my mental faculties returned, I questioned his words, doubting that they were true, but how could I know? Suppose they were true? But why would any demon be after me? It would be Tenzin they would be after because of his intelligence and abilities. My mind was in such a state of confusion that I felt it safer to trust Zerdan, just in case there was the danger of a demonic interference. I had to take whatever precaution I could to protect myself and Tenzin.

In the days and weeks that followed, I vacillated between believing Zerdan and thinking he had deceived me, exerting control over my mind and causing me to believe things that inside I knew to be untrue. I felt trapped. He clearly had powers and I feared how he might use them. If I cut off all ties, would he harm Tenzin? That was my greatest concern, and as that thought arose, I realized that I would make any sacrifice, even my life, to safeguard my son.

I began selling the jades, scrolls, and other precious items Yeshe had brought back from the Song Empire. Although I tried to sell them quietly, word of my activities reached Sonam and he called for me. When I reached his home, I found him in a distressed state, but I was not the cause of it. Bakhtiyar Khalji's campaign to invade Böd was progressing. His elite force of ten thousand men had reached our lands. Our once powerful empire was now fragmented among a number of warlords, and we had no central army to counter theirs, although our tribes were organizing and attempting to resist. It was indeed a very tense time, and as Sonam described our situation, my concern for Tenzin grew. If Khalji succeeded, the monks of Samye would be endangered and would need to flee, but to where?

"Although the military situation is very much on my mind, I have not called you here to discuss that, Padma."

"I know, Sonam. You are concerned that I am selling the treasures the Yeshe had collected over the years."

"Are you in need of funds?" he asked. "If so, I will give you what you need."

I shook my head. "I want to simplify my life, Sonam. Those things never meant as much to me as they did to Yeshe."

"You should keep them in the family, Padma," he urged. "Your children may want them."

I tried to smile. "Yeshe brought them many gifts. It is time for me to detach myself from these material things." He looked at me skeptically. My brother knew me well enough to know that I was not being honest, but he didn't protest. Rather, he told me again that if I needed funds, if I needed anything, I should let him know. Trying to change the subject, I asked him how likely it was that Khalji would reach Lhasa. Sonam, like Yeshe, had channels to government officials and often had information that the rest of us didn't have.

"Khalji's army has reached the Chumbi Valley, but they are being met with fierce resistance by the tribal warriors, who have come together to repel this attack," he replied in a worried tone. "Our advantage is that they are not used to our terrain, but I have heard that the battle is ongoing and brutal, the outcome uncertain. If they make it through the valley, they will reach here."

"He has conquered the Sena Empire. Is that man so greedy that he wants our lands as well?" I asked bitterly.

A sardonic laugh escaped his lips. "Is there an end to man's greed?" he asked. "He wants to control the lucrative trade routes, Padma. His army needs an ongoing supply of horses, and we control the horse trade. But if he manages to reach Lhasa, what happened to Nalanda could also happen to our monasteries."

"Should I take Tenzin and flee?" I asked with great urgency.

"Flee to where, Padma? To the Song Empire, which is being threatened by the Mongols? I don't believe it will come to that. Our tribal fighters are employing strategies and tactics that will counter Khalji's army."

Over the years, the horse trade had become a more prominent part of my family's business activities. While Yeshe and his family had focused on trade with the Song Empire, Sonam and his son had developed profitable relationships with the Sena Dynasty, now conquered. In its place stood the newly established Delhi Sultanate, under Bakhtiyar Kahlji's control. And they were at our doorsteps.

Sonan continued, "The battle has reached a critical stage, and now is the time we must pray to Guru Rinpoche that the tribal fighters will succeed." He paused and then added, "And we must pray to the Bon gods and goddesses, who have protected this land since ancient times." I nodded in agreement, but instead of calling upon Drablai Gyalmo, or Nam Tsho Chukmo, or Dalha, recalling what I had recently heard about Zerdan's spiritual efforts to protect our land, I resolved to return to his monastery, believing that he had the power to defeat our enemy. Even if he used his powers for personal gain, perhaps this once he would use them to protect Böd.

Before I left, Sonam pressed a pouch of gold coins into my hands. At first, I refused, but then he said, "It will make me feel better. Keep this in case of an emergency. Take it as coming from Yeshe. It is what he would have wanted me to do."

I took the gold coins and looked sadly at my brother, knowing that I could not keep the promise I had made to him—the promise to stay away from the man who was now dominating my life.

CHAPTER 13

Descent into Darkness

Who has not experienced at one time or another the slippery slide into the mind's cavern of delusion? Who has not been tempted to discard discrimination in favor of a more seductive but illusory version of truth? Had I recognized my dilemma as a trap that even the most faithful can be subjected to, I might have had more compassion for myself. My inner struggles only increased with time, as I saw the blatant fallacy of Zerdan but could do nothing to prevent myself from falling under his sway and berating myself for my weakness.

I could not explain what kept drawing me back to him. He now increasingly occupied my mind. On some days, I told myself that he was mentally chasing me, seeking to lure me into his lair, but I knew this was not completely true. I was entering willingly, surrendering my mind and willpower, in addition to whatever wealth Yeshe had left me. Although the thought of his prideful tone and self-assured gaze disturbed me, when I was in his presence, I could only do his bidding. Occasionally I would hear in my mind Bhasundara's words about surrender and wonder if this was what she meant. Was it a good thing then that I willingly gave up everything for this man?

No longer did I fall into that dazed state that had overtaken me when I first met Zerdan. When in his presence, I was quite alert but unable to contradict him or resist his demands. He had found my weak point,

Tenzin, and never failed to take advantage of this, ever so subtly implying that his protection was needed for my son's safety. I told myself it was for the sake of Tenzin that I kept returning to the monastery, but I knew this was not the full story. There was something else, but I couldn't understand what it was that kept me from severing all ties.

Despite the power he exhibited over me, I didn't hate Zerdan. I feared him, but I couldn't bring myself to admit anger toward him. My animosity was directed at Lobsang, who I came to realize was Zerdan's money man. He was the one who spread stories of his master's grandeur to solicit donations. He was the one who cajoled me and repeated what I knew to be lies about my need for protection from demonic forces, alluding to the dream as evidence of this. Khalji's army was defeated, and the memory of the nightmare drifted away from me, as it had in the past. Whether or not any of this could be attributed to Zerdan, I didn't know, but it was possible, or so I told myself. I lived with an underlying anxiety of what he might do if I completely withdrew from him, what might happen to Tenzin or to Samye Monastery, with which he seemed to be in intense competition. Many people in Lhasa shunned him, and I knew never to mention his name to any member of my family. But he was also gaining a significant following, including among some reputable people, and I was not alone in succumbing to this questionable man.

I cannot explain why at this time Dalha was absent from my thoughts. I didn't call on her, and I didn't pray to her or to any of the goddesses for help or direction. They seemed to have disappeared completely from my mind, and this was as much a mystery to me as everything else to do with this most painful and inexplicable situation. I didn't even seek out my dear friend Bhasundara, but this was due to shame. I knew that she would be aware of my mental state, and this was something I tried my best to hide from everyone. How could I let her know the darkness into which I was rapidly descending?

By now I had sold all my precious possessions and given the funds to Zerdan. "This is for the protection of Böd," I said as I lay the silver and gold before him. He looked at me thoughtfully, a slight smile playing around his lips. "This time Böd has been spared, but dangers still remain. Your donations will strengthen this monastery's ability to protect our land, and to keep you and your son safe. You haven't had any more of those frightening dreams, have you?" I shook my head. "You see. I am protecting you from that demonic force. You must have more faith in me."

I nodded. I had learned from Sonam that our tribal fighters had inflicted such heavy casualties on Khalji's army that they had been forced to retreat. The tribes continued their attacks, chasing the army on its route home. Of Khalji's ten thousand elite soldiers, only a few hundred survived, and the brutal general himself died, which was a relief to all of us in Böd.

"Padma Tshomo, you should now come live here and assist me in my work," exclaimed Zerdan in a grand manner during one of my visits. His personality was so imposing that when he spoke, he expressed himself with his whole body, gesticulating with his hands and arms, and even lightly swaying his torso in an almost rhythmic manner. Some might have found this impressive, but to me it was unnerving. At this invitation, I stared at him, wondering what more he wanted from me. I knew to be on guard against him and so didn't respond. The home I had shared with Yeshe was all I had left, and it was my most precious possession, filled with memories of my life with him. "It is time for you to free yourself of worldly goods. What need do you have for a house? Sell it," he instructed me in that authoritative tone with which I was all too familiar, one hard to resist. "Why do you need it? You are alone. If you come here, I will find a place for you near the monastery, where you can devote yourself to spiritual matters. Then we can meet more often, and I can teach you the secrets of tantra."

"Rinpoche, I am a Bonpo," I reminded him quietly. But as soon as those words escaped my lips, I knew that I could no longer describe myself as that. I didn't know what I was anymore, but by saying this, I could maintain a line separating me from Zerdan and his monastery.

He laughed. "What does that matter? You are now one of my major supporters. It is time for you to free yourself by selling your home."

"Sell my home," I murmured in a pained voice.

He nodded. "Why do you need such luxury? The funds would be put to better use to support the monastery so that we can continue to protect Böd and your son." Those last words were ones he never failed to add, and every time he mentioned Tenzin, I trembled inside. It was as if he wanted to remind me that he held power over my son's fate. He continued, "One danger to Böd has been resolved, but another will crop up. We are surrounded by potential invaders, eyeing our resources, and our efforts are helping to protect this land," he said in a firmer voice. "If you come here, you can be part of something greater than yourself."

I didn't answer, but the very idea of selling the home disturbed me, and I knew that I needed time to think it over. I didn't stay long at the monastery and when I reached home, Tenzin was there waiting for me, pacing the floor. I had never seen my calm and demure son in such a restless state. He seemed to know that I was making donations to Zerdan and although he wouldn't say, I soon realized that Sonam had arranged for someone to watch over me, so my family knew my comings and goings. Tenzin wasn't angry at me but at the one he called "that man."

"Did your *agu* (uncle) send for you?" I asked in a resigned tone.

"He is too sick to come here himself and so he sent a messenger to get me. Ama-la, he is worried about you, as we all are. You promised him you wouldn't see that man again, and yet you keep going. Why?"

Trying to calm him, I told him that Zerdan had been praying for the protection of Böd, and that his students claim that he had helped make possible the defeat of Khalji's army. He looked at me wide-eyed in disbelief.

"You are not attributing Khalji's defeat to that man, are you?" I didn't respond. "So he is claiming credit for this. Unbelievable." He shook his head. "What about the brave tribal fighters, who fought fiercely and risked their lives for our protection? They are the ones to whom we should be grateful. Besides, every monk and spiritual aspirant in Böd has been praying, the most highly advanced ones staying up through the night in meditation for days on end. Ama-la, do you realize that it was on the tenth night of the waxing moon that Khalji began his retreat? That night one of our monks saw a faint image of Guru Rinpoche in the sky. He seemed to be smiling. It was Guru Rinpoche who prevented Khalji's advance, because of the attunement with him of so many devout Buddhists. What has come over you, Ama-la, that you would believe anything that man says?"

"Tenzin, I know your feelings about Zerdan, but many people respect him," I claimed defensively, unhappy to be reprimanded in this way by my son.

Tenzin's voice rang with exasperation. "Those people are taken in by him. Ama-la, can't you see that he is an imposter? No, worse than that. He is a dangerous man."

I was thoughtful for a few moments and then asked, "Tenzin, how can we judge? How can we tell who is a fraud and who is authentic?"

"Ama-la, there are always, at all times, in all communities, people who engage in arduous spiritual practices and attain certain powers, but who present themselves to be far more advanced than they truly are, because their egos are still strong. If there is no ego and no desire for power or a large following, for recognition of any kind, those people are authentic. I find that man to be a bit pitiful really because he has such an inflated view of himself. He is seeking recognition and credibility and entrapping people who can grant him that. True teachers are not like that.

"Don't you remember the story about Buddha Star that Apa-la used to tell me? He repeated that story over and over so that I would not be impressed by spiritual powers. Buddha Star taught while levitating and attracted many students because of this. He also had a hold over people, and many thought him to be a highly advanced master. But the great Rinchen Zangpo saw through him right away, and all he had to do was to point a finger at him while Buddha Star was levitating, and that man came tumbling down from the air in front of all his students. The purpose of that was to cut down his ego and someone needs to cut down Zerdan's ego."

I smiled. "Your grandfather also used to tell me that story and others like it."

Tenzin was quiet for a few moments and then added in a less agitated tone. "There are still those like Rinchen Zangpo here today, but that man is not one of them. The monk I most admired, the one who was killed at Nalanda, Norbu Dorje, was the wisest, most compassionate but also the humblest man I have ever met. Two years after I entered the monastery, one of the other young monks who had entered at the same time as I did become gravely ill, and no medicine could bring down his high fever. The doctors had given up on him. His family lived far away, and he kept calling out for his mother in the night. My room was next to his and so I heard him, but everyone was hesitant to go near him because his illness was contagious, everyone except Norbu Dorje. He stayed with him day after day, making sure he drank liquids and the medicinal soups that were prepared, and he meditated through the night by his bedside. After many days of this, that young monk awoke one night and saw a tremendous light streaming from Norbu Dorje's meditating body, filling the whole room. He thought he was dreaming and turned over and went back to sleep.

"The next morning, he was so much improved that he could get up from his bed and eat a normal meal. He recovered quickly after that and told everyone that Norbu Dorje had healed him, but Norbu Dorje would take no credit for it. 'It was Guru Rinpoche,' he said, 'who had come in the night.' Once he was fully recovered, the young monk asked to be assigned to serve Norbu Dorje, but he accepted no service from anyone. He was always cheerful and smiling, and all the monks young and old adored him because his very nature was compassion itself. No task was too small for him, and everyone received his full attention—from the workers who served at the monastery to the most highly advanced monks. He was a true man to follow.

"His age was beginning to slow him down when we traveled to Nalanda and the Abbot, who was quite protective of Norbu Dorje, didn't want him to go. But he insisted, saying that he wanted to be there to help our monks. When we arrived at Nalanda, I saw how many students from faraway places came to him for teachings and counsel. I never understood how they had heard about him, but I think they could feel his tremendous love and compassion and humility.

"When I returned to Nalanda from Vikramshila and saw what had happened and learned that he had been killed, I was struck with such sorrow. Again and again, I asked, why him? He was a man who only gave and gave and sought nothing in return. Then one of the monks from Gyagar told me what had happened. Norbu Dorje seemed to know in advance that Khalji's army was coming, and he managed to help many students leave the grounds in the days before the army's arrival. It was he who suggested a week earlier that I and a few others from Samye take a trip to see the remains of Vikramshila, and in this way he not only saved our lives but spared us from having to witness that tragic event. He remained at Nalanda and tried to save many of the monks who were being attacked. Some he saved, but others died, and in the end, he was also killed while trying to prevent the army from attacking the library. I realized that he had sacrificed his life for the sake of others and for the dharma, but through his death he left us a great teaching about service, one that will remain with me for my whole life. He is a man to follow." Tenzin stopped speaking and I could see that the memory of those events awakened deep feeling in him. Then looking at me questioningly, he asked, "Ama-la, who is the humblest person you have ever met?"

"Dalha, of course," I responded without hesitation. "To this day, few people know about her, and even those who do, don't realize how extraordinary she was; she knew things and did things I didn't think possible, but always quietly so that no one would notice." As I spoke her name, something in me stirred, and I realized that I was keeping myself away from her. It was not she who was absent but I.

"You have told me of her spiritual powers, her magic. Is this what drew you to her?"

"Not at all," I replied hastily. "It was her love. Even when I didn't think of her, she was caring for my wellbeing. Her life was all about love."

"She is a true teacher, rare to find," said Tenzin quietly. "Ama-la, why have you traded gold for ash? Promise me you will stay away." I nodded, knowing somewhere inside that it was another promise I would not be able to keep.

Tenzin's words stayed with me for many weeks. I didn't sell the house and I didn't go see Zerdan. I was determined to stay away, but I could not get him out of my mind. I would ride to the place in the forest where Yeshe and I used to visit in his last months, sit there by the stream and ponder, whispering, "Why do you have such a hold over me? What is our karmic connection? Why did you threaten me with a demonic possession, when deep inside I know that is not the meaning of the dream?"

Sonam's hacking cough was becoming more frequent and deeper, causing his whole chest to convulse when he coughed, and he was growing weaker, making it difficult for him even to rise from his bed on some days. He hardly ate and had grown very thin. His condition weighed heavily on me, and I tried to spend as much time as I could caring for him. I had sent for Bhasundara, but after creating numerous herbal combinations, she told me that his condition was incurable, that it had progressed too far and his lungs were now damaged. But she gave him medicine to ease his cough. It was during one of her visits that she asked if we could meet somewhere to speak alone. I told her that as soon as I could get away, I would ride out to her cottage.

I had purposely avoided visiting Bhasundara, so sure was I that she would scold me for having been taken in by Zerdan. When I told her that I would come to see her, she took me aside and said, "I want you to recall now what you told me about your last meeting with Dalha."

"My last meeting? You mean at the horse market in Amdo?"

"Do you remember what she told you?"

"Of course. She spoke of love and finding the goddess inside and told me to keep my mind on her."

"If you had followed her counsel, you would not be in this situation." At her words, I looked away ashamed. "I say this not to make you feel badly. That is not the point. The point is to call upon her again and again. Only then can she guide you. It is Dalha who will help you understand that dream, not Zerdan. Only by going inside will you find the answer. And you know, of course, that this has nothing to do with Tenzin. That man has no power over him. Tenzin has all the protection he needs at the monastery."

"But Bhasundara, he has powers and can be vindictive. I have seen that. He could harm Tenzin . . . ," my voice began to tremble.

Taking me by the shoulders, she shook me gently, "Wake up, Tshomo. This has nothing to do with Tenzin. There is some old samskara between you and that man. Finish it. See him for what he is and sever all ties." I didn't answer, and she added, "Come see me and we will perform a ceremony."

As many times as a dear one tries to wake up a person, it will not happen until the person is ready to wake up, and I had not yet reached that point. There was still further to fall. Had I been more aware, I would have reflected more deeply on Bhasundara's words and called upon Dalha, but I was too ashamed to call out to her, and my mind quickly reverted to concern over my ill brother. Weeks passed and I hardly left Sonam's side. Pumo had also come to stay with him, and we took turns caring for our eldest brother.

The thought of my brother's death left me feeling dejected and depleted, too exhausted to think about anything else, and so I didn't visit Bhasundara. I hardly ventured out. It was in such a state that Lobsang Rinpoche found me one day. I had returned home after a night of caring for my brother, worried and feeling helpless as I watched my brother day by day grow weaker, and he was waiting there for me. I cringed at the sight of him but invited him in anyhow. Seeing my distressed condition, he told me that Zerdan had sent him. "He knows all about my brother's condition and is praying for him continually. If you allow him, he will cure your brother's illness."

"What do you mean if I allow him?" I asked in a tired voice.

"He is aware that you don't want to be indebted to him."

"I would give anything to have my brother cured," I replied simply.

"Anything?" he asked. I looked at him without replying. He nodded and smiled, and then left. A few days later Sonam's condition began to improve noticeably, and I called for Bhasundara.

"The medicines are having an effect," she said. "But I have to warn you, Tshomo, it is only temporary. I can make him more comfortable, but your brother does not have long to live. The medicine can keep him alive perhaps a few weeks longer, that is all." Before leaving, she reminded me that she wanted time alone with me, and I assured her that as I soon as I could, I would come. Looking at me sadly, she asked in a lowered voice, "What has happened to you, my dear friend? I know you are avoiding me, and you won't ride out to my cottage. I will have to come find you, but don't worry, I will."

Dismissing her words, I chose not to believe her diagnosis of Sonam, since I saw him gaining strength day after day, until he was able to get out of bed and do small chores around the house. Once again, he became his old cheerful self, making jokes, refusing our services, shooing us away, instructing me and Pumo to go back to our lives now that he was recovering. At his insistence, Pumo returned to the monastery where she and Tashi were working on murals. It seemed like a miracle, and I attributed my brother's improvement to Zerdan. The least I could do was to thank him. Forgetting my determination not to see him again, I rode out to the monastery.

"Will you trust me now?" he asked with an alluring smile when I entered his room. "Since you have witnessed how I was able to heal your brother, now is the time to sell your home and come work with me. I will use the money to expand the monastery and build a place for you to live nearby."

I nodded, so grateful for Sonam's recovery. Soon after I returned home, I set about quietly selling the only valuable possession I had left, keeping my decision from my family. It was days after the house had sold and I had arranged for the funds to be delivered to Zerdan that my second brother arrived at my home to tell me that Sonam had died in the night. He had had a sudden relapse and this time none of the medicines could help.

I was shattered, totally heart-broken at the loss of this brother who had been like a father to me. But his death also served to wake me up. It took weeks for the shock of Sonam's death to pass. Tenzin and my two daughters in Amdo had come to stay with me, and after they left, I realized that I had only days left to vacate the house, and still I had not told anyone what I had done. Now I would have to face the situation alone, having no place to go.

Tenzin had told me that the Abbot was sending him to the Song Empire with a delegation of monks to help with translation. He didn't know how long they would gone but they would be visiting several monasteries and might be away for a year or longer. He was hesitant to leave me, but I assured him that I would be fine and had his sister Yara to help me through the difficult mourning period. I was glad for him to travel again to the place where he had gone with his father. With him away I would be able to focus more fully on my immediate challenges, and I assumed that by traveling he would also be out of the reach of Zerdan. No matter what happened to me, at least he would be safe. Despite the assurances of the Samye Abbot and Bhasundara, I could not free myself from the thought that he might cause harm to Tenzin if I were to withdraw myself. But I had nothing left to give him. What more would he want from me?

The next many days I spent reviewing my last conversations with Sonam. When he was too ill to rise from his bed, and as he had begun to recover, every time I visited him, he warned me about Zerdan. I had broken my promise to him, just as I has reneged on my promise to Tenzin and continued to submit to that man when I knew I should not have. Bhasundara had warned me that Sonam would die, but Zerdan had said that he had cured him. Who had I chosen to believe, giving away the last of my possessions for the sake of my brother? Despite everything though, I could not bring myself to hate the man who had taken everything from me. It was Lobsang Rinpoche whom I blamed, and more than anything I wanted to be free of them both. That was my most pressing desire.

With no home and no possessions, my only recourse was to go live with Samaya in Amdo. But first, I had to make sure that he would not entrap me again, that he would not harm Tenzin or anyone else in my family. I knew there was a Buddhist practice of offering prostrations while reciting a mantra, and this practice suddenly entered my mind. I had seen

Buddhist monks doing this along the routes to temples. I was desperate and could not think of any other way of freeing myself. So I decided to offer 1008 prostrations along the route to his monastery, taking Dalha's name as my mantra, pleading for release, but I would have to disguise myself. I had already caused enough shame to my family through my association with the one Tenzin called "that man." My humiliation was already almost more than I could bear.

I waited until the house and the last of my possessions were out of my hands, leaving me only the pouch of gold coins that Sonam had given me, coins that I knew I could never part with. Then, to disguise myself as a poor village woman, I rummaged through a giveaway box at one of the monasteries and found some simple old clothing and tore them so that I would look impoverished. Covering my head with an old woolen hat, I rode out with Anpu on the road toward Zerdan's monastery. Stopping a short distance away, I climbed down from Anpu, and looking into his eyes sent an image of what I was about to do. Wait here for me. I hope to return before sunset, I said as I held his face between my hands. I had stopped along the way to spend the night so I could arrive very early in the morning, thinking that after a few hours I would be done. I had my plans set. I would then stay with my daughter Yara in Lhasa until Samaya could come to get me. I hadn't yet decided how to tell them about the house, but I would think up some story.

Without any hesitation I began the prostrations, chanting silently all the while, calling upon Dalha for the first time in nearly two years to help free me from Zerdan. The hours passed and my knees grew sore and began to ache; my body became faint from lack of food. So preoccupied had I been with disguising myself, that I had not thought of taking any food along with me. I had only a small jug of water strung around my waist, enough to wet my lips every twenty prostrations. Despite the weakness coming over me, I kept going, stumbling forward little by little. It was the warmest season, and as the sun reached its noon zenith, I thought I would pass out due to heat and fatigue, but I pushed myself to continue. I had to reach the goal I had set, or the whole practice would be in vain,

I told myself. But as time passed it grew more and more difficult and I began to lose count. One hundred prostrations, two hundred, three hundred, I didn't know any more how many I had done, but I kept going, reminding myself that I had no other recourse. I knew of no other practice that would yield the result I sought—freedom from that man. I had performed numerous rituals over the few years since he had entered my life, but they had not served to free me.

I continued on, four hundred, five hundred, I was halfway to my goal—or so I thought—but by now I was making up numbers. The pauses between prostrations grew longer, my feet became unsteady until at a certain moment my knees gave in, and I collapsed onto the ground. Too physically and mentally worn to move, I surrendered to my body's plea for rest and lay there motionless in a stupor-like state for I don't know how long, until I heard someone call my name.

"Tshomo, get up," the voice said gently. "I have come to take you home." I didn't answer or look in the direction of the voice. I told myself that I had to get up and continue the prostrations, but I didn't have the strength to lift myself. Again, I heard the voice call my name, but I had no will to respond, and so I lay there, my face turned to the ground. "There is nothing you have to do to free yourself," the voice said softly. "You are already free; you just don't know it." I lay there unresponsive until I felt arms lifting me. She turned me gently and I looked up into the face of Bhasundara and saw my faithful horse Anpu standing by her side.

CHAPTER 14

A Debt Repaid

Bhasundara helped me onto Anpu, and together we rode to a nearby tent community where she arranged for us to spend the night. I was in no condition to ride back to Lhasa, and I had no home to return to. It was not until I had taken some food and a medicinal drink and settled down in the tent provided for us that I had the clarity of mind to ask in a subdued voice how she had found me. Had it been anyone else, I would have been deeply ashamed of my appearance and weakened state. I had disguised myself so that no one would recognize me—the woman, who in my mind, had brought shame to her family.

"It was Anpu," she replied. "In the night I had a terrible feeling about you and thought you might have gone to see Zerdan. At the first light of dawn, I began to ride toward the monastery. When I was a short distance away, I saw Anpu wandering aimlessly as if he was searching for someone. As soon as he saw me, he let out a loud sound and shook his head fiercely. Then he led me to where you were doing the prostrations. Even he was aware of your mental state." She sighed. "Tshomo, I have been trying to speak with you for over a year, but you have avoided me. Why?"

Looking directly into her eyes, I did not try hide my pitiful condition. "I was too ashamed to see you. Ashamed for what I have done to my family, and if Yeshe ever knew what has become of me, perhaps even he would stop loving me . . ." my voice fell off as the thought of my distinguished husband was too much for me.

Bhasundara leaned over and hugged me, whispering in my ear, "Love is not like that. It is unconditional. There is nothing you could do that would make Yeshe, or me, or Dalha or anyone who truly loves you, stop caring for you."

Wiping my moistened eyes, I began again. "Since coming under his influence, I have not been able to think straight. He has some power over me that I can't understand. I have not been able to stay away from him and have watched myself sink into this deplorable condition," I said wistfully. "I could not explain my actions, and I didn't want you to scold me. I have had enough of that from my family. Bhasundara, I have given him everything I have, and yet I am not sorry. It is as if I owed him a great debt and have now paid it off, but I don't what that debt is or why he has such a hold over me."

"You know I would never scold you," she replied in a gentle tone. "From me, of all people, how could you hide your difficulties?" I looked at her blankly. Then she hastened to add, "It doesn't matter now. I have found you. I knew what you were going through and that is why I wanted to see you. I knew something was wrong and that you had become entangled with that man. It is one thing to give him money, but another to let him control your mind."

"Bhasundara, I have nothing left, except some gold that Sonam gave me. I don't know what will become of me now."

"Nothing left? What are you saying? You have everything except a few paltry possessions, which in the end mean nothing. You have freed yourself so that you can move on."

"I have not freed myself," I murmured, "and I don't know where I can go since I have no home. I had thought to go live with Samaya, but that is not what I want." I turned my eyes to the ground.

"What do you want, Tshomo?"

I was quiet for a few moments and then lifting my eyes toward hers, I replied slowly, "I want to be mentally free of him, and then perhaps I will be able to think clearly. I don't want to think about him anymore; when I am alone at night, I don't want to hear internally his sarcastic laugh or see his alluring eyes, which only try to entrap me. That is why I thought to do the prostrations. I have seen monks do that to realize an ardent prayer."

"Prostrations alone will not free you. You must get to the root of the problem. You are tired. Let's rest tonight and we will be able to plan more clearly tomorrow. I will help you, no matter what is entailed."

"You are a good friend, Bhasundara," I replied gratefully, my voice still blanketed with sadness. "I could have gone to Pumo, but I am her elder sister and couldn't bear to have her see me in this state."

"I understand," she replied. Comforted by her presence, I lay down and quickly fell asleep.

It was during the early pre-dawn hours that I awoke with a start, in a fit of fear. "He has found me," I whispered. Getting up and wrapping the blanket tightly around me, I quietly went to sit outside, trying not to disturb Bhasundara, who was still fast asleep. The night sky abounded with stars. When Yeshe and I had traveled and slept in tents, we used to sit outside until late, comforted by their presence. But even they could not comfort me as I sat recalling the dream that had awakened me. Zerdan had entered my dream world and asked what more I would donate. I told him that I had nothing left, and he replied, "You have this strong, beautiful white stallion. He can be your offering." Crying out, I wrapped my arms around Anpu's neck, gripping him tightly, and told Zerdan that I would never part with this horse. He was my gift from Dalha and I could not let him go. Then he looked at me with those wide magnetic eyes and said, "You can give me your future wealth, whatever is destined to come to you in your next birth." I nodded and said I would and then woke up. It was the first time he had come to me in a dream, and it felt so real, like an actual experience.

"He will pursue me into my next life," I whispered in the still night air. I began to weep quietly and didn't hear Bhasundara come out of the tent and sit beside me. "Did you have a disturbing dream?" she asked gently, putting her arm around me.

I nodded, and suppressing my tears, asked, "Bhasundara, are dreams real?"

"Some of them are, but some are also just expressions of our fears and anxiety. I also had a dream last night, a beautiful one of Dalha."

"You are fortunate then. My dream was of him. He is still pursuing me. Will I ever be free?" My voice was almost desperate.

"When I kept asking you to come meet me, I wanted to tell you that this life is not your first meeting with the one called Zerdan. You have known him before, and it was a very troubled, complex relationship. I don't know the details, but I also felt that you owed him a debt. You have now paid that, but you still allow him to entrap you, and he is not free of you. There is some obsession. Both parties must make peace for this matter to end. He was seeking something from you, and I don't think it was really money. There was something else.

"When I saw Dalha in the dream last night, she indicated that you have a choice to make. You are at the crossroads and must decide which way to go. One road leads you away from Lhasa to your daughter in Amdo, where you will live the rest of your life comfortably, without encountering that man again, at least in person. I have met Samaya. She is a good daughter and will take care of you, and you will be out of Zerdan's physical reach. You will have no more to do with that man in this life, but you may have to meet him again in the future to resolve this issue."

She paused and I asked hesitantly, "Where does the other road lead?"

"It goes back in time so that you can unravel that relationship and bring it to conclusion, by finding the source of the difficulty. The next part of the message was not clear—something about a frightening dream that she suppressed in you years ago but has emerged again. It seems that man sparked a memory in you of something from your past."

"I suspected as much," I murmured. "He told me it was a vision of the future, but deep inside I knew it was a memory from the past. He told me that what I was seeing was a demonic possession, but I didn't believe that to be true. It isn't true, is it?" I asked with pleading eyes.

"If he said that, then he doesn't truly know who you are," she replied with a chuckle. "With all the protection you have around you, no demon would dare approach. Tshomo, you don't have to decide tonight. Going back to the root of your conflict with him may be painful. I don't know how to advise you, because sometimes it is better not to see disturbing things, but then you will have to face those issues at some point. I will bring you to my cottage and let your family know that you have sold the house and are going into retreat for an extended period. Your family trusts me. Don't rush in deciding your next steps."

"Bhasundara, if I do decide to go back in time, how will I do that?"

"I don't know. That was not part of the message. We will have to wait and see. I am sure the answer will come."

"Just receiving a message from Dalha is comforting. Although I lost sight of her, she did not not lost sight of me."

"If we don't receive an answer to our prayers, it is because of our lack of attunement. There is always a response, but because our minds are so restless or clouded, we can't always hear it."

"I am ashamed to admit that during this time my mind has been in such a state that I have not even called out to her. It is only in the last day that I have begun to turn my mind to her while doing the prostrations."

"Perhaps that is why you feel her response now. Keep her in your mind and she will guide you. She will never lose sight of you, Tshomo. She worked through Anpu and led me to you. And I will not let you go until we have an answer. You are safe with me now."

I looked at Bhasundara gratefully, unable to find the words to thank her. Neither one of us felt like trying to go back to sleep, and so we sat out under the expansive sky and watched the darkness gradually give way to the earliest signs of day, as the first hues of pink peaked over the horizon. The dream I had had in the night lingered with me, but Bhasundara's presence helped to steady my mind, and for the first time in several years I felt Dalha with me.

Bhasundara insisted on giving me the back room where she normally slept and set up a sleeping mat for herself in the front room, which served as a kitchen and sitting area. I thought I would be there for only a few days and didn't protest because my mind and body were so very weary. When the days stretched into weeks, I became uncomfortable, knowing that I was imposing. She was away much of the day, caring for people in the city, and I tried to make myself useful by tending to the garden and collecting medicinal plants from the nearby forest, but I was becoming restless and felt I had to make a decision. Bhasundara kept telling me to allow things to unfold in their own time, but I had to know whether to send a message to Samaya or . . . or, I didn't know what the alternative path was. Would I choose a life of ease with my daughter, or would I dare to tread back into the unknown past, which could be filled with untold sorrows? And if I did, how would I do that?

One afternoon as I was gathering plants in the forest, I sat down and realized that I didn't trust myself to make any decision. I no longer had any faith in my judgement. I knew that I could not live with Bhasundara forever, and yet I was still so indecisive. An hour passed and soon I heard Bhasundara's cheerful voice calling out to me. Catching sight of me, she came to sit on the ground beside me.

"What are you thinking about?" she asked.

"I don't trust myself to make any decision," I replied dejectedly. "I have been stripped of all I thought was mine and shorn of all confidence in myself."

"Tshomo," she began haltingly, "your judgment was clouded due to an old samskara, a karmic relationship between you and Zerdan. Perhaps unknowingly, you allowed yourself to be deluded in order to repay a karmic debt." She looked at me as if she expected me to understand, but I didn't. Nothing she said could counter my sense of deep shame and insufficiency.

She was quiet for a few minutes and then whispered almost more to herself than to me, "When hope departs, new possibilities arise."

"What do you mean?" I asked, wondering if there was any relief for my pitiful state of mind.

"Sometimes the ego needs to be crushed. Humiliation can lead to great spiritual growth. There was a time when I also fell into a deep, dark hole, and Dalha was not here to pull me out. It turned out to be one of the greatest lessons of my life."

"You have never told me."

"It is not a story I am proud of, but it may help if I share it with you now. I was about twenty years old and had settled in Lhasa only a year or two earlier; I had begun treating people who were ill. One day without any notice, Dalha told me that she was leaving and would be away for quite some time as she was going to a distant village in Zhang Zhung to help with some problem. At that time there was a young man in Lhasa, about five years my senior, who was also treating patients, and one day we met at the home of an ill man. We had both been called there—I, by his wife, and he, by the sick man himself. I watched as he mixed certain herbs and administered the medicine, and I was impressed with his knowledge. We both came several times to the man's house and watched over his recovery, and during that time we became friendly. He was a good-looking, well-spoken man, but what drew me to him was his knowledge of the plants. I was intrigued by his intuitive knowing of which mixtures to make for different conditions.

"After we had seen each other a few times, he invited me to a shop where he kept his medicines in the back room, telling me that he would teach me about some of the rarer plants. He knew things that I didn't know, and I was grateful for the time alone with him. I was naturally naïve, as I had little experience with the ways of the city or the ways of young men, having spent most of my life in remote villages or traveling with Dalha. I trusted him, and it didn't occur to me that there might be something wrong in meeting this man privately. I went several times to his shop and learned about the healing properties of some plants that

I hadn't known before. Because I was learning so much, I kept visiting him, but soon I realized that there was something else drawing me. After about two months, we were alone in the back room, and he began to talk about how deeply he had grown to care for me. During this time, I had also begun to care for him, attracted by his knowledge, but also by his tender ways with the patients." Bhasundara briefly looked away bashfully. "And I began to have expectations of a life with him. I believed that he was sincere, and well . . . you can imagine what happened next. I thought that we loved each other, and he kept saying that as soon as he was in a better position financially, he would marry me. This went on for a year and then I discovered I was pregnant."

Seeing the look of shock on my face, Bhasundara paused before she continued. "I know, you are surprised by this. Let me finish. I told him I was pregnant, and I assumed we would then marry, but right after that, this man disappeared. I asked around and looked everywhere for him but was finally told by an acquaintance that he and his wife and young child had suddenly moved to another town. He had never told me he was married. That was the worst part. When I heard this, I became frantic and didn't know what to do. I didn't know when Dalha would return and had nobody from whom I could seek counsel. I was pregnant and alone and deeply ashamed of my naivety. I thought I really loved this man, and now I can hardly remember his name or what he looked like."

"What did you do?"

"I knew which plant medicine to take to end the pregnancy, and several weeks after I ended it, Dalha returned. She didn't say a word to me, and I was too ashamed to tell her. I assumed she would be so disappointed in me, but in subtle ways she let me know that she was aware of what I had been through. She stayed with me for some time, caring for me as a mother would, making me rest, feeding me special foods to nourish me, cheering me up with stories, and then one day she said to me, 'When a child is first learning to walk, that child stumbles a lot. If the mother rushes every time to pick up the child, that child will never learn how to pick himself up and begin again. So the mother must watch and wait for the child to learn, even though it means enduring many stumbles.'

"I burst into tears when she told me this, but she simply looked at me lovingly and said, 'You must learn to distinguish between love and passion. Love is never self-serving; it only cares for the wellbeing of the other. Eventually you will know that love is a state of being, not an emotion, not a feeling.' She left soon after this and didn't come back for about year.

"Just after she returned, she woke me up in the middle of the night and told me in a hurried voice to ride out to the home of a certain pregnant woman whom I knew. 'She is going into labor and there is nobody to assist her,' she said. I protested, saying that I knew nothing about delivering babies, but she looked at me sternly and told me to go. I, of course, listened to her and went straight to that woman's home. It was a difficult birth because the baby was in the wrong position, and for a while we didn't know if the baby or the mother would live, but I put everything I had into that delivery, calling upon Dalha the whole time. Both mother and daughter survived, and when I held that baby in my arms, I felt such joy, such overwhelming contentment.

"I had worked through the night and day and when I returned home in the evening, I was exhausted but also exhilarated. Dalha met me in the doorway. Smiling, she said, 'You have saved a life and given that child a good home. She will have a better life with that family than had she been born to you. You have paid off the debt.' That was the first open acknowledgement I had from her that she knew about the pregnancy.

"I looked at her in astonishment and exclaimed, 'Dalha, was that the child . . .' I didn't finish. She nodded and nothing more was said, but it was through this experience that I first gained some understanding of how she helps us work through samskaras. I began to reflect in the months that followed, and I came to realize that when a being in the world between lives seeks to return to earth again, that being finds an opening where conception can occur. If you abort that child, a debt is incurred, which you must repay in some way. Dalha was able to find that being and guide it to another opportunity for human birth in a good family. By delivering the child safely, I paid off that karmic debt. Do you see the complexity of karma, Tshomo? It is amazing, isn't it?"

"Beyond what I can comprehend!" I replied, still shocked by my friend's revelation.

"The beautiful part is that I am still close to that family. The child, who is now a young woman, has been drawn to me since she was young. Her parents have told her that I saved her life, and she feels a kinship with me, often visiting to share with me things about her life. In my darkest moment, I never could have imagined that it would work out this way. Do you see where trust comes in? Do you understand the degree to which we are looked after?"

As I sat there listening to her, I realized that Bhasundara was sharing with me a very personal trial. Previously, I hadn't truly understood that she, like the rest of us, encountered such challenging situations. She had always seemed so steady and unshakable, even in the face of great uncertainty. I had always regarded my friend as being above such trials, as always knowing what to do, the right course to take, but now I was hearing that she was like the rest of us, with only one difference: she had ultimate faith in Dalha. But even then, she was tested. I had always had her to counsel me and to provide words of wisdom, but in her most difficult hour, she had nobody to turn to, no one to provide the comfort we all need. As a mother of four children, I could only imagine what a difficult decision it must have been to end a pregnancy, and a surge of compassion arose within me. I looked at her with new appreciation, and said, "Your story has inspired me. Thank you for sharing it."

"My feelings at that time were much like yours, Tshomo. Up until the time when I delivered that baby, I lived with such a deep sense of shame. It was not the judgment of others I feared, but my own judgment of myself. I chided myself continually for my lack of discernment, for my naivety. I lost all confidence in myself. I told myself that I had the blessing of living with Dalha, of receiving her teachings, of engaging in spiritual practice, and yet I had allowed myself to be so deceived by that man, believing that he loved me. It was a most humbling experience.

After the child was born, those feelings quietly departed. I had no idea how I was able to deliver that baby and save her life, but I gained a new sense of my worth and my feeling of shame disappeared.

"Every now and then, though, for some time afterwards, I would think of that man and wonder why I had fallen victim to him. What was the karmic cause? I am not able to see my past and so I didn't understand what had caused me to be so drawn to him and to believe his words. When Dalha saw that I hadn't been able to free myself mentally from him, she asked me if I wanted to see my past relationship with the man, but I shook my head vigorously. I pretended that I didn't care, but deep inside, I held anger toward him, which I never mentioned to Dalha.

"One day, when she unexpectedly showed up at the cottage, she casually asked, 'Who suffers when you burden yourself with anger? You had an unfinished matter from the past with that man. It is done now. Let it go. You are free of that relationship, so why like an old stubborn mule do you keep lugging around this anger, refusing to put down your heavy load, when I have offered to take it from you?' When I heard this analogy, an image of an old mule came before me, and I could not help but laugh. Then she broke into that bubbling laughter of hers and neither of us could stop laughing for quite a while. I think it was her laughter that chased away my anger. After that I felt only compassion for the man, for I know that his lust did not end with me, and lust is no friend to anyone. It is a disease of the mind, like anger.

"When Dalha first asked me what the root of anger was, I told her that I didn't know, and she replied, 'Unmet expectations, thwarted desire. Don't have any expectations of anyone and anger will not arise.' She told me this many times until I finally took her words seriously and began to practice that."

I was quiet for a few moments and then replied slowly, "What I want most is to be free of Zerdan, but I also want to understand why he has such a hold over me. When I think of him, I don't feel anger, but rather fear, a gripping sensation, as if he would kill me if I don't obey him. I need to see the past so I can know where this comes from."

"What are you afraid of, Tshomo?"

"I don't know the answer to that, Bhasundara. If I knew, perhaps I could free myself."

"What is the worst that could happen? Death? If you die, you will be reborn. What is terrifying about that?"

"I don't think I am afraid of death. I want to know what he has done to me, or what I have done to him to create such a reaction in me."

"Seeing the past may not be what you think, Tshomo. It may not be comforting, or easy." I sighed and didn't respond. "But if that is what you need, that is what you will receive. Tshomo, Dalha helped me and she will help you. You must have faith in her. She helped me climb out of the deep ditch I had dug for myself, but she did it all discretely, with no fanfare or lectures. Never once did she chide me or make me feel as if I had done wrong. That is the mark of a true teacher, a true master. Eventually, I developed gratitude for that painful episode in my life because it helped to clarify for me what I truly want. And what I want is the treasure that Dalha has to offer, that unspeakable treasure which is far more precious than anything in the world."

She then added gently, "You must also get over judging yourself. In the long run, giving up your possessions and your house is not such a big deal, for at the end of life it is what we all must do anyhow. Perhaps it has happened this way so that you can enter a new stage in your journey. You know what you need to do now, Tshomo."

Nodding, I replied pensively, "I have to pull myself out of this pit. I am determined to work through this karma with Zerdan, so I know that I cannot go to Amdo and live with Samaya. I have made that decision. But now what? How can I work through that samskara without meeting him again?"

"Patience," she replied. "The path will become clear."

"Perhaps I can find a Bon shaman to help me . . . or a Buddhist." I looked at Bhasundara hopefully one morning, several weeks after our conversation in the forest. We were sitting together in the kitchen area sipping a hot cup of po cha. "Surely there must be a powerful shaman somewhere in Böd who can lead me back into the past."

"You have experienced what it is like to submit to someone who is not a true master. I have met many shamans, both Bon and Buddhist, but nobody that I would trust like Dalha."

"We can ask around, can't we?"

"The only one to ask is Dalha and I have been asking her. Tshomo, when no answer comes, that is the answer."

"You speak in riddles, like Dalha herself," I replied, unhappily.

"I mean that the answer is to wait. While we are waiting, I have been wanting to say something to you, although I didn't want to hurt your feelings. But we are close enough now that I can say it." She drew in a deep breath and I looked at her questioningly. "You have not been tending to yourself, and perhaps this is what you need to do now. You have always been an attractive, refined woman, but your appearance now reflects your dejected state. You must pull yourself back together, and now is the time to do it. Look at you. You are wearing the same old clothes every day; your hair is untended. You used to wear such beautiful jewelry, and now you wear no ornaments, not even in your hair or your ears. I am taking you to the market today to fix you up."

"Why?" I asked with a frown. "There is nobody to see me and nowhere to go."

"I am here to see you!" she exclaimed. "Don't I count? Besides, it will help lift you out of these doldrums."

"I can't risk being seen by my family, so I can't go to the market, and the only money I have is that which Sonam gave me."

"Then I will go to the market for you," she insisted. "And don't use that money. This will be my gift to you. Remember I once told you that rivers must flow freely, without any dams. It is the same with money. It must flow from one person to another, and I am in a comfortable position now so I can let whatever I have flow through me." She smiled. "Besides, I will have fun dressing you up."

Bhasundara returned home that evening with a basketful of fine, colorful woolen clothing, skirts and jackets like the ones I used to wear, in addition to silver and turquoise jewelry and ornaments for my hair."

"Why these fancy things?" I asked in surprise.

"We are going to meet someone, and you must be dressed as my dignified Padma Tshomo has always dressed."

From then on, I got up and dressed myself properly, braiding and tying up my hair as I was accustomed to doing. Still, I waited, busying myself with chores around Bhasundara's cottage. A few weeks later, she came to serve me tea one morning and said that we were going on a ride to the Yarlung Valley.

"To Samye Monastery?" I asked in dismay. That was not a place where I wanted to be seen. Tenzin was away in the Song Empire, but I didn't want to meet the Samye Abbot or any of the other monks. I was too ashamed to show my face there.

She shook her head. "We are not going to the monastery. Actually, I am not sure where we are going, Tshomo, but last night Dalha showed me the faces of a man and a woman, and I knew immediately that they are the ones who can help you. As I was coming out of the dream, I heard the words Yarlung Valley, and so there we must go in the hope that they will show themselves."

"We are going there with no further information, no names, no indication of whom to ask for?" I inquired, doubtfully.

"Right." When I continued to look at her in disbelief, she said quietly, "This is the meaning of trust, Tshomo, and of surrender. What Dalha shows to me, that I do whether or not I understand it, whether or not I agree with it, whether or not I desire it. If I fail to follow her guidance, I have not surrendered, and without full surrender, I cannot come to know who I am. It is not for her sake that I surrender, but for mine, to free myself from the trappings of the ego, from thinking that I know better."

"Then let us go," I murmured uneasily.

The Yarlung Valley was a place I knew well because of my many visits to Samye, but we didn't take the path that led to the Champi Valley where the monastery was situated. Instead, we kept riding, passing a few isolated temples and monasteries, and every now and then an old castle presiding over a hill peak. It was the warmer months and many patches of wildflowers blanketed the valley, but the scenery consisted mostly of large swaths of low brush, and rocky mountains lining the valley on all sides. We spent several days riding back and forth looking for clues about whom we were seeking.

Yeshe had once told me that the valley was dotted with caves in which hermits lived in solitary retreat, and along the way we passed some of those hermits. As we rode through the valley, we could not help but stop the horses and pay our respects to Mount Sotang Kangbori, the abode of the powerful mountain god Yarlha Shampo, the protective deity of the region.

"When Guru Rinpoche first arrived here many centuries ago, the great deity Yarlha Shampo took the form of a frightening giant white yak, and with lightning flaring from his eyes, the yak charged toward him," remarked Bhasundara as we began to slowly ride again, side by side, gazing at the majestic mountain. "The great Guru was unmoved and saw through the disguise right away. Grabbing the yak by the nose, he whirled him around and threw him to the ground, at which moment, the yak transformed into his true form and bowed before the great Guru, realizing who he was. It is said that Guru Rinpoche beseeched him to remain in the area and help the spiritual aspirants who would come in the future to realize the awakened mind. To this day Yarlha Shampo remains here to fulfill that task. You should invoke him, Tshomo, while you are here." I nodded, although I felt far too intimidated to think of invoking that powerful deity. Besides, I was not seeking the awakened mind, only to free myself from what I felt was an occult bondage.

"There is a cave somewhere in this valley where Guru Rinpoche first meditated and subdued the troublesome spirits," she continued. But he knew he could not finish the work and so he called his celestial consort

Yeshe Tsogyal to take birth to assist him. He returned to his homeland, and she took birth in Böd. At a young age, she fled her home to come here. You know that story. Her cave is also somewhere nearby, where she spent twelve years in solitary meditation, completing the work Guru Rinpoche had begun." Bhasundara smiled. "Dalha always said they were a supreme example of how the gods and goddesses work in concert, two aspects of a single whole."

"But they are not gods," I noted in surprise.

"Who is to say, Tshomo? What is a god or goddess, and who are we? I have told you many times that to know the answer to our questions, you must first know yourself."

"There you go again, speaking in riddles," I gently chided her. Bhasundara began to ride with greater speed, but I called out for her to wait. Halting and turning to me she asked what was wrong. "What day is it?" I suddenly asked her. We had been wandering around the Yarlung Valley for three days, and I was beginning to lose hope, but last night as we sat outside our tent, I felt strangely drawn to keep staring at the moon as if it would provide some clue for us. It was not a full moon, far from it, but even in its decreased state its radiant light kept me entranced for quite a while.

At first, she didn't understand my question, but then a faint smile peered out from her lips as she realized the reason I was asking. "You are right. How did you know? I have calculated that today is the tenth day of the waxing moon, the day when Guru Rinpoche provides special blessings. Surely today he will provide an answer."

Bhasundara began to speed up her trot again and I followed behind her, with no indication of where we might find the people we were seeking. At one point, Bhasundara stopped, jumped down from her horse, and spoke to a monk who was walking along the path. Then without a word she got back onto her horse. I followed on Anpu, trusting her to lead the way. After riding a bit longer, Bhasundara caught sight of a stone structure jutting out from a low mountain ridge ahead. It appeared almost to be part of the mountain itself and one could have easily missed it. It was a very short climb from the valley. A narrow path led up the sloping mountainside and Bhasundara gently prodded her horse to climb over the stony path to reach it. I did the same. As we came closer, I could see that the structure was longer in length than it appeared from below, with a door and a window facing the valley. In the doorway stood a woman. Pulling the reigns of her horse, Bhasundara halted his steps, and I heard her say, "She is the one. I am sure of it. The one who appeared in my dream."

Without a pause, she jumped down from her horse as I hesitantly followed. Before us in the doorway to the stone structure stood a stately woman, smiling as if she was expecting us. She was slender, taller, and with a fairer complexion than the people of our local tribes, causing me to wonder if she was a foreigner. It was hard to tell her age, but I thought her to be quite a bit older than I. For a moment I stood staring at the unusual looking woman, whose abundant mane of white hair flowed loosely around her waist, not braided like most of the women in Böd. Her delicately carved face held large, clear eyes, and her skin was as smooth and clear as sanded stone, not in any way damaged by the searing rays of the sun. She struck a somewhat exotic appearance. As I drew closer, I noticed subtle creases around her mouth and eyes and etched across her forehead, indicating an elderly status.

Bhasundara introduced us and mentioned that she had been directed by her teacher to bring me there. The woman seemed to know all about it and agreed that yes, Bhasundara should leave me in her care. She said that she had come for that, but she didn't introduce herself, state her name, or say where she had come from.

After looking at me for a few moments, she commented, "How elegant you are, my dear. I am so happy to see you. Then she invited Bhasundara to come in for food and drink before leaving, and I glanced nervously at my friend, wondering if she would really leave me there alone with this stranger.

We entered the hut, which was larger and more comfortable inside than appeared from the outside. It consisted of one large room with a window facing the front, now open to let in the bright afternoon light, but with thick wooden shutters to keep out the cold night air. Near the entrance at the front of the room were a small stove and a low table with cushions for seating. In the back of the room, which seemed to be dug into the mountainside, was a single bed made of a thick mat placed on the ground, covered by a copious quilt. The floor of the hut was dirt, but it was covered by several small carpets and cushions, making the hut seem quite comfortable, even cozy. A sweet scent filled the air.

After we were seated and were sipping the tea that had been offered, I asked her, “By what name shall I call you?” She didn’t reply right away but looked at me tenderly and then said, “You may call me Ama-la (mother). I think that is what you would call me here.”

“Ama-la?” I asked. She nodded. “But what is your name?”

She laughed. “I have many, but Ama-la will do.” Bhasundara took hold of my hand and squeezed it, indicating that I should press no further. But if I was to stay with her, I had to know something about her.

“Are you a Bonpo?” I asked.

“A Bonpo?” then she quickly replied, “If that is how you see me, then that is what I am.”

She speaks in riddles as Dalha does, I thought to myself. Unsatisfied with her answers, I felt anxious about staying with this stranger alone, so far away from everyone, and whispered to Bhasundara that I wanted to speak with her privately. She nodded and whispered back that I should wait outside, saying that she wanted to have a few words with the woman. Several minutes later, she joined me.

“Bhasundara, we know nothing about this woman. She doesn’t look like one of us. I don’t know if it is wise for me to stay here without you.”

“Do you trust Dalha?” she asked in a firm voice.

“Of course. But what does that have to do with this?”

“It was Dalha who led me here. Without question, she is the one I saw in the dream. This woman is of high spiritual stature. Can’t you see the light emanating from her?” I shook my head. “She is the one you have been waiting for. Now is the time to test your faith.”

"Didn't you say there was a couple? Where is her husband?"

"I asked her about that. She said he will come soon." Seeing my hesitation, she added, "But you can change your mind, Tshomo, and return to Lhasa with me. I will send for Samaya to come get you if that is what you want." I shook my head. She paused and then began again, "No step on the spiritual path can be taken without courage. Are you afraid of this woman or are you afraid to face your past?"

"Can't you stay here with me?" I pleaded.

Taking my hands in hers and looking directly into my eyes, she said firmly, "This is a path you must walk alone, with the help and guidance of this woman. I have helped you to find her, but there is nothing more I can do. You have decided, and at any time, if you want to change course, send Anpu for me and I will come. But I truly believe that you will find what you are seeking here in this hut. Tshomo, this valley is incredibly blessed. Guru Rinpoche meditated not far from here, as did Yeshe Tsogyal. The monasteries are filled with meditating monks and there are hermits scattered throughout, engaged in advanced spiritual practices. The mountain gods protect this valley. It is one of the most sacred places in all the world. No harm can come to you here. The only danger is in your mind, and that is the one you must confront. What a blessing for you to stay with this woman who is a sage, an adept. What a gift Dalha has given you."

"Do you really think so?" I asked meekly. She nodded. "And you will inform my family?"

"I will tell all of them that you have gone on an extended retreat with a woman Bonpo in the Yarlung Valley, who will help settle your mind. They will understand. But, Tshomo, don't think in terms of time. You must be patient. Let the days and weeks and months pass without you getting anxious."

"Months!" I exclaimed. "I can't stay more than a few weeks at the most."

"She has assured me that you will know when you are ready to leave."

"But will you be alright, Bhasundara, riding back to Lhasa alone?" I asked, vaguely hoping for even a hint that perhaps I should accompany her.

"I will spend the night with the family where we slept last night. I have already told them to expect me."

There was nothing more I could say, and we went back into the hut, where Ama-la was waiting for us with sweet snacks. I sat quietly as Bhasundara engaged in light conversation with her, and then I walked Bhasundara out and watched sadly, suppressing my tears, as she rode away into the dimming light of another declining day.

CHAPTER 15

Trust

I was not to surrender myself readily to the care of the one called Ama-la, but after Bhasundara left, we got off to a positive start when I saw her tender care of Anpu as she gently led him to food and water and a place to rest, with me following close behind. When I heard her speaking to him as she would to a person, I momentarily relaxed. One can tell a lot about people by the way they treat animals, but still I could not easily let down my guard.

"What a beautiful creature you are," she murmured as she stroked his back. "I am happy to meet you. I will not tie you as I know of your devotion to your master. You are free to come and go, and please let me know your needs." Her voice was melodious, gentle, and pleasing, and he responded by making low sounds that I recognized as acknowledgement of her attention. He had warmed up to her immediately, something I could not do.

I could not deny an innate resistance, not knowing who she was or how she could help me. A determination arose to remain reserved and alert, and sensing this, she suggested that I rest on this first day of my arrival. When we re-entered the hut, she told me that the sleeping area was for me, and she showed me clothing that she said she had made especially for me—beautiful, colorful chubas of fine silk and the softest wool. Passing my hands over them to feel their texture, I wondered how she could have gotten such expensive material, and what need I would have for them while on retreat. Sensing my thoughts, she replied, "It is something I have wanted to do for you, *Bumo* (daughter). Rest now, while I prepare the evening meal."

Uncomfortable with her addressing me in such an intimate way, I reminded her again of my name, but she only smiled. As I was to discover, no matter how many times I told her that she could call me either Padma or Tshomo, or Padma Tshomo, to her I was only Bumo.

Before beginning to cook, she swept her hair up into a knot on top of her head and I watched her graceful movements as she began to prepare the meal, refusing my assistance, saying, "Today, you rest." I told myself that there was nothing to fear, but I remained watchful and spoke little, scanning the hut, alert for any hints of danger. No longer did I have the trusting nature that had once fitted my character; Zerdan had destroyed that.

Every now and then Ama-la would turn to me and ask with apparent sincerity if I needed anything. As darkness began to descend, she closed the wooden shutters and lit many lamps around the room and then told me to come eat. She watched as I drank the soup and ate a simple but delicious fare of dumplings with dried cheese.

"Aren't you eating?" I asked when I saw that she had set no food for herself.

"Not today," she replied with a smile. "Tomorrow I will share a meal with you."

After the meal was finished and everything put away, I began to feel very drowsy and lay down on the bed she had arranged for me, covering myself with the thick quilt she had laid out. I asked where she would sleep and she replied, "Not today. Tomorrow I will sleep." I wondered how she could stay awake all night, but my mind would not let me ponder this matter for long, because within no time at all I had fallen into a deep sleep, not waking up until mid-morning. It was the most refreshing and peaceful sleep I had since the death of Yeshe. By the time I awoke, the window had been thrown open, bathing the room in streams of sunlight as well as the cool morning air. Ama-la's smiling face greeted me and she said she had prepared a bath for me. She led me out of the hut to another small structure, just large enough to hold a tub for bathing. I drew in a deep breath, believing I would have to lower myself into freezing water, but when I bent to touch it, I found the water to be alluringly warm.

"How did you heat it?" I asked in surprise.

She simply smiled and replied, "Come back when you have finished, and we will have meditation and the midday meal."

I thanked her and then eagerly sank into the deep tub of soothing warm water. It was not only the heating of the water that amazed me, but how on earth did she fetch the water with no servants to help? I knew there was stream nearby, but did she carry buckets of water by herself? It was at that point that I told myself not to wonder at her actions, but to accept them. She was a mystery, no doubt, but it was unlikely that she would cause me harm. If I truly trusted Dalha and Bhasundara, I would have to trust this woman.

When I returned to the hut, she said to me gently, "When the mind is full of worry and stress, this passes into the body and causes illness. You need to heal and strengthen your body while you are clearing your mind. Bathing helps with that, and so it is something you will do every morning before meditation while you are here with me. Come now, let us sit together in meditation." She asked if I knew any meditation practices and any sacred sounds, mantras. I told her that I knew a few Bon mantras, but that when I meditated, which I hadn't done since Yeshe died, I kept my mind focused on my teacher Dalha.

"That is all you need," she replied. "Concentrate on her."

I was so relaxed from the bath that I was able to sit quietly for a time, which was unusual for me. When she felt me getting restless, she rose and told me to come eat. She had prepared a delicious meal of tsampa and root vegetables, with some cheese on the side, and this time she ate with me. The meal was so delicately spiced that I wondered where she had found the herbs. After the meal, she suggested we go for a walk.

It was late summer, but the rains had mostly passed, and the daytime temperatures were still mild.

As we walked along the mountain paths, she told me something of the history of the area. This sacred valley once had a temperate climate, with an abundance of fruit trees, she said as we passed through a patch of alpine brush. “It has become drier now, but the cloudless skies enable one to draw closer to the sun and moon and stellar beings. Come, let us sit and look down at the valley below.” Taking my hand, she led me to a place where we could rest on a large boulder that seemed to have been hewn from the mountain side.

“When the one you call Guru Rinpoche was here in meditation, after he subdued the troublesome spirits, thousands of celestial beings came to greet him. Some took physical form, and others came in their light bodies. It was a most magnificent sight because the light from their bodies illuminated the whole area. Day or night it didn’t matter, the whole valley was filled with a supernal light. His celestial consort came as well, and it was here that he asked her to take physical birth. Consenting, she said that she would come to this very place to continue his efforts of embedding sacred vibrations in this valley so that all who came would benefit. Wherever the gods and goddesses and the great masters have touched the earth, that spot is forever blessed.” I didn’t respond, but I thought to myself, so she is another Bonpo like Dalha who knows about Guru Rinpoche and Yeshe Tsogyal.

“We will sit out here one evening, and I will show you the light that lingers throughout this area,” she added in a quiet tone. “No matter what happens in the future, no matter what,” she said, emphasizing those words, “that light will continue. Nothing can erase or diminish it.”

She rose and we began walking again. I watched the delight on her face as she stopped often to admire a rock, a bush, or a flower, to run her hands caressingly over them or to look up at the bright sky, as if seeing it for the first time. I had to admit that I was intrigued by her, captivated by her attention to everything great or small, which seemed to equally delight her.

"I have been many times to this valley to visit the monastery where my son stays, but I never realized that this area has been blessed by the gods," I remarked. "I never imagined that the gods came to this place."

"During your time here, you will see many things that you didn't see before," she acknowledged with a glimmer in her eye. We walked a bit further before returning to the hut. Telling me to rest, she began to prepare the evening meal. After consuming the noodles and vegetables she cooked, I began to help her clear away the meal, but she insisted that I rest. When she was done, she asked that I join her in meditation. Within a short time, I grew sleepy and went to bed, leaving her in the silent sitting position. Filled with a peace I hadn't experienced in quite some time, I easily drifted into a deep and restful sleep.

And so passed the days: eating, walking, meditating, bathing, with a limited amount of talking. I didn't think to ask her where the food came from, how she drew the bath water and heated it, or about so many other unexplainable things. We seemed to have everything we needed, with no deprivation. I allowed her to do everything for me as I realized how desperately I needed to be cared for; how my mind and body needed to heal from the turbulent emotions that had been coursing through me the last few years. It was not only my encounter with Zerdan, but also the loss of Yeshe, from which, I now realized, I had never really recovered. It was perhaps this vulnerability, the loneliness that had set in, which had left me open to Zerdan's deceptions. As the weeks passed, slowly the oppressive weight that had clung to me began to lift, and as I began to emerge from my self-absorption, I noticed the joy she took in doing even the smallest act of care for me. Who was this woman and how did I intuitively know not to ask any questions, not to enquire about her background or life?

Two months passed before I began to speak more openly about personal matters, before I began to truly let down my guard. She seemed to know much about my life, but she asked for more details about my family. Since my arrival, she had treated me as a mother would treat a child, and I allowed this because it brought me a comfort that I desperately needed. I was still young when I lost my own mother, and Ama-la's care made me realize how much I missed that motherly love. One day when she was preparing the evening meal, for the first time I got up to help her. She began to tell me to rest but I responded immediately, "Ama-la, a grown daughter is not served by her mother; rather, she serves with her mother." She smiled at that response and after that allowed me to help with all the meals.

Another time she asked me if she could comb and dress my hair. Laughing, I told her it would be my pleasure. As she ran her fingers through my long hair, she commented, "You have such beautiful thick hair, Bumo."

"That is what my husband used to say. He loved to run his hands over it when I brushed it out at night. But it is not nearly as beautiful as yours, which shimmers like freshly fallen snow when struck by sunlight. My hair is now becoming a very dull grey, as I become an old woman."

"To me you are young," she responded quietly. "The streaks of grey complement the black. It is very dignified, my dear. Age brings a different kind of beauty, not less valuable than that of youth. We should wear our age proudly."

"You remind me very much of my mother. She died when I was a young woman and there were many conversations that I was never able to have with her."

"You were close to your mother?"

"She was everything to me when I was growing up. She was a very wise and caring woman, a true Bonpo, unlike me."

She cracked a smile. "What do you mean, unlike you?"

"She truly lived with the goddess every day. The goddess was a living presence for her. She would take me into the forest, talk to the nature spirits and listen to their counsel, but the one to whom she was most devoted was the goddess of the sacred lake, Nam Tsho Chukmo. I was never able to feel that presence. The goddess has not become a reality for me."

"Perhaps she has, but you don't know it," she replied quietly. "I know your past, and you have a long history of devotion to the goddess. But in the past, you sought her external form; now you must find her internal presence. Forms come and go. The internal presence never leaves, for it is your very Self."

"You sound like my teacher Dalha and my friend Bhasundara," I said, struck by the similarity of their words. She began to draw my braids onto the top of my head, winding them together and fastening them with a turquoise hair pin, and I thought of how my mother used to do that to her own hair. "My mother has been gone many years, but her teachings have not left me. It is she who instilled in me my Bon beliefs."

"You earned such a mother. It is not in every birth that one comes into such a family. You have been brought up in both the Bon and Buddhist ways, have you not?" I nodded. "They are but different expressions of the one truth."

"That is what my teacher used to say. You also remind me of her."

Many such discussions filled our days, and slowly I was beginning to feel close to the one I called Ama-la. Although I learned nothing of her background or history or where she came from, I was coming to know her, and I was often struck by her simple wisdom. She didn't speak grand philosophical truths, as I had often heard in the conversations between Yeshe and Tenzin. Her wisdom was conveyed through brief comments at unexpected moments, often when she was speaking about a very practical matter; her words were few but carefully chosen, and no matter what, she always wore a cheerful face. It was impossible not to be uplifted by her presence, and slowly a bond of trust began to form. Although Bhasundara had spoken of the light surrounding her, that was not what I saw when I looked at her. I saw a very loving, mother-like figure who attended to my everyday needs. This warmed my heart, a heart that had begun to turn cold. During the years since Yeshe's death, and especially after meeting Zerdan, my spirit had begun to wither, suppressing anything akin to happiness; that withering was slowly but surely now being lifted.

Once a month we would ride to a small market where Ama-la would purchase food staples and some root vegetables. She used her own funds for this and would never accept or let me use the gold coins that Sonam had given me. She must be a woman of means, I said to myself one day, but why was she using her funds to support me? That was a mystery. Later, I discovered that sometimes in the early morning, while I was still sleeping, she would ride to one of the monasteries and get milk and cheese from the monks. From the milk she would make yoghurt. Surprisingly, there never was any lack when it came to food, and I was amazed by the diversity of the meals she supplied. Some days she would eat, but there were many days when she would not, and she would be as energetic on the days without food as the days with. She was most resourceful, and I never ceased to be amazed by her most unusual ways.

More months passed, but I was hardly keeping track of the time. I soon found myself living in an unbounded frame of mind, almost forgetting the reason for which I had come. A contentment had settled over me, and I was happy to continue as we were. I felt my strength return as well as my positive attitude and cheerfulness as Zerdan retreated from my mind. I had forgotten how to laugh, but in Ama-la's presence, laughter returned. I had no concern for the future. Each day was a lifetime in itself, and all I thought about was what that day would bring. She and I spent all our time together, enjoying the gathering of food and wood, the preparation of meals and tidying up. Her impulse was still to do everything for me, but at my insistence she came to accept my sharing in the chores.

Then there were the meditation hours, every morning and evening, which I gradually began to look forward to, something I had never done before. My mind had not reached the clarity of one of our sacred lakes, but the sediment was settling enough to allow, every now and then, a momentary glimpse of the place where thought cease to be. Those brief moments of deep peace were awakening in me a thirst for more, and my attention began to shift from the external world to the internal one, wherever or whatever that is.

It was after such a moment of resting in the thoughtless realm that the image of Lhamo La-tso arose before me, and I became aware of the absolute stillness of the water, protected and sheltered by the surrounding mountain gods. As the image of the lake became more vivid, I felt myself being drawn into the powerful presence of the goddess herself, Palden Lhamo. Her magnetic intensity drew me deeper and deeper into the depths of the lake, until I felt myself being sucked through the vortex of time, unable to resist. Losing all sense of the present or bodily awareness, I was swept into the interior spaces of mind, where I found myself in another place, another time period, speaking a different language, wearing a different body. It was the body I had seen before so many times in dream, and I knew she was me.

CHAPTER 16

End of the Eleventh century, Gaul (France)

I was born in one of the many small farming villages in the southern part of the Duchy of Burgundy, not far from the grand alpine mountains. The area around our village abounded with forests of beech and oak trees, and from an early age those forests beckoned me to enter their richly scented pathways. Further away there were the pine and spruce forests, but I never saw them as a child as my mother was afraid of the spirits that she said lived among the trees. In the village square there stood an old yew tree near the village church. As a young child, I would run to the tree on our way to Sunday mass and stand under it, looking up at the sunlight filtering through the hairy canopy of leaves, but my mother would always hasten to pull me away. One day, the tree was cut down. When I asked why, my mother replied that the yew tree was the tree of death, inhabited by evil spirits that would place a curse on the church and the people of our village. In many ways she tried to instill in me a fear of forests, but her words only made me more eager to explore.

Mine was a poor family and my parents worked hard to feed my two older brothers and me. They were strict believers in the church, which in our village was presided over by a severe and intimidating older priest.

For as long as I could remember, I shied away from him and the others who controlled the giving of the sacraments. They all instilled fear in me, talking of sin and other such things of which I had no knowledge.

My father was a strict disciplinarian and ensured that my elder brothers worked hard in the fields, and that I helped my mother with food preparation and care for the animals. The atmosphere in the home was austere, with little time for pleasures, except for the occasional outing after church on Sunday, when we could mingle with the other villagers. Despite the hard work, I was a cheerful child. My greatest pleasure was sneaking off to the small forest that abutted our farm. I had to steal away because if my mother discovered these forbidden outings, she would scold me, saying, "Spirits and devils live there. Creatures that would eat you alive. You are not allowed to go there, Claire, do you hear?" How often I heard that refrain, but I would seek refuge in the forest anyway, less afraid of what might inhabit it than of the village priest. I firmly believed that only good spirits lived in the forest, and I wanted to see them. I don't know how I came to this conviction because nobody in my family ever mentioned such a thing.

I was eight years old when I began seriously to search for those spirits, whom I thought of as small, beautiful fairies hiding among the moss and wildflowers that peered out from the forest floor. On an early morning when my mother had gone to the village to buy some goods after instructing me to feed the chickens and collect their eggs, I ran to the forest in search of the fairies. After I entered the wooded area and looked behind trees and bushes, my search was interrupted by a voice singing a tune I had never heard before. Abandoning my search, I approached the sound and caught sight of a lovely woman and a girl about my age. I stood there watching as the older woman sang and the child danced. As I began to slowly inch closer, the woman noticed me, stopped singing, and with a smile motioned me to approach, which I hesitantly did. The young girl was about my height but stockier, a pretty girl with a rounded face, large, bright eyes, and flowers woven into the dark braid that hung down her back. She was neatly dressed in a clean flowered red skirt and top. I felt a bit embarrassed because my hair was unkempt, loosely held together behind my head by a string, and my old clothes were drab and more than a little tattered.

"What is your name?" the older woman asked.

"Claire. I live on the farm beyond the forest over there," I pointed in the direction of my home.

"And we live on a farm on the other side of the forest," she said, motioning in the direction of her home. "My name is Gabrielle Beaufoy and this is my daughter Elise. We come here every Tuesday to collect plant medicines, and while we are here, we invite the fairies and angels, the forest spirits, to appear. Then we sing and dance for them. Would you like to join us?"

"You invite the fairies!" I exclaimed with wide eyes. It seemed my search might be over. "Have you seen them?"

She laughed. "Of course, Claire. If you truly love them, they will come to trust you and may show themselves to you. I have seen them many times in this forest. But if you fear them, they won't show themselves."

"I don't fear them," I claimed with determination. "And I have always wanted to see them."

"Then dance with us." She began again to sing a most melodious tune and Elise started to dance. I was shy at first and stood there watching, but after a few minutes, I began to follow the steps that she was making. I had never danced before, and it felt so freeing, so joyful, that I couldn't stop. Elise and I danced and danced until her mother's voice grew quiet, and then she gathered both of us in her arms and hugged us. "The fairies and angels came to greet us today. It is because you both have danced so well." I looked at her happily. Even though I hadn't seen them, I was glad to know that they had come.

"We will be here again at this time next Tuesday, Claire, to collect plants. Come join us," said Elise. I nodded and then I asked if she had any sisters. She shook her head.

"I also don't. In fact, I don't have any friends, except for older cousins who never play with me," I added.

"Then we will be sisters, you and I, Claire."

I nodded and watched as they walked toward their farm on the other side of the forest, then I sped back to mine. My mother had already returned from the village and had been searching for me. I made up some excuse and cheerfully helped her prepare supper for the family. I had met someone who saw the fairies and forest spirits and that was enough to make me feel very happy.

The next Tuesday, under the pretext of checking on the animals, I raced toward the forest and soon caught up with Madame Beaufoy and Elise, who were busy collecting plants. I watched as Madame Beaufoy carefully selected and then examined each plant before placing it in her basket.

"Can you teach me, Madame Beaufoy?" I asked after greeting them.

She smiled. "If you are to be Elise's sister then you mustn't be so formal with me. Call me Gabrielle. Whatever I know I learned from my grandmother, and I can share her knowledge with you. She never taught me the official names of the plants, and I doubt she knew them, but I learned to recognize them. Do you see this one? I call it the small yellow bud plant because of the way it looks. If you boil it and drink the liquid, it can ease any stomach ailment. This one I call the long stalk plant and it brings down fevers. This one with purple buds is for general wellbeing, to restore one's strength after an illness or fall. I don't know their fancy names, but I can tell you what their properties are. If you come collect the plants with me, I will teach you as we go along, but . . ." She didn't finish the sentence.

"I want to learn," I said decidedly. I saw Elise and her mother exchange glances and sensed that something was wrong, so I asked if the plant medicine was secret.

"Not secret," she replied. "But one must be cautious. Elise's father doesn't like that I give people medicine, and he doesn't like that I collect these plants. But how can I not help people when I know how? You also must be aware that in our village, many don't like it that women have this ability. If your parents find out, they may not be happy."

"I would never tell them," I hurried to assure her. "I can't even let them know that I come to the forest. My mother believes that devils and dangerous spirits live here."

Gabrielle laughed when she heard this, and seeing the serious expression on my face, said it was time to sing and dance and call the fairies, nature spirits, and angels to us. Once again Elise and I danced while Gabrielle sang in her beautiful voice. No wonder the angels and fairies draw near, I thought to myself; she sings like a heavenly angel. As we were getting ready to leave, I asked Gabrielle what the difference was between the fairies, forest spirits, and angels.

Sitting me down beside her, she began to explain. "Everything is alive," she said. "There are spirits that live in the rivers and streams and there are those that live in the trees, the soil, and the air, only we can't see them with our normal eyes. We must develop spiritual sight to see them. They maintain the harmony of the natural world. They are very sensitive to our thoughts, and when we mistreat nature or have harmful thoughts, they are disturbed. That is when we get droughts and floods and storms and other such things. People call these spirits by many names—some call them fairies. Angels are different. They are celestial beings who can come near to help us in times of trouble. But the one to really call upon is the Great Mother goddess. She is far above all the others in her benevolence. She is pure love itself." Her voice softened when she spoke of the goddess, as if filled with a special feeling, and I could not help but note this.

"A goddess," I murmured. "I have never heard of her."

She smiled and then said it was getting late and I better return home. I had completely lost track of the time. When I emerged from the woods, my second brother was frantically looking for me. He saw me walking through the field next to the forest and hurried over to me.

Mama has been looking for you for a long time and she is angry, he said as he took my hand and pulled me along. By the time I reached the kitchen area, my mother was in too much need of my help to ask many questions. I was sure for the next few days to stay always within her sight, and I didn't go to the forest the next Tuesday, but I went the week after that.

"We missed you last week, Claire," exclaimed Elise when she saw me. "And I think the fairies missed you as well because it wasn't the same without you."

"My mother was watching me closely," I replied apologetically. "I may not be able to come every week, but I will come whenever I can."

I had brought with me my hairbrush and summoning my courage, I asked Gabrielle if she could fix my hair as she had done for Elise, who every time had different flowers in her braid. My mother never attended to my appearance, so I had never learned how to make myself attractive.

"You have such beautiful wavy golden hair, Claire. I think when you can, you should keep it loose, but brushed and tidy, and put flowers in it. I will show you." I squirmed in discomfort as she pressed the brush through my knotted hair, but finally she made it smooth and almost silky and then placed a woven string of flowers on my head like a crown, making me feel almost like a fairy princess. After she was done, she took my hand and said, "Come, Claire, let me show you a magical plant that heals almost anything. Often when the plants are combined and boiled together, they produce a stronger effect. This large-leafed one can increase the potency of the other plants. I add it to many medicines. I call it the large leaf miracle," she chuckled. "Since I don't know their official names, you will have to remember the appearance of the plants. Run your hands over this one so you will remember it. Often, I find it by streams. There is a stream on our side of the forest and that is where I go to collect this one."

"Does this forest have many healing plants?" I asked looking up at her.

"It has some. I try to visit the other forests near our village where I find different plants. But healing plants can also be found in fields, almost anywhere. The goddess has provided everything we need. If you come to our home one day, I will show you many plants and teach you their properties. But Claire, not everyone can heal with plants. You must develop a relationship with them and speak with them as if they are your friends, because that is what they are."

"Do you speak to them?"

"Always. I never pluck a plant without first seeking its permission and asking it to infuse itself with healing power. I tell them it is to relieve pain and bring comfort to people."

"And does the plant respond?"

"Of course," she replied with a smile, "but not in the way you think. I feel it internally, in my heart, because plants communicate not through words but through feelings. Sometimes I receive a message, a feeling, that a particular plant is too young, and I should let it to grow and select another plant. I always listen. Sometimes I hear that the plant is more powerful when mixed with another specific plant, but I must determine the exact proportion to mix when I boil them. In this way the plants play with me and I with them. They are like my children. But come, let us sing and dance before you must return home."

When I reached our cottage that day, my mother looked at my smooth flowing hair crowned by flowers, and with a frown asked, "Who has done this to you, Claire?" When I didn't answer, she asked again in a sterner tone, taking tight hold of my arm.

"I did it to myself," I replied, lowering my eyes. "I wanted to look pretty."

"You are too young for that," she scolded, as she tied back my hair with a string and threw the flowers on the ground. "Better think of your chores and how to help your parents run this farm. I don't want to see this nonsense again, Claire." I made sure after that to tie back my hair and take out the flowers before leaving the forest.

I went as often as I could to meet Gabrielle and Elise, and the hours spent with them were the happiest times. Elise became the sister I never had, and eventually we became so close that she and I began to spend some of the time together sharing incidents in our lives. I told her about my harsh mother, who often scolded me and on occasion when she was angry enough pulled my ear so hard that I squirmed in pain, and she told me about her father who sometimes took his hand to her mother, making her fearful for her mother's safety.

"It's not so bad because we have each other, Claire," she said to me one day as we watched Gabrielle collect her stock of plants for the week. She had just finished telling me of her father's anger when he discovered the place in one of their old barns where her mother made the medicines. "He threatened to burn it down, but she threatened to burn herself along with her plants. They fought, but in the end she prevailed."

"You are so lucky to have Gabrielle as your mother," I remarked. "I so wish I had a mother like her, but she is my teacher and that is almost as good. I am grateful to have such a teacher."

"But I can't protect her, Claire," she replied mournfully. "When my father's anger erupts, there's nothing I can do to keep her from getting hurt. She always sends me away, so I won't see what he does to her, but every night I pray that he won't harm her."

"Whom do you pray to?" I asked curiously.

"The goddess," of course.

"Why doesn't the goddess protect her? Your mother loves her so."

I once asked my mother that and she said that we each have free will and the goddess can't interfere. It is my father's choice to treat her like that, and it is her choice to stay. She could run away, you know, but she doesn't, and I believe it is for my sake. I feel guilty about that. But she also told me that she is not angry at my father. She feels badly for him because he doesn't know the goddess. I think even though the goddess can't change my father's behavior, she brings my mother much comfort and that seems to be more than enough."

"I wish I could protect her, Elise. What you have told me makes me sad, very sad for what she must endure."

After that conversation, we began to speak more about the goddess than of the nature spirits and fairies. I began to ply Gabrielle with questions, asking her where she had learned about the goddess. She told me that her grandmother had been a priestess, a Druid, who performed ceremonies to the goddess, but she had to do so in secret because almost all people had forgotten about her, and that was why there was so much suffering in the world. I had never heard that word Druid before and asked what it was.

Smiling, she replied, "They are people who honor the goddess, and their places of worship are the forests, not churches. It is in the forests that they commune with the nature spirits and work with them to keep the balance in the natural world, to keep the rains coming on time and in the right amount to maintain the health of the plants. It is these nature spirits who give us the plant medicine, and we must express gratitude for that. This is what Druids do—express gratitude to the world of nature. Some of them can also see the future, and they work not only with the spirits of the earth and the forest, but also with the spirits of the sun, the moon, and the stars."

"They also have spirits?" I asked in surprise.

She nodded. "Of course, my dear. The whole universe is alive, and we are part of that vast living being called the Great Mother, the one who brought forth all of this and who takes care of it. That Great Mother is the goddess we must seek."

"The Great Mother is kind and caring, not mean like your mother," Elise hastened to whisper to me.

"She is above all pettiness and only wants what is best for her children," continued Gabrielle. "And it is not only we who are her children, but the animals and plants, the trees and mountains and rivers, the stars, and moons. To her, we are all the same, children to be respected and loved. That is why we must give love to all, even to those who seek to harm us."

I thought about her words long after. It was easy to love the trees and plants, but I found it hard to love my mother when she was scolding me. Nevertheless, I took Gabrielle's words to heart and tried not to hold on to resentment or anger.

I was learning so much from Gabrielle, and my time with her and Elise brought joy to my life, a feeling I did my best to hide when I was home. I knew to keep the relationship and my forest visits secret, but often I was afraid of being discovered, knowing that my mother would not take it well. I had been meeting them for about four years when my parents announced that they would be away for the day. I was to be in charge of preparing supper for when they returned. After spending the morning tending to the animals, I decided to quietly slip away. It was not a Tuesday, and I knew that Gabrielle and Elise would not be in the forest, so I decided to visit their house for the first time. It was an easy path through the forest and once I arrived, I found Elise alone outside.

At the sight of me, her whole face brightened. "Claire!" she exclaimed. "What are you doing here?"

"I've come to visit you. My parents are away for the day and my brothers are working in the field. I have a few hours before I must return. I want to see where your mother makes her medicine."

"She is working there now. My father and brothers are also in the field. I will take you there. She keeps the place locked so my father can't enter. It is a source of continuing tension between them."

Gabrielle was surprised and pleased to see me. Hugging me, she said, "My two daughters. I am so glad you have each other. Come, Claire, let me show you the medicines I am making." Elise didn't have much interest in medicine so she sat there quietly, waiting patiently for us to be done so that she and I could talk privately together. I was amazed at all the plants Gabrielle had gathered. She went through them one by one, telling me of their properties and where I could find them.

"What is this one," I asked, picking up an evergreen branch with bluish leaves and yellow flowers. "It has a bitter smell."

"You don't need to know about that one," she said taking it from me and placing it back on the table.

"Tell us, mama," insisted Elise, who had drawn closer.

"It can be toxic and is not to be used lightly," she replied hesitantly.

"What is it for?" I asked innocently.

"Well, I suppose you girls are old enough. The name of this one I know. It is called ruta. When rubbed on the skin, it can be used to treat inflammation, but when ingested it can end a pregnancy. But it can also be toxic and cause serious illness. All of these over here can be used to end pregnancy. I know their names because some women from our village and neighboring towns have secretly come to me pleading for these plants. That is why I keep them here. This one is called mugwort, this is angelica, and that is yarrow," she said as she pointed to the plants lying next to the ruta on the table. "They are often combined but must be handled with care or harm can come to the woman. You can also add parsley, arnica, and pennyroyal. It is strange but I only know the official names of these plants because they are in such demand, and I have had to learn them."

Looking at her inquisitively, I asked in a serious tone, "Why would anyone want to end a pregnancy?"

"Sometimes it is necessary," she said quietly. "It is never an easy decision to make, but if a pregnancy is forced or unwanted, it may be the better choice."

"Oh," I said, moving away from that part of the table. Then turning to look at her, I added, "I hope I never have to use those plants." In a more cheerful tone, I exclaimed, "There is so much to learn. When I am older, I want to come study with you all the time."

She laughed. "We will see what tomorrow brings. Your parents may have other plans for you. But there is no end to learning about the plants because they are always changing, just as we are. We grow from childhood to youth and then old age. Similarly, the plants have a life cycle, and one must learn how these changes affect their healing properties. Plants also migrate. They travel as people do. Plants found in one place one year may be in a different place the next year. These plants like to be near water. Those on that table like the mountains where the air is cooler. I had to climb a nearby mountain to find them. By spending time with these various plants, you come to know them. They become part of your family."

I spent hours that day learning about the different healing properties of the plants while Elise sat patiently nearby. Finally, Gabrielle said, "Enough for today. Spend some time with Elise. I have to go prepare for supper." So entranced was I that it didn't occur to me that I also should head back; it was such a rare occasion to be able to spend time with my friend at her home. We sat in the kitchen and chatted while her mother prepared food. It was only when I saw darkness approach that I realized how much time had passed and said that I had to leave immediately.

I had stayed far too long. My parents would soon be returning, and

I had done nothing to prepare the supper. I would be in for a scolding for sure. What I hadn't imagined was that my brother and mother would be waiting for me by the edge of the forest. My parents had returned early and, when my mother couldn't find me, my brother suggested we look in the forest as I sometimes went there. She refused to enter the forest for fear of the devils who might be lurking around, so they waited by the edge. When they saw me emerge, my mother slapped me harder than she had ever done before, and taking hold of my ear, she pulled me across the field into the house, ignoring my cries of pain.

"Are you possessed?" she asked, looking angrily at me. I didn't respond. "How many times have I warned you not to go into the forest, and yet your brother tells me that you pay me no mind." Her voice was cutting.

"I go to meet a friend, that is all," I protested tearily.

"A friend? What friend?" she asked in a raised voice.

"Mama, her name is Elise. She is the daughter of the farmer on the other side of the forest. She is my age and we like to talk."

"How many times have I told you what can come over you when you enter those woods? Perhaps she is also under a spell. Who is her mother?"

I hesitated but when pressed again replied quietly, "Madame Beaufoy." My father had just entered the room when I spoke those words. He stood there listening and then said to my mother, "I hear she is something of a sorceress. We shouldn't have anything to do with that family."

"Did you hear that?" my mother's eyes flashed. "You are not to go there or see them anymore. If you do, I will have to deal more harshly with you."

Nothing, not even my mother's threats, could prevent me from going to see Elise and Gabrielle. I felt that somehow the goddess they spoke of would protect me. After all, wasn't she the Great Mother? I didn't venture to go to their home again and would only meet them on some Tuesdays for a very brief time, hiding my family situation the best I could. The demands of daily life kept my parents and brothers fully occupied, and as long as I didn't stay away for an extended time, they seemed not to notice my absences. My relationship with Gabrielle and Elise deepened until I came to regard them as my family, people who understood me more than my blood relatives.

It was on a Tuesday when I went to meet them that I found Elise there alone sobbing. She had been waiting for me, hoping that I would be able to get away.

"What is wrong?" I asked in alarm as I put my arm around her.

Wiping away her tears with her hand, she explained the situation. "Claire, mama is in danger. She helped a young unmarried woman end a pregnancy. Mama gave her a dose of the medicine and instructed her on how to take it, but she was so frightened that she insisted on receiving a second dose, in case the first one didn't work. Reluctantly, mama gave it to her but told her to wait a week before taking the second dose. Instead, the girl took them both at once and started to bleed heavily and became very ill. Her parents were frantic. They didn't know about the pregnancy, and the girl blamed everything on mama, saying she felt ill and came to mama who gave her some medicine. The family now accuses mama of being a sorceress and casting a spell on the young girl. Now my father is so angry that he burnt down the barn with all the plants she had gathered. I pray he doesn't kill her."

"A sorceress," I murmured in confusion. "That is ridiculous. Your mother is the most loving person I have ever met, who goes out of her way to help people."

"The priest came to see my father. Claire, I am frightened. I am so afraid of what they will do to her." At the mention of the priest, my chest tightened. He was far more of a sorcerer than Gabrielle ever could be.

"What does your mother say?"

"She is in a difficult spot and doesn't say much. Even though the young woman has turned on her, she doesn't want to reveal that the girl was pregnant."

"I am sure this will pass, Elise. She doesn't force anyone to come to her for treatments, but she does the best she can for all those who come. Those who say mean things about her should simply stay away."

A few days later, when the family was sitting together having our supper, my mother stared at me for a few moments and then spoke in an icy tone. "It's a good thing that I stopped you from meeting that girl. Everyone in the village is now talking, saying that the mother is a sorceress. It was probably she who put a spell on you and kept you going back into the forest." I was stunned that this accusation had gone so far and was now spreading among the villagers.

"She is not a sorceress!" I exclaimed, standing up from my seat at the table. "How can you believe such things? She helps people through her knowledge of the plants."

"Look at her!" exclaimed my father. "Defending a sorceress. Your association with that family could get us into trouble. I don't know what will happen to the husband. He is a decent farmer, but unless he gets rid of her, who will buy his crops?"

"Let the priest take care of it," replied my mother. "He will know what to do."

For the next few days, I was on edge, wanting desperately to go see Elise and Gabrielle, but knowing that I could not escape my mother's hawk-like watch, I waited impatiently to hear that everything had been resolved.

Instead, a few days later, my mother dragged me by the arm to the church in the village square. "Why are you taking me there?" I asked nervously.

"I want you to see what happens to women like her."

What could a child's mind imagine about punishment? A flogging perhaps? Public insults? A harsh scolding? I thought perhaps they might denounce her or beat her, and as sad as that would be, she would still live, and I would somehow be able to meet her again. But what does a child know about the world and human cruelty?

As we drew closer to the square, I saw Gabrielle in front of the church tied up to a large pole. "No, Mama, I don't want to see it!" I cried out, pulling back, thinking that they were going to hit her. I knew beatings could be brutal, and I didn't want to see her suffer or be disgraced. I didn't want to witness the humiliation of the one whom I regarded as my teacher being struck in public.

"You are going to watch this, so that you never forget. Never." She spoke harshly as she pulled me along, gripping my arm so tightly that I moaned in pain. I didn't want to see her being beaten. I began to cry, resisting and pleading with my mother to take me away.

Many people had gathered. Some were shouting, "*Brûlé la sorcière, brûlé la sorcière*" (burn the witch), while the priest stood by the church door watching. Pushing people aside, my mother drew me up close, but I put my hands over my eyes so as not to see.

"Open your eyes, Claire," commanded my mother sternly, firmly pulling away my hands. "You must never forget what you see here today."

In terror and in a state of disbelief, I watched a man approach Gabrielle with a burning torch and set fire to the wood at the base of the pole to which she was tied. First her skirt succumbed and then the lunging flames rapidly moved to engulf her body. Gasping in horror at what I was witnessing, I could not help but cry out as I frantically looked around for the people who would surely come forward to put out the fire. But no one came. I wanted to run up to her, but my mother firmly gripped my arm, holding me in place. I could no longer see Gabrielle's body as it was soon covered by smoke and flames. My chest was heaving, and I felt the world crashing down around me, and then I lost consciousness.

I woke up at home and wondered if I had dreamed the whole thing, but I was not to be so fortunate. A short while later my mother entered the room and said sternly, "Now you see what happens to women like that. The same will happen to you if you mix with the devil. You are never to see that girl, her daughter, again."

I cried until I had no more tears left. What Elise must be going through now, I couldn't imagine. They had killed her beautiful mother for no reason. Then and there, a fierceness arose in me that I didn't know existed, and I made a vow that I would never step foot into a church again, that I would be a Druid like my friend Gabrielle, that the forest would be my place of refuge, and from that moment on I would only follow the way of the goddess.

CHAPTER 17

Healing an Old Wound

"Bumo, you have been crying for so long. Open your eyes." The gentle voice of Ama-la brought me back to the present. But even with open eyes, I couldn't suppress my pain. I was too shaken. "You are here with me in the Yarlung Valley. You have visited the past, and it is time to return to where you are now. It is very late in the night. You have seen enough for the time being."

With searching eyes that sought answers, I looked into Ama-la's caring face. How glad I was to have her here beside me! A soft glow from lamps lit the room. "I know everything that you have experienced," she said gently. "We will talk about it tomorrow. Now I want you to drink this soothing tea I have prepared. It will help you sleep. You need to refresh yourself before we speak." Without a word, I took the cup she handed me and drank it all and then went over to the sleeping mat to lie down. There was nothing to be said, still burdened as I was with the emotions of the young girl Claire. I was sure that I would not be able to sleep, but after a short while my eyes grew heavy and I drifted into a dreamless rest.

I awoke the next morning to bright sunlight streaming through the open window. The warm months had passed and normally it would be too cold to open windows, but somehow our little hut stayed warm, even with cooler air pouring in.

"You are awake," said Ama-la when she saw my open eyes. I nodded, still interiorized and reluctant to speak. Rising from the bed, I went to the bath hut and refreshed myself. A tub of warm water was waiting for me. Sinking into it, I could not prevent the emergence of images from what I had witnessed the night before, and I broke into sobs.

From outside the bathing hut, I heard Ama-la's words, "You are remembering events from one hundred years ago. Of what use are your tears? Come, and I will show you where your friend, your teacher from that time, is now. There is a happy ending to this saga."

Rising and drying myself, I went back into our hut where Ama-la was seated in meditation. "Come, sit down and quiet your mind." I did as she instructed. Her voice was soothing as she intoned certain sounds and my emotions subsided. Then with closed eyes I saw an elderly woman, her skin bronzed, her dark hair braided, her face lined with age. She was teaching a group of women about which plants to use for different ailments. Then someone who looked like the village chief came and folded his hands before her. With a downcast head, again and again he expressed his gratitude to her for healing his daughter. Other people came and she dispensed medicine to them. The scene continued, and I saw that she was greatly respected, admired by the community.

Coming out of meditation, I asked, Ama-la, "What am I seeing?"

"You are seeing your friend Gabrielle as she is today. She lives in a village in Bharat, the region you call Gyagar. After her death, she was taken to a realm where she could recover from the tragedy, submerge the memory of it, and imbibe more knowledge of the healing arts, and then she was born in a place where her gifts would be valued. She has had a wonderful life, a husband who respects her, children and grandchildren, and she has been able to heal many people openly, not in secret."

"But why did she have to suffer such a terrible death?"

"That is not for us to know. Some people choose to pay off a great deal of karma through a traumatic event, like an intense purification you might say. Some make a sacrifice, consuming a degree of collective karma, taking on the burden of others. Unless you know her past and what her deeper intention was, you cannot understand what happened. What you witnessed was the beginning of what is becoming more commonplace in that part of the world. It was rare then for women to undergo such a tragedy, but now and in the future many will have to face it. I know you will ask me why. Those who commit the terrible deed may have to undergo it themselves. Perhaps they will be reborn as women who will face the burning stake, so that by undergoing such suffering, they will never inflict it again. The cycle continues—burn and be burned—until the cycle is broken through an awakening process."

"I think I understand," I replied quietly.

"That lady Gabrielle made such an impression on you that when deciding where to take birth next, you found a woman much like her, didn't you? Wasn't your mother in this life just the kind of mother you yearned for then? She was dedicated to the goddess and knew the plant medicines, but unlike Gabrielle, your mother was very much respected and appreciated by the community."

"You are right, Ama-la," I replied pensively. "Do we choose our parents then?"

"Of course, but perhaps not consciously. The higher Self knows to choose a family that will provide the environment needed for the next step on the journey toward awakening. You chose your parents in Burgundy to experience the restrictions of formal religion, and the harsh conditions that some women have to endure. Those were important lessons for you.

"As the young girl Claire, you were just coming into womanhood when you had to witness the burning and killing of your friend and teacher, a woman you so admired. It left a very deep imprint in your mind, so deep that you carried it from that life into this one. That is why you had those dreams, or nightmares, I should say. They were repeats of a memory that refused to lie dormant as most memories do, but there was a purpose to that."

"Ama-la, I can't believe that I was actually that girl, Claire."

"Why do you say that?"

"She was a simple village girl, unsophisticated and uneducated." I looked at her in disbelief.

"And willful and determined—and disobedient." She smiled. "Don't you see any similarities? Lifting my brow, I gazed at her without answering. "You have only seen the early years. There was much more to that life."

"What happened to her after?"

"You will have to find out for yourself. For now, you must make peace with what you have seen, so that the memory will not haunt you in the future and you will have no more of those nightmares. Come let us eat and then we will walk by the river."

We spent much time by the river that day. I asked Ama-la if we could perform a ritual to invoke the river deity. She requested that I conduct it, and I did as I had been taught. Then we sat and watched the rushing water as it hurried by us. The river was so different from the lakes, and it didn't awaken in me that stilling, reverential feeling. But nonetheless I had grown to love it, probably because it reminded me of Yeshe. The great Tsangpo sped along as if needing to get somewhere quickly, creating turbulence in its wake.

"Look at the river, how fast it is flowing, like time itself," reflected Ama-la. "In a brief span we emerge into this world of physicality many times, one life after another in quick succession, and so it continues. As one wave subsides it gives rise to the next, each incarnation feeding the following one. But there is a choice. One can live reactively to whatever comes one's way or learn to make good use of those experiences and not fall into the cycle of repetition. How would you make good use of the scene you witnessed as Claire?"

"The burning of Gabrielle?" I asked. She nodded. "I can't imagine what good would come of that," I murmured.

"Think more deeply, Bumo."

I was quiet for some time as she waited patiently. "Claire was deeply stirred by what she witnessed and made an inner determination to seek the goddess," I responded thoughtfully. "Is that what you are referring to?"

She shook her head. "Whether you are called Claire or Padma Tshomo or hundreds of other names, the goddess has been known to you since ancient days. I am referring to something else. Can you guess what it is?" I shook my head. "Seeds were watered. Seeds that had been sown long ago were further nurtured by that event, to such a degree that it is assured they will bear fruit in the future." Her voice was quiet. I frowned, wondering what kind of seeds she was speaking of, and she caught my drift. "In time, Bumo, perhaps the far future, you will take up the cause of women as a result of what you witnessed. Perhaps that was the purpose for you to be present during such an event, which will stay with you for lifetimes, consciously or unconsciously, as a prod to action. The timing and means of such action are yet to be determined. You will have to find your way."

"The cause of women? What do you mean by that, Ama-la?"

She studied me for a moment and then replied, "You will have to find the answer to that yourself."

For several weeks, I thought about that phrase "the cause of women" without understanding it. What cause did women have, I wondered? In my mother's Sumpa heritage, women had often been the leaders, strong, independent, and free, but perhaps this was not true in other parts of the world. After a while I stopped wondering about this. That phrase disappeared from my mind, as I assumed it was not something to worry about now, but something for the future.

Often during the night, I would find myself reviewing the scenes I had witnessed as the young girl Claire, and while the image of Gabrielle burning filled me with sorrow, gradually that sorrow began to fade away. Having a glimpse of that woman's current life as a respected healer did much to erase my sadness.

Several months were to pass before I was to return to the life of Claire. During that time, the days were filled with walks, talks, meditation, and deeper bonding with the one I called Ama-la. I was in such a state of mental retreat that I hardly thought of the outside world, of my family, or Lhasa or even Zerdan. Then one day, quite unexpectedly, when my pain over Gabrielle's death had fully subsided and I had achieved a deeper state of peace, I found myself traveling back again through the tunnel of time and place. Although I saw no form or face, I was very aware of the presence of that powerful deity Palden Lhamo, as she drew me deeper into the still lake of mind. Once again, I was there in a small farming village very far from the sacred Yarlung Valley.

CHAPTER 18

Escapes

My relationship with my family deteriorated after the death of Gabrielle, exacerbated by my refusal to attend church with them on Sundays and holy days, but my position was non-negotiable, and I suspect they feared the embarrassment of bringing a screaming child into that austere place where all the villagers gathered. Eventually, they stopped trying to convince me, making excuses that I was unwell, and, indeed, they thought me quite unwell mentally. I knew my mother believed that Gabrielle had cast a spell on me, but even her threats of eternal hellfire didn't deter me from my commitment never to enter a church again as I blamed Gabrielle's death on the priest who had visited her husband and had stood there watching her agony as she was set afire. Somehow, I knew that he had sanctioned that horrible deed. I had to admit to myself that I never liked the church anyway. It had always made me uncomfortable to sit before the figure of Christ on the cross. The forest was my holy place, and, after Gabrielle's death, I knew myself to be a Druid in search of the goddess.

"You'll end up going to hell, burning like that sorceress, that you will," my mother threatened time and again. But in my mind, I would rather go to hell, wherever that was, than attend the very church in front of which Gabrielle had been set afire. My father's solution was to seek a marriage for me.

"Let a husband deal with her," he said one day to my mother. I was fourteen when Gabrielle was killed, sixteen when I was sent away to another village for marriage. It wasn't easy for my parents to find a man who would agree to marry me without my having to step foot inside a church. Under those circumstances, an ideal husband was not to be found, but I didn't care. I wanted to get away from my family, and I reasoned that any husband would do. A compromise was reached, and a marriage ceremony took place with an older man from a neighboring village, outside on the steps of his village church.

I didn't expect much happiness from marriage, but I was glad to be free of my family and their overbearing ways. My husband Michel was a farmer, twenty years older than I, with a son Jacque, who was only a few years younger than I. Michel's wife had died when the boy was young. He had married again, but that wife had died during childbirth, along with the infant. I entered into a family already burdened with many problems. A cloud of sadness hung over Michel. The loss of two wives meant no more children, no more sons, whom he very much needed to help with the farm work. So he married me, a much younger woman. His son Jacque was adamantly against another marriage and resented me from the start. Jacque was a tall, slender, average-looking boy, with a somber expression and sand colored hair that flopped over the side of his face. His suspicious eyes studied my every move, making it difficult to be comfortable in his presence. It was not easy to escape his watchful glare, and no matter where I went in the house or on the farm, he was always there, observing me from a distance, as if he feared that I was going to steal something of theirs. Navigating father and son was to take an emotional toll on me.

Michel was not an unattractive man. A bit stocky, with a rounded face and a mess of tangled greying hair always pulled back and tied with a string, he mostly wore a tired expression as if life was too much for him. But he was kind, and I came to regard him almost like an older brother. He defended me from Jacque's subtle but constant attacks, and often told me to forgive the boy, saying that he had never gotten over his mother's death, but I saw that his hostility was more than that. He was undisciplined and there was a meanness about him that made me want to keep my distance. At first, I did my best to win his favor. I cooked his favorite foods, but he picked at the food and walked away from the table. I mended his clothing, but he would soon rip whatever I had mended and be sure to let me know that my sewing was insufficient. Within a short time, I came to feel that he hated me, but I told myself that I would have a child of my own and would be less concerned with winning his acceptance. Whatever the difficulties, my life was far better than what I had experienced at my childhood home.

There was no pressure to attend church and I could walk to the forest whenever I wanted, where I would try to remember all that Gabrielle had taught me. There I would look for the nature spirits, but I could never see them. I had made a commitment to be a Druid, but I didn't know what that meant, and I had no one to guide me. All I knew was that the Druids sought refuge in the forest, spoke to the spirits and worshipped the goddess, and so the forest became my place of devotion.

I was grateful for the degree of freedom that I had, and life was tolerable for a while. After a year of marriage, I went home to visit my parents and thought to stop in the village market before returning home. It was there that I ran into Elise. I hadn't seen her since before her mother had been killed. After that, I had not been allowed to leave the house and had no word of her, so I was overjoyed to meet her again. After a long embrace, we strolled to a place where we could sit and talk.

"Elise, what happened to you after that horrible day? I wasn't able to leave home to find you, but I never stopped thinking about you." She had not been there to witness the burning of her mother and was spared the searing of that image into her mind.

"My father remarried very soon after to a younger woman and now has a baby with her. My brothers seemed not to care that mama was gone. They said she had brought shame to the family, but I descended into a deep depression, unable to function until mama came to me in a beautiful dream, Claire, and that changed everything.

"In the dream, she said the goddess had come for her that day and had taken her to a place where she could truly learn the art of healing. Then she told me that she had found a good husband for me, and she was glad that I would have a happy life. It was such an uplifting dream that it helped to bring me out of my stupor. Soon after I was with one of my brothers in the village. He was buying something for the farm at a shop next to the bakery. I waited outside while he made the purchase. While I was standing there, a young man came up and introduced himself, saying that he had wanted to approach me for some time but had been too shy. I recognized him as the baker's son, and we chatted for a while. He asked if he could visit me, and I nodded, so pleased." She looked down and then at me again. "Papa had told me that nobody would be marry me because of mama, and I had begun to believe him, but this young man didn't care about what other people said. Claire, he is the handsomest man in the village. Do you remember the baker?" I nodded. "Francois is his eldest son. What really moved me is that during our first conversation, he told me that he would never forget mama's kindness. She had once taken care of his sister when she was ill, and the family felt indebted to mama. He spoke so warmly of her, and that was a sign to me that he was the one mama had chosen."

"I do remember him," I mused. "A very good-looking boy. I met him a few times but never really got to know him."

"After we met in the village, he visited my home twice, and on the third visit asked my father for my hand in marriage." She lowered her voice. "Papa was so convinced that nobody would marry me that he readily agreed, with no questions asked. Claire, I could not have asked for a better husband."

"You are in love, aren't you?" I asked, as I gazed at her beaming face.

"In love and with child. Sometimes I feel guilty for being so happy. How can I be happy after what happened to mama?"

"Elise, your mother arranged for this. Perhaps it was her time to die and if the goddess took her to a good place, we should be at peace." Although I spoke those words to soothe her, in my heart I didn't feel at peace and wondered if I ever would. I smiled and added, "And so you are married to a baker. That is perfect. The breads you baked were always the best."

She laughed and asked, "What about you, Claire? So often I wanted to meet you but knew I could not, seeing how your family felt. I heard that you left the village to get married. Are you happy?"

"Happy?" I murmured. "I am not sure what that means. But he is a kind man, not demanding, and doesn't give me any sort of trouble. It is a relief to be away from my family. Perhaps it was a means of escape. But I don't know what it means to love a man, Elise." I looked at her forlornly, not wanting to reveal the isolation and loneliness that I felt.

"Perhaps he will grow on you, Claire. Sometime love comes immediately, and at other times it develops more slowly. That is what mama taught me. She said love must be cultivated patiently."

I sighed. "She was a wise woman. It is a loss for us that she is not here to guide us anymore."

It was comforting to know that Elise was happy, and when I shared with her my worries about my relationship with my stepson, she smiled and replied, "How can you expect him to treat you as a mother when you are only a few years his elder. Treat him as a younger brother. It is not your responsibility to discipline him, Claire. That is a task for his father."

We chatted for a bit longer and as I was about to get up to leave, she leaned over and whispered to me, "Claire, we must keep to ourselves whatever mama taught us and not tell anyone about the goddess, the spirits in the forest, the Druids, or anything else, if we want to have a happy life. We should forget all of that. I try not to think of it anymore." I nodded but knew it was not the course I could follow. How could I forget the times that were the happiest for me, the woman who helped me to see the world in a new light, one which felt so real and true?

I did try to follow her advice about Jacque and treat him more as a younger brother than a stepson, but to little avail. His resentment of me seemed to grow year by year, turning into near animosity. It got to the point that I tried to have as little interaction with him as possible, even taking my meals separately. Although Michel desperately wanted another child, when after three years I didn't get pregnant, he resigned himself to his fate. He was now frequently falling ill with bouts of stomach ailments, and this concern took precedence over all else.

As his heath declined and his ability to work the farm decreased, my husband told me that we would need to hire help. Jacque was not interested in farming and used every excuse to avoid the hard work. Due to our need for money, Michel allowed me to assist in a shop that sold medicinal herbs so that we would be able to pay for the farm help.

An older man ran the herb shop. He was respected in the village and was glad for a little assistance. Although he said it was most unusual to have a young woman assistant, he accepted me, asking that I stay mostly in the backroom, chopping and compiling the herbs, so as not to be seen. I would go every morning for a few hours and help him grind and sort out the plants. As I placed them in various bags, I would ask him questions about the herbs, and in this way, I came to know them by their proper names and gained greater knowledge of their usage, learning about a much larger variety of plants and the effect of various combinations.

"For a young lady, you catch on quickly," he said after I had been assisting him for several months. "Not many girls show an interest, or perhaps they are not allowed to study the plants. Did you learn from your mother or grandmother?"

"I had a teacher," I replied quietly. But then I thought to myself, she treated the plants as friends and spoke to them. She was different. It was not the same studying under this man, but I was glad to be able to learn more and to be away from the steely eyes of my stepson, who was becoming worse even than my mother in terms of the hostility he displayed.

On one occasion, I took Jacque aside and asked him why he had such an attitude toward me, and he replied that it was because of the influence I had over his father. "It's like you have a cast a spell over him," he said resentfully. Those words made me tremble, but I tried to laugh it off. "Don't be silly, Jacque. He treats me as any husband would treat a wife."

Shaking his head, he contradicted me. "Since you came here, he has changed. You have done something to him, I know it." I couldn't think of what to say to dissuade him, and so I decided to keep greater distance.

After I had been working in the shop for about a year, the shop owner was called home due to an emergency, and he asked me to tend to the shop while he was gone. He said he would be away for only an hour or two. I was hesitant to take on such responsibility, but there was no choice and so I agreed. I didn't feel comfortable dispensing any medicines and desperately hoped that nobody would enter the shop. It was early in the morning and the first two hours were quiet. I was anticipating that the owner would return any minute when a young man entered, who looked to be a few years older than me. He was an attractive man with fine features, well-built, of medium height, with neatly combed, wavy dark hair dusting his shoulders, a shallow cropped beard, and deep sea-blue eyes that were the highlights of his slender, oval shaped face. But it was his warm smile that drew me. He was looking for medicine to bring down his mother's fever. I knew what to give him, but I suggested that he wait for the shop owner, who would soon return. We chatted as he waited, and he asked me about various herbs. I told him about their special properties and usage. With my guard let down, I mentioned what combination I would use to help his mother. "But I am not properly trained," I hurried to add. "It is better to wait."

"You know quite a bit about medicine. I trust you," he responded with an engaging smile. "I will take what you recommend."

Just at that moment, the shop owner returned and confirmed what I had told the young man. Thanking me and the owner, he left with the medicine. It was also my time to leave, as it was close to noon, and I had to hurry back to prepare the afternoon meal. After I left the shop, I saw the young man standing there, as if waiting for someone. It was about a twenty-minute walk to reach the farm, and he approached me as I headed in that direction.

"I was waiting for you in the hope that you would soon leave."

"Don't you have to get home to give your mother the medicine?" I stammered, embarrassed.

"I do, but I haven't learned your name, and I can't leave until you tell me."

"Claire," I replied simply. "I didn't give my last name, because I didn't want him to ask around and learn that I was married."

"I am Stefan. Can I walk you home?" I shook my head. "Then can I meet you again? Do you work here every day?"

"Every morning," I hastened to reply. "But I really must go now." How I wanted to stay and walk with him, but I was also afraid of being seen, so I hurried away without another word. When I reached home, Jacque verbally attacked me for being late. "Papa is waiting for his meal. You know he is not well."

"The shopkeeper had to go away and left me in charge of the store," I replied defensively. Just the little time I had spent with Stefan had cheered me, although I tried not to show it. Normally I would have responded to Jacque's harsh tone with bitter words of my own, asking why he hadn't begun preparations instead of waiting for me, but I said nothing, not wanting to get into yet another fight with him.

The next morning when I left the store, Stefan was waiting, requesting that I allow him to walk me home. So pleased was I that I didn't refuse. As we walked, he told me about his family. His father had died, leaving his elder brother in charge of the family's mill, but he had other aspirations and was hoping to leave the village to explore the larger world. As he spoke, a hope entered me that I hadn't felt before, a hope that it was possible to escape the narrow confines of village life. When we were a short distance from the farm, I told him that we had to part there, and reluctantly I left him to continue home alone.

The next day, and for the next six months, it was the same. He spoke and I listened as he filled my head with thoughts of what might lie beyond our village. All this time, I told myself that he was a friend, as Elise had been, and there was nothing wrong with spending time with a friend, even though he was a man. I told myself this so often that I truly believed it. I shared nothing about my personal life and never revealed that I was married, until one day he asked me to leave the village with him. "We will go far away, Claire, and begin a new life." I was stunned and didn't respond.

"What can the village offer you, Claire? I know you want to leave as much as I do."

"It is true, Stefan. I would love nothing more than to get away from here, far away," I replied quietly as I looked off into the distance. Then turning my eyes to him, I added, "but I can't leave. It wouldn't be right. There is much about me that you don't know." Embarrassed by the fact that I had kept my marriage from him, I cast my eyes downward. He had taken me to a place to sit away from the village square, as he often did when he walked me part way home.

"I know you are unhappily married, and I don't blame you for not telling me. You were young when your parents sent you away, but you shouldn't stay in a such a situation, Claire, when you have an alternative."

My eyes opened wide as I looked up at him. "For how long have you known?"

He smiled. "Soon after we met, I wondered why you never invited me to your home to meet your parents, so I checked around and heard about your ill husband, a much older man, and the stepson who gives you so much trouble."

"And yet you continued to come even though you knew my situation?"

"At first I wanted to offer you friendship, knowing you would be in need, but then my feelings changed, Claire." His voice grew quiet and tender. "I want you to come with me and leave this village behind."

My emotions were in a turmoil. "Give me time to think," I replied, confused.

When I reached home Michel was in bed with a fever. As I sat beside him, he asked that I not go to the shop anymore. I was needed at home to care for him. When I asked how we would manage, he said Jacque was taking on more of the farm work and we wouldn't need a full-time helper. I should spend my time looking after the two of them, he requested. I didn't know what to do. That evening, I went outside to have time alone to think. Jacque found me there.

"I know about the man you are secretly meeting," he said angrily. "This afternoon I stopped by the shop and told the owner you would not be able to come anymore. You are to stay here and care for papa and not leave the house again. If you do, I will tell papa you are having an illicit affair and call in the priest. You know what happens to adulterers. Remember what happened to that sorcerer lady in your village. It's the same for those who are sinful." At the mention of the priest and Gabrielle, my heart froze. Jacque knew of my fear of churches and priests and often used this to get what he wanted. I didn't answer him, knowing there was no point in defending myself.

Days passed and I could not get away. Finally, after a week, I escaped and rushed to the shop in the hope that Stefan would be waiting. He was there, standing a short distance away in the place where he always waited. I had never been so happy to see anyone. For the first time, I allowed him to take me in his arms.

"I knew you would come," he said, joyfully. "You are leaving with me, aren't you?"

I shook my head. "I just wanted to see you once more." After many minutes of back and forth, he sighed and said, "I will come back for you. Wait for me, Claire." With a sinking heart, I watched as he walked away, wondering if I had relinquished my last chance for happiness.

How many times I chastised myself in the following months for not pursuing my heart's desire! It was fear that had paralyzed my will and kept me in that unhappy home, so sure was I that Jacque would send the priest after me, that I would be accused of adultery and end up like Gabrielle. Jacque knew he had the upper hand on me now and his hostility was inescapable. The next few years were most unhappy for me as I was once again a prisoner at home.

I had almost given up the idea of ever seeing Stefan again when I heard Jacque say to the occasional worker who helped us on the farm, "That treacherous man I once told you to watch out for is back in town. I heard he returned to see his dying mother. Keep any eye on him and let me know what he is up to."

I knew instantly that he was referring to Stefan. "Stefan is back," I whispered to myself. He returned for me, as he said he would. Jacque kept a close watch on me, and I wasn't able to get away until a week had passed. He had gone out on an errand, and I rushed to the place where Stefan and I used to sit and talk, but nobody was there. How foolish of me, I thought, to think he would be waiting here day after day. Then the thought came to me that perhaps he had forgotten me or married someone else. After all, three years had passed. Just as I was about to leave and head home, I saw him rushing toward me.

Out of breath, he explained that his sister had seen me walking in the village and hurried home to tell him. "Stefan, I want to leave with you. Take me far away from here."

Smiling, he put his arms around me. "That is what I was hoping you would say."

"I heard your mother has been ill. How is she?" I asked after I had returned his embrace.

"She passed away soon after I reached home, ten days ago. I need to be here another few days. This Sunday, when all is quiet, at ten in the evening, when everyone has gone to bed, meet me here. Don't bring much. We will leave then."

I nodded and he hugged me again, this time more tightly. Then we parted. Over the next few days, I was fearful that Jacque might discover our plan. My stepson had grown into a large, muscular man, with an intimidating presence. If he were to encounter Stefan, there was no question who would win the fight. But Stefan was exceptionally clever, and I believed could talk his way out of any situation.

Over the next few days, I tried to take special care of Michel, whom I knew was dying. The doctor had told me as much, and there weren't many months left. Again and again, Michel had told me that Jacque would take care of me after he was gone. "He is rough around the edges," he said, "but his heart is good." I knew that to be untrue. Before Stefan returned, I didn't know what my fate would be. When Michel died, where would I go?

During the last few years, I hadn't thought much of the goddess, although I had committed to following her, but now it seemed clear to me that Stefan's return was due to her workings. She was looking out for me. The timing of it all could not be a mere coincidence. He had returned in time to spare me from years of torment alone with Jacque. "I will dedicate myself to you now," I said silently to the one about whom I knew so little.

As the appointed hour approached, I slipped out the back door and made haste to our meeting place. I had never been out at that hour and the night sounds frightened me— the hooting of an owl, the incessant barking of a stray dog, and the howl of a larger creature—but I didn't let that deter me. When I reached the meeting place, Stefan was already there waiting with two horses, and I managed to escape once more from a hostile environment, not knowing what lay ahead.

"Where are we going, Stefan," I asked after we had been traveling for several days.

"To Bohemia, to Praha (Prague)," he replied in an excited tone.

"Where is that?"

"Over the mountains, to the east, where a great river flows." Stefan had told me that when he first left the village, he traveled to numerous towns in our region seeking out those who knew about science, his area of interest. One man directed him to a growing city called Praha, saying that the city was attracting interesting people from faraway places, men of invention, scientists, astronomers and alchemists. Stefan had been getting ready to travel there when he had a foreboding dream of his mother, which was why he returned to our village. "I want to go where there are men of invention, Claire. Praha lies at a crossroad where men from the east and west come to exchange knowledge. I have heard about one inventor, a Master Vaclav, living in Praha, who is accepting students. You can work in a medicine shop, while I study with him."

I didn't really care where we were going as long as it was far away, so I nodded my assent, realizing that I didn't have much say in the matter anyhow. I had not gone to see my family before leaving, and I knew that once I traveled far, I wouldn't see them again, but that didn't bother me. My mother had died a year earlier, and I had pretty much broken off relations with my father and two brothers, so I was saying goodbye to the past for good.

My thoughts turned to Elise, and I was sorry that I hadn't had a chance to say goodbye to her. I had seen her a few times in Stefan's absence and had come to accept that we had drifted into different worlds. With two young children and a newborn to raise, she had no time to dwell on other matters; a sisterly warmth remained between us, but little more. I was only twenty-four, still young enough to begin a new life, and I didn't want anything to hold me back.

During his three-year absence, Stefan has sustained himself by taking odd jobs, and he had saved some money for the journey. I had taken whatever money I could find in the house without feeling guilty, since I told myself that I had supported the family through my work at the shop. We had enough to last us until we reached Praha. We rode through the day, staying at guest houses and inns each night. Presenting ourselves as a married couple, we shared a room and before long became lovers. It was not unwanted, and I found comfort in his physical embrace, feeling for the first time in my life that someone truly cared for me. I told Stefan that I didn't want to marry again, because I wanted nothing more to do with priests or churches and how else could we marry? He had reluctantly consented saying that he hoped I would change my mind.

When we arrived in Praha, I was at first overwhelmed by the scenes that met me. Not having left the village before, I had never been among so many people and of such different appearances, and I didn't know where to place my eyes. I had never seen such crowded and busy markets with such fine objects, so many varieties of foods, entertainers and singers in the streets, and the noise and commotion were almost too much to bear. We found a small guest house in a quiet section of the city, and over the next several weeks I became accustomed to the sheer volume of life there, and even grew to like it. But there was one thing I didn't like; Praha was overrun with priests. There were far too many of them roaming the streets, and instinctively I tried to hide myself whenever I saw one.

As soon as we were settled, Stefan set out to find Master Vaclav, while I went to seek employment in a medicine shop. He was more successful than I. After going to several shops, I realized that nobody would employ me because I was a foreigner and didn't speak the language. With his quick mind, Stefan was able to pick up the language and was soon assisting Master Vaclav with his projects, receiving some compensation for his work.

For the first time, I was beginning to feel that my future would be a happy one, when my quiet contentment was disrupted by the appearance of a very attractive woman knocking on our door one evening. Stefan was with Master Vaclav, where he was spending most of his time, when she asked if she could enter. Nodding, I opened the door and invited her in. After a few awkward moments, she explained that she needed some herbs to end a pregnancy. At first, I didn't respond, surprised that she had come to me. How could she know of my interest in medicinal plants?

"Who sent you here?" I asked suspiciously. "I am not trained and am not able to help you."

"It was the Master who told me to come to you." I looked at her in shock, wondering how he knew of my knowledge of the plants.

Stammering, I asked whose child it was. She didn't answer, so I told her that I wouldn't help her unless she revealed the truth about the pregnancy. Between sobs, she told me that her husband was a student of Master Vaclav and that it was he, the Master, who had gotten her pregnant. I looked at her confused, unable to fully grasp what she was saying. I had heard only praise of the Master from Stefan.

"I have three children with my husband, but several months ago, the Master sent him to another city on an errand that would take him away for a while. It was during that time that this happened. When my husband returns, he will be furious if he finds out, and I could never tell him who got me pregnant. He thinks so highly of the Master. I can't let him know."

I was stunned and didn't know how to respond. At which point, she dropped to her knees and said she would have to take her own life if I couldn't help her end the pregnancy. I told her to return to me in two days and I would have what she needed. I knew only too well which medicine to get, but I trembled when I realized what I was doing. This was exactly what had ended Gabrielle's life.

I didn't say anything to Stefan that night as I didn't want to discuss the matter. I thought the less said the better. I knew it must have been he who had told Vaclav of my work with the plants. I was sure that he had done so out of pride, his high regard for my knowledge and abilities, which he thought to be greater than they actually were. When the woman returned two days later, I gave her the medicine I had prepared and instructed her on its use. "Come to me in a week's time to let me know that you are okay," I requested. That night, I couldn't sleep. I hadn't thought of Gabrielle for a while, but now she was much in my mind as I remembered her words about how sometimes it is necessary to end a pregnancy. I recalled my words to her, that I hoped I never had to do so. Worry about the woman's condition kept me tossing that night, as I fretted that perhaps I had not given her the right amount or that she would not follow my instructions. I knew that I would not feel easy until she returned to me. As dawn approached, I quietly got out of bed and went to a corner of the room that I shared with Stefan where I tearfully called upon the goddess, making an inner promise to repay that innocent soul in the woman's womb.

The woman returned at the set time, and when I saw that she had suffered no ill effects from the medicine, I breathed a sigh of relief. "Stay away from that man," I warned her. Life went on, and six months passed when another attractive woman appeared at my door. Stefan was again not at home, busy with the one he called Master. It was the same story. Vaclav had sent her to me after he had impregnated her. The woman's husband, his student, had been sent away on some excuse. She had no children as she was newly married and was frightened, tearfully pleading with me to help her.

"Do you love your husband?" I asked, astounded at her confession. She nodded. "Then why did you do such a thing?"

Between sobs, she told me, "The Master called me to his workshop one evening after my husband had left and told me that my husband had no gift for alchemy and would be sent away unless I complied. It is my husband's greatest dream to study under him."

Foolish woman, I thought. I was of a mind to send her away, but she was pitiful, and I could not help but tell her that I would give her the medicine on one condition, that she never meet that man alone again. She nodded her head in agreement. Two days later she returned, and I gave her what she needed and asked that she come see me after ten days.

Once again that night, I called upon the goddess and made another promise to in some way help that soul who was being so harshly sent away. I still had not discussed the matter with Stefan, but I was annoyed that Vaclav was sending women to me and wondered whether Stefan knew of his master's abuse. I dared not say a word, because I saw how Stefan was flourishing in this new environment. Previously, I had not recognized the extent of his intellect and abilities, but now they were coming to the fore, and I didn't want to do anything to impede him. At home, Stefan spoke warmly of Vaclav and the potential for inventions that would greatly improve life. I would smile and say nothing, but inside I was tormented.

As time went on, an unacknowledged distance began to creep between us. At one point, I asked Stefan when we would be able to leave Praha, and he replied that he wanted to spend the rest of his life working on inventions under the Master. So engaged was he in studying the sciences that he didn't notice my increasing dissatisfaction.

Then the day came when a third woman appeared at my door with the same request. Inviting her in, I asked her how this had happened. She wasn't married and was in love with the Master. Although she knew he was married and had children, he had told her that he would leave his family for her, and that was why she had yielded to him. The relationship had been going on for many months when she found out she was pregnant. When she told him about her condition and asked when he would take her away, he found one excuse after another.

"How could you think he would leave his family?" I asked incredulously. She didn't respond but looked at me with desperate eyes. "I am sorry for you, but you are not the first woman who has come to me in this state. Who sent you here?" I asked, already knowing the answer.

"It was the Master," she replied quietly. "He assured me that you would help me. I know that you are the wife of Stefan, whom I hear is the finest student of the Master. I trust no one else but you." She began to cry.

Two days later I gave her the medicine and told her to return at a certain time. I was shaken by what I had heard, by the thought that I was becoming the cleanup woman, the one to take care of the master's misdeeds, and he was taking no responsibility at all. Again, I prayed to the goddess to help me fulfill a promise to pay back what I had taken from that unborn life. I was angry and for the first time this anger was directed at Stefan, for being blind to Vaclav's true nature.

"Your Master Vaclav is no Master at all. He is a monster, defiling these vulnerable women," I stated in a raised voice after I had treated the third woman. For the first time I told Stefan about the women to whom I had given medicine and how difficult it had been for me. At first, he didn't believe it and questioned whether it had been Vaclav who had impregnated them. "Perhaps it was other men, and they are blaming him for their misconduct," he replied, trying to find any excuse to clear the man he greatly admired.

When I was able finally to convince him that it was Vaclav himself who had committed the misdeeds, he seemed as conflicted as I. "Give me some time to think," he requested in a subdued and steady voice, in a tone that I normally found comforting, but which was not soothing to me now.

"After I give those women the medicine, I can't sleep for days worrying that something might happen to them. The plants are strong. My teacher once nearly harmed a woman by dispensing the medicine, and for this she herself was murdered. Don't allow him to put me in this position ever again. Promise me, Stefan."

"I will tell Master Vaclav that he must find another way to deal with his personal matters."

"Find another way? He must stop his behavior or one day I will expose him."

"We should not get involved in his personal life. You are right, Claire. I will speak with him." His tone was serious, leading me to believe that he understood the difficult situation I had been placed in. I knew how hard it would be for Stefan to bring up such a sensitive subject with a man he so respected, and I felt terrible for putting him in this position. His relationship with Vaclav was only about science and inventions. I didn't want to involve him in matters that would detract from their work together, but internally I could not resolve the conflict that I felt.

The next few months were quiet, and I made every effort to forget about the women who had come to me. Stefan was increasingly excited about his work, and I tried to make peace with the life we had, believing that I would no longer be involved in anything to do with Vaclav. I had made clear my feelings about the man and so we hardly mentioned him. Stefan was away much of the day and often at night, but I had made a few friends and often went for walks with them in the nearby forest, where I searched for medicinal plants and tried to think about the goddess. After several years in Praha, I had come to realize that the city was less of a draw for me than the forests. I knew that it was in that pristine setting, rather than in the bustle of city life, that I would find the One I was seeking.

The months passed and another attractive girl showed up at my door—this one frailer and younger than the others. My heart sank when I saw this girl of fourteen and heard her predicament. She had gone to Vaclav to pick up something for her father, who was his student, when he attacked her. She tried to resist but couldn't, and she was now pregnant. As soon as she entered my home and I closed the door, she began to shake with fear. She couldn't tell her parents as they would never believe that the Master would do such a thing. They would think that she had had an affair and would send her away to the convent, which she dreaded. And of course, Vaclav sent her to me. Although I had never asked Stefan whether he had spoken with Vaclav about his sexual escapades, I assumed that he had, since nobody had come to me for medicine for nearly a year.

Now, as I saw the plight of this girl, I didn't know which emotion was stronger in me, anger or compassion. Promising to help her, I asked her to come back in two days. Then I hurried to the same medicine shop that I always visited. As soon as I entered, I heard a familiar voice, but I didn't recognize the person as his back was turned to me. He was dressed in the clothing of a priest, and I wondered how I could have known him. I had never been acquainted with any priest and yet I recognized the voice.

Drawing my head cover tightly around me and keeping my back to them, I listened as the priest said he was looking for a woman, an adulterer whom he heard had come to Praha and would most likely have visited the medicine shops. His description of the woman was very much like how one would portray me, but this didn't strike me at first. After a brief pause, the shop keeper said that a woman who fitted that description did visit the shop every now and then, but he asked why the priest was so interested in her. And I heard the words, "She betrayed my father, her husband, took his money and fled with another man; she and I have unfinished business to settle." I had to cover my mouth to prevent myself from gasping in disbelief. Quickly leaving the shop, I hid myself while I waited for the priest to leave. There was no mistaking. It was Jacque. How could he have followed me to Praha, and did he really become a priest in the years since I had left? I wanted to run back home but knew I had to purchase the medicine, so I waited until the shopkeeper stepped out and his assistant took over before going back into the shop to buy what I needed.

Stefan didn't come home that night until I was already in bed, so we didn't speak. The next morning the young girl anxiously appeared at my door, and I carefully instructed her about what to do and asked that she return in ten days. I was far more disturbed this time than previously, upset by the girl's young age and that the relationship had been forced on her. She had been raped, and I was more worried about her health than I had been with the other women. After she left, I once again appealed to the goddess to guide the soul in the young girl's womb to where it needed to be. I was now distraught on two fronts. Jacque was here in Praha, and so I had to leave, and quickly. When Stefan came home that night, I told him I had seen Jacque, who had become a priest and was searching for me.

"Praha is a big town. He will never find you here," he said trying to comfort me. "And besides, you have my protection and that of the Master."

Neither his protection nor Vaclav's meant anything to me now. They were no match for Jacque. Stefan and I were living as husband and wife, yet we not married, and I knew that the church considered this a sin. I could not risk being discovered by Jacque.

"He is determined to find me," I murmured between tears.

"I will make sure that he doesn't," he replied in a voice I could no longer trust. "Look at you, you are trembling. You must get over your fear of priests and of Jacque. You must learn to face your fears and not run from them. You are not guilty of anything, and you have nothing to be ashamed of. We love one another and are as good as married."

"No matter what we think, in the eyes of the church, we are unmarried, and that is regarded as a sin."

"Then we should get married," he replied with a smile. "Then no priest will dare harm my wife. We couldn't marry when your husband was alive, but he must be long dead by now." How could I tell him that Gabrielle had been married and that her husband had not been able to save her? He didn't seem to grasp the depth of my anxiety, and I knew he valued his work more than anything. When I realized that he would not flee with me, my disappointment grew, amplifying the crack that had emerged in our relationship.

In my fearful state, I began to question whether I had given the young girl the right proportion of medicine, and I waited apprehensively for her return. All I could think of was Gabrielle's words about how strong the plants were and how they could harm one. If something were to happen to that young girl, I knew I would never forgive myself. As the days passed, I began to berate myself for giving her the medicine in the first place. When she didn't appear after the allotted time, I hurried to her home, introducing myself to her parents as Stefan's wife.

"She is sick with heavy bleeding and a fever," the mother explained in a baffled tone. "We don't know what is wrong, and she refuses to see a doctor."

"I have some medical knowledge. Do you mind if I tend to her?"

The mother led me into the room, where the young girl was lying, pale and faint from loss of blood, and most likely an infection. I told the mother which medicines to purchase and stayed by the girl's side until the mother returned. Then I boiled the plants and helped her drink the mix. It was a combination good for nourishing the blood and bringing down fever, which I had learned from Gabrielle.

"If you don't mind, I would like to stay here until she is out of danger."

"Why is she like this?" the mother asked worriedly.

"It sometimes happens to young girls," I lied. "Please let me remain with her".

I stayed by her bedside throughout the day, and when in the middle of the night her breathing slowed, I feared she wouldn't make it. At that moment, I prayed as hard as I had ever prayed to the goddess to preserve this young life, promising that I would give up that which was most dear to me if she could be saved. That was the sacrifice I would make. By morning, her color returned, and she had enough strength to sit up in bed. As soon as I saw she was recovering, I departed and went home.

Stefan had already left to be with his teacher, and I sat alone that day pondering what to do. If I stayed in Praha, I would have to hide, and I didn't want once again to have a confined life, to live always in fear. I couldn't do that anymore. It was inevitable that I would one day run into Jacque, who was now a priest, a man of power, especially power to decide the fate of women. It was impossible for me to remain there. I knew that Michel had most likely died soon after I had left the village, and my stepson would have blamed me. He would also resent me for having taken the money for my journey. Somehow, he had tracked me down, and now I had to leave.

I knew that Stefan wouldn't abandon his teacher, no matter what. He was thriving in Praha and it was in his best interest to remain. We would not find another city as stimulating with so many possibilities. I told myself that if I truly loved him, I should not interfere with his work, which was of utmost importance to him. He would be better off without me, I sadly reasoned.

Love called me to stay, but fear called me to flee. For two days I sat with indecision, until the image of my burning friend arose in my mind and fear got the better of me. In the middle of the third night, I got up and whispered to Stefan, who was fast sleep, "I love you and am grateful that you saved me from a terrible fate. I am sorry that I cannot stay here any longer. You helped me escape once, but this time I will have to do it on my own." Leaning over, I kissed him gently several times, my tears dampening his cheeks. The flicker of a smile spread across his face as he stirred in response. Drawing in a deep sigh, I tried not to think of how my departure would affect him. After staring at him for a few moments and struggling to restrain the sobs that were threatening to break, I mumbled in a barely audible voice, "It is painful to leave you, Stefan, but I have no choice."

Getting up, I took a pouch packed with a few changes of clothing and quietly left our home, taking a small handful of coins with me. Dawn was an hour or so away. Climbing onto my horse, I rode through the gates of the city, with no idea of where to go. It was early spring and the warmer weather made my journey easier. Day after day, I rode west in the direction of Burgundy, often slipping into barns at night for rest, or sleeping out in an open field, trying to preserve for food what little money I had. As the days went by, I felt myself at times being overcome by nausea, but at first, I attributed this to fatigue and my disturbed mental state. It was on the tenth day, when I was far from Prague, overcome by faintness and a fluttering stomach, that I had to pause my journey and, in a state of disbelief, had to accept that I was pregnant.

CHAPTER 19

Promises Made & Kept

Slowly I opened my eyes and saw Ama-la stirring a pot on the stove. I sat there quietly watching her. "You've returned," she said simply without turning to look at me. "I have prepared a soup with herbs that will help you sleep tonight. It is very late. You should get some rest." I didn't speak, but I watched as she ladled the soup into a bowl and brought it to where I was seated in the meditation corner. "Here, drink." Taking the bowl, I lifted it to my lips and took a slight sip. It was hot and I placed the bowl down next to me on the floor.

"Bumo, you mustn't get lost in the life of Claire. It is useful to see, but not to let the emotions of that life overcome you, because it is finished. You are no longer that girl." I nodded as I lifted the bowl again and took another sip. "Is there anything you want to ask me?" she inquired. I shook my head, too interiorized to speak, as I began to spoon the soup into my mouth, realizing how hungry I was. "There is much to speak about tomorrow. For now, you should rest," she said in that soft gentle voice of hers. I finished the soup and went over to the sleeping mat and lay down, hoping the images I had seen would not continue to rattle my mind, but soon they faded into some corner of my consciousness and I fell asleep.

I awoke at the first crack of dawn and, not finding Ama-la in the room, went into the bath hut to see if she was there. As I stood in the doorway, I saw her put her hand into the empty tub and watched as it magically filled with water. Then I watched her stir her hand around the water and saw the heat rise. So that is how she does it, I thought to myself in a very matter-of-fact way. Magic no longer surprised me. During the many months that I had been with Ama-la, I had often asked her if I could help bring the buckets of water from the stream to the tub, but she had always smiled and replied, “No need.” I often felt guilty having an older woman do such strenuous work on my behalf, and it never occurred to me that she might have other means. I never asked her how she heated the water, but somehow none of this surprised me.

“You are here,” she said when she saw me standing in the doorway. “Your bath is ready.”

After the bath, I returned to the hut, and we sat for meditation. I tried to keep my mind on the present and not let it drift back into the past. For a while I was successful, but as I found myself slipping away again, envisioning those last days in the city called Praha, Ama-la called me and said the morning meal was ready. I hadn’t spoken at all since the night before and now I sat and ate in silence. “We’ll ride down to the river and sit there and talk,” she said quietly. I nodded.

Once we arrived at the river and found our usual place to sit, the silence that had enveloped me since the night before continued. It was Ama-la who broke it. “Do you remember, when you first went to see the one you call Dalha, she said she wouldn’t receive you until you had fulfilled three promises you had made. Do you now understand what those promises were?”

Turning my eyes from the river to stare at Ama-la, I asked in amazement, “Could it be?” She nodded.

“Each time, you helped to end a pregnancy, you prayed to the goddess and promised that soul that you would repay it in some way, and you did. They were born as your three daughters. You deprived those souls of a human body and then gave them one. But more than that. It is normally the mother who takes on this responsibility, to complete the karma that is incurred. Instead, without even knowing it, you took it on yourself, helping those mothers. But your guilt was such that you had to experience for yourself what it was like to lose a child. Dalha helped you with that when you had the miscarriage early in your married life.

"But Claire's pregnancy . . . ," I blurted out. Interrupting me, she placed her fingers over my lips.

"You haven't seen the end of that story yet. Claire thought she couldn't have a child, but several years after her marriage to Michel, she did become pregnant. She didn't know that her stepson Jacque had been adding an herb to her meals that prevents pregnancy, and in Claire's case it created a miscarriage when she was married. She never realized what had happened. That very same soul again entered her womb when she was with Stefan, and that is why, without knowing the reason, she couldn't bring yourself to abort. She had some karma to bring that soul into the world.

I was quiet, knowing not to ask her what happened to Claire when she discovered she was pregnant, although her words indicated that Claire did, indeed, give birth to the child. But how and where? By now I knew Ama-la well enough to understand that she wanted me to find things out for myself and would for the most part only clarify what I was experiencing. Her refrain was that whatever I needed to know would come to me naturally. My mind now turned to Jacque, and I recognized that this very stepson who had once so troubled me had been reborn as Zerdan. My sentiments when in the presence of both men were similar. I didn't hate either one, but I feared what they might to do me and resented the hold they had over me, not understanding why they pursued me with such intensity.

"You are right," she said quietly in response to my unspoken thoughts. "Jacques was reborn as Zerdan."

"I don't understand, Ama-la, why Jacque hated me from the moment he saw me. What was the cause of that?"

"Perhaps it was not hatred as much as hurt and anger," she replied gently.

"Why would he be hurt? What had I ever done to him?"

"That you will have to discover on your own. It was not your first meeting with that soul. You will have to go further back in time to find the source of the conflict."

I looked out over the river, wondering if I had the stamina to go back further. The two visits to the past had depleted me emotionally and physically. A faint smile crossed Ama-la's lips when she saw me frown.

"Don't worry so much, Bumo. You spend too much time in your mind. Let's enjoy the river before we must head back."

I expected that I would be drawn back into the past to see the rest of Claire's life, but the weeks sped by with no further experiences. One day as we were walking collecting sticks for the fire, I blurted out, "What a pitiful life she had."

"Not pitiful at all in the end," she responded.

"She was tossed around from here to there and did not take control of her life," I said in a judgmental tone.

"She was a woman of conviction and could not be dissuaded from her beliefs," she replied in defense.

"She was driven by fear," I said firmly, getting up from my bent position and looking directly at Ama-la.

"She had the courage to act," she replied as firmly. "It takes courage to flee, with nobody and nowhere to flee to." When I didn't answer, she added, "Stop judging yourself, Bumo. Each life brings a different lesson. Each life can be a step forward, and each life brings circumstances that demand courage. By demeaning Claire, in reality, you are demeaning yourself because of what happened with Zerdan, but you don't yet have an understanding of that relationship. It will come."

Every now and then I asked Ama-la a question about Claire's life, since I knew that she was aware of all the details of my past lives and the present one.

"Do I know Stefan in this life?" I asked as we were preparing the evening meal many weeks later. She shook her head. "Will I know him again in the future?"

She nodded. "But it will be different. There is a debt you owe each other. You fled from him without explaining, took money and his unborn child. He did not heed your concerns and was not sensitive to your needs.

That all must be sorted out at some time in the future when it will benefit you both. Don't concern yourself with this matter."

Another time I asked her whether Jacque had stayed in the place called Praha after I had fled. She smiled. "Now you are asking me not about your history but his. I will tell you briefly. He became a priest for the sake of power. At that time, in that place, the church was a very powerful institution and had a strong hold over people's lives. When he couldn't find you, he returned to one of the larger cities in Gaul and became a rather important church official. Later in life, he became interested in the occult for the sake of gaining more power. Although obsessed with finding you, he was unable to locate you in that life. He took birth in Böd to continue his search and to gain the occult powers he couldn't attain in his life as Jacque. Karmically, it was necessary for the two of you to meet in this life to complete what had been left undone. I hope you realize once and for all that this matter has nothing to do with your current son. Zerdan only used your concern for him as a tool to reach you and strengthen his hold over you. He found your vulnerable spot and used it to his advantage."

"What was left undone?" I asked perplexed. "I still don't understand the relationship."

"That you will have to discover." Another unsatisfactory answer. No matter how hard I pressed, Ama-la would tell me no more than she deemed fit at that moment.

The months passed and I lived much of the time in silence as I reviewed again and again different scenes from Claire's early life. Some silences between people are awkward, causing much discomfort, but the silence that encased Ama-la and me was a most gentle and comforting one as she seemed to know exactly what I needed and allowed me the space to dwell in the interior realms that beckoned me.

It was spring again and wildflowers decorated the valley, bringing it back to life. Since my last journey into the past, I had begun to spend more time in meditation, aside from the morning and evening hours Ama-la had set aside. Often during the day, I would be drawn to sit in the meditation corner, trying to return to the life of Claire so that I could see the rest of the story. I knew my intentions in meditation were not pure, and Ama-la was aware of this. "Don't have expectations," she told me. "The more you try to see, the more you will not see. Let it all unfold naturally in the right time. And meditation is not for that purpose, not for reliving a life already lived." But once more her answer didn't satisfy me.

A year had passed since I had first come to Ama-la. I had partially discovered what I had come to uncover, something of my past relationship with Zerdan, but I didn't feel ready to jump back into the world and into my life. There were still answers not yet had. One day as I was returning from gathering wildflowers, from a distance I saw a woman standing in front of the hut speaking with Ama-la. By the time I reached the hut she had already mounted her horse and ridden away.

"Who was that?" I asked, unaccustomed as we were to visitors.

"Your friend, Bhasundara."

"Why has she come here and why didn't she wait to see me?"

"She didn't come to see you, but to check up on you. Your sister has made her promise to come every so often, and she has been here already twice, but I have always sent you out in advance so that you would not meet her. It would disrupt your inner work to meet her now."

"Is everyone in my family well?" I asked hesitantly. The mention of my sister made me realize how far I had flown from my present life. She nodded. As much as I cared for Bhasundara, I was relieved to have missed her, as I knew I wasn't prepared to see anybody from my current life. I was still too much identified with the personality of Claire and wasn't ready to become Padma Tshomo again.

Two more months passed, and the rainy season was nearing its end. The first nip of cold air greeted us one morning. This meant taking out our heavier woolen jackets. Ama-la and I had just finished the noon meal when she asked me to go gather more sticks and brush for the stove fire. This was a chore we always did together. She had never asked me to gather wood alone before, but I didn't hesitate. Although the morning had warmed into a bright sunny day, there was still a hint of chillness in the air. Drawing my woolen jacket tightly around me, I walked down the shallow incline into the valley where a small gathering of low trees stood and began picking up fallen branches and placing them into the large basket I had brought along. Suddenly the weather turned as it often did in this valley. Without any notice, dark clouds appeared threateningly in the sky, shrouding the sun as gusts of wind began to gather speed. An unusual end-of-summer storm was upon us. I hurried to fill the basket with as much wood as I could as the clouds released the first diamond-shaped droplets, followed by sheets of snow. It was not the season for snow, but soon wild white flakes were whirling around me, blocking my vision. The wind was so strong I could hardly maintain my balance, and I knew I had to make haste back to the hut with whatever I had gathered.

As I attempted to retrace my steps, my feet grew heavier, and I had much difficulty moving. Unable to see ahead, I wondered how I would manage to climb the short distance back to the hut. Determined to return before the storm worsened, I made great effort to take a step, when suddenly a roaring gust of wind swept me down, and I tumbled into a blanket of freshly fallen snow. I felt my face against the cold wet ground, and as I lay there, the memory of another snowstorm awakened within me.

CHAPTER 20

A Visitation and More

I stopped at a town and purchased the medicine I needed to end the pregnancy. My funds were nearly gone, but I had enough to stay at a roadside inn that night, where I asked the innkeeper's wife to help me prepare the medicine. I told her it was for a stomach ailment. For hours I sat in my room and stared at the bowl of medicine, unable to bring myself to take it. I had very much wanted a child in my early married years and had to make peace with the fact that I was unable to conceive. Now I was pregnant with the child of the man I loved, but I didn't see how I could bring this child into the world. As much as I told myself it was best to end it, I could not bring myself to drink the medicine. Finally, I had to admit that I wanted to give birth, and in a fit of tears, I threw the medicine away. In my distraught state, I did not consider returning to Praha. Perhaps it was fear, or due to the feeling that I had already said goodbye to that part of my life.

The next morning, I got up and rode out of the town, past farms and villages, at a loss as to where to go. I was not well enough to think of sleeping outdoors or to slip into barns as I had been doing. Fortunately, I was able to find a family to put me up on the first night and also the second. Each night I prayed to the goddess for a sign, but with the arrival of day no sign came. A few more days passed in this way, traveling from village to village, finding a farmer's wife who would have compassion on me and invite me to stay the night. When I reached the point when I knew that I could not continue, I remembered Gabrielle's words about the magic of the forest, about the benevolent spirits and angels who visited those sacred places. Surely, I thought, I will find help there, some sign as to what to do, where to go. My mind was a bottleneck of confusion, and I couldn't think straight. This, coupled with a melee of emotions, left me in really a deplorable state.

In what seemed like the middle of nowhere, I caught sight of a forest off to one side of the road. I entered and tied my horse to a tree. Then I began to walk in search of a stream. Gabrielle had always said that streams and rivers were sacred, inhabited by protective spirts, but as I walked, snow began to fall, bringing an unusual spring storm. I wasn't prepared for the abrupt change to the weather. Invoking the goddess, I paid no heed to the winds that swept around me, brushing snow into my face and eyes, blinding my vision. I was determined not to leave that forest without a response as to where I was to go and what I was to do. With much difficulty I trudged a few steps through the accumulating snow, but my feet were so frozen that it was difficult to walk. Heavy curtains of snow were now raining down on me, making it nearly impossible to move. Through the howling wind, I heard the cracking of a branch and felt something hit me hard on the head. As I crumpled into the snow on the icy cold ground, the scene before me darkened, the sound of the wind dimmed, and I lost awareness of my surroundings.

I awoke to a gentle voice calling me back to the world. Opening my eyes, I saw that the sun was shining brightly, and a woman was standing over me, seeking to awaken me. She appeared like an angel, or a goddess, and I wondered if she was the answer to my prayer. I was quite dazed and confused, but as she helped me to a seated position, I remembered that I had fallen during the snowstorm. Looking around I saw that I was still in the forest on the snow bedded ground. Touching my head, I felt a swelling and realized that I had been hit by a branch. Gazing into the face of the kind young woman who was now helping me to rise, I wondered how she had found me.

After a few moments I dismissed the thought that she might be a heavenly being and assumed she was a village woman who had by chance come across me in the forest. She was quite pretty, about my age with wavy golden hair like mine, and a delicate face with fine features and large blue eyes. Seeing that I was unsteady on my feet, she took my arm and said, "I know a place for you to rest and recover." I didn't argue, thinking she would take me home and allow me time to consider my next steps. Even if she wasn't a heavenly creature, I felt that the goddess had responded and sent her to me.

She guided me to my horse, where her horse was also standing, and helped me mount. Then she led the way along a stretch of the road out of the forest, off a side path to a small structure that looked like a deserted barn. After she climbed down from her horse, she helped me descend and led me inside the rather dilapidated structure. I had not said anything about my condition but had told her my name before leaving the forest. Somehow, she knew of the pregnancy because she quietly told me, "Claire, this will be your home until you give birth to the child growing inside of you."

"How did you know I am with child?" I asked, still dazed.

Without responding to the question, she looked at me caringly and said, "It was not hard to find you, but had I found you earlier, I never would have allowed you to suffer so."

"How did you find me and who sent you?"

Rather than answering, she asked, "When was the last time you ate?"

"Yesterday, I think," I mumbled.

"Then I will go find food. You wait here."

She started to leave, but fearing that she might abandon me, I called out, "Wait! You haven't told me your name or where you are from. Are you from the next village?"

"You may call me Catherine. I am from a place far away, but not so far after all."

"Will you promise to come back?" I asked anxiously.

"You are safe here, Claire. Of course, I promise that I will stay with you until the birth of the child."

After Catherine left, I began to look around at the place that would be my new home for the next many months. My head was throbbing, so I sat down. Although the outside of the structure was quite dilapidated, inside it was not so bad. In one corner were stacks of hay that could be used for bedding. In another was a pile of wood that would make a good fire. A straw broom was near the wood. After sitting for a while to regain my strength, I got up and began to sweep the place. Then I spread out the hay, making two beds out of it. It was hardly a home, but with no funds, I had no alternative, and how could I complain when my prayer for help had been answered?

Catherine returned with jugs of water and enough food for several days. Over the next weeks, we worked together to make the place comfortable. When I told her that I had no money, she had smiled and said, "Money is not of much importance. We will have everything we need. She must have had means of her own because every day she went into the village to purchase necessities, such as cloth to place over the hay for a bed, and blankets, items for cooking over our open fire, and other such things. On occasion she would bring me back milk from a nearby farm, saying it was for the baby. I was amazed at her resourcefulness and cheerfulness, how she made do with so little, never issuing even a single complaint. I wondered why she sacrificed so much for me, obviously using her own funds to care for me, and the only answer I could think of was that the goddess had sent her.

While she was away, I would wander into the nearby forest to collect wood and forest edibles, which I had learned to recognize from Gabrielle. Gradually our small, abandoned barn became a cozy home. We lived much of the time in silence, and I was grateful for Catherine's quiet ways. Under her attentive care, I felt much comforted and at ease, and this gave me the opportunity to reflect on my life—my childhood struggles, my marriage to Michel, the conflict with Jacque, and the few good years I had spent with Stefan. My heart still ached for him and at moments I was overcome by guilt for taking his unborn child from him, a child he would never know he had.

Catherine asked me no questions about my past, and I asked her none; it was as if we had an unspoken agreement not to inquire. Instead, we focused on the needs of the day—where to get food, the preparation of the meals, where to get water for washing, and such daily matters. It was this, and her continual cheerfulness, that kept me from slipping into a depressed state overcome with fear for the future.

As my belly grew, she began to refuse my assistance for the daily chores, taking on more and more of the work herself. When I protested, she would smile at me and say, "I want you only to rest and not do anything that might risk the health of the child." Who was this woman and why did she show such care for me?

In utter wonderment I watched as the baby began to kick and move about within me. I became acutely aware of what a gift motherhood was, yet I knew all along that this child was a treasure I would have to part with. The time of my delivery came, and Catherine made ready to go in search of a midwife, but I clung to her hand and would not let her leave, fearing that the baby might arrive in her absence. So it was she who safely delivered the baby girl into this world.

For days after the baby's arrival, I held her and tried to feed her. Catherine said nothing about the future, but two weeks after the birth, I whispered to the baby, "We must now find a good home for you. If you stay with me much longer, I will not be able to part with you, and I must."

"What should we call her?" Catherine asked.

"Let her mother name her. I am only a vehicle for her to come into this world. Now I must send her to her mother."

"Wait until you have recovered, Claire. You are not ready yet to move about."

I shook my head. "We must go soon, in the next day or so."

She tried to dissuade me, but I stubbornly insisted. Finally, she relented, saying quietly, "Then I will let you find the mother."

It was the winter season, days before Christmas, but we were in a relatively warm spell, and I thought it the right time to go searching for a mother. Bundling up the baby in a blanket, I tied her to my chest, and we rode through one village after another. Finally, toward the end of the day, I saw a small path leading to a farm and indicated to Catherine that we should follow that path. A few minutes down the path, we came to a lovely looking cottage, and I spoke words that I didn't know how I knew.

"There is couple there who have been longing for a child. The wife is a good woman, but she cannot conceive. Let us give her a daughter."

Nodding, Catherine helped me down from my horse and after hiding them among a small group of trees, we took the bundled baby and left her at the door, knocking loudly. Then we withdrew and watched from behind the small grove. A woman came to the door and, seeing the baby, called out to her husband. They spoke for a few minutes, then lifted the bundle and withdrew into the cottage. As they did, I remembered my words as I sat praying fervently during the night by the side of the fourteen-year-old girl, whose pregnancy I had helped to end; I had promised the goddess that I would sacrifice that which was most dear to me if the girl could be saved, and this is what I had just done. "Words become deeds," I whispered to myself, realizing I had fulfilled that commitment.

"They are the right couple, Claire, good people."

"I don't know how I knew, but I did," I replied sadly, as pangs of separation shot through me. "It was as if their yearning for a child led me here." It was then that I was struck by the fact that I had nowhere to go. During the time of my pregnancy, I had not allowed myself to think of the future, but now the future was staring me in the face, and it was a blank stare.

"Claire, you are not well. We have been riding for hours, and you have not yet recovered. I fear you will soon come down with a fever. Let me take you to a place where you will be cared for."

It was true. I was feeling dizzy and faint, and the separation from the baby now hit me hard, as if a part of me had been ripped away. I had not allowed myself to cry, but I could no longer hold back my tears. Putting her arms around me, Catherine comforted me, saying, "You have passed through much struggle, Claire, but you have a bright future ahead. Let me take you to where you need to go."

"I must find someplace that will take me in as a servant. That is the only future I can see for myself," I managed to say as I gained control of my emotions. I was struggling not to fall into despair, but in my weakened state, I couldn't think straight. Then the thought came to me that I had trusted Catherine all this time, and I had to trust her now, so I added, "If you know a place that will take me in, I will go there. Perhaps they will need a servant."

Climbing back onto my horse, I followed as Catherine led the way. We rode for another hour or two and as the time passed, my condition grew worse. I began to shiver, and several times I nearly fell off the horse. I was not dressed warmly and the cool spring air began to seep into my bones. Seeing my state, Catherine grew concerned and slowed our pace.

"We are not far away, Claire. Can you hold on for just a little bit longer?"

I nodded. Another hour passed and I clung onto the horse as best I could as the world began to spin around me.

Finally, we arrived at an enclosed structure, encircled by a rather tall wall. Catherine descended from her horse and helped me climb down, holding tightly onto me and steadying my steps as we approached the enclosure. Standing before the gate, she said, "When you enter this place, you must ask for Marguerite. She will take care of you and give you the medicine you need. I must leave you now. You will be in good hands."

"Catherine, you are leaving?" I could barely get out the words. I didn't want her to go but I didn't have the strength to protest. It took all my will to be able to stand and walk the few steps to the gate.

"I must leave you now, my dear Claire. You have no more need for me." With those words, she loudly rang the bell and then quickly mounted her horse and rode away. I was left there watching her, unable to call her back as much as I wanted to.

A woman, dressed fully in black like a widow, opened the gate and invited me in.

"I am here to see Marguerite," I managed to say in a weak voice as I took a few steps into the courtyard.

"Do you have an appointment?" she asked sweetly. I shook my head.

"Then, my dear, I am afraid you will not be able to see her today. Come back another day after you have made the proper arrangements."

I looked at her confused for a moment and then turned to go, but as I took a step toward the gate, a burning sensation came over me, and I stumbled and fell onto the ground. Another voice called, "Sister, help me carry her into my room," and I felt myself being lifted.

Sometime later, I woke up in a bed. Two women dressed in black were by the bedside speaking quietly, and I heard the words of one of the women as they drifted to my ears. "She is burning with fever. We should call the priest to confess her sins in case she dies."

"We must inform Sister Marguerite first," said the other.

"No priest," I called out in a faint voice, and then asked, "Where am I?"

"You are in the Convent of Our Lady," the first woman replied gently.

"Is this a church?" I asked in a barely audible voice. She nodded. With great difficulty I tried to lift myself to a seated position. "I can't stay here. I must leave right away," I whispered.

At that moment, another woman entered the room and asked the two women to leave. She was also dressed in black. She is one of them, I thought, again making a motion to get up.

"I can't stay here," I murmured.

Sitting down beside me, she helped to prop me up against a pillow, "My dear, you are very ill with an infection. I have made this medicine myself to bring down your fever. Once you are well, you can leave if you want." Then she told me what plants she had combined to take the heat out of my body. It was exactly what I would have prepared.

I took the bowl of medicine and drank it, and then allowed her to help me lie down again. Before getting up from my bedside, she asked gently, "Now tell me, why do you say you can't stay here?"

"I don't believe in the church or in sin," I said weakly.

"Neither do I," she replied gently.

"I won't see a priest. I don't like them."

"Neither do I," she repeated.

"I follow the way of the goddess," I added, sure that she would now understand why I couldn't stay there in the convent.

"So do I," she replied in an almost whispered voice.

"Are you Marguerite?" I asked, looking up into her kind eyes. Although she was dressed like the other women, there was something distinctly different about her.

"I am. And I have been expecting you, Claire."

"Then she has led me to you, the goddess I mean," I murmured as I closed my eyes and fell back to sleep.

CHAPTER 21

A Teaching on Love

The snow had stopped falling and the sun now peered out from behind the clouds, streaming down on the glistening white ground. I had slipped and drifted into something of a reverie, which had drawn me back into the past. One snowfall had stirred the memory of another, and I suspected that it was Ama-la who had changed the weather and created the conditions to help me return to the past. Looking around and getting up, I found myself in the present again, in the Yarlung Valley. I picked up the wood that had fallen when I had slipped and carefully made my way up the icy incline into the hut. Without speaking, I lay the bundle of fallen branches by the stove and removed my wet clothing. Ama-la stood by the stove stirring a soup. After gazing at me compassionately for a few moments, she began spooning a portion into a bowl and set it on the table. I knew it was for me and I sat down to eat. Neither of us had spoken a word since I had returned. My mind was still very much interiorized. After I finished, I went over to the meditation corner and sat down against the wall, closed my eyes, and spun back time to the moment when I lay in bed, sick with fever, being cared for by the one called Marguerite.

When I awoke the next morning, my temperature had come down, but I was still feverish and weak. Marguerite waited by my bedside to feed me more medicine. I had many questions, but she cautioned me not to speak, to rest until my strength had returned. I slept most of that day and the next, waking only to take medicine and some liquid. On the fourth day my fever fully subsided, and I was able to sit up in bed and eat solid food.

A woman I didn't recognize had brought my meal, and when she began to clear the food away, she asked my name. Then she plied me with questions about where I was from and why I had come. I didn't answer and looking up saw Marguerite standing in the doorway.

"You may leave now," she said quietly to the woman. As they spoke for a few minutes in the doorway, I noticed the respectful way in which the woman responded to Marguerite and realized that she had some authority in this place.

"You are better today, my dear. I am pleased to see this. For a while there, we thought we might lose you, but you have a strong will to live," said Marguerite, after closing the door behind her and coming to sit by my bedside.

"It was you who took care of me, wasn't it?" I asked in a weak voice. She nodded and I thanked her. I was now able to take note of her for the first time. Marguerite seemed a number of years older than me, perhaps in her late thirties. Her face showed the first signs of age with faint creases around her eyes and mouth. I couldn't see her hair color as she wore a black head covering that came down over the top of her forehead, as did all the other women I had seen in that place, dressed as widows would.

Taking off her head covering, she smiled at me, and I saw an abundance of dark cropped hair descend to her chin. Brushing it back off her face with her hand, she said, "You are in my room and in here we can speak freely. Claire, let me help you get up into a chair." Taking hold of my arm, she assisted as I rose from the bed. Then she continued. "I know that you have recently given birth and found a home for the child." I nodded. "When you arrived here, you began to hemorrhage, and an infection set in. That is why you had such a high fever. I imagine that you have been through some difficult emotions, and this was your body's way of purification. But you should be fine now. Do you have a home to return to?" I shook my head. "Then you may stay here."

"Marguerite . . . is that what I should call you?" I asked, recalling that the other women who had tended me called her "sister."

"That is my name," she replied with a smile.

"How did you know my name and that I had given birth?"

"About a week before you arrived, I had a dream in which I saw a woman who looked like you enter our gate. She was in much distress, so I knew to expect someone. There was a note stuck in your pouch that fell out when you fainted. The note told me your name and mentioned the birth and asked that I take care of you. It wasn't signed by anyone."

I sighed. "You saved my life, and I am grateful, but I don't see how I can stay in a church. Years ago, I made a vow never to step inside of one, and I plan to stick to that vow."

She chuckled. "This is not exactly a church. Besides, I am in charge here, and if I tell you that the only rules you need to follow are the ones you set for yourself, would you then be able to stay for a while, until you receive an indication of where to go next?"

"Is it possible then that I don't have to mingle with the others and follow their routine, and that I never have to meet the priest, not even to take the sacraments?"

She nodded. "You will be my assistant and stay close by me. There is a chapel here on the grounds, and the women go every morning for prayer. A priest comes on Sunday to conduct the mass, and I must attend but you do not. I promise that you will never have to step foot inside that chapel or meet the priest unless you decide otherwise. I will respect your decisions and make sure that the others do as well."

I thought for a moment, wondering how I could be her assistant. "Marguerite, I don't know how to read or write. How can I assist you?"

"That is of no importance. I oversee this convent of many nuns, and there are many other matters you can help me with aside from writing letters."

I looked at her gratefully, realizing that I had no other place to go. "Why are you being so kind to me?" I asked, hesitantly, knowing that she was making an extraordinary exception by taking in a woman who was hostile to the very ideals of that place.

"Claire, you and I are not so different from each other. I was young when I came here, and there was nobody who understood me as I understand you, and so I have learned to live a life of disguise. But I made a commitment early on that I would rise to a position where I could offer protection to all who came, no matter their beliefs or background. I have been able to do that. Among the women are a number of unwed mothers who have had to give up their children and have had no place else to go, women who have ended pregnancies, women who have been raped and thrown out by their families, and those who seek escape from an unwanted marriage. And then there are those who come purely out of love for their God and the desire to serve. They each have a story, and, yes, most have turned to the church for comfort. Religion is a personal matter and I allow each one to approach their God however she wants. There are no set rules, but we cannot say that openly, or I will get into big trouble with the bishop." Smiling, she added, "In order to give these women shelter, I must keep up my disguise for their sake."

Over the next few days, we were to have many such conversations, and as I slowly regained my health, I began to trust the woman I now considered my new friend. Often, I thought to ask Marguerite about her story, how she had come to the convent, but I was a bit awed by her and still too shy to enquire. Upon my arrival, Marguerite had given up her room for me, but once I had begun to recover, she moved me into a room next to hers, and I spent most of the first weeks between these two rooms, hardly venturing out, eating all my meals with Marguerite in the small sitting area that adjoined her bedroom. I began to notice that for many of the women, her room was a place of refuge, where they could unload their burdens, where they would find a listening ear and receive care and understanding. They came to her with all sorts of problems, and she always listened patiently and offered her counsel. One day she called for me. When I entered her room, I found a young nun in tears kneeling before her. I thought to withdraw but Marguerite motioned for me to stay, and I stood there listening.

"Mother, I have sinned," sobbed the young woman.

Marguerite bent over and taking hold of her hands, helped her rise to her feet. Putting her arm around her waist, she said, "There is no such thing. You have fallen in love, that is all, and I will help you realize your dream. Gather all your belongings and in one hour go to the front gate, which will be unlocked. I have asked your beloved to wait for you at the end of the path." Then taking a small pouch from her desk, she placed it in the young woman's hands, and said, "This money should help you go far away with him and begin a new life. Love is a gift. Treasure it."

The young nun could hardly believe what she was hearing and asked if it was true that her beloved was waiting for her. Marguerite nodded and after a few minutes the nun hurriedly withdrew. When she was gone, Marguerite sighed and said to me, "That poor girl. She fell in love with a man whom her parents didn't approve of, and when she refused to marry the man of their choice, they sent her here and forced her to take vows. She has been miserable, and I was determined to find that young man and unite them, but it wasn't easy," she chuckled. "He is a good and responsible man, and she will be happy with him." This was the first time I witnessed the ways in which Marguerite quietly helped each woman according to her need, but there were to be many, many examples of such assistance.

As the weeks went by, I saw that the other nuns kept their distance from me, and some even looked at me suspiciously. Although I wanted to remain apart from them, I began to feel as if they scorned me. Perhaps it was because I never went to the chapel. Perhaps they knew I was not truly a Christian inside. Perhaps they thought I was an infidel and didn't know why I was here, or perhaps they knew I was a poor uneducated village girl. Each interaction with a nun made me feel self-conscious. After one incident when an older nun harshly upbraided me in front of the others and addressed me in a scornful manner, I hurried to Marguerite in tears, thinking it was time for me to leave, but I still had nowhere to go. Marguerite listened as I shared with her my sense of humiliation.

"Are you afraid of scorn and humiliation, my dear?" she asked. When I didn't answer, she continued. "Those two are good teachers." I looked at her questioningly. "If you are to stick to your principles, you must have the courage to face this. If you can withstand it, you may gain humility, the most treasured of all the virtues." I was quiet as I sat pondering her words. "But I have a suggestion. You have kept yourself apart from the other women. Perhaps they think you believe yourself to be better than they are. Reach out to the women and be of service, despite how they treat you. Everyone has personal struggles, my dear. You can become a listening ear." I left Marguerite that day determined to no longer hide from the other women and not to fear how they might regard me.

Every morning I began taking walks through the hallways and into the gardens, which were just beginning to burst into flower. When I encountered the other nuns, I greeted them cheerfully and asked if they needed help with their chores. This did not come easily to me, but it was something I forced myself to do out of respect for Marguerite, whom I had come to greatly admire.

The weather was warming and I was glad to have some time each day to go outside into the fresh air. I noticed that each Tuesday in the afternoons, Marguerite would disappear for several hours. It was on a such a Tuesday that I happened to meet her as she was getting ready to depart, her horse laden with several bags attached to the side of her saddle. I assumed that Tuesday was the day she went to the market to pick up supplies for the convent and asked if I could accompany her, not having left the convent since I had arrived months earlier. After a moment's pause, she nodded.

Calling for a horse for me, she said she would take me to a special place. We rode for nearly thirty minutes, but not in the direction of the market. Soon we approached a forest and at the edge, our horses came to a halt in front of a little hut. Descending, Marguerite lifted the bags off the horse and entered the hut, with me following close behind. I had no idea where we were or whom we were going to meet, but I was glad to be away from the confinement of the convent. A solitary man was inside seated at a table writing. As soon as he saw her, he rose and smiled, but then he noticed me and asked who I was.

"This is Claire," said Marguerite, introducing me. "She is one of us. I have taken her as my assistant. We can speak freely in front of her."

"Claire, are you a nun?" he asked. I shook my head vehemently.

"Don't mention that matter to her," chuckled Marguerite. "It is a sensitive subject. As a young girl she took a vow never to enter a church, and she has stuck to that. But she lives in a convent, at least for now." As soon as we had entered, Marguerite had thrown off her head covering and cloak, and I did the same.

"A wise vow," he commented, amused.

"Claire, this is Brother Bernard. He once lived in the monastery further down the road but lives now as a hermit copying manuscripts and translating them. This brilliant monk knows Latin, Greek, and Hebrew," she said proudly, "but sadly, the church didn't appreciate his knowledge and sent him here to live a solitary life."

"Marguerite, enough about me," he replied in an embarrassed tone. "I want to hear about your week. I wait eagerly for your visit, but not for the food."

"Of course, not for the food," she said teasingly, as she set her packages on the table, carefully setting aside his manuscript.

Turning to me, he added, "It is my good fortune that I have been sent away to live in this forest among the trees and animals. It is far better than living among men."

I smiled, thinking this is a man to my liking. Brother Bernard was a slim tall man, with dark hair falling just past his shoulders tied back neatly with a string. Subtle strands of grey sprinkled the hair at his temples and dotted his thin cropped beard, giving him a most distinguished appearance. His slender face bore no sign of age, but the grey in his beard made me think he was around the same age as Marguerite. His eyes were a deep green and lit up when he spoke. From the moment I stepped into the hut, I felt a lightness, a carefreeness that I had not felt in a long time, if ever.

I helped Marguerite unpack the various food items she had brought—freshly baked bread, butter, cheese, and a variety of vegetables—putting them away in the small corner that served as his kitchen. Then she began tidying up the place. The one room hut was small and bare, with only a bed on one side and a table near the kitchen area. The wooden floor had one thin rug in the middle. Lamps lit the room, casting a soft glow. There was one window near the kitchen area, but the shutters were closed. Going over to the window, Marguerite threw open the shutters as she said, "Must I remind you each week to let in the fresh air, even on cool days." He watched her with amusement as she went about organizing the small hut.

"Enough, enough," he finally said. "I didn't invite you here to work."

"Did you invite me, or did I invite myself?" she teased. Back and forth they bantered, until after a few minutes, he turned serious and asked about her week. She shared with him some of the troubles faced by individual nuns. He seemed familiar with many of them because he asked specific questions and gave her counsel. They spoke for some time, and after they were done, he picked up a lute and went outside. Marguerite followed and I did the same. Their interaction revealed a familiarity and closeness that struck me as being most unusual and made me wonder about their relationship.

Once outside, he went around to the back of his hut and walked a short way down a path, where he seated himself on the forest floor and began to play the instrument. Marguerite sat down beside him, closed her eyes and after several minutes began to sing in an enchanting, almost haunting voice. The notes of the lute mingled with the tones of her voice in an elevated combination of sounds. I closed my eyes and felt myself carried back to the days when I used to dance in the forest to Gabrielle's singing. She had sung folk songs, suited for children, but Marguerite's chanting was of a totally different nature. It awakened a deep longing that lay undiscerned in the heart. When it ended, we sat in silence for a long time before Marguerite said we had to return to the convent.

Once we arrived back, Marguerite told me that if I liked, I could accompany her to visit Brother Bernard on the next Tuesday.

"Marguerite, if I could . . . I have been happier today than I have been in a long time." She nodded and smiled. I went with her the next Tuesday and the ones after that. It was always the same. Each week, Marguerite brought food for him, cleaned up the hut, and then we sat outside while he played the lute and she sang. I didn't speak much, still shy in the company of this monk who hardly seemed to fit my image of a monk, and I continued to wonder about their relationship, becoming more curious as the weeks went by. After several visits, she told me that I could come with her each week.

"I think Brother Bernard enjoys your company, Claire, so you may join us. But now I will let you do the baking," she said with a sparkle in her eyes. I wondered what she meant when she said that Brother Bernard enjoyed my company. I had never shared with him my inner thoughts and most of the time I did nothing but sit there smiling, thoroughly enjoying the lightness and closeness those two exhibited, a closeness I began to envy.

Since my first visit to Brother Bernard, I found myself waiting all week until the next Tuesday in anticipation of leaving the convent, but now I had another reason to eagerly await the day of the next visit. I would bake a cake for him. Monday night I was busy in the kitchen until late, baking two loaves of bread and a fruit cake. As a child, I had learned from my mother how to bake bread, but I had never made a fruit cake before and had to ask several nuns for recipes. I was excited to try my hand, but more than that, I was eager to offer something to this man whom I was growing fond of.

Although there was clearly a familiarity between Marguerite and Bernard that I didn't understand, they always addressed each other formally in my presence. This broke down on the fifth visit. As Marguerite was putting away the food that we had brought, she set down on the table the cake that I had made, saying, "Beau (pronounced Bo), Claire baked this cake especially for you."

"Margot, you are giving her extra work," he remarked with feigned severity.

"The cake was her idea," she protested. It was then that I realized that this stately woman, who garnered the respect of everyone, became like a young girl when in his presence. Turning my eyes from one to the other, I stammered, "You two . . . you are brother and sister, aren't you?" They looked at one another and smiled.

"Margot is my dear younger sister, but most people don't know that. The bishop looks the other way and pretends not to know that she visits me regularly, which is against the rules, because he is our uncle."

"The bishop is your uncle!" I exclaimed.

They both nodded, "But not necessarily a friendly uncle, at least to me," remarked Brother Bernard quietly.

"With the exception of Sister Anna, the other nuns are unaware, Claire," added Marguerite. Sister Anna was the other assistant who helped Marguerite and was about my age.

"I will never say a word," I assured them. Why did it make me so happy to know this about them? Had I secretly feared that they might be lovers, and why would that have disturbed me?

"Come, let us go sing in the forest," urged Bernard.

As I sat on the forest floor listening to the uplifting sounds, something came over me, a happiness, the joy of being with these two people who were fast becoming dear friends. Getting up, I took out the pins that held my hair in a tight bun behind my head, and shaking my head back and forth, allowed the golden waves to fly freely over my shoulders, reaching down to my waist. Then I began to dance, not the child's dance that I had once done with Elise, but another, more sophisticated version that came naturally, as if the music was directing me, streaming through my body, lifting my limbs. When the music stopped, I dropped onto the ground and laughed. "I couldn't help myself," I exclaimed. "The music was too beautiful."

I felt Bernard's gaze upon me and heard him say to Marguerite. "Claire has such beautiful hair. You mustn't ever let her cut it." Embarrassed, I took the pins and tidied up my hair again.

It took me a few more visits before I was calling Bernard "Beau" and Marguerite "Margot," when I was alone with her. Several months later, I learned their story. I was sitting alone with Margot late at night after she had been tending to many pressing matters. I could see how tired she was, and I was about to leave her room when she began to talk about Beau. She mentioned how she often worried about her brother and wished she could do more to care for him. After she had expressed her concerns, I ventured to ask her how it came to be that they had both entered monastic life.

"Our story is not a happy one," she began. "Our father comes from a powerful aristocratic line and our mother from a merchant family. Their marriage was arranged because she had wealth and he had title, but they were mismatched from the start. They had two children together; first Beau and then two years later I came along. As a young child, I couldn't pronounce Bernard and so I called my brother simply Beau, and the name stuck. Our father was very strict, which didn't suit our mother's independent nature. She began spending more and more time away, saying she was visiting her family, but he didn't believe her. He became suspicious, bitter, and oppressive. Our father's family was a religious one and his brother had just become bishop. Accusing our mother of adultery, he convinced the bishop to annul the marriage and excommunicate her, and she was forced from our home. Much later, we found out there was another reason. She had been drawn to a small hidden Druid community that lived in a remote forest many hours from the city where we lived. She fell in love with the forest and began to feel confined by city life with our father. My uncle, the bishop, found out about this and threw her out of the church. They said that she had had an affair. Beau and I never found out if she really had a love affair or whether they used this as an excuse. But she did leave and go live in the Druid community, and eventually she got together with a man from there. Years later, when I grew older, I began to meet her secretly and it was she who taught me about the goddess.

"I was eight and Beau was ten when she left. I knew it was difficult for her because I remember her crying in the weeks before she was forced to leave. Our father remarried soon after to a very religious woman, another aristocrat, and had more children with her. She didn't like Beau because he challenged her, and she convinced our father that in order to cleanse Beau of the pagan influence, he should be sent to the monastery. We were both well-educated and our uncle, the bishop, consented, saying that with Beau's knowledge and intellect, he could rise eventually to become a high official in the church. Beau was only sixteen at the time. He didn't want to be a monk, but he had no say in the matter. After he entered the monastery, he didn't get along with the abbot and refused to abide by rules that didn't make sense to him. Beau makes his own rules and doesn't follow orders very well. He is too smart for most.

"After many years of a troubled relationship, the abbot sent him off to be a hermit. At first the bishop objected, but Beau finally convinced him to let him live as a hermit monk on the outskirts of the monastery grounds. They still restrict him in many ways. Once a week, on Fridays, they bring him food that is hardly fit to eat. That is why on Tuesdays I bring him real food. They also bring him manuscripts to transcribe and translate, which has satisfied his intellectual hunger. I have seen my brother make peace with his situation, and I know he is content living the life of a hermit, but that doesn't stop me from worrying about him. As you get to know my brother, you will see that he is very special, very precious indeed.

"I was heartbroken when Beau was sent to the monastery. He had been everything to me, my protector, my best friend, my confidant, and my teacher. It was because of him that I was educated, and where there was a lack in my education, he always filled in. After he had left home, our father, at our stepmother's insistence, tried to arrange a marriage for me with her nephew. I am sure that she was thinking that she would be able to control me through this marriage. The nephew was a very religious man, with set ideas about women that I could never accept. After hearing about this proposed marriage, I ran away to the monastery where Beau was living. For a week, I hid myself in his tiny room, where we had long talks about what I should do. I wanted to enter a nunnery near him so that I could look after him. Religion was not on my mind, but my brother was. He never cared much for his material needs and I feared for his health. Beau tried to discourage me, saying that I didn't realize how strict the rules were, that I might not be able to see him at all. But I insisted, believing it was the only way I could think of to be near him. Eventually, he spoke to our uncle, asking that I enter the nunnery not far from him. The bishop was so pleased that he said he would help me, and he convinced my father to let me go. That is how I was brought here, and why I have risen in such a short time to be in charge of this place.

"Beau never had a good relationship with our uncle, but I have learned how to please him and he is very fond of me. As a result, I am able to do what others can't do. Claire, sometimes it is more effective to work from within the institution. What do I care about the church or its rules, about the dogma, the blind belief? I care about the women who have taken refuge here. By serving them, I have found deeper purpose to my life, and over the years I have come to love very deeply the one called Jesus. You must ask Beau one day to tell you the story about him."

"I know all the stories about Jesus," I replied with a frown. "I was also born into a religious family."

She chuckled. "You may know the stories that the priests tell, but not the ones that Beau shares. They are as different as night and day."

"What about your mother?" I asked curiously. "Did she become a Druid?"

"What do you know about the Druids?" she asked with a faint smile.

Finally, I confessed to Margot what I had never dared to say out loud before. "I am one." She looked at me in surprise and then I told her for the first time that Gabrielle had been my teacher. "The woman I told you about who was burned, Gabrielle, she was also one. I believe that is why they killed her although they found some excuse for her murder. I learned a little about the Druids from her, about how they commune with the nature spirits. It was she who first told me about the goddess, whom I vowed to follow. After her death, I decided that I was a Druid, although truthfully, Margot, I don't know what that really means."

Margot smiled. "There is not so much difference between a true Christian and a Druid. These are only names. As you get to know my brother better, you will understand this. It is the church that makes a distinction. After my father remarried, distance grew between him and me. I hadn't seen my mother for a number of years. But after I entered the convent and Beau had gone to live in the forest, I received a note telling me where I could meet her. I went to that place and found her waiting. At first, she wouldn't say much about her life, except that she was happy. When I saw how she glowed with an unusual joy, I began to ask her questions. I had not taken an interest in religion before, but when she spoke of the Great Mother, something in me stirred. I was already living in the convent and so had to integrate what I was learning from her into my life here. Fortunately, I had Beau to help me.

"After that meeting, my mother started sending me money every month, instructing me to use it to take care of Beau and to serve the many villages around here, to help families during difficult times. She came from a wealthy family who didn't care much about religion, and she was left with significant funds, although she lived very simply as is the way of the Druids. That was many years ago, and every month the money never fails to come. Every now and then I receive a note and I go meet her. In this way, she has remained very much part of my life, much more so than my father. It is because of her that I have a degree of independence. All the ways in which we help the villagers, that is due to my mother. I tell the bishop that the money comes from an anonymous donor."

"Is Beau also able to see her?"

"When he was sent to live in the forest, he had to take a vow not to leave the hut. That was the compromise they reached. He is an honorable man and has lived up to that. However, I have brought my mother to him a few times, disguised as one of the nuns. She has encouraged him not only to copy and translate the manuscripts but also to write his interpretations. But I doubt any of the church officials will understand what he writes. My brother is far ahead of our times."

"Margot, when I first came, I told you that I follow the way of the goddess and you said that you also do. What did you mean?"

"One cannot truly know Jesus without knowing the goddess, and it was Beau who helped me understand that." I was quiet, perplexed by her response. "Claire, you have asked me many questions, now let me ask you one. What does it mean to you to follow the way of the goddess?"

I stared at her for a few minutes, not knowing how to respond. Finally, I murmured, "To believe in her, I suppose."

She shook her head. "Belief is not enough. You must know her, Claire. Then you will understand how to follow her."

Margot's words left me speechless that night. How to know the goddess? I had no answer to that. And I couldn't imagine what connection there could be between Jesus and the goddess. Were they not in opposition? Didn't the church burn those who believed in the goddess? Then again, Margot seemed to imply that whatever the priests claimed, that was not the true story. How was I to understand it all?

"Perhaps you can enlighten Claire," said Margot casually as she and I were sitting in the forest with Beau behind the hut one afternoon.

He chuckled and replied, "It is Claire who must enlighten me."

"What do I know?" I asked in surprise, looking at him questioningly.

"You know about matters of the heart," he replied fondly. I turned my eyes away, wondering if he perceived my growing feelings for him, feelings that I had never expressed, not even to Margot, that I dared not admit to myself.

"Claire cannot disassociate Jesus from the church. She sees them as one," Margot explained.

"What has the church to do with Jesus? Claire, you must separate them in your mind. Many speak in his name, but few know him."

"The church rejects the goddess, and so I assumed that was his teaching," I ventured to say.

Beau laughed. "Whomever rejects the Mother of the Universe, rejects him as well. That is the irony." Then in a more serious tone, he added, "Do not blame the teacher for the poor understanding of those who claim to be students, and even the close disciples themselves. Most cannot grasp the true meaning of the teacher's words or know what the teacher has come to accomplish."

"Beau, you must explain to her. Tell her the hidden story."

"What do you mean hidden story?" I asked. "I grew up in a religious home and know inside and out the story of Jesus' life."

"Do you?" asked Beau, with a teasing expression on his face. "Then I will tell you a story that perhaps you haven't heard." I waited eagerly, knowing that Beau would have a different interpretation of events. After exchanging glances with Margot, he began, "Not long after I had been sent to live here in this hut, a wandering ascetic in need of shelter appeared at my door and asked if he could spend the night. Naturally I invited him in, prepared a meal for him, and started to lay out blankets for a bed on the floor. He said he had no need for sleep and went to a corner of the hut where he entered a deep state of contemplation. Eventually, I went to bed and awoke early the next morning to find him still in that unmoving state. When he finally emerged, he was quiet for some time before he began to speak.

"He told me that he was returning from travel through distant lands in the east, where he had spent years wandering through the great mountains and meeting the sages of that region. Finally, he came to a place called Kashmir, where he met an old woman sage, and she told him this story. She said that when Jesus was born, the three sages who came to him were from *Inde* (India) and they were sent to impart certain knowledge to him. They whispered sacred words in his ear, words that would stir his memory and set him on his spiritual journey. Then they returned home. As he grew up, those words never left him. When he was a young man, he left home and traveled east to find those sages. Soon his search turned in a different direction. After spending some years in contemplation in remote mountain caves, he came to the place called Kashmir and there he entered a cave, which the locals call Amarnath. Again, he entered a state of contemplation and awakened to a deep truth.

"This traveling sage told me that the people in the whole region of Inde believe that the Divine One takes human form again and again to help humankind. Jesus, he said, was one of those forms, one among many, and in parts of the east he is regarded as an emanation of the divine power they call Shiva. Shiva has a feminine counterpart, a consort you might say, who is called by many names—Parvati, Uma, Bhavani, so many names. She is considered to be the Mother of the Universe. Eons ago, she incarnated on earth in search of Shiva, not realizing that he and she were already one, that they were inseparable. Entering a cave high in the mountains, she spent many thousands of years in contemplation until she awakened to the fact that she herself was the Mother of the Universe, already in complete union with Shiva. This took place long before Jesus appeared on earth.

"Now Jesus sat in that very same cave, experiencing within himself the force called Shiva, remembering the intense yearning of that consort, which had spanned so many millennia. He recalled her condition at that time when she didn't eat or sleep and suffered every bodily deprivation and mental struggle possible. In the process, she absorbed into herself much of the world's suffering; her purpose being to show that no matter what the condition, humans can realize union with the Divine. The intensity of her yearning for Shiva had stirred the whole universe, and many divine beings approached Shiva, pleading with him to ease her suffering. He knew she didn't want or need his intervention; what she was to achieve had to be done by her alone to serve as a model for all humankind. He waited and waited, yearning for her as much as she yearned for him, until she had achieved on her own the realization of her union with him. Once she had awakened to her true nature, flooded with unspeakable bliss, she was able then to perceive her beloved consort, who in reality had never been apart from her. The vision of that whole cosmic episode was experienced by the one called Jesus.

"As Jesus sat in that cave, she appeared to him in her cosmic form, and there in that cave the illusion of separation lifted. Soon after, Jesus got up from his contemplation and walked away, fully united with the Mother of the Universe. As he was descending from the mountain, the old Kashmiri sage approached him and asked where he was going.

He replied that it was time for him to return to where he had come from. After a moment's thought, she told him, 'They will kill you if you return.'

"He replied, 'How can they kill the one who is united with the Mother of the Universe, and how can I not fulfill the purpose for which I have come?'

"She advised him, saying, 'Speak in veiled tongue so only those who are ready for your message will hear it. You carry within you her presence, for you are one with her and there is no need to speak her name.'

"Jesus returned to Palestine, so filled with love that his only thought was to spread that love and ease the suffering of those he met. The love he embodies is the love of the goddess. So you see, Claire, those who reject the Great Mother, reject him . . . for they are inseparable. Over time, as patriarchy grew stronger and suppressed the intuitive wisdom through which the Mother speaks, she was replaced by the Father. The goddess grew silent. That is the condition in which we find ourselves today, but in the turning of time, this will change once again."

"Is your story really true?" I asked in astonishment.

Smiling at me, he replied, "That is the very question I posed to the wandering ascetic who visited me. He told me, 'Look inside yourself to find the truth. Just as the goddess resides within Jesus, and their union is complete, so she resides within you.' His words changed everything for me. I saw the gift that I had been given when I left the monastery and was sent to live here alone. He gave me practices to deepen my contemplation, which I have done regularly since then.

"Jesus lived during a very dark time, when much of the world was in chaos and ignorant of spiritual truths, and that time has not yet passed. The doctrines of the church, all the texts written about him came much later. There were a few during his time and in the centuries after who understood his teachings, but they had to live hidden lives or they would be persecuted. I don't blame those who misunderstood him, but we mustn't get caught in believing the doctrines they preach, doctrines born of ignorance."

"What a touching love story," I murmured. I had never heard that story of Jesus. So he also was a follower of the goddess, I thought. Hearing that opened my heart to him for the first time.

"All of life is a love story," replied Margot. "You can only know the goddess through love. Love is the force that reveals her, and love is not an emotion, Claire, but a state of being. Jesus saw the Great Mother in every person, and treated every person as her, because, in truth, we are all her expressions. We are one with her, not separate, but we don't know it yet."

"Once you find the goddess inside, Claire, you will see her everywhere," added Beau.

"And you two, have you found her?" I asked timidly.

Margot answered for them. "Claire, we are not so different from you. We are still seeking."

Beau's story stayed with me for long after, a story so radically different from the one I had heard since childhood, the one that had created fear in me, and Beau's version made much more sense. The more I thought about his words, the more my feelings changed. Months passed and that conversation still reverberated in my mind. I had been searching for the goddess for so long; was I to find her here in the convent? The very thought turned my world upside down.

It was Christmas eve, and the evening singing reached my ears. For days the atmosphere in the convent had been most joyous and I could see how much the celebration meant to the nuns. Christmas had never meant much to me, but on this Christmas eve, I quietly crept up close to the chapel entrance so I could hear the singing better, and then hurried away at the first sign of nuns leaving the chapel. It was widely known and accepted that I didn't participate in church events. I doubt anyone understood why, but none dared to question Margot's allowance of this.

That night, something came over me, and I couldn't sleep. It was in the pre-dawn hours, when I knew that everyone would still be fast asleep, that I quickly dressed and quietly went to the chapel, one I had never entered. For quite a while I stood outside the door, remembering the moment when I had made the vow not to enter a church again. Then something came over me and I heard myself whisper, "For love, I will break one vow and make another." Gently pushing open the door, I tiptoed into the chapel. For a few moments, I stood there trying to overcome an innate resistance, which over time had become such a powerful force inside of me. Then I slowly walked up to the altar and dropped down on my knees. I looked up into the face of Jesus hanging on the cross, an image that had always frightened me, but now when I looked at him, I saw only love for the goddess, and I said in a determined voice, "My vow is to forever love and serve the goddess, whom you also adore, the Mother of the Universe. I know that you came to serve her children, and that I will also do." A tremendous feeling of upliftment came over me as I spoke those words, a joyous wave. Closing my eyes, I rested in that feeling for quite some time before rising and leaving the chapel. When I closed the door behind me, I found Margot waiting outside for me.

"How did you know to come?" I asked in a whisper.

She smiled. "Don't forget, your room is right next to mine. I heard you leave and knew where you were going. I was also unable to sleep tonight. Come, sit with me in my room for a while."

Once we had reached her room, we sat in silence for a few minutes and then she began to speak quietly. "Claire, I know what is in your heart." At her words, I could not prevent a look of pain from crossing my face. The love for Beau that I had been trying so hard to suppress burst forth, and tears welled up in the corners of my eyes. "You have fallen in love with my brother, and he with you. I am most grateful, for you have opened his heart. This gives me great happiness, but I also know that it will cause suffering for you."

"But Margot, I know that a relationship is impossible. I wouldn't do anything to harm him."

"There were many teachings in that story Beau told you. Do you remember him saying that the goddess endured many thousands of years of yearning before she could realize her union with her beloved? She is a goddess; we are only human. You will not have to wait so long. What did

Jesus do in that cave when he had the vision of the goddess? He expanded the love for her into love for every human being. That is the teaching. Your love for Beau can be expressed by loving and caring for all who come to you for help. Love is not meant to be confined to one person. It is to be given freely to all. This is the universal love that the great ones experience, and it brings immeasurable joy. This is what we must strive for."

"Then you are not angry at me?" I asked, meekly. I had long wondered if Margot would be upset if she knew of my feelings for her brother.

"Angry? When have you ever seen me angry? My brother has struggled for so long and his difficulties have been my greatest regret. My only wish is that I could have done more for him. I have never seen him so happy as when he is with you. Whether or not you ever consummate your love is of no concern to me. That is between the two of you, but I know that my brother is unlikely to break the vows he took. Let me advise you that there are many ways to express love. Physical intimacy is only one way, and it may not be the best way for either of you now."

"I know this," I whispered.

"On our last visit, you asked Beau to teach you to read and write. Use the Tuesday visits for this. I am overwhelmed with work now, and it is often difficult for me to take so much time away, so I will not always accompany you on those visits." I nodded, catching the drift of her words. She wanted to give us time alone. Then she added quietly, "I leave my brother in your hands, Claire. Take good care of him."

On most Tuesdays, Margot did not accompany me on the visits to Beau. She packed up the food on my horse and began adding some extra items, a blanket, a new cloak that their mother had made for him and other necessities. Beau spent much of the time teaching me to read and write. I was smart, he said, and learned quickly. I had never expressed to him or Margot why I was so eager to learn, but it was for the purpose of being able to be of greater assistance to her. She had so many letters to write and answer, and the nun who had assisted her for so many years was suffering from failing eyesight. Within a few years I was able to relieve her of this work.

On many of those treasured Tuesdays, after organizing the food Margot had sent and spending time reading and writing, Beau and I would sit in the forest and I would listen as he played the lyre. At times I would dance, and at other times I would sit there quietly with closed eyes as the music lifted me into a beautiful realm. I often felt as if I had entered the world of the Druids, where the spirits and fairies and heavenly beings lived. Sometimes I thought that I was beginning to know the ways of the Druids, and it was Beau who was helping me gain this understanding. Then there were days when we simply talked, and I shared many things about my earlier life. Beau listened and offered insight about what I had gained from those experiences.

"All of life is a teaching," he said. "You have grown much stronger and determined through those experiences, Claire. It takes courage to leave an unhappy situation, but how can we gain courage if we are never tested?" I had never viewed my past suffering as tests, but now I was beginning to see it in this light; Beau was teaching me to leave behind my regrets. In fact, I was learning to be grateful for all that had come to me, even for witnessing the burning of Gabrielle, for he said that I would someday use that experience to bring benefit to others.

On one occasion, as we were seated in the forest listening to the bird sounds, I began to speak as Gabrielle had once spoken to me, about the life in the stones and trees and streams and everything around us. Beau smiled and replied that this was exactly what his mother had taught him when he was very young. "You and Margot and I, we are Druids, Claire. I see no contradiction between a Christian and a Druid; it is only the church that makes it so. But it is also true that in the same way as superstition has crept into the church, it has made its way into the Druid beliefs and practices as well. None of these religions as they are practiced today follow the true ancient ways; so much has been lost in the passage of time. It is up to us to take the best of each and to integrate whatever sounds true to us from both paths, not allowing ourselves to be boxed in and forced to call ourselves one thing or the other."

"I live in a convent but can still be a Druid," I remarked, amused at the irony. "I can still believe that the stones and trees speak to me and I to them, that the rivers are alive..."

"Of course!" exclaimed Beau. "Claire, we must learn to live without these identities that society imposes on us."

"You are something of a rebel, Beau," I commented admiringly. I had never met anyone quite like him before, who was so free of societal restrictions and so at peace with himself.

Then he added in a gentle, slow stepping tone, "And I can be a monk and you can be a nun, if that is the path you choose, and there can be a deep love between us. We mustn't deny or be afraid of that. Love in any form is a gift. We mustn't feel guilty about our feelings for one another. In the true spiritual life, there is no place for guilt, especially when it comes to love. How grateful I am to have you in my life." He was quiet for a few moments and then added softly, "But we also mustn't grow greedy and seek more than is given."

This was the first time he had expressed his feelings for me, and I gazed into his calming green eyes without replying. I had not taken the vows of a nun and the thought of becoming one was still very distasteful to me, but I was in love with a monk, and a serious monk at that. What was I to do?

Increasingly, the days apart from Beau were becoming painful for me as I waited eagerly all week for the few hours I could spend with him. More than anything it was his presence I yearned for, a presence that always brought spiritual upliftment, a presence that made me feel alive and vibrant and appreciative for every little thing. But the joy I felt by having him in my life was accompanied by a growing ache, and as I listened to his words, I wanted to say how much more of him I wanted and needed.

There were times when I desperately wanted to embrace him but didn't; when I wanted him to press his lips against mine but knew that he couldn't; when I longed to speak of my feelings but said nothing. One day as we were seated outside, those feelings nearly overcame me.

Sensing this, he took my hand and helped me to my feet, and said it was time for me to return to the convent before darkness set in.

We walked to where my horse was waiting. I hesitated before mounting and turning to face him began to speak, but he put his fingers over my lips and said, "Some things are too precious for words and are better left unsaid. I know your heart, Claire. That is enough. We must be grateful and happy for what we have and not seek what we cannot have."

I rode back to the convent that late afternoon, knowing that if I pressed for more, I might lose him. I was in a quandary unlike anything I had experienced before. Having Beau in my life brought me happiness, and yet the limitations imposed on the relationship brought me pain. Hastening to my room, I found Margot waiting for me, and before she could say a word, I tearfully rushed into her arms.

She seemed to know my sentiments because I heard her whisper as she hugged me and stroked my head. "Love is not an emotion. It is a state of being. One day you will know this. In the greater universal love, there is no sadness because there is no grasping. With the more limited love, there is both joy and pain, for they are two sides of the same coin. Expand your love and you will remain undisturbed, steady in your being, unshaken by whatever comes."

I heard her words, but I didn't understand them. I couldn't imagine that love of which she was speaking. She continued, "All separation is imagined. Think of the suffering of the goddess when she struggled for thousands of years to unite with her beloved, only to find that they were never apart. Why did she have to undergo that, when she is the Mother of the universe? To help us bear what little suffering we must endure. You will not have to wait thousands of years, my dear. Of that I am certain."

CHAPTER 22

The Unshaken State of Being

I had much to learn about love. I had thought of love as the fulfillment of desire, but what happens when desire can't be fulfilled and yet the bond between two people continues to grow? This was new territory for me, a territory I could not enter without great inner struggle. I continually had to resist impulses—simple things like brushing Beau's hair out of his face when strands would loosen from the string that held it in place, or wanting to press his hand against my cheek in a show of affection, or lay my head against his chest. I had to find other ways to express my feelings. When I was with Beau, he kept my mind on spiritual matters; he told me more stories of the god Shiva that he had heard from the wandering ascetic and gave me new understanding of events in the life of Jesus and what came after. He read to me his interpretations of the manuscripts he was translating, interpretations that never made their way into church canon and which I could barely understand. In this way, he calmed my desires and did not let them disrupt our relationship. I didn't know whether he struggled as much as I and thought it better not to ask.

I had been living in the convent for more than five years when one morning the monk who brought the week's food to Beau sent a message to Margot that her brother was seriously ill but was refusing to be moved to the monastery infirmary for care. I was with her when she received the message.

"The bishop is coming, and I am unable to leave here today, Claire. What should I do?" There was panic in her eyes, and for the first time she turned to me for counsel.

"You stay here. I will leave immediately, Margot," I hurried to assure her. "Help me gather food and medicine.

"Whatever he has may be contagious, Claire . . . ," she began.

I cut her off. "Whatever he has, I will also have. I must hurry and not delay."

When I arrived at the hut, Beau was burning with a high fever. He tried to tell me to leave so that I would not get sick, but I hushed him and prepared the medicine. "I am not going anywhere until you are fully healed," I said quietly. He slept most of the time, and I only roused him every few hours to feed him the medicine and soup I had brought with me from the convent. I had told Margot that I would spend the night at the hut and the night after, if need be, and she had consented. I slept sitting up by the side of his bed, waking at his every movement.

The next morning, his fever seemed to have abated a little, but I could see that his body was aching so that he could hardly move. I kept feeding him medicine and soup throughout the day. That afternoon I went into the forest searching for the plants that Gabrielle had told me would bring down fevers. How glad I was for all she had taught me. Fortunately, I was able to find what I was looking for. At night, his fever spiked again, and I fed him the medicine I had prepared. Once more I slept sitting up by his bedside, waking every hour or so to wipe his face. This went on for four days. Finally, his fever broke, and he was able to sit up and eat a small meal of solid food. I looked at his colorless face, which had always been slender but was now thinner from lack of eating, and I could only feel gratitude that I was able to tend to him. He might have died had I not been there, and the very possibility shook me to the core.

"Claire, you haven't slept in days," he said, looking at me affectionately.

Taking one of his hands and for the first time pressing it against my cheek, I murmured, "How could I sleep, knowing how sick you were?" After going through the illness with him, I felt freer to display my feelings.

Margot had come to see Beau the day after I arrived. It was during a brief respite when his fever had somewhat subsided, but I told her then how ill he was and asked if I could stay until he fully recovered. She nodded and thanked me for being there. Then she said, "I have told everyone that you have come down with the illness that is going around and that I have sent you home for a month to recover. So, there is no need to rush back, Claire. You can stay as long as need be to care for Beau."

A few days later, I began to feel feverish, and it was his turn to care for me, although he had not fully returned to health himself. Thankfully, my illness was less severe, and I recovered in a few days, although Beau's ill health lingered on for some time. There we were in that small hut caring for each other, and this allowed us to express our affection in a way we had not dared to do before. Despite our affliction, those days were happy ones because we were able to be with one another continually. He had moved to sleep on the floor when I became ill, giving me the bed, but once I recovered there was an awkwardness as to where to sleep.

Beau broke the awkwardness by saying, "Claire, I will remain on the floor, where I am quite comfortable. It is enough for me to have you here for this time, to see your face before I sleep and when I awake in the morning. I ask for nothing more." I understood then that he would keep to his monastic vow and so nodded. It became a comfortable situation. Later I realized the gift Margot had given me. For the rest of my life, I would treasure those four weeks where we could eat all our meals together, walk in the forest, and sit together in silence for hours on end, day after day, with no thought of having to rush back to the convent. We could together see the sun rise and set and bid each other goodnight. On occasion I would take his hand and he would smile at me. What comfort that was. What a precious time we had. At the end of the four weeks, he said to me, "We mustn't be greedy. We mustn't cause any trouble for Margot."

I realized how concerned he was that my time away might reflect badly on her, and I nodded, saying, "I know. It is time for me to return."

During my stay at the hut, every Friday morning I would go into the forest for a few hours alone so as not to be seen by the monk who brought Beau his weekly food, but one day I returned just as the monk was leaving and could not avoid meeting him outside the hut. Embarrassed, I quickly wrapped up my hair and explained that I was Sister Marguerite's assistant and that she had sent me to deliver medicine to Brother Bernard.

He smiled and replied, "Do you know how much the monks admire Brother Bernard?" I shook my head, surprised to hear this. "Many of us are aggrieved by the way the abbot treats him, but we can do nothing. It is his sister who has protected him all these years, by developing such a close relationship with the Bishop. Without her, he would have endured much more hardship. She is a strong woman and I have great admiration for her. I am glad that she has sent medicine for him, something the abbot did not think to do."

After returning to the convent, I strangely felt that Beau was with me more than ever before. Something had happened during that month together that had cemented our relationship, a deepening of the love. Beau never quite returned to full health. He developed a persistent cough that flared up whenever the weather was cold and damp, and none of the medicine I tried could eradicate it. I continued to visit on Tuesdays and my facility with reading and writing enabled me to be of great assistance to Margot. Aside from my worries about Beau and my constant yearning for more time with him, my life was moving smoothly along.

It was on a Tuesday after I had finished reading a translated manuscript that Beau had set before me that he surprised me by saying, "Margot wants you to succeed her when she is no longer able to take care of the convent. She has already spoken to the Bishop about this."

Turning my eyes away from the manuscript, I looked at him in utter surprise. Margot had never said a word to me, and this was the furthest thing from my mind. I had never even taken the vows of a nun. Both she and Beau knew of my continuing distaste for all things relating to the church. Seeing the shocked expression on my face, he continued with a slight smile. "There is nobody more capable than you, and nobody that Margot trusts more with the women. Their lives will be in the hands of whomever succeeds her."

"But why is she speaking of that now? She is in good health."

"Claire, I have passed the age of fifty, and Margot is not much behind. You are younger than us. She has to think of succession. Otherwise, the Bishop will choose and that would be a disaster for the nuns, and for you as well. Without Margot there, who will protect you?"

"I can't bear to think of either one of you leaving me," I blurted out, suddenly becoming despondent at the very thought.

"Friends part for a brief time and then meet again. It will be the same for us. Never doubt that." I didn't answer. "Margot has been hesitant to bring this up with you because she knows your feelings."

"It will mean taking the vows of a nun, something she has not asked me to do in all these years."

"For you to have a more visible role, it will be necessary. Nobody can force you. It must be your choice. But think of it as putting on an armor to shield the women from the assaults of the world and the church. Remember your friend, Gabrielle," he said quietly. "If not for Margot, some of the women in the convent might have suffered the same fate. You can be their protector. I know that my sister is most concerned about what will happen to the nuns after she is gone. You see how the convent is growing, how many women have come in search of peace, solace, and love. You can give them that love, Claire, because you know that you are a child of the Mother, and her love will flow through you. Perhaps in this place, at this time, becoming a nun and taking charge of the convent is the best way to serve her, and you have dedicated yourself to that service." I looked at him reluctantly, struggling internally. If this was how best to repay Margot for all she has done for me, how could I not do what she was asking? Seeing my hesitation, he added, "This is a decision you must make, Claire. I don't want to press you. I am only suggesting that this is one way to serve the Mother, by protecting her daughters. Think about it. You don't have to decide now."

"Will anything change between us if I take the vows of a nun?" I asked him hesitantly.

He chuckled. "What can change? I have taken the vows of a monk, and we have both accepted the limitations imposed by that."

Because Beau asked this of me, in my heart I knew I would accept this fate and consent to it, but I still hadn't made peace with it. Margot had done so much to protect Beau over the years. How could he not try to ease her concerns over this matter? The devotion between this brother and sister often moved me to the point of tears. How rare was such sibling care.

Although while sitting with Beau I had made my decision, it took me many days of internal debate to fulfil what I had decided to do. A week later, before retiring for the night, I went to find Margot in her room, going through a pile of correspondence. As soon as I entered, I noticed her worn look and signs of extreme fatigue on her face. The demands on her were great these days. "Margot, why are you working at this late hour? You should let me take care of the letters tomorrow."

Instead of answering, she asked in a tired voice, "Why are you here, Claire, so late at night? You should be resting."

"I am here to ask you to officially ordain me as a nun," I replied in a determined voice.

She laughed softly. "You have already taken the vows, have you not?" I looked at her questioningly. "In the chapel that Christmas eve some years ago. You took a vow to serve the Great Mother, didn't you? You have given your life to her, haven't you?"

"Don't I need something more formal?"

"If that is what you want. Get down on your knees, Claire, and make your vows."

Dropping to my knees, I looked up at her and said quietly, "I vow to offer my life as a servant of the Universal Mother and to care for these nuns, who are her daughters sent by her into our care. I will protect them with my life and love them as you have taught me, Sister Marguerite. My hope is that they will find solace in love for Jesus and in love for the Great Mother. It is the same."

"Now stand up, Claire. You are officially nun Sister Claire. Do you feel any different?" I shook my head. She laughed and said, "The Church makes such a fuss over this. What nonsense, but now I don't have to worry about the Bishop. I told him long ago that you were ordained because I considered it so. I will train you to take over more of my responsibilities so that I can step back. I am tired, Claire, so very tired. You have come to me at just the right time."

That night in bed, I wondered at the irony of my life. I had once vowed never to step inside a church, and I had once fled from priests; now I would have to deal with both. I, a Druid, would become head of a convent. I laughed out loud and then turned over and went to sleep.

A few Tuesdays later, Margot and I went together to visit Beau. As we were sitting in his hut, Margot suddenly turned to her brother and asked, "Beau, if you could do it all over again, what would you do differently?"

He was thoughtful for a moment and then replied, "Perhaps I would become a trader and travel the world and meet the sages from various places. I would go to that kingdom called Kashmir and learn about that god called Shiva."

"What else?" she asked.

"I have wanted to have a son. That desire has never left me. If I had a son, I would take him to see the world, and I would ensure that he had the best education possible. I would give him every opportunity and make every sacrifice for his sake." He was quiet for a few moments and then asked Margot what she would do differently. She simply shook her head and replied, "Wherever she places me is where I want to be. I have no other desire." It was my turn next, and Margot and Beau waited expectantly.

At first, I didn't speak, but when Margot prodded me, I replied thoughtfully, "I would be born in a place where women don't have to hide behind walls to find their freedom, where they could openly declare their love for the goddess and speak of the spirits that inhabit the forests and rivers. And . . ." I didn't finish the sentence. Beau and Margot continued to watch me. "I would give Beau the son he wanted. That would make me very happy." We were all quiet for a few moments and then I broke the silence by saying, "But this is all speculation, isn't it?"

"Perhaps not," replied Beau quietly. "Perhaps we are creating our future."

"Future?" I asked. "What future? We are all getting old now, aren't we?"

They didn't answer, but I saw Beau and Margot exchange glances and smile.

Beau didn't live much longer after that. It was as if he had lived just long enough to help Margot pass on the responsibility of the convent to me. During his last weeks, Margot sent me to stay with him, telling me that she would make some excuse for my absence. Once again, I was able to care for him as I had always wanted to do. This enabled me to be with him when he died, but I can't say that I didn't tearfully cling to his hand and plead with him not to leave me. In all that time, I hadn't learned to love without clinging. But he was free of clinging. With a smile, he told me that we had already laid the foundation for the future. I saw no future, but he did, and this left me wondering for the rest of my days. His last words to me were, "You must be unshakable, Claire, firm in your being."

"I don't know how to be that," I whispered to him, but he smiled back, a faint almost imperceptible smile.

As I sat in the hut watching him fade from life, I thought to myself, a love that could not complete itself was yet a complete love, of a deeper nature than I could have imagined, one that truly nourished my soul. My early life had been filled with such difficulties, but it had in the end brought me to Beau, and how grateful I was. Without a doubt I would go through it all again, and much more, if it meant finding him. Then I thought of that great Goddess, who had endured so many thousands of years of the harshest austerities to realize her union with her beloved. In view of that, how minor are our human challenges.

For months after Beau's passing, a cloud of dejection hung over me, and I tried to hide it by throwing myself into the work of overseeing the convent. Margot had had several bouts of ill health, one after another, and I was surprised one day when she told me that the two of us were going on an outing.

"Where to?" I asked, knowing that she was trying to cheer me up.

"It's a surprise," she replied, her weary eyes lighting up.

We rode for several hours before we came to a village that seemed vaguely familiar. Margot seemed to know exactly where she wanted to go and led me down a narrow path toward a small farmhouse. A girl was playing outside, as her mother, seated nearby, watched her.

"Here we are," Margot said cheerfully as she alighted from her horse.

I now knew exactly where we were, but I was too shocked to speak or to get off the horse. Before me stood the farmhouse where I had left my daughter after giving birth, and the girl in front of the house would then be that very daughter, now fourteen years old.

Walking over to me, Margot stood by the side of my horse and said very quietly, "Don't you want to see what has become of her."

"Margot," I murmured, my eyes brimming with tears. "How did you know where to find her."

"Come," she said without answering. Climbing down from the horse, I followed as she approached the woman. Seeing us dressed in the garb of nuns, she hurried to greet us. Margot explained that we had been riding for hours and in need of water. Could she offer us a drink? Eagerly she invited us into the home and asked us to join the family for the noon meal. Once inside, she introduced her husband and her daughter, who was named Clara. The girl was quite pretty, with long golden hair woven into two neat braids, tied by colorful ribbons. She was neatly dressed in a colorful floral skirt and top. The farmhouse inside was well decorated, leading me to believe they had a comfortable life.

After the family meal, Margot played with the child while the mother took me aside and told me that an angel had left the baby for them weeks after her birth at Christmas time. "For years, every month, we receive a secret gift of money to help care for Clara, so we have been able to give her the best," she explained. "We don't know who sends the money, but it makes us think that she is a blessed child. And it is true. She is such a cheerful, smart girl, so curious, so interested in learning, so quick to pick up on things. We don't know where she got that from."

"She is a beautiful child, and I believe there is an angel looking out for her," I replied, greatly moved by the scene. I knew immediately that Margot was that angel. As I gazed at the fair-haired girl, I thought how much like her father she was—so clear eyed, so well-spoken and intelligent, just like him. Controlling my emotions, I requested, "When it is time for marriage, let her choose her husband. Let it be a marriage of love. She deserves that."

The mother smiled and replied, "My husband says the same thing."

We stayed for several hours with the family and then took our leave. Before getting back onto our horses, I looked at Margot and asked, "Are you supporting them with the money your mother left you?"

She seemed embarrassed that I had discovered this. "How can I not help a sister when I have the means to?" she replied, turning her eyes away as she mounted her horse.

On the ride back to the convent, I thought about what Margot had done. I had to admit that I had not thought much about the child since my arrival at the convent, but Margot hadn't forgotten that I had given birth. Somehow, she had tracked down the child, and I realized that there was a purpose to our visit. Margot wanted me to stay in touch with the family when she was no longer here. I was able to see Clara twice more, at her wedding and then again after the birth of her first child.

A few days after going to the village to see my daughter, I went to Margot's room. She had been unwell and was resting. Getting up from her bed, she went over to her writing table and from a drawer took out a folded piece of paper and handed it to me.

"What is this?" I asked.

"It is the note that fell from your pouch when you first arrived here."

The note was addressed to Sister Marguerite and read: "Her name is Claire and I place her in your hands. I know you will care for her. She has just given birth. Here is where her daughter lives. I leave the rest to you." On the bottom of the page was a map with the name of the village. But the note was unsigned.

"Somehow, I knew that whoever wrote this note was connected to the dream I had before you arrived," explained Margot.

"You saved it all this time?" I murmured, my voice tinged with emotion.

"I assumed it was written by the woman who had brought you here, and I thought she must have meant a great deal to you, but you never spoke of her and so I never asked. I saved this, thinking perhaps someday you might want to see the note."

"Her name was Catherine. She was a stranger sent by the goddess to save my life. I would have died without her."

"Then I am most grateful to her," she replied with a smile.

I was so touched by her thoughtfulness that I could not help but blurt out, "Margot, how I wish I could be like you."

"I wouldn't want you to be like me," she replied, casting me a loving look. "I want you to be like you."

"You know everyone's need before they even know it themselves. It is as if you can see into their souls. How can I ever repay you for all you have done?"

"You have more than repaid me. You are taking over this place and will soon be in charge, and I know that is the last thing in the world you wanted to do. I am well aware of that."

I chuckled. "You are right. I am doing it for you and for Beau."

"Don't do it for us, Claire. Do it for the women. Learn to love them as you have loved us. I once asked you what it means to follow the way of the goddess. That is the way to follow her."

A year or so later, Margot passed very peacefully in the night. It had been more than fifteen years since my arrival, and I felt as if I had become a completely different person. I was no longer the fearful young girl Claire who kept running away, for I had learned that there was no place to run to. As Stefan had once told me at a time when I couldn't hear it, one has to stand and face one's fear. That is the only way to overcome it.

I never made peace with the church or the priests who sought to impose their version of truth on others. I knew I would not forgive an institution that ripped away the lives of women, condoning their sacrifice. The image of Gabrielle burning no longer haunted me, but it was also not to be forgotten. Over time, the resolve that grew in me, with Margot's help, was to protect women from those who sought to control their lives. Ironically, I found myself as the head of an organization, part of an institution against which I had fought all my life.

In the years left to me I never made a decision or acted without first considering what Margot would do. I saw myself as standing in for her, knowing it was her work that I was completing. She was continuing to oversee the convent through me. How often in my remaining years did I step back and laugh to myself at the strange twist of fate that had brought me to that position.

I was never able to resolve the question of where to find the goddess. How many times Beau had told me to look inside, but sometimes the most obvious place is the one most obscured. Remembering Margot's words to me in her last days, and not knowing where else to turn, I sought to find the Great Mother in the faces of the women who came seeking a place of refuge, trying to treat them as if they were her, hoping that someday she would reveal to me her true self. I do not know if I was successful in my care for the women as I did not have the patience or sense of self-sacrifice that Margot had. My last years were lonely ones, as I never truly reconciled myself to institutional life. Often, I doubted myself, especially when the women came to me for spiritual counsel. How could I guide them when I did not have the answers myself and knew I could not share with them my true beliefs? The one thing I could do was to give them freedom, not impose on them any church doctrine. They could believe what they wanted and pursue the practices they felt beneficial. This was the least I could offer.

I often wondered what Beau meant at the end of his life when he began to speak of a future. I had no knowledge of what came after this life, but I knew that whatever it was, it would include Beau, and this is what brought me peace in the end.

CHAPTER 23

Past and Present

Weeks or perhaps months sped by, I hardly knew, since I was living in a timeless realm where past and present converged. My outer life had become a mostly silent one, but the interior space was filled with people and conversations unseen and unheard by the exterior world as the memories splashed across the screen of my mind. I went through the motions of daily life: I ate the food that Ama-la prepared, meditated, and slept, hardly leaving the hut except for the morning bath—all the while totally engrossed in that other time. I left the present reality at the door to my inner world. When I witnessed the scene of Beau dying, I was right there with him. I cried out and could not stop myself from weeping, heaving, and sobbing. Ama-la's arms were around me, holding me gently. She didn't speak. She held me until the crying stopped, then released me and I returned to meditation. Finally, when I saw the end of that life, I opened my eyes to the present. Emerging from meditation one evening, I asked Ama-la if I could help her prepare the evening meal. She welcomed my offer and together we began chopping vegetables.

"I know that Beau was reborn as my husband Yeshe Dorje," I said quietly as I chopped away. "So why was I crying? Why did I experience such pain at his loss?" I paused and glanced at her from across the table. I never needed to explain to Ama-la what I was experiencing. It seemed that whatever I saw, she saw as well.

"The one who cried was not Padma Tshomo but Claire, who didn't know that a short while later, in her next birth, she would marry the man she loved and they would have a happy married life together, with many children. She would give him the son he so wanted, a very special son, and he would be able to give that son the education of which he dreamed."

"Who was that man Jesus?" I asked, pensively. "I have heard of the Christian religion, but don't know much about it."

"In Buddhist terms you would say he is the Buddha of Compassion," she replied gently. "And yes, there are still Druids, hidden away, but mostly they are disappearing as Christianity takes hold over that whole region."

"He is also said to be somehow related to the god Shiva, isn't he?" She nodded. "Yeshe once spoke to me of Shiva, but he seemed to imply that Shiva is the totality of all that is. In his younger days Yeshe was able to visit the Kingdom of Kashmir and had a powerful experience of Shiva. It was the ascetic who had once visited Beau who implanted in his mind that wish. So many desires from his previous birth have been fulfilled," I stopped speaking and then added thoughtfully, "There are so many different names for the gods, aren't there?"

She laughed a quiet, gentle laugh. "Don't we all have many names. And yes, all desires are fulfilled at one time or another. A form of the one called Lord Shiva is said to abide at Mount Tise, also called Mount Kailash by his devotees. His consort Parvati is said to be connected to Lake Manasarovar, also known as Tsho Mapham. Some say Palden Lhamo is an emanation of Parvati. Between Gyagar and Böd there are many close connections, a long and ancient history."

"Who were the Druids?" I asked.

"They were the people who followed the old ways in that part of the world. Many of their ancient practices and beliefs are much like Bon. There was a time when there were no boundaries or borders, and the wise sages from many regions all around earth conversed with one another and shared wisdom. That is why we find so many similarities among the ancient traditions.

"Because of the landscape of Böd, the people here find their gods and goddesses in the mountains and lakes. The region where the Druids live is filled with ancient forests and that is where they find their deities. They live close to the forces of nature and conduct rituals and ceremonies to maintain the harmony and balance of those forces. But over time, much knowledge has been lost, and the Druids began to disappear, existing only in secret pockets as the newer religion began to spread. Like in Böd, there was tension between the new and the old and few were able to integrate the wisdom of both. Superstition and rigid belief find a way into all religions, Bumo, and that is why one has to go deep inside to find the answers. The greatest masters don't preach doctrine but show you how to search internally to pierce illusions and find what is."

I was beginning to understand Ama-la's words, and my excursions into the life of Claire were beginning to shed new light on my current life. I thought much of Yeshe in the days that followed, realizing what a happy life we had had together and feeling much gratitude for it. No wonder he loved to travel, I realized one day. In his past birth, he had been confined to a hut and could only engage in journeys of the mind. It was also no surprise that he remained something of a rebel, refusing to become a monk as his parents had wanted. But he must have overcome that resistance because he encouraged our son to enter the monastery; yet it was a different kind of monastery where Tenzin could travel and engage with sages of other places. These ruminations about Yeshe helped to catapult me back into the present.

At times my mind also reverted to Stefan. After leaving him in Praha, Claire never saw him again, but she often thought of him and wondered if he was happy, fulfilling the mission he had set for himself. One day I asked Ama-la what had happened to him.

She didn't answer right away, but when I persisted, she finally revealed, "A few years after you left, he married and was able to accomplish much. Had he fled with you, he would not have been able to fulfill his dharma."

"He had a happy life then. I am glad," I murmured and then asked somewhat sheepishly, "Who did he marry?"

She smiled. "Why do you need to know that, Bumo?" And she would say no more.

In the days that followed, I thought of Margot's counsel to me about the teaching of humiliation. Bhasundara had told me something similar when I mentioned how humiliated I felt for giving all the wealth Yeshe left me to Zerdan. She had responded, "At one time or another we all must experience the descent into darkness. Humiliation awakens compassion, and it cuts down the ego. It is a great teaching." So, I had to experience that again in this life, I thought. I was beginning to see how the inner struggles Claire underwent had in many ways prepared me for my current life. Claire's search for the goddess fed into my search, a search which had not ended.

The next weeks were a time of return for me. I was able to move around more, taking walks outside and talking with Ama-la, but in the quiet moments I continued to review and relive many of the scenes I had experienced in meditation and connect them to my current life. I felt sentimental about the time I had spent time with Beau, and I relived the tender moments with him again and again, connecting them to scenes of my life with Yeshe, which were also mere memories now. Beau had taught Claire to read and write and interpreted for her sections from manuscripts he was translating. Yeshe had loved to tell me stories of Buddhist masters and to connect them to Bon. Both lived beyond the doctrines of their tradition and found their knowledge through their own inner search. Both had lived disciplined lives, something that I could not emulate in either of my births. Claire's desires that couldn't be fulfilled with Beau and that had caused her pain were completely satisfied with Yeshe. The intimate part of my life with him had been most fulfilling. It seemed that one life took off where the previous life ended and continued what had been begun. But what of Jacque and Zerdan? I still didn't understand that relationship.

"You continue to identify with the personality of Claire, and that is why you haven't been able to let go yet," Ama-la explained as she told me to be patient with myself. "That identity will soon dissipate because you are no longer her."

Another day she found me seated outside reliving a scene from the past and quietly counseled me, "It is time to close the door on the life of Claire and return to the life of Padma Tshomo. It is in this life now that you must do your work."

Nearly two years had passed since my arrival, and one day it occurred to me that her husband had never come, and I began to wonder if there was a husband.

"Ama-la when I first arrived, you said that your husband would soon come. But he hasn't come in all this time."

"He will come soon," she replied simply.

Instead of doubting her, I asked, "What does soon mean to you?" She laughed without replying. "I don't feel ready to return to my life," I murmured, "and so I will wait for him."

"You are not ready yet, but you soon will be."

I had come to realize that the word 'soon' meant different things to us. But I was content to remain with Ama-la and not seek to see anything further of my past. It was enough to reflect on what I had seen, and to try to understand how the past had shaped the present; how the influence of Gabrielle had brought me to the mother who gave birth to me in my current life; how my search for the goddess had led me to Dalha, and how the restrictions of institutional life and my affinity with the Druids had led me to identify so strongly and openly as a Bonpo. In the past I had had to hide my Druid affiliation, but in my current life I was able to proudly proclaim my Bon beliefs.

"Ama-la, I have seen many things, but still I haven't found the origin of Jacque's anger toward me or the source of Zerdan's power over me. Perhaps I don't need to know that anymore, I said to her one day as we were walking.

"To understand that, you will have to go back further in time."

"I don't need to. I don't really want to see anymore. The experience of revisiting an earlier life is an exhausting one. I don't know that I can emotionally manage another return to the past. I have shed so many tears these few months; first it was Gabrielle's death, then leaving Stefan, and finally the loss of Beau and Margot. And the fear of Jacque was powerful. I experienced all of that already when I lived as Claire, and I have had to go through it all again."

"That is why life is constructed in such a way that people do not remember. For most it is not necessary or useful to relive a life that has already been lived. But you have sought answers. Deep inside, you already know the cause of your troubled relationship with that soul who has taken birth as Zerdan. Whether it comes into your consciousness now or not is up to you."

"I don't really want to see any more. I will never meet him again, so that relationship is done."

"Not quite done," she replied firmly. "If you don't resolve the problem, it will emerge again, if not in this life, then another. Do you think he will let go of you so easily?" I was quiet. "By seeing your past, you have freed yourself from the frightening memory of witnessing your friend Gabrielle being burned alive. You will never have that nightmare again. You have also come to appreciate your relationship with Yeshe in a new way, haven't you?" I nodded. "And you understand that your love for the goddess has been with you for a long time, hasn't it?" Again, I nodded. "Through your recollections, you have recalled profound teachings about love that we need to hear in every lifetime. Was that not worth the tears?" Once more, I nodded. She smiled. "Don't worry. Whatever visions you see will be for your healing and growth. I am here to help you through it, and there is a deeper purpose to my presence, which you will soon understand." Then she asked, "Have you thought about Catherine? You have known her before."

"She must have been very dear to me in an earlier life because we became close so quickly. She seemed to know and understand me so well."

She nodded and for the first time offered information that I hadn't discovered on my own. "Just before your life as Claire, you were born in the Duchy of Normandy, married to a warrior, called a knight, of the great King William, who conquered England and firmly established Christianity there. You went with the knights to England and gave birth to a very special daughter, who died before she reached the age of twenty. She was both very devoted to the one called Jesus and to the goddess, finding much affinity with the wisdom of the Druids. She was guided by William to help people integrate the old and newer religions, which was William's work in that life.

"Most people saw William only as a powerful knight who became king and they didn't know of his inner work. That daughter of yours walked through the villages and found people who were secretly worshipping the goddess. She tried to help them integrate the wisdom of the ancient Celtic people with the teachings of the newer religion. In many ways, the ancient beliefs and practices had become distorted and had devolved into superstition, with unsound practices like animal sacrifice. She sought a return to the higher Celtic wisdom and to show that it was compatible with the teachings of Jesus. In that life, you began to feel the tension between two streams of knowledge, feeling them to be different although their source is the same; you felt a contradiction between them where there is none.

"That daughter was dearer to you than life. Few understood her and you had to protect her against those who thought her mentally unfit. She was different from the others, so absorbed was she in the spiritual world and indifferent to material matters. In your next life, you were born as Claire, and she came to you as Catherine in your time of greatest need. Had she not appeared, Claire would have died during the pregnancy because she had lost the will to live. Remembering the love that the mother of her previous birth had once showered upon her, she helped Claire to survive the birth and find her way to the place she was destined for.

"Before your life in England, you lived in the Tang Empire (China) as a Daoist woman poet named Shu, married to a renowned poet. You had a teacher, whom you called Shifu, and Margot is the rebirth of one of the Daoist nuns in her center, where you spent much time. Her name was Ying and the two of you became the closest of sisters. Although you never became a Daoist nun, later in life, you helped her manage the center, which is why, without knowing the past, she intuitively had such confidence in you and trusted only you to succeed her. You both had helped each other in that earlier life, and in the life you have recently recalled. Do you see why she had such confidence in you and wanted you to supervise the nuns after she departed?"

"I also lived in the Tang Empire," I mused. "I am not surprised, not at all. When Yeshe invited me to go along with him and Tenzin to visit the Great Song, which came after the demise of the Tang Dynasty, I felt strongly not to go, having a sense that I already had been there. It was a place familiar to me and I didn't feel the need to see it again, but when Tenzin returned, he often recited Tang poetry in the Han language. Although I didn't understand the words, I loved to hear him recite the poems."

"The story of that life is a tale unto itself that you don't need to revisit now. Bumo, this is the third life in which you have felt torn between two traditions, resisting one while clinging to the other, struggling to reconcile them. In England, the tension you experienced was between the older Celtic ways, where they worshipped the goddess, and Christianity, which suppressed that worship. In the life of Claire, this conflict again erupted, and your intense resistance to the church became almost an abhorrence because you were exposed to a false understanding of those teachings. Then again in your current life, you have struggled to integrate what you believe to be the different Bon and Buddhist views. I believe this tension has been resolved now." She looked at me with a playful smile.

For many days, I thought about what she had said. Although I didn't remember anything of the life in England, I understood what Ama-la was saying about the tension between two traditions, something I had felt since early childhood when I proudly declared to the rest of my family that I was a Bonpo, not a Buddhist. Wasn't that the same sentiment that Claire had felt? Now I recognized how, over the course of my life and my marriage to Yeshe, this tension had dissipated, and I no longer felt the need to define who I was and what I believed.

A few days later, Ama-la suggested that we take a ride along the Yarlung Valley. Coming to a place not far from the turn off to Samye Monastery, she stopped. "Why are we here?" I asked, anxiously, hoping we were not going to ride all the way to the monastery. I assumed that my son Tenzin was still away in the Song Empire, but I didn't want to chance running into the Abbot or any of the other monks.

"I wanted to show you this place." She pointed in the direction that led to the monastery.

"What is special about it?" It looked no different than any other part of the valley.

"Guru Rinpoche came here during the time when he was meditating to subdue the unruly spirits. There is a story about that time. After meditation, one day he came out of the cave. When he began to walk along the valley, he noticed a cow following him. After some time of walking, he turned around and told the cow to go back to where it had come from. Heeding his words, the cow walked up to a boulder and entered it, disappearing. As soon as he did, the word 'Ma' appeared on the boulder. It is still there, but we won't ride all the way up to see it. When he saw the letters appear, Guru Rinpoche knew that a monastery must be built on that spot. Then he heard the voice of his consort Yeshe Tsogyal, who had not yet taken birth, telling him to create a place for women. To emphasize her message, she sent her dakini daughters to dance around him. That is when he decided to build a monastery for women. Do you see that monastery in the distance?"

I looked around but couldn't see anything. "There is nothing there, Ama-la. Just brush and rocks, lots of rocks."

She smiled and replied quietly. "You must look into the future to see it, Bumo. It is already created in the ethers but has not materialized yet. It will one day. It may be fifty, or a hundred or a thousand years, but it will be built because Guru Rinpoche has decreed it. The timing depends on the readiness of men. Just as one can see the past, one can also expand one's vision to see the future." With those words, she turned around her horse and began riding back to our small hut perched on a low cliff above the valley.

The weeks passed and over time I was able to assimilate my memories as they receded into pockets of my mind, much as memories from childhood do. Still, on occasion, I would find myself speaking with Beau or with Yeshe, whom I felt closer to than ever before. Remembering his last words to me before he left for Amdo—that he would find me again—I thought to myself, when Beau died, it wasn't the end, and Yeshe's passing is also not the end. We have a future ahead of us.

I had for the most part put to rest the life of Claire and was settling into a peaceful state of mind when memories were again stirred, and I felt myself being pulled back through the vortex of time to a far older era. I tried to resist, as intuitively I knew the memories would be painful, but the pull was too strong; there was nothing I could do to retain my hold on the present. I was back in the Han Dynasty (3rd century China) as it was collapsing, not a peaceful time by any means, but one defined by intense competition and fighting between ambitious warlords. It was there in that troublesome mix that I was to find the source of my conflict with the one I knew as Zerdan.

CHAPTER 24

Healing an Ancient Sorrow

My Daoist family was among a small group who had left their homes in an effort to create an ideal state founded on the principles of Daoism, a state called Hanning. But very quickly, the vision that had inspired us was compromised by ambitious people seeking their own advancement, my husband being one of them. He had secretly learned to control people and events through sorcery, and he instilled fear in me. The situation at home became tense and I repeatedly sought refuge in the forest cottage of my grandfather, whom I called Yeye, one of the last of the old Daoist sages of our community.

Thoughts of fleeing entered my mind, but I had two children. The younger one, a boy, had been ripped from my arms at an early age by his father, who would not let me nurse him, saying a son should not be dependent on his mother. As an infant, when he would cry in the night, his father would lock his door and not let me go to him no matter how much I pleaded. Eventually, I learned to unlock the door quietly when my husband was sleeping and creep into my son's bed, which was the only time I could hug him, but even in his sleep he would turn away from me. It was a struggle from the start to have a normal relationship with this son.

As he grew older, he increasingly gravitated toward his father and his sorcerer ways, finding fault with me over small matters, and asking all sorts of questions of his father about how to contact spirits. The breakdown in our relationship, or the lack of one, was a source of great pain. When I discovered the sorcery of my husband, he used my son to get back at me, telling this young boy that I was a sorcerer who sought to harm our family, and that he, the father, was the only one who could protect us.

"Your mother will be the cause of Hanning's downfall, inflicting immeasurable harm on the family and the whole community if she doesn't begin to obey me," he told the boy. It was during one emotional outburst, a painful exchange, that I learned the degree to which my husband had turned this child against me by convincing him that I was the evil one. My daughter understood the true situation, but not this son. I had uncovered my husband's harmful occult practices, including performing animal sacrifices, which were forbidden in the community, and my discovery had aroused his wrath. When he realized that I was aware of his actions, he threatened me, and in a state of panic, I fled, taking my son and daughter to Yeye's cottage in the woods. But he tracked me down and took the children away. As we were forcibly parting, I saw anger, near hatred, in my son's eyes, as if to say that I was responsible for breaking up the family. That look was to haunt me for the rest of my life.

That night I sat with Yeye under a bright moon, distraught, believing that if I returned to my husband, he would kill me and my children would lose their mother. If I ran far away, as I longed to do, I would never see my children again, and they would also lose their mother. Either way, my children would suffer loss. Overcome by fear, I decided to flee. My decision, once taken, would not be able to be undone. Yeye comforted me in the night, speaking of the Goddess of the Moon, a goddess he said that I would one day come to know. "If you turn to her, she will guide and protect you," he quietly counseled.

"Yeye, what will happen to my children?" I asked fearfully as we sat there in the forest, bathing in the moon's quiet light.

He was silent and didn't respond at first, but when I prodded, he revealed something of their future. Your daughter does not have a strong relationship with her father. In fact, like you she fears him, and she has a deep connection with you. She is a true Daoist. When she comes of age, she will leave her father and begin her search for you, but she will not find you in this life, and that is necessary for her growth. When conditions are right in a future life, she will be born again to you. What is left undone will be completed at that time. Your son is a different matter. His spirit is aligned with his father, and he will seek powers through sorcery. His anger toward you will not be abated in this life. I am afraid you will have to meet him again to help him resolve his anger. But it is not your fault, Chunhua. You are not to blame for his lack of discernment, for what will become his obsession with power. Each person has a choice as to how to live, and we ourselves determine our future by the choices we make. He will have a rough road ahead and suffer many insecurities. I saw this in his personality from a young age, but when the two of you do meet again, I hope it is at a time when you won't fear him, when you will have gained enough strength in yourself so that you can help him overcome anger and hatred.

"I have to take some responsibility for this," he confessed, "because I did not oppose your marriage strongly enough. And now I am not discouraging you from fleeing. My own emotions have gotten in the way. I can't bear to see my dear granddaughter further hurt by that man, your husband, even if it means in some way you will have to make it up to your children in the future." Looking into my eyes, he said, "When the time arrives, Chunhua, for you to make peace with this son of yours, I will come to you. No matter where I am in the universe, I will come to you."

Yeye's words brought me little comfort. My whole being trembled at the thought of returning to my husband, something I knew I simply could not do. Overcome by fear, I fled from our community, led away by Yeye's close student Yu Yan, who accompanied me to a safe place far from Hanning. The image of my son's eyes filled with anger and rage never left me, and I never healed from the grief of losing my children. Yu Yan became the hidden gift my grandfather gave me. His words, spoken through her, kept his presence with me as a guiding hand, although I didn't see him again in that life. She was a solitary, quiet woman and we never developed the close friendship I had hoped for, but she continually sought to awake in me a relationship with the Goddess of the Moon, the One she adored.

Years later, sensing my ongoing sorrow, Yu Yan offered to go look for my family. Although no longer young, she undertook the long journey back to where many people from Hanning were now living after its fall and takeover by the war lord Cao Cao. Returning, she told me what she had discovered; my daughter had left home when she came of age to search for me, but she was evasive about my son. One afternoon, as I was returning from a walk in the forest, I overheard her speaking to a neighbor who had come to bring us some food. When this woman asked about the fate of the people who had lived in Hanning, Yu Yan described the condition of some of the leaders. Then she repeated what she had told me about my daughter. After a pause, she added, "Chunhua's son is now well known in that community as someone pursuing occult powers. Without revealing my identity, I spoke with him, and he told me that his father, before his death, had made him vow to take revenge, and that when he does find his mother, whenever that will be, he will make her pay for what she has done. He blames her for the breakup of the family, and even for the fall of Hanning. Nothing I said could dissuade him. He spoke with such conviction and certainty. It made me sad. Fortunately, he will never find us here and so Chunhua is safe."

Her words, not meant for my ears, created such a disturbance in me that fear of my husband now turned into fear of my son. What had possessed him? Why had he turned so against me? I never found the answer to those questions. With the death of that body, the unresolved relationship with this child submerged below the surface of my mind. The ocean of time kept moving, and four lifetimes later, I met him again in the form of Jacque when I was born as Claire. In that life, I fled not from his father, but from him.

"So that is how it is," I murmured to Ama-la days after I had experienced a brief memory of leaving my children behind during the time of Hanning. We were sitting outside, relishing the heat of the sun, as we were now in the warmer months. Taking a deep breath, I relayed to her what I had seen. "Zerdan was that son of mine. That is why I have not been able to be truly angry at him, out of guilt. I think I pushed my anger onto Lobsang, blaming him for what has become of me." After a few minutes of quiet, I sighed and commented sadly, "I abandoned my children. What kind of mother would do that? I should have remained even if it meant death."

A subtle shadow momentarily flickered across Ama-la's face, like a faint dewdrop of sorrow. Had I not been so attuned to her, I would not have noticed, and I wondered if I had said something amiss. But it quickly passed, leaving me to believe I had imagined it.

"It was not your abandonment that sent him in the wrong direction, although that was the excuse he told himself," she replied in a sympathetic tone. "Like his father at that time, he thirsted for power to make himself feel important. Underneath was a deep insecurity that came from an earlier life, which had nothing to do with you. We are not responsible for the decisions our children make. But you did abandon your children and had to pay the price. That daughter was born to you again as a daughter when you lived in the Tang Empire as the poet Shu, two lifetimes later, and she was very bonded to you. That son had several lives where he quested for power in one way of another, but he didn't gain much occult power until his birth as Zerdan, when he found a tantric teacher who could give him what he wanted. He wasn't interested in truth, but rather in manipulating the world to gain what he desired. More than anything he wanted to be recognized as more than he is.

"When he was born as your stepson Jacque, you fled from him out of fear that he would kill you, unconsciously repeating behavior that had developed during your last association with him. The old pattern of fear resurfaced. Still seeking control over people, he became a priest because in that society this was a position of power. When he was born as the one called Zerdan, as soon as he came into a position of power, he sought you unconsciously, not remembering the past. In his mind, it was because you were the wife of Yeshe Dorje and would give him credibility, and you had a brilliant son, of whom you were so protective. He found you, drew you to him, and took away everything you had, leaving you destitute. That was his revenge for your abandonment. See how differently your two children from that time responded. Love for you increased in your daughter and she didn't give up until she found you. Your son fell into the trap of anger, a trap that ensnares too many people.

"You have repaid the debt you owed him, but you still fear him. The guilt over once having abandoned your children, hidden within you, weakened you and allowed him to take over your mind. That is why you could never explain any of this to your family, or even to yourself. Lying dormant was a guilt of which you were not aware."

"What possessed him?"

Ama-la smiled and looked off reflectively. "What brings people to anger?" she asked as she shook her head. "Extreme anger is a demonic energy, which opens the door for distortions to take over the mind so that one can no longer distinguish right from wrong. It leads to the desire to possess, unsatiated greed, crudeness, indifference to others, all the negative emotions. They are the demonic forces that people unleash on the world."

I was thoughtful for a few moments and then said, "I feel sorry for him now. I never wanted to hurt him. I only wanted to be free. But I also don't want him to do to others what he has done to me."

"You have freed yourself of fear. Now you must rid yourself of guilt and anger. Then you will truly be free."

"Anger? I have no anger towards him," I muttered almost inaudibly.

Looking at me fondly, Ama-la chuckled and asked in an amused tone, "Is that so?" I didn't answer. She went on. "Let me tell you a story of something that happened long ago. It is a complicated story, but I will make it simple and brief. Once a powerful being took birth in the eastern region of what is now Gyagar. He was a king and conquered many of the surrounding kingdoms. In his early life he had undergone great austerities and received a boon, a blessing. The blessing that he asked for was that he could not be killed by anybody except his mother. It was a very strange boon to request, but he knew what he was doing. As soon as he received this boon, he killed his mother and thought that he was now immortal.

"What he didn't realize was that a mother from a past birth could kill him. As it happened, a great soul named Krishna had taken birth also in Gyagar, an incarnation of a powerful god called Narayan, who is akin to Shiva. One of his wives had been the mother of this demonic king in a past birth, but she herself was not strong or wise enough to kill him. A whole chain of events had to unfold for her to come into her own power, so that she could eventually kill him and free the many people whom he had taken captive."

When she ended the story, I looked at Ama-la and asked nervously, "Why are you telling me this story?"

Seeing the anxious expression on my face, she hastened to say, "I am not telling you to kill Zerdan. The opposite really. You will save him. And perhaps that wife of Krishna didn't really kill the demonic king but rather transformed him into a benevolent being. What she killed was the darkness that had infiltrated him. That was an extreme example, because that man was very dangerous and caused much suffering in the world. To save Zerdan, the pride and arrogance in him must die, and that process has already begun."

"I don't need to save him, just to free myself," I mumbled. She smiled and didn't say anything more.

Only days later, an eruption of anger took hold of me, of an intensity that I had never experienced before, and it was directed at the one who had once been my son. I had thought that I was free of anger, but anger would not let me be free. To release myself from its hold, I would have to confront it head on. I would have to let emerge so many suppressed feelings, and I would have to find the means to slay them – to rid myself of the negative emotions, if I was to be truly free.

CHAPTER 25

Battling Anger

I was seated quietly in meditation when anger first began to show its fiery face, anger toward a son of long ago, to whom I had once been so devoted, but who had turned against me. It was an anger born of guilt, a guilt that had long been suppressed because of the deep pain it caused. This anger was amplified by the stepson who sought to harm me, and further magnified by Zerdan, who took advantage of my vulnerabilities and deceived me, leaving me bereft of everything I had. Getting up from my seat in an agitated state, I went out into the cool night air. I could not stop asking myself why. He turned on me even before I fled Hanning, choosing to side with his father from such an early age. As Jacque, he never gave me a chance, taking a dislike to me from the beginning. And as Zerdan, he sought me out, using my anxiety over Tenzin as a way to dig his tentacles into my mind. The more I thought about it, the angrier I became. I sat outside for quite some time as I rationalized my anger by telling myself that I had every good reason to be upset, when Ama-la came out to offer me a warm drink.

"It will help you sleep tonight," she said tenderly as she handed me the herbal tea. I took a sip and realized it was a kind I had not tasted before.

"Have you used special herbs?" I asked. "I don't recognize this tea, but it is very tasty." Earlier in the day during our walk I had noticed her collecting plants along the way, but I had been too preoccupied to ask what she was gathering. She nodded and sat down next to me without speaking while I drank the tea. In the silence, my mind reverted again to my anger.

"Ama-la, it was not only that son of mine who was angry. I felt betrayed by him. You are right, I am very disturbed by that man," I admitted. "All this time, I thought I was not angry at Zerdan, but that is untrue. That anger was hidden, and I wish it had stayed hidden."

"How can you free yourself if you don't even recognize what is there? Let it come up, face it, scream at him, fight him, do whatever you need to do, and then let it go. And finally, you must release your guilt. Whatever happened in the past is finished and you have paid whatever debts you have owed. Now you are Padma Tshomo and you are no longer Claire or Chunhua. Cut your identification with those personalities. It is past time to let it all go. That is the way to free yourself."

"Fight him," I murmured. "How can I? He is far too powerful."

"There are many ways to battle and many types of battle, not all in the physical realm," she responded quietly. "The most important battles are the mental ones, which destroy harmful patterns of thinking."

"Mental battles? I don't understand what you mean."

"You soon will," she replied simply.

Whenever Ama-la spoke words I didn't understand, I would tuck them away somewhere in the background of my mind for later reflection. I knew she would never explain herself, because whenever I pressed her, she would say that it was for me to find out. Now I did the same, filing away her words in a corner to dwell upon later. The only battles I knew were ones with weapons, and I had never even held a sword, let alone know how to use one.

As I sat there, a story Bhasundara had once told me came into my mind. When she was holding on to her anger toward the man who had seduced her, Dalha had told her that she was carrying around her anger like an old mule too ignorant and stubborn to let down its burden. It was the same with me, I mused as I smiled at the image. Dalha had said then that she was trying to lift that burden from her mind. Would she do the same for me now?

"Your anger will dissipate. Have patience," Ama-la counseled and then added, "You know one must also have compassion on oneself."

Suddenly I felt the need to express myself and to share feelings I had not previously acknowledged. "To be honest, from the moment I met Jacque, I didn't like him. Something in him repelled me, but as Claire, I would never admit that. I blamed our sour relationship all on him, but it was me as well. I had carried over that fear of him, a fear that was perhaps unwarranted. Perhaps he never would have done me harm. Perhaps it was all in my mind. When I was born as Chunhua, I also bear some responsibility for what happened to that son. I never explained myself to him. I never said a word to him against his father, although that father was engaged in harmful occult activities that threatened the very security of our state. I never explained to that son why I had to leave. I kept telling myself that he should have understood me, that he was my son as well as his father's, and he should have known that I wouldn't flee unless I had to." I spoke in a rapid tone as if I had to get it all out, and Ama-la listened without responding.

For the first time I was ready to admit my role in shaping the relationship with the one I knew as Zerdan. I continued, "I went to Zerdan of my own free will. I could have stayed away as I was warned to do so many times. I even lied to my brother and son, hiding my inability to refuse whatever that man requested. Yes, he manipulated me and found my weak spot, but I also bear some blame." On and on I went rehearsing old events again and again, until Ama-la finally stopped me.

"What good will it do to continue reliving the past? It is gone. It is important to see your role in all of this and to take responsibility for what has come to pass, Bumo; to see your weaknesses so you can correct them. But your focus now should be the present and the future. Wish the best for that soul and bear no ill will. Don't be like an old mule carrying around a useless burden." When she spoke those last words, she winked at me, and I opened my eyes wide, gazing at her in amazement. How could she have known those words spoken by Bhasundara to me in private?

After a few minutes, I asked, "Ama-la, how long will it take to dispel this anger? I don't want to carry it around with me."

"It will soon be gone, for I see you gathering your will power to free yourself. Nobody can do it for you."

"Soon," I murmured. The only thing I understood was that soon could mean any amount of time, a few days, a hundred years, or perhaps a thousand. There was no time limit to soon. Changing the subject, I sought to find out how she knew so much about me. How could she have known about that private conversation with Bhasundara? After all this time, she was still very much a mystery. Soon after arriving, I stopped asking Ama-la questions about herself, as I realized it was no use; she would share no details of her life. At first this bothered me but eventually I came to accept it.

"Ama-la, have we known each other before?"

"I would not be here now if we had not."

"Was it long ago?" I asked.

"That depends on one's perspective, Bumo. What might seem long ago to you, may seem a short amount of time to me."

"How do you know so much about me, about my thoughts and private conversations?" She smiled and didn't answer. "Have you come from very far away?"

"Very far, but not far at all," she replied evasively. "Again, that depends on one's perspective."

She is obviously from another kingdom, I thought, and that is why she looks different from our people. Trying to get more information, I asked, "The place where you come from, is it very different from here?"

"Very different, but not so different."

"You are like Dalha," I murmured. "Speaking in riddles, giving me no information." I looked at her in exasperation.

The crack of a smile crept across her face as she asked, "What good will information do you?" Then she added, "Soon you will understand it all."

As the days passed, anger strode with me wherever I went and consumed my mind no matter what I was doing. About a week later, I had a frightening dream, where I was battling a form that seemed much like Zerdan, although I couldn't make out the details of the face. The next night I had the same dream, and then again, the following night. Each time, I saw some protective force shielding that form from my blows, as I was seeking to fight him with my bare hands, screaming insults as loud as I could.

"Something is protecting that being, whomever he is," I mumbled to myself upon awakening after the third dream.

Ama-la was preparing the morning meal and hearing me, she replied, "It is your higher Self protecting him. You don't really want to hurt him; you are simply seeking to release your anger."

"My higher Self," I muttered as I got out of bed, worn out from the night's battle. "I don't know what that is."

Later that day, Ama-la suggested we ride out to the forest.

"You know, there is no real forest near here," I said looking outside at the landscape, filled with low brush and a sparsity of trees.

"It is not exactly a forest, but it will do," she replied. Retrieving our horses, we rode quite a way until we came to a small, conifer rhododendron forest, hardly a forest by the standards of Lhasa, but it was the best we could find in the valley.

"This place must be very beautiful when the bushes are in bloom," I murmured as we walked through a patch of large rhododendron.

"Let us sit for a while," she said, finding a small clearing. When we alighted from our horses, she took off from the back of her horse the blanket she had brought and laid it out for the two of us to sit on. As soon as we did, Ama-la closed her eyes and I did the same. Within a short time, I felt myself transported back to Hanning, where I was sitting in a forest with Yeye, having taken refuge with him after a terrible scene with my husband.

"Nature's words are few," Yeye said, quoting the Daoist sage Laozi. "And yet Nature has so much wisdom. Chunhua, what do the animals and plants teach us?"

I answered as I had so many times before when I was a child. "From the birds we learn to be free; from the tigers we learn to be fearless; from the trees, inner strength and patience."

"Remember, my dear," he responded, "if you are strong inside and of pure intent, no human or demon can harm you. The Dao is the ultimate protection."

As I sat in the forest beside Ama-la, I cracked open my eyes, but not fully returned to the present I heard myself ask, "Yeye, what is the Dao and where can I find it?"

And I heard his reply. "It is the natural flow of the universe, unimpeded. There is nowhere to go and nothing to find, for you are that and that is you."

Half in a daze, I asked, "Where then does anger come from? Is it not also part of the Dao?"

"It is the Dao impeded. Anger blocks the flow as a dam prevents the free movement of the river. Anger comes from unfulfilled desire, unmet expectations. Have no expectations, no desire, and anger does not arise. Where do you find anger in the natural world, Bumo?" The words were no longer those of Yeye but those of Ama-la, who spoke quietly. She was answering my internally asked question, and for a moment the inner and outer worlds converged. It was as if we were all seated together in that forest of olden days—Yeye, Ama-la, and me.

Opening my eyes fully, I turned to look at her. I had thought I had been speaking with Yeye, but now I realized I was no longer Chunhua and she was not Yeye. She continued, "Animals experience suffering, but not in the way humans do, because they live fully in the Dao and have no expectation of anything to be different from it is. They live in the consciousness of 'what is,' not 'what could be' or 'what should be.' Do you understand, Bumo?" I nodded slightly and she continued. "Now your anger is directed at Zerdan because of your past with him, but anger can pop up again at any time, and one must be watchful not to have expectations for things to be other than they are.

"When anger accumulates in the collective, that is when wars break out as an outlet for negative emotions. Each one of us plays a role in building that collective, and so we have a responsibility to more than only ourselves. To be in the Dao, to live in the Dharma, is to not let these emotions that arise take root in our mind. They may pass through the mind, but let them flee as quickly as they arrive. Don't give them credence; don't make them real. See them as illusionary, as having no substance. That is the way to contribute to a balanced world."

I was silent for quite some time. Not understanding her words about anger, I changed the subject and asked, "Ama-la, when I first came here, I thought you were a Bonpo, and then I thought you were Buddhist. Are you now a Daoist?" A broad smile broke across her face and a gentle laugh. I continued, "I think that Daoism is much like Bon. When Yeshe took Tenzin to the Song Empire, he wanted him to meet the Daoist hermits. When I asked him why, he had replied that he wanted him to understand Daoism and to see the unity of all religions. I didn't understand him then, but I do now. Daoism and Bon seem very much alike."

"They both contain perennial wisdom," she replied. "When Tonpa Shenrab was on earth, he and the sages knew how to maintain harmony in the natural world, so there would be no droughts, no floods, no violent storms, no excesses of any kind. It was the same with Laozi. They knew how to use the vibration of sound to maintain the balance among various forces. Man's mental powers are very great and affect the external world in many ways. Violent thoughts create violence in the external world, and a calm, loving mind helps to bring about harmony. Every one of us contributes in some way to these external conditions. If only man understood the connection between the inner and outer worlds. That is why your Yeye always sent you to the forest to maintain your peace and mental calmness. Your mother in this life did the same.

"Tonpa Shenrab also knew how to channel the energies of the benevolent ones called the deities, who emit such an abundance of love, and how to transmute the negative energies of the ones called the demons—forces that generate anger and fear. What the Buddha and Guru Rinpoche did was to refocus the human mind on the internal rather than external conditions. Rather than seeking the deities in the external world, they can be found inside where all things exist, in the realm of the mind. It is a matter of refocusing. After all, the external is a projection of the internal. The deities are without but also within. Do you follow what I am saying?"

"Sort of," I replied, with a confused expression.

"It was your Yeye who taught you about the goddess of the lunar worlds. In two successive lives in the Tang Empire, you were devoted to her. But when you took birth in the Duchy of Normandy and lived in England, you could not find her in that newer religion, and dissatisfaction arose. Then again in your life as Claire, you sought her, resisting the religion that had suppressed the goddess. It was Beau who tried to help you integrate the two, but you had to take birth in this sacred land of Böd to find her. That you did."

"But I haven't found her, Ama-la," I confessed.

She smiled. "You have. You just don't know that you have. Soon you will know."

I wondered how many more lifetimes would pass before soon became a reality. She continued in a gentle, explanatory voice, "In this sacred land of Böd, the ancient wisdom has found new expression. A deep integration has taken place and the wisdom from here will reach all corners of the world, but for that to happen, many sacrifices will be made. Even from this point in time where we now stand, I can see that. But what is time? There is no suffering in the timeless realm, which is where the true Böd exists." Her voice trailed off. She had lost me and so I didn't respond. We sat for a while longer in silence and then returned to the hut.

A few nights later, a fierce battle exploded in my mind. During a shallow but restless sleep, I found myself fighting that being who had been visiting me, the one I thought to be Zerdan, only this time I was battling him not with bare hands but with a sword. Swinging the long weapon back and forth, I could not pin him down as he evaded every attempted slash. The more he evaded me, the more aggressive were my swings. I woke up in the middle of the night sweating. Looking over at Ama-la, I saw her seated in meditation in the usual spot. Getting up, I decided to go outside so as not to disturb her. As I reached the doorway, I noticed a sword standing next to the door, still in its sheath. In all the time that I had stayed in the hut, the sword had never been there before, and I wondered where it could have come from. Without dwelling on the matter, I lifted the sword from its sheath and went outside.

For a few moments, I stood in the dark night, lit only by a half moon, and then I remembered the story Bhasundara had told me about when she and Dalha had gone to Mt. Tise and visited the woman ascetic; how she had heard and seen Dalha engage in a sword fight with some invisible being. The image of Dalha rose before me, and I called upon her. I imagined her hands wrapped around mine as I tightly gripped the sword. Muttering to myself, "I will resolve this once and for all," I lifted the sword with two hands. It was heavy, but despite its weight I began to swing it around as if I were attacking someone. As I did, I saw an undefined dark shadow in front of me, flitting about from one place to another, and I began to thrust the sword at it with all my might. Within minutes the sword had grown lighter, far easier to handle, and I spun around, sword in hand, attacking the image again and again. Before I knew it, I was leaping, twirling, jumping, swinging, dancing with the sword as if it were a partner, attacking the presence, the dark shadow of a being, who was stealthily moving around me. This went on and on, and although heaving with exhaustion, I couldn't stop. It was as if some force within me was driving my movements, directing my arms and hands, or was it Dalha engaged in the battle through my body?

After a time, the sword seemed to become weightless and I was swinging it with one arm, moving forward and backward with my feet, flowing to an unheard rhythm. The steps became a cosmic dance, in harmony with the swaying of the cold night breezes, with the inflowing and outflowing of my breath, the inner and outer winds that had become indistinguishable from one another. My feet refused to stop; the sword would not pause its cutting motion. On and on we flew together, until I could no longer see the dark outline of a form that had drawn me to itself, an impression that had dissolved in the night air, or perhaps had dissolved into my being.

When the first peek of dawn appeared on the horizon, suddenly everything halted. Calling up the last of my strength and using both hands, I dug the sword deep into the earth with a forceful motion. Exhausted, I fell onto my knees, and with a racing heart struggled to catch my breath. I didn't know exactly what I had done or why I had done it, but I felt that something significant had transpired.

Once I was able to breathe normally, I looked up and saw Ama-la standing in the doorway, a slight smile on her face, and she spoke in a gentle, loving voice, "Long, long ago, you were a dancer, and you became known for dancing the part of a great goddess killing a mighty buffalo demon. This past night, you not only danced the part, you also killed the demon, the demon of anger within you and him."

Helping me to rise, she looked at the sword and commented, "I thought you might need this and so beckoned one for your use." Leading me inside, she told me to rest while she prepared the morning meal.

I was so worn out that I fell asleep immediately. When I awoke several hours later, she indicated that food was ready, and I silently took the bowl of tsampa, vegetables, and yoghurt that she had set on the table. After I was done, she placed before me a pouch of herbs and said quietly, "Zerdan had a heart attack in the night. At this moment, he lies in a painful place between life and death. This medicine that I have prepared can bring him back to life."

"Did I kill him last night?" I asked in dismay.

She shook her head. "It was his own actions that brought the heart attack, but last night you freed yourself and him as well. It is up to you now whether he lives or dies. Without these herbs, he will die in a matter of days. But why would you save him, the one who caused you such suffering?" she asked, looking intently at me.

"Surely, the monastery must have the same medicine . . . ," I began, but she shook her head.

I was silent as I took in the import of her words. His life now depended on me. How many times I had wished that he would die and free me from whatever hold he had over me, but I now understood that death does not provide relief. Whatever we do, we carry with us from one life to the next. I wanted him to live, to give him a chance to mend his ways.

"Of course, I must go to him," I said in a quiet voice, turning my eyes to her.

"You will need to stay with him for ten days, feeding him the broth from these herbs every few hours." I nodded, not hiding how reluctant I was to leave her and return to the monastery from which I had fled two years earlier.

"I will come back here after the ten days," I affirmed.

"Yes, you must. There is still more for you to see." Her voice was quiet and tender.

"I will leave then now." There was hesitation in my voice.

"Take your bath, Bumo, and change your clothing. I will pack a few things for you."

I went into the bath hut and found the tub filled with heated water. My body ached from the battle of the night before, and the warmth soothed my sore muscles. I didn't stay long in the bath and, after changing into new clothing, I saw that Ama-la had tied a bag of fresh clothing with the medicine on the back of Anpu. But I wasn't ready to ascend the horse yet, and I stood outside, gazing for several minutes at Ama-la smiling in the doorway. I had never expressed to Ama-la my love and appreciation for her and still felt shy now to do so, but I was determined to let her know my feelings when I returned. How much she had helped me, I could not even begin to say.

"I don't want to leave you," I said sadly. "But I know I must go."

"Yes, you must complete this cycle. It is for this I have come. Don't be sad, Bumo, you will return here."

I started to walk toward Anpu, but she called me back and told me not to ride too fast. Nodding, I walked away again, but she called me back once more and said that she would ensure that Zerdan would survive until I arrived there, no need to hurry. Nodding again, I turned and began walking toward Anpu. As I was about to climb onto the horse, she called me back a third time. Again, I approached her, and as I stood there looking into her face, she reached out and hugged me tightly, holding me for a long time, something she had never done before.

"I will return in ten days," I whispered as I returned her embrace. Then I walked away again, mounted the horse, and slowly rode off, stopping only once to look back at the hut, but Ama-la had already withdrawn.

"She will wait for me," I thought to myself. "Surely, she will wait."

CHAPTER 26

A Cycle Completed

It took all the strength and courage I could muster to return to the place that had been the scene of so much pain and humiliation for me, but I was aware that if I allowed my mind to dwell on that I would never enter the monastery, which I knew I had to do. To help me, I kept my mind mostly on Ama-la, reviewing her words to me of the last many days, and this allowed me to maintain my calm. In fact, it made the whole return seem like a dream to me, an otherworldly reality. As I spoke to the monks and moved around the monastery, I was present, but I was also not. My mind was in another place.

At first, I was greeted with shock and gratitude. As soon as Zerdan's assistant Lopsang heard that I was there, he hurried to receive me, exclaiming, "Padma Tshomo, you are the last person I expected to see here. I am glad you have come, as I know the Master would want to see you before he dies. But I am afraid it may be too late. I don't think that he will last the night." After a pause, he asked, "How did you know to come? Word of his condition could not have spread beyond the monastery."

As soon as I saw Lobsang, I stiffened as the memories of his uncaring behavior toward me returned. Instead of answering, I instructed him calmly, "I have brought a rare, powerful medicine. Boil these herbs and I will feed him the broth. If you do as I say, he will survive." I don't know why he trusted me, but he did. I suppose because there was no alternative. After a moment's hesitation, he took the pouch I handed him and went to heat up the medicine, while I asked another monk to take me to Zerdan's room, so that I could sit by the bedside of the man whom I regarded as both friend and foe. When I entered the room, I was shocked to see the change that had come over him in the two years that I had been gone. Once an attractive and dynamic man with a full face and piercing eyes, the unconscious man lying on the bed before me was thin and pale with far more grey in his stubbly hair than I remembered.

Sitting down on a chair by his bed, I silently spoke to the one I once knew as my son, then as my stepson Jacque, and now as Zerdan. "I am sorry that I hurt you long ago," I whispered internally. "I am sorry that you once felt abandoned by me, that you believed I harmed your father. I am sorry for all the ill you heard about me, but none of it was true. I am sorry that you became obsessed, seeking revenge in one lifetime after another. I was never a sorceress, never sought to be one or to exert power over others. The choices you made, I don't understand them, but I hope that one day you will achieve your aspirations, whatever they may be. Let there finally be peace between us."

Lopsang returned and watched as I dropped a small spoonful of medicine between Zerdan's slightly parted lips. "It happened in the middle of the night," he explained to me quietly. "He had been having restless nights for the last many days, unable to sleep, so I was staying outside his room, listening for any sounds. Last night he awoke shortly before dawn with a terrible pain in his chest. When I heard him cry out, I rushed in only to hear him whisper that it felt like someone had struck him hard on the chest. By the time the physician reached here, he was already unconscious. We tried all the known medicines, but nothing has been able to revive him."

"I will stay by his side and feed him this medicine every few hours," I said curtly, without explaining what the medicine was or where I had gotten it. Just make sure I have a constant supply of broth from the herbs I brought."

"Why are you doing this?" he asked quietly. "He has taken so much from you and treated you so harshly."

"Why?" I murmured. "I am not sure I know the answer to that."

"He was tough on you, Padma Tshomo, more than on the others. He seemed singularly focused on taking away everything you had. Are you not angry at him for that?" I shook my head. "Then I will tell you what happened after you left Lhasa. When we learned that you had passed out while doing prostrations along the path to the monastery, he began to have a change of heart and sent someone to find you. When he couldn't locate you, Zerdan himself went to your relatives, to your two brothers and daughter in Lhasa, but they refused to see him or to convey any message about you. Then he went to Samye Monastery and asked to see the Abbot, who also refused to meet him. He continued to search for you, and finally he found a man who told him that he had heard you had gone on a long retreat and could not be reached. This person said there was no way of knowing where you were or when you would return, that even your family didn't know.

"I asked him why he wanted to meet you again when he had already taken all your possessions and funds. He had once told me that he had even taken your wealth from your next birth, if that is possible." Lopsang shook his head and muttered, "Who would ask for such a thing? But this is how fixated he was on you as if he wanted to punish you for something you had done to him. You had nothing more to give, so I asked him why was he still pursuing you? He replied simply that it was not over yet. Every now and then he would send another monk to a place where he had heard a woman might be in retreat, but he was not able to receive any word of you. And now you show up at this crucial hour."

"He was right," I replied quietly. "It was not over then, but now it is. I will stay by his side and feed him the medicine until he recovers, and then I will disappear again."

"I will withdraw and leave you here. A monk will refresh the medicine every few hours. But where will you sleep?"

"In this chair by his bedside," I replied wearily. I hadn't slept much the past week and my body was greatly fatigued, so I didn't think I would have much trouble sleeping while sitting up. I waited a few hours until I received another dose of medicine to drip between Zerdan's lips, then I allowed myself to fall into a shallow sleep, listening for any movement of the immobile body lying on the bed beside me.

Over the next few days, I began to feel the presence of the one I called Yeye, the grandfather I remembered from my life in Hanning. He came to me in dreams, and I felt him standing by my side as I slept upright in the chair by Zerdan's bed. At one point I heard him repeat a teaching from the Sage Laozi: *Without desires, all is peaceful/ And the world settles itself.*

"That is the message of the Buddha, Yeye," I whispered as I partially awoke to those words and briefly opened my eyes. Closing them again, I saw his smiling face and understood what he was showing me: the teachings of Laozi and the Buddha were the same.

Looking at me steadily, he repeated the words, *No matter how great or how often, / Repay injury with De.*

"What is De?" I had asked when he first recited those lines to me long ago.

"It is the Dao in action," he had replied. "Harmonious action, acting out of virtue, out of love. That is De."

Coming to full wakefulness, I heard myself whisper, "Yeye, what you describe is Dharma. I had thought that Daoism is very much like Bon, but now I realize it is also much like Buddhism. Are all three of them related?" I asked him internally.

"Why do you separate them, my dear? They speak of a wisdom that predates religion, a wisdom that the ancients of all lands imbibed although they expressed it differently. A feature of all manifestation is diversity. We should not be deceived by the apparent differences in the outer garments."

I had already come to understand that the division I had created between Bon and Buddhism was a false one. I knew that it was my own limited mind that had made this distinction, a leftover belief from previous births. But hearing Yeye's words helped me to grasp more firmly this truth of unity. Yeye continued to speak with me. At one point I sat up abruptly, having realized that our conversation was not a memory of the past but an exchange of the present. Yeye was there with me, only not visible to the outer eye.

"You had said you would come when I would face that son again, and you have," I whispered to him internally.

"Promises are not forgotten, but the timing for both of you had to be right for peace to be made," he replied.

"So many centuries have passed. What has this son of mine gone through to make him such a power-hungry man?"

I heard Yeye chuckle. "His trajectory has been as long as yours, but while you continued to search for answers, he sought to impose his own vision on others, which he finally achieved in this life. He gained a large following, but now is a turning point for him. You have helped him more than you know, and he will soon come to replace the thirst for power with a yearning for acceptance and love. It may take him a few more births, but he will find that love, which in truth is what he has always unconsciously been seeking."

"Has he forgiven me, Yeye?" I asked internally.

"Have you forgiven yourself?" he asked in response. With a sigh, I replied that I had. My battle of a few nights earlier had freed me of the last remnants of guilt that I had been carrying.

The days by Zerdan's side were filled with assiduous care for the man, feeding him medicine and liquid food every few hours, but the nights were filled with such conversations with Yeye, sometimes in dream, but mostly in a half sleep state. They brought me much comfort. During this time, Lopsang came to sit with me on numerous occassions.

"I am the only one left with him. Everyone else has deserted him, and it happened so quickly," he commented sadly one day. When I didn't respond, he continued. "Since you have been on retreat, you probably haven't heard." I turned my eyes from Zerdan to look at him directly.

"Not long ago, a number of Atisa's students gathered and demanded that he sign a statement admitting that he had knowingly lied about being the reincarnation of that great master, that he had fabricated the whole story. At first, he protested, saying he had shown signs of occult powers, but when they asked him questions about Atisa's life, he couldn't answer. Finally, a few weeks ago, he signed the statement, which became public. There was an uproar here at the monastery as so many had believed him. The senior monks came together and appointed a new abbot, a good man, who went over all the financial details of the monastery and found many instances of misuse of funds. The monastery then insisted that he leave."

"When did all of that happen?" I asked curiously.

"In the weeks before the heart attack. If he had not become gravely ill, he would be gone from here by now, and if he recovers, he will have to leave immediately and cut all ties with the monastery. Nobody here will associate with him anymore." As he spoke, I realized that Zerdan was going through that trial at the very time that I was battling him in my dreams at night.

"Where will he go?" I asked in a detached tone. Truthfully, I didn't care anymore what happened to him, as long as he survived. Lopsang shook his head and replied that no decision had been made, but no monastery would take him. "What about you? Will you stay or go back to your family?" I asked. Lopsang had been Zerdan's enabler, doing the dirty work for him, clawing money from people. He had originally come from a wealthy family, one known to my brother Sonam, who had told me that early on Lopsang had tricked his family into donating large sums to Zerdan, but they had eventually turned on him and cut off all relations.

"I have nowhere to go," he replied despondently. The monastery won't let me stay and my family shuns me."

"Each of us must pay for our deeds," I replied coolly. I had to admit that I wasn't sorry to hear of his misfortune. I had forgiven Zerdan because I understood the cause of his behavior, my role in it, and our long history together, but I couldn't forgive Lopsang, whom I blamed for pressuring me and conniving to convince me of many falsehoods.

On the fifth day, Zerdan opened his eyes. It was midday and light streamed in from the window, whose shutters Lopsang opened every morning and closed every night. The air was still warm from the late summer sun, but the nights were getting cooler.

"You are finally here," were his first whispered words.

Nodding, I replied quietly, "I have been here the whole time, feeding you medicine."

Closing his eyes again, he drifted back to sleep. Several hours later he woke up and I fed him the medicine. "Five more days of this medicine, and then you will be well," I remarked as I spooned the liquid into his mouth. Lopsang helped him rise in bed, but as soon as he took in the medicine, he reclined again, still weak from his illness.

I heard him utter, "Thank you, Padma Tshomo, for coming," and then his eyes closed and once more he was asleep. The next few days passed in this way, with brief waking moments and the exchange of a handful of words, and gradually he began to return to life. As I gazed at the pitiful man lying in the bed next to me, I realized that both my fear of him and my anger were gone. I didn't want to be the cause of any more suffering for this man. I wished him well on his onward journey.

Ten days had passed, and I had hardly left his side, only withdrawing to take care of the barest necessities. On the tenth morning, he seemed to be resting quite comfortably, and I went to wash and put on fresh clothing. When I returned to his room, Zerdan was seated in a chair, eating solid food for the first time. As soon as he saw me a smile crept across his face, but it was not like before. It was not a controlling or alluring smile, but a sincere one of gratitude.

"At first, I thought that I had dreamed you were here, but you actually came," he said in a subdued tone.

"I came as soon as I heard," I replied.

"You left your retreat for me?" he asked with a surprised look on his face. I nodded. He looked down and didn't respond right away. A much-humbled man sat before me. After a few moments he spoke again, continuing to keep his eyes cast down. "I don't know what to say to you.

I have been looking for you this whole time, and now that you are here, I don't know what to say."

"There is nothing to say. I came because I want you to live," I replied with a touch of emotion. "Despite everything, I didn't want you to die." I was about to say more, to tell him about my retreat with Ama-la, but I decided to say nothing. I realized that this would be our last meeting, and there was a certain poignancy to the moment. I understood that between us there was nothing more to say or do. "Once you recover fully, where will you go?" I ventured to ask.

He sighed and replied sorrowfully, "I must leave this place, which I have devoted so many years to building. A new abbot had been chosen and I will go on retreat, like you. Only my retreat will last the rest of my life. I have much to ponder over and many regrets." I could see that our brief conversation was tiring him, but he seemed to want to continue talking. "Where will you go Padma Tshomo, now that you have no place to live anymore?"

Th question surprised me because since going to the Valley, I hadn't thought of the future. My mind had been in the past, and I hadn't given any thought to what lay ahead for me. But suddenly the answer came. "I will go live with my sister Pumo," I replied with conviction.

"I am sorry," he said faintly, with downcast eyes. How different he was from the arrogant and unapologetic man I knew before. He had experienced the difficult teaching of humiliation, something I had also experienced, and I could see that it was having its desired effect. Most would view him as a broken man, but I saw him as one reborn.

At that moment there was only gratitude in my heart. If he hadn't taken everything from me and propelled me into such a state of despair, I would never have met Ama-la or recaptured so many memories from my past, which were far more valuable than any material possession. So I answered, "There is no need to be sorry. It has all worked out for the best. You have helped free me of many attachments, and I am more grateful than I can say." Seeing how our conversation had fatigued him, I suggested he return to bed. Once I saw that he was asleep, I packed up the few things I had brought and went to find Lopsang.

"You are leaving?" he asked when he saw that I was ready to depart.

"There is no need for me to stay any longer, and there is something I must attend to." I had told Ama-la that I would return after ten days, and I was eager to get back. Something inside told me that she would not be with me much longer, and I wanted to see her again to express my feelings for her, my great love and appreciation.

Lopsang gazed at me steadily for a few moments. We were standing outside by the entrance to the monastery. "Before you leave, let me share with you why he was so eager to find you these past two years. The funds that you gave him from the sale of your home and the last of your possessions, he never did anything with it. He never used those funds. After he heard that you had disappeared, something came over him, and he couldn't bring himself to use that money. I tried to convince him to use it to support one project or another but each time he refused, saying that the funds did not belong to him. I don't know what created this change in him, but he became more reflective, more withdrawn. He probably didn't mention it to you now because he is not yet thinking clearly, but as soon as he recovers, I am sure he will ask the new abbot to return the money, as it was given under false pretense."

I was quiet for a few moments and then replied, "I have no use for it now and so don't need it back."

"Are you sure, Padma Tshomo?" I nodded. "How would you like the monastery to use it then? If you tell me, I will speak with the new abbot and try to ensure that your wishes are respected, although I don't think I will have much say here any longer." I didn't answer right away, and then I remembered Ama-la taking me to the spot where she said Guru Rinpoche had envisioned a nunnery. She had said that it had not materialized yet. At that time, I wondered why she had taken me there, because I knew that everything she did had a deeper meaning. Then I remembered the nunnery that Margot had overseen, where I had lived in my life as Claire, which had offered a safe place of refuge for so many women.

"If the monastery truly wants to respect my wishes, then use some of the money to support Zerdan in his retreat, for food, and use the rest to build a place where women can pursue a spiritual life," I replied firmly.

"For women?" he asked in surprise.

"Yes, women also need a place to do their spiritual work, a place of retreat from the world. That is what I would like to help manifest here in Böd."

Turning his eyes from me to look off into the distance, he seemed thoughtful for a few moments and then replied. "I will do my best to fulfill your wishes, Padma Tshomo, but once I leave here, my voice may not count for much." We were both quiet and then he asked, "Will you visit him again?"

I shook my head. "From here, our paths will diverge and follow different directions. I am sure that Zerdan will recover, and I hope he uses his remaining years to reflect on his misdeeds and truly serve the Dharma."

"Then we will not meet again, you and I, will we?"

I looked at this man, whom I had long resisted, and replied quietly, "One never knows what the future holds." With those words, I tried to smile and put aside my lingering dislike. Then I retrieved my horse and rode away.

CHAPTER 27

A Very Ancient Tale

I rode as fast as Anpu's speeding feet would carry me back to the hut I shared with Ama-la, fighting off a sense of foreboding. In my mind lurked the thought that she might not be there when I returned. She wouldn't leave me, I repeated again and again to myself. But in my heart, I knew my work was done; I had accomplished what she had come to help me do. As I sped along the valley, I remembered the way we had parted, how she had called me back several times and then held me tight—something I had not made much of at the time in my hurry to get to Zerdan. Now as I remembered that moment, I spurred Anpu to ride faster, knowing that he was very much in tune with my thoughts and would also not want to miss seeing Ama-la again. I had to find out who she was to me, and where she had come from. This would now be the focus of my meditation. Without these answers, my mind would not be at rest.

During the two years that I had been living with Ama-la, I had grown very attached to her. I recognized my feelings as similar to those that I had toward my own mother in this life. Was it because I missed my birth mother, who had died when I was young? Had I transferred those feelings onto Ama-la, who treated me as her own daughter, even calling me that. After first meeting her, on several occasions I had repeated my name to her, thinking she had forgotten it, but each time she had simply smiled and replied, "You have had so many names. I know them all, but I think of you only as Bumo."

I could see that the ride was tiring Anpu and I had to stop midway to give him water and rest. Along with me, he was also growing older. "Forgive me, Anpu," I whispered as I stroked his mane, "but I can't give you long to rest. I must return before Ama-la leaves. I have a feeling that she won't remain long with me, and I haven't even thanked her yet. I don't know what would have become of me had she not appeared in my life. You understand, don't you?"

He looked directly at me as he so often did when I spoke to him, but only silence followed. "I know you want to say something," I added sympathetically. "In your next birth, you will speak."

Within a short while we were again hurrying along the valley. A part of me was afraid that the hut wouldn't be there, that it would have magically disappeared. Ten days of mingling among people, seeing Zerdan again and the monastery, had propelled me back into another reality that I didn't want to return to, not yet. I wanted to remain a little longer in that sacred space with Ama-la, even if it was an illusion, even if it existed only in my own mind.

When the hut came into view, I sighed in relief. It was still there. I could re-enter that world again, but as I drew close an uneasy feeling came over me once more. Jumping down from Anpu and hurrying to the door, which was slightly ajar, I pushed it open. It was late in the day and the shutters were closed, leaving only the open doorway to allow in shafts of light. At first glance, I didn't see anyone. Perhaps she went for a walk, I thought. Surely, she knew I would return today. As I was debating whether to go in search of her or to wait for her return, I caught sight of a man sitting in the meditation corner. Somehow I hadn't noticed him when I entered.

Slowly he opened his eyes, and rising, he approached me. I stood there transfixed, thinking perhaps this was her husband, who was supposed to come soon. He was a dignified older man dressed in a dark blue silk robe, tied by an embroidered belt, looking almost like an aristocrat or government official. His dark hair, laced with many streaks grey, was multi-braided and wrapped on top of his head. A single long earring hung from his ear. For several minutes, I stood there without speaking, wondering who he could be, and then it hit me. I had to peer through his current appearance to recognize the one I knew well and so dearly loved. No longer did he look like the sparsely dressed forest hermit grandfather from Hanning. He wore a new form, but his presence and the light gleaming from his eyes were the same.

"Yeye?" I asked in a startled whisper, opening my eyes wide in surprise. Nodding, he smiled. This was not the image of Yeye I had in my mind—not the man I saw in my memory, not the one who spoke to me as I sat by Zerdan's bedside these last few days. How I knew it was him, I couldn't quite say. But I knew.

"Where is Ama-la?" I asked in confusion, wondering what my grandfather from Hanning was doing there.

"She has returned to where she came from. She could not stay here any longer. That is the way it is," he replied quietly.

"What should I call you?" I asked meekly, wondering if he was some high official.

"Yeye. That is how you know me."

"I am confused," I muttered, unable to reconcile the man before me with the Yeye of my memory.

"Come, let's walk in the forest. You will find clarity there." At the mention of the forest, I smiled. My Yeye had been a hermit living in the forest. How many times he had me sit quietly there and connect my *qi* to the *qi* of nature. Those recollections had recently revived for me.

"Yeye, there are no forests here like we had then," I murmured.

He chuckled. "Then we must create one." I looked at him doubtfully, and he hurried to say, "We will sit by the river. Nature can speak to us there as well as in the forest. But first you must eat. She left food for you, enough for a few days." Sitting at the table, I allowed the one I had known as Yeye to serve me food, then we went outside, where Ama-la's horse was waiting beside Anpu. I had not seen it when I arrived, but there the horse was, waiting for us.

We rode down to the river, where I led him to a place where Ama-la and I had often sat together. After watching the water rise and fall as it rushed by in ever renewing waves, Yeye began to speak in a serious tone, "To understand who she is to you, I have to begin with my own story." He was quiet for a few moments, and I waited eagerly. The Yeye that I had known so long ago used to fill my mind with tales of magical events, and as we sat now by the side of the river, I recalled those stories, and I became a young girl again, resting by the side of a much beloved grandfather.

"The story begins before the melting of the ice, so many, many millennia ago. I was born to parents from a small mountain tribe not very far from here, further west, in the place today you would call Gyagar. There were no countries then, no borders or boundaries. The land was open to all, and the tribes moved freely from one place to another, because the concept of ownership of the land was unknown. The earth was our mother and she fed us, providing for all our needs. How could we think to claim her, to fight over her? There was plenty for everyone. The population of humans was much smaller than it is today, and there was a great diversity of animals. There were no religions to separate us, no fighting for territories, no conflict. We lived in tight tribal communities, eating whatever we could find in the forests and valleys. Food was plentiful and there was no lack, no need for cultivation, because the earth provided and what she provided was shared. It was a time when great sages were studying the skies, mapping it and tracking the passage of time. They could foretell future events by watching the movement of the stars and the relationships of the planets to one another. At that time, we viewed the stellar bodies as our elders who taught us much about the universe. We spoke to them, asked questions, and they responded in a way we could hear.

"As I grew into manhood, I met a sage who inspired in me the desire to peer deep into the heavens and understand the heavenly configurations. He told me that if I traveled toward the rising sun across the great mountains, I would reach a high plateau where not many humans were living. That was the best place to view the heavens, he said, because the water was frozen, the sky clear of all humidity, the air rarified, and the view of the stars unmatched. He also said that sometimes the deities, beings from nonphysical realms, came to that place because it was so remote and unpopulated. It was a place where they could experience physical embodiment undisturbed, which they sometimes liked to do. This gave them insight into the nature of material life and enabled them to better assist the process of human development.

"This sage taught me how to generate an inner heat so that I wouldn't suffer from the cold. I left my tribe and traveled toward the rising sun, walking over vast mountain landscapes, then traveled north until I came to the place near what today you would call the Kunlun Mountain Range. I found a large cave to live in and spent most of the nights studying the skies. The stars were my elder guides, and I learned much from them. The air was so rarified that the moon and the stars seemed much brighter and closer than they had when I lived on lower land, and I was entranced by their beauty. I found that in the cold climate, I didn't have to eat often, but the air was so dry that I was frequently thirsty. Very close to the cave where I lived was a large field of ice, and I would chop it with a stone so I could bring it inside by the fire to melt and drink it. The water had many nutrients and minerals, and I didn't need much else. Often, I heated the water in a stone pot I made and added small plants that I found. That was how I lived.

"After a few years, I found that what the sage had said about the deities, whom you call the lha, was true. I couldn't see them, but I could feel their presence. When gazing at the stars at night, I sometimes could feel one of the lha around me, as if observing me, and on occasion I would be aware of one directing my vision toward a certain part of the sky. I had many such experiences. The years passed, and I was deeply contented. Then one night as I was sitting outside by the ice sheet, I caught sight of faint lights flitting across the frozen water. This intrigued me. After a few nights of watching, my attention began to shift from the stars to these flickering lights that appeared, sometimes briefly and sometimes longer, and then disappeared. Gradually I began to see that those flickers were really light bodies, female forms, and what had seemed like a flickering was actually a well-composed dance. They were dancing on the ice. I was intrigued, mesmerized by what I was witnessing.

"This went on for several months, and little by little I saw that the ice field was beginning to turn into a lake, a large beautiful blue lake. The light forms continued to dance every night over the melting water. One evening as I watched them late into the night, my attention was drawn to one of the light forms. As I stared, it approached, coming closer until it stood in front of me. Within a matter of minutes, it became more and more defined, as if the light particles were condensing, solidifying into a discrete form, until finally it assumed a physical body—that of a most beautiful young woman. She was tall and slender, clothed in a thin white diaphanous dress that brushed around her when she moved. Her long dark flowing hair was loose and reached her waist. Her face was pale and thin, with refined features. Her eyes large and oval shaped; her expression gentle. I had never seen such a beautiful woman and I couldn't tear my eyes away from her.

"I had been living alone in the cave, with no human contact, and now there was this beautiful woman before me. I fell in love instantly. After a few minutes, she disappeared with the others, their light forms dispersing into the night sky. The next night, for the first time in many months, they didn't appear, and I wondered if it was because they had noticed a human watching them. For the next several nights, I hid myself in the hope that they would return, but they didn't come back. Yet I couldn't get that beautiful woman out of my mind, and I began to yearn for her as I had never yearned for anything. Every night I would go out to the lake, calling out to her—the one of whom I had caught only the briefest glimpse and for whom I had no name.

"Then one morning, when I emerged from the cave and went to get some water, I saw her sitting by the side of the lake, dangling her feet in the water. She was a human woman, but I knew instantly that she was the same one I had seen dancing, who had transformed from a light body into a physical one. She could speak my language, and it was as if she immediately knew human ways. But when I asked her name, she didn't respond. When I asked where she had come from, again she didn't respond. Then I asked her if she would stay with me, and she nodded. The language that I spoke at that time was different from the language here in Böd today, but I ended up calling her the words for deity and lake because I knew she was from another world, and because she and the others had created that lake. In your language today her name would be Lha-tso.

"Those light forms dancing on the ice were *dakinis*, celestial dancers, and it was their movement over the ice that had melted it and formed the many sacred lakes in this region. That is why it is said the goddesses live in the lakes or are associated with them. The memory of that time is instilled in the collective mind of the people of this region."

Yeye paused and I asked eagerly, "What happened after that?"

He continued. "She lived with me for a while, and it was like living in an ideal world. I knew that she had come from someplace else, and I considered her to be one of the lha that I had heard about. She didn't distinguish between cold and heat, had little need for eating or sleeping, and had a most joyous, uplifting spirit. Everything she saw and touched pleased her, and I realized that she was experiencing the physical world for the first time. She was in awe of everything. She loved to look at the stars at night, to gaze into the sun during the day, and she had a deep affinity with the moon. She would gaze up at it affectionately for a long time at night when it appeared in the dark sky, showing us its face, like a lone light blessing the earth.

"After a year, she became pregnant, and we had a daughter. That changed everything. She doted on this daughter but couldn't care for her as a human mother would. She didn't realize that the child needed to eat several times a day and would forget to feed her. She didn't realize that the child needed so much sleep and couldn't withstand the cold, and she would keep her outside for hours at night and speak to her about the stars. She would take her to a new ice field, not far away, and call her to dance on the ice, saying, 'Come dance with the dakinis.' This alarmed me. She would point to the air and say, 'See their light forms dancing there,' but the child couldn't see them.

"Our daughter was very attached to her mother and wanted to do all the things she could do. One day when the girl was about four years old, against my objections, she tried to dance on the ice with her mother and fell and broke her arm. I was very attached to this child, and in a moment of forgetfulness, I scolded her mother quite harshly, something I had never done before. I told her that the child was not a dakini but a human girl and couldn't dance on ice; that the child had to eat and sleep and be protected from the cold, and that she didn't know how to be a human mother. The next morning, the child's arm was healed but her mother was gone. And she never returned. I was beside myself with grief and remorse."

He paused and I asked hesitantly, "Is that the end of the story?"

"Stories never end," he replied with a faint smile. "They are ongoing—the end never in sight. For several years I remained in that place in the hope that she would return. My daughter would cry at night for her, and in the day gaze longingly at the lake or the ice sheets and say that she wanted to dance with the dakinis. I was afraid that she would enter the water and drown or hurt herself again on the ice, so I knew that I had to take her away. I realized that my daughter needed to be part of a human community. She couldn't live in isolation, as I could.

"One night my dakini wife came in a dream and told me to take our daughter back to my tribe. 'You will find a husband for her there when she comes of age,' she said. Seeing my deep regret at having lost my temper at her, she conveyed to me that she didn't leave because of that, but because had she stayed any longer in the physical world, she would have become caught in the cycle of rebirth. As it was, she said, she had overstayed her visit, and had formed a relationship with me and the daughter that would need to find fulfillment in the future.

"As I reflected on her words in the dream, I realized that when such beings from other worlds come into ours, to avoid the cycle of rebirth, they do not stay long, unless they are of a very high consciousness. Then nothing touches them. But for the younger ones, once their attachment begins to grow, they incur samskaras and will go through the process of death and rebirth, which they seek to avoid. They leave their beautiful world for ours to experience physicality and to help evolve the human species and other life forms. During the melting of the ice and afterwards, many such lha visited us to help guide the cycle of time. Knowing all of this did not ease my yearning for her as we had bonded so deeply. Yet there was nothing I could do. I realized that she was not coming back, and I didn't know how to reach her. Not until much later did I realize that her visit was not accidental. It served to create in me an aspiration for something greater. I was determined that nothing would stop me from trying to reach her world, that I would search the whole universe until I found her." Yeye paused as he turned his eyes away from me and looked off into the distance.

"What happened to the daughter?" I asked meekly.

Without turning his eyes to me, he replied gently, "She wanted to dance with the dakinis, but she could not. After all, she was only a human child. Her mother left a deep impression on her, and I knew that her memory of that mother would lead to a search for the supreme Goddess. But I wanted her to forget about the dakinis, so we began the long trek back over the mountains in the direction of the setting sun. Fifteen years had passed since I had left the tribe. My parents had died, but my brothers and sisters were there with families of their own. When they saw my daughter, they asked about my wife, and I said that she had died, and that this was the reason for my return. This is what I also told my daughter, but I knew that she didn't believe it. She knew that her mother had returned to where the dakinis live.

"I left my child with one of my sisters and her family, and I went off to seek a way to reunite with my beloved. I vowed never to forget her and never to stop searching for her. I knew that my wife's prediction would come true and that my sister would find a good husband for my daughter."

"Did you find that dakini again?" I asked quietly.

A slight smile crossed his face as he turned his eyes back to me and replied, "I didn't find her in that life, and I didn't see that daughter again after I left. That was another great regret. I was so consumed with searching for my beloved that I left my only child, not realizing that my prime responsibility was to care for her and give her the love that her mother was not there to give. At the end of that life, I suffered from deep remorse and vowed to make it up to that child.

"The search for my beloved was a long one, in human time. It took me many, many lifetimes and much striving to be able to reach her world. I have heard other stories of situations like that, where a celestial being comes into this human world, mates, and then disappears, leaving the partner longing and dedicating many lives to meditation to attain that higher state. It was not such an uncommon story, especially in those days."

"Did you ever find that daughter again?"

A gentle chuckle escaped his lips as he looked at me with wide eyes and replied, "She is seated beside me now."

Looking at him in amazement, I asked, "Is that a true story?"

"That is a question my granddaughter Chunhua always used to ask, and I would always reply, 'I would not tell it to you were it not true.'"

I was silent, unable to respond. It was impossible for me to peer that far into the past, but at least one part of the story definitely rang true. Ama-la had been a mother to me, a mother from whom I had been separated, a mother for whom I had yearned and who finally had found me again, who had come to me in a time of great need, perhaps a turning point in the journey of lifetimes. There was no doubt about that.

Tears began to form in the corners of my eyes, and I shut them, trying not to let my emotions flow. Instead, I brought my attention to the present moment, to the environment around me. And I became aware of a tickling breeze brushing against my face. Breathing in deeply, the fresh river air flooded my being, enabling me to almost taste the clear water. The sound of birds flapping their wings and swooping down onto the waves crowded my ears. Yeye had carried me into a distant past, but now I was very much aware of what my senses were experiencing in the moment, and this carried me back to the present. Evening was not far off, and I became conscious of the waning heat of day. Before he had been my grandfather, I thought, he had also been my father, and she truly was Ama-la, a mother who had left me but returned so many millennia later, perhaps in her world the time span of only a few days. What is time truly, I wondered? Ama-la kept referring to events in the future as 'soon,' and I had guessed that she lived in a different dimension of time, where the passing of days was but minutes, and the passing of years but days. After some time of silence, I asked, "Why did she come to me now after so long?"

"It was the one you call Dalha who found her and sent her. You had prayed to Dalha and she responded. This mother from ancient days had been waiting for the time to meet you again, a time when you would need what she could offer. She could open the door to the past for you. But there was another reason. When we lived in Hanning, and you were Chunhua and I your Yeye, I had been struggling with how to guide you, knowing that whatever choice you made, whether you fled or stayed with your family, suffering would follow. Then one night in sleep I felt a presence and heard a voice telling me to help you flee. I didn't know whose voice it was until much later, but I understood that by fleeing you would be spared the pain of seeing a son, to whom you were quite attached, become so consumed by anger and hatred. You did not have the inner strength or awareness then to help that son, and even as Claire, you were unable to face him. Only now, in this life, with great assistance, could you do that. In addition, the one you know as Dalha helped her fulfill her long held desire to meet you again at a time when it would benefit you, when she could be of great service."

"Dalha knows Ama-la." I whispered. "She made this possible."

Once again, the question of who she was came into my mind and Yeye hurried to say, "Never mind that. The important thing is that your mother of long ago had some unfinished matters to complete, and Dalha saw that this was the time when she could be who she has long wanted to be to you, when it would help you the most. Since you knew her last, that dakini mother has also grown in understanding and wisdom. Just as humans grow and learn through the cycle of rebirth, beings in those other realms have their own way of advancing. In these two years she was able to be the mother to you that she could not be in that earlier time. You see, many things have come to completion."

"But she left before I was able to thank her," I murmured. "I owe her such a debt of gratitude." In the short time that I was with Ama-la, she had turned my world around and I had come to love her deeply. I had learned so much from her. I would miss her and wouldn't forget her for the rest of my days.

"There is no debt to a mother, and the heart says what words cannot express. She was able to witness a complete change in you, a time of great growth. That is the only reward needed. Now, what lies ahead for you, Bumo, is to learn to access everything you need by going within. You can reach Ama-la anytime you attune your mind to her, for the reconnection has been made."

At that moment, I could think of nothing more to ask. We stayed a while longer by the river until the lowering rays of light spilled across the water, casting a most beautiful glow, and Yeye indicated that we should return to the hut.

When we arrived back, Yeye said that he would prepare the food, as Ama-la had done, while I meditated. Before going over to the meditation corner, I asked, "Yeye, do you live here in Böd now?" He shook his head. "But this dress . . . you look like some official."

"She left these for me," he replied with a chuckle. "I found them here when I arrived and so I put them on. I thought you might be more comfortable seeing me dressed as the people from this region."

"Did you meet her here at the hut before I returned?"

He shook his head. "I had other matters to tend to and came when I had finished. She was already gone."

I didn't ask anything further, although there was so much more that I wanted to know. Where did Ama-la come from and how did she get here? Where did he live now and were they united? The story he had told me was far more than I could comprehend, but I didn't dare doubt his words. It seemed to be more like the legends of old than real life, but my birth mother had always told that me that the legends were true, only difficult to fully comprehend with our limited intelligence. Since my youth, she had filled my head with stories of godly beings, the lha, who had first lived in ancient Böd before humans came, but those stories had not seemed real to me then. Now I had to rethink everything she had told me.

After the evening meal, Yeye said that he would sit outside during the night to commune with the stars; it was a treat to see them from the vantage point of earth. Instead of sleeping, I insisted on sitting out in the open with him, realizing what precious time this was. I knew he would soon disappear, as Ama-la had, and my limited time with them would become dream-like. As we sat under the stars, he asked if there was anything I wanted to know. After a few moments of thought, I remarked quietly, "I have been wondering what that place where Ama-la lives is like."

"There are many, many worlds in this vast universe, reflecting different levels of consciousness. That world where she lives is composed of light, not condensed matter, and it is here right now, only human senses are not refined enough to perceive it. In that realm of light, there are many planets, like in this physical world, and many, many beings, more numerous than on earth. In the higher realms, they assist with maintaining harmony and balance throughout the worlds. Some of those beings can cross into this world, although it is rare for physical beings to cross into theirs. They are called the lha, the gods and goddesses, but even among them are very different levels of consciousness."

"Is her world one of the Buddha realms?" I asked.

"You might say that, for there are buddhas, or enlightened beings, who reside there. But again, there are so many degrees of awareness. Everybody, when they die and leave their physical form, crosses into another dimension of reality. For those who are still materially minded, they may experience a sleep-like or dream state and remain semi-consciousness until they take rebirth. Many others recall that their true nature is not a material one, and they experience a much more joyous and expansive state of being, finding those they have known and loved in the past, until latent samskaras compel them to take birth again."

"Could I have met Ama-la between human births?" I asked curiously. "I don't remember anything about those times."

He smiled. "Most of us don't remember our time in the worlds between births. But I do not believe that you met her there. The time frame in that world is very different from the one here. Ten thousand human years is but a few years in the more elevated worlds, and to her it probably seems that it was not long ago when you were born to her as a daughter. One thing I know about the dakinis, or *gandharvas* as some of the heavenly beings are called, is that they have long memories and do not forget as we do. They can see into the past and future and attune themselves with someone with whom they are very close, and they can experience their memories as well. That is how she was able to know so much about you."

"And you, Yeye, where do you live now?"

"After you knew me as Yeye during the Han Empire, I took only one more human birth, but I come into this world every now and then for special reasons. There are some still here for whom I have taken responsibility, and I come for them. I had promised that I would help you make peace with that son of long ago, and I was meant to be here with you these last two years helping you to recover your memories, but she requested that I delay my appearance, and I agreed. I understood her reasons. But I will not be here long, my dear, as I have other matters to which I must attend."

I was seated on the ground outside of the hut next to Yeye. Since his arrival I had not shown him any physical affection, feeling too shy before this form of his with which I was not familiar. How vividly I recalled laying my head against the shoulder of the hermit grandfather whom I had known in the past, when I was the young woman Chunhua. How often I had hugged him and rested with his arm around me. But I was no longer that young woman and couldn't behave as if I were. He seemed to understand and looked at me affectionately, and in the dim moonlight I perceived a faint smile.

"You cannot be Chunhua again, nor the Tang poet Shu, nor the nun Claire," he said softly. I looked at him in amazement, wondering how he knew about those other lives. Now you are Padma Tshomo, and soon you will be someone else. Don't be attached to any of it. Learn from all that comes to you, both the good and the bad, for there are teachings in both, equally valuable.

"In this life, not only have you made peace with that son of long ago, but you also have been shown how to transform negative energies and emotions, something you will have to put into practice again and again and again. That is the way to progress. Anger and fear are part of the human experience, but they impede growth and disturb the processes of life, affecting much more than the one individual, impacting the balance and harmony of the whole. Through spiritual practice, you can dispel negative emotions, but you also must carry the fruits of your meditation into your daily interactions. The deeper spiritual work is to watch the mind moment to moment, not only when you are in meditation. A good part of spiritual practice takes place while one is fully engaged in the demands of life. Only then can you tell how far you have progressed.

"Remember, my dear, each step you take, each lifetime, brings you closer to the goal of knowing who you are. Take what you have learned and the love you have experienced and carry that forward. You will meet your Ama-la again when the time is right. So much depends on timing.

"One lesson I had to learn over many lifetimes was to expand my yearning for my consort into a yearning for full awakening, to living fully in the Dao as I once would have said to you. The more earnestly I sought after her, the farther away she seemed, because I was grasping, acting from a place of desire, of wanting, not realizing that what I was thirsting after was already with me. As soon as I let go and found myself living naturally in the Dao, without any expectation or wanting, she was right beside me, and I understood that separation is an illusion, a shadow cast by an uninformed mind. Never had we been apart; it was I who had failed to perceive her." After a slight chuckle he added, "And as a matter of fact, I see her now. She is here with us, smiling at our conversation. You can't see her because she has slipped behind the thin etheric veil that shields that world from your sight."

As the night wore on and I listened to Yeye speaking, my eyes began to droop from fatigue. It was well into the darkest hours, with dawn still a distance away. Seeing my tired state, Yeye's voice grew quieter, almost like a subtle background hum. "In you, I still see many characteristics of Chunhua. You have grown in experience and understanding, but I still see her in you, such an endearing child. Memories never die. They lie dormant somewhere, ready to be roused at any time." He continued to speak, but I could no longer distinguish the words as I drifted into a most peaceful repose.

I awoke hours later to find the morning sun flowing in through the window. The shutters had been thrown wide open as Ama-la had done when she was there. I turned over and closed my eyes, not yet ready to rise, but then I remembered that Yeye was with me, and I shouldn't waste the precious time sleeping away the day. Quickly rising, I saw that he wasn't in the meditation corner. Going outside, I glanced around, but he wasn't anywhere in sight. Returning inside again, I found a bowl of tsampa and vegetables on the table. Clearly, Yeye had left it. Perhaps he has gone for a walk, I thought.

Before eating, I went to the bath hut and found the tub filled with hot water. He has the same abilities as Ama-la, I said to myself with a smile. Sinking into the tub, I felt my body relax from the exertion of the day before. It was only yesterday that I had returned from Zerdan's monastery, and the ride had tired me out. That was why I fell asleep, I thought, but how did I get into my bed? The last I remembered, I was sitting outside by Yeye's side, listening to him talk.

After the bath, I went to the meditation corner and sat for a while. Then I ate the food that Yeye had laid out, hoping that he would soon return. Although the warmer months were in the last days of their decline, the weather was still quite pleasant, and I decided to wait for him outside the hut. For many hours, I sat there on the ground, watching the few people who passed by in the valley below, continually looking out for him, but Yeye didn't come. Night arrived, but no Yeye. There was still some food in the pot on the stove, and I ate half of it for the evening meal and went to bed, thinking perhaps he would return the next morning. When I woke up many hours later, day was breaking. No food was laid out, but the tub was filled with warm water. He must still be here somewhere, I said to myself.

That day, I did what I always did when Ama-la was there. After the bath, I meditated and then ate the food remaining from the night before. Afterwards I went outside to wait.

For hours I sat on the ground outside the hut, taking in the scene around me, hoping for Yeye's return. As the day passed, I began to review the many things I had experienced when Ama-la was there. After recalling the life of Chunhua when I had fled from my family, I had said to Ama-la, "What kind of mother would abandon her children?" Now I felt terrible for having uttered those words, and I wondered if she had taken it personally. But she never indicated that she had. Not for a moment had she spoken from a place of guilt or regret. Perhaps those are only human emotions, I thought. Perhaps she understood that in time all would be made right. There is nothing to mourn, nothing to celebrate, for everything comes into balance in its own time. Wasn't that the lesson she was trying to teach me?

I had greatly mourned Beau's death, but then we met again and had a happier life than we could have had in that place at that time. It worked out better than anyone could have arranged. And I knew that I would meet Yeshe again, of that I had no doubt, in a future that awaited me.

The pain and guilt I had felt about abandoning my children in the life of Chunhua, the fear I had of that son when he was reborn as Jacque, and the power Zerdan held over me, all of that had now dissolved. What was left was only love and gratitude. I had given that reborn son of mine all that I had to give, but what truly mattered was that I gave him a new beginning, an opportunity to amend his wrongs. I had been able to save his life. What more could a mother ask to do?

And the goddess I had been searching for, had I found her in this life? This question perplexed me. Suddenly the image of Dalha came to my mind and the words she had once spoken returned to me. Didn't she tell me to find the goddess inside, and wasn't that also the guidance of Beau and Yeye?

The day's light was fading, and I went into the hut, realizing that Yeye would not return that day or any other. After cooking the last of the root vegetables that had been stored away, a fare that could not compare to what Ama-la used to prepare, I went over to the meditation corner and sat there with an unfocused mind adrift in so many memories. I tried not to dwell on them but couldn't help getting caught in the emotions of the scenes that were emerging. I decided to persist and wait for my mind to empty itself.

Much time had passed when slowly the darkness of shuttered eyes gave way to a subtle light in the middle of which sat a fierce blue female form, gazing directly at me with fiery eyes open wide, her many hands wielding deadly weapons. Abundant, flaming hair streamed wildly in all directions. She was not adorned with beautiful jewels or flowing robes, but rather her half-naked body seemed more like that of a rugged ascetic than a heavenly figure. Strangely, despite the utter intensity of her presence, at the sight of her a great calm washed over me as if cleansing me, accompanied by a deep sense of wellbeing. In her eyes, I saw the merging of all duality. She was the awakener of fear and the means to overcome it, the arouser of anger and the subduer of it, the obstacles and the overcoming of them, the agony and the joy that relieves the pain. In her rested the opposing forces and the harmonizing of those forces. She encompassed the totality—what we view as the good and the bad. Her very presence bestowed a sublime experience and enabled me to ascend to the state of mind where dualities meet and are transcended. As I stared internally at the powerful form, fear became a distant memory and anger a forgotten emotion. She washed them away, purifying me of their negative imprints, and replacing them with a distinctive, expansive love.

The image remained clear in my sight only for a brief time and then faded away, replaced by the darkness of closed eyes, leaving in my mind only the whispered words: "Palden Lhamo, the pacifier and great protector." For a long time that night, I was unable to move, overcome by gratitude for the visitation and the teaching it conveyed. Is she an internal or external reality, my mind asked? Both, my heart replied. If she lives within you, there is no need to search outside.

This was not the image of the goddess I had envisioned and long sought, but somehow it was the form I now most welcomed—the protector, the awakener of strength and conviction, the destroyer of evil and all negativities. She was the one who released me from my past. For so long, through multiple lifetimes, I had thought I was seeking the beatific form of the goddess—the gentle, smiling face, richly adorned—but it was her fierce face that she showed me, with flaming eyes and hands wielding powerful weapons, because that was the form I most needed. It was in that form that I found the great overflowing of love.

The vision was still with me when I awoke the next morning. It seemed to have stayed with me throughout the night, carrying me in sleep to a place I had never been before, at least not in my memory. I didn't know if what I had seen was my imagination or a real experience, but it didn't seem to matter. Something had transpired that had changed me inside in a way I couldn't quite articulate or even understand. I lingered in bed, not wanting to leave that peaceful state. When I finally arose, I went to the bath hut, but seeing that the tub was empty, I returned to the main hut and whispered to myself, "They have now really left." Going over to the meditation corner, I sat there for quite some time. The vision of the night before didn't return, but a glow from the previous night remained with me as well as the upliftment I had experienced.

After meditation, I went to the kitchen area, but there was not a morsel of food left. I checked all the water jugs and there was only enough to fill my small traveling jug for the journey back to Lhasa. For the first time the house felt empty, and I knew it was a sign that it was time for me to leave, but I was loathe to depart from the place that had given me so much. Without them, I thought, this is only an empty hut, but then why was it so difficult for me to leave it behind?

I sat outside for a while. Although I realized that I could not stay any longer, I was unable to make myself climb onto Anpu and ride away. I was in this indecisive state when I heard Ama-la's voice inside of me. "Your work here is done, Bumo. Go now to your sister. She needs you."

"Pumo needs me?" I whispered. Then I thought, I don't even know where to find her. She and Tashi could be at any number of monasteries in Böd painting murals. The next thought was to go to Bhasundara. She would have word of Pumo. Suddenly, concern for my sister arose within me, and I felt an urgency to see her. In that moment I knew that I had returned to the life of Padma Tshomo.

CHAPTER 28

The Return

I looked around the hut for the last time, wanting to take something from that place that would retain the memory for me. All I could find were the few silk chubas that Ama-la had given me, so I packed those into my bag along with the items of clothing that I had brought. Without further delay, I climbed onto Anpu and rode away, stopping only once to gaze back at the stone hut tucked into the low cliff above the valley.

It took me two days to reach the city. As I drew closer to Lhasa, anxiety over my sister grew stronger. For the first time, I prayed to the goddess who had visited me in vision, to Palden Lhamo, that Pumo was not dying, that she would not leave me. Only days earlier I had told Zerdan that I would go live with her. She could not die, not now. I had to see her again.

While riding back to Lhasa, I could not help but note the irony of my situation. Throughout my life I had wanted to see the goddess. But it wasn't any of the goddesses I had heard about from my mother—not Drablai Gyalmo nor Nam Tsho Chukmo, who had come to me, but rather Palden Lhamo, goddess of Lhamo La-tso, and I understood the meaning. It was Ama-la who had finally integrated for me the two traditions that I had lived between, so that I could become a Bon Buddhist and never again feel torn between these two spiritual paths. I now knew that in the ultimate sense they were one. She had accomplished this for me. While working to help me resolve samskaras from the past, she had also guided me to a deeper spiritual understanding of a profound truth: the forces in the universe that we call deities have many, many names, as do we. In these two years, I had experienced being the different faces of Claire, Chunhua, Padma Tshomo, and Bumo, all at the same time. Those personalities and forms continued to live within me, so it must be the same with the deities.

During the ride back to Lhasa I came to truly appreciate the teachings that I had received over the last two years. When I reached Bhasundara's forest cottage, it was late in the night and all was dark, yet I felt she would be expecting me, that she would know I was returning. When I pushed open the door, I found her in the entry room seated at the table with her head resting on her chest, fast asleep. Quietly calling her name, I expected her to immediately rise and embrace me, but her response was somewhat different. Slowly lifting her head and opening her eyes, she stared at me for a few moments without speaking, then quietly in a sleepy voice said, "You are not the same Tshomo that I left at the hut in the Yarlung Valley two years ago."

"You are right," I replied with a faint smile. "Did you know I would be returning tonight?"

"Dalha usually gives me a hint of what lies ahead, and I had an inkling that you would return sometime soon, perhaps this week. So, I have been waiting. Come, sit and eat what I have prepared. You must be hungry after the long ride."

At the mention of Dalha, a warm feeling arose in my heart, and I realized that she was also responsible for the change that had come over me. It was she who had shown Bhasundara in a dream the face of Ama-la, and that is how we had found her. It was she who had found Ama-la in her celestial world and sent her to me. As I ate, I noticed a somewhat somber expression on her face and asked if anything was wrong.

"At Pumo's insistence I visited Ama-la a few times to check on you, but you were always out when I came, and I never stayed long. When I visited last, Pumo had returned to live in Lhasa. Her husband Tashi was losing his eyesight and could no longer paint. I explained this to Ama-la, and she said . . ." Bhasundara didn't finish her sentence. Putting aside the food I was eating, I gazed at her steadily and asked her to continue. "She said that he would not live much longer, and that she would see to it that you returned before he died. That is why I have been waiting for you, every night cooking food for you, and sitting here until I couldn't stay awake any longer. Tshomo, Tashi is very sick. I have been tending to him, but I don't think he will live more than a few weeks at the most."

I felt myself become pale. "Tashi," I murmured. "Tashi, dying?" My awareness began to drift as if my feet had slipped off a ledge of a mountain, and I was tumbling through the air. I had been in such an elevated state these past two years, and especially the last few days, and now to think my sister was suffering such a loss while I was away, and not there to support her. Tashi, who was so dear to me and all the family, he was leaving us.

"Tshomo, your challenge now is not to lose what you have gained. I see what a change has come over you. It is evident in your face, in your very appearance. But it is one thing to feel joy and peace when in retreat, and quite another to maintain it during times of great heartache. If you allow yourself to sink into sorrow, you won't be able to help Pumo, who is going through a difficult time."

"I must go to her now," I said, rising from the seat.

"Tshomo, it is the middle of the night!" she exclaimed. "You can't go anywhere now. I have made a bed for you. Get a good night's sleep and come with me first thing in the morning when I go to bring him medicine."

I nodded, realizing how tired my body truly was. I fell asleep almost immediately but awoke early and found Bhasundara sitting outdoors, wrapped in a light woolen jacket, watching the dawning sun. The first signs of the changing seasons were upon us: a cooling crispness in the air accompanied by distinctive scents, a harbinger of the dry season that lay ahead.

I had so many questions, but I knew that now was not the time. All my thoughts had to be on my family. But before seeing them, I had to learn how much they knew about where I had been during the last two years.

"Bhasundara, does my family know about Ama-la?"

She shook her head. "Only you and I know about her, and it will stay that way, Tshomo. Even I don't know much, except that hers was the face that Dalha showed me in a dream, and she was there in that hut when we went searching. It is better that you don't speak of your time there, even to me. Such sacred experiences are meant to be kept wrapped in the heart. Speech will only degrade them." Rising she came to hug me and with a slight giggle added, "I was reluctant to embrace you last night, when I saw how different you look. But although you have changed, you are still my dear friend Padma Tshomo."

"And will always be," I replied, returning her hug.

Bhasundara quickly prepared po cha and millet and, after gathering her medicines, we left for Pumo's new home. Indicating that she would go around to the back where she kept additional medicine plants for Tashi, she left me at the front door. After knocking, I pushed the door open and to my surprise found my son Tenzin standing before me. We both spoke at the same time, each of us wearing a look of shock on our face.

"Ma, you have returned."

"Tenzin, you are back."

"It was not a time to express joy with our Tashi so sick, but for a moment we stood gazing at one another, and then came a long embrace. A few minutes later he was leading me by the hand into a sitting room where we could speak privately. I will take you to see *Ani-la* (aunt) after we talk," he said.

"How is your *Agu* (uncle)," I asked with a pained look.

"A little stronger today. Ani-la is with him, helping him to eat."

"When did you return from the Song?"

"A few weeks ago," he replied. "After I returned, the abbot sent me here, saying that he had heard that Ani-la had moved back to Lhasa and that her husband was very ill. I have been staying here, helping out. What about you, Ma? I thought you were still on retreat. You look different, more stable than when I last saw you."

I smiled at him. "My retreat also ended a few days ago. It was a wonderful retreat with a very advanced woman teacher. I have learned a great deal. Now I will have to apply what I have learned."

"Is she a Bonpo?"

"A Bonpo and a Buddhist," I replied with a slight laugh. "A Bon Buddhist, as I am."

"I have never heard you say that before," he replied, amused.

"You will hear me say things you have not heard before. Now take me to see my sister. I am very worried about her. We will have time to catch up later."

We didn't have a chance to even rise from our seats. Looking up, I saw Pumo standing in the doorway with watery eyes. Rushing over, she bent over and hugged me as I began to rise, and I heard her whisper somewhat sternly, "Padma Tshomo, you are never to leave me again."

"And I never will," I whispered back.

Days later I was seated with Tenzin and my two daughters, who had arrived from Amdo. My youngest daughter Yara was also there, as well as Pumo's two sons and her daughter. Tashi seemed to have gained back some of his strength and was able also to join us, and we were in a somewhat celebratory mood. It had been a long time since our two families had gathered in this way. It was then that Tenzin brought out the gifts for the family that he had carried back from the Great Song. Lush silk robes for his sisters; a painted scroll of mountains for Pumo and Tashi, and smaller gifts for Pumo's children and his nieces and nephews. He had brought other gifts for my brothers and their families, which he had already given them. After handing out the gifts, Tenzin sat back with a sly smile on his face, taking pleasure in seeing how satisfied everyone was with the objects he had brought back.

"Didn't you bring anything for Ama-la?" asked Yara in surprise.

"I don't need any gift," I hurried to say. "I am happy to have my son home and the family together. That is the only gift I want."

Turning his gaze to me, Tenzin remarked cryptically, "I was trying to think of what to bring you. You had sold or given away all the precious items that Apa-la had brought you over the years, so I knew that you wouldn't want any more of those. You had told me that you were simplifying your life, freeing yourself of material possessions."

"That is all true. I don't need a gift, Tenzin."

"But I wanted to bring you something. Then I remembered when Apa-la and I had traveled through the Song Empire, he had searched for books of poetry to bring you. He had told me then that you loved poetry and that great poetry was written during the Han and Tang Dynasties. Although we looked at scrolls and books, he decided that it would be too difficult to translate them, and so we never brought any back. During that trip, he mentioned that if I ever returned to the Song and knew enough of the Han language, I should get a book of poetry and translate it for you, and he recommended a few poets he had heard about. In the years since, I forgot about it. But before returning home from the Song Empire this time, I met a Daoist, who handed me this book of poetry; it happened to be poems by one of the poets Apa-la had recommended. So this is a gift as much from him as from me. I translated all the poems for you." As he spoke, Tenzin took out of his bag a book and handed it to me.

"Who is the poet?" I asked, my eyes moistening. When he mentioned his father, suddenly I felt Yeshe there in the room with the rest of us.

"His name is Li Bai, and he is much loved by people throughout the Song Empire for he wrote about the common people and their struggles. There are many interesting facts about him. For one, he was married to a woman poet, but her poems have been lost and nobody knows much about her."

"What else?" I asked in a teary voice, very much touched by the gift.

Although he was Daoist, he also knew much about Buddhism, and it is said that he integrated both traditions. He was devoted to the Goddess of the Moon, called Chang'e in the Han language. I thought that would be meaningful to you. They say that one night while riding in a boat drunk, he saw the reflection of the moon in the water and, reaching out to embrace what he thought was the Goddess of the Moon, he fell into the water and died. It is just a story, but it shows his love for the goddess."

Hugging the book to my chest, I replied, "You could not have found a more meaningful gift for me."

"Apa-la would be happy that I could translate the poems for you. Translating poetry is not easy," he replied with a slight laugh.

The improvement in Tashi's condition was only temporary and, a few weeks later, he lay dying. How glad I was that I could be with Pumo to help her through this time of loss. The days after his passing were busy with family. My daughters from Amdo were still in Lhasa, and my two brothers were also very much present, along with their children and the children of my eldest brother Sonam, who had died a few years earlier. And then there was Tashi's family.

Since my return, I had had to put to one side thoughts of Ama-la and Yeye, the vision of Palden Lhamo, and my remembrances of the past. If I allowed myself to return mentally to the hut, I would not have been able to be present for the others.

At Pumo's insistence, as soon as I returned, I shifted from Bhasundara's cottage to her house. "This is your home now," she had told me firmly as she ushered me into a small guest room, which was fitted with a small rug and cushion, a low bed, and a chest for clothing. Walking over to one corner, I was startled to find a small, lifelike painted scroll of Palden Lhamo. I recognized her immediately from the vision I had experienced.

"Is this Tashi's painting?" I asked admiringly, going close to examine it. "It is so powerful and beautiful."

"I painted it," she replied modestly. "Tashi has not been able to paint for some time. It is of Palden Lhamo. Remember the goddess of the lake Lhamo La-tso we once visited? She is a rather fierce goddess, and perhaps I should put a painting of Tara here instead."

"No, no," I hurried to say. "This painting is perfect, exactly what I need. I love it."

"Are you sure, Padma? You can make any changes to this room. It is yours. And if it is not suitable, you can choose another room. I want you to feel at home."

"I am at home," I replied quietly. "And everything is just as it should be. There is nothing I would change."

"If you like, I can paint a scroll of a Bon goddess to hang here?"

I shook my head and replied, "Palden Lhamo is the one I want."

A few weeks had passed since Tashi's death and Tenzin was preparing to return to the monastery. As I accompanied him on a walk around Lhasa, he began to describe the cities of the Great Song. "There is so much activity in the towns there, so much economic and cultural life, and so many people, crowds everywhere in the larger cities, with many markets."

"Did you like the Song, Tenzin?"

"I was amazed how in certain areas they are very advanced. I like the Song very much, but I like Gyagar equally."

"How do those two places compare with Böd?" I asked tentatively, wondering if he felt as I did about our land.

He was thoughtful for a moment and then replied, "It is said that the feet of Guru Rinpoche and his consort Yeshe Tsogyal have touched every corner of this land, and so I guess that makes Böd very special."

"Your *Momo-la* (grandmother), whom you never met, used to tell me stories of the ones who first came to this land. They were called the lha, godly beings. That also makes this place special. No matter what happens in the world, I believe the lha, Guru Rinpoche, and Yeshe Tsogyal will always protect this land."

Tenzin then added reflectively, "Ama-la, while that might be true, there is another view, which states that Böd is not necessarily a geographical place, but rather a state of mind. In that case, it would mean that Guru Rinpoche and Yeshe Tsogyal have touched all corners of the mind, awakening it fully. When I was in Gyagar, I heard the same said about Bharat, the old name for Gyagar. The word Bharat means one who is engaged in the search for knowledge. Anyone seeking truth lives in Bharat, and I believe the same can be said for Böd. Anyone seeking to awaken the enlightened mind lives in Böd. Now we think of it as a geographical region, but borders change, people migrate, empires come and go. Nothing stays the same, except that which is unchanging. So, I believe Böd is a state of mind, and I hope to always live there."

I smiled and thought how wise my son had become. He sounded so much like his father.

The day before Tenzin was to return to the monastery and my two daughters were to return to Amdo, we had a last meal together with Pumo and her children. During the gathering of the family, Pumo had restrained her grief, but I knew that once everyone had left, that would be the time she would need me most, and I was trying to prepare myself. But I was also longing for solitude where I could continue to recall the many experiences that I had while I was with Ama-la. Pumo and I were both in a reserved mood as we listened to the chatter of our grown children.

Turning to me suddenly, she said in a very quiet tone, "Tshomo, I want to return to Nam Tsho. I have not been back to the lake in many years. Now that Tashi is gone, I want to sit by the side of the goddess once more."

"It is not an easy ride, Pumo, and we are old now," I replied in a half whisper so that our children wouldn't hear. I knew that they would encourage anything that would lift Pumo's spirits, but I was not sure that I was up for the journey. Suddenly, the conversation among our children ceased, and they all turned their eyes toward us as they had clearly overheard our words.

"Ani-la, Ama-la, I will take you," declared my eldest daughter, Samaya. "I have never been to the lake." My two other daughters chimed in that they wanted to go as well.

"Let us take our daughters," urged Pumo. "Our mother would have liked her granddaughters to see the sacred lake and greet the goddess there."

Tenzin looked at us in mock indignation. "Why just take your daughters? The sons would like to go as well." Pumo's sons concurred, and so it was agreed that the whole family would go once the warm weather returned and before the rains descended.

CHAPTER 28

Reunion

For several weeks I stayed by Pumo's side, hardly ever leaving her, trying in every way to distract her and cheer her up.

"I didn't stay with you for long after Yeshe died," she said to me one day in an apologetic tone. "I am very sorry about that."

"What are you talking about? You were with me for weeks, until I finally chased you away."

"I guess you are right. I forgot," she replied with a slight laugh. "And now I must chase you away. You have not had a minute to yourself since you returned from your retreat. Go visit your friend Bhasundara. I am fine, really."

Bhasundara had come regularly to treat Tashi before he died, but I had not had any time alone with her, and then she stopped coming after his passing. I yearned to see her but had been trying to put aside my own needs to tend fully to Pumo. Now was the opportunity.

After telling Pumo that I would spend the night at Bhasundara's and return the next day, I rode out to the cottage. My friend was not at home when I arrived, so I sat down at the table and waited, thinking that she might be in the city tending to some sick person. When she didn't return after some time, I decided to walk in the small forest that abutted her cottage. The cooler weather had already arrived, but there might still be a few edible plants left amidst the yellowing forest growth, and I decided to search for them for the evening meal.

As I strolled through the slightly cleared paths, I caught sight of Bhasundara seated in meditation in one of her favorite spots. Going over to her, I saw that she was deeply immersed and wouldn't hear me, so I sat down beside her and entered meditation. Ever since my time with Ama-la, the peaceful state came to me more easily, but I couldn't say that my meditations were long or deep. Often, I found myself reliving a scene from the past, revealing nuances I hadn't noticed before.

As I sat there, I gradually felt myself slipping away from the external world, a state with which I had become familiar, and I found myself back in Hanning, in Yeye's forest cottage, the night before I was to flee accompanied by his student Yu Yan. Yeye and I had stayed up talking late into the night, but before the first hint of dawn he had told me to get some rest because the journey would be long and arduous. I lay on the floor mat unable to sleep, fitfully tossing about. Finally, I must have slipped into a light sleep state but was awakened by a woman weeping in the next room, quietly crying, "How can I leave you, Shifu." *Shifu* (master)was what Yu Yan called my grandfather, and I knew that it was she struggling to muffle her cries.

"I am too old to take her away myself, and there is nobody else I can trust," he explained gently. "I must put her in your hands."

"But Shifu, who will take care of you?"

A quiet laugh escaped his lips. "Yu Yan, do I need anyone to take care of this old bag of flesh?"

She continued to weep but then I heard her ask mournfully, "I will not see you again, will I?"

"Are you that attached to this aged form?" he asked in a gentle tone, and then his voice became sterner. "Many times, I have told you that this body has become a hindrance, of little value to me. Whether you stay or go, this body will soon be gone. I am asking you not only to take Chunhua to safely, but also to guide her through the difficult years ahead.

As you have cared for me, you must care for her now. A student must one day become a teacher, and you can be that for her."

"I can't be her teacher, Shifu," she replied as she restrained her sobs. "Only you are that. I am just a poor forest dweller, your servant."

He answered in a loving tone. "That is not how I see you. Not at all. It is time for you to become who you truly are—a strong spiritual warrior, who can withstand all difficulties. This is a test for you as well. You have spent many years with me and now is the time to spread your wings and fly on your own. And I know that you can and you will. I am sending you away for a purpose."

"Shifu, I cannot be her teacher, but I can be her friend, and that I will be."

Her voice was now calm and steady, and I heard him ask, "Is a teacher not also a friend? You have within you all the wisdom you need to guide her." He sighed. "A student must one day leave the teacher in order to realize her potential. I want to see you fly, Yu Yan."

"I want to fly with you," she replied in a constrained voice.

"And so you will. Wherever you are, I will be beside you. I will never let go of the hand of those who come to me for guidance. Whenever you enter a forest, you will find me there walking among the trees. When you look up at the night sky, perhaps you will see me passing between the stars. When you quiet your mind and peer inside, into the vast trove hidden within, that is where you and I will be together. I won't lose sight of you, my dear Yu Yan. That is my promise. And when the time is right, you will see my physical form again, but perhaps a newer version." Then he posed this question to her. "What is the meaning of Laozi's words—*The sage travels all day / And never leaves his supply wagon?*"

Her voice was firm, and I heard her say in a determined tone. "You have recited those words to me so often. They mean that everything I need is within me. No matter where I go, no matter how far I travel, no matter what I go through, no matter what trials come, I am in the Dao and the Dao is in me."

"Then there is no need for tears, is there? This simple teaching is all you require, but it cannot remain in the realm of thought and words only. It must become a lived reality. I want you to continue reflecting deeply on these words during your times of cultivation (meditation). You will now have a chance to put into practice all that I have taught you." His voice became quite gentle and loving as he counseled her, "Yu Yan, when you lose the awareness of oneness with the Dao, turn to Chang-e, look to the Moon Goddess. She will help you regain that attunement. You have served me well all these years, now serve my granddaughter. A time will come when you may go in search of her children. Sadly, the son will follow the way of his father, but you mustn't let her know the full extent. Shield her as much as you can. When she is stronger and more settled in the Dao, then she will resolve that relationship."

Their voices quieted and I couldn't hear them any longer, but for the first time I felt what Yu Yan was going through on my behalf, what it was like for her to leave her beloved Shifu, whom she had served for so many years. I had been so caught up in my own feelings those last few days that I hadn't considered the sacrifice she was making for me. She was leaving the one she loved most in the world, her Shifu. Tears came into my eyes as I thought of her sacrifice and the love between her and Yeye. Was this the quality of love between a student and the master? I understood the love between grandfather and granddaughter, but this was something different, or was it? I had not gotten to know Yu Yan well over the years, because she had always maintained a background presence when I visited my grandfather. Now I wanted to understand this one who was so completely devoted to him.

Bhasundara's surprised voice abruptly hurled me back into the present. "Tshomo, what are you doing here, and why are you crying?"

My eyes had moistened when I realized the tender love between my Yeye and his student. Now I opened my eyes and gazed into Bhasundara's cheerful face, recognizing her immediately as that very Yu Yan, who was now my dearest friend, truly my teacher in this life, sharing with me her experiences and the teachings she received from Dalha. She must have noticed the shocked expression on my face because she immediately asked me what was wrong, but I shook my head without speaking and tried to smile.

We walked back to her cottage in silence. I remembered her telling me not to talk about my inner experiences with anyone, not even with her, so I kept quiet about what I had just witnessed. Later, when we were preparing the evening meal, I asked if she remembered anything about her past. "I mean the distant past," I clarified. "An earlier life."

With a mysterious smile, she replied, "Tshomo, I see the future, not the past. Why look back when we are meant to move forward?"

"You see the future?" I asked in amazement, putting down the chopper I was using to cut the plants I had gathered in the forest.

"We'll talk about that another time," she replied simply.

Stopping my work, I went over to the low table and sat down on one of the floor cushions. "Come sit and talk with me for a few minutes. We have hardly had a chance to speak since I came back." We hadn't exchanged many words since returning from the forest a few hours earlier, except about what to prepare for dinner. She came over and sat across from me. "Do you remember the dream you had before you took me to meet Ama-la?" I asked.

"Very vividly."

"What did the man in the dream look like?"

"Why do you ask?"

"It's important for me to know."

She didn't respond right away, but then she began to describe him: "He was quite elderly, thin, slightly bent over. His straggly white hair was drawn up on top of his head in a bun, held together by a pin but not very neatly." She smiled. "Many thin strands were falling down over the side of his face and even to his shoulders. Although he was elderly, he did not seem old to me. His face and eyes had an illumined look. There was such a sparkle, a light in his eyes." As she went on to describe him, I realized that the form she had seen was the man who had lived in Hanning, the Daoist sage Yeye, not the form of the distinguished man who had come to me in the valley hut. I wondered why he had taken a different form when he appeared to me. She continued, "Tshomo, I wasn't going to share this, but now I will. I met that man, rather that adept, I should say, while walking in the forest one day while you were away in retreat."

"You met him?" I asked looking intently at her. "In the flesh?"

"Of course, in the flesh."

"What did he say to you?"

She looked down at the table and didn't respond. I pressed her several times and finally she replied, "Some things are best to keep hidden in the heart, Tshomo. He was not an ordinary man." Then looking up at me, she added in a tone of surprise, "He called me by my name, as if we were on familiar terms."

"Which name?" I asked in an almost breathless voice, hoping that he had called her the name she had had while living in Hanning.

"What do you mean, Tshomo? I only have one name—Bhasundara."

"He called you Bhasundara?" I asked. She nodded as she looked at me with a strange expression.

"What else did he say?"

"I wondered what to call him. He wasn't dressed like a Buddhist monk, and somehow I didn't think he was a Bonpo, but he was clearly a man of great spiritual knowledge so I simply called him Rinpoche. We spent so many hours in the forest that day talking about spiritual matters and meditating. He seemed to know of Dalha and much about my life with her, how she had found me, our travels together, my difficult times. He also seemed very caring of me and asked about my wellbeing, whether I have enough to take care of my material needs. I was touched by that.

"I insisted that he come back to the cottage with me so that I could prepare a meal for him. I have never done that before with a stranger, but this was different. He didn't seem a stranger at all." She paused and smiled as she reflected, "There was such a strong urge in me to serve him, one that I couldn't resist. Then I pleaded with him to spend the night. He agreed to whatever I asked, with such a tender look in his eyes. I prepared a bed for him, but he said that he would stay out during the night looking up at the sky, and he did. I didn't want to leave him so I sat outside watching him, and every now and then he would say a few words, words of great wisdom. During the night such a swelling of love arose in me—a state of love, of complete wellbeing and wholeness that was not directed toward anyone or anything. I had only experienced that state of overwhelming joy once or twice with Dalha, and it came to me again with him.

"When morning arrived, I was so reluctant to let him go that I pleaded with him to stay a little longer. He ended up spending a few days here, mostly meditating outside, but in between those times of silence, his words, always few and carefully chosen, tapped something deep within me. I still didn't want to let him leave after those few days, but I dared not ask him to stay any longer, thinking that would be greedy. Strangely, in that very short time that we had been together, a surge of emotion had emerged in me, a deep attachment to him that I couldn't explain. The thought of him leaving made me very sad.

"Sensing my difficulty in parting with him, he spoke these words to me and told me to reflect on them: '*The Sage travels all day / And never leaves his supply wagon.*' I didn't know where those words came from, whose teaching they were, but I understood his meaning right away, because it was the same message that Dalha had always given me. After he spoke those words to me, he added, 'Why cling to an old rag when a jewel shines inside?' Hearing those words, I no longer tried to detain him. It was as if something in me snapped, freeing me." As she finished speaking, she became reflective.

"What do you mean, something snapped?" I asked, pensively.

"I don't know how to explain it, Tshomo, perhaps an old attachment. I felt myself becoming somewhat detached from everything, and as I looked into his eyes, I simply smiled at him and said, 'Rinpoche, I understand.' He smiled back and replied, 'Only be attached to that which is unchanging,' and then he walked away, just like that." Bhasundara was quiet as she gazed at me, her face shining with a sublime joy, something I had not seen in her before.

"Bhasundara, you have also changed," I said quietly. "Something is different about you."

"That meeting with him affected me deeply. He must have been my teacher in the past, because after he left, many realizations came to me, aspects of Dalha's teachings that I hadn't understood before. I believe he came to break my attachment to all external sources and to make me realize fully that Dalha and he and all the wisdom I seek are already within me. I believe she sent him. Or perhaps he sent her to me in the first place, I don't know. What I do know is that my connection to him is long and deep, as it is to her, and they will both continue to guide me. The truth is that all we need exists within us. Since she left her physical form, my relationship with Dalha has become an internal one. More than before, I hear her speaking to me from inside. And since I met that Rinpoche, it is the same with him. I feel his presence, and his words have been going through my head again and again ever since that time. Whenever I sit to meditate, I see him before me, and I often hear that phrase he spoke before leaving. That brief time with him left a permanent imprint, and just as you have changed, so have I, Tshomo." After a pause she asked, "Is he the consort of that woman in the hut? Did you ever get to meet him?"

I nodded. "What you saw was an earlier incarnation of his. He appeared to me in a body that looked quite distinguished and refined, a stately man really, not elderly but rather ageless."

"That is odd. Why would I see an earlier incarnation?"

"He didn't show you anything of the past?" I asked inquisitively.

"He showed me the future, not the past. But why do you ask?"

"For no reason," I replied and then changed the subject, realizing that what I had seen was meant for me, not for Bhasundara or anyone else.

That night I lay awake, reflecting on what had come to me in meditation in the forest hours earlier. Hundreds of years earlier, Yu

Yan had led me away in my flight from Hanning, taking me far from Yeye, the grandfather I would not see again in that life. Now it was she in the form of Bhasundara who had the vision of him and who led me to the hut where I would meet him again. So many centuries later, she had come in another form to lead me back to him, to help me resolve the matter with my son of that time. Is this how the universe unfolds and balances itself, I wondered? Is this how the law of cause and effect operates in the realm of time, ignoring the passage of centuries as an irrelevance?

Was she not truly still serving her Shifu, even though she didn't realize it? Bhasundara had dropped everything to take me to the hut in the Yarlung Valley, not knowing where we were going or what awaited us. That was her trust. She had said it was her trust in Dalha, but wasn't it also her trust in the man she had seen in the dream, Yeye? Even though she didn't remember him, her higher Self, as Ama-la once had said, knew it all. Then what was the connection between Dalha and Yeye? The fact that those two might in some way be related was something I had never considered. Both Bhasundara and I had forgotten him, but he hadn't forgotten us. I had lost sight of Ama-la, burying her memory in the deepest, most veiled corner of my mind, but she hadn't lost sight of me, although so many millennia and lifetimes had passed, so many changings of bodies and names. Was that the nature of an awakened being, to maintain the awareness of it all?

I didn't get any sleep that night, and after hours of trying unsuccessfully, I rose to greet the slowly opening eyes of dawn. Bhasundara was already seated outside, wrapped tightly in a woolen cape, watching the first rays of sunlight appear on the horizon. I went and sat quietly by her side, hugging my wool jacket around me. The morning air was quite cold, an indication of the frosty days ahead. Neither of us spoke for some time.

"I will go prepare the po cha," she said after a while. I followed her inside while she heated the water and prepared millet and vegetables for the morning meal.

"Bhasundara, Pumo and I are taking our children to Nam Tsho when the weather warms. Will you join us? I have never been there with you, and I am quite sure this will be my last visit."

"It sounds like a family affair. I don't belong there, Tshomo."

"You are my family," I insisted.

"You know, I am a solitary person."

"As I am. Please come with us."

"Let us see when the time arrives."

The cold months lumbered by, increasing our yearning for the warming sun. Many weeks after my visit to Bhasundara, Lopsang came to see me. I can't say that I was happy to see him or to hear news of Zerdan, but I was polite and listened patiently as he described the plight of the man who was once his master and who had been sent to live in a broken-down hut not far from Lhasa. As I had requested, the monastery sent food every now and then, but Lopsang told me that it was not enough to meet his needs. Even he refrained from visiting, and so nobody really knew his state. He explained that Zerdan never fully recovered from his illness, and surely the conditions under which he was now living would adversely affect his health. "He has been greatly humbled. He has fallen from a great height to the lowest of low places," he said sadly.

"Why are you telling me all of this?" I asked, after hearing of Zerdan's current plight.

"I know that deep inside you care," he responded, hopefully.

"I care about what happens to him long-term. If he must suffer now to prevent a worse situation in the future, it is well worth it, no matter what he must go through. If he had continued along the path he was on, he would have accrued many more debts and a very troublesome future for himself. This is far better. I truly hope that he has learned from this experience. There is no room for deception in the spiritual life."

"I believe his remorse is sincere," replied Lopsang, hoping to melt my hardened stance.

I was quiet for a few moments, then added gently, "What Zerdan was lacking is love. Never did I hear him express a word of care or compassion for anyone. I don't think he knows the meaning of those words. I saw the way he treated the other monks—and even you. He wanted only their submission, and that is what he got. Now everyone has abandoned him because they did not feel that he cared. I hope that in the future, his heart will awaken. That is the best that I can wish for him. What I learned on my retreat is that love is the essence of spiritual life. Without that, one has gained nothing, no wisdom at all."

We spoke a little longer and then he left. As always, Lopsang's presence made me uneasy and brought up a host of unpleasant memories. I didn't want to think about him and truly hoped that I wouldn't have to meet him again. That night in my meditation, I revisited the life of Claire. I remembered how I felt when I learned that Margot had been sending money each month for so many years to the family of the daughter I had given birth to, even though the responsibility was mine, not hers. I remembered how I felt when I learned that the mother of Margot and Beau had been secretly sending them what they needed to serve others, when she could no longer be part of their life. I thought about how Ama-la had supplied all the food during the two years I was with her, knowing that I had no funds to give. Even if I had had funds, I knew she would not accept anything from me. Was I also not to learn from my past experiences?

When I had returned from the retreat, my youngest daughter Yara had taken me aside and said that she no longer needed the money from one of our family stores that had been meant for me. I remembered having asked my brother after Yeshe died to give my portion to her, when her family was not doing so well. Now they no longer needed assistance. I accepted her offer since I very much wanted to help support Pumo's household. But after hearing of Zerdan's plight, I began to discretely set aside a small amount every month and send a package of staple foods anonymously to him. I didn't want him or anyone else to know. I had fulfilled all my responsibilities to him and believed that I had resolved any remaining karma. Now my act was simply one of compassion.

Several months later, the family gathered to travel to Nam Tsho. We were a rather large group. Pumo had her daughter and two sons; their spouses and children were to be left home. It was the same with my three daughters. Tenzin was also coming. Samaya had made all the preparations and had arranged for several servants to accompany us. I had seen Bhasundara sporadically since I had invited her along many months earlier; each time I brought up the trip, but every time she refused to commit to joining us. I took one last visit to her cottage and implored her to come on what I viewed as my last sacred journey.

"Why are you so insistent?" she asked as we sat outside enjoying the warming breezes.

"I don't know. I think I just want to experience this last visit to the lake with you, my dearest friend."

She sighed. "You know it is difficult for me to refuse you, yet I don't want to be part of the entourage. I have so much to take care of in these upcoming weeks, but perhaps I will meet you there. Try to find some time to sit by the lake alone. Send the rest of the family off to explore the nearby caves. I am not saying that I will come for sure, but I don't want to disappoint you." That was the best I could get from her, and I had to be satisfied with a perhaps.

We traveled slowly through the path that led to Nam Tsho, taking several days to reach the vicinity. Pumo and I had no desire to speed along, and our children, despite the eagerness of their younger years, ensured that our ride was gentler than it might have otherwise been.

Samaya had arranged for us to stay with a Drokpa family, who had several tents for guests. It was the first time that our two families were having such an adventure together. For me and Pumo, visiting the lake was a sacred experience, and it recalled for us memories of our mother. For my daughters, and I suspected for Puma's children as well, it was a trip to a place of exquisite beauty. What it meant to Tenzin, I couldn't be sure, as he often kept his feelings to himself. As we walked down to the edge of the lake and touched her waters, I could tell that he was greatly moved, but whether it was her beauty or the spiritual presence that touched him, I couldn't tell, and we had little time for private talk together.

We stayed for five days with the Drokpa family, each morning riding to a different part of the lake, spending a few hours by her side. My daughters and their cousins spent time in chatter, while Tenzin was often absorbed in quietly whispering mantras. Then they would all go off to explore different scenic spots, leaving me and Pumo alone.

On the first day as we sat together looking out over the azure blue waters, I told them about their grandmother's love for the lake and the goddess associated with it, Nam Tsho Chukmo.

"None of you knew your momo-la," I said as I looked around at my mother's grandchildren. "She was a great collector of stones. She always said they spoke to her, that she could feel a presence in the stones. When she was a child, she came here often to stay with her maternal grandmother, who lived not far from here. She would always bring back home small stones that she found from around the lake and in the neighboring areas, ones that called out to her. She liked to think that the stones bore the footprints of the goddess, that Nam Tsho Chukmo had walked over the stones, leaving blessings for whomever picked them up. When Pumo and I were growing up, she kept many stones that she gathered from here on the rooftop of our home where she conducted her Bon ceremonies.

"There is one stone in particular that she gave me, and for years I have always carried it with me wherever I have gone. I took out from my pouch the small rounded bluish stone that my mother had given me when we had come to the lake together. "I keep this with me because it reminds me of my mother. It helps me to feel her presence.

Pumo looked surprised when she saw me pull out the stone that she remembered from childhood.

"You still have that?" she asked in amazement. "I remember you sleeping with it after Ama-la died."

"It is one of the few things left from all my possessions," I replied with a smile, recalling how I had kept it when almost everything else had been taken from me.

"Let us all go find some small stones to take home," said Tenzin, when I finished speaking. For the rest of that day and the next, this was an activity that engaged them. On the last day of our visit, Pumo and I were sitting quietly alone, while our children were seeing another part of the lake.

"What are you thinking?" I asked, turning my eyes from the lake to her.

"I am thinking of Tashi," she replied with sadness. "He would have enjoyed coming here. For so many years all he did was paint, and he didn't get to travel much. He didn't get to go to the places he wanted to see."

"Where did he want to go the most, Pumo?" I asked.

"To Kashmir, of course," she replied lovingly. "He had heard so much about that place from his grandmother when he was young, and his father had said that he would take him one day, but that day never came. His father never got to travel there and neither did Tashi. It is a place that I also very much wanted to visit."

"Yeshe had special feelings for Kashmir as well. When he was traveling through Gyagar as a young man, he went there and had a powerful spiritual experience, where he felt himself expanding to encompass the whole universe. He became one with it all." I didn't say it but as I spoke, I remembered the story Beau had told me of the one called Jesus, who had traveled to Kashmir and had a vision of the all-powerful goddess. Kashmir seems to be a special place," I murmured.

"It would have been nice to visit the land that meant so much to our husbands," she replied.

"Then let us go together, Pumo," I murmured, looking at her with a smile. She laughed, and I hurried to assure her, "Not with these aged bodies, but sometime in the future, you and I will go together."

She looked at me with a serious expression. "Do you mean that?" I nodded. "Then we will do that, Padma Tshomo. You and I will surely go." After a pause, she asked, "Where would you like to be born and what would you like to experience in your next birth?

"I don't know. I don't care really," I replied without thinking. Then as I cast my eyes over the scene before us, they fell on the snow-topped mountains in the distance, and I mused. "That is not quite true. I very much want a taste of the experience Yeshe had when he went to Kashmir, just a taste of that expanding awareness. I think that is the goal of the Buddhists and Bonpos, and of those who worship Lord Shiva as well."

"Perhaps you will have a taste when we go to Kashmir," she replied dreamily. I looked at her without answering. At that moment, I saw our children returning to us with eager expressions. Breathless, Samaya told us they had discovered a wonderous cave that we must see as well.

"You go with them, Pumo. I want to sit here alone for a while, and I saw some of those caves when I came with Yeshe years ago." Nodding, she got up and followed them. This was the last day of our visit and with a sinking heart, I had to acknowledge that Bhasundara would not come, but I could not quite accept that. She had given me an indication, sort of. This was the first occasion for me to sit alone by the lake, and if she were to come, it would be now.

Looking out over the calming waters, I realized how much this sacred lake had meant to me over the years, since I had first come with my mother. My mind then wandered back to the story Yeye had told me on that last day at the hut, a story of ancient times, of which I had no memory. Had it been Ama-la, a mother who could dance on water and turn ice fields into lakes, who had first inspired me to seek the magic of her world, I wondered? And could Nam Tsho have been one of those lakes that she and the dakinis had created out of the fields of ice. As I sat there, I tried to visualize what it must have been like to see the dakinis dance on the ice, and I wondered if they were still dancing in some other world, creating lakes in another place far from earth.

My ruminations were interrupted by the sound of footsteps, and as I looked around, I caught sight of my dear friend approaching me. After prostrating to the goddess of the lake, she seated herself beside me, and I exclaimed in a pleased tone, "You came after all!"

"I always keep my word, Tshomo, but why were you so eager for me to meet you here?"

"I wanted to experience Nam Tsho with you, and I wanted you to tell me about your visit to Nam Tsho with Dalha. You once told me that you had a magical experience with her here, but you never told me the details."

"Did I say that?" I nodded, and she laughed. "I could have told you that story while sitting in the cottage."

"It would not be the same," I replied, looking out over the sacred waters. It was known that the atmosphere around Nam Tsho was very fickle, and often clouds would suddenly appear, dampening the scene and dimming the color of the lake, but I had never experienced that. On each of my visits to Nam Tsho, the sky had been eminently clear and allowed an effulgence of light, which made the water shimmer and shine in the deepest of blues. Today was much like that. During the few days of this visit with the family, varying degrees of wind had swept over the lake, but today the winds meandered gently, causing the water to rise and fall in shallow wavelets. The high-pitched whistling of a bird drew my eyes away from the water to the sky, where I caught sight of a lone eagle swooping down overhead. It made me think of Dalha and I wondered if she had come close to listen.

"Several times I came here with Dalha," she began. "I must have told you some of those stories, but there is one story I know I haven't shared with you, because I haven't told anyone."

"I think that is the story I need to hear now," I replied, turning my eyes and attention to her.

She was quiet for a few moments and then began. "This happened around the time when Yeshe had taken Tenzin to the Song Empire and you were staying with your daughters in Amdo, but before I found the gems in the forest. Do you remember that story?

I nodded. "I haven't forgotten anything you have told me about Dalha."

"I hadn't seen Dalha for a long while, when one night she arrived at the cottage and told me that I had to leave immediately with her for Nam

Tsho. There was no time to pack anything. She appeared so suddenly and, even though I had gotten used to Dalha's ways, this was most unusual. Rarely did we begin a journey during the night. I knew not to question her, so I got on my horse and followed. It was one of those nights when the sky hosted a large full moon, creating enough light for us to travel. She kept urging me on, saying that we had to ride faster. We sped along more quickly than I had ever traveled, as if the wind carried us forward. I worried about the horses, but they seemed to obey her command, much like I did. We rode through the night and the next day with only brief stops and arrived at the lake in the late hours of daylight. We had come to a part of the lake where you could see an island in the middle.

"Leaping off her horse and pointing to the island, she said, 'I must go there. Wait for me here, by the side of the lake.' I looked around. It was the warmer months, and all the ice had melted, so it was impossible to walk across the lake. I told her that I would go find a boat, but she immediately responded, 'I have no time for a boat.'

"'Will you swim?'" I asked in amazement." Bhasundara paused and smiled. "Even though I had known Dalha for many years, she continued to confound me. That never stopped. She turned to me and said in a hurried tone, 'There is no time to swim.' At that moment I saw her speed across the lake in a flash of light. From my vantage point, the small island looked deserted, and I wondered why she wanted to go there. What was so urgent?

"As she had instructed me to do, I sat down and waited. The hours passed, and I wondered when and how she would return. The night arrived, and then another day and night, and still no sign of Dalha. I spent much of the time in meditation. We had brought very little food and not much water, and I ate and drank sparingly, saving what we had for when she returned. On the second morning, I was seated in meditation when I felt my consciousness transfer to that island and into a stone hut that was not visible from the shore." Bhasundara closed her eyes as if to recall the scene before continuing. "Inside the hut sat a hermit in meditation, and in front of that hermit sat two luminous beings, also in meditation position on the ground. One I knew immediately to be Guru Rinpoche. Dalha had described him to me numerous times and that is how I recognized him, but the other was a woman I had never seen before. She was a beautiful young woman, with long wavy black hair that hung loosely around her chest down to her waist. She was dressed simply in a white cloth wrapped around her—as he was. I could not only see them but could also hear them as if I were present in the hut. Together, they were giving profound teachings to this hermit, teachings that I heard as well. As I listened, I became completely absorbed in what they were saying, lifted into another state of awareness, and I lost all sense of time and place. It was a most joyous, expansive experience, and as I sat there, I became filled with an overwhelming abundance of love. It is hard to find the words to describe that heightened awareness. Remember, I told you that I had experienced this state with that adept I met in the forest not long ago. Well, this was one of the other times I had experienced it some years earlier in the presence of the great Guru.

"Intuitively, I knew that the two of them were bestowing this state of consciousness on that hermit, teaching him how to transmute negative energies into beneficial ones through the power of love. For some reason, which I didn't understand at that time, I was brought there and allowed to witness this and partake in it myself.

"By nightfall, I found myself back in my body on the shore. I had been magically transported to that island for a while, and now I was returned. For most of the night, I sat by the side of the lake reflecting on what I had heard and seen. The only people in that hut were the hermit, Guru Rinpoche, and that beautiful woman. So where was Dalha, I wondered?

"Sometime in the early pre-dawn hours, I lay down and fell asleep. When I awoke, Dalha was beside me, preparing food. I looked at her in a way I had never looked at her before. Smiling, she said to me, 'You finally got to see the great Guru. I wanted to fulfil this desire of yours before I depart.' Immediately, I prostrated myself in gratitude, but I hesitated to ask the questions that perplexed me: Who was that woman in the hut and where had she, Dalha, been?

"In answer to my unasked question, Dalha looked at me with a slight smile playing around her lips and reminded me quietly, 'Rather than ask who she is, ask who you are. That is the only question to pursue. Once you find the answer to that, everything will become clear.' She had repeated those words to me so many times over the years, but on that day, I finally grasped her meaning. It was as if her life teaching to me was summed up in those words."

"But did you ever find out who that woman with Guru Rinpoche was?" I asked curiously.

Disregarding my question, she continued. "This experience held great significance for me, Tshomo, especially now, after having spent some time with Rinpoche."

"Rinpoche, who is Rinpoche?" I asked perplexed, forgetting that the one I called Yeye, she called Rinpoche.

"Don't you remember, the adept I met in the forest while you were in retreat. I told you about him not long ago."

"You mean, Shifu?" I asked.

"Who is Shifu? Is that what you call him?"

"No. No. To me, he is Yeye," I replied impatiently.

"Tshomo, whom are you speaking about?" Her voice was as impatient as mine. "I am referring to the old ascetic I met in the forest just before you returned from retreat. Have you forgotten about that already?"

"Never mind what we call him, go on. How is he connected to this?"

"He showed me the future," she replied cautiously. "My personal future and the future of Böd." I looked at her expectantly while she paused, as if debating how much to share. "Just as it is better not to speak of the past, it is also wise not to speak of what will come because what we see are potentialities—the likely unfolding of events according to karmic patterns that have been set. On a personal level, he showed me that I will take several future incarnations in Böd as a Buddhist monk; my current life has been a preparation for that. He indicated that I will be part of the changes coming to our land, the new religious structures, and that I have been training for such a role through many lifetimes." She muttered to herself, "I had to experience being a true Bonpo in order to become a proper Buddhist of Böd." Then her voice grew louder. "Because of this future, Dalha thought it important for me to witness those esoteric teachings of Guru Rinpoche. Even though I may not remember that incident in my next birth, at a deeper level the teachings will remain with me, and I will be able to pass them on. Nothing is really lost when we move from one body to another." She paused and then blurted out, "But you, Tshomo, will take birth in Gyagar to complete certain matters." She stopped abruptly and I knew that she felt she had said too much.

"In Gyagar," I whispered. "Is that what he said?"

"I am sorry. Those words slipped out. Don't press me for any more. What is to be will come to be in the natural course of things." She was quiet for a few moments and then added, "I have told you that meeting Rinpoche had a great impact on me. I believe that he is linked to Dalha, but I am not sure how. Perhaps it was he who sent me to Dalha in the first place. I used to believe that I had met her quite by accident, but there are no accidents in this world. I don't know what my relationship was with him in the past, but whatever it was, he seemed to have taken a strong interest in me and perhaps he sent me to her for training.

"That hermit who was in deep meditation in the hut on the lake island holds great importance for the future of Böd, and that is why the great Guru appeared to him. Dalha could have come on her own without me, but she didn't. She wanted me to witness that scene because of how it would help me in the future. Everything changed after that trip to Nam Tsho, and I didn't see Dalha again. That was the last time. When I began to review many of the experiences I had with her, I came to see them in a new light. She was and is even now actively guiding so many people. For so long I had viewed her as my own, not realizing her grander role."

I stared at Bhasundara, wide eyed, trying to absorb what she was saying. Finally, I asked, "She is so close to Guru Rinpoche. Do you think Dalha could be an emanation of Yeshe Tsogyal?"

She laughed and replied, "Tshomo, how can we know? It is said that Yeshe Tsogyal is an emanation of the great Goddess Sarasvati. Dalha appears to me as an emanation of the Moon Goddess. She always has, and that is why, unconsciously, I gave her that name. I feel that in the past I must have been very devoted to that goddess. But to you she may appear as something else."

"An emanation?" I asked thoughtfully. "So, you never found out who that beautiful woman in the hut with Guru Rinpoche was?

She smiled and replied, "Who do you think?"

I was quiet as internally I began to re-hear a conversation from long ago, when Yeye was telling Yu Yan to keep her mind on Chang'e, the Moon Goddess. 'She will always protect and guide you,' he had said. If what Bhasundara had told me was true, then that goddess had come in the form of Dalha, or at least sent her, to guide her devotee of an earlier time. The very thought astounded me. I knew that I also had some relationship with that goddess when I lived as Chunhua in Hanning. Our whole community had worshipped the Lunar Goddess.

Hearing laughter in the distance, Bhasundara suddenly rose and said, "Your family is returning. I have found out where you are staying and have made arrangements to spend the night there. I will return now to that Dropka family and join all of you for a meal tonight before departing in the early morning.

"Bhasundara, thank you for coming." I rose to see her off.

"No need to thank me. I wanted to see Nam Tsho once more as well, and besides, we are friends after all." She began to walk away and then turned back to look at me, saying, "Tshomo, I will leave first, but you will soon follow."

Bhasundara hurried away and the family arrived back moments later. While they were busy talking, I fell into something of a reverie, thinking about Yu Yan, who had become my dearest friend, Bhasundara. When we had fled Hanning, I had hoped to get to know this student of my grandfather's, but we never really became close; she was withdrawn and used to a secluded life, not much given to social conversation. Now Bhasundara had become such a close friend, an important support for me through so many difficulties. She was someone with whom I could share my personal life, and I knew that she felt the same about me. I didn't know what I would have done without her. She had become for me the teacher that Yeye said she would be.

Was this all Yeye's doing, or was it our karma that had brought us back together? I couldn't dwell in the past because Pumo's question returned me to the present. "Was that Bhasundara who was here with you?" I nodded and said she would join us later. I didn't think much of her last words to me about leaving first. It was only later that I came to understand her premonition.

I didn't see Bhasundara again after our trip to Nam Tsho. Two months later she died, on the tenth day of the waxing moon, that special day when Guru Rinpoche spreads his blessings.

CHAPTER 30

A Final Teaching

Bhasundara's departure was yet another blow. In her death, I saw my own. When we had been at the lake, I had interpreted her words to mean that she would leave the lake before me, but when she died, I realized that she had been referring to her death and mine. She had used that word "soon" again, which could mean anything.

I was nearing my sixtieth year and the journey to Nam Tsho had made me more conscious of the creep of age. Physically, it had been a difficult trip, and since my return from the retreat I had come to accept that there were many things I could no longer do.

I had not been able to see Bhasundara again following our meeting at the lake, but several weeks after her death, I went one last time to her cottage in the forest. I had heard that a student of hers was now living there and was surprised to learn that she even had students. But as I was to discover, there was much about Bhasundara I didn't know. When I arrived at the cottage, for several minutes I stood outside, recalling the many times I had sought refuge there. Catching sight of me, a young woman emerged, introduced herself and invited me in for po cha.

"I recognize you," she said. "I met you here once or twice. You are an old friend of hers, aren't you?" Nodding, I followed her into the cottage.

"I didn't know Bhasundara had students," I said hesitantly, as I sipped the tea she served me. In earlier days, I would have asked this woman if she was a Bonpo, but now the question did not even arise.

She smiled. "People came from all over to see her, didn't you know?"

I shook my head. "Did they come for healing or to learn about medicine?"

"Much more than that," she replied. "She was our connection to the one she called Dalha and told us many stories about her. But we all soon learned that Bhasundara had great wisdom, and she guided so many people through difficult struggles in life. She was more than just a teacher really. Her humility hid her true stature." She continued to speak about Bhasundara with great regard and love, making me realize how much about my friend's life I didn't know. I was reflecting on this when she suddenly asked, "You have met Dalha haven't you? What was she like?"

I smiled as I remembered fleeing from Bhasundara's cottage so many years ago when I recognized Dalha as the one who had turned her hat into a bird during my visit to Nam Tsho with Yeshe. How could I explain what she was like? "With Dalha, one had always to expect the unexpected. She had great humor and was most playful, most joyous, the emanation of love itself," I replied. "I don't believe that she has died, and so one day you still might meet her. Only you have to look for her in the most unlikely of places."

"That is what Bhasundara once told me." After a pause she asked, "Do you want to take something from here as a reminder of your friend?"

I shook my head. "All the reminders I need are tucked in here," I replied, tapping my chest. Then, changing my mind, I added, "But perhaps I will take a stone from the garden. Bhasundara knew that I loved to collect stones, and it would be nice to have one from here to join my stones from Nam Tsho and elsewhere."

After finishing the tea, I went outside and walked around the side of the cottage to the garden. I sat down to meditate before choosing a stone to take home with me. As I did, the image of Yeye came before my mind, and I recalled the last memory I experienced while sitting in the forest with Bhasundara many months earlier. I understood that in that earlier era, in Hanning, Yeye had tried to awaken in her the teacher that she would become. In her life as Bhasundara, that potential had been realized, although in the humblest of ways. As Yu Yan, and again as Bhasundara, she would never acknowledge to be anything more than a simple woman in search of truth, and that humility was what Yeye loved about her.

A pang of regret shot through me as I realized that I had not truly appreciated who she was. Often I had spoken to her casually, complaining, sometimes not heeding her counsel, treating her just as a friend, when so many of the teachings that had come to me had come through her. It took this young woman, her student, to make me realize what she truly meant to me and how much she had shared and given. "Bhasundara, forgive me," I whispered. Immediately, I heard her quiet laugh inside and suspected she was conveying that she would not have wanted it to be otherwise.

She had been the living example of Dalha's love; giving and giving without expecting anything in return. Despite my occasional neglect and my despondence, she never lost patience or gave up on me; her love never stopped flowing.

It was difficult for me truly to grasp the nature of such love. Then the memory came to me of Margot, of her quiet, unseen acts of compassion. I remembered saying to her that I wanted to be like her. I thought about how Bhasundara had found me and cared for me in my time of great desperation after I had sold the last of my possessions. The image of Ama-la came into my mind, and I thought of her incredible, selfless generosity. I had all these models before me, and yet I didn't think that I had lived up to any of them. The thought entered my mind that I would keep trying, keep aspiring to be as they were, to live in the shadows and perform whatever helpful acts I could.

Then I remembered that in a dream I had offered to Zerdan all the wealth that might be destined to come to me in my next birth. How often since that time I debated with myself, thinking I had been foolish and should find a way to undo that offer. Now with closed eyes as I sat in Bhasundara's garden, with great clarity I resolved to keep that commitment in the hope that it would bring him some benefit. It was the last act I could do for him. Thank you, Bhasundara, I whispered, accepting this moment of clarity as a parting gift from my dear friend. I knew that in my forward journey, I might not recall the details of my past experiences, but I also knew that the teachings would never leave me.

Getting up from my seat on the ground, I selected a small stone from the area where Bhasundara had conducted her ceremonies, and after saying goodbye to her student, I climbed onto Anpu, and returned to the city.

Many months later Tenzin came to visit. He had been very much on my mind since returning from Nam Tsho. After spending so many days with him, I had seen how much intellectual knowledge and philosophical insight he had gained, and I saw how greatly his siblings and cousins respected and admired him, but I worried that he lived too much in his head and not enough in his heart. Yeshe had once told me that he would ensure his mental development but that I should care for his emotional wellbeing. My son was a man who kept much to himself, and many of our interactions were confined to either light conversation or deep intellectual discussions at a very mental level, but I wanted to know whether he was internalizing what he was learning. I had been concerned about this when he appeared one day at Pumo's home with little notice. After giving him time to rest and recover from the journey, I asked him why he had come to Lhasa.

To visit you, of course, he replied. We had seen each other not so very long ago, and I knew something else was on his mind. It took several days for me to discover the reason for his visit. The abbot was sending a delegation from Samye Monastery back to Nalanda, to what remained of the Mahavihara, to recover some of the texts and bring them back to Böd. Initially, the abbot had included him in the delegation, but he had refused this opportunity. The monks were leaving in two weeks, and the abbot sent him to speak with me before making a final decision about whether he should go.

"Why have you turned down his request?" I asked, trying to hide my feelings. I knew that the time left to me was limited, and the journey to Nalanda would not be a short one. It could be months or years. The thought of my son going so far away once more, perhaps not seeing him again in this life, filled me with anxiety, almost panic, but I also didn't want to stand in the way of this opportunity, knowing how much Nalanda meant to him.

"I don't want to leave you," he replied quietly. "I have been away too much. Perhaps if I had not traveled to the Song Empire, I could have helped when you were going through the difficult time with that man."

"There is nothing you could have done," I assured him. "It was something I had to work through myself. Tenzin, more than anything, I want you to fulfill your potential, to contribute what you can. If the abbot feels that you are needed, that you or Böd would benefit by you going, then you must be part of that delegation. I don't want to stand in the way. These are the instructions that your father left me. He was very clear about that. I believe that when he first sent you to Nalanda, in some way he knew that he would not live to see your return, but he also knew how much you would gain and that was uppermost in his mind. The same is true now. This may be your only opportunity to return to Nalanda, and I know what that place of learning means to you. I understand what it would be like to find your old teachers again. There are efforts to restore what remains of Nalanda, and I am sure that you want to be a part of that. If you don't go, you may regret it later."

"I would very much appreciate meeting some of my old teachers again, if I can find them," he mused. "And my Sanskrit would benefit, but what about you, Ama-la?"

I smiled, covering up my reluctance to part with him. "I have Pumo here with me. We take good care of each other. And my brothers are still in good health. I also have Yara in Lhasa and her children. There is plenty of family around."

"Then you don't mind me leaving?"

"Of course, I mind!" I exclaimed immediately. "But I won't let that interfere. Until you return, I will pretend that you are at the monastery. All I ask is that you take good care of yourself. The occupiers of Gyagar are violent, and I pray that you stay safe and away from them."

His face lit up with a smile. "Then I will return to Samye and tell the abbot that you have given your permission."

"Tenzin, you are no longer a young man. You don't need my permission anymore."

"I will always seek it," he replied quietly.

Before he left to return to the monastery, I told him that I would ride with him part way. I wanted to take him to a certain place before he returned to Samye. A few days later we were riding along the Lhasa River to the place where it met the Tsangpo. From there we turned off down a small path and a little further along the way I stopped Anpu. Lopsang had told me where Zerdan was staying, and I had arranged for the monthly supply of staples to be delivered at the time when I knew we would reach there.

When we arrived at the broken-down hut that was hardly a hut at all, we stayed far enough away so that Zerdan would not notice us as he came out of his hut, but close enough to get a glimpse of him. Hiding behind a small assembly of bushes, I watched as the box of food was delivered to him, and I saw Zerdan emerge from his hut and accept it.

"Who is that old man and why did you bring me here?" asked Tenzin in a baffled tone. Earlier, he had asked why we were leaving the main route and without explaining, I had told him to follow me.

"That old man is Zerdan, and that box of food is what I send him anonymously every month." Tenzin looked at me in surprise and disapproval. I had decided to share something of my experience with Tenzin in the hope that it would awaken compassion in him.

"See what a broken man he is, Tenzin? It was his pride and thirst for power that brought him to this state." I could see that Tenzin was unhappy that I had brought him and so I said, "Let's sit by the river and I will explain."

Getting back onto our horses, we retraced our steps and found a spot near the Tsangpo. It was a place where Yeshe and I often used to rest during our journeys to Samye. After descending from our horses, we sat in silence for several minutes as I reflected on how to begin, what to say and what not to say. Tenzin broke the silence. "Why do you send him food after all that he has done to you and to our family, and to Buddhism?" his voice rang with agitation.

The words of Yeye came to my mind and, without hesitating, I recited them: *"No matter how great and how often, repay injury with De."*

"I know the teachings of Laozi," Tenzin responded quietly. "But how do you know them?"

"Never mind that. What is important is not only to know the teachings, Tenzin, but to put them into practice, and that is what I am trying to do. During the retreat, I tried hard to let go of anger and of judgment. When I think of the struggles, the humiliation I had to endure because of Zerdan, I realize how much benefit that whole experience brought me, and I am grateful."

"What benefit? I see only the hardship he caused you," he replied bitterly.

"Had I not met Zerdan, had he not sent me spiraling down into such a deplorable state, I would never have met that great woman in the Yarlung Valley who helped me to heal an old karmic wound, and who gave me such extraordinary experiences and insight. With the proper attitude, suffering can be the gateway to wisdom. During my retreat I learned how important it is to have the right attitude. It is quite a teaching to have everything ripped away from you, even your self-respect. I had to fall into a deep pit of shame and learn to pull myself out, with a lot of help. After it was over, I came to realize that obstacles are in fact a great blessing. Of course, when in the midst of a difficulty, it is hard to see it that way, but after the trial is over, if we look carefully, we can see how much was gained. It is not enough, Tenzin, to be able to recite the teachings, to know the words and to explain them; they must be lived, and this is what I came to understand when I was in retreat. I learned that when we hold on to anger and resentment and fear, we ourselves are the one to suffer."

"You sound like the abbot."

"Does he say the same thing?"

He nodded. "When I heard that you had donated a great deal of funds to Zerdan, who I knew to be a fraud, I was very angry, and I was ashamed to meet the abbot. I had gone to see you and you had promised not to meet that man again, but you broke your promise. Realizing that you were still supporting Zerdan, I kept avoiding the abbot and the other senior monks, fearing that they had heard of your contributions. Finally, the abbot came to my room and sat down with me.

"I began to apologize for what you had done, but he interrupted me, saying, 'Your mother has done no wrong. Do not judge her. It is you who have misunderstood the situation. She is working through an old relationship with Zerdan, and you should not interfere.' Then he added, 'There is no room for anger in the human heart. It will only harm you and all those around you. There will always be forces seeking to disrupt the balance of the world. They have a purpose. Progress is made by countering these disruptive forces, and this is the battle in which your mother is engaged. Do not disturb her efforts. Do not further burden her with your own emotions.'

"After this conversation I decided not to mention anything more to you, but still I was angry. When I came home next, I didn't say anything, but when I saw how many of Apa-la's treasures were gone, I knew what had happened. I tried to introspect to see what was causing my anger, and I realized that I felt you were betraying Apa-la, who himself had lived a rather austere life so that he could contribute significantly to Samye Monastery and provide for the family. He made such an effort for me to be accepted by the monastery, and I felt that by supporting Zerdan's monastery, you were not honoring this."

"Do you still feel that way?" I asked, looking at him intently. He had turned his eyes away from me to look at the river, but now he turned back to me.

He shook his head. "My anger toward you, Ama-la, was misplaced. It was really anger toward Zerdan, but it wasn't only personal. He was harming the Dharma, misleading people. It was due to these emotions, in addition to my knowledge of the Han language, that the abbot sent me to the Great Song along with the other monks. The purpose of the trip was to engage with the Buddhist teachers there, but several times when I wandered off alone into the mountains, I encountered an old Daoist sage. I met him in different places, which I thought was very strange, and each time, he would repeat to me the words of Laozi. On my last encounter with him, he gave me a copy of Laozi's teachings and I studied them. By reading his words, I felt my anger dissipate, replaced by a deep sense of acceptance and contentment.

"During my last encounter with him, he spoke words that had a great impact on me. He said, 'What happens here affects the whole world.' We were in the Song Empire and so I assumed that he meant what happened in the Song affected every place else. I asked him if that was his meaning, and he shook his head and repeated those words to me. When he saw my perplexed expression, he pointed to the heart. I asked him to clarify, and he responded, 'What is in the heart will shape your experience of the world. The outer world is but a projection of the inner. To cleanse the outer world, cleanse the heart.' Then he added, 'The oppressed becomes the oppressor and the oppressor becomes the oppressed, and so it will continue until the heart awakens. When the heart awakens, there is nobody to oppress, and there is no oppressor. Be generous like the wind spreading seeds of goodness everywhere. Every kindness is returned in equal measure.'

"His words stayed with me throughout the rest of the journey and even now I continue to reflect on them. When I returned with the other monks to Samye Monastery, the abbot came to see me and asked if I was still angry. I replied, 'Why would I be angry?' I had completely forgotten about those feelings toward Zerdan that had possessed me before I left.

"The abbot replied mysteriously, 'Ah, then he has done the work for me.' Several days later, he called me to him and asked if I had encountered

Guru Rinpoche during my travels. Not understanding his question, I looked at him blankly without answering. He had sent me to the Great Song, what was he speaking about? Then he addressed my unspoken thought, saying, 'Do you think he doesn't live in the Song?'

"I was perplexed. Guru Rinpoche had died so many centuries ago. What did he mean? When I expressed this, he replied, 'Who has died? How can the great Guru die?' After speaking those words, he told me to go back to my study, but I couldn't keep my mind on the texts. I kept wondering if that wandering sage had been Guru Rinpoche. I never found the answer to that question, but that is what the abbot seemed to imply. Ama-la, I thought all my anger was gone, but when I saw Zerdan now, I realized there are still some embers left, which need to be put out."

"Tenzin, anger can adopt any cause and crop up at any moment. It has taken me many centuries to work through this complex relationship with Zerdan, one filled with anger on both sides. That is why one must be vigilant and address the negative emotions in their seed form before they take deep root, and that is where the wrathful deities can help. They can be our armor, shielding us from the negative emotions that seek to take hold.

"Another thing I have learned is that Guru Rinpoche can speak through any form. It was he who taught you through the mouth of that Daoist sage you met in the Song Empire, and he helped you to release your anger. He will never abandon those of us who even for a short time have passed through this sacred land of Böd. He was present before he was Guru Rinpoche, and he will be here when we no longer remember that name.

"During my time in retreat, I was able to see far into the past, and I recalled many instances when I could have but did not repay injury with De, and that is why I send food each month to Zerdan. It is a lesson I hope to take with me into the future, but whether or not I will remember, well, that is another matter." I ended with a slight chuckle. Then I added, "All the knowledge you have gained, Tenzin, is of great value, but you mustn't overlook the wisdom of the heart, for the heart knows things that the mind can't grasp. The mind and heart must be in balance; everything depends on this balance."

"Ama-la, where did you learn all of this?" I had never spoken to Tenzin in this way, and he was surprised to hear such words from me. He still thought of me as a Bonpo in the conventional sense, one committed to doing my rituals in the effort to commune with the nature spirits, and he knew little of my feelings for Guru Rinpoche and Yeshe Tsogyal, but we had been apart for a long time and I had never shared my inner experiences.

"Everything I know, I learned from Dalha, Bhasundara, and during my time in retreat," I replied quietly. "Bhasundara was not the simple village woman she projected herself to be, but a woman of spiritual stature that even she would not acknowledge. And what can I say of Dalha, except that she is the one who brought me to Guru Rinpoche. Her love for him is beyond description. And I believe that on the tenth day of the waxing moon, it is she who plays with him in the fields of the manifest worlds, bringing blessings to all who are open to receive them."

"I guess we can't tell who anyone is," he replied thoughtfully.

"That is exactly right," I affirmed with a nod of the head. "Tenzin, you will soon leave for Nalanda, and I will not be able to stop myself from worrying about you, no matter how much I try. Promise me that you will listen to your heart as you continue your studies. Don't live only in your head."

He smiled. "I will do my best, and I am sure that even when you are not with me, you will keep reminding me."

"That I will," I said as I took his hand in mine and held it tightly.

A few minutes later I noticed the progression of the sun and realized that I had to head back to Lhasa if I was to reach the city before darkness. "If you are not coming with me all the way to Samye, you should return now, Ama-la."

I nodded and he helped me rise. We were loath to part with one another and walked slowly to our horses. "I leave in two weeks, Ama-la, but I will not stay long in Gyagar."

"What does long mean?" I asked with a slight smile. "When you are gone from me for even a few months, it seems long."

"Then are you telling me not to leave?" he asked questioningly.

"If I did so your father would chastise me, and that I won't have." I stood by the side of Anpu, gazing up into the face of my now grown son, feeling that he was in good hands and that he had all the guidance he would need in life. It was time to let go, if possible. I watched Tenzin climb onto his horse and then I did the same. He turned his horse in the direction of Samye and I turned Anpu toward Lhasa, and we both rode away.

Several weeks later, I was walking in the market alone when I came across a poor beggar seated by the side of the road. I passed him by and then turned around, thinking I should offer him some of the food I had purchased. As I drew closer, to my great shock, I saw that it was Lopsang. Standing before him, I extended my hand and offered him a package of food as he looked up at me with pitiful eyes. At first, he didn't take it, but as I kept my hand extended, he took the food and turned his eyes downward before quietly thanking me.

Sitting down beside him on the road, I asked how he had ended up in such a state. He gazed at me for a long time before answering. "I am paying off my debts," he replied in a bitter tone. "For deceiving people—you included."

"Your family would not help you? I asked, trying to show some sympathy, but really feeling that his condition was very much deserved. I knew that they had cut off all ties with him when he was with Zerdan, but I wondered how his wealthy relatives could allow him to become a beggar on the street.

"Why would they help me? I took advantage of them, squeezing them for all I could get," he muttered. "When they cut all ties with me, they told me I brought them shame and said they would have nothing more to do with me. I have had to learn the hard way the value of family."

I sighed and replied, "I am sorry your family abandoned you. I don't know what I would have done without my family after I lost everything."

In truth I didn't care much about what happened to Lobsang but felt the pain of what it would be like to be abandoned by those who had once loved you.

His eyes had been staring at the ground but now he turned them to me and asked in a timid voice, "Padma Tshomo, can there be peace between us? You have made peace with Zerdan, why not with me?"

I didn't know why I couldn't make peace with him, but I knew that I was not ready. Standing up, I mumbled, "Someday I hope I can forgive you, Lopsang. Perhaps someday we will be reconciled." As I gazed down at him, a bud of compassion stirred within me, which made me place beside him the bag with the rest of the food I had purchased. "Lopsang, did you truly believe in Zerdan, or did you know all along that he was lying and deceiving people?" I asked suddenly. I had assumed that he had been part of the deception, fully aware of how Zerdan was misleading people.

He replied immediately without a moment's hesitation in a sorrowful voice. "I believed in him fully. Like you, I sacrificed everything for him. I don't think I can believe in anyone or anything again. He has destroyed my faith."

"Then you are far worse off than I am," I replied quietly. "I hope that one day you regain your faith." He didn't respond and with those last words, I walked away. Over the next many days, I wondered why I could not make peace with Lopsang. I no longer harbored any ill will toward Zerdan; that relationship felt as if it had completed itself, but the same was not true with Lopsang. Why was it so hard with him? I didn't know the answer and decided not to dwell on it.

It was not long after this encounter that I came down with an illness, which sapped much of my energy and kept me home bound. I had been ill for several weeks when the abbot from Samye Monastery came to visit, which he had never done before.

"What are you doing in Lhasa?" I asked in surprise as Pumo ushered him into the room where I was resting. She helped me rise from the bed and sit up in a low chair, where she could serve us po-cha and snacks.

"I came on monastery business and also to visit you," he replied with a smile. "I heard that you were ill and didn't want to miss the opportunity to speak with you."

After what Tenzin had shared with me during our last meeting, my appreciation of the abbot had grown, and I had come to see him in a new light. I had not had much interaction with him previously and had regarded him more as a religious official than a man of true spiritual wisdom. But that had now changed.

"I want to thank you for giving us Tenzin at such a young age, and for allowing us to send him on so many faraway missions. He has greatly aided the monastery and the work of the monks."

"It is I who should be thanking you for taking such care of his spiritual growth," I replied quietly. "I have seen who Tenzin has become, and I owe this to you. He has great respect and admiration for you."

He laughed softly. "I can't claim any credit for that. All I have done is give him the opportunity to realize his potential."

"That is what his father so often said that we must do. Give him the opportunities."

"Ah, Yeshe Dorje was a great friend of Samye Monastery. I used to wonder why he didn't become a monk himself, but then one day I stopped wondering."

"Why was that?" I asked, mentally saying to myself that I knew the reason. In his last birth he had been a monk, but it had not been a path that he had happily chosen.

"Your husband once asked me who had more freedom—a monk or a lay person. I looked at him and asked in return, 'What is freedom?' He didn't answer, and I reframed the question, 'Who on earth is free?'

"'Guru Rinpoche,' he replied immediately. 'And he was not a monk,' he added. 'But he might be now,' I responded to him with a laugh. "A monk becomes a lay person who becomes a monk again, and so it goes round and round, until we realize that freedom does not depend on any external conditions. So, your question has no answer."

"I have a question as well, and perhaps there is also no answer," I hesitantly said.

"Ask," the abbot replied with an expectant look.

"The last funds I gave to Zerdan were never used. When I returned from retreat they were offered back to me, but I didn't want to take them, feeling they had already been sullied. But I asked that it be used to create a retreat place for women. No nunnery has been built or even planned, even at Samye. The monks have their place, why don't the women?"

A serious look crossed his face, and he was quiet before responding. "There is no good answer to your question. But I will say this, freedom is not found in a monastery or nunnery any more than it is found in the marketplace. The one called Dalha lived neither in the monastery nor in the market, and she is one of the few who can be said to be free."

"You know of her?" I asked in surprise.

"Who among us does not know her? There were times when the monastery was in great need of funds and donations did not cover our expenses. It was she who turned up just at the right time with just the right amount. This happened on two, no three occasions. I didn't know who she was. She was dressed like a poor, simple village woman, and the first time I saw her, I asked, 'who has sent her.' I wanted to know where the funds were coming from. She replied mysteriously, 'The one who rides on the wind.'

"I asked her who that was, and she responded, 'He is the one who makes way for her.' I was still perplexed and so I asked her, who is he making way for. She replied very quietly, 'The One who will make all well but who will never be known, for She does not wish to be known.'

"After those mysterious words, she hurried away. She came twice more to provide relief, but with few words."

"That sounds exactly like Dalha," I replied lovingly with a faint smile.

"I know that I have not answered your question," he replied, "but I will leave you with this thought. Perhaps when she is known, more care will be given to the training of women monastics, or perhaps when more care is given to the training of women monastics, that is the time when she will become known. That is something worth fighting for, Padma Tshomo."

A small laugh escaped my lips. "I have little time left."

"You have all the time in the world, and you are already becoming a spiritual warrior, are you not?"

I nodded and murmured, "I guess I am."

This conversation brought a certain closure to my life and much comfort in those last remaining weeks. I had begun my life in a divided world, struggling to define myself as either a Bonpo or a Buddhist, but I was ending my life with an identity that transcended both. The words of the abbot remained with me, and I heard Dalha's voice in them. I knew that they were her last teaching for me, at least in the life of Padma Tshomo. I had to keep trying to become the spiritual warrior that Ama-la had sought to awaken in me, so that I could better serve and help make known the One who has no desire to be known.

CHAPTER 31

Between Earthly Lives

I had been staying in the forest for many days, for it is the place where the mind truly settles without any stirrings, where it can become like the still deep of a lake. It is the place where I could most easily see and feel Tenzin, although the gulf between us now was one I couldn't easily cross. It is difficult to express in language the view from here, where we can at moments observe from a distance the lives of our loved ones who have not yet left their physical forms. But unable to be seen, we cannot embrace them or be embraced and can only speak through whisperings to their internal selves, hoping they are attuned enough to hear.

This forest is well known to me. It is one I have come to in the past to relive old memories, a place where I can more easily access the mind's expansive storage house. Although the forest is thick with trees of many varieties, light permeates the area, bringing clarity to a clouded mind. Whether the radiance comes from the sky above, or from the trees, or the ground below, I don't know, because everything here shimmers with luminosity.

This forest houses no debris, no fallen branches or decaying plants. It lives in a forever spring, filled with the greenest of newborn greens. Quilts of moss warm the ground, sprinkled with small tender buds of pink and yellow with a scattering of blue, and shades of colors not yet named.

I came for the solitude it affords me, although the presence of my beloved Satya is never far, kept in the background by a preoccupied mind, by a gaze inward bound. Waiting patiently, not interfering with my continual returns to the life of Padma Tshomo, he understood the ties binding me to Tenzin, filaments that death could not unwind.

As I sat there, seeking the guidance and wisdom of the elder trees, Satya's presence became more visible, and even through closed eyes, I saw his precious form appear before me. I was here in the world I called home, and the image of Tenzin was fading away. Gently, Satya unleashed the grasping of my mind, and I had no choice but to let go.

"Usha, it is time to awaken fully to where you now are. You must release that life." His gentle voice stirred my consciousness.

"Release it," I whispered as I opened my eyes. "How long has it been?"

"You have been here ten days, hardly leaving the forest."

"Ten years in earth time," I murmured. I had stayed by Tenzin's side during his long period of grief over the death of his mother, my death, and then a few years later the death of the abbot. Both were severe blows. How could I leave him?

"A woman has come into his life, and it is time for his mother to step away, knowing that he is in good hands," he continued with a smile.

"A woman?" I asked in surprise. "I have not seen that. He is a monk—how can that be?"

"And will remain one in this life. But a woman has come, the daughter of a patron of the monastery. It was her father who funded his last trip to Nalanda. The father has now passed, but the daughter continues to fund projects for Tenzin. A modest, unmarried woman, a devout Buddhist, she has fallen very much in love with him. But he is naïve, unskilled in these matters, and doesn't understand such love."

"How could I not have seen that?" I asked, bemused.

Satya's sweet laughter rocked the air like a newborn breeze. "A mother sees what she wants to see. But you must put aside your mother role, for your next interaction with him will be different."

"I want to see her, that woman," I implored, still identified with the role of mother.

"Focus your gaze and you will find her assisting Tenzin in so many matters. He has become a senior monk, a teacher to the others, selecting those who will go to near and far monasteries for debate. He is no longer the young man whom you nurtured."

Turning my gaze inward, I saw a woman about his age, modest in appearance, clearly well educated, lively and even dynamic, sitting with Tenzin as they discussed the needs of the delegation of monks who were to travel to the Mongols for dialogue. It was obvious she was funding the trip, and his look was one of gratitude and appreciation. A wave of satisfaction passed over me as I witnessed the scene and realized that Tenzin had emerged from his difficult period, perhaps due to her entry into his life.

Satya's voice drifted to me quietly, almost as an internal one. "She is too proper to declare her love for him, and he is too ensconced in his role as senior monk to notice it, and that love will not find fulfilment in their lifetime. Their connection is a deep and old one, but this life is not the right time for them. They will marry in their next life, and you will be the one to bring them together."

"I will meet Tenzin again," I murmured in relief.

"Sooner than you think," he replied softly, "and you will be best of friends. Their meeting now is a preparation for a future union. You have wanted to see the opening of his heart, and she will be the one to do that. In your next birth, he will take care of you. That was a commitment he made when he returned from Nalanda and learned that you had passed—a commitment to find you and to take better care of you in your next birth. Although unwarranted, he feels guilt for all that you went through and the fact that he was not there to help you, and for that reason he will draw you to him."

Rising from my seat on the ground, I looked around at the forested land, which had provided shelter as I adjusted to my separation from all I knew as Padma Tshomo, and I told Satya that I was ready to leave.

Taking my hand, we continued to communicate through thought as he led me along flowered pathways until we emerged into the open fields.

She has been waiting for you. I knew immediately he meant the one who had guided and cared for me in the Yarlung Valley. Within moments, as quickly as the rising and falling of a breath, we were there.

Standing before an elegant home, carved with fine details and set among vast sea gardens, she stood expectantly, looking not quite as I remembered her. Her long strands of white hair were more luminous, shimmering with touches of gold; her face bore not even the subtlest hint of age; she was youthful, radiant, and exuberant with joy. Dressed in a flowing robe colored like the clearest sky and tied by golden strings around her slender waist, she began to converse with me through thought, describing how she had first come to be my mother, a story I had heard from Yeye but which I had wanted to hear from her.

The beautiful jewel of earth was known to her world, a gem among the many physical planets that harbor life. In an exploratory mood, she and her companions decided to cross through the etheric film that separates the realms of light from the denser worlds. Selecting a remote place where humans did not dwell, a place where vast fields of ice were encircled by mountain heights, they thought they could descend and dance unseen. They would watch what happened when their feet touched the frozen surfaces. To them, it was a form of play. On one such day, she realized they were not alone. At the edge of the ice field stood a human man observing their light forms, watching their dance with great curiosity. He had come to that place searching, but he was not looking for them, as he did not know of their existence. He was seeking beings from faraway star systems whom he viewed as elder guides. He knew they sometimes came to watch the unfolding of life on earth. With that intention, he had journeyed alone to that remote place, believing they could teach him about the stars. He didn't meet any such being, but he did see the flickering lights cast from the dakinis as they danced on the ice.

The moment she noticed him, he also saw her. Looking into his eyes, she was surprised to find knowledge there, an unexpected, awakened awareness, and her curiosity was piqued. She had recently learned to condense her field of light and had gained knowledge of the mechanics of matter, and the desire arose to experience the density of the atomic world. She did not realize that she would have to leave behind the wonderous realm of light from which she came. He could not enter her world, but she could enter his, and so she did.

For some time, she was trapped between two worlds, unable to leave him and the child she bore, but unwilling to extend her stay indefinitely, a stay that could involve multiple returns. Experiencing the struggles of the heart, she came to understand the human plight. Longing for the realm of light, yet held by human ties, she lingered for some time, until a being came to release her, the one known by some as Dalha.

"In time, this man will reach the world where you abide," Dalha told her. "That will be his goal and aspiration. Your visit has served this purpose for him and for the daughter. And in time, I will bring this daughter to you when she is ready to receive you. Hidden among so many memories will be the memory of the dance of the dakinis, and of you."

Ama-la paused and then added, "Many lifetimes later, this daughter did dance, but not on ice. I have already told you that in a growing city by the sea, you became known for dancing the part of the great goddess who killed a vicious buffalo demon. All of that was preparation for the dance you did that night in the Yarlung Valley, which freed you from an old samskara with a wayward son."

Ama-la stopped conversing. She, Satya, and I were sitting on the lush greenery beside a garden of vibrant flowers. Changing the subject, Satya told me, "When you were together with Ama-la, she told you stories of the ones known as Guru Rinpoche and Yeshe Tsogyal. I can also share with you a story of them, one that took place not in the physical realm, but in the realm of light."

"Do you know of them, Satya?" A surprised look crossed my face.

He looked at me with equal surprise. "Did you think I didn't know them?" I didn't respond and he continued. "In the cycle of time when people on earth entered a period of spiritual decline and deeper descent into materialism, the one known as Guru Rinpoche became concerned. After much meditation— decades, centuries or millennia, it doesn't matter—he knew to call upon the hidden One. To reach her, he had to traverse innumerable Buddha realms, realms where the *devas* (gods) and *devis* (goddesses) live, and there he found her, meditating in the center of it all as universes swirled around her, the wonderous Mahadevi Sarasvati. He beseeched her to send her emanation into the world to spread the teachings that prod awakening, to keep alive the sacred knowledge embedded in all creation.

"But there is another way of telling the story. Some say that it was she who first called him. As he was immersed in the blissful state of fully awakened awareness, she approached and requested him to take birth in the human world. It was only after he agreed to do so that he appealed to her to accompany him. It does not matter who initiated the call because both are manifestations of the limitless love and compassion that flow through the worlds.

"There he stood, pleading with her to enter the earth realm for the sake of humankind. Smiling, she consented and sent forth her emanation, who was born as the very Yeshe Tsogyal and who continues to spread the teachings of tantra throughout the land you call Böd and beyond. You know the rest of that story." Daring not to express my ignorance, I silently wondered about the nature of an emanation. It was something I had heard about in the past and again during my life as Padma Tshomo, but I could not say that I fully understood it. Catching the drift of my thought, Satya responded.

"When deities project a part of their consciousness into the material realm, or anywhere else, that is called an emanation. It is rare for a full incarnation to take place; less rare for the devatas to send out emanations. But let me continue. It is also said that it was she, Sarasvati Devi, who sent her daughters to dance on the ice. The ancient *rishis* of Brahmavarta (ancient name of India) claim that throughout the Himalayas, they also saw her guiding the melting ice in its flow down the mountains into the plains, forming rivers where the clans could gather and foster new societies. It was the same in the region known as Böd. The formation of rivers and lakes needed a knowing hand, and the dance of so many unseen dakini daughters."

Ama-la laughed when she heard Satya's account. "I had not heard the story told that way, but you are right," she said as she gazed lovingly at him.

"Do you two know each other?" I asked, hesitantly. I had thought this visit was on my behalf only, not thinking that they might have met before. Smiling at each other, they exchanged knowing glances, and that was my answer.

We stayed for some time longer and then Ama-la rose, as did Satya, and I heard her say internally to me, *Remember the power of the sword, Bumo, the sword of wisdom and discernment, and remember the dance that night under the stars. Through that dance you dissolved your anger and subdued the anger of Zerdan. But anger can find any cause to latch onto and will no doubt creep up again. That is when the sword of discernment is needed, a discernment that must never sleep. Anger freezes the heart; dance melts it. Always remember the dance of the dakinis, which you witnessed in the past, and which you too now have danced. Store that memory in your heart.*

While she and Satya stepped away for some exchange, I sat there for a while longer with closed eyes, and for the first time, relived memories that I hadn't recalled before: memories of light forms dancing on ice fields; memories of a childhood in a remote place with a mother who one day disappeared and a father who never got over that loss. I sat unmoving as I watched the scenes float across my mind. Where had I stored them for so long? Why had they never emerged before now? How had I forgotten this mother whom I had once cherished?

Opening my eyes, I saw Satya standing alone a few steps away, waiting for me to emerge. Ama-la was gone but I heard her voice internally. *There was a purpose to that forgetting*, she communicated. *I was a young dakini, not schooled in human ways, and you were still young in your evolutionary journey, oblivious to other worlds. We both receded from each other's minds so that we could continue growing according to our determined courses, but I never fully lost sight of you. In this realm, many worlds remain in view, although on earth, other worlds recede from sight.*

Ama-la's voice became muted, and as he held out his hand to help me rise, Satya explained, "It was during the turning of the cycles, the end of the ascending Satya Yuga and the beginning of the descent. Every turning brings changes to the earth, physically and spiritually. In the Satya Yuga, a time of greater harmony, numerous celestial beings roamed the earth. Some, entranced by earthly pleasures, became trapped in samsara, falling into the cycle of rebirth. But for those who have reached a certain level of awareness, they can come and go at will, with discretion, not for their own enjoyment but for the benefit of others."

I didn't ask where Ama-la had gone as this is the way it is in that realm. People appear and disappear at will. Changing the subject, Satya said, "You and I first met not long after your birth to your dakini mother."

"It was not so soon, Satya. Many millennia passed in between."

He smiled. "You still have your earth mind and think in terms of earth years. In many ways you and I have had parallel journeys, which is why we bonded so quickly when we met. Around the time when you were born to her, I was born to a woman from a mountain tribe who had fallen in love with a young *gandharva* (a celestial being), who had appeared temporarily in human form. He disappeared soon after my birth and that mother never stopped seeking him. Eventually, after many, many births, she found him in the gandharva world.

"After that time, both you and I separately spent many lifetimes in tribal clans in different parts of the world and then were born in the area of Bharat. That was when we met. You remember our meeting, don't you?"

A smiled broke across my lips as I nodded. How often Satya liked to remind me of that first meeting. He knew that when in human form, I never recalled him or anything about our lives together. The past is hidden from view when experiencing a life on earth, except when someone helps to pull away the veil, as Ama-la had done.

We sat down and Satya entered meditation. As he did, I thought to myself, he is right, I have not fully left my human mind behind. There were people I wanted to find. Perusing the inner skies and penetrating the etheric veils that separate worlds, I found the mother who had birthed me in Böd. She had taken birth again in Böd into a nomadic family and was now a mature woman with children of her own. Although she looked different, I recognized her right away. Changing appearances does not mask identities. Further scanning the skies, I saw my father, now a young man in the Song Empire. And I saw that Yeshe was now a young child in the Song. I knew that I would meet Yeshe again, as he had made that promise to me. As the thought of Yeshe arose, I said to myself internally, *to me he is an emanation of Satya*. As that thought passed through my mind, I tried to suppress it, hoping Satya would not catch it in this place where little could be hidden. The thought brought joyous laughter from Satya, bringing him out of his meditation. Opening my eyes, I saw that mirth had taken over the one seated beside me, but he said nothing.

Embarrassed, I looked away and murmured, "I have heard that Yeshe Tsogyal saw her beloved consort in all beings. Perhaps it is the same with me." Then in a soft tone, I added, "Satya, I don't want to think any more of the life I just left."

"Then don't," he replied, adopting a serious tone. "Much time has already passed. Why spend your days here thinking of what has already become a dream? Too soon you will again be gone from here."

We got up and began walking again, and I gazed in wonder at the striking scenery before me, scenes that poets stretch their imagination to describe. This was a beautiful world for sure—a world where every conceivable joy could be created. But how many times had Satya spoken of the innumerable higher realms, even more precious than this one. "This is not the end of the journey," he had often said.

"Satya, there is so much I don't understand," I remarked as we slowly walked along the neatly carved paths lined with many varieties of flowering grasses.

"There is so much I also don't know," he replied in a matter-of-fact way. I looked at him in amazement. It seemed to me that my Satya knew all there is to know. When he saw my surprise, he explained, "The knowledge of the hidden workings of the universe is embedded in all things, and we can access that knowledge because it is in us. But there is no end to that knowledge. Usha, there is no end to knowing, as there is no end to the expansion of consciousness. It is not like one arrives, and that is the end. The journey is an ongoing one, ever expanding into new levels of awareness. One can be seduced into enjoying the beauty of this world and the many worlds like this one. And we are meant to enjoy them, but we should not become so entranced that we fail to seek the reality beyond the phenomenal world, to keep seeking, and to a greater and greater degree become one with it all, where there is not even the slightest ripple of separation."

I looked around at the many light beings who were passing by, knowing that some never left this elevated world; others would return to earth like me, and still others would move into a subtler realm of being, further along in their journey toward greater knowing. Satya's words were now internally conveyed. *You and I are no different from the great ones. It is just that they are more awakened to the reality beyond the phenomenal world. We are all the many expressions, projections of that one reality, and we must dissolve all the illusions that keep us separate. Like you, I have not achieved this yet.* Satya paused and then asked with a slight smile, *You have wanted so desperately to know who she is. Do you now know?*

I was aware that he was speaking of Dalha, and I nodded. Looking up, I gazed into the grand expanse of sky. A brilliant ethereal effulgence was emanating from the sun, not the physical sun but a sun nonetheless; from the moon, seated nearby, a paler, more subtle but equally beautiful array of radiating rays was streaming forth.

"She is an emanation of the Moon Goddess," I replied quietly.

"You have a history with that lineage." I nodded again. Things that had once perplexed me no longer did, as I realized more deeply how one incarnation links to another and then another in a long chain of action and reaction. I understood now that the abandonment by my dakini mother had in fact brought me much benefit, as it had inspired my desire to find her and her world, leading to my long search for the goddess through so many births and deaths and rebirths. Many times I had been born to a people who worshipped the Goddess of the Moon, and that eventually led me to Dalha.

"I have learned one thing in my life as Padma Tshomo," I said out loud as I turned my eyes to Satya.

"Only one thing?" he asked in a playful tone.

"Many things," I corrected myself with a slight laugh, "but perhaps the most important was to perceive the hidden blessings in the obstacles that arise. They can bring much benefit if understood in the right way and received with the right attitude, although that is not always easy to remember."

"Nothing in this universe is construed to harm us," he replied. "It is a matter of who we think we are. If we think we are the body, then yes, the body suffers. If we think we are the mind and emotions, then yes, the mind suffers. But if we know who we truly are, nothing can harm us; difficulties are there to awaken us. If we have a weakness, we will receive a situation to bring out that weakness so that we can work to overcome it. If we don't overcome it, another situation, another opportunity will be given. It is hard to understand this amid suffering, but it is the way the universe works. We call to ourselves what we most need. You needed to make peace with your son from the Han era, to free yourself of anger and fear, and he needed to get his revenge so that he could finally make peace with you. All has now been cleared."

As we continued to walk, we fell into silence. Then we sat down on a soft stretch of mossy greenery, and with closed eyes I took in all that Satya had said. Many hours or days passed, depending on how one calculates time. Then we rose and visited sages and dear ones I had known from earlier times, taking meals with them, foods of the most delightful nature. With the passage of time came a freeing from earthly concerns and much contented enjoyment, feeling the presence of the different forms of the Supreme Mother I had experienced over numerous lifetimes, especially those forms most dear to me. That presence is far more palpable in this world, and it brought me deep happiness.

Then one day as I was sitting with Satya by the sacred body of water not far from the cottage where we lived, he mentally conveyed, *Usha, one cycle has been completed, but a new one is arising for you, one for which you have already begun to prepare.* His words made me realize that a return to earth was imminent. The life of Padma Tshomo had been long ago put to rest. I was no longer her. Was another personality beckoning me?

You will find that son Tenzin again, make peace with someone whom you have resisted, and have a taste of the experience of Mahadev (Shiva) that you desired. These thoughts were already implanted in your mind, and you must return to fulfill them… and there may be some surprises.

"What surprises?" I asked, furrowing my brow.

"Life on earth and everywhere else is always full of surprises," he replied out loud with a slight laugh.

The light was dimming, casting a soft glow on the water as the sun began to set; another day passing, another year on earth. My eyes caught sight of a mountain, worlds away. Cradled on one of its cliffs was the one I had known as both Bhasundara and Yu Yan, deep in meditation training, seated next to her Shifu, her Rinpoche, the one I had known as Yeye.

Turning my eyes inward, I caught sight of Dalha in a small tent community in the place once known as Zhang Zhung. She was speaking to one of the children, with a broad smile on her face, and I murmured, "She is still there."

She never left, was Satya's mental reply.

Turning to my companion, I said, "Let's go home, Satya."

"We are home, Usha. Home is wherever you are."

The scene changed and we were now seated on the ground in front of the cottage where we lived. Satya could travel freely through the many universes and never be away. For me, each leaving was a going away. Earth was a place I visited, a place I had grown to love, but deep inside I knew it was not my true home. But when there, my mind was wiped clear of all memories, and it became the only home I knew.

"There is still time, Satya, isn't there?" I asked hesitantly. "Still days left?" He didn't respond. Once back in the cottage, I lay down and rested for a long time, unaware of Satya's comings and goings. His activities were still a mystery to me, as he could be with me and away at the same time, in so many places all at once. I was content to be there with him, even if it was only a part of him.

More days passed, and the time finally came for the restricting of consciousness into the world of matter, for the imposition of limitations. I saw the blueprint of a life taking shape, where I would find Tenzin and others from times past; a mother who would bring back to me the love I once knew for the one called Krishna; a father who would teach me about the great all-pervading deity called Shiva. I was to take birth in Bharat, not Böd, but those two places were now twinned in my heart and mind, and I would bring to Bharat the learning I had gained in Böd.

The world of earth had changed since my last journey out. The Song Dynasty had been conquered by the Mongols and a new dynasty established, known as the Yuan, under the rule of Kublai Khan. Böd was now also increasingly under the influence of the Mongols. In Bharat, the place I had called Gyagar, the Turkic invaders had expanded their power, solidifying the Mamluck Dynasty of the Delhi Sultanate, as they continued to destroy temples and places of knowledge. This would be my new battlefield. No longer contesting with a personal foe, I would have to face a collective one, and I wondered if I had the strength and wisdom to do so. It was into this environment that I was to take birth.

One day as I was seated outside, the light of the luminous world began to fade away, and with it, Satya's form, and mine. The cottage, the wonderous landscape, the love that vibrated in the air, filling all with a joy not known on earth, became like dreams lost somewhere in the folds of time. The great forgetting had begun. Several decades after the death of Padma Tshomo, I left my home in that realm of light to enter another physical form, with a new name and a new identity. Padma Tshomo was to become Devaki, born in a small village into a poor community of laborers.

PART 11

Late Thirteenth Century, Bharat (India)

CHAPTER 32

Another Tale of the Moon Goddess

I was born in a remote village a few days ride to the north from the age-old city of Patna, which had been part of the Pala Empire but had been conquered by the Delhi Sultanate not long before my birth. On a clear day, when the sky appeared as a pristine blue lake, one could see the snow-draped mountains in the distance, a reminder of the proximity of our devatas (gods) who blessed the area. In ancient times, the place where I was born had been part of the kingdom of Mithila, the sacred birthplace of Sita Devi. Much had changed since then, but it was said that those who loved her dearly could still feel her presence in our land.

My village was far enough away from the centers of power and insignificant enough to be immune from the destructive activities of the Sultanate, so I grew up with little awareness of the transformations occurring in the region. Village life went on with little notice of the happenings in the political realm. My family belonged to a community of laborers, including those who took in clothes for washing, but there were also those who cleaned the streets and helped with the many manual chores needed to keep village life humming along. Then there were those who were able to lease small plots of land to farm, allowing them greater self-sufficiency.

We had very little in way of material possessions, but that hardly mattered as we were a contented family. Our two-room mud hut was enough for my parents and six children. The real wealth of my family lay in the devotional nature of my parents—my mother for Lord Krishna and my father for Lord Shiva. The back room was where the children slept on thin mats on the floor. The front room served as the place for everything else. It was where my parents slept and where we ate and spent much of the day when we weren't outside. In one corner of the main room sat a small, standing *murti* (statue) of Lord Krishna and next to it was a small Shiva *lingam* (representing the formless aspect of Lord Shiva). Early morning hours would often find my parents in that corner, my mother offering a *puja* (ritual) to the murti, and my father sitting silently before the lingam. I grew up hearing stories of the two devas and naturally felt great reverence for both.

The first of the children was a daughter, Lalita, followed by three sons, Bhadra, Mahesh and Keshava, then another daughter, Uma, and after that I was born, the youngest child. My oldest sister Lalita was married when I was still an infant, and a close relationship never developed between us. The oldest of my brothers, Bhadra, had a bitter nature and quick temper, and resented the hardships our family underwent. I learned early on to keep a distance from him. My second brother, Mahesh, died when I was still young, before he was ten years old, after eating contaminated food during a village festival. This was a tragedy that my family never forgot, and we were forbidden to eat street food after that. His death left only four of us children at home as I was growing up. My closest relationships were with my third brother Keshava and my second sister, Uma, who was only a few years older than I.

My oldest brother, Bhadra, often complained about the continual shortage of food and other necessities, but my parents took in stride his dissatisfaction. After a particularly difficult period when our meals were limited and Bhadra had loudly protested, my mother took him aside. She told him that when she was young and her family was suffering from the lack of many necessities, her mother had told her that if she worked hard and performed good deeds, she would be born in a better material position in her next life. "But I firmly refuted her," my mother gently explained. "I was only twelve when I told her that I wasn't interested in material wealth, but rather in gaining the wealth of devotion. Gladly would I give up meals if I could gain greater devotion to the lord in my next life. Son, you must steer your heart in that direction." Sadly, her words were wasted on this brother of mine. Bhadra sneered and mumbled something I couldn't hear, but I was touched by my mother's story. That was her character. Everything she did was for the purpose of gaining greater devotion to her Krishna.

I was six years old when my mother began to take in laundry to help the family get by. My two older sisters would assist with the work and on occasion I would go down to the river and help as well. Washing clothes in the river was an opportunity for the women of our community to gather and talk, to tell funny anecdotes of their husbands and children, to gossip about their neighbors and chatter about one thing or another. It was a time for the women to share their lives with each other, but my mother never participated in their discussions. I once asked her why and she told me that when she worked, she kept her mind on Sri Krishna. "I pretend I am in Vrindavan," she explained with a smile, "the mother of one of his childhood friends, washing the clothes that I know he will wear when he goes to meet his friend Krishna. The clothes must be clean and well cared for so he will look his best when he meets him."

"Do you think Lord Krishna knows that?" I asked innocently.

"Of course!" she exclaimed. "He knows everything in my mind and heart, for I have given myself to Bhagavan (the Lord)." I wondered at her words. What did it mean to give yourself to Bhagavan?

My father had similar feelings for Lord Shiva. Once he returned home from work with tears in his eyes and refused to speak, going to sit in front of the Shiva lingam, not moving for quite some time. Only later did my mother reveal what had happened, which she learned from a neighbor who had witnessed the incident. My father was cleaning the street that day and by mistake his broom hit the shoe of a man. That man had spit on my father and pushed him away with his shoe. My father, a man of great dignity, wouldn't speak of the matter.

When I asked my mother whether he was upset about this insult to him, she shook her head and replied, "No, Devaki, he doesn't care what is done to him for he has given his life to Lord Shiva. Your *pitaji* (father) is sad because this man spit on a devotee of the Lord. Such an act will bring ill upon that man. To spit upon a devotee of the Lord is no minor matter." Again, I was left wondering what it meant to give your life to the Lord.

"He must have been a *brahmin* (priestly caste)," retorted Bhadra angrily, overhearing our conversation.

My mother turned to him and replied calmly but with firmness, "There are no higher or lower *varnas* (castes) in the eyes of the Lord. There are only two types of people in this world; those who love and serve the Lord and those who don't. Nothing else is relevant." At those words, I wondered into which category I would fit. Was I to be like my parents, fully devoted to their devatas, or like my brother Bhadra who had distrust for that type of devotion? In my heart I thought I knew the answer, although I had no idea how to gain such love.

Despite the physical hardships we had to endure, I considered myself very blessed to grow up in a home where the devatas were a living presence. Many times, I remembered my father's words: "Whatever I do, I do in the sight of Lord Shiva, so I must do my very best no matter what that activity is." On occasion, especially around Maha Shivaratri, the sacred day for devotees of Lord Shiva, he would tell us stories of the Lord. One story he liked to repeat over and over was the story of the creation of the sacred shrine of Somnath. He always told it in a slightly different way, so it was like hearing it for the first time. All the children except Bhadra would listen attentively. Inevitably, my eldest brother would get up and leave our home when either parent began telling stories of one of the devatas.

On one Shivaratri night, my father began to speak of the Lord: "There are many shrines for Lord Shiva, the most sacred pilgrimage, of course, being to Mount Kailash (Mount Tise), but it is unlikely that a poor devotee like me could ever travel to those faraway places." My father chuckled softly and added, "But Lord Shiva once made a promise. He said that those devotees who could not travel to him, he would come to them, so Lord Shiva has had to visit me in our very modest home. What does he care whether a home is small or large, poor or wealthy? He doesn't even notice because he only sees the heart."

At that point, Bhadra, who had been busy in another part of the main room, left the hut, slamming the door behind him. My father seemed not to notice and continued. "One of the stories I love most was told to me by my grandfather, an ardent devotee of the Lord. It is the story of the Somnath Shrine. I think it is the place I would most like to visit. It is by sea, and I have long wanted to catch a glimpse of that great body of water. There are many versions of this story, but the one I believe is this:

"Many eons ago, the Goddess of the Moon, the one we call Rohini Devi, caught a glimpse of Lord Shiva and became totally enamored of him. After that one glimpse, she began to see him in all things. Everywhere she set her eyes, no matter where she looked or what she did, all she saw was Shiva. At all times, her mind was fully immersed in him and love for him overwhelmed her heart. Her consort Chandra, also called Soma Dev (God of the Moon), saw this and became jealous. Jealousy is a very human emotion and is practically unknown among the devatas, but sometimes a seed of emotion develops, and the Lord, out of compassion, will help to uproot this. Like us, the devatas are tested at times because they also aspire toward perfection, and any imperfection, any impurity, affects the celestial worlds as well the physical realms. Mahadev (a name of Shiva) often helps the devatas overcome their minor shortcomings.

"Every time Soma Dev saw his consort Rohini, her mind and heart would be fully engrossed in Lord Shiva. Eventually, he became so upset that he confronted her and asked why she didn't adore him, who was after all her consort. Confounded, she replied that she did adore him, but that she did not distinguish between him and the Lord. She saw them as one. She had realized the reality behind the appearance. Her answer only angered him more, and the thought entered his mind to distract her from her devotion, to take her mind away from the Lord, which he tried unsuccessfully to do. Her single-minded absorption in the Lord disturbed him even more. Sensing that this was a problem not easily resolved, Rohini appealed to Lord Shiva to help her husband overcome the illusion of jealousy. Another issue had arisen because of this situation. Soma Deva's unstable mental state was dimming the radiance of that world and affecting other parts of the universe. Something had to be done.

"Lord Shiva realized that Soma Deva had not yet fully awakened to the reality behind appearances and that a journey into the physical world would benefit him. Being unable to free himself from the human emotion of jealousy would require him to experience a human life. But due to his beneficence, Lord Shiva shortened his stay on earth, enabling him to manifest a human body for a brief time without going through the process of birth."

My father then added with a smile, "This world is a testing ground not just for us humans but sometimes even for the devatas themselves. But back to the story. During his short stay on earth, Soma Dev encountered many forms of jealousy among men and women and saw the unnecessary suffering this troublesome emotion causes. What he witnessed in others, he also experienced himself, and this caused him great pain. He recognized that jealousy is a projection, an illusion cast by the human mind that comes from unfulfilled desires, insecurity, and greed, but he knew himself to be a deva, above those conditions. He wondered what had come over him to be jealous of Lord Shiva, whom he also adored. Then he realized that he had been given a test for the sake of lifting the final veil of separation, an illusion that made it appear as if he were separate from the Lord. Rohini had torn away that thin covering, but he had not yet done so.

"That test was also to help him understand the human condition so that he could better serve the world. Realizing this, he humbled himself before Lord Shiva, who told him that before returning to the celestial world he must purify himself by bathing in the sacred Triveni Sangam, where the Sarasvati, Kapila, and Hiran rivers converged and flowed into the western sea. He did this and then returned to the lunar world.

"As a result of this trial on earth, his devotion to Mahadev increased, equaling that of Rohini Devi. At moments he saw himself as inseparable from the Lord, but at other times he saw himself as separate but filled with an overwhelming love. Soon after he had bathed in that sangam, a *jyotirlinga*, a lingam of light, appeared, and much later a shrine was built by the sea to house that lingam. Devotees who go to the Somnath Shrine with a sincere heart receive the blessings of Soma Deva, Rohini Devi, and Lord Shiva, and it is said that they will never experience the harmful emotion of jealousy. I have heard that the lingam appeared in such a way that when the sea rises up, it washes over the lingam, bathing it, and this is seen as evidence that Soma Deva continues to serve Lord Shiva. It is also a reminder of the purifying effect of bathing in a sacred *sangam* (the confluence of rivers).

"Rohini Devi was extremely grateful for the change that had come over Soma Deva, but Lord Shiva wanted to give her a special boon and asked her to make any request of him. Do you know what she requested?" My siblings and I, who were gathered around my father, along with my mother, all shook our heads. "Her request was that she never leave Shiva's side, and that is why Lord Shiva is always seen with a sliver of the moon in His hair, an indication of her union with her beloved Lord."

My father ended his story, his face beaming with joy, as if he was experiencing what the Devi herself had experienced. When my father told such stories. it was as if another voice spoke through him, so engrossed and carried away did he become. We were all quiet, not quite sure of how to respond. Finally, my sister Uma broke the silence by asking in a curious voice, "Pitaji, is there really a Goddess of the Moon?"

My father smiled and replied, "Of course, Uma. But not the physical moon, which is only a symbol of a spiritual reality." Turning to my mother, he said, "You know that Sri Krishna was born into the Chandra Vansh (lunar dynasty)." My mother nodded. "There is a story behind that," he noted and, before anyone could stop him, he had already begun.

"The beginning of that dynasty was said to have taken place long ago when a young Devi from the lunar world, known as Lla, mated with a human man called Budha, giving birth to Pururavas, and from him descended the lunar dynasty. Many legendary heroes were born from that line, but over time, ignorance spread, corrupting and dividing that lineage. As tensions grew, they built up to a looming conflict, one that could cause massive suffering. Lla approached Lord Vishnu with great urgency, requesting the Lord to take birth in that lineage to save it from total destruction, and this he did. That is when he was born as Sri Krishna. The great war that took place during that time nearly destroyed the lunar dynasty, but Krishna was able to save it—as he had promised Lla. But that is another story entirely.

"Children, when you look up at the moon, think both of Sri Krishna and Lord Shiva and remember that the moon, like everything else, is most sacred. There are many teachings in these stories. Most importantly, never be jealous of anyone because the Lord has given you exactly what you need to have a happy life."

Bhadra had just re-entered the hut. Hearing those last words, he couldn't help but interject with a touch of haughtiness, "Not everything, Pitaji. Why should we be content and accept less than others?" His face hardened as he spoke.

"It is not wrong, Bhadra, to seek to better oneself and one's situation, but not out of anger or envy. Everyone, no matter what one's status in life, should aspire to improve. That is how we progress. Contentment doesn't mean giving up. It means being grateful for what one has."

"I don't agree. I won't accept that our condition cannot be changed." At that point my mother stepped in to end the discussion. Bhadra, now fourteen, was increasingly challenging my father in a way that disturbed the family harmony, and I could see how much it pained my mother, although my father was unruffled, aways patient and understanding. "It is his right to question," he told my mother on several occasions. "He must learn in his own way, in his own time."

"But not with anger or disrespect," she always replied.

My oldest sister Lalita was a devotee of Lord Krishna, like my mother. She always listened attentively but questioningly to my father's stories when she visited. Bhadra was hostile to spiritual matters, believing that the devatas, if indeed they did exist, did nothing to improve our lives. Before his death, my brother Mahesh had been indifferent. My third brother, Keshava, loved most to hear stories of Krishna, while my sister Uma was drawn to Shiva, but I considered myself to be a devotee of both and felt no need to choose. Often, Keshava and Uma would argue over which devata was greater, each recounting stories that one of our parents had told to prove their point. I thought this silly and on one occasion asked why they were arguing. My siblings each responded that I had to choose and could not follow both devatas, but I insisted that I saw them as one. This was my belief from early on. My only question was how I could gain the devotion that I saw in my parents.

A year later, on the next Maha Shivaratri when my father repeated the story of the Somnath Shrine, I ventured to ask, "Where does the Devi of the Moon live?" I was now nearly eight years old and beginning to think about these things for myself. Previously, I had remained silent and listened to the questions of my older siblings.

My father chuckled and replied, "I don't know the answer to that, Devaki. There are many things I don't know, but I suspect it is a world that our human eyes can't see, a beautiful world, I am sure. And I suspect that she helps Lord Shiva, guiding his devotees in this world and many others. You might encounter her in disguise one day and not know it is her. That is why we must treat all people as if they are one of the devatas in disguise— because they very well might be."

A few days later, I was helping my mother prepare food when she turned to me and said with a slight smile, "When you were a few years younger, maybe four or five years old, you and I were sitting outside one night when you suddenly looked up at the sky, and in a very matter-of-fact manner told me that the Moon Devi was your friend. I asked you which devi, and you replied that you had forgotten her name."

"I don't remember that at all," I replied, embarrassed.

"You were very young, but that was not the only time you referred to her. On several other occasions you told me that you had seen her and talked with her, and that she was your friend. But gradually you stopped speaking of her. As a child we remember things that we forget when we grow older."

I was always uncomfortable when my mother referred to things I said when I was younger, so I replied, "Perhaps I made it up."

"I don't think so, Devaki. Although you were so young, you spoke in a very serious tone. I thought perhaps she had come to you in a dream. Often children see things that adults don't see."

During my growing up years I wondered how my parents knew so much about the devatas since they could not read or write and had no exposure to the learned people in our region or to religious texts. They both said they had learned all they knew from their grandparents, who had learned from their grandparents.

Once when I had questioned my mother, she had replied, "Do you think knowledge only resides with those who can read the texts? These are stories that each generation passes on to the next. That is how they have survived. Long before writing and reading came about, these stories were preserved by being told and retold, each generation narrating them a little differently, according to their understanding, which added to their richness. There is no end to the telling of these tales."

Once my father overheard my youngest brother Keshava and my sister Uma arguing about which of the devatas was more powerful. Keshava was naming all the demons Sri Krishna had conquered, stories he had heard from my mother, and Uma was arguing that Lord Shiva had conquered even more. I was quietly sitting by their side, thinking they were silly to argue over such a matter. After several minutes, my father interrupted. "You two remind me of a story I heard regarding the creation of the Trimbakeshwar Jyotirlinga. Do you know what makes that lingam so special among all the others?" They stopped arguing, looked at my father inquiringly and shook their heads. Pleased that he had caught their attention, he continued, "It is because that lingam contains the faces and the combined power of Lords Vishnu, Brahma, and Shiva—all three. Why do you think that is?" Nobody responded.

"There was a time when the devotees of Lord Vishnu and Lord Shiva were arguing over who was the supreme deity, just like you are now. Even some of the sages and learned people got involved in the debates, and this created a great division in society. The followers of Lord Vishnu would not mingle with the devotees of Lord Shiva, and vice versa. There was one city in particular that held a number of these debates, and outside of this city lived a poor simple farmer who worshipped all three deities because he saw them as different aspects of the One. He heard about these debates, but he didn't believe anybody who truly understood or loved the devatas would engage in such foolish thinking.

"One night he had a dream in which Lord Shiva was worshipping Lord Vishnu. The next night he had a dream where Lord Vishnu was worshipping Lord Shiva. And the third night he had a dream in which they both were worshipping Lord Brahma. He woke up from those dreams so overcome with love for all three that he went to the place where the learned people were debating and tried to get a word in, but nobody would let him speak. After all, he was only a poor farmer, who didn't know much about philosophy or the sacred texts. That night he went home and prayed to all three devatas, asking them to help people understand that the very concept of competition among the devas was a falsity created by the human mind. He didn't receive a direct answer to his prayer, but the next day there was quite a buzz in the town. Everyone was talking about the images of all three deities that had appeared on the Shiva lingam, and the wise men of that place took this as a sign. After that, there were no more debates about who was the supreme deva and that was how the Trimbakashwar Jyotirlinga came into being. It was a message important for that time and equally crucial for us today. We keep forgetting and need to be reminded again and again of the love between these three equal expressions of the supreme One." After my father told this story, there were no more discussions about this matter in our family.

When I was nine, we encountered a year of difficult harvests and food was scarce. Since my oldest sister was living with her husband's family, and one brother had died years earlier, my mother had only me and my three siblings to feed, along with her and my father. My eldest brother, who was now a rapidly growing young man, had a voracious appetite and never seemed satisfied. For three days my mother went without food so that everyone else could eat. After the first day, I asked her why she hadn't taken her meal, and she replied that she wasn't hungry. On the second day it was the same, and yet I saw her doing all the work she normally did. On the third day I erupted angrily at my eldest brother for taking such a large portion, blaming him for eating our mother's share. Taking me aside, my father explained the situation.

"Three days ago, your mother had a dream of Sri Krishna, in which he said, 'You have fed me for so long, now I will feed you. For three days you will need no food.' The dream became true. She has not been hungry or fatigued or weakened at all during this time. In fact, she has told me that she has more energy than ever. So, you see, Devaki, Bhadra is not to blame. She is being fed by Krishna and has no need to eat. After today, she will take food again."

"Still, Bhadra eats too much," I protested, defensively. My relationship with my eldest brother had never been good, but as I grew older it became even more troublesome as I found fault with everything he did.

My father smiled. "He is a growing boy. I know that he annoys you, but you must learn to have compassion for your brother and see his good qualities." I could not fathom why my parents always defended him when he had no good qualities that I could see.

I was ten years old when my father became ill. He was a thin man to begin with, but now he began to waste away, and my mother turned all her attention to him. I watched as he aged very quickly. In a short time, his cheeks hollowed and his hair turned fully grey. Every morning, before the day's work began, my mother would go to the well and fetch two buckets of water, one for drinking and the other for soaking my father's feet. When he developed a fever, she would continually wipe his face, neck and arms with a cold cloth and send me to the nearby forest to collect special medicinal plants. She taught me early on about the medicinal plants and edibles that hid themselves in the neighboring forests. It was during this time of my father's illness that I began going to the forest each day to collect whatever food I could find, since my father was no longer able to work.

Late one night I couldn't sleep and went to open the door to the main room. I had only cracked the door open when I heard my mother say to my father in a tearful voice, "You are most precious to me. How can I bear to part with you?"

And I heard his reply. "It is Krishna who is most precious. You will find me again in him. Cling to him and you will never be alone."

I didn't want to hear any more, so I quietly closed the door, returned to my mat on the floor and muffled my tears. Several months after he had taken ill, he passed away, leaving my mother to care for those of us who were still at home. For me, as well as the others, his loss was a huge one. He had been such a calming and stabilizing force in our family. Nothing disturbed him and for every difficult moment, there was a story about Lord Shiva to see us through and to bring a smile to our faces. Where would I find the Lord now without him to guide me? I cried for weeks after, but my mother shed few tears, quickly assuming the role of both mother and father. She would say, "Lord Shiva is still here with us. He has not abandoned us," and she would remind us of one of my father's stories.

Each day when I went to the forest, I would ask Sri Krishna and Lord Shiva to help me find food, and inevitably I would return with a basketful of wild grains and root vegetables. One day when I was out searching for food, I walked further than normal until I came to the edge of the forest. Peering out, I saw a large house, backed by a lush garden filled with beautiful, carefully tended flowers. I couldn't help but try to get a closer look. Placing on the ground the food I had gathered, I thought perhaps I could take one flower home to my mother, a rare gift for her. As I drew closer to the house, I noticed a rather large basket nestled on the grass not far from the door of the house. Right next to the basket on a low table was a bunch of bananas. I was terribly hungry and tempted to take one banana, but I hesitated as my mother was strict about us not taking what didn't belong to us. As I was gazing longingly at the fruit, I saw two large monkeys approach the bananas and the basket on the ground. Without thinking, I grabbed a large stick and ran over to the monkeys, shooing them away. They ran immediately, but as I peered into the basket, I saw that it contained a small baby, and I couldn't help but stare at him and smile at how adorable he was.

As I did, he opened his eyes and seeing my beaming face hovering over him, he smiled back at me. Then he reached out his tiny arm. I wanted to take hold of his hand, but my hands were dirty from digging in the ground, and he was so clean and neatly wrapped in a white blanket that I resisted. He continued to stare at me. His smile grew broader, and I found myself greeting him, introducing myself. At my words, he began to squirm and move about and then he let out a rather loud squeal. It was not a cry, simply a high-pitched sound, and I took it as an acknowledgement of my greeting. I could not help but giggle when I heard it, but then I realized I was in someone else's home, uninvited and most likely unwelcome. Uneasiness came over me at the thought of what might happen if I was discovered. I told myself to hurry away, but an inner urging caused me to stay, cementing me in place and making it impossible to pull myself away from the beautiful baby lying before me.

"Who are you?" I whispered as he continued to squeal at me. As I stood there peering into the basket, I heard a door open and the sound of footsteps approaching. It was too late for me to run. I would have to face whatever consequences awaited me.

CHAPTER 33

A Forgotten Son

"He is adorable, isn't he?" The gentle voice of a woman startled me and I swung around, certain that I was in for a scolding. I found myself face to face with a matronly woman. She was plumper than my mother and her coal dark hair, wrapped up behind her head, was not streaked with grey, as was my mother's. She was beautifully dressed in a brightly colored skirt and top, so different from the plain, faded cloth my mother always wrapped around her body.

"I was standing by the window when I saw the monkeys approach him, but I couldn't get outside quickly enough. I am grateful that you shooed them away." Glancing around, she murmured, "I don't know what happened to Sarita, the woman who watches him. She is never supposed to leave his side." At that moment a younger woman emerged from the doorway. Seeing the older woman there, she immediately began to apologize, saying that the other son had called her. Feeling awkward, I began to back away, when the older woman turned to me and asked, "What is your name?"

"Devaki," I replied meekly, wondering if she would now scold me.

"And your surname?"

I hesitated and then murmured, "Dhobi."

Handing me the bunch of bananas, she said, "Please take these and give them to your mother, in gratitude for protecting little Shankara."

I hesitated again but she pressed the bananas into my hand. I took them and ran away as fast as my legs could carry me, afraid that she might ask for the bananas back.

When I arrived home and Bhadra saw the bananas, he immediately grabbed them and began eating one.

"They are not for you," I cried, trying to get them back. "They are for *Amma* (mother)." At that moment my mother walked into the hut and asked where I had gotten the fruit. I didn't tell her the whole story, only that I had shooed away a monkey from an infant and this was the reward. She accepted that.

A few days later I was home alone with my mother when the woman who had given me the bananas knocked on the door of our hut. My mother stepped outside to speak with her, telling me to wait inside. When she didn't return after some time, I became worried, wondering if that woman would ask my mother to punish me for wandering into her garden. When she finally did re-enter the hut with a basket in hand, she wore an expression of concern on her face.

"What did that lady want?" I asked anxiously.

"She wants you to come help look after her little son." At those words, my heart leapt, but I tried to restrain myself as I knew that my mother had not yet given her approval. "She has given me these clothes for you to wear when you go to her home." Seeing the excited expression on my face, which I could not fully hide, she cautioned me in a somber tone, "I have not yet agreed but she insisted that I take these clothes. I don't know if it is a good thing, Devaki. I must enquire about the family. They are brahmins, and I worry about how you will be treated. I told her I would let her know in a few days." Her expression softened as she asked, "Is this something you want, Devaki?" I nodded enthusiastically. "Let me think about it and ask Krishna. He will guide me to the right decision."

Anxiously, I waited for my mother's approval. I knew it wasn't the big house, the food that would await me, or even the relief from helping my mother do the washing that was drawing me. There was something else, something that made me smile every time I thought of that infant.

On the third day, early in the morning, my mother rose from her seat in front of the murti of Krishna, offered pranam to the Shiva lingam, and told me that it was fine for me to go help with the baby on the condition that we accept no payment from the family. That was more than okay with me. What did I know or care about payment?

"I have inquired at the temple about them," she explained. "The Banerjees are a good family, devotees of Lord Shiva. The child's father is a well-known Sanskrit scholar who spends most of his time in Patna, and the mother very generously donates to the temple and feeds the brahmin students. They are based in Patna but have a home here. There are two older boys in the family; one is away studying and the second is still at home but will soon go to the city for study as well. This third son, the mother wants to raise here in the village. You will be his playmate, Devaki. It is a good arrangement. I will miss your help with the wash, but we will get by." She smiled at my eagerness.

She continued. "Bhadra will walk you there in the mornings and Keshava will pick you up at the end of each day. But you must wash every morning before going, mind your manners, listen to instructions, speak little in front of adults, and don't make yourself too visible. Stay in the background, Devaki."

It suddenly occurred to me that I would no longer be able to go to the forest to find food. "Who will gather food, then?" I asked.

My mother smiled. "That is no longer necessary, Devaki. With both Bhadra and Keshava working, we will have enough. I only sent you there so you would know where to find food in the event of an emergency. It is important knowledge for you to have. The devas and devis have supplied everything we need through Vasundara Ma (earth goddess), and we must know how to live through her generosity."

My mother must have conveyed her consent to the family, because the next morning she awakened me early with a bucket of water for me to wash. "These are the clothes she has given, two pairs of fine quality," she explained, as she laid out the new cotton skirt and top. Then she combed my hair, something I rarely did, and carefully braided it, tying my hair with a ribbon that the woman had also left.

My walk with Bhadra was mostly one of silence. He was not happy that he had to walk me the distance to the big house, and angry at my mother for not accepting payment for my work.

"I am not going to work, Bhadra," I told him, angry that he was interfering in my life. "I am going to play with the baby."

"You are too big for play, Devaki. It is time you also contributed to the family."

But play was indeed what Shankara's mother, whom everyone called Panyaji, had in mind. I soon learned that Sarita, the young woman who was assigned to watch Shankara, was most attentive to his older brother, often leaving Shankara alone. That was why his mother wanted another person to attend to him, one who would not only take care of his needs but also keep him entertained. And that is what I did.

I knew nothing about toys as I never had any, but I knew about things in nature that amused a baby. I would show him how to build with sticks and leaves and stones, then knock them down and make him laugh. I made funny faces that caused him to smile. I held his hands and ran them over my face and told him the word eyes when he touched my eyes and ears when he touched my ears. I knew he was too young to understand, but it was my way of entertaining him, and he seemed to enjoy it because before long he was laughing with me. I was so engrossed with keeping Shankara happy that the days flew by.

At the end of each day before I was escorted home, Panyaji would hand me a package for my mother. The first time when my mother opened the package, she sighed and murmured. "I told her that we would accept no payment, but I didn't say that we would take no food, and so I must accept this. I will accept it as a gift from Lord Shiva." My mother was a proud woman and would never accept what she called charity. But Bhadra was pleased that there was some reward for my work, especially since it involved food items that we had never tasted before. I could see that my mother was cautious, not wanting us to get used to things that were beyond our reach. She told Bhadra on that first day when I brought home the package of food, "The only reward is knowing that we are pleasing our deva."

"Which deva?" asked Bhadra sarcastically.

"Both!" exclaimed my mother, displeased with his tone.

"It is not Krishna who will put food in our stomachs," retorted Bhadra rudely.

"Who else has fed us all these years?" she asked, casting him a stern look. Bhadra was about to respond but held back. The tension between him and my mother had grown since my father's death, which my brother blamed on the hard work he had to endure so the family could eat. As a result of his growing dissatisfaction, my brother had begun to associate with a few other young men, who also complained about the inequities of life.

Since my father's death, Amma had become stricter with Bhadra, and I knew that this caused her great pain, a pain which she couldn't quite hide behind the veil of her eyes. It wasn't in her nature to scold him or any of her children. I knew how much she loved him and how hurt she was by his refusal to even look at, let alone approach the corner of our home where Sri Krishna and the Shiva lingam rested. She never cared which one we loved, only that we took one of the devatas as our own.

My evenings were filled with trying to navigate between my mother and eldest brother, listening to their nighttime arguments over the marriage my mother was trying to arrange for him. But my days passed joyfully, taking pleasure in each advance of little Shankara, as he first learned to roll over, then to sit up and grasp whatever I held in front of him.

Shankara's second brother was sent to Patna for study and the woman in charge of the children, Saritaji, took over more of the household responsibilities, overseeing the other servants, and I quickly saw how negligent she was of little Shankara. There were several other servants in the household, who took care of cooking and cleaning. Saritaji's job had been to look after the children, but she didn't seem well suited for this work. I soon found out that there was a family connection because no matter how negligent she was, Panyaji would not send her away. I knew that Panyaji was relieved by my presence as I watched Shankara's every movement, not leaving him alone for even a moment, except when he was asleep. Even then, I often would sit by his side watching over him, making sure that he was resting comfortably.

"You will make a good mother, Devaki," she said to me one day.

"I don't want to be a mother. I want to look after Shankara always," I replied without thinking as I helped him rise to a standing position.

She laughed and said, "You are still so young. That will change in time."

"Look at him stand, *mahashani* (great lady)!" I exclaimed. "He learned this only today."

"Devaki, you must call me Panyaji like the others." I nodded. She had told me that many times, but I still couldn't bring myself to address her by her name. "You take as much joy in my son as I do. That makes me very happy."

A year passed. Bhadra was walking me to the big house one morning when he suddenly asked, "Don't you envy them? It seems unfair that they have so much while we have so little."

"Envy whom?" I asked innocently.

"The Banerjee family of course."

I stopped walking and looked at him. "Bhadra, do you remember nothing of what Pitaji taught us?"

"Taught us what?" he asked as he also stopped walking.

"The story of the Somnath Shrine. That was a story he told us again and again, about not allowing the poison of envy to enter our minds."

"You believe that story?"

I stared at him without answering, but when he started to laugh, I retorted angrily, "So now you are doubting Pitaji," and began to walk away.

"I don't want to be fooled or deceived," he replied bitterly. When I didn't answer, he called out after me, "Fine. From now on, you can walk yourself to that fancy house. Devaki, don't think you are better than us because you work there."

His words pained me deeply. I didn't care at all about the house or the fine things the family had. I didn't even care about the fancy foods. All I cared about was Shankara. If it weren't for him, I would rather be home helping my mother, as I knew my absence meant more work for her. How often I had debated what to do, but my heart kept telling me again and again that I couldn't leave Shankara.

One thing I learned was that the big house had as many problems as my family had, only the problems were of a different nature. They didn't worry about having enough food, but rather about having the time to tend to the children. Even Panyaji was too busy at the temple to have much time for Shankara. His father was in Patna, as were his older brothers, and there was no one fully devoted to him. As young as I was, I made it my purpose to be that person.

My third brother Keshava took over Bhadra's responsibility and began walking me to and from the big house each day. He and I were much more similar in temperament, and I liked this arrangement better, even though it meant more effort on his part. My relationship with Bhadra deteriorated further after that exchange, and I couldn't help but retort to each of his caustic comments when I was home. My mother would cast a disapproving glance at me but say nothing. One evening I lashed out at him and grabbed his food, saying that if he was so opposed to the Banerjee family then he shouldn't eat the food they sent. Taking hold of my hand and leading me outside, my mother scolded me for those words, which I wanted to retract as soon as they slipped out of my mouth.

"I expect more from you, Devaki," she said sternly. "You must have patience with your brother. You see that he is struggling with many things, and we must have patience with him. If he needs occasionally to vent his frustration, we must allow it. Someday everything will improve for him, I am sure, and he will then have a better attitude."

"He has been like this his whole life and will never change," I blurted out tearfully.

"He will. Every night I pray to Krishna about him, and Krishna has never let me down. But it may not happen quickly. It may take a lifetime, and that is okay. As long as he makes peace with himself before he leaves this world, I will be satisfied." After that scolding, I learned to hold my tongue, at least when my mother was around, but my feelings for this eldest brother didn't change.

I had been going to the Banerjee home for near two years when Saritaji began to instruct me to take up other chores, saying that I no longer needed to hover over Shankara all the time. I didn't protest because I saw myself as a servant of the house, but soon after this began, I overheard a conversation between her and Panyaji.

"Devaki is not a servant here," Panyaji began. "I have not brought her here for that. She is Shankara's playmate, and you mustn't give her other tasks to perform. She is to spend every moment that she is here with him."

Sarita didn't answer right away, but after a few moments she replied with a touch of haughtiness, "I don't understand, Panyaji. Why would you bring a girl like that into this house to care for Shankara? She is even eating with us. She is a…"

"Hush!" exclaimed Panyaji before she could say the word. "I don't want to hear this from you again. She is the daughter of Rupendra Dhobi, a great devotee of Mahadev and known in the village as a saintly man. His parents were also devoted chelas of Mahadev, and that is why I brought her here. It doesn't matter whether you understand or not. These are my orders." I didn't hear any more of the conversation, but I wondered how she knew of my father. Had she inquired about my family, just as my mother had inquired about hers? For the first time I wondered if it was Lord Shiva who was protecting me because of my father's devotion. Was it he who had arranged for me to stay near Shankara, a child to whom I had grown very attached?

Shankara was a most precocious child and learned to walk and speak early. Before he even learned to say *amma*, he learned the word *didi* (sister), which is what he called me. Soon I was running after him, picking him up when he fell on the ground, and dreaming up all sorts of games to keep him occupied. At the same time, the situation at home began to fester. Amma had found a good marriage for Bhadra with a girl from our community, with a family that had a little more than ours, which was what he wanted. At first, he said he would build an additional room onto our little home, but one night after he made a caustic remark to my mother, I couldn't prevent myself from lashing out at him. "Bhadra, if you are so unhappy here, why don't you leave. We would all be better off without you."

My two other siblings looked at me in horror, and my mother had no time to say anything before Bhadra shouted back at me, "I will leave, Devaki, and let you take care of the family!" He stormed out of our home, slamming the door behind him, and didn't come back that night.

I feared that my mother would scold me, but she didn't. Turning to her, I muttered, "We would be better off," it is true, hoping that she would come to my defense, but she didn't respond. She didn't speak to me that night, but the next morning as I was getting ready to go to the Banerjee house, she said, "You will not go there today. You will find your brother, apologize, and ask him to come home." She sent Keshava to tell the family that I wouldn't be able to come, while I unhappily went out to look for Bhadra. Not long after, I returned home without finding him.

"You cannot go to the Banerjee's today or any other day, Devaki, until you find him and apologize." That brought tears to my eyes, but it made me realize my mistake in not restraining my anger. I left home again to look for him, checking the huts of his few friends, but I was no more successful this time. Finally, I sat down by the side of the road, discouraged, and tried to imagine how my father would advise me. Then I remembered something he had once told us. A year or so before he died, after we had finished the evening meal, pitaji told us a story following one of Bhadra's outburst when he had stormed out of the home.

"Some time ago in a village, there lived a very irritable hermit, who had a nasty temper, making many people in the village afraid to approach him," explained my father "Everyone kept their distance. If someone crossed his path, this man inevitably reproached them over one thing or another, found fault with that person, or yelled at them for no good reason. He was unmarried and seemed to have no family, and everyone thought he was a bit crazy. It got to such a point that when the village elders gathered, they discussed asking him to leave the village. Many of the village elders were devotees of Lord Shiva, and they even mentioned that this hermit seemed to have disdain for religious ceremonies since he never came to any of the festivals or celebrations, and he never went to the temple. Having an irreverent man in their midst could harm the youth, one of the elders said.

"The village chief was an ardent devotee of the Lord. He was the one who always arranged for the many rituals and ceremonies to be performed by the brahmin priests at the temple, and his advice was much valued. He agreed with this elder that the irascible hermit could disturb the religious sentiments of the youth and said that something had to be done about him. That night the village chief had a dream in which Lord Shiva appeared and asked him, 'Why do you wish to send away my beloved *chela*(disciple)?'

"Much surprised by these words, the man responded, 'But Prabhu (lord), he is not a chela at all. He opposes you at every turn.' Whereupon the Lord smiled and showed him all the good works the man anonymously performed, leaving food by the doorway of those most in need, providing medicine for those who had been taken ill. 'You do not recognize who he is, so how can you judge him?' asked the Lord. After that dream, the village chief could not send the hermit away. Nothing changed. That man never participated in any of the religious festivals or ceremonies or visited the temple. He remained an irritable and unfriendly man, but he continued to help the villagers anonymously." After finishing, my father looked at us and asked what lesson the story held.

"Never to judge," Keshava replied quietly.

"That is correct," said my father. "We must realize that we only see half the story, perhaps not even half, and we can't really understand what is behind a person's actions or words, or who they truly are."

As I sat by the side of the road, my father's words came back to me. Immediately I jumped up and raced home, thinking to ask my mother to come help me search for Bhadra. Now I was worried that something might have happened to him in the night, and it would be my fault. When I pushed open the door, I found my elder brother sitting quietly talking with my mother. As soon as I saw him, I began to cry and between sobs asked his forgiveness.

"Don't make such a fuss, Devaki," he replied in an emotionless tone. "We both needed time to cool off."

My mother was not going to let the matter pass. "Come with me," she said as she took me firmly by the hand. Leading me around to the back of the hut, we walked a short distance into a small, forested area, until we came to something that looked like a small shrine, although not a religious one. There was no Shiva lingam, no murti, only a small covered clay pot surrounded by flowers and leaves and carefully mounted piles of small stones. "This is your brother's special place. When he didn't come home for the noon meal, I thought he might be here, and this is where I found him. This is where he spent the night."

"What is this place?" I asked, looking around at how carefully the area had been arranged and maintained.

"After your brother Mahesh died, Bhadra was inconsolable. He blamed himself since he was at the festival with your brother that day and had bought him the contaminated food he had eaten. He cried for a week, and finally your father decided to do something that was most unusual. He brought a small portion of your brother's ashes, which are in the pot there, and your father told him that whenever he missed Mahesh, he should come here and talk with him. Every morning Bhadra comes here before going to work to greet your brother, and whenever he storms out of the house or is upset, he comes here to sit with him and to pour out his heart. I don't know why I didn't think to look here last night, but by afternoon I realized where he must have gone. I have been very touched by Bhadra's continued devotion to his brother." Her voice grew quiet when she spoke those last words.

"I didn't know," I murmured.

"There is something else you should know. Every night when you bring home food from the Banerjee house, Bhadra sets some aside. Do you know why?"

"I assumed that he was taking an extra portion for himself," I replied. "Saving it for later."

She shook her head. "After the meal, he takes it to your sister Lalita, who is pregnant. He worries that her husband is not able to take proper care of her. Sometimes they don't have enough to eat."

"Lalita is pregnant again?" I asked in amazement. Nobody had told me.

"I am telling you this so you won't judge your brother so harshly. He has many fine qualities. Don't see only his rough edges. Before your father died, I asked him why Bhadra was indifferent, even hostile to everything religious. Your father told me not to worry about that because his way of serving the devatas is by serving people. He knew that Bhadra would devote himself fully to the family, making sure that everyone had enough food and all the basic necessities, and your father was right. He also felt that Bhadra had suffered a deep hurt in the past, perhaps had been greatly deceived and that was why he had turned away from religion. Lately, Devaki, I have begun to wonder why you are so bitter toward him. Why do you attack him over every little thing?"

As the conversation turned to me, I began to defend myself, but she interrupted me. "Hush, Devaki, and listen to me. It is you, not Bhadra, who is resisting. Many times, he has tried to make peace with you, but you have always refused. I think he may have hurt you in the past, but it is time to forgive him for whatever he might have done. Let go of your anger."

"I am not angry, but I find him annoying," I murmured meekly. Rarely did my mother rebuke me as she was doing now, and I felt it unfair but dared not contradict her.

She continued, "What Krishna sees and cares about is his heart, not whether he offers *pranam* (reverential salutation) to the murti or even whether he acknowledges Krishna's existence. That is what we should see, his heart. You must be more concerned with yourself, how to control that tongue of yours when you get angry."

"It is only Bhadra who gets me upset, nobody else," I replied quietly.

"I will tell you a story. Your father and I have told you many times about the great war that took place long ago." I nodded. "You know about Arjuna, the hero of that war, and Duryodhana, the villain." Again, I nodded. "Before the war, both *kshatriyas* (warrior caste) came to Krishna to invoke his help. Krishna looked at them and told them that one of them could have his counsel, but he would not use any weapons or fight, and the other one could have all of Krishna's army, which was one of the mightiest at the time. Do you know why he asked Arjuna first which one he would choose?"

"Isn't it because he saw Arjuna first?"

My mother shook her head. "He wanted Duryodhana to see for himself Arjuna's devotion so that perhaps he would choose the same. Arjuna said that he would far prefer to have Krishna by his side than that mighty army. When it was Duryodhana's turn to choose, he picked the army. Krishna asked him three times if he was sure, giving him three chances to make the right choice. Had Duryodhana also said that he would prefer to have Krishna over the army, the war would have been averted. In his ignorance, Duryodhana did not understand the opportunity Krishna was giving him.

"In the end, when Duryodhana was killed, Krishna stood before him and gave him another chance to appease his anger, but Duryodhana died in a fit of rage, which then determined his future birth. At that moment when he lay dying, Krishna spoke quietly to him, affirming, 'My love for you is no less than my love for Arjuna. The only difference is that you would not receive it. I will come to you again and again until you are ready to take me into your heart.'" I could see that my mother was carried away by the story and her eyes teared. "That is the promise of the Lord. We mustn't give up on anyone, Devaki, and certainly not your brother."

How many times my mother had told me to see Bhadra's good qualities, to look beyond the rough edges. I knew she was right, but I was unable to do so. I was unable to keep myself from getting irritated at him over minor matters and my irritation only created a reaction in him that generated a cycle we seemed unable to break. Internally, I acknowledged the truth in my mother's words, and I knew that I was a large part of the problem, but I also didn't know how to change my feelings toward this brother of mine.

Later that evening I asked Uma why nobody had told me that Lalita was pregnant again. "Devaki, when you are here, all you talk about is Shankara: what he did that day, what he said, how smart he is. Your mind is only on Shankara. You never ask about the family and so nobody offers any information."

"I don't mean to be like that," I murmured.

"Just don't forget that we are your family," she replied in a gentler tone.

A few weeks later, Panyaji came to my mother to ask whether I could live at the Banerjee house and not return home in the evenings. Shankara was four and was asking for me at night, wondering why his Didi didn't live with them. I was fourteen when I went to live with the Banerjees. It was a relief to be away from Bhadra, but also sad, because I was deprived of my mother's constant counseling. The daily packages of food turned into weekly deliveries, which allowed me to continue feeling that my family was gaining some benefit from my time away.

Panyaji did all she could to make me feel at ease, giving me a room right next to Shankara and treating me as part of the family. For the first few months I hardly went home, only going back for a few brief visits. On each return, I listened to talk of a marriage for Uma, but nothing had been decided. I knew that she had her mind set on a particular boy, but that my mother opposed the marriage. There was not much I could do and so I didn't get involved. Several months later, I received word that everything had been arranged for Uma's marriage, which was to take place in a few weeks. Panyaji agreed to let me go home for that time, and Bhadra came to pick me up.

As soon as I saw him, I asked why Keshava had not come to get me. "He has been ill," Bhadra replied curtly.

"Why didn't someone come get me sooner?" I exclaimed.

"He is better now, but needs rest," he replied, ignoring my question. I knew what he was thinking—that I was drifting further away from the family. Not wanting to get into another argument with him, I didn't respond, and we walked the rest of the way in silence.

Once I saw Keshava, I was shocked by his pale and thin appearance, but everyone in the family seemed to brush it off. Taking Uma aside, I asked her what had happened. "Keshava came down with a high fever and was shaking for two days. No physician would come, but Bhadra borrowed a horse and spent the night going from village to village until he found a woman who would treat him. It is because of Bhadra that Keshava has recovered, but he won't let Keshava work again or leave home until he has regained his weight."

"He was fine the last time I saw him. Uma, why didn't someone tell me? I could have asked Panyaji to send her doctor."

"You are busy with your life at the big house, Devaki. We didn't think to involve you."

"If something happened to him and I wasn't here, I never would forgive myself," I replied in an annoyed tone. "You must promise to let me know when there is trouble in the family." She nodded. "Now tell me, how did Amma finally give her consent to this marriage for you. Last time I was here she was so opposed."

Uma smiled. "Again, that was due to Bhadra. Amma opposed the marriage at first. You know how traditional she is. She didn't like it that Kashi had asked me directly, instead of having his parents approach her about a marriage. She thought he was a brash young man and felt it boded ill for the relationship. I think she was afraid he was too forward and might abuse me, but she was wrong about him. He is a very kind and gentle man. Bhadra found me crying one day and when I told him my feelings, he went to Kashi and arranged for him to speak with Amma directly. They had a long talk, and after that, everything was set aright." She paused before saying, "Devaki, I know you have always resented Bhadra, but he is most devoted to our family. We mean everything to him."

None of my other siblings shared my feelings about this eldest brother, and to them his devotion to the family came as no surprise, but it was a quality I had always chosen to overlook. I had long regarded him as selfish, but the others didn't see him in this light. As Uma began to praise Bhadra for what he had done, I thought to myself, perhaps Amma is right. Perhaps he hurt me in the past and that is why I hold something against him. But how could I free myself from something of which I had no memory?

I remained with my family for the preparation and celebration of the marriage, keeping away from Bhadra and spending as much time as I could helping my mother. Soon it was time to leave again. Our home now consisted only of Amma and Keshava, who still had not regained his strength, with Bhadra and his wife living in an extended part of the hut. The family left at home was shrinking, and my life was taking me further away.

As Shankara grew, I became more and more engrossed in watching him progress, both physically and mentally. From an early age he showed a keen intellect and curiosity, asking questions about everything, most of which I could not answer. Instead of sending him to Patna for his education, his mother insisted on bringing tutors to him, as she was loathe to part with this last child of hers, or to leave their beautiful home in the village for city life.

His study of Sanskrit began when he was six, and he quickly picked up the ability to write and speak in the language and to memorize long texts. Once he asked me if I wanted to learn to write, but I shook my head and said I had no need. In truth, I very much wanted to learn but was prevented by a growing sense of guilt. How could I have or learn more than the rest of my family? There was a limit to how far I would remove myself. But I asked him to write in Sanskrit the names of Lord Shiva and Sri Krishna, thinking I would show the writing to my mother.

On the next visit home, I took out the paper Shankara had given me and showed my mother how her Lord's name looked in writing. "It is beautiful!" she exclaimed as she ran her hands over the written word.

"And this means Shiva," I explained, showing her the second paper. Just then Bhadra walked in and saw the writing.

"Don't think you can become a brahmin because you can write now," he scoffed.

"Why must you always misinterpret, Bhadra. I don't know how to write, and I don't want to be a brahmin. This is Shankara's writing. He is only seven and look at his beautiful writing, so meticulous." My face glowed as I spoke of my little friend.

"Everything is always about Shankara, Shankara, Shankara," he sneered as he left the room.

Smiling, my mother consoled me. "Don't pay him any mind. Writing is a wonderful thing. It would not be bad for you to learn, Devaki." I shook my head and told her I had no need. Later, I wondered if I felt that way because of Bhadra. Did I feel guilty because of his criticism of me?

The subject came up several times with Shankara and he even asked if I wanted to study Vedic philosophy with him. I replied, "All the wisdom I need for life I learned from the stories my parents told me. I have no need to read any sacred texts. He then asked me to share with him one of the stories. When I told him my father's account of the Somnath Shrine, he was thoughtful and remarked, "That is not the way I have heard the story, but I like your father's version much better. It makes more sense. I wonder how he came to hear that account."

"My father was a very wise man," I replied with a smile. "Often, he told me that he heard the stories from his grandparents, but on one occasion, he said that it was directly from Lord Shiva himself. It is the same with my mother. It is Krishna who speaks to her. I am fortunate to have such parents and I do believe them, for the most part."

By now Shankara knew that I had another family, as he called them. A few years later, when he was ten, he asked me which devata I worshipped. "You have told me that your father was a devotee of Lord Shiva and your mother of Lord Krishna. What about you, Didi?"

"I love and worship both of them equally," I replied simply.

"All my family and teachers are devotees of Lord Shiva. I would like to meet your mother because I don't know any devotees of Lord Krishna," he remarked casually.

"What are you saying? You know me!" I exclaimed. I didn't think much about the conversation, but a few months later he said to me, "You know my family, but I don't know yours. That is not how it should be among friends." I didn't answer, but this was the first indication that my relationship with Shankara was shifting into one of friendship. Even though I was ten years older, he had a maturity that made it easy to speak with him as a peer. Since an early age he showed more interest in discussing serious matters than in playing childhood games, and he had always regarded me as his companion.

I didn't pursue the matter, but he did with his mother, and she agreed to let me take him to meet my family. Warning him not to expect much hospitality from my eldest brother, we set off in the family's bullock cart. As we drew closer to my home, I saw that he seemed not to take much note of the impoverished conditions of the area in which my family lived. When he entered my family's hut, the first thing he noticed was the small Krishna in the corner by the side of the Shiva lingam. My mother was in the kitchen area preparing food. I had sent her word to expect us, and as she began setting out snacks, I saw her eyes follow Shankara as he went and offered pranam to Krishna and Shiva. He then approached her and bent to the ground to touch her feet. I was surprised to see my very humble mother allow this.

Sitting him down, she asked him as her eyes lit up, "Do you know the story of how the devotees of Vishnu and Shiva came together?" He shook his head and asked her to please tell it.

"There was a time when the devotees of Lord Vishnu and Lord Shiva were arguing as to who was the greatest. The wise people of the community came together and had a great debate, each side presenting the unique qualities of their lord. The discussions went on through the night and into the next morning and the next night, but there was no clear winner. Nobody could convince the other side to change their views. Finally, after several days of debate, Lords Vishnu and Shiva appeared before the gathering. Each side expected that their lord would be pleased with how their devotees had spoken, but something strange happened. As Lord Vishnu's devotees went to touch the feet of their lord, his form turned into Shiva, and as all the Shiva devotees went to touch the feet of their lord, he turned into Vishnu. Lord Shiva then bowed before Vishnu and praised his glorious deeds, while Vishnu bowed before Shiva and praised his glorious deeds. Then the great devas disappeared, leaving everyone confused.

"Instead of realizing the truth, the people began to argue with one another about what had just taken place. There was one child at the gathering. He had come to learn from the elders but all he heard was adults arguing and acting like children. Among the adults were scholars, priests, and respectable people, but they seemed to be all confused. He wondered what they could possibly teach him. Why were they competing instead of loving one another as the devatas taught them to do? As this child was looking at all the confused people, he saw in his spiritual eye the forms of Vishnu and Shiva merge into one great, sublime light, which filled the whole area and then expanded until it reached as far as he could see, and he let out a loud joyous laugh. Everyone turned to look at the child who was laughing while they were engaged in serious, contentious discussion.

"Instead of explaining why he was laughing, he simply looked around at his elders and asked them, 'Which of your parents and which of your children do you love the most?' Leaving them with that question, he walked out, but his brief message had an impact, and the people went home and reflected on what he asked. That child eventually became a great sage, earned the respect of the people, and helped to keep the peace in that town.

"So Shankara," my mother concluded. "You may have more wisdom than many teachers. Trust your wisdom and learn to interpret what you hear for yourself. Don't accept anything blindly. You are a devotee of

Shiva, and he will speak directly to you. He will teach you all you need to know."

"I am a devotee of both Shiva and Krishna, like Didi," he replied with a smile.

"She is wiser than she knows," my mother chuckled.

We spent a few hours that day with my family, but before leaving Shankara asked my mother if she could share another story. She was thoughtful for a few minutes and then replied, "I will tell you of something that happened to me personally.

"After Devaki's father died, I was very sad. All my life, I had clung to Krishna, but at that time even He could not take away my sadness. I tried not to show it, but nothing could replace the husband who had been by my side for so long. "About three months after his passing, I had a dream in which I saw Krishna standing with my husband. The Lord smiled at me and thanked me. I was wondering why he was thanking me, and he answered my unasked question. 'Thank you for letting me bring home my devotee. He has been away for far too long.' At those words my husband smiled, folded his hands in pranam, and I heard him say to Krishna, 'How could I be away, Prabhu, when you have always been with me?' Krishna smiled and replied, 'Shiva has taught you well.'

"I awoke from the dream and the words that stayed in my head were, 'How could I be away when you have always been with me?' Those words made me realize that my husband was not away. He was with me, just as my Krishna is. That dream brought me much comfort and helped to chase away my sadness."

"Wasn't Devaki Didi's father a devotee of Lord Shiva?" Shankara asked when she had finished speaking.

She nodded. "That is what was so beautiful about the dream. I have heard that sometimes when one prays to one devata, another responds. The purpose is to show that they are in truth one. Krishna was letting me know that he and Shiva are but different aspects of the One. If you truly worship one, you are worshipping the other as well. Shankara, the Lord speaks to us through our hearts, not through our minds. I have heard that you have great mental gifts, and you should use them to serve humanity, but the way to know the Lord is through your heart. That you must open, and nobody can show you how. That is for you to discover."

On the way home, Shankara was quiet, but as we approached his house, he said thoughtfully, "I learned a lot from your mother today." Then in a light tone, he added. "But I don't understand why you speak ill of your brother Bhadra. I like him very much." I sighed in relief, glad that Bhadra had been on his best behavior and had even joked with Shankara. He had not spoken a single sarcastic or harsh word in Shankara's presence.

A few days later I was sitting with Shankara outside his home in front of a large Shiva lingam, when he suddenly asked, "Didi, do you know what the lingam represents?"

I nodded. "I once asked my father that very question, and he replied, 'Long, long ago, people wanted to find a way to worship Lord Shiva, but they knew him as the unmanifest, infinite consciousness out of which everything comes. How could he be represented? But they were human, and humans need something to help connect them to the supreme reality. They didn't want to use a human form, because that would not suffice to indicate his infinite, transcendent nature. Yet they wanted something before which they could perform rituals because rituals are a powerful way to connect to the devatas. They choose a simple rounded stone as the best way to represent the infinite, and that is how the lingam came to represent Lord Shiva. There are natural lingams everywhere, in the mountains and rivers, the ocean and soil, indicating that Shiva is everywhere."

He laughed. "Your father described it better than my teachers. I will remember that."

Three weeks passed and I went to see my family again. For the first time, I noticed the change in my mother's gait, which was slower and more tentative than usual. I asked Bhadra about it, but instead of responding to my question, he looked at me intensely and replied with a touch of anger, "Instead of tending to your past family, why don't you tend to the one you have now?" Not understanding his question, I looked at him blankly, but just then my mother walked into the room, and I couldn't ask the meaning of his words. They stayed with me though and festered, making me decide to visit more regularly.

Each year, Panyaji had resisted sending Shankara to Patna for further education, but when he turned twelve his father insisted, and she could no longer refuse. They would have to move to the city, at least for most of the year.

"You will come with us," said Shankara to me as his mother made plans to depart. It was a statement, not a question.

"Of course, Devaki will come," insisted Panjyaji, who, much to her dismay, would also need to shift to the city for a while.

I looked at the two of them and nodded, but in my heart, it didn't feel right. My mother was getting older and frailer, and I worried that something might happen to her in my absence. On the other hand, I couldn't bring myself to part with Shankara, and for days I struggled over what to do. Finally, I did what I had rarely done before—I prayed to Krishna for an answer. But the one who responded was Shiva. Internally, I heard a voice, and I knew it was his. "Why would you leave when I am sending you someone who will bring you to me?"

I didn't depart with the family for Patna, but I didn't return home. At Panyaji's insistence I was to stay in the big house to oversee the household affairs, and a new chapter in my life was to open.

CHAPTER 34

Meeting the Kashmiri Pandit

"I don't understand what you are asking of me, Panyaji," I finally ventured to say in protest, shaking my head. As she was getting ready to depart with Shankara for the city, she had asked me to oversee the food donations to the temple which were used to feed the brahmin pilgrims. It was a responsibility that usually fell to Saritaji, who every week brought many baskets of food to the temple, but unlike me, she was a brahmin. Since I had turned down the request to go to Patna with the family, Sarita was to accompany Panyaji, while I stayed behind in the village.

"What don't you understand, Devaki? I am asking you to bring the donations each week to the temple." She knew what I was referring to, but she chose to avoid acknowledging that I was from the laborer community. How could I bring food for brahmins? It was enough that she had me oversee the preparation of food for the family, much to the consternation of the servants. "Devaki, you are like my adopted daughter. When you arrive at the temple, ask for Nalini and say that you are coming from the Banerjee family, sent by me personally. No one will question you."

"But if someone should recognize me . . ." my voice resonated with uncertainty, almost fear of being discovered. Panyaji often introduced me to others as her adopted daughter, but this always made me feel uncomfortable, as if I were ashamed of my family, or denying them, and I could not imagine anything worse than to reject the parents who had given me so much.

"There is nobody else whom I trust with this responsibility," she insisted patiently. "Don't make this into a bigger issue than it need be. In our own quiet way, we are breaking taboos, and it is high time to do so." There was nothing more to be said. The family had been more than kind to me, making no distinction between the family members and me, something unheard of in our society.

It was with some trepidation that I packed the baskets of food into a cart at the start of the week and rode with one of the servants to the temple, one I had never entered before, as my community had its own place of worship. For several minutes I stood before the white stone structure, which shimmered in the early morning sun, before daring to enter it. I did as Panyaji requested and asked for Nalini. A woman dressed in white, looking like a widow, came to greet me. She was rather plump, middle aged, with a cheerful round face. "Are you Devaki?" she asked. I nodded. "Panyaji told me that you would be overseeing the food distribution while she and Sarita are away." Again, I nodded. She hesitated and then said, "I have a request to make." I looked at her inquiringly. "If you don't mind, would you take this basket of food to Panditji, who lives in a cottage with his wife not far from here?" Saying that I would be happy to do so, I took the basket, as she briefly described the couple. "Saritaji often took food to him and his wife, a Kashmiri couple who have lived in that cottage for a number of years. His wife has lost much of her sight and so we send them food as often as we can. They are a very special couple, and the husband adores the wife, treating her as a devi. I am sure you will enjoy meeting them." She told the servant where they lived, and we rode off in that direction.

The cottage was at the foot of some low hills by the side of a forest, with no other structures around. I intended to drop off the food and then return immediately to the Banerjee home, so I was not prepared for the reception that greeted me. When there was no response to my knocks, I quietly pushed open the door and peered inside. Both husband and wife were seated in meditation. The cottage was cozy, nicely decorated with numerous rugs on the floor and a low table surrounded by many lush cushions. At the back of the room was a door that must have led to another room for sleeping. In one corner, where the couple was meditating, stood a prominent Shiva lingam, surrounded by lamps and flowers. The shutters were closed, the only light being from the lamps, which gave the room an unearthly, mystical feeling. The atmosphere was peaceful, and not wanting to disturb them, I quietly crept into the cottage and unpacked the food, laying all the items out on the table. Nalini, the woman at the temple, had sent enough for several days. I was about to leave when I heard the man's voice call to me.

"Come closer, so I can see you." I approached and bowed in front of him, folding my hands in pranam. "Sit down," he said quietly as he peered out of half opened eyes. I obeyed. His wife, still with closed eyes, made a slight movement, indicating that she was emerging from meditation. His eyes now opened fully, and for a few moments he stared at me without speaking, finally murmuring more to himself than to me, "So it is you who have come."

Surprised, I studied the man, whom I had never seen before. His appearance was elegant, indicating a man of refinement. His complexion was on the lighter side, his face slender with high cheekbones and a narrow aquiline nose. He looked to be in his mid-forties, with quite a bit of grey in his neatly cropped beard. A checkered hat hid whatever hair he had, and he wore a simple grey woolen outer garment, like a robe, not normally worn by the people of our region; the dress of his wife was more colorful, with hues of red and pink, of a style similar to his. Her braided hair peered out from under a floral head covering, which came down over her forehead and was drawn back behind her ears, hanging loosely over her shoulders. She was a pretty woman, also with a light complexion but a face rounder than his. A slight smile wrapped around her full lips as she opened her sight impaired eyes.

"I am glad to see you," he said as I sat there gazing at them, so sure I had never met them before. Assuming he had mistaken me for someone else, I introduced myself, saying that Nalini from the temple had sent me with food from the Banerjee home. He nodded and then introducing me to his wife, told her with a chuckle that he and I were old acquaintances. I didn't correct him, because I assumed that either his eyesight was also failing or perhaps his memory was faulty. Either way, I would not contradict him.

I offered to set the food out for them as it was approaching mealtime, but he insisted on doing it himself and invited me to stay for the meal. This was something I would not consider, so I lied and said I had already eaten. I knew little about Kashmiris, but I knew he was a brahmin. Even at the Banerjee home, I most often ate alone, not wanting to go against traditional restrictions, even though Panyaji had strongly objected. But I accepted the tea he offered and, realizing that my visit would not be a short one, I sent home the servant with the cart who was waiting outside.

When he asked me to tell them something of myself, I spoke about the devotion of my parents, not mentioning the community from which I had come, and told of my life with the Banerjee family, whom he knew a little about. But he seemed less interested in them than in me, which was baffling.

"Just the name Kashmir stirs something in me," I mentioned during a pause in our conversation. "I can't say what or why."

"What do you think of when you hear the name Kashmir?" he asked, gazing at me with interest.

I was quiet for a few moments and then responded, "I think it must be a place where one can experience Lord Shiva. I grew up in a home where we worshipped both Krishna and Shiva, but I know Krishna better. Shiva is still very much a mystery to me, and someday I would like to experience that great One."

He smiled and replied, "And so you will."

As we were speaking, I watched the way he cared for his wife, whose name was Sulabha, helping her eat as her eyesight was much diminished.

I was touched by his tenderness. "Why did you leave Kashmir and settle in this village?" I suddenly asked him.

"We came initially for my wife," he replied, looking at her lovingly. "For several years after our marriage she had been looking for a teacher of tantra. She went to visit one teacher after another, but nobody satisfied her. Then one day she had a dream in which Sita Ma visited her and told her that she would bring her to the teacher she was seeking, and she directed her to head in this direction. We traveled for some years, passing through different kingdoms, towns, and villages before we found that teacher, who was living in a remote cottage in the mountains not so very far from here.

"This teacher immediately recognized Sulabha as her student from the past and accepted both of us. We stayed with her until she passed away. Around that time, Sulabha began to lose her eyesight, and it was difficult to remain in such a remote location, so we moved here to be close to the village. I wanted to go back to Kashmir, but she insisted on staying, saying that she could not leave this place, which was part of Mithila, the ancient kingdom of Sita, because Sita had directed her to come here."

"Did Sita Ma really appear to you in a dream?" I asked, turning to look at Sulabha, who hadn't spoken much.

She nodded. "After many lifetimes I finally found my gurudev again, and it was Sita who brought me here. How could I leave this region which is still imbued with her presence."

"But Sita lived so long ago!" I exclaimed. "How did she know your teacher?"

Sulabha smiled. "What is long ago in divine time? It is but a flicker of an eye. Sita is a living presence, with us always. The guruji she sent to me had been a student of a great woman sage named Maitreyi, whom Sita knew well. Sita saw that this student was now in human form, well advanced in her meditations, and had become a sage in her own right, a teacher of tantra."

I looked at her, perplexed, and Panditji explained on her behalf, "Sulabha had also lived in Mithila at that time and had some brief encounters with our teacher, who in that birth of long ago was not ready to take on her own students. In a later life, Sulabha again met her, and this time asked to be accepted as her chela. Over time, this one, whom we call Ammaji, had advanced greatly through tantric practices and was now able to transmit to us many blessings. Behind her is the power of the great sage Maitreyi, and behind her is the great Mother, Sita Ma herself. Surely, Devaki, you have heard of Sage Maitreyi?"

I shook my head, but then smiled and replied, "Of course, I know of Sita Ma. Who doesn't know of her? I think I may have heard of tantra, but I can't be sure. What is it?"

He smiled and was quiet before beginning. "It is difficult to explain tantra, but to put it simply, it encompasses esoteric or advanced practices that lead to the realization of the Self, practices which, when done faithfully and sincerely, with full concentration, lead one to *moksha*, liberation from *samsara*, the cycle of death and rebirth. These practices awaken one to the nature of reality. Regular practice changes the brain, the patterns of thought and the emotions. The root meaning of "tan" is to expand and "tra" signifies instrument, so the meaning of tantra is an instrument for the expansion of consciousness. It is rare to find a teacher truly capable of guiding one in these esoteric practices, and that is why we traveled all the way from Kashmir to find and follow such a one."

"Will tantra give one the experience of Lord Shiva?" I asked curiously. He nodded. "Then it is something I would like to learn."

"It demands complete dedication," he replied gently. "It is not to be taken up lightly because it involves sacrifice. It is not something one can do half-heartedly because it will consume your whole life."

"Sacrifice," I murmured as I reflected on his words, unsure if I was ready to make such a commitment. "I must think about that." The word "tantra" sounded familiar and I tried to remember where I might have heard of it. I was sure that my father never mentioned it. He had loved to tell stories of Lord Shiva, but he never revealed how to experience him, and I wondered if he knew about that. I was so young when he died, but perhaps had he lived longer, he would have shared with me how to have the direct experience. "How do I find Lord Shiva?" I suddenly asked.

He smiled and replied, "It is Sri Krishna who will lead you to him." I looked at him questioningly and he continued. "It was Krishna, after all, who sent Arjuna to Shiva before the great war. There is an important message in that. Can one truly know Lord Shiva without knowing Lord Vishnu? Can one truly know Lord Vishnu without knowing Lord Shiva? Approach one and you will find the other."

"You sound much like my parents," I remarked with a smile.

"You are fortunate to have such parents then. Most people do not realize this and thus there is religious competition, which is such foolishness."

"Can you tell me about Kashmir?" I asked.

"What is it you want to know?"

"Anything at all," I replied.

"Srinagar, where we lived, is the main city and it sits in a large valley embraced on all sides by mountains. In ancient times, as the ice began to melt, the valley became completely consumed by water, and *nagas* and *asuras* (demons), unruly creatures, began to inhabit that place. Eventually, the few human clans who lived nearby desired the area for their growing community, so they prayed to Lord Shiva and Parvati Ma to make the region more hospitable for humans. Parvati Ma had a fondness for the mountains in that area because long ago it is where she had engaged in intense *tapasya* (spiritual discipline) to realize her union with Lord Shiva. In response to the prayer of the clans, she went to the valley, accompanied by Rishi Kashyapa, and together they drained much of the lake, reducing its size and creating a fertile area suitable for human habitation.

"After the place became livable, the Uttara-Kuru clans moved in, and a new society began to flourish. The region was named after that ancient *rishi* (sage), and that is why the area is called Kashmir. Over time it became a crossroad for many cultures and is known for its religious tolerance. Shaivites, Sufis, and Buddhists live together peacefully and engage in profound philosophical exchanges. Many places have been influenced by our culture, including Tibet. There was a time when numerous Kashmiri sages and artists traveled there, bringing the esoteric teachings of tantra and Kashmiri artistry to that land. To this day, Kashmir is permeated with the presence of Lord Shiva and Parvati Ma. Sometimes she emerges as Durga Ma, and you can almost see her riding a mountain lion across the peaks and through the forests. She is a powerful presence. Sarasvati Ma also has had a keen influence on Kashmir, and through her it has become a center of learning. Kashmir is indeed a special place, truly a magical land."

I had heard of the Buddhists, but I had never heard of Sufis and asked about them. "The Sufis are *bhaktis* (those on the path of devotion), very much like the lovers of Krishna. They view divine reality as their beloved and sing and dance to that One," he explained.

"They are Krishna devotees then?" I asked.

"Not exactly," he smiled. "They call their god Allah, so they are a kind of Muslim, but to me they often appear as Krishna Bhakts."

We had been talking for so long that I didn't notice the passing of time. As Panditji and I were engaged in conversation, Sulabha had made her way to one of the windows and threw open the shutters to let in the air. Glancing at the light streaming in through the window, I saw that the sun was declining. I had a long walk home and told Panditji that I had to hurry back. Sulabha returned to the meditation area and entered a state of withdrawal.

"You will come again?" he asked. I nodded and folded my hands in pranam as I bowed and took my leave.

My visits to Panditji and Sulabha became the highlight of my week, an event I very much looked forward to. Each time after I laid out the food, I would sit and watch while he and his wife ate, and then we would talk before I returned to the Banerjee home. Sulabha was quiet much of the time, but her face shone with great peace and inner joy, and he seemed to dote on her.

After I had been visiting for several months, I commented on how much I admired his devotion to his wife. "You are a model of how a husband should be," I replied as I thought of my own father, who had exhibited some of the same tendencies.

He laughed and replied, "I was not always this way."

"What do you mean?"

"I will tell you a story."

"I love stories," I replied eagerly, remembering how I would hungrily absorb the tales told by my parents, stories that always had a message for how to live. Soon after meeting Panditji, I asked him if he would be my teacher, but shaking his head, he replied that he would be my friend, not my teacher. Secretly, I regarded him as my teacher and initially kept a certain formality between us, but after a few visits our relationship became more informal, and I felt more relaxed speaking with him.

"Quite some time ago," he began, "there lived an irritable Shaivite hermit named Dattadri, who was somewhat arrogant." Chuckling, he corrected himself, "No, he was very arrogant. He had lived alone in a mountain cave for many years and thought he was very advanced spiritually. One day he made the acquaintance of a sage and his wife who lived nearby. On occasion he would visit them, and the wife would ask him to stay for a meal. He didn't think much of the wife, but he had great admiration for the sage and wondered why he had married the woman, whom the hermit felt was spiritually far inferior to his friend. But it wasn't only her for whom he had disdain. It was all women. He felt them to be impediments, their only value being to serve their husbands and families.

"Now, that wife, she didn't like him one bit either. Every time she saw him coming for a meal, her back would stiffen. She was always polite enough, but she couldn't fool him, although she did her best to hide her dislike for the sake of her husband. Many times, the hermit asked the sage to go on long pilgrimages with him to the Himalayan shrines, but the sage always declined, saying he could not leave his wife and the journey would be too much for her.

"In truth, Dattadri was jealous of their relationship, but he disguised his jealousy as contempt, and he treated the sage's wife rather rudely.

He was a rough character, unkempt, inconsiderate, and abrasive. What angered Dattadri the most was the respect the sage accorded his wife. Every time Dattadri and the sage would have a philosophical discussion, the sage always insisted that his wife participate, often asking her opinion. This angered Dattadri because he didn't think the wife knew much about anything, and the tension between him and the wife grew to the point that he eventually stopped coming to visit. Before that, the sage had taken him aside and with a deep sigh said, 'One day you and she will have to sort this out for yourselves.'" Panditji paused and gazed at me in a way that made me slightly uncomfortable.

"After the hermit stopped visiting that couple, he became very defensive and blamed the rupture in the relationship all on the wife, on her attitude toward him. Then one day he was standing outside his cave when a young attractive woman ascetic approached him and asked if he could direct her to a nearby cave where she could engage in tapasya. There were a few other male ascetics in the area, practicing long periods of meditation, and he thought she would be a disturbance, so he abruptly told her to leave. He said she would only be a nuisance to the other yogis and that she should find some other place for her meditation. She looked at him intently, repeated her request, and again he told her to leave in a more aggressive tone.

"'A nuisance,' she murmured, staring at him. As he turned to walk back into his cave, he heard a thundering voice ask, 'When has the Mother of the Universe ever been a nuisance?' He swung around to look at her again, but she had disappeared. She was nowhere in sight. It was like a jolt of lightning awakening him. He knew that he had turned away Parvati Ma herself. He was deeply disturbed and, as he sat in meditation, he heard an inner voice say, 'By disrespecting my daughters, you are disrespecting me.'

"One of the women of whom he had spoken disparagingly about over the years was the great sage Maitreyi herself, whose student has now become my guruji." He paused and closed his eyes, folding his hands in pranam as he mentioned his guruji. My eyes widened as he told this story, horrified that the hermit would have turned away Parvati Ma.

"This set off a long period of self-reflection," he continued. "The sage's wife was a devotee of Narayani (Lakshmi Devi), and he had disrespected that wife because at that time he thought women were distractions for men, of little intelligence, and could teach him nothing. He had not even truly respected his own mother. Now he remembered all the harsh words he had spoken to her in his early years, and he felt deeply ashamed and remorseful. By the end of that life, he vowed to take birth as a woman and to compensate for the wrong attitudes he had held. He vowed never to forget how respectfully and lovingly the sage had treated his wife, even though she did not have a high level of realization at that time. That did not matter at all to her husband. After several lifetimes the hermit took birth as a man again and began seeking a consort, whom he vowed to treat as the Devi herself." Panditji fell silent and for a few moments nobody spoke. I looked over at Sulabha and saw that she was smiling.

Finally, intrigued by his tale, I asked, "Is this a personal story?" He nodded. "And were you the sage?" He shook his head. "I can't believe that you were that hermit!" I exclaimed in disbelief.

He nodded. "Indeed, I am ashamed to admit that I was that man."

I stared at him, doubtfully, but his eyes lit up, a playful smile curled around his lips, and at that moment, I thought perhaps it wasn't a story about him at all. Perhaps it was a teaching story like those my father liked to tell.

Breaking into joyous laughter, I remarked, "Panditji, you almost fooled me. You are the most devoted and respectful husband I have ever seen. I can't believe that you were that hermit at all. But perhaps such a man did exist and there is a lesson in your story. All women should be treated as daughters of Parvati Ma."

"Do you think the sage's wife would forgive Dattadri were she to meet him again?" he asked in a serious tone.

"No doubt. Why would she hold on to something that happened so long ago?"

He smiled and replied quietly, "Then all is settled."

As I got up to leave, I thought of the words that had just slipped out of my mouth and the image of Bhadra came into my mind. My mother had once suggested that he may have hurt me in the past and that may be why I had such a hard time with him. I wanted to change the relationship but didn't know how.

"Panditji, if someone has hurt you in the past, how do you make peace with that person?"

"You just told me the answer yourself," he replied with a slight smile. "By not holding onto it, by living in the present." I nodded, thinking that those words were easy to say but hard to implement. Then he added, "You are speaking of your eldest brother, aren't you?" Again, I nodded. During an earlier visit, I had shared with him and Sulabha my troubles with Bhadra. "See the good that he does and pay no mind to the things that irritate you. Forgive him for whatever he had done in the past."

"How can I forgive him for something I don't even remember?" I asked as I looked into his eyes for answers. Just the mention of my problems with Bhadra created a tension within me.

"Ah, that is the gift of forgetting," he replied quietly. "You don't need to remember to forgive. You can begin anew. Start your relationship from right now. We have all made mistakes in the past and should not be judged for them."

"I will have to seek help in this matter," I mused, knowing how hard it was for me to restrain from judging Bhadra.

"Well, Devaki, you know whom to call upon."

"Will it be Krishna or Shiva?" asked Sulabha with a chuckle.

"Both," I replied firmly. "I will need the help of both to heal this troublesome relationship."

CHAPTER 35

Coming to Shiva

"Panditji, I am from a community of laborers," I said somewhat hesitantly, telling him my surname. After visiting him and his wife Sulabha for over a year, the thought that I might be deceiving them weighed heavily on me, and one day I felt impelled to disclose my background. I had told them a little about my parents and family life but had never told them where I lived or what my parents did. He showed no surprise. Instead, with a smiling face, he shared a story.

"Once there were two ardent brahmin devotees of Lord Shiva, both professing that they would renounce everything for him. They approached him and declaring their love and devotion asked for the ultimate realization. He told them to go find a certain woman, saying, 'Accept her as your guru. She can grant you what you seek.'

"Eagerly they sought out this woman, but when they found her, she was not at all what they expected. She was a simple woman from the poorest, uneducated community, but her eyes shone with love for the Lord. Upon arriving, the first brahmin said, 'Aha, Lord Shiva is testing us. There is no way we can learn anything from an illiterate *shudra*,' and he walked away, thinking he had passed the test. The second brahmin exclaimed, 'Aha, Lord Shiva is testing us. He wants to see if we can pierce illusions and see the reality of who this woman is. She is clearly a realized one,' and he stayed and found what he was seeking.

"The first brahmin returned to Lord Shiva, expecting to be praised for his discernment, but the Lord asked him, 'You were not satisfied with the teacher I sent you?' The man replied proudly, 'I knew you were testing me, Prabhu, and you will now send me to a proper teacher.' The Lord smiled and told him to go find a certain man. That man was very refined and scholarly, knew all the texts and rituals, and this devotee was satisfied. He studied under him for the rest of his life and gained much knowledge, but he never attained the realization he sought. The second brahmin never learned the proper rituals or texts, but he was soon swimming in the bliss of the Lord.

"Your father, Devaki, was a man of such discernment. You were young when he passed and so might not be aware of how he was regarded."

"How do you know about my father?" I asked in surprise.

"The true Shaivites in this region know of your father. He was a most humble man, living in the shadows of life, unseen and unheard by the world, but he was one blessed with the rare gift of a visit by the Lord himself."

"What do you mean?" I looked at him curiously, wondering what he could know about my very modest and humble father.

"Do you remember an incident when a brahmin kicked and spit on your father, when your father was cleaning the street and by accident brushed against the man's foot?"

"Although I was young, I remember that incident very well," I murmured. "It caused a lot of pain to my family, especially for my elder brother, who became so resentful after that. How did you know?"

"Our guruji told us that story. Before she left her body, Sulabha asked her if there was anyone in this region who had actually seen the Lord, saying that we would like to visit such a precious devotee of Lord Shiva. Our guruji thought for a while and then mentioned your father but said he had already passed on. She told us that story, but there is more to it than you may know."

His words baffled me. "How did your guruji who lived away in the mountains know of my father, who never left the village?"

He chuckled. "What did she not see? She told us about that incident and how your father had prayed that no stain fall upon the brahmin who had kicked and spit upon him. Because your father recognized no reality apart from Lord Shiva, he had taken it as an insult to the Lord himself and was much aggrieved over that. A few days after the incident, your father went and left a bundle of fresh wildflowers by the door of the man who had kicked him. As he was leaving that place, an ascetic appeared and asked why he had left the flowers.

"'After explaining what had happened, your father said, 'I want to appease the man's anger so he will never insult the Lord again.'

"The ascetic looked at him curiously and asked, 'How has he insulted the Lord? He only kicked you.'

"Your father replied with downcast eyes, 'My life belongs to Lord Shiva. I have no existence apart from him. When that man spit upon this body, who was there to affront but the Lord himself?' Hearing those words, the ascetic smiled and, after gazing at your father, he turned and began to walk away. Realizing who stood before him, your father began to weep, and falling to the ground he prostrated himself in the shadow of the One he recognized as his own Beloved. Very rarely does Shiva show himself in form, but your father was blessed with that vision. So, who, dear Devaki, is a shudra and who is a brahmin? Who is the servant and who is the teacher? These divisions are human fabrications, and the only laws that matter are the divine ones."

"My father never mentioned that. Did Lord Shiva really appear to him?" I asked as tears gathered in my eyes.

"That is almost exactly how our guruji told this story. She loved to tell accounts of others who had seen the Lord. The Lord also appeared to her once, but that is a story I will tell you another day."

I left Panditji and Sulabha that afternoon in an emotional state. The story he had shared about my father made me miss him terribly and made me feel as if I had never truly appreciated him, never knew his real character. To me, he had only been a wise and loving father, devoted to his Lord, who told stories with lessons for life. It had been many years since I had mourned his loss, but that day as I walked back to the Banerjee house, I wept the whole way for a father I never really came to know.

Hearing the story about my father directed my footsteps back to my family home with a visit to my mother a few days later. I hadn't gone home in many weeks because I was trying to avoid my brother. A marriage for me had become almost an obsession for him. Several times over the last few years he had found what he considered to be a suitable match, but to his consternation I had rejected it each time. Instead of visiting for a few hours, I decided to spend several days with my mother, hoping to end the conversation of marriage once and for all. By the second day of the visit, the topic came up when Bhadra announced another prospective marriage. After I replied with a definitive no, he erupted at me, saying that I was already too old for marriage and my choices were now limited to those who had lost their wives. It was true. I was twenty-five years old, well past the age of marriage, but Bhadra had found an older man whose wife had died and who was eager for more children.

"Why does she have any say in the matter?" my brother asked my mother angrily. I listened silently to his tirade until my mother interrupted, asking Bhadra in a stern voice to please leave so that she could speak with me alone. Slamming the door behind him, he left her part of the hut. Once we were alone, she drew me close to her and with a pained expression said quietly, "Many years ago, when the lady of the Banerjee home came here to ask for you, I was unsure of what to do. I was worried that you would find yourself between two worlds, unable to return to our community but also unable to find a place for yourself in theirs. My fears have come true." Shaking her head, she sighed, "How can I leave this world before I see you settled?"

"I don't want you to leave this world, Amma, and I am already settled. I am happy the way I am," I murmured.

Taking hold of my hands, she continued. "I didn't want you to go there to the big house, but that lady was so insistent. I asked her why? Why you? She told me that there was a woman she consulted about spiritual matters and that this woman had indicated you were the one to look after her precious son, that nobody would take better care of him than you. I still didn't know what to do, so I sought that woman out. Do you know what she told me?" I shook my head. "She told me that Shankara had been your much beloved son in your previous birth, and that you had endured years of separation from him and didn't see him before you died. Deep inside, you continued to long for him. That is why you found him again in this life. Hearing this, how could I object? But I thought if that were the case, we could not accept any payment for your service. I knew it was Krishna who had led you to that son of a previous birth, and I am grateful that this unfulfilled wish of yours could be satisfied. But Devaki, you must think of your current life and your future. Shankara is now gone for his studies and will grow up and get married and will not need you in the same way. Perhaps a husband and children of your own . . ." At the word husband I burst into tears. "Why these tears?" she asked gently, wiping my eyes and cheeks with the cloth that hung over her shoulders.

Struggling to control my sobs, I sought to express feelings that I had never given voice to and explain what I didn't truly understand myself. "It is not that I haven't given thought to marriage, Amma. But the truth is that I feel as if I have a husband, a most wonderful husband, whom I love dearly. Only he is not here, and I don't know where to find him. But the thought of him is with me and this gives me comfort. I cannot marry anyone else. I simply can't."

"My dear, my dear," she whispered, pulling my head against her shoulder and stroking my hair as my sorrow bubbled forth. "How often you would tell me this when you were a child, but I was sure those feelings would pass. Most likely, you are remembering someone from the past, now hidden behind the clouds that shade the mind. It is not in every life that we are blessed with such love for a husband. I had that with your father, but I know how rare it is, and I would not wish for anything less for you. My advice to you then is to take Krishna as your husband. Let he be the one with whom you live. He will take care of you and my heart will be at ease."

Pulling away, with tear-soaked eyes, I looked into my mother's face, lit with a soothing joy. She had had an extraordinary husband in my father, but I knew that Krishna was the one who governed her heart. "Take Krishna as my husband," I whispered as I stared into her loving eyes.

She nodded and replied quietly, "In him you will find the one you are missing."

A few days later I walked back to the Banerjee home, wondering why I was becoming so emotional these days, so easily brought to tears. It was unlike me. For months now, some sorrow hung over me, making me feel as if something was amiss. Normally I would unburden my heart to Shankara, but he was away. Every few months or so, he would return home for a short stay, and I was always relieved to find that nothing had changed between us. If anything, our relationship had deepened as we freely exchanged thoughts and shared experiences. But he would not be back until the monsoons, which were still many months away.

Several weeks passed and we were approaching Maha Shivaratri, a big festival in our village and in my home as well. I had told my mother that I would not join the family for the celebration as I wanted to spend it with Panditji and Sulabha. She was happy when I told her about my newfound friends and encouraged me to spend as much time with them as I could. "I miss hearing your father's stories of Lord Shiva," she said to me. "I am glad you have found people to bring Mahadev into your life, as your father used to do." I replied that one day I would bring her to meet the couple. As I walked to Panditji's cottage, I made a mental note to make that visit happen sooner rather than later, as I could see my mother was growing increasingly frail.

When I arrived at the cottage, I saw that Panditji was preparing for a journey. When I asked if they were leaving, he told me they were going into the mountains for Shivaratri, for one last visit to the cottage where their guruji used to live. He explained that Sulabha had recently had a dream of their guru and felt called to be there for the sacred night of Shivaratri.

By now I had lost all shyness with him and blurted out before I could contain myself, "Do you mind if I accompany you?" I had never left the village and wasn't sure why I was asking. Perhaps it was due to the emotions coursing through me; perhaps I thought that in the mountains I might find some remedy for the unsteady state in which I found myself, with much uncertainty about my future and an eerie feeling of convergence of past and present. After meeting Panditji, at his insistence I had begun an attempt at meditation, but my efforts were unsatisfactory with little result. Several years had passed in this way and I felt myself at a crossroad. Despite my mother's advice to keep my mind on Krishna, he was as far from me as ever, and Shiva was a complete unknown. I had no idea how to come into a personal relationship with either, as my parents had been able to do.

"Of course. Come with us, Devaki. That is a very good idea. By going to the place of our guruji, you will receive the blessings of Mahadev."

Returning to the Banerjee home, I made preparations and a few days later we were on our way. It was to take several days of travel by horse for us to reach our destination. Because of her failing eyesight, Sulabha sat on Panditji's horse with him, and they looked to be a most beautiful couple as they rode together. There is something very special about couples in their middle and elder years, when they seem to grow together into one being, like intertwined branches, knowing what the other needs and wants without having to inquire. Such it was with these two, and it gave me great comfort to be with them, since they reminded me of another precious couple, my parents. As we began to ride and these thoughts passed through my mind, I smiled, remembering his description of himself as once being disrespectful to women. He is such a loving man, I thought; it could not possibly be true.

After we had passed through the plains and low hills, my enthusiasm grew. Each turn of the path was a new adventure, revealing previously unseen landscapes, expanding my horizon, my view of the world. I had grown up in the shadows of the mountains, which from the village on a very clear day could be seen towering up from the earth in the distance. Now as I rode along the narrow ridges for the first time, I could feel in my body the presence and power of those magnificent peaks, which rose and fell and rose again. As we climbed higher, the scenery morphed into alpine forests and frozen landscapes. The few villages spread over the plains below retreated into miniscule forms before disappearing completely.

By day we trekked on our horses up and over mountains, and at night we found a lone mountain farmer or hermit to host us for a few coins. On the fourth day we reached the remote abode where Panditji and Sulabha's teacher had lived. A lone student maintained the small cottage, and he warmly greeted us. The night of Shivaratri was two days away, giving us ample time to get settled. My father had always celebrated the special night of Shivaratri in solitude, sitting alone by the lingam in our home, while my mother took us children to the village temple where there was great celebration lasting well into the late hours of night. I knew that this Shivaratri in the remote mountains would be a quiet one, with no parades, no chanting, and no festivities, and that was exactly what I needed and wanted, time to reflect, to go inward.

The night before Shivaratri, after helping to clear away the evening meal, I found Panditji and Sulabha sitting outside, wrapped in multiple woolen blankets shielding them from the cold mountain air. He was looking up into the night sky, while she was seated nearby with closed eyes. I went to sit beside her. After a few moments she asked if it was me, and I replied that it was.

Opening her eyes, which veiled much of the outer world, she reached for my hand and asked quietly, "Who is Shiva?"

"I don't know," I replied, startled by her question.

"That is the question my guruji asked me the last night I was with her before she left the body. I replied as you did, and this is how she responded to me. I have thought about her words again and again. She told me, 'Shiva is pure being without any attributes, the essence out of which everything comes, the compilation of all that is, before it becomes and after. He is infinite infinities.'"

"What does that mean?" I asked, furrowing my brow.

A slight chuckle escaped her lips. "I also asked her that and she replied, 'He is the supreme unmoving, undifferentiated consciousness before he moves into becoming, resting in his own blissful awareness. Eons pass without a ruffle of desire stirring the still lake of consciousness. But eventually through his will, he initiates the subtle creative impulse, called *spanda* or vibration, and the slightest step of division begins, imperceptibly. That is *Shakti* (the divine feminine energy) separating herself from him. She is the impelling force, containing all attributes and holding within herself the entirety of creation until the will to manifest arises, and the One initiates the becoming of the many. With her separation from Shiva, time and space come into existence. You might say that Shakti is Shiva knowing himself. When Shiva and Shakti are united, there is no dichotomy between the observer and the observed, but as soon as Shakti separates, the observer comes into being, as well as that which is observed, the objective world. Out of Shakti's own power she manifests herself as the cosmos. For that, she must impose limitations and contractions on herself, which begin the instant she separates from Shiva. These contractions are what cause all that is observed to appear as distinct and separate objects. This is the great illusion to which we are all subjected." She paused and I sat in silence trying to grasp what she was saying.

She continued. "The world we see is Shiva's reflection and that reflection is Shakti. Together they play and dance, bringing forth all that is—creating, evolving, transforming. Every aspect of creation reflects the interaction between Shiva and Shakti, a playful love sport that creates delight and desire, the vacillation between yearning for union and the desire for apartness. You might say that all creation is the play of Shiva and Shakti.

"Before the material world comes into existence, the *gunas*, the fabric of creation, are in perfect equilibrium, but with manifestation, the gunas are thrown out of this state of equilibrium and this stirs the manifestation of the material world, held together by opposing forces of harmony and chaos, light and shadow. They arise together and one cannot be had without the other. Realizing the inseparability of opposing forces helps us transcend the material world . . ."

"Sulabha," I whispered, interrupting her. "You have lost me completely. I don't understand a word you are saying." Somewhere midway in her talk, she seemed to be speaking less to me and more to herself, almost as if it were her guruji speaking through her.

"What don't you understand, Devaki?" she asked gently.

"I can accept that Shiva is everything, the totality of all that is. But how is it then that my father saw the Lord in a human form?"

She smiled. "That is his sublime mystery. If he is every atom of creation, can he not manifest a human body? We speak of him, but no words describe him. We form concepts of him, but concepts cannot define him. The human mind and the human senses are limited to a very narrow framework. But through *anugraha* (grace) we can experience him because we are his reflection, or her reflection. We are no other, and that is the realization your father attained. When we realize that, he appears and we know him as our eternal Self. With that knowing comes indescribable bliss because that is his nature, our true nature."

I shook my head slightly. "I can only go one step at a time. If I can take one small step toward knowing Shiva, that will be a lot in this lifetime." The biting night air was making me shiver and, sensing this, Sulabha suggested that we retire into the cottage for the night.

Despite the cold mountain wind that whistled through the cracks in the walls, I slept soundly, wrapped tightly in the thick woolen blankets I had brought from the Banerjee home. The next day we fasted as I had been accustomed to do in my childhood and with the Banerjees. By nighttime, the night of Shivaratri, a most uplifting calm permeated the area. We had hardly spoken that day, but Sulabha's words of the night before continued to drift in and out of my mind. I tried to sit with them in meditation, but after some time of restless thoughts, I went to bed, leaving my two friends alone to watch the passing of this most sacred night, a night devoted to meditation on Shiva. I tried not to feel discouraged as I lay in bed, wondering why I had such a hard time controlling my mind and the constant urge to move about when I was trying to sit in meditation. After a few years of attempted practice, it was hard not to feel disheartened. As I lay there, I turned my mind to Krishna and prayed that he help me experience a small taste of the reality of Shiva.

Soon after, I fell asleep, but somewhere in the middle of the night or early morning hours, Sulabha's words again rang in my mind. "He is the supreme, unmoving, undifferentiated consciousness before It moves into becoming." As I heard those words, my sense of self, of Devaki, dropped away, disappeared, and I had no consciousness of "I" or me. The "I" was no longer there. Only the All existed, and my perception was the consciousness of the totality. There was no other, no separate me; the planets, stars, and moons were spinning within this awareness. It was a most wonderous state, beyond description, but then the thought of "I" returned, calling me back as fear emerged—fear of the loss of self, the loss of separate identity—and I felt myself falling as if from the sky, back into my own limited awareness, back into being Devaki. I awoke, overwhelmed by this most beautiful experience, but also aware that it had a feeling of death to me. Thinking that it had been a partial experience because it had been abruptly ended by my fear, I got up from the sleeping mat on the floor and quietly stepped outside, where dawn was beckoning. The air was frigid, so I retreated into the cottage, where Panditji and Sulabha were just stirring from their meditation.

I sat down across the room from them, glad for time to be alone to revisit my experience, which I knew to be sacred and best kept to myself, but I needed help in understanding it. When Sulabha emerged from meditation, I went to sit by her side and quietly attempted to describe my dream, or vision, saying, "I felt myself dissolving as if the "I" was no more, but then the fear of this brought me back. I nearly lost myself."

"No," she replied quietly but firmly. "You nearly found yourself. Had fear not overcome you, you would have expanded until you encompassed the whole, a most blissful union with Shiva, one with all that is. This yearning for union is what drives all human desire and aspiration. The memory of that state resides in all of us because that is who we truly are. You took the first step, my dear Devaki, and he blessed you on this sacred night of Shivaratri."

Gathering my courage, I gazed into my friend's face, her eyes half closed due to lack of outer vision, and I asked, "Sulabha, do you know Shiva?"

Smiling, she replied, "Devaki, there is no end to knowing."

CHAPTER 36

A Marriage

The experience of that Shivaratri night left a deep imprint on me, one that would remain with me throughout my life and beyond, but it also raised many questions. What was the fear that had prevented further expansion, that had cast me back into the awareness of my limited self? If that all pervading consciousness was Shiva, then who was Krishna? This question percolated in my mind until I finally sought an answer from Panditji.

I found him sitting alone outside his cottage one late afternoon when I came to deliver food. Sulabha was resting inside. "If Shiva is the All, then who is Krishna?" I asked with a confused expression, after I sat beside him on the soft ground, padded with lush grasses and warmed by the spring sun.

He chuckled. "Why do you distinguish between them? After all, these are merely names. The One is the One, no matter if you call that One by the name of Shiva or Narayan or Krishna or something else."

"But Krishna has a distinct form, a most beautiful one," I protested.

"That all-encompassing One also takes the form known to us as Shiva. Didn't Sulabha explain this to you that night?"

"To be honest, I didn't understand her."

He smiled. "Then let me try. Within the formless exists the potential for all forms, infinite in number and expression. When the unmoving initiates movement, the first emergence is the subtle realm of thought, sometimes called the ideational or causal realm, because it is the cause of all the rest. From this realm further concretization takes place. Thought creates light form and finally matter, the densest of the realms. The first forms to emerge were the supreme *mahadevatas*, the controllers of the forces of creation, and from them emerged the beautiful worlds they inhabit. These mahadevatas were needed for further manifestation to take place, as they oversee the cosmic laws that govern the manifest worlds. They initiated further movement and other devatas came into being, furthering the process of separation and individuation to oversee different cosmic functions.

"One can take a piece of clay and divide it into innumerable pieces, but it is still clay and can rejoin with other portions of clay to be reunited into its original whole. From the subtlest causal or thought realm, further densification created the etheric or light worlds, which are far more expansive and beautiful than the physical universe. Finally, further densification or crystallization led to the emergence of the physical world, the realm of atoms. Each of these realms is a matter of degree of densification, or concretization of thought.

"Your explanation is no easier for me to understand than what Sulabha said," I replied with a touch of exasperation.

"Devaki, it is like freezing water into ice. That ice is still water, only in frozen form. The absolute permeates all the worlds because they all exist within it. The One is projecting itself through Shakti, creating the appearance of separate entities. Krishna, as an avatar of Narayan, is also the absolute. Didn't you read that in the *Bhagavad Gita*? Krishna explains it all there."

"Panditji, you have forgotten that I don't know how to read," I replied in a quiet voice, casting my eyes downward, somewhat embarrassed by this lack.

"No matter. I suspect your father never learned to read and we have told you of his realization."

"My mother always says that Krishna conveys to her whatever she needs to know. What He doesn't convey, she doesn't need to know. I suppose it is the same with me."

He laughed. "In the Gita, even the great Arjuna is fearful when he experiences the reality of Krishna, and he pleads with that overwhelming All to return to the familiar human form. Our human mind can best relate to that formless consciousness through a form, and so it takes a form through which we can come to know the true reality. Form and formless are but two sides of a coin. Both are the coin.

"Until one reaches a certain stage of awakening, fear is natural. The small self doesn't easily relinquish its separate identity. It likes its confinement, that is until it experiences the grandeur and bliss of its true nature. But that takes time, innumerable lifetimes and much prodding. It is like a caged bird who momentarily hesitates to fly away once the cage door is open. Habit and familiarity keep the bird there for a moment. It is the same with us. It takes time to let go of confinement and get used to unlimited freedom.

"Devaki, don't worry about what you can't understand now. Take whatever is useful, and don't bother with what is not useful. You have had a taste, and that is far more valuable than all the reading in the world. It is not reading that brings the experience."

"What brings it then, Panditji?"

"Anugraha (Grace). And do you know what brings anugraha?" I shook my head. "Love," he replied in the gentlest of tones. "Love is the doorway to both Krishna and Shiva. Do you know why in our ancient stories, Shiva is always granting boons, even to rascals who show a little bit of devotion?" I shook my head. "It is because he cannot resist love, even imperfect and conditional love, which is all that most humans can offer."

Despite my most uplifting experience, I could not remain absorbed in the inner world for long as the demands of outer life were calling me. The monsoons had come and Shankara was home for an extended stay. As usual, he shared with me all his studies, his readings of the Vedas, the Upanishads, his study of mathematics, logic, and science, most of which went in one ear and out the other. But when he mentioned the *Bhagavad Gita*, my ears perked up and I began to question him.

"I can read and translate it for you, Didi, if you like. It is not very long." So began what I thought would be a simple exercise, but which turned out to be far more complex than I could have imagined. I understood only a fraction of what he read, but he patiently explained the text, and by the end of his stay, I had listened to most of it.

"It will take a lifetime to grasp the meaning," I blurted out when he had finished reading.

"That is why I keep reading it again and again, and I don't know how many more times I will need to read it." As he spoke those words, I remembered what Panditji had told me. It was only anugraha that brought the experience, and it was love that brought anugraha. During Shankara's visit home, I noticed how he was increasingly living in his head, in his mind. That had always been his nature because he had such a keen intellect, but now it was even more apparent. It was hard to find him not fully engrossed in some text, oblivious to the world around him.

While he was thus engaged, his parents were discussing marriage for him, and this concerned me greatly. Although he was only seventeen, already a marriage proposal had been put forth by a friend of the family. That monsoon season, this family visited and I knew that the young, attractive girl was not the right one. Shankara seemed immune to the marriage talk that swirled around him, but when his attention was finally caught, he came to me with a sense of urgency, asking what to do.

"You are still young, Shankara, devoted to your studies. Tell your parents that the time is not right and reject the proposal. That girl is not for you." He nodded in agreement and the matter was put to rest.

Over the next few years, several proposals were put forth and each time Shankara approached me and asked what he should do. Each time, I told him to reject the proposal. Finally, I had to ask myself whether I was acting in his best interest or mine. Did I not want him to marry? Was I fearful that a wife would come between us? As I reflected, I knew that this was not the case. Deep inside, I felt there was someone waiting for him, and it had to be her and no one else. He must have known this as well because at one point he told me that he would only marry a woman of my choosing.

My dear Shankara had grown into a most attractive and dynamic young man. Tall and slender, with features finely formed, a much-admired intellect and a promising future, it was no wonder so many families sought an alliance. Shankara had asked his parents to put aside talk of marriage until he had finished his studies. They were not pleased but decided not to press the matter. He was now twenty years old and had begun teaching, and I knew that talk of marriage would again crop up.

Shankara was home for the monsoons. I found his mood demure, even somber, which was unusual for him, and initially he wouldn't confide in me. After pressing him, he told me that he had visited the remains of Nalanda Mahavihara and had been deeply disturbed by accounts he had heard of its destruction nearly a century earlier.

"You once told me the invaders had destroyed that place, so why would you visit?"

"I traveled to all three universities destroyed by Muhammed bin Bakhtiyar Khalji," he replied solemnly. "Nalanda, Vikramshila, and Odantapuri, these ancient great centers of learning, were all destroyed and only a few remnants are still standing. There have been attempts, although somewhat feeble ones, to rebuild Nalanda, and I wanted to see what I could contribute. Many of the great texts had been saved, rescued by a group of Tibetan monks and taken back to their monasteries. Someday I would like to go there and study those texts. Many prominent brahmin pundits were at Nalanda, teaching Sanskrit, the Vedas, philosophy, and science."

As it turned out, Shankara had been invited to Nalanda by one of the brahmins currently teaching in the restored part of the Mahavihara. That monsoon season this man and his daughter Bhavani visited the Banerjee family at their village home. Their plan was to stay for just a few days. Shankara eagerly engaged in discussions with the man but seemed oblivious of the daughter. I watched her carefully and took note of her comments during the discussions. She was bright, knowledgeable, and seemed to have an intellect on par with Shankara. She was also modest in appearance, wearing little jewelry and plain cotton clothing, with no color added to her eyelids and lips, indicating that she paid little attention to her looks, unlike the other girls who had come to visit in the past. She exhibited a rare maturity for a girl of seventeen, and I could discern her feelings for Shankara. Her eyes followed him admiringly whenever we were all together, and she attended to his every word. It was clear that she was enamored of him, and I knew that this was the reason for their visit, but Shankara seemed not to notice, so engaged was he in discussions with her father about the possibility of restoring Nalanda. It seemed that Nalanda was all he cared about, but at a certain moment I knew that she was the one and that I had to intervene.

After five days, the father indicated that he had to return to Patna, and his daughter looked on desolately as the family said their goodbyes. I watched as they climbed into their *shigram* (horse-drawn carriage) and began to head down the narrow path that led to the main road. Taking Shankara aside, I chastised him, telling him that he had acted rudely to the one who was destined to be his wife. He looked at me in shock. I, myself, didn't know why those words came out of my mouth, but they did. "Are you going to let her leave like this?" He didn't answer. "Go bring her back!" I insisted loudly. He didn't move, and, in desperation, I ran out after the shigram. When they saw me chasing them down the path, the vehicle came to an abrupt halt.

Turning to Bhavani, I spoke in a breathless voice, "Shankara has sent me after you to ask if you would stay longer. He has hardly been able to spend time with you and would like to do so. You will be under my care, and I will get you back home safely in a few weeks' time." Her eyes lit up when I spoke those words, and she cast a pleading look at her father. Acquiescing, he instructed a servant to bring her things back to the house.

As she and I walked down the path leading to the Banerjee home, I apologized for Shankara. "He is sorry that he devoted so much time to your father and couldn't get to know you better. You know that the rebuilding of Nalanda means a great deal to him."

She smiled. "I know that from our trip together to Nalanda. He sought out every story he could find about what happened to the mahavihara and especially the library, which he said was one of the greatest in the world. I was hoping here in the village we would have more time to get to know one another. He is someone I admire immensely." As she spoke, I thought to myself, yes, you admire him, but how do I help him admire you?

For the next many days, I spent all my time making sure the three of us went on outings together, and then making myself scarce so that they could have time alone. After a week, I saw that Shankara was feeling more comfortable and speaking more freely with Bhavani. Again and again, I told him, "Don't only talk to her, Shankara. Ask her thoughts and opinions and listen to her. She is a young woman with much to say. Value her thoughts."

Toward the end of the visit, Bhavani approached me and asked shyly, "May I call you Didi, as Shankara does?"

"You may," I replied with a smile.

"I know it was you, not Shankara, who called me back, and I want to thank you."

Looking at her thoughtfully, I replied. "He is like a younger brother to me, and I know him perhaps better than anyone. Nothing would make me happier than to see the two of you together, because you complement one another. You have an intellect to match his—remember that. But you also have something else that he needs."

"What is that?" she asked curiously.

"What he needs is to have his heart opened, and I believe you can do that. My dear Shankara lives too much in his head, and I am hoping that you can open his heart as no one else can."

"You and I think alike," she replied with a smile. "Had you not called me back, I would have asked my father to forget about arranging a marriage, because I would never impose myself on anyone and he didn't seem interested. Now I see that I have misunderstood him. Didi, for some reason, Shankara has closed his heart, but I believe, if given a chance, I can pry it open."

I took her hand in mine and squeezing it gently, replied, "We will work on that together."

Shankara's marriage with Bhavani was arranged and planning for the ceremonies had begun. There was much fanfare at the Banerjee home, involving weeks of preparation. The wedding was to be a grand affair, with relatives coming from many parts of the region. Panyaji asked me to be her main support and I had little time to see my family, but my mind was much on them due to my mother's failing health. I tried to push concern for her out of my mind so that I could focus on the upcoming ceremonies, but it was difficult.

Before the wedding, Shankara approached me as I was sitting outside alone, eager for a quiet moment of reflection. I was truly happy about the marriage and felt as if something had been completed, as if a matter of great importance to me was being fulfilled. Asking if he could join me, he sat down beside me. "Are you happy about the marriage, Didi?" he asked cautiously.

"So happy," I replied with a smile. "She is the perfect woman for you."

"Nothing will change between us, will it? You will come live with us."

"What could change?" I asked looking at him intently. "We are best of friends, aren't we?" He nodded. "But my mother is not doing well, and neither is your mother, and she has indicated to me that she wants to stay here in the village. Both need me now. Perhaps in the future I will live with you and Bhavani, who knows." My voice trailed off as I spoke those last words. He seemed satisfied with my response and then went on to tell me how close Bhavani felt to me, as if I were her sister as well, and how she wanted me to live with them. "If she is your wife, then I am her didi," I replied quietly, and the matter was left at that.

Days of celebration left me exhausted, but I had no time to rest. My mother was ill and once again I had to spend much time at home with her. I felt her slipping away, but I was determined to do everything in my power to keep her alive. I could not bear the thought of losing her.

"I am old, Devaki. It is time for me to go."

"I won't hear of that," I replied tearfully. "I won't let you leave us."

She sighed. "If your mind was on Krishna, you would not be so sad."

"I don't have your devotion, Amma."

"Of all my children, you are the one who holds Krishna most dear."

I sighed as I looked at her frail form lying on her sleeping mat on the floor. She had been unable to get up for days now. My siblings all came around, taking turns caring for her, but I was the one who stayed with her at night, when we could have our quiet conversations.

"Your friends came to visit me," she said to me one night when we were alone. "They are fine people."

I looked at her in surprise and asked which friends, assuming that she meant some of the village women with whom I was acquainted.

"The couple from Kashmir," she replied.

"Panditji and Sulabha came here? When?"

"While you were busy with the wedding, they came and stayed with me for a whole afternoon. We spoke some, and then while I slept, they meditated in the corner by the murti and lingam."

I hadn't seen Panditji and Sulabha since before the wedding, weeks earlier, and was surprised that they would come on their own, without me. "Did they say why they had come?" I asked curiously.

"I was sure they had come looking for you, but when I asked them, Panditji replied that they had come to meet me. Then they told me a story about Krishna, and it filled my heart. For days after, I felt Krishna's presence so strongly. You must go to them and thank them for me."

"Amma, what story did they tell you?" I asked, still unable to quite believe that they had come to our very modest abode. They had never told me any stories of Krishna, only of Shiva."

"Devaki, I have told you many times the story of Krishna playing with the *gopis* (milkmaids devoted to Krishna) and how he replicated himself, making many multiples of himself so that every gopi could have a Krishna of her own." I nodded, saying that I remembered well that tale. "That is not simply a child's story. There is great truth in it. Your Panditji told me that something similar happened after the great war (Mahabharata War). There was much sorrow in all the kingdoms, and Krishna, being the heart of all beings, felt that sorrow as his own. He is both apart from and within his creation, and as part of his creation, he feels the joy and sorrow of everyone and everything. Feeling that sorrow, he went and sat with every family, not only in Dwarka, but with families in other kingdoms as well. Most people could not see him. Only those with love in their hearts were able to see Krishna coming to sit and comfort them, and they received much relief from their sorrow, but he was equally present to the ones who couldn't perceive him and tried to bring them comfort as well. The ability to perceive Krishna rests with us, not with him, because he is everywhere, equally available to all, if we but open our eyes and hearts.

"This was the reason that the whole region was able to recover so quickly from such a great war, which had caused so much death and devastation. Krishna's presence permeated the whole of Bharat. Panditji explained that this story is not only one of the past, but it is also true of our current time. For every assault against us, he is here to take away our pain. That is what we must remember, Devaki. After Panditji shared this story, I felt the presence of Krishna so strongly, and I thanked your friend. Then his wife spoke, and she told me of the meeting of her guru's guru, Sage Maitreyi, with Krishna during the time of the great war."

"Do you know of Sage Maitreyi?" I asked in surprise.

She smiled faintly. "I don't know much, Devaki, but I may have heard that name. It is a beautiful story. According to your friend, during the great war, the powerful negative vibrations released on the battlefield reached even into the celestial worlds, causing much unsettlement. What happens here affects there as well, in the same way that what happens there affects us here. Sage Maitreyi, who was living in the celestial world, felt the vibrations of suffering and grief. Overcome by the desire to alleviate the pain, she flew to the battlefield in her body of light to see what could be done. There she saw Krishna standing beside each dead and wounded warrior, unseen by most, pouring out his love. The sage dropped to her knees and cried out, 'Prahbu (Lord), so much suffering!'

"Turning to her, Krishna replied calmly, 'You have come. Go now to Rukmini (Krishna's wife). She is waiting for you. Together you can dispel this destructive power.' Rukmini was in Dwarka, deep in meditation, helping to counter all that was being unleashed. Sage Maitreyi went to her and together they did as Krishna had asked. This was just before Arjuna's son Abhimanyu was killed and the battle turned a critical corner.

"When your friend was narrating this story, she closed her eyes and at the end said, 'I heard this story from my guruji, who is a chela of the great Maitreyi, and I asked her why Krishna had sent Maitreyi to Rukmini. Wasn't he dispelling the violent energy? And my guruji replied, 'There is Shiva and there is Shakti, Narayan, and Narayani. Part of what is done is by him and part by her. They each have their roles to perform and work together in perfect harmony. In truth, they are one and only appear to be separate.'"

Amma paused for several moments and then added, "You don't know how their visit and stories uplifted me. Devaki, you must go thank them for me."

"I will go once you are better, Amma," I replied sorrowfully as I saw my mother making a great effort to speak. Just the brief conversation we were having was taking its toll.

"No," she said. "You must go tomorrow, and you mustn't go empty-handed." Pooja (Bhadra's wife) made some food for me, but I have no appetite and have no wish to eat. Bring the food to them as my offering of gratitude."

The next morning, she insisted I go to meet Panditji and Sulabha that day. I resisted but she would not hear of me staying with her. "You must thank them for me or I will feel a great lack. It is an honor that such people came to my home, to see me, a poor, simple village woman," she whispered.

"I will go quickly then and return," I replied, unable to disobey my mother's command.

She nodded and whispered, "If you keep him in your heart, there can be no sorrow."

As I left the back room and reached for the door of the hut, she called me again to her. Looking at me with glowing eyes from her bed on the floor, she whispered, "Devaki, you must make peace with your brother. Promise me. He has a good heart."

"I know, Amma, and I will," I replied, holding back my tears. "Wait for me. I won't be long." I left her room again and, as I walked to the door of the hut, I failed to see the package of food on the table that Pooja had left that morning; my mind was in such a state of heightened emotions that I overlooked that part of my mother's request.

I made my way as quickly as possible to Panditji and Sulabha's home. When I asked them why they had gone to visit my mother, Sulabha replied quietly, "We went for *darshan* (being in the presence of a deity or revered person)."

"It was a great honor for us to meet such a devotee of Lord Krishna," Panditji began, at which words I burst into tears. "Sulabha saw immediately that your mother had lived in Dwarka during the time of Krishna and Rukmini, and her devotion comes from that lifetime. We wanted to touch her feet but did not want to embarrass her."

"Devaki, I want you to know that I felt Krishna himself standing by her. His presence was palpable." Sulabha added caringly. "She is not alone."

"She insisted I come here to thank you, but I must return home right away," I blurted out between sobs.

"Devaki, come to us whenever you need to," replied Sulabha as she reached out to hug me.

I hurried home as fast as I could, believing that through my will alone I could keep my mother alive. In my presence, I knew she would not leave, but by the time I reached home, it was too late. My mother was already gone, and I suspected that she had sent me away so that I wouldn't hold her back.

CHAPTER 37

The Temple of the Heart

There are no words to describe the desperation I felt upon losing my mother; she was not only a mother to me, but my conduit to Krishna. When I arrived home, it was my weeping brother Bhadra who held me and tried to comfort me. For several days I remained in an immobile state, barely able to rise from the bed my mother had slept in. Even in the weeks that followed, I didn't leave home, as I tried to recall every story that my mother had told me about the one she so loved. Sulabha and Panditji came to see me several times, but even they could not lift me out of my state. Word was sent to the Banerjee home about my condition, and finally, Shankara and Bhavani came to try to comfort me. A month had passed since my mother's death, and I was just beginning to recover.

I spoke to them extensively about my mother, sharing with them the last stories she had told me, still unable to focus on anything else. After listening patiently, Shankar made a proposal. "Didi, we are going to Mathura to visit Bhavani's brother. It is the birthplace of Krishna. Come with us and you will feel his presence and that of your mother. We will also take you to Brindavan, where he spent his childhood."

I didn't answer right away. Bhadra, who had entered the room and overheard the conversation, encouraged me to take up the offer. "If you stay here, you will only wallow in sorrow. It is time to return to life, Devaki." Nodding, I consented. I had only left the village once, to go to the mountains with Panditji and Sulabha, and visiting the cities would be a totally new experience. I believed it would also help me continue to feel my mother's presence. What she would have given for a chance to visit Brindavan, where the childhood adventures of her Lord had taken place, I thought. On the other hand, I reasoned, she had no desire to go anywhere because Krishna had come to her. She had once told me, "He finds his devotees, no matter where they are." I hoped that by visiting Brindavan and Mathura, I would finally be able to establish my own relationship with Krishna and not need my mother to feel his presence in my life.

It took many days to reach our destination as we traveled at a leisurely pace with two shigrams. We first visited Brindavan and my spirits were lifted at the sight of the Jamuna River. We walked through the market and visited temples. Being in such a large town, compared to my village, was a novel and somewhat startling experience, and there were many things that attracted my attention. Shankara watched my moods carefully and did everything he could to bring a smile to my face. After a few days we left for Mathura, which was also situated along the banks of the beautiful Jamuna. By the time we reached Mathura, I had already become accustomed to the busyness, the clutter and chatter of the towns, a far cry from the life of my small village. I wasn't yet sure if I liked the crowded streets, jammed with sellers and buyers of goods, but I was beginning to adjust. The temples, which were larger and grander than anything I had ever seen, greatly appealed to me and kept me quite entranced.

Bhavani's brother and his family received us warmly, and after they saw the closeness between Shankara and me, they began treating me as if I truly was his elder sister. But as was always the case with new acquaintances, there was a slight hidden fear that they might find out about my background, and this led me to maintain my customary reserve in their presence.

It was the brief conversations in the market, with the servants in the household and overhearing discussions between Shankara and Bhavani's brother, that gave me a glimpse of what was taking place in the cities of our region. Fear of the Delhi Sultanate was gripping people, an uncertainty over what tomorrow might bring. They could be forced to flee; their temple could be destroyed; there could be killings. They were living with an anxiety unknown in my village, and I tried to block it out by thinking that this was a sacred city, the birthplace of Sri Krishna, and that no harm could come to it or the people.

After a week's stay in Mathura, I had a dream in which I found myself standing before a magnificent temple to Lord Krishna, admiring all the exquisite details of the building. Entering, I walked through the various shrines where murtis stood made of gold and silver with precious stones encased in them. I never imagined such a glorious place existed and I wondered if it was a celestial temple, but then I heard the words: "The grand temple of Mathura, built on the birthplace of Lord Krishna." I awoke from the dream greatly elevated and wondered if the dream had been Krishna's blessing to me on behalf of my mother because of her great devotion. Then the thought came to me that if there was such a temple in Mathura, I must find it. I wondered why Shankara hadn't taken me there, but perhaps that was to be a surprise saved for the last day.

By the time I came out of my room that morning, the family had all gone out on an excursion. A servant told me that Shankara had asked her not to awaken me as he said I needed the rest. Grateful for some time alone, I decided to go on my own to find the Krishna temple I had seen in my dream. I set out with no idea of where to go or how to find the temple. The only thing I knew was that it was built on the place where Krishna had been born. After walking through many streets and markets, I began asking people. Most of them looked at me baffled, but finally one man pointed ahead and said, "If you are looking for the place of Krishna's birth, it is in that direction, down that street." I headed there but could find no temple. Again, I asked a man, and he pointed down the road a bit, saying over there is the place where Krishna was born. A large structure stood in that spot, but it didn't in any way resemble the temple I had seen in my dream.

"Where is the temple?" I murmured.

"Temple? What temple?" he asked.

"The one built on the place where Sri Krishna was born?" I replied somewhat impatiently, thinking that surely all the residents of Mathura would know of it.

He laughed scornfully. "That was destroyed long ago. There is a mosque in its place now."

"A mosque?" I asked, looking at him in surprise. He nodded, and I stumbled away, more than a little confused. I had seen the temple in my dream. It must be real. As I approached the large building, a voice began to chant blaring words I didn't recognize, and suddenly a rush of men began to walk in that direction. I turned around and around in a daze, wondering what to do, when one of the men accidently knocked into me and, losing my balance, I stumbled onto the ground. He reached his hand out to help me rise but then was shoved away. Getting up on my own, I tried to steady myself when I felt a kick to my leg and was knocked over again. Falling back harder onto the stone road, I lost consciousness.

When I awoke, I was in a strange room and a woman was standing over me, patting the side of my head with a wet cloth. Her head was covered so I could hardly see her face. The memory of falling returned, and I realized that someone had carried me to their home and was treating my head wound.

I sat up but felt faint and dizzy. Realizing that I was with strangers and should leave immediately, I didn't lie down again. The woman withdrew from the room without a word, and a man about my age entered and introduced himself as Aamir. He explained that he had seen me being knocked to the ground and had carried me to his home not far away so that his wife could treat me. The realization that this strange man had lifted and carried me made me shrink back in dismay, but he seemed not to notice my discomfit. He asked my name and I told him "Devaki," but revealed nothing more about myself, despite his questions.

I demurely thanked him, then told him that I had to go home. I didn't know anything about this man, and the whole situation was most uncomfortable. I wanted to leave immediately, but he would not hear of it and insisted that I eat and drink before departing. Despite my resistance, he took hold of my arm and helped me to stand. My leg was sore and my head was pounding, so I agreed to stay for a short time until I could gather my strength. He called for the woman who had treated my head wound and asked her to bring food and tea. Then he guided me to a cushion on the ground next to a low table and sat down opposite me. Until then I had kept my eyes down, but now I raised them to get a good look at the man, who was quite attractive, with a neat dark beard, carefully cropped; his hair was short as well. His features were nicely formed, his face on the thin side, his eyes welcoming, but I was in too much distress to make much of his appealing appearance.

"The place where I fell, is that a temple for Muslim people?" I asked after a few moments of silence.

"It is a mosque," he replied with a smile and a nod. "I was on my way there for the afternoon prayer when I saw that you had accidently been knocked over."

"Then you . . . you are a Muslim?" I asked tentatively. He nodded. I didn't want to be rude, but I felt compelled to leave and was debating internally how to do this without insulting the man who had rescued me. I had never met a Muslim before and didn't know what to expect. As I sat pondering what to do, the woman, who turned out to be his wife, re-entered the room, bringing tea and some snacks. After setting everything on the table, she disappeared again behind the door without a word. I sipped the tea and listened as he spoke, telling me more about his life than I cared to know. He mentioned that he had a shop in the market and was doing quite well. As I listened and drank, taking a few bites of food, I felt my strength returning, and I began to seek an opening to bid this man goodbye. After a while he fell quiet and I felt his eyes upon me, which caused me to look away.

Glancing around the room, I saw that it was nicely decorated. I had been lying on a low bed with many cushions spread across it and now saw that it served as a seating area. This must be a reception room, I thought. Rugs were strewn on the floor in a nice arrangement and many decorations hung on the walls. It was far more decorous that the simple hut where my family lived.

"I can tell by your name that you are not Muslim," he said. I shook my head and he continued. "None of my grandparents were Muslim either. It was my father who converted and then, of course, my mother had to as well to marry him."

"Convert?" I asked, putting down my tea and gazing at him. "You mean he abandoned the devatas?" He didn't respond. "Why would your father do that?"

"We were from the shudra community, and in Islam there are no varna distinctions. That was appealing to my father and so he became Muslim, a rather strict one at that. We are now in a good social position, much better than we were before."

"He became Muslim because of that?" I asked, perplexed. He nodded. "You mean he abandoned his religion to rise in social status?" I asked again in disbelief. The discussions I had been hearing at Bhavani's brother's home suddenly hit me. This was what was happening to our people. They were changing their religion, either through coercion or by being offered some benefit.

"By the way you are dressed, I can see that you are not from the shudra community, and you may not know what it is to live like that. It is a most unfortunate lot, with no means of betterment."

The impact of his words sunk in and slowly rising, I replied, trying to control my indignation, "I am most certainly from the shudra varna and know very well what it is to be born in that community, and I would never seek to be anything else. To do so would be an insult to my parents, who are great devotees, among the finest people you will ever meet." Then, no longer able to submerge my emerging anger, I lashed out at him. "I would rather sweep streets and clean dung for the rest of my life than abandon the devatas who have sustained me and my family." With those words I turned and limped out of the room, without saying goodbye.

Rising quickly and following me, he called out, claiming that he didn't mean to insult me, but it was too late. As I reached for the door, opened it, and stepped outside, I turned, and in a fit of rage, spit at him as he looked on in shock. Then with a limping leg, I did my best to hurry away.

I was able to find a palanquin quickly and returned to the home of Bhavani's brother. Bhavani was pacing the walkway outside her brother's home when I arrived. When she saw me step out of the palanquin, she hurried over and hugged me, saying that they had been so worried when they returned home and found out that I had been away for most of the day. "Shankara is looking all over the city for you. He is beside himself with worry and is reproaching himself for not taking you with us this morning." Noticing the bruise on my forehead, she touched it and asked what had happened.

"Let's go inside and talk," I replied in a trembling voice. I needed time to quell my anger and I waited for Shankara to return before explaining to them what had happened. I told them about the dream, describing what I had seen in detail, and said that I had gone out to find the temple that was built on the spot where Krishna had been born.

Interrupting me, Shankara looked at me in surprise, and said, "You are describing the temple initiated by the great-grandson of Sri Krishna, one of the great temples of the world. That was destroyed by Mahmud of Ghazni over two hundred years ago, didn't you know?"

"How would I know that, Shankara?"

"It was built over many centuries with hundreds, no thousands or even tens of thousands of artists and workers. You are blessed, Devaki, to have had a vision of it in your dream. Most of us can only imagine what it might have looked like. It is said to have been the richest and most magnificent temple in all of Bharat. Muhmud of Gazni destroyed it all over a period of twenty days, and then he smelt the gold and silver murtis for booty, and he burned much of the city, which has since been rebuilt. This was part of his campaign to break the spirit of our people, but all that destruction has not broken our spirit. If anything, it has fortified us."

I told them what had happened, about the mosque where I had been knocked down and that I had been rescued by a man, but I didn't tell the rest, as I was too embarrassed by my behavior. How had I had the audacity to spit on anyone, let alone a man who had rescued me? That is an act I will regret for the rest of my life, I thought. After Bhavani saw how shaken I was, she said that I should stay close to the home for the rest of the visit and not wander out.

"Bhavani, there is nothing I want more right now than to return to the village. I have seen enough of Mathura. Krishna has been so desecrated here in this town of his birth that it pains me to remain." Shankara said that he understood and would arrange for a shigram to take me and one of the servants back home the next day.

"Devaki, when I first saw the remains of Nalanda, I felt the same. Such massive and unwarranted destruction. Great anger surged within me, but as I thought about it, I realized that we mustn't waste energy focusing on what has been destroyed, but rather focus on what has not yet been destroyed and make a commitment to save that. Don't spill tears. Build resolve. Knowledge can never be destroyed, only the outer displays. I made a commitment to do what I could to preserve the essence of Nalanda, its wealth of knowledge, whether we can rebuild it in the same way or not."

On the ride back to the village, which lasted for several days, I could not get my behavior out of my mind, and again and again internally I apologized to that man. I felt that an apology was something I would have to do in person one day, although I doubted that I would ever see him again. The matter weighed heavily on me, almost as much as hearing of the destruction. I kept reminding myself of Shankara's words that I had been blessed to see the temple in a dream. Was that Krishna coming to comfort me after my mother's death? Did he know the effect the visit to Mathura would have on me?

As the shigram drew closer to the village, I had to acknowledge that all my mother's stories and urgings, knowing her supreme love for the Lord and his presence in her daily life, none of that had been able to anchor him in my heart. Somehow, it was standing in the very spot where destruction had taken place, where a mosque had been erected on his birthplace in the attempt to erase his memory, for some reason, it was that experience which made Sri Krishna real to me. And I knew that on that day I had become a devotee.

When I reached home and Bhadra saw my depressed mood, he asked why the journey had not uplifted my spirits. I didn't dwell on the matter of the temple but rather on my behavior with the man called Aamir. "I was pushed onto the ground by a crowd and got hurt and a man saved me, took me into his house and fed me. And what did I do, Bhadra? I got up in anger and spit on him."

"You did what?" he asked in astonishment.

"I spit on him. And I, of all people, should not have done that after what had been done to Pitaji," I replied mournfully.

"That is so unlike you, Devaki." He shook his head in wonderment. "What led you to do such a thing?"

I explained about the conversion and the long-ago destruction of the temple and the city of Mathura and ended by saying quietly, "Bhadra, you have directed your anger in the wrong direction. The brahmins are not the enemy. They have preserved our knowledge and culture through many thousands of years. The enemy are those who are seeking to destroy what we have fought so hard to preserve. You strike out at the brahmins because they are near, in our midst, and the invaders seem far and inaccessible. But they are here, slowly poisoning our society, turning our own people against our history and beliefs. We can't see that in the village but go to the towns and cities and you will see what they are doing." He didn't reply, but I could see that my words struck a note.

Coming home to my mother's small abode was a huge comfort, and for the first time, in the mornings I would sit before the small murti of Krishna that my mother had worshipped, not out of any sense of loyalty to her but out of the desire to know him. After a few days when my mind began to settle, I realized that there was another matter to which I had to attend. My mother's last wish of me was to bring food to Panditji and Sulabha as her way of thanking them for their visit, and I had failed to do this.

Telling Bhadra that I would spend the day visiting my Kashmiri friends, I made a small package of food that I had cooked and went to their cottage, about an hour's walk away. When there was no answer to my knock on the door, I pushed it open. Sulabha was seated in meditation in her usual spot, and Panditji was reading. He didn't greet me with his usual warmth but when I entered, he told me that he was expecting me. Then he asked a question.

"Devaki, where is the temple?"

Putting the package of food on the table, I offered pranam and looked at him questioningly. He asked the question again, and I responded by asking, "Which temple, Panditji, are you referring to?"

Instead of responding, he asked another question, "Where did you have that sublime experience of Lord Shiva?"

I knew what he was referring to and replied, "In the mountains that time with you and Sulabha during Shivaratri, at your guruji's cottage."

"Did you need a temple for that? Did you need a murti?"

"No," I replied softly, catching the drift of his words.

"So why have you been so disturbed?"

"Panditji . . ." I began to object and then sank onto the cushion beside him.

Then I heard Sulabha's voice as she emerged from meditation. "Do you understand what Panditji is saying? That grand temple existed for thousands of years, but it too was impermanent, as is all material manifestation. Nothing is this world is exempt from the continual flow of time ever bringing change. There are karmic reasons for what is taking place. If you become too dependent on outer form, that outer form will be ripped away."

I turned my eyes from one to the other. This was not the reception I expected. I knew they both were sensitive to my various emotions and could peer into my inner life, and so speaking with great feeling, I told them all that had happened to me, all that I had experienced. "While I was in Mathura, I spoke with people and saw what is happening there because of the Delhi Sultanate. One woman told me she fled from Delhi, where a trail of destruction followed: destruction of places of worship, killing of our people, and conversions. I couldn't help but get angry," I said. After explaining this, I expected some sympathy from my friends, for them to say that I had every right to be angry. But this was not what I received.

"It was your anger that knocked you to the ground unconscious, Devaki, not any man." Panditji's voice was firm and unemotional. Becoming defensive, I turned my eyes to him and asked, "Isn't it right to be angry in the face of evil?"

In a gentler tone, he continued, "The cosmic law of cause and effect takes care of all matters. None can escape it. Our anger is not needed. Devaki, those who destroy will themselves in time be destroyed. The universe maintains its balance and equilibrium, but in divine time, not human time. What we must focus on is building the temple of the heart, the only true place of worship, a temple that no outer force can destroy. It is this love and devotion which will ensure that for every outer temple torn down, a new one will be built. Was not the Somnath temple also destroyed and rebuilt?"

"That was also destroyed?" I asked in alarm, remembering how dear that temple had been to my father, who had never even seen it.

"The same man who destroyed the great Krishna temple of Mathura also sacked and looted the Somnath temple, and killed many people who were resisting, but the temple was quickly rebuilt. Those temples are places of great power, and the invaders think that by destroying the outer temples, they can assail the spirit of our people." He let out a sarcastic chuckle. "That is the folly of men, taking pains to destroy what can easily be rebuilt, because with every assault the resolve of the people grows stronger.

"Your experience in Mathura affected you deeply, didn't it?" I nodded. "Perhaps that was the purpose of the visit. Your mother had departed, and Krishna had to find another way to reach you. He gave you a vision of that celestial temple, stirred a memory, and then allowed you to see the birthplace, which was not a very lofty place at all. It was, after all, a prison where his uncle had locked up his parents. That is where he was born, and the minds of men are still imprisoned there. Don't dwell on that prison. Free yourself from the outer world so that the Lord can reach you, and you can reach him, any time, any place. That was the purpose of your visit."

"But I am angry, Panditji. They have attacked our devatas. Are we to do nothing?" My voice trembled with emotion.

"Then do something about it," he replied, looking at me intently.

"What can I possibly do?" I asked, feeling utterly helpless.

"You can anchor him deep in your heart, so deep that nothing can disturb your devotion, so deep that you see him everywhere, in all beings. That is what you can do to counter all of this."

A slight smile crossed Sulabha's lips as she added, "So Krishna has finally come to you, like Shiva had that night in the mountains. You are truly a child of your parents, Devaki. You may feel sad and disturbed, but that is not how I see you now. Something has changed, and I see the love beginning to bloom in your heart."

Their words calmed me. Laying out on the table the food I had brought, I said quietly. "This is from my mother. It was her last wish and request for me to bring you food to express her gratitude to you for honoring her home with your visit."

Folding her hands in pranam, Sulabha lowered her head and replied, "This is prasad (offering) from the Lord himself because she is now in him."

CHAPTER 38

Journey to a Forgotten Land

A seed had embedded itself in my heart and a newfound devotion to Krishna awakened in me. It was as if the preservation of his memory and living presence depended on my love, and I knew I had to nurture it and protect it as one does any newborn seedling.

The wise counsel of Panditji and Sulabha subdued but could not eradicate my anger. I packed it away in a corner of my mind, but I knew it would revisit me time and again. A defiance I had not known I was capable of had stirred within. One night I had a dream in which I was throwing stones and breaking apart that mosque in Mathura, and I awoke with a terrible feeling. Where had this anger come from, and with such ferocity? I reasoned that it couldn't be only over the destruction of the temple; there had to be a larger issue that I couldn't yet identify.

I was spending most of my time at the Banerjee home, as Panyaji's health was failing. My home situation was also a cause of concern. My eldest sister Lalita, with whom I was not very close and whom I didn't see much of, was ill. Bhadra was devoted to her and was spending much time caring for her. On occasion I brought her food but didn't think to do much else. On days that I would visit Bhadra, I would ask him about

Lalita, but I didn't notice that he was growing thinner, and his appearance was more solemn.

I hadn't visited in over two weeks when I managed to get away. Upon entering my mother's part of the hut, I found Bhadra seated on the ground, his head bent down. "I am here, Bhadra," I said casually, as I went about unpacking the food I had brought from the Banerjee home. Pretending to ignore his obviously depressed state, I began to speak about various things. He was quiet. After several minutes of his silence, when I didn't hear his usual caustic welcome, I finally asked him what was wrong.

"You haven't asked about Lalita," he said quietly, lifting his head and gazing steadily at me.

"Is she doing any better?" I asked hesitantly.

"She died a few days ago," he replied mournfully.

I was stunned and went to sit by Bhadra's side. "Why didn't someone come for me?"

"Why didn't you come home to inquire?"

"I didn't think she was that sick." My voice trembled. He got up and walked out, leaving me riddled with guilt. For a long time, I sat staring into space, wondering if what Bhadra had always accused me of, neglecting my family, was in fact true. Had I been so absent these past many years that I was oblivious of the struggles they endured?

After her marriage, my sister Uma had moved to another village, and over the years I had hardly seen her. We had been close in our younger years, but when I saw her during the last weeks of my mother's life, I realized how far apart we had drifted. Lalita was sixteen years older than me and we had never been close. She married when I was still an infant. Keshav, who had once been dear to me, was now working on roads some distance from our village and returned home occasionally. Only Bhadra was left. Whenever I came home, the tension between us arose again, despite my intentions to make peace with this brother. I had promised my mother to do so, and also Sulabha, who had advised me on several occasions to put aside any lingering resentment, but I could not, and I didn't understand why. Why was there such a blockage?

My escape was the Banerjee home, where Panyaji treated me as an adopted daughter, or at least a friend, and nobody criticized me or made me feel as if I were abdicating a responsibility.

My negligence of my eldest sister brought up a guilt that had emerged every now and then over the years, and sending word to the Banerjee home, I decided to stay several days with Bhadra and make every effort to devote more time to him and his family. I could see that the troubles of my siblings were wearing him down. While home, I learned that he was not able to work very much and that Keshav, through his work on the roads, was helping to feed his family. But Bhadra was also looking after Lalita's family, helping her six children since her husband was not a very capable man. The burden on Bhadra was overwhelming, and I was becoming increasingly aware of this. Taking some comfort in my newfound devotion, I would walk to the nearby forest, where my mother used to take me, and sit there inwardly calling out to Sri Krishna for some relief for my family. But this was not to last. As soon as I saw that my brother had begun to recover from his grief over our sister's death, my mind returned to the Banerjee home and to caring for Panyaji.

Several years passed when one evening Keshav arrived at the Banerjee home urgently asking for me. When I saw the look on his face, I knew something had happened: Bhadra was gravely ill. Taking whatever medicines I could find, I hurried home with him.

When I saw my eldest brother lying on a sleeping mat on the floor of my mother's part of hut, I was deeply moved. "We moved him here," Keshav informed me, "so he could rest without being disturbed by his family."

"I will stay with him, Keshav, you go home." I could see how weary this third brother of mine was, and nodding, he left.

Kneeling beside Bhadra, who was sleeping, I whispered to him tearfully, "You better not leave me, *bhai* (brother). I am not ready for that." For the next several days, I wiped down his heated face, boiled medicine, and fed it to him. Every now and then he would mumble words and momentarily open his eyes, but he seemed not to be aware of my presence. At times, he called out to my mother, apologizing for allowing two of his siblings to die, for not doing a better job in caring for the family. Until that moment I had not realized the extent of the guilt he was carrying, and how much, in some odd way, I depended on him. He was the family to which I could return. Somehow I knew he would always be there for me. After four days, his fever subsided, and his delirium passed. When he fully awakened and saw me, a slight smile crept across his face. “I didn’t expect you to come, Devaki,” he said in a weak voice.

“You gave me quite a scare,” I replied in a feigned scolding tone. “Never do that to me again, bhai.”

“I think this is the first time you have called me that,” he responded. I helped him sit up and then assisted as he tried to eat the food his wife had prepared.

“Your family is beside themselves with worry, but I don’t want them to see you until you have regained some strength. You look awful, Bhadra, truly awful.”

He smiled faintly. “That is more like the Devaki I know.”

A week later my brother was much recovered, and I was thinking about returning to the Banerjee home, but Bhadra was loathe to let me go and made one excuse after another, until I finally said, “I will stay with you another week, but then I must return. In any case, I am sure you will be happy to be rid of me.” He didn’t respond. During his illness I had spent more time with Bhadra than I had in many years, and I could see his depressed state. Losing Lalita had taken a toll on him, but I didn’t know what to do. I had other responsibilities, and he had his wife and children.

Before it was time for me to leave, Keshav came and asked to walk with me in the forest. As we walked, he said, “Of all of us, you and Bhadra are the closest. I have always known that, which is why I went to get you when he fell sick. I knew he would not die if you were there.”

I stopped walking and replied with a slight chuckle, “Bhadra and me? We have always fought. He has always tried to control me, and I have resisted since I was young. I can’t stand when anyone tries to control me.”

"You have misunderstood him, Devaki. He has looked out for all of us but worries about you the most. He has told me this many times. One thing about him has confused me though, and that is his rejection of the beliefs and values of our parents. Recently I asked him why and do you know what he told me?" I shook my head. "He said that he doesn't want to be deceived and that he can't trust what anyone says about religion—or the devatas. I think that at some point in the past he must have been badly deceived, and that is why he has put up a wall around himself. After hearing this, I began to have compassion for him, Devaki, because he can't bring himself to believe in anything."

"Amma once told me the same thing about him," I mused. "The rest of us all have some connection to either Krishna or Lord Shiva. Bhadra alone rejects it all. Something has made him bitter, Keshav, but I don't know what we can do about it."

"You can spend more time with him, Devaki. I believe what he needs is for you to be more present in his life." I had heard this before, but this time Keshav's words stuck, and I said to myself that perhaps now was the time to make greater effort to fulfil the promise I made to my mother on her deathbed—to make peace with my brother once and for all.

A day before I was to return to the Banerjee home, Shankara came to visit me at the hut. I suspected that he had come to retrieve me, but his purpose was something quite different. Bhadra had returned to living in his part of the hut and I was alone in my mother's section when he arrived. I could see that something was on his mind. He inquired about my brother's health, I asked him why he had come to the village. He and Bhavani now had two small children and were living near the partially rebuilt Nalanda where he was teaching.

"I've come to bring my mother to Patna. My father is insisting that because of her health she can no longer stay in the village. But I have another matter to talk with you about. Didi, I need your help."

"My help? With what?" I asked curiously.

"After Nalanda was destroyed, monks from Tibet and elsewhere came to salvage some of the sacred texts and bring them back to their country. A small delegation is now going to Tibet to view these texts, and I have been invited to go as well. It is a great honor, and I am very excited about it."

"You are going to Tibet, so far away," I murmured, not knowing whether to be happy or sad about this news. "How long will you be gone?'

"Many months at least, perhaps a year. I am not worried about the trip. It is a journey many have taken. That is not the problem. I need your help because Bhavani is insisting that she accompany me, and I have insisted that she stay home with our children. She is determined and bursts into tears whenever we discuss this. She will listen to you. You must convince her to stay at home with the children."

"I will do my best," I murmured, still dazed by this news. Shankara was leaving, going to Tibet, so far away. The very thought made me uneasy. Living in Patna was one thing, but to take such a long journey, that was another.

The next morning Bhavani arrived alone at the hut. Before I could say a word, she looked at me with pleading eyes and said, "Didi, I need your help. You must help me convince Shankara to take me with him to Tibet. I will not stay behind, and I have made all the arrangements for the children to stay with my brother."

"Can you really leave the children, Bhavani?" I asked, wondering now what I was to do.

"They will stay in Mathura, and I hesitate to ask, but I am hoping that you will also go there to help care for them. They know you much better and will feel secure with you there."

Putting that aside for the moment, I pressed her, "Bhavani, why do you feel so intensely about going? Is it that you fear for Shankara's safety and don't want to be separated from him?"

Her eyes began to tear. "It has nothing to do with that. I want to go for myself. I feel such a longing. Since I was young, I have wanted to meet a real Bon master, and I can only do that in Tibet. If I don't go on this trip, there won't be another opportunity."

"What is a Bon master?" I asked curiously.

"Bon is the original religion of Tibet and is very ancient, as old as the Vedas, they say."

"Bhavani, you are a devotee of Parvati Ma. Why do you want to meet a Bon master?"

Her voice cracked as she spoke. "Years ago, my father took the family to the kingdom of the Malla Dynasty (Nepal). There we met a Bonpo family who had come from Tibet, and the mother told me many stories of Bon masters, who would perform magical feats. She said that in Tibet there are still such people. When she described the landscape of that place, I felt such an urge to go, but over time I put that desire to rest, never expecting to have such an opportunity. Now this has come, and I can't pass it up. I must go, and besides I want to experience it with Shankara."

"How do you know you will find a Bon master if you go? The visit is to the Buddhist monasteries."

"I have faith that Parvati Ma will fulfil this desire of mine."

"Have you told this to Shankara?"

She shook her head. "He is too concerned about my safety and the children, I know, and won't understand my yearning."

I was moved by her words and hugged her as I whispered. "I will try to convince him. Don't worry. I will do my best to see that you go with him to Tibet."

Pulling away, she looked at me and said gratefully, "It is because of you that I was able to marry Shankara, and I trust that you will also soften his heart so that he will take me with him."

After she left, I realized that I had a difficult task before me and wasn't certain that I would be successful. Shankara was quite firm in his determination that Bhavani must stay home. He and I had never been at odds before, but now I felt it my duty to take her side on this matter. Later that day I went find him.

As soon as he saw me, he looked away and said firmly, "I know that Bhavani has gone to you to plead her case. The answer is no, a definite no."

"Look at me, Shankara." He turned his eyes to me. "You have no right to deny her this opportunity. Before you married Bhavani, I told you that you must respect her thoughts and feelings. She is not asking to go so that she can be with you. It is not because she fears a separation from you. She has her own past, and it may have been in Tibet. Perhaps there is something unfinished that is calling her to return. You have no right to stop her from going."

"No women are coming on this journey," he remarked.

"Let her be the only one then," I replied.

"It will be a very difficult trek," he retorted.

"She is a strong woman and can manage whatever you can," I responded in an equally firm tone.

"We have two small children. How can they be away from both of their parents?" His angry tone had turned into a pleading one.

"I will take care of them in Mathura at her brother's house. I promise you. Do you not trust me?"

"You hate Mathura. Why would you go back there?"

"I don't hate Mathura and I would welcome the chance to return. I am doing this for you, Shankara, as well as for Bhavani, for the sake of your marriage. If you don't take her with you, I am afraid she might not forgive you. If you trust me, you will listen to me. Just as you feel the need to travel to Tibet, she feels it also, for her own reasons. You mustn't deny her this opportunity. Perhaps there is something important for her to discover there."

He sighed. "I have never been able to say no to you. Why do you make it impossible for me to deny your requests?"

I laughed. "Because I am your favorite didi."

"My favorite and my only didi," he replied with a smile.

"Then it is settled?" He nodded.

As I thought about returning to Mathura, I realized that this was something I had to do. Somehow, I had to find and apologize to that man whom I had insulted years earlier. Perhaps he had forgotten, but

I had not, and I would never be able to face my father again in the life after earth if I did not rectify this matter. I would have to bring flowers to Aamir as my father had done to the man who had spit on him. Only then could I release my guilt.

I told Bhadra that I had agreed to go to Mathura for what might be a long period of time, but that afterwards I would leave the Banerjee house and come live with him and his family permanently. He looked at me skeptically and didn't respond. In my heart I made a commitment to do this. Two months after Shankara's visit, I went back in Mathura with Shankara's two young children, to the home of Bhavani's brother and his family.

As I said my last goodbyes to Shankara and Bhavani, I implored them to take care of each other. I hadn't been able to express my own anxiety over their journey because I was also enthralled by the idea of their expedition. "I will go with you in spirit," I told them quietly, and in some way, I did. Not a day would go by when I did not try to imagine all they might encounter on their journey to that magical land.

The three children of Bhavani's brother were only a few years older than Shankara's children and the combination of these young ones kept everyone very busy, but several times a week I found time for myself and went out into the streets in search of Aamir. He had told me that he had a shop, and I began looking for him in the markets. As I wandered, whenever I found any sign or indication of the power of the Delhi Sultanate, my insides churned, making me realize that my anger and defiance were still there, although much tempered.

Often, I would find myself at the place of Krishna's birth, as if all roads led there. Something kept drawing me back and at one point I made the decision not to see the mosque at all, but to close my eyes and visualize the celestial temple I had seen in my dream. As I envisioned that temple, I saw myself entering and standing before the beautiful murti of Sri Krishna. Folding my hands in pranam, I offered prayers for the safety of Shankara and Bhavani. This helped to ease the anger lurking in the corners of my mind. On other days, I would wander along the Jamuna and sit beside her flowing form, sometimes gentle and sometimes fierce, and offer the same prayers for the safety of my loved ones, offering those prayers to Lord Shiva. How fortunate I felt to have a relationship with those two great mahadevas!

I had gone to the site of Krishna's birthplace perhaps a dozen times, when after I had finished praying, I heard a man's voice from behind inviting me into the mosque. Without turning around, I replied, "I see no mosque here, only a temple, a grand temple to Shri Krishna." He walked around to face me, and my eyes opened wide at the sight of Aamir standing before me. Age had not in any way diminished his attractive appearance. If anything, the slight touches of grey in his beard and at his temples made him look more distinguished.

"Devaki!" he exclaimed. "I have been searching for you for over five years, and here you are."

For a moment I was taken aback and didn't say anything, but then I replied, "I have recently come to Mathura and have been looking for you as well."

"Then you must come to my home for tea," he insisted.

"I cannot come today, but will come tomorrow," I replied, wondering if he still lived in the same place and if I would be able to find him again.

He pointed to a nearby street and said it was the same place where he had taken me after I had been injured. "You will come, for sure, won't you?" he asked. I nodded. After he left, as I began to walk back to the home of Bhavani's brother, I summoned up the image of my father bringing flowers to lay on the doorstep of the man who had insulted him and decided to bring Aamir flowers from the banks of the Jamuna.

The next day in the early afternoon, after the children were settled for their nap, I walked along the Jamuna gathering flowers, thanking Krishna for helping me to settle this matter. I had no other intention than to apologize to that man for spitting on him in a fit of anger and then to leave, having fulfilled my mission. When I arrived at Aamir's home with a bunch of flowers, he appeared excessively pleased.

"This is a peace offering," I said with a smile, as I handed him the flowers. "Since that day some years ago, I have been wanting to apologize to you for my behavior. It is not in my character to spit at anyone."

"There is no need for an apology," he replied. "I admired you for sticking up for your beliefs."

As he ushered me into the room where I had previously rested, I noticed a small murti of Krishna on a table, something I had not seen the last time I had been there, although at that time I had been quite dazed. Going over the table, I lowered my head and folded my hands in pranam. He waited respectfully as I stood there for a few moments and then said he would go make tea and bring some snacks. I sat down and waited for him, immensely relieved that he had accepted my apology and received me now quite graciously.

"Last time when I was here, I had not noticed you had a murti of Krishna," I remarked casually.

"It was not here last time." I looked at him questioningly and he explained. "It belonged to my grandmother. When my father converted, he made her throw away all the religious objects she had. She was a devotee of Krishna and hid this one statue. I used to stay with her on occasion, and one day I found her praying to it. Embarrassed, she told me that she kept it hidden, but sometimes took it out when nobody was around and prayed to it. She made me promise not to tell anyone. After she died, I retrieved it from her belongings but also kept it hidden. I had to wait until my wife died last year before I could take it out, because my wife was a very religious Muslim and would not abide by any "idols," as she called them, in our home."

When he spoke those words, I didn't feel anger as I had last time but rather compassion. "It is sad that your grandmother had to worship in secret. That is something I would never tolerate." He didn't respond, and I asked, "Then are you a devotee of Krishna?"

He shook his head. "I am not a religious man at all. I go to the mosque for appearances sake, but my only interest is my shop and my family. Long ago I decided to keep this statue in memory of my grandmother, and now because it reminds me of you. I usually keep it hidden because my son and his family live with me now, but I displayed it today because I knew you were coming." I appreciated his honesty, but his words embarrassed me, and I looked away, wondering why he had wanted to remember me at all.

"When I met you, something about you reminded me of my grandmother, whom I greatly loved," he continued. "When my father converted, she was deeply saddened but dared not say a word to him because he was such an overbearing person. I believe that of all her grandchildren, she wanted me never to forget my heritage. That is why my meeting with you touched me."

"And that is why you have so easily forgiven me," I replied with a slight smile. He didn't respond but went on to describe how lonely he has been since his wife's death. His oldest son was encouraging him to remarry, and he very much desired to do so.

"Surely, there are women in your community who would want to marry you," I remarked, suddenly feeling very uncomfortable.

"We will see," he replied with a slight smile. Soon after, having finished the tea, I politely told him that I had been away too long and had to return home. He nodded and said he would see me again. I had no plans to visit him anymore, as I had accomplished what I had set out to do, but I nodded, not wanting to be in any way impolite to this kind man.

The next time I went to pray before my celestial temple, he was there waiting for me. Telling him that I couldn't accompany him for tea, I agreed to allow him to walk me most of the way back to where I was staying. On the way, he chatted about his shop and his children. I listened half-heartedly, wondering why he was taking such an interest in me. And so it was that whenever I went to that spot to pray, he would find me. The only time I could get away from the family was when Shankara's two small children were taking their afternoon nap, so I could not change my schedule. I began to find the man annoying and stopped going to the place of Lord Krishna's birth. Instead, I would walk by the Jamuna River. But he would show up there as well, and I began to wonder if he was spying on me.

After several months of this, I asked him why he continued to seek me out. Bashfully, he told me that it was because he wanted to marry me. I was stunned and asked how he knew that I wasn't already married.

"You are always out alone," he replied. "No husband would allow that."

"In fact, I do have a husband," I told him with some hesitation, seeking a way out. "But he is not here."

"Has he died?"

"Not exactly," I murmured.

"But you are separated from him?" he asked.

"For now," I whispered. This was the narrative I had told my family so many times and one I deeply believed so I didn't feel I was lying.

I kept finding different routes to the Jamuna and sat in different parts of the riverbank in the hope of avoiding him, but Aamir kept finding me. For some reason he didn't believe that I had a husband and kept bringing up the subject of marriage. One day he said to me, "Devaki, you would have to convert in name only. I wouldn't ask you give up your worship of Krishna." We were seated by the Jamuna. Astonished by his presumption, I rose from the ground, my anger beginning to arise again. As I prepared to leave, I looked at him and said quietly but firmly, "Aamir, if you bring up the subject of marriage one more time, I am afraid I will not be able to see you again. I consider you a friend, nothing more. Please don't have illusions about this friendship." I walked away, leaving him speechless and leaving me with a sorry feeling that I had hurt him once more. He was a good man and I had been reluctant to reject him so openly, but I felt he left me no choice. I stayed at the house for many weeks after that and did all my praying for Shankara and Bhavani in the little room assigned to me.

Six months had passed since Shankara and Bhavani had left. Before departing, they said they would be gone for at least six months, but perhaps as long as a year. I was waiting eagerly for their return, not because I was unhappy in my situation, as I had grown very close to the children, but because I was eager for some words about that mystical place to which they had gone. I knew little about Tibet, having only heard of it when

Shankara described to me the destruction of Nalanda and the flight of the monks, but now my curiosity was awakened. I would repeat the name of Tibet to myself before going to sleep and try to visualize what they were experiencing. Had Bhavani found the Bon master she was seeking? Had they been able to travel to Mt. Kailash as they had hoped? I had asked Bhavani to keep a diary of their travels, and now I impatiently awaited their return so I could hear it all.

Three more months passed. One morning I awoke at dawn feeling greatly uplifted. Seeing that the sun was only beginning its ascent, I decided to go to the birthplace of Krishna before the children awoke, while the streets were still empty. I quickly dressed and quietly left the house. It had been months since I had last visited that spot, as I was trying to avoid meeting Aamir and I knew his shop was nearby. Standing before the stone structure of the mosque and envisioning the celestial temple I had once seen in dream, I folded my hands in pranam. As I did, I recalled the dream I had had just before awakening that morning, which had left me in such a joyous state. I hadn't remembered it until that very moment. As sometimes happens when supernal experiences are given during sleep, it can take time for them to filter through the many levels of consciousness before reaching the thinking mind.

Now those images rose before me, images that were all too vivid. I saw myself seated by the side of a large beautiful blue lake, unlike any I had seen before. An elderly woman was seated beside me, someone who seemed very familiar and dear to me. Suddenly she turned to me and said, very gently, "Your anger toward your brother is left over from the past. It is an old wound. He has forgiven you. Now you must forgive him. He has suffered enough, and it is time to make peace with him." As the memory of the dream returned to me and her words resounded in my inner ear, I let my hands drop to my side from their folded position and stood there staring blankly ahead, struck by her words and knowledge of my life. Try as I might, I could not recall the details of the woman's appearance. I just knew that she appeared to be elderly and had a most loving presence and imbued me with more joy than I had ever felt before, and that she had worn a strange looking red hat. That much I remembered.

So many times my mother had pleaded with me to make peace with Bhadra but I had not been able to, for reasons I couldn't understand. Now this woman appeared for that very purpose, only this time something shifted in me, as if a great blockage was cleared, lifted from my heart, freeing me. She confirmed what my mother had implied, that my anger was a result of a past hurt. But who was she? I had been praying to Krishna and Lord Shiva, but she turned up. The whole experience was beyond what I could comprehend, and the only thing I understood was that she was taking away my anger or resentment, or whatever it was that prevented me from loving Bhadra as I knew I should.

After a few minutes I began to walk slowly back to the house. As I walked, I remembered more about the dream. After she had spoken, the woman looked at me and smiled so sweetly. Then she took a few steps into the lake and turned into a beautiful white bird and flew away, leaving me with such a feeling of elevation that I felt I could fly away with her. Was there such a person in real life, I wondered, who could turn into a bird, or had the dream simply been a creation of my imagination? But if it was only my imagination, why was it that I felt so different, so at peace, so eager to return to Bhadra and care for him as I had never done before?

The one indication I had that the experience was not a mere creation of my mind was the joy it left, joy that was to fill me for many, many days.

CHAPTER 39

Return of the Goddess

Over the next many days, my mind kept reverting to my brother, and I began to feel restless and eager to return home. When I realized that I had never prayed for his welfare, I berated myself, saying internally that I had been an indifferent sister. He had been right about me. I had ignored my family and only taken an interest in Shankara. In the years left to me, I resolved to make up for it.

A few more months passed before we received word that Shankara and Bhavani had returned to Nalanda and were coming to retrieve me and the children. My heart sang. They were back home safely.

For days I listened to stories of their travels. I wanted to hear everything and told them not to leave out any detail. They spoke about the long journey through the awe inspiring mountains, and I listened eagerly to their description of Lhasa, where they visited several monasteries. I heard their description of the Brahmaputra River, also called the Tsangpo. "We rode often to the river to sit on the sandy banks," explained Shankara, "and we rode to the Yarlung Valley, where we visited Samye Monastery, a very old monastery founded by the great Guru Rinpoche, who is considered an enlightened master. After the destruction of Nalanda, some of the monks from there came to save the sacred texts and bring them back to Tibet. We tried to catalogue the texts taken, but there were too many."

"Did you bring them back?" I asked.

He shook his head. "They are safer there. Whatever we rebuild here is likely to be destroyed again. That is the sad condition of our land. Tibet was able to protect itself. The same man who destroyed Nalanda tried to conquer Tibet, but the Tibetan tribes defeated his army. The Mongols have a growing influence there now, but they are Buddhist and would not destroy the places of learning."

We were still at the home of Bhavani's brother, and I had been listening to them for days describing so many aspects of their journey. It seemed they had exhausted their store of tales when Bhavani said to me as we were sitting together one afternoon, "But we haven't told you the most extraordinary part of our visit to Tibet." At those words, Shankara smiled and sent Bhavani a knowing glance. In the few days since they had returned, I could see how much stronger their relationship had become. They always had been a loving couple, but Tibet seemed to have bonded them in a very special way.

"You tell it," said Bhavani to Shankara.

"No, this story is for you to tell," he insisted.

I looked from one to the other, wondering what it could be. She again asked him, and he again told her to tell the story. Finally, I turned to Bhavani and implored her, "Don't keep me waiting any longer. I am eager to know whether you found what you were seeking."

"Under the strangest of circumstances, we met a Bonpo master, a woman."

Shankara smiled and turning to Bhavani said, "She was a Shaivite. Don't you remember all the stories she told us of Lord Shiva? I thought it very strange to find a Shaivite in that remote area of Tibet."

Leaning over to me she whispered, "She was a Bonpo master, but he doesn't know." Then in a louder voice, she continued, "This is how we met her. After Shankara had spent many months going over texts and giving advanced classes in Sanskrit, our hosts invited us to join them on a visit to a lake sacred to the Tibetans called Lhamo La-tso. They told us that when one peered into the lake, sometimes one could see the past or the future. They described the lake as a very special and most sacred place, so we eagerly accepted their offer. We traveled for two days, staying in tents along the way, and when we arrived early one morning I was struck by the beauty. The lake was a pure crystal blue pearl set low, embraced on all sides by mountains. The morning we arrived the weather was beautiful, with a clear sky that was reflected in the water, which at times appeared blue and at other times a beautiful shade of blue-green. I could feel the magic of the place. We were traveling with a group of four other people, and we all sat down to meditate by the side of the lake.

After a time, Shankara and I got up and decided to climb one of the hills abutting the lake. One of our hosts had opened his eyes and we told him of our intention. With much effort we managed to reach the top of the hill and stood there admiring the scenery, when the weather took a sudden turn. At the approach of threatening clouds, Shankara said we should return to our group, but before we could, high winds swirled around us and the sky released torrents of rain, making it impossible to see ahead. At that moment, seemingly out of nowhere, an elderly woman appeared and asked us to follow her. She led us down and through a mountain pass, where a tent was waiting. 'Stay inside the tent until the rain passes,' she advised us. We had no choice but to obey and were grateful for her assistance.

"I was anxious about our hosts, knowing they would worry when we didn't return, but the woman assured us that she would let them know that we were safe and would meet them in the morning. After a while, the rain stopped, but night was upon us and there was no way we would be able to find them in the dark. That evening, she stayed with us and told us many stories of Lord Shiva, which is why Shankara believes her to be a Shaivite." She paused and Shankara took over.

"She also told us there had been an ancient connection between the people of Tibet, which she called Böd, and the people of Gyagar, which is what they called Bharat, and that Mt. Kailash, which they called Mt. Tise, had been the center of their earliest societies, where the ancient masters had gathered and a few great ascetics still live. One of the stories she told us about Shiva goes like this:

"When humans were still in an early stage of development, some of the devatas, whom they call the lha, from various realms appeared on earth to mate with the humans and in this way advance their development. Before coming, they invoked Lord Shiva, asking him to manifest himself on earth to help with this process, but his radiance was so bright that he sought to shield the world from the intensity of his light. So, he entered the interior of Mt. Kailash and remained in meditation for eons, helping the advancement of life on earth. After they had fulfilled what they had come to do, the Iha departed, and a race of demons called the dud took over. Feeling the intense power emanating from Mt. Kailash, they sought to make that their base. Shiva knew that if he showed himself, the power of his energy would obliterate them, and this was not his intention. They had to be transformed into benevolent beings. The power of the dud grew until one day a high being called Tonpa Shenrab took birth. Shiva appeared to him and informed him of the *leela* (play) that was about to unfold.

"The most powerful of the demons was looking to engage in a battle so he could destroy Shenrab. To challenge him, this demon kidnapped Shenrab's beloved daughter and stole his beautiful horses, which he adored and which were also like his children. The demon knew of the power emanating from Mr. Kailash. Seeking to capture that power and make Kailash his base, the demon lured Shenrab to that sacred mountain where Lord Shiva was in deep meditation in the mountain's interior. Facing a large array of demons, Tonpa Shenrab engaged in one of the fiercest battles that had ever taken place on earth. Unlike the demons, Shenrab knew how to harness Shiva's power for the greater good, and Shiva knew that Shenrab was a man of great compassion who would not destroy any being. During the battle he was able to successfully transmute the dark destructive energy and transform the head demon into his disciple. Many great sages, men and women, rallied around

Shenrab and established a new culture and society with Kailash as its center. That is how the ancient religion of Bon was born.

"After telling us this story, the woman insisted that we must visit Mt. Tise. I explained that we had very much hoped to go, but that our hosts had called off the planned trip because of weather. She laughed and said that the changing weather was only Guru Rinpoche's play, and she would see to it that we traveled there safely. She directed us to a certain hermit living outside of Lhasa who, she said, was soon to embark on that journey.

"Looking at us intently, she then told us, 'You have come to the sacred lake hoping to see your past or your future. I will share with you what may be helpful.'" Shankara was quiet for a few moments before continuing. "Turning to me, she said, 'The hermit I speak of was your mentor in your past birth, someone very dear to you. He died in the attack on Nalanda, trying to save the monks and the sacred texts. You were a student at Nalanda at that time and witnessed the destruction. That is why the place is so important to you. A few of his former students have found him again, but he remains partially hidden in this life. You must go to him for his blessing.'

"Turning to Bhavani, she explained, 'That hermit was a great friend of your father in your past birth. Your father of that time funded many of the trips to Nalanda undertaken by the monks. He will be happy to see you again.' Then she added with a grin and a sparkle in her eye, 'It is very good, my dear, that you have accompanied your husband so that you may also receive the blessing of this very great ascetic.'"

Shankara paused and looked away, and I could see how moved he was while recounting this event. After several moments he returned to his narrative. "After talking to us for quite some time, she suddenly left the tent and told us to wait inside. It was quite dark by now, and we knew we would have to spend the night in the tent away from our hosts. A short time later she called us to come outside where we saw her preparing a meal for us. I have no idea where she got the food because there was nothing and nobody around. We were in a very deserted place. After we had finished eating, she told us to go inside and sleep. Two thick woolen blankets were laid out for us, but she remained out in the cold even though she was dressed in only a thin woolen jacket and wool skirt, and the high mountain air was bitter at night. When we awoke in the morning she was gone."

Shankara stopped speaking and for several minutes there was silence until I finally asked, "Is that the end of the story?"

Quickly glancing at Shankara, Bhavani replied, "No, not the end. I awoke in the middle of the night and decided to go outside to tell her to come into the tent because it was so cold. She had not told us her name and I wanted to remember her. After all, she had rescued us. Several times during the evening I had asked her name and each time she had replied, 'I have many names and no name at all.' "When I went outside, I found her seated in an immobile state, and even though the air was bitter cold, when I came near her a soothing warmth enveloped me. I sat down beside her and at that moment realized there was something extraordinary about this woman. With still closed eyes, she spoke to me, saying, 'Your love for this man has finally been fulfilled. It is a love you have sought through three births. Treasure it now.' Then opening her eyes and smiling at me, she continued, 'In your past birth, your grandmother was a Bonpo, a close friend of the grandmother of your current husband in his last birth. That is how the families came together, because of the friendship of those grandmothers. Now you are a devotee of Lord Shiva. There is a long and ancient association between these two traditions, both centered on the sacred mountain.'

"I was so touched by her that I again asked her name. The moon had just come out from behind the clouds and a stream of light was beaming down from it. It was a sliver of moon, like the one dressing Shiva's hair. Looking up at it, she let out a joyous laugh and replied, 'Call me whatever you like. There I sit, adorning his hair.' Turning her eyes to me, she said very lovingly, 'The greatest magic lies within, my dear. You will find it there. Don't seek it in the external world.' Then, as quickly as a streak of lightning, she rose and disappeared into the night. As she merged into the darkness, I saw a beautiful white bird rise and fly away, leaving me spellbound." Bhavani's voice became very quiet as she finished speaking, so that it was almost difficult to hear her, and her eyes assumed a dreamy look before closing. And once again, silence fell over the room.

After what felt like many minutes, Shankara broke the quiet by saying, "I did not experience that, but Bhavani did. She then came back into the tent and fell asleep again. When we awoke and found her gone, we began to wonder how to find our hosts. As we were debating what to do, we saw them ride up on their horses. I asked them how they had found us, and they replied that the day before a woman in a red hat had come to them and led them away from the lake as the rains started to pour down. She led them to a tent and stayed with them through the night, filling their ears with stories of Guru Rinpoche. She said she often finds him sporting in these parts and comes to join him. In fact, she had just seen him helping some travelers who had gotten lost. Our hosts said that she spoke to them well into the night and, assuring them that we were safe, told them where to find us. By morning, they said, she was gone.

"Didi," exclaimed Shankara, "isn't that one of the most extraordinary stories?"

I was speechless and couldn't respond. Then Bhavani said something that left me even more speechless, if that were possible. "That night when we were with her, at a certain moment she turned to Shankara and said, 'I have a message for the one you call Didi. Tell her to make peace with her brother. It is high time now, and he has suffered enough. After that, her anger will subside.' She asked me to write down the words so I wouldn't forget them," said Bhavani, "and I wrote them in my journal."

I was listening intently to Bhavani, and after a few moments I asked her to describe the woman. As she did, the image of the elderly woman who had appeared to me in dream but whose features I hadn't previously been able to recall, suddenly came into focus and I saw her very vividly. Immediately I knew her to be the same woman whom Shankara and Bhavani had met. The red hat was the giveaway. My heart began to beat rapidly, and I asked Bhavani when this all took place. After thinking for a moment, she told me the date, and it was around the time that I had had the dream. I was confounded. I looked away so that Bhavani and Shankara wouldn't see my confusion, and again wondered who this woman was and how she knew about my life.

Oblivious to my reaction, Shankara went on to speak about their trip to Mt. Kailash. As soon as they returned to Lhasa, their hosts introduced them to a Buddhist monk who then told them they could join a hermit living outside of Lhasa who was preparing to travel to Mt. Kailash. "Remembering the woman's words, we quickly agreed," continued Shankara. "We went immediately to find that hermit, who was about the age of my father. He was not a Buddhist monk, but lived like one, and there was an immediate connection between us. Along the way, he inquired a great deal about the rebuilding of Nalanda and about my spiritual life and told me that I must study less and meditate more." Shankara laughed. "I told him that it was not my nature to meditate, and he replied that I should make it my nature. He is a man I will never forget, and I will try to follow his advice."

"This hermit was also very attentive to me," mused Bhavani. "He told me stories about Parvati Ma, and I wondered how a man living in Tibet knew so much about her. He also revealed that many people believe that Palden Lhamo, the goddess of the lake we visited, is an emanation of Parvati. Palden Lhamo has a fierce form, perhaps more like Kali, but she is dearly loved by the Tibetans. The night we visited Lake Manasarovar near Kailash, I had a dream in which I felt the presence of Parvati Ma. It might have been because that hermit spoke of her so much to me. In the dream, I didn't see a form but experienced a vast loving presence, and I knew it was her. Perhaps it was due to the blessing of that mysterious Bonpo woman, I don't know. She is without doubt the most extraordinary person I have ever met, and the journey was well worth it if only to meet her."

After they had finished speaking, I sat thoughtfully for a while, then remarked, "I feel as if I went on that journey with you. Thank you for bringing me along."

"I felt you there with us, Didi," commented Bhavani. "You were very much in my thoughts, especially the time we spent at Lhamo La-tso with that Bonpo. When she mentioned the message for you, I felt as if you were seated there beside us. It was eerie, really. In fact, it didn't seem like she was speaking to us at all. She addressed what looked like empty space as if she were talking directly to you."

I turned my eyes down and didn't respond. For some reason I didn't feel like sharing my own experience of her, perhaps because I didn't fully understand it. "We don't know what to call her, do we?" I asked in a quiet voice.

"I call her Devi," replied Bhavani. "Although she appeared to us as an older woman, for a moment before she disappeared into the night, I thought I saw a most beautiful devi figure standing there, but perhaps it was my imagination. They say often the devis come in disguise, and I think perhaps that is what she is. At other times I think she is a Bonpo master like the ones I heard about in childhood."

"Why do you think only the Bonpos can perform supernatural feats?" intervened Shankara looking at Bhavani with a grin. "In any case, Tibet is a magical land for sure."

Our discussions continued over the next few days and then it was time for me to depart. Shankara and his family were returning to Nalanda, and he pleaded with me to come live with them. "The children have grown so fond of you, Didi. They will miss you if you don't come. Why return to the village? Amma is now in Patna with Pitaji, and so the house will feel empty. Please, come live with us."

Shankara seemed always to forget that I had another family. Despite his pleadings, I had made up my mind to return to the village, to Bhadra. "The Devi's message to me, Shankara, was to make peace with my brother, and that is what I intend to do. He and I have been at odds ever since I can remember, and I know that he needs me now. He has been carrying all the burdens of our family alone. I can't let him do that anymore." Reluctantly, he consented and said he would send me back with one of the servants.

The morning I was to leave Mathura, I walked one last time to the place of Krishna's birth, to the place where I, and perhaps I alone, saw that grand temple as if it hung in the ethers just beyond our sight. After I had finished praying, I began to walk back to the house when I heard my name being called. I recognized it immediately as the voice of Aamir. Hurrying over to me, he told me that he came every day in the hope of seeing me, but that I had stayed away, and he asked why. I told him I had been busy and that I was returning to my village that day. He asked when I would visit again, and I replied that I didn't know, although I was quite sure that this would be my last visit to Mathura. He pressed me again about marriage, and not wanting to offend him, I replied with a smile, "Aamir, you are such a kind and attractive man. Surely you can find a wife from within your community."

We came to the junction in the road where I told him that we had to part, as I had to head down the lane leading to the home where I was staying. We paused for a moment and then bidding him goodbye I began to walk, but I hadn't gone far when I heard him call after me in a loud and confident voice. "Devaki, I will marry you one day! You can be sure of that."

At an earlier time, his self-assuredness might have incited my anger, but now I found his persistence somewhat charming, after all no other man had pursued me like that. I had to admit there was something that drew me to him. Turning around, I smiled at him and waved, realizing there was no point in answering. I knew that his desire could never be fulfilled, at least not in this life. I strolled the remaining way with a glow on my face, acknowledging silently that I had come to like Aamir, but he was not of my community, not a devotee of either Krishna or Shiva, and as I always had said, I already had a husband, even though he was not here.

CHAPTER 40

The Question

Bhadra was surprised to see me. After so many months had passed, he had given up waiting for me and assumed I had gone to live with Shankara. Although I had promised to return to live with him, he had not believed me. When I announced that I would no longer go to the Banerjee house, he looked at me in disbelief and asked why. At first, I thought to explain that Panyaji would not return to the village but would stay in Patna; that Shankara's eldest brother was taking over management of the house, and that he and I had never quite gotten along. But then gazing at my brother, I suddenly changed my mind and told him that it was time for me to return to my family, to help him carry the burden that he had borne for so long.

At first Bhadra was doubtful, and even after several weeks had passed, he kept asking when I was leaving. But his tone, always edged with a touch of sarcasm, no longer annoyed me. Ever since my return, I felt very warmly toward him, and sometimes I would even affectionately take hold of his arm, something I had never done before. The first time I did so, he looked at me in surprise and asked, "What is this?"

"You know that despite our differences, you have always been dear to me, dearer than I realized when I was young and obstinate." That brought a smile to his face and I hugged his arm more tightly. After that he began to relax and accept that I would be a permanent fixture in our humble home.

I was now living full time in the two rooms in which my mother had lived, where I had grown up. Her presence was still tangible. After I had settled in, I thought often of my promise to her and wondered why it had taken me so long to fulfill it. Why had I made little or no effort over the years? It was something I couldn't do on my own, I realized. I needed the help of the Devi to lift me out of the hole I had dug for myself.

Most evenings, despite my objections, Bhadra would bring me food that his wife had cooked for the family. One evening, after delivering the food, he lingered in the doorway as if he wanted to say something. Instead of speaking, he stood there bashfully, almost like a schoolboy who had done something wrong and had come to apologize.

"What is it, Bhadra?" I asked, looking up at him from my seat on the floor. He didn't respond. I was about to tell him that I was tired and that he should go back to his wife, when he suddenly blurted out, "Devaki, I am sorry. I am sorry for whatever I have done to make you unhappy with me."

"Bhadra, that has all passed now. Both of us bear the blame, but let's not think of that anymore. You are my dearest brother and I will make up for all the time I was away." When I saw that he still hesitated in the doorway, I went over and taking hold of his arm laughingly asked, "Why has it taken us both until middle age to heal our hurts?" Until that moment, I had not realized how much our conflictual relationship had weighed on him. And I couldn't say for sure that I would have been able to reach this stage and fulfill the promise I had made to my mother had the Devi not come to me and lifted that festering burden from my heart.

Months passed. One night I awoke sometime between dark and dawn and felt my mother's presence as if she were seated beside me. Sitting up on the sleeping mat, I rested my head on my raised knees and remembered a story of hers, one she had told me years earlier that I hadn't paid much attention to because it didn't have any meaning then. Now it did. Recalling it was like hearing it for the first time.

"I had a most unusual experience when I was pregnant with you," she had told me. "I was seven months pregnant. Food was scarce, so I had to continue taking in laundry. Your father had wanted me to stop working, but we wouldn't have been able to survive. I would go down to the river with a basket of clothing, do the wash, and dry some of it there, then carry the load back home to distribute the next day. One day as I was leaning over to scrub the clothing, I must have twisted my back, and I could barely stand up. This sixth pregnancy was the most difficult one, since I was no longer young. Although your sisters often helped me, this day I was alone. Other women were there by the river, but they didn't notice my difficultly and I hesitated to draw attention to myself. I managed to stand up but, as soon as I lifted the load, a searing pain shot through my back. I waited a few minutes and then with difficulty I took a few steps. As I did, I heard someone call me from behind.

"Turning around I saw an elderly woman approaching. She said that she had come to help me carry the load of laundry. I had never seen her before and knew by her dress that she was not from our village or any of the neighboring ones. It was a hot day and she was wearing a woolen skirt and jacket and a strange hat, as if she had come from the high mountains. Seeing that she was elderly and a small woman, I politely declined, but she insisted. When I again refused, she asked me, 'Did you see Krishna here by the river today?' In a matter-of-fact tone, I replied, 'Of course. He is always here.' She smiled and said, 'It is he who has sent me to carry your load. Will you refuse him?'"

"As soon as she spoke those words, I handed her the load of laundry and sighed in relief. She gave me a walking stick she had been using and with the help of that stick I was able to manage the short distance home. When we arrived, only then did she set down the basket. Taking my hands in hers, she examined them, and I could see how touched she was by the sight of the raw and rough skin on my hands, which were red and irritated by the constant washing. There were even a few sores that had turned bloody. I was embarrassed and tried to pull my hands away, but she held them for a few moments. Before leaving, she put her hand on my protruding stomach and said, 'This daughter, you will bring to Krishna.' I asked her to come in so that I could serve her some food to show my gratitude, but she said that Krishna had already fed her. Chuckling, she hurried away. I never saw her again, and my hands were never chapped again. They remained smooth as sanded stone no matter how much washing I did, and I had no more back aches during that pregnancy. I often found myself wondering about that woman, who she was and where she had come from. I wondered how she had found me at a time when I was suffering, and how a woman, who was not from our region, had spoken so intimately about the Lord."

When my mother told me that story years earlier, I had dismissed it. There were so many people in the surrounding region who loved Sri Krishna, and I assumed she was merely a good-natured visitor from one of the mountain villages who saw my mother's struggles and took pity on her. But now that story assumed new meaning for me. Lifting my head, I sat up straight as the thought came to me that she might have been the same woman who had appeared to me in dream in Mathura, the same one who had appeared to Shankara and Bhavani by the sacred lake in Tibet. By my mother's description I could only conclude that it was her, but then it made no sense. How could she have appeared in our small village, and at the very time when my mother had been in desperate need? If she was that woman, that would mean that she appeared to Bhavani as a person of the Bon tradition, to Shankara as a Shaivite, to their Tibetan hosts as a Buddhist, and to my mother as a knower of Krishna. Was there a message in that, I wondered? Was she all of these, and if so, how could that be?

With these questions pursuing me, I felt a pressing desire to seek an answer from Panditji and Sulabha, whom I hadn't visited in many weeks. I had seen them just a few times since my return and only briefly, as my whole attention had been on trying to adjust to life with my brother and his family. It never occurred to me that anything would have changed with my Kashmiri friends, since we often make the misconstrued assumption that life stands still for us, however much evidence to the contrary we encounter. I had passed the age of forty and my friends were a decade or more older than I, but they had both been in good health, or so I thought.

When I reached the cottage, Panditji was seated outside reading. A broad smile broke across his face when he saw me, and he immediately rose to greet me, saying that Sulabha was inside sleeping. "Let's wait out here until she awakens," he said sitting down on the ground again. I seated myself beside him.

"She has not been well," he said quietly after a few moments of casual conversation. "In fact, she may not have many days left. I believe she may have been waiting to see you again before departing."

His words surprised me, and I asked, "Departing? Where to?" Noticing his serious expression, I stared at him, unable to accept what he was implying and mumbled, "She was fine when I was here last."

"She was not so fine," he replied calmly. "These last months have been difficult for her, and her life force is slowly ebbing away. She is hardly able to eat anything. Perhaps seeing you will awaken her will to live a little bit longer. Now tell me, have you made peace with that brother of yours?"

I nodded. I had not told him before about the Devi who had come to me in dream, or about her meeting with Shankara. Now I told him those stories as well as my mother's experience with her. "She seems to appear to each one of us when we are in need, but who is she truly," I mused.

Panditji didn't respond right away but then explained, "That experience you had in the mountains, that vision, we told you that what you had a glimpse of was Shiva. Someone else might have called that Krishna, and the Buddhists would have another name for that primordial consciousness. There are many names, Devaki, but the experience is one. That was her message to you. The devatas and masters know how to speak to each person according to their temperament and ability to understand. There is great diversity among people and that is why there are different religions, but there is only one truth, one ultimate reality."

As he spoke, Aamir came into my mind, and I wondered if this was true of his religion as well. Panditji seemed to pick up on my thoughts and he asked, "Have you thought any more of that man Aamir, the one who wants to marry you?" I shook my head, unable to admit that every now and then I did think of him.

"Leave him to the future," he said. "For now, you have ended your troubles with Bhadra. That is a big accomplishment."

"But what was the cause of our conflict, Panditji? I could never understand why I resented him so."

Panditji laughed and replied, "There is no point in digging into the past or trying to envision the future. It is enough to tend to that which confronts you today, Devaki."

My mind then turned to Sulabha and I asked in a concerned tone, "Is she really that ill?"

He nodded. I wondered why he didn't seem shaken, and he responded to my unspoken thought by saying, "I am very grateful for the life we have had together. For me, something has also been completed. She has healed me of my past and I have been blessed with a woman more spiritually aware than I am."

"But she is leaving you now," I replied sadly.

"There is no leaving, Devaki. You must rid yourself of that notion. It is simply a change of costumes." His voice trailed off and I heard Sulabha call to him. Panditji immediately rose and entered the cottage, as did I.

Sulabha was sitting up on a low bed and as soon as she heard me greet her, her face brightened. But my face paled when I saw her thin, frail form, much deteriorated from a few weeks earlier.

"Devaki, help me get up." I went over to her and helped her stand and take a few steps to the low seat by the table. "I am glad you have come. I was hoping you would," she said in a weak voice, after I had helped her lower herself onto the seat.

Trying to mask my dismay over her condition, I pretended that nothing was amiss and repeated to her the stories of the Devi that I had told Panditji. I ended by saying, "I cannot help but wonder who she is and why she came to me in a dream when I have never met her."

Sulabha smiled and said she would tell me a story of her guruji. "Soon after we had first met her and gone to stay with her in the mountains, she stared at me one day and asked in a most serious tone, 'Who are you?' even though I had introduced myself days earlier. Thinking she was a bit forgetful, I stated my name again, but she shook her head. Then I mentioned my family background and where I come from, and she shook her head again. I told her of my spiritual practice and went on and on describing all the many aspects of who I thought I was, but she continued to shake her head. I was perplexed. Every time I would come before her, she would ask me the same question. Panditji seemed to be amused by this exchange and watched the whole interaction as it unfolded over several days.

"Finally, she said to me, 'Clearly, you don't know who you are. Go find out.' She sent me into a tiny hut in a pine forest not far from her and told me not to emerge until I had discovered who I am. She said food would be provided each day. I went into that hut and stayed as the weeks turned into months. A year passed. During that time, I saw many of my past births, until I found the one where I had sought to be her chela during the time of Sita Ma when she was with her guru, Sage Maitreyi. That was a beautiful remembrance, and I recalled that her guru had asked her the same question, sending her off for a lifetime of retreat until she had found the answer. After this memory returned to me, I had a dream/vision, much like the one you had, Devaki, when we were at my guruji's hut for Shivaratri. In that vision I dissolved into the whole and experienced the most intensive explosion of joy and bliss. That was my experience of Shiva, but it didn't last. When I came back to my normal consciousness, I was myself again, Sulabha, but I didn't want this identity anymore. I wanted to be that, not this," she said as she pointed to her body. "Unlike you, I did not experience fear or resistance. I wanted to live in that sublime consciousness all the time, but I didn't know how to achieve it again.

"Soon after, my guruji came to me. I looked at her sadly and said, 'Guruji, I still don't know who I am.' Then I recited all the names I had had in the lives I had remembered, the many births, but I knew that none of those were my true identity. I was no longer that one personality or the other one, and I didn't any longer identify with Sulabha, so who was I? She looked at me compassionately and told me it was time to come out of the hut. I wondered why when I hadn't yet discovered who I was, but she explained, 'You briefly experienced your true Self but didn't realize that is who you are. Meditate on that which you perceived. It doesn't matter when you attain the full realization as long as you keep asking the question. This will guarantee that one day you will know.'

"Before she left her body, my guruji called me to her and asked me again, 'Who are you?' This time, I looked at her and smiled, but I didn't respond because I had no name for that which I am. She chuckled and told me to keep meditating. Now, Devaki, how does this relate to you? You want to know who that woman in your dream is. First find out who you are, and then you will know she is."

"Who I am?" I murmured.

"There is no other question to ask," added Panditji. "One must ask again and again and again, until one knows."

"Perhaps I don't need to know the answer," I mused. "Perhaps I am comfortable just being Devaki, happy the way I am."

"Are you?" he looked at me with a strange gaze. "Then you will keep returning with different personalities and bodies to keep searching, going through the rounds of birth and death, joy and pain, all the polarities. That is okay. We each progress at our own speed, in our own time, one that we ourselves determine. Most people are content as they are and seek no further, but one day each person must ask, what is this life about and who am I truly?"

"To know the answer to that question is our purpose and yours, Devaki," Sulabha replied tenderly. "You would not have come to us were you not traveling the same road."

I looked at these two dear friends and smiled, realizing what a gift their friendship was. Their words struck a deep chord and could not easily be dismissed because, on a profound level, I knew them to be true.

Panditji urged me to spend the night with them, but I felt pressure to return to Bhadra. Realizing the fragility of Sulabha's condition, I said I would return the next day if I could. Panditji began to protest but Sulabha intervened, saying the most important thing for me right now was to assure my brother of my care for him. Hugging me as tightly as she was able, she whispered into my ear, "You and I will meet again." Hugging her thin frame, I helped her walk back to her bed and took one last glance into those eyes whose vision had dimmed to the outer world, as I assured her that I would return the next day.

When I reached home, Bhadra seemed surprised to see me. "You've returned from your brahmin friends. I thought you might spend the night," he commented.

"I am going nowhere, Bhadra. I am here with you," I replied with a smile. I knew my friend was slipping away, and I couldn't help but sink into a deep sadness that night. After my father's death, I had felt keenly the absence of Shiva in my life, but Sulabha and Panditji had restored him to me, making me feel whole again, as I had during childhood when in my home there were daily stories and continual prayers to both Krishna and Shiva, my two mahadevas. I wanted to maintain this connection to both and resolved to do so.

The next morning, I went around to Bhadra's part of the hut and told him that I would return to Panditji's to check on them. When he didn't reply, I told him that my friend Sulabha was dying. "I don't know how many more days she has left," I said quietly. With a relaxed expression he asked if he should walk me there. I shook my head, and he told me to go then and to stay as long as need be.

I quickly made my way to the cottage. When I arrived, Panditji was seated outside in meditation. As I reached for the cottage door I heard him say, "She is not there. She has already left." I stood frozen at the entrance. Rising from his seat on the ground, he looked at me with the faintest smile and said, "She left in the night while in meditation, as she had hoped to do. It was a peaceful departure. Her last words were, 'Guruji, you have come.'"

I didn't answer but turned to gaze at him. Seeing the sadness on my face, he put his arm around me. "You will never see her again," I murmured.

"Never? There is no such thing," he replied quietly. "I will see her quite soon."

I didn't understand his words as my mind was too distressed. For me, her death meant not seeing her loving face, not hearing her wise counsel or her joyous laugh, not listening to her stories of Lord Shiva or her guruji. For me, it was a great loss, the end of something very precious.

"In every loss there is gain," Panditji said quietly. "When something or someone is taken, something or someone else is given. One has only to look closely to recognize what is given. You will not be left alone, Devaki, I guarantee that. You have never been alone. Didn't you tell me that your mother once had told you to take Krishna as your husband. Take him now as your friend and speak with him as you have spoken with Sulabha and me."

I looked up into his face. This had always been the counsel given to me, but how to do it? That had never been explained.

CHAPTER 41

The Making of a Vow

Panditji did not remain long in the cottage after Sulabha's death. A few weeks later he was also gone, returning to Kashmir to transfer their properties and tie up all their worldly affairs. On that last day, I stood before him with tears in my eyes, while he looked at me fondly and said, "We have had good times, Devaki, and have grown dear to one another. Our common friend has been watching from afar and is very pleased. I have looked after you on his account." I didn't know which friend he was referring to, but it didn't matter. He was leaving me, and that was all I understood. Seeing that his words brought me no comfort, he reminded me of what he had said after Sulabha's death, "Remember, when something or someone is taken, something or someone else is given." I tried to smile but could not.

As always, Panditji's words held true. Once he had departed, leaving me with an aching hollow inside, my attention was forced to focus on an emergency that had arisen in my family. My deceased eldest sister Lalita had several children, one of whom, a daughter, had died a few years earlier, leaving a four-year girl. This daughter's husband had remarried and now had a young child with the new wife leaving my sister's granddaughter very much alone and often mistreated. My two brothers were discussing the matter. Even my sister Uma had come from her village to see what could be done. Lalita's other children were in no position to take this little girl, named Sarita, whom I had met on several occasions and for whom I had developed quite a bit of affection. As I listened to them discuss the matter, something impelled me to offer to have her come live with me in my mother's hut. I had never been close with Lalita, but I felt that by taking in her grandchild I could make up to this eldest sister for my years of neglect or indifference. All eyes turned to me when I made this offer, as I was so often judged as being inattentive to the family.

"You take her?" asked Bhadra in amazement. I nodded. "Devaki, you have never raised a child. You don't know the effort involved."

"That is not true," I replied defensively. "Don't forget, I raised Shankara and have cared for his children."

He was thoughtful for a few minutes, as both Keshav and Uma inserted that this was a perfect solution. Sarita, now seven years old, could come live with me in my mother's hut. Funds were scarce as Bhadra and Keshav, who for so long had supported the extended family, were now in their elder years. It was their sons who were working to support them and me as well, laboring long hours on plots of land they had leased.

"It is settled then," I said, ending the conversation. I was pleased, because the few times that I had seen Sarita, she had been very drawn to me, even physically affectionate, asking if she could call me *Dadi* (grandmother). My sister Lalita had been the prettiest of my mother's daughters, and like her, this granddaughter was an attractive girl with a sweet disposition, but the neglect was beginning to show. Since her mother's death, her clothes were rarely washed, her hair untidy and her appearance, once adorable, was often now disheveled. It had weighed on my heart to see my sister's granddaughter descend into this condition, and I was relieved that I could do something about it.

Little did I know that among all my mother's grandchildren and great-grandchildren, she was the most like her, with a strong attraction to Krishna. Once she arrived at the hut and saw my mother's murti of Krishna, her whole face lit up. I thought she would be sad to leave her father and the only home she had known, but she seemed delighted to live with me in her new home. Bhadra had a grandson about her age and they soon became fast friends. It was an easy transition for me from living a somewhat solitary life to having a child to look after.

Each night before bed, Sarita would ask for a story about Krishna, and I would narrate all the tales I had heard from my mother. After I had told her those stories many times, I began to make up new ones. When she had been living with me for nearly a year, she said one day with a small laugh, "I feel that Krishna is living with us here, and that is why I am so happy to be with you, Dadi." This caught me off guard as they reminded me of Panditji's last words: "When something or someone is taken, something or someone else is given." I knew that Sarita was that someone else. I had always felt that I had received so much more from Sulabha and Panditji than I had been able to give to them, and now I had an opportunity to give what little I had to this young girl and make her life better. It brought much fulfillment, filling the emptiness I had felt when my dear Kashmiri friends departed.

About a year after Panditji had left his cottage to return home, a man from Kashmir appeared at my door and handed me a rather large, tightly wrapped box. Introducing himself as a servant of Panditji's family, he told me that before he died, my dear friend had instructed him to hand deliver this package to me. He had traveled all the way for this purpose.

"Panditji died?" I asked in dismay. I couldn't say that I was surprised because he had indicated as much, but somehow the world felt darker without his presence in it. Inviting the man in for a cup of tea, I inquired into the details of Panditji's passing and asked him about his relationship with my dear friend.

He told me that his family had been long time servants of Panditji's family for many generations, and he went on to speak of their prominent position in Kashmiri society. "They had no children," he explained, "and so their wealth and possessions have been distributed to family and society, as he wanted, except for this box, which he expressly said was for you."

"I had no idea of their status! They had always presented themselves so humbly," I exclaimed, never considering that my friends had been people of means. "What is in the box?" I asked.

He smiled. "Panditji never told me. He mentioned that you would know what to do with it. He also left you a letter." As he held out the letter to me, I had to admit bashfully that I couldn't read, but fortunately, this servant was able to read it to me. In the note, Panditji asked me to accept the gift as coming from the husband whom I always said was not here. "He is here," the letter said, "only you cannot see him, at least not yet. I have been looking after you on his behalf." I smiled as I listened to Panditji's words. He was the only one, aside from my mother, who took me seriously when I said I had a husband who wasn't here.

"You traveled all this way to give me this precious gift," I remarked, deeply touched by this messenger's devotion.

"My family owes a great deal to Panditji. There is nothing I would not do for him."

I didn't open the box until the man had departed, and when I did, I was left speechless. The box was filled with pouches of gold and silver coins. With trembling hands, I immediately carried the box to Bhadra and presented it to him.

"What is this?" he asked as I handed him the box.

"My friend Panditji has left this for us upon his death. Open it."

Bhadra's eyes shot wide open when he unwrapped the package and saw what was inside, and he looked at me in bewilderment, unable to utter a word.

"I have no need for this, Bhadra, and so I am passing it on to you. Do whatever you think fit with these coins. But one thing I know for sure, it will make life easier for you and Keshav now, and it will allow us to provide dowries for all the girls in the family and to make sure everyone has enough to eat."

"We can't keep this," he said when he had found his voice.

"What should we do with it then?" I asked, looking at him questioningly. "My friend has died." Since a young age, I had the feeling that money and all the things it could buy were not for me in this life. When I went to the Banerjee home and Amma refused any payment, this feeling was confirmed. Wealth was not to be my companion.

"It must be distributed to those in need," he replied slowly. "There are so many in our community with not enough food and medicine."

"I leave that in your hands," I said. "Do whatever you think is best, Bhadra. I trust you to make the right decisions." As I said this, I looked directly into his eyes to show my sincerity. Since that evening when Bhadra had stood in the doorway and we had both apologized to one another, an unspoken bond had developed between us, a complete healing of whatever had hampered our relationship. I didn't know quite why I was handing over to my brother the treasure I had received; it was an almost instinctive act. Little did I realize then that by generously dispersing the funds, Bhadra would negate some of his negative actions from the past and at the same time help set his future course. As I was to later learn, in his past he had taken from others; now he could return what he had taken.

As I was about to leave, I hesitated in the doorway and turning around said to him, "I will take one coin as a keepsake, a reminder of my dear friend." Before leaving for Kashmir, Panditji had given me the floral head covering that Sulabha had often worn and so I had something to remember her by, but I had nothing from him. This coin would serve that purpose. From then on, I would always carry that coin with me, often tucking it away in my clothing. It was my way of keeping Panditji with me.

Shankara and Bhavani visited several times a year. His mother had died soon after Sarita had come to live with me. I had said my goodbyes to Panyaji when she had left the village to spend her last days with her husband in Patna, and her death came as no surprise. For years, her health had been declining; yet it was another departure of a dear one. Since Shankara was not close with his brothers, and his father was very elderly, he clung to me as his dearest relative. Instead of us meeting at the Banerjee home, he and Bhavani would visit me at my mother's hut. We would walk into the nearby forest and spend hours exchanging details of our lives. Sometimes they would bring their children, who would play with Sarita.

Several years after Panditji's departure, Shankara and Bhavani were visiting when I noticed that Shankara was in a particularly somber mood, and Bhavani was trying to cheer him up. We were sitting in the forest, with Sarita quietly listening to our conversation. After asking Shankara several times why he was so serious and quiet, he finally informed me that the Somnath Temple had once again been attacked. "Alauddin Khalji's army sacked the temple (1299)," he replied solemnly. "They defeated the Vaghela King Karna, and that kingdom may now be gone, occupied by the Sultanate. It is the same story, Devaki, that we have heard again and again. Hundreds of towns have been destroyed, thousands massacred, and many temples and palaces looted and brought to ruin. Dwarka, the region where Krishna once lived, is now under Muslim rule."

"What happened to Somnath?" I asked in dismay. I knew that it had already once been destroyed and then rebuilt.

"I heard that two Vajra warriors stood in the doorway trying to defend it, but they were killed and then the temple was demolished. The wealth was looted and the main murti taken to Delhi where it was destroyed. The fragments were scattered on the ground in front of the mosque for people to step on when they enter the mosque." His voice was bitter.

"Somnath destroyed again," I murmured. "Why so much death and destruction? Do they hate us so much? What have we ever done to them?"

"There is no rationale, Devaki. When man is consumed by greed, he abandons all value for life."

Bhavani had been quiet this whole time, but now she interjected in a firm tone, "For every temple destroyed, a new one will be built, because they can't destroy the temple of our hearts. Somnath exists inside of us, and I have no doubt that its physical expression will come again. If our devatas live in our hearts, they can never conquer us. We must build our resolve. That is the only way we will survive this onslaught. Khalji came with a massive army, but armies can only destroy stone and brick, not our devotion. Shiva is untouched. Krishna is untouched. That which is divine can never be destroyed. We must not forget that."

I had never heard Bhavani speak so forcefully and I looked at her in gratitude. Her words awakened in me the same defiance I had felt during my first visit to Mathura when I realized that the grand temple I had seen in vision had been destroyed. Panditji had consoled me with words similar to those she had just spoken—to nurture the temple inside. Only then will the external temple be rebuilt.

In a gentler voice she turned to Shankara and said, "I know that you can never forget what happened to Nalanda and you are seeing history repeat itself, but one day there will be an end to this destruction and a grand revival and rebuilding will take place. It must."

"It is the feeling of being helpless in the face of such evil, Bhavani, which has pained me. It is strange, but I am remembering the words that the Tibetan hermit told me while on the journey to Kailash. He said that in the future my dharma will lead me to study and excel in military strategy. Those words made no sense to me then, but perhaps that is something I must pursue. Perhaps we have been weak in this regard and that is why we are being defeated."

"You, study military strategy?" I exclaimed. "Shankara, you are a scholar, not a kshatriya."

"He was looking into the far future, Shankara, not this life. That was clear," inserted Bhavani. "He also said the Yuan Dynasty (China) would fall and another would rise. I am certain he was not speaking of this lifetime."

"Perhaps you are right, but the desire has been stirred in me. Our defenses are poor. Our kingdoms are not united. All depends on the Rajputs now."

"The Rajputs, why them?" I asked.

"They are fierce kshatriya and have the will and means to defend their land. Only they can prevent the Delhi Sultanate from conquering more and more of Bharat."

This conversation stirred within me a strong resistance, something I thought I had settled years earlier after my experience in Mathura. Later that night, as I was putting Sarita to bed, she asked if I was sad about the destruction of the temple. Nodding, I told her that the temple was very dear to her *mahaan daada* (great-grandfather). Sitting up on her sleeping mat, she looked at me with lit eyes and said decidedly, "Then he will be reborn there and help rebuild the temple, won't he?"

"I hadn't thought of that, Sarita, but I think you are right. Wherever he is, I am sure he will want to be born again to help rebuild that temple which meant so much to him. Did you hear everything that Shankara and Bhavani spoke about?" She nodded, and I felt sorry that Sarita had heard so much. Shankara had vividly described the destruction, the massacres, and the fate of our beloved murtis. How would this information affect this young girl who lived such an innocent life?

As she lay back down again and turned over, I heard her whisper, "Dadi, I want to learn to read and write."

"Why is that, Sarita?" I asked softly. Nobody in my family had ever thought to ask this before.

"I will be able to do more then," she whispered. Smiling, I replied that I would ask Shankara to find a teacher for her, but I doubt that she heard me because she was already asleep.

I couldn't sleep at all that night. My ruffled mind reviewed again and again the plight of our temples and the people who simply wanted to pray to their devas. What could a poor village woman like me do to reverse the fate of our land and culture? We were all helpless in the face of such an onslaught. I couldn't understand what *karma*, what collective past actions, had led to this. Getting up before dawn, I walked the short distance to the river and tried to make sense of it. Often in the early morning I went to the well to fetch water before Sarita awoke, so I knew she wouldn't be frightened if she didn't see me when she got up.

As I sat before the river in the awakening light, I thought of my father and wondered if he knew about the fate of the Somnath Temple in whatever world he might now be inhabiting. He would not be angry, that much I knew. Rather, he would pray for those who had undertaken such misguided and unholy actions, actions that would surely someday rebound. But I did not have his wisdom and took the destruction very personally, as an attack on my father himself. Trampling on the broken murti of Lord Shiva was the same as trampling on my father. How many more people like him would suffer because of that destruction? How many people had lost their lives trying to protect their right to worship the deva they loved? The grand temple to Krishna in Mathura was destroyed before my time, but this destruction was taking place now, in my time, while I was alive. I was here living through it and could do nothing. I was not angry, as anger had departed from me as soon as Bhadra and I had reconciled, but a deep, deep sadness and a feeling of total helplessness swept over me. It was as if all I loved was under attack and I had no means of defense. I sat there for some time until gradually a determination arose within me, a resolve that in the future, a future I could not now know, I would not allow myself to be so helpless. I would be born in a place and into conditions where I could do something about it, no matter the sacrifice entailed, and I made this resolve, this vow, in the name of Krishna.

As I sat there staring into the river, I heard Sarita's voice calling out to me. Turning around, I saw her small body running to me. She had had a nightmare and, not finding me when she awoke, became frightened and was looking all over for me. Quickly I rose and took her in my arms to calm her. "It is alright, Sarita, I am here with you." As I had suspected, hearing about the massacres had scared her. "We are far away from all that destruction. Here, nobody can harm you." Taking her hand, I told her with a smile, "Let us make a vow together, you and I, that nobody will ever touch the Krishna or the Shiva who lives in our heart." This brought a smile to her face and she nodded.

That day, in the early morning hours before the busyness of village life got underway, a determination was made. I didn't know how it would manifest in the future, but I believed without a doubt that it would.

CHAPTER 42

When the Past Becomes the Future

With his newfound ability to help our community, Bhadra was a reborn man. He never revealed to others, except the close family, that he had access to such a large amount of funds, but people in need knew to come to him, and he gave generously for the distribution of food and medicine and to meet other needs. I was so happy to see the change that had come over him and proud to see this charitable side of his character, which served to ease his anger toward those whom he deemed more privileged. Our closeness became a source of comfort, as he confided in me everything he did with the money, often asking my advice. I knew that whatever from our past had led to the tension between us was now fully resolved, and this brought me much peace.

A rare disagreement between us arose over my insistence that Sarita learn to read and write, as she had requested. Shankara found a teacher for her who would meet her at the temple every morning. At first Bhadra protested, saying it would be difficult for her to fit in with our community if she acquired these unnecessary skills, but I knew that her future would not be in our community. I had already asked Shankara to bring her to Patna when she grew a little older and to help arrange a marriage for her, if that was her desire, and he had agreed. After a few respectful discussions, Bhadra yielded. "You have taken responsibility for her, and so her future is for the two of you to determine," he finally affirmed with a smile one day. How my brother had changed! I wondered if it was due to the respect he was afforded by the community or to my return to the household, or perhaps both.

The years passed. Several times Sarita's father tried to bring her back to his family, but he now had several children with the second wife, and Bhadra and I knew they only wanted her so that she could take care of the young ones and perform household tasks, and we resisted. When I asked her if she wanted to go back to her father, she shook her head vehemently and replied, "This is where Krishna lives, and I want to live here with him."

"How do you know he lives here?" I asked with a smile.

"Because I see him." This young girl continued to surprise me in her similarity to my mother. She had a maturity about her that made me wonder who was the adult and who the child. If days went by without me mentioning the name of Bhagavan (the Lord), she would say something that would bring my mind back to him. In many subtle ways she kept reminding me, much like my mother had done.

As I grew older and the aches and discomfort of age began to pursue me, I was determined to get her settled before my death. Shankara was dividing his time between Patna and Nalanda and agreed to have Sarita live with Bhavani and him until he could find a suitable marriage. Bhadra, much weakened by age, did not object, but Sarita was loathe to leave me.

"I would go with you if I could," I said to her one morning. "But . . ."

"I know, you cannot leave the family. I know that, Dadi. And I want to go to Patna . . ." Still, she vacillated.

"You will bring Krishna with you wherever you go," I said to her on another occasion.

"I know," she affirmed. Another year was to pass before she finally left the village for the city at the age of seventeen, and I was glad for the new opportunities that awaited her.

Another year passed. I had gotten adjusted to living alone again, although my life was hardly solitary as Bhadra's part of the home was always bustling with activity. But I could come and go as I pleased and retreat to the corner where my mother's murti and my father's lingam still stood.

It was a hot sultry day in the pre-monsoon season when I went to the village well to get a bucket of water. Of late, Bhadra's daughter-in-law had been drawing water for me, but I wanted to get some air and walk around. The day had advanced and not many people were out in the heat. After drawing water from the well, I began to slowly make my way home. As I passed through an area of the road that was deserted, I saw a man who looked to be an ascetic walking toward me from the opposite direction, performing strange antics. I didn't think much of it and kept walking. As he came closer, I could see that his unusual behavior was due to a severe limp, and a wave of pity came over me. He suddenly stopped right in front of me, and I had no choice but to halt. For a moment he stared at me and then asked for a drink of water. The cloth wrapped around him was very worn and torn in parts, so I assumed he was a poor wandering ascetic. Without thinking I filled the cup that I was carrying with water from the bucket and handed it to him. Then something impelled me to look at him more closely, and I thought this poor, strange man might not have eaten that day and might not know where to get food. I had never seen him before and knew he wasn't from our village. Instinctively, I took out the gold coin that had come from Panditji, which I always kept tucked in my skirt, and handed it to him, saying, "Buy some food with this," and I pointed in the direction of the market.

Taking the coin, he smiled and replied as he folded his hands in pranam. "Thank you, *Rani* (queen). I will remember your kindness."

Chuckling, I told him that I was no rani and that my name was Devaki Dhobi, that the coin had been a gift from a dear friend but that he had more need of it than I. "I live ahead in that hut in the distance," I said pointing in the direction of the hut. I wanted to clarify that even though I had a precious gold coin, I was not a woman of means.

"I have been searching for the Rani, knowing that the one who gives me a gold coin will be her," he replied with a broad smile as he stood up straight. "She will need my assistance in the future."

Chuckling again, I replied, "Swamiji, you are mistaking me for someone else." Surely, I thought, either this man is not in his right mind, which seemed very likely, or he had a vision problem. Anyone could tell by my appearance that I was a common village woman.

He laughed, "Why see only what appears today? The future is already here. The destruction of temples, who can stop that but the Rani herself? You have made that vow, have you not?" As he spoke those words, an ominous feeling came over me, and I looked at him a bit fearfully, wondering if I had done something to set in motion an untoward event that I would later regret. Touching my head in blessing, he added quietly, "Do you think Bhagavan does not see and hear? Know that I will be there to help you." Then quickly turning, he walked away at great speed with no limp at all, leaving me to stare after him and wonder at what had just transpired.

The brief interaction unsettled me, and as I continued walking, I wondered if the man was mocking me for the vow I made at the river not long ago. But how could he have known of that vow? There had been nobody nearby that morning and I had made the resolve silently. When I arrived home, I absentmindedly went about preparing some food, but the image of that strange man kept popping into my mind. That evening when I went to take off my clothing, the gold coin that I gave him fell to the floor. I picked it up in amazement and stared at it, going over again in my mind everything that I had done and said to that ascetic; I had given him water and handed him the coin, and he had taken it. I had no doubt that I had given the coin to him, and he had not given it back. So how did this coin now appear in my clothing, in the same place where I always kept it? Did I imagine that I had given him the coin? I was becoming increasingly forgetful these days. I was aware of that and was doing my best to hide it from the family. The thought that I might have imagined the whole exchange made me fear that my mind was becoming foggier than I wanted to admit.

A few days later, I began to experience extreme fatigue. In the mornings, I could hardly pull myself off my sleeping mat and going into the village was now out of the question. I could barely get myself around the hut to take care of my daily needs, never mind walking anywhere beyond. Bhadra noticed my tired state and several times mentioned it to me, giving me medicine to enhance my strength, but I brushed off my condition, assuring him that it would pass. I had always been healthy. In the past, his daughter-in-law often cooked for me, but now she began to supply all my meals and water. As the days flew by, I waited for the fatigue to pass, but it didn't.

Shankara surprised me with a visit one day. A week earlier Sarita had awakened in the morning and insisted she had to see me; nothing could dissuade her. The two of them had taken horses and come to the village as quickly as they could, straight to my hut. When he saw me, I could tell by his expression that he was shocked to see the change that had come over me. I was hardly eating, and I assumed that I must have looked drawn and worn, but I hurried to assure him that I was okay, only in need of rest. He insisted on calling his family doctor, who came and told me it was my heart, but I tried to make light of it.

"A few weeks ago, I was carrying a bucket of water from the well in extreme heat," I told him with a smile. "Perhaps I wore myself out." Changing the subject, I asked about Sarita's upcoming wedding. I knew that she and the son of a shopkeeper in Patna had fallen in love, and that Shankara had arranged the marriage. As he began to explain that he and Bhavani were preparing the dowry, I interrupted him, knowing that Bhadra with his pride would never allow this.

"There is no need, Shankara," I told him. "For some reason that I can't understand, when he died, Panditji left funds for the family." I told Sarita to go spend time with her cousins and to send Bhadra to me. When Bhadra entered my part of the hut, I told him about the need for a dowry. I knew that he would insist on providing one for the granddaughter of a sister he so cherished.

Shankara and Sarita spent a week in the village before returning to Patna, with Sarita sleeping beside me, and Shankara staying at his family's home. I realized that the time alone with Sarita was precious as she was soon to be married, and I made a point of saying to her all that I wanted to say, giving her whatever counsel I could for her future. With Shankara, it was more difficult to express my feelings; my relationship with him was long and deep.

The rains had come, providing a good excuse for us not to take our usual walk to the forest. I didn't want Shankara to know that I never left the hut anymore. As he was sitting beside me on a monsoon drenched morning, I suddenly blurted out, "Shankara, what I cared about most . . . ," I paused for a moment to calm my swirling emotions and then continued, "was to see to your marriage with Bhavani and to make possible her trip with you to Tibet. I am happy that I could do that for you."

Hearing the deep feeling in my voice, he didn't answer right away, but then he replied, "You have done all of that for me, Didi, and more but what have I been able to do for you?"

"What are you talking about, Shankara? You have always looked after my welfare. In addition, you brought me to Brindavan and Mathura, something I could never have done on my own. And you will look after Sarita for me, I know that. You have given me your friendship. Nothing has been more precious to me."

"Didi, if you had allowed me, I would have looked after you better. Even now, I beg you to come home to Patna with me where your life will be easier. Bhavani and I miss you, and so do the children."

I smiled at him and didn't reply. He knew I would never leave the village, and in my condition, I was no longer able to go anywhere. I looked at my friend fondly, his hair now sprayed with hints of grey, but he was the same Shankara. He was more than a friend really, more than a brother even. I felt as if we had come into this world knowing each other and would find each other again, even though our situations might be vastly different. Somehow, we would find one another.

Before they left to return to the city, I took Sarita aside and gave her the wedding gift I had planned for her, my mother's murti of Krishna. "If my mother were alive, she would want you to have this."

She hesitated, "Dadi, it belongs here with you."

I shook my head. "Not anymore," I told her. I also took out the gold coin from my clothing and handed it to her. This is not to spend, but to keep with you always as a reminder to be steady in your devotion. It was given to me by a dear friend before he died, and it has seen me through some difficult times. The murti is from your *dadi ma* (great-grandmother). This coin is from me."

Their visit did much to cheer me up and by the time they left I had regained some of my strength, but it still felt like a goodbye, and my strength didn't last long. Soon after, I was confined to bed, only rising for the meager meals I was able to take. My aged brother was much worried about me and came throughout the day to check on me. I found myself telling him what to do with the hut after . . . I didn't say after what, but he knew what I meant and kept telling me that I would recover. After all, he would say, he was quite a bit older than me and should be the one to go first. I would look at my bent over brother who now used a walking stick and smile.

I had kept my mother's hut exactly as she had left it, and I knew that Bhadra would do the same. Neither of us wanted to disturb her memory. Once I was gone, he and his wife would move into my part of the hut where she had lived, leaving the rest to his eldest son and his family, who had been living with them. Almost unaware, I found myself thinking this way, planning for how it should be when I departed.

I smiled to think that Bhadra would now live with our father's lingam, which had such a powerful presence. So many times, I tried to get him to sit before the lingam, but he always resisted, saying that he didn't trust anything otherworldly, that he was afraid of being deceived. I always wondered what he meant by that. The Devi had said something about wounds from the past and that he had suffered enough. He had been born to such devoted parents and yet he had blocked out everything to do with religion. What he cared most about was the suffering of those in his family and community, and I respected him greatly for that.

In the weeks after Shankara left, I felt myself preparing to depart and I didn't cling to anything. Death came slowly, bit by bit taking away what was left of my identity. One morning I awoke and didn't know where I was. It was only when I sat up and really looked around that I remembered I was living in my mother's hut. A few days later I woke up and couldn't remember my name, but it wasn't a frightening experience at all. In fact, it was rather freeing. I had to chuckle when I recalled that I was Devaki. Then I remembered the words of a friend, whose name I had forgotten, when she asked me who I was. She had startled me with that question. I had thought I was Devaki Dhobi, but I wasn't so sure anymore. My days were now spent in silence as I lingered between life and death, and then one evening as I was sleeping, gently and ever so quietly, with no clinging to anyone or anything, I left behind the body I had been inhabiting.

Each death is different from the ones before, but there are certain experiences that are the same—a review of the highlights of one's life as people and events pass through the mind. And so it was that as I was making the transition from the physical body to the body of light, Aamir came into my mind, for what reason I didn't know. He had not played an important role in my life, at least I didn't think he had, but it was a premonition of the past becoming the future.

CHAPTER 43

Home Again

I was acutely conscious of Bhadra's grief as he stood over my newly vacated body, and I found myself traversing time back to the origins of the tension between us. In that awareness all points of time converge, and one can see behind and ahead, although in truth there is no behind or ahead, only the eternal now. Lobsang was not the first form of his I had known. Much earlier I had known him as Chao during the Han Empire, when I was Chunhua, the mother of the boy whom I would later know as Jacque and then Zerdan. As a very young woman coming of age, Chao and I had fallen in love, but he was from a small tribal community and the consent of my parents would never be given. After we became lovers, I promised to flee with him, but my mother discovered this forbidden love, and a marriage was quickly forced on me with the son of a prominent family, among the founders of the ideal Daoist state Hanning. I abandoned Chao, he protested, and fearing he would reveal our illicit relationship to the authorities, I sought the intervention of Yeye. Chao's family was quietly sent away, a deed for which he would hold me accountable, and I grew to resent him, fearing he would divulge our relationship to my overpowering husband. Ours was a love turned sour, not really a love at all but rather a passion disrupted. When expectations and desires are not met and disappointment sets in, passion can lead to resentment, anger and even hatred. So was our fate.

The karma of Chao and my son from that era brought them together centuries later as Lobsang and Zerdan, both seeking revenge, united by their anger toward me; one an abandoned son and the other a spurned lover. Anger and hatred have a binding quality, and what we oppose we often draw to us. In my life as Padma Tshomo, debts were paid and lessons learned. Peace was made with Zerdan but not with Lobsang. Then I, as Devaki, and he, as Bhadra, were given a new opportunity to forgive and heal our wounded relationship, but it took a whole lifetime and the intervention of Dalha to achieve this. I had to gain a deeper understanding of love, the teaching that she sought to impart again and again and again.

In my life as Chunhua, I had deprived the man I knew as Chao of love, causing him and his family to lose their home and be sent away. In his life as Lobsang, he had conspired with Zerdan to take from me all I had to give, including my home. Was that not justice? But in the life I had just left, with the gift Panditji had provided, I had been able to offer Bhadra the resources to begin a new chapter in his soul journey, to find fulfillment in helping those who struggled. His future direction would lead him to fight for those less fortunate, to work for social reform. What a welcome twist of fate.

Now, as I witnessed my brother's grief and saw his future course, I wanted to embrace him but could not with arms that no longer moved, which no longer heeded my command. But I could embrace him with my heart and that is what I did, surrounding him with waves of ever-expanding love as his image and the rest of the scene faded away.

Sweet floral fragrances stirred my senses as I awoke to find myself lying on the soft padded ground, vibrant with color and life, outside the cottage I knew to be my home. It took me a few moments to become fully aware of my surroundings. Sitting up, I saw the forms of the ones I had known as Panditji and Sulabha slowly become visible, seated near me in meditation. I also entered meditation and, as I did, I realized that the one I called Panditji had been known to me as the irascible ascetic Dattadri, the one who had scorned me and whom I had scorned in my life on earth as Usha more than a millennium earlier. Now he had become my dearest friend.

I saw that after his life as Dattadri, he had taken several births as a woman, enduring many difficulties and much prejudice as he tried to pursue a spiritual life. Then he had taken birth again as a man and encountered an aspiring woman yogi, an earlier birth of Sulabha, with whom he fell in love, but she was a celibate, a free soul refusing to be encumbered by married life. He had to cultivate patience to attain her, and finally they were united as Panditji and Sulabha, an ideal couple pursuing their spiritual goals together.

But what of Sulabha? When or where had I known her? She was familiar to me and yet the memory of an earlier encounter was locked away, closeted somewhere in my mind. I had to go back much further in time and clear away the filaments of mental debris that cloud events of long ago. Then the images appeared. I had been a servant in the household of Janak Baba in the ancient kingdom of Mithila.

Sage Maitreyi had brought some of her students to visit Janak Baba's daughter Sita, whom we called Mata. One of those students brought a young woman in her care named Dhara, who became ill as soon as they arrived at the palace of Janak Baba. Mata instructed me to care for the young woman and see to all her needs. Having been given this task, I brought her food and medicines throughout the day and tried to comfort the disappointed young Dhara, who could not attend the dialogues for which she had come. She had been so eager to listen to Mata's wisdom and to be blessed with the viewing of the sacred bow, said to belong to Lord Shiva, which was under Janak Baba's care. Dhara knew that Mata would bring the women to the temple where the bow lay, but she was too sick to join them. On the last day of the visit, before the women were to return to their homes, Mata took them all, except Dhara, to one of her favorite places in the nearby forest for deep meditation. It was then that the young Dhara pleaded with me to take her to the place where the sacred bow was kept. But I was just a servant, not able to take such a bold step.

Although I had served my whole life in the palace, I had never entered that temple, so fearful was I of the power of Lord Shiva. I had heard stories of how after entering, some people had fainted or suffered some ill effect, so I had always kept my distance and never dared to ask. That day, young Dhara pleaded unceasingly, saying that she could not return home without receiving Lord Shiva's blessing.

It was a great dilemma for me. I searched for Mata to seek her permission, but she had not returned from the forest. Janak Baba also could not be found. How could I bring the young woman to the special temple without receiving permission? For hours I debated and debated within myself. Mata had instructed me to tend to all her needs. Was this desire one of those needs? How often Mata had told me to use my judgment, but I had not understood what that meant. Never would I make an important decision without first consulting those of greater knowledge, seeking their consent. Now, for the first time, I had to decide on my own, and the very thought troubled me. Perhaps the power of the bow would kill the young woman and I would be responsible, but if she left without seeing the bow, perhaps she would not forgive me. The group was leaving very early the next morning, and there was no knowing when Mata would return from the forest.

Finally, seeing the young girl's distress, and unable to resist her pleading, I decided to take her to the place where the bow lay. I didn't dare enter myself and stood guard outside the door. When I explained to her why I could not enter, she smiled and replied, "You fear the power of Lord Shiva? His power is only that of love. How can you fear that?" Still, I would not enter.

An hour passed and when she didn't emerge from the room or respond to my quiet calls, I knew that I should peer inside to see whether something had happened to her. Yet the thought of entering the temple frightened me. I was debating what to do when one of the students of Sage Maitreyi arrived in a hurried state and said that Mata had sent her to retrieve the young woman who had fainted upon touching Shiva's bow. Quickly she entered the temple and called out for me to come help carry the young woman to her room. I hesitated, unable to overcome my fear. A second time she called out and then a third, in a more urgent voice. I ran to see if I could get help, but none of the other servants were nearby, leaving me no choice but to enter the temple room. Keeping my head bowed low, I anxiously entered and helped lift the young woman and carry her to the room. Assuming that I would be severely reproached by this student of Sage Maitreyi, I stood by the door of Dhara's room, waiting for her to revive. After uttering some mantras, the woman was able awaken her.

When Dhara recovered, she described what she said was the briefest glimpse of that all-pervading blissful consciousness called Shiva, but I didn't understand any of that. What I understood was that I had acted on my own and caused this disturbance, news of which would soon spread throughout the palace. I was responsible for the young girl fainting and I felt terrible. Apologizing profusely, I was convinced that I had overstepped my bounds by taking Dhara to view the bow.

When she saw my anxiety, Maitreyi's student smiled at me and replied, "Mata wants you to learn to use your discretion, to make decisions on your own. She told me this when she sent me to you. That is why she put Dhara under your care, knowing that the girl would ask you to take her to the sacred bow. You responded to her yearning for the Lord and did no wrong. She could not contain the power but having had a glimpse of that all-pervading consciousness called Shiva, she will begin her search in earnest." Then she added gently, "Fear blocks love. Perhaps that is the lesson for you. You entered the room where the bow lay but could not feel Shiva's overwhelming love because of your fear."

I didn't grasp the meaning of her words. What did she mean by discretion and wasn't it natural to fear things one didn't understand? What was Mata trying to teach me? Before leaving the palace, Dhara told me she would not forget my kindness. Again, I didn't understand her. I had caused her to faint. What kindness had I shown her? Hadn't

I been wrong to bring her to the bow? A few days later, Mata took me aside and explained that I had followed instructions for so long, and it was now time for me to cultivate judgement, to know what to do under difficult circumstances when there was no one to direct me. Still, I didn't quite grasp her meaning. I was a servant. Wasn't I meant to follow instructions, not to make decisions on my own?

Millennia later, I now understood. Mata had given me the opportunity to bring the young Dhara to the experience of Shiva, knowing the fruit it would yield in the far future. In my life as Devaki, Dhara, now born as Sulabha, had brought me to the place where I could also have a taste of that vast, all-knowing, all-pervading consciousness, at a time when I was better able to grasp it. She had returned the favor. Sulabha's guruji had been that student of Sage Maitreyi who had brought Dhara to Janak Baba's palace, and we had all formed a karmic bond at that time. What had seemed a very minor incident, quickly forgotten in the flow of time, had seeded events that were later to have great import for me—orchestrated through the knowing hand of Sita Ma.

As Devaki, the fear I experienced in the mountains on that night of Shivaratri was of a totally different nature than that experienced by the servant in the household of Janak Baba. No longer was I afraid of the power of Shiva. I was now fearful of losing myself, my separate identity, of merging into the One. Although I had gained enough knowledge to realize that this was the goal of life, I was not yet ready to take that step.

As the memory of these events awakened within me, internally I heard Mata's voice: "There is no loss, only gain for that is your true Self. One day you will know this." Echoing vibrantly in my mind, those words brought with them the clear presence of Sita Ma and I whispered my gratitude. I didn't need to see her form to know that she was there. With her presence came a great elevation, another momentary glimpse into the vastness of the awakened mind.

When I eventually opened my eyes and looked over at Sulabha, I saw that she was emerging from meditation after sharing those memories with me. Her eyes once dimmed to the outer world were now able to take in all the sights. She smiled as her gaze fell on me, and I smiled back, wondering at the amazing convergence of karmic ties that had brought Panditji and Sulabha together with me in the place on earth that was once the ancient kingdom of Mithila. As soon as this thought arose, my two friends disappeared. There was no clinging on my part. What was meant to be done had been done: Samskaras had been cleared.

As my friends' forms disappeared, Satya manifested, seated in meditation beside me. I knew he had been there the whole time but had not become visible. My eyes took in his form, so dear to me, before I entered meditation again. I knew he was helping me to understand the karma that had led to the birth of Devaki. I saw that my father, Devaki's father, had been reborn into a brahmin family in the western part of Bharat and was helping to rebuild the Somnath Temple. He would become the priest taking care of the lingam, and I remembered my dear Shankara's words, "For every temple that is destroyed, a new one will be built." In his life as Devaki's father, he had revered that temple but had never been able to see it. Then it was destroyed. His devotion led him to take birth in a family living near the temple and to be part of its restoration. Of course, it would be that way . . . what a beautiful unfolding, I thought.

I could not find my mother, but I saw that she and I had an old connection from the time I had lived in ancient Dwarka, a dancer who had been taken into the care of Rukmini Ma after suffering a great tragedy. Satya transmitted to me that she was now in a realm of Krishna devotees and that he would take me there to meet her. My husband from my previous life as Padma Tshomo, Yeshe Dorje, had recently left his incarnation in the Yuan Empire (China) and was deep in meditation in one of the buddha realms. *You will also visit him*, expressed Satya.

Shankara, still in his earthly incarnation, was gaining much repute as a scholar, now teaching the correlation between Buddhism and Shaivism, which he had come to understand more deeply after his journey to Tibet. There was no more clinging to him, as had been the case during my last return home. The woman who had entered the life of Tenzin in later years had been reborn as Bhavani, the wife of Shankara. I had seen him lead a fulfilling married life and develop his intellectual capabilities, and I was satisfied, but I knew that our karmic ties would continue and that one day we would meet again.

And Zerdan, what had become of him? I saw that he had taken birth in the Yuan Empire into a well-to-do family. He had no spiritual aspirations and many internal struggles as he was continually being manipulated and taken advantage of by others. His was not a happy life, and I knew it would take several births before he returned to the spiritual path. Eventually he will, I thought, when his store of negative deeds is depleted.

Beings from previous births passed before my inner eye and I could see where they were now, some in earthly incarnations and others in various realms, continuing their journey of awakening. All became visible. The thought of Yeye passed through my mind and immediately I saw that he was still in deep meditation with the one I had known as Bhasundara. He was preparing her for her next birth as a monk in the Sakya lineage of Tibet, where that monk was to play a role in the religious re-organization of that society.

Then the thought of Aamir came to me, creating unwelcome ripples in my consciousness as I saw that he was still mentally pursuing me, and this made me want to hide myself. Perhaps due to a premonition of what lay ahead, I looked away, not caring to know where he was and not wanting him to find me. Instinctively, I shut down my seeing faculty and my many acquaintances faded from view.

Opening my eyes I looked again into the beautiful face of Satya, his luminous colorful eyes wide open. Gazing at me lovingly, he responded to the weight that still oppressed me, the pain of the occupation and destruction taking place in Bharat. *Disunity, internal factions, and the focus on material wealth and power, create internal weakness, depleting the store of merit and allowing outside forces to invade. This is the situation in Bharat. But there are now and always will be hidden awakened ones generating protective and positive energies that will eventually repel the negative forces. Bharat will not be destroyed, due to the efforts of these beings working now for the future, a future that may seem distant in earth years. You mustn't live only in earth time, Usha. You must expand your horizon of time.*

Every obstacle and challenge offers the possibility of a positive outcome, if lessons are learned. Destruction gives rise to rebirth and the emergence of the new. It stimulates transformation, and without transformation, there is no advancement.

Each individual holds some responsibility for the collective fate. A person's adherence to dharma increases the unifying, beneficial forces; one's deviance from dharma adds to the harmful, divisive forces. Yet most often people think only of their immediate needs and desires; they live in the moment without seeing the long-term effects of their actions and thinking.

In many of your births, Usha, you have had to experience that which is called sacrifice, as all people do. As Padma Tshomo you had to sacrifice wealth, and as a mother, you had to give up your desire to keep your son near you. Those were forced sacrifices, but there is another kind of sacrifice, one that is chosen for the greater good. At one time or another in our sadhana, we are all called to make this type of sacrifice willingly, joyfully, for the sake of others. You will know this more fully in your next birth.

"Sacrifice," I repeated, speaking the word out loud as I recalled a teaching I had learned from my Daoist master centuries earlier in the Tang Empire. "To give up the lesser for the greater."

He nodded and reverted to spoken words. "What we deem as sacrifice is, in fact, no sacrifice at all; to give up small desires and ego consciousness for the consciousness of the all-pervading, all-knowing, how is that truly a sacrifice? Only the unenlightened mind thinks it so. There is no need to dwell on this now, Usha, for it is time for you to be here and not think of the future. I was simply planting a seed that will germinate later."

Standing up, he held out his hand to help me rise. As we began walking, he continued, "Leave behind the life of Devaki, one more role you have played among so many. You completed what needed to be completed and came to know something of that which is called Shiva, the vast, luminous awareness beyond concept and thought, beyond all manifestation, out of which everything emerges. One glimpse will lead to another glimpse, then to another and yet another, until you are eventually stable in that awareness, one with it. It could be the next lifetime or a hundred lifetimes from now, what does it matter? It was Sita Ma who began this series of events for you, when as a servant you led a young woman to the place where Shiva's bow rested. It was Mata's quiet inner prodding that helped you to make that decision, and this led to you forming a karmic tie with the one you recently came to know as Sulabha. Events begun at one time sometimes find their fulfillment thousands of years later in earth time, when the conditions are ripe."

A deep contentment and peacefulness came over me as I walked hand-in-hand with Satya. The scene before us was luscious, brimming with many varieties of both plant and animal life, forms not seen in the physical world. My eyes took in the landscape of gently undulating waves of hills and valleys, brightly lit with an inner light, but as we walked the scene suddenly changed and we entered a more softly lit world, colored by gentler hues. I saw her standing a few steps away and my feet suddenly halted. Satya's quiet laughter filled the air, vibrating with the joyous sound of love if love can be said to have a sound. Before me stood the one I had known as Dalha, but she was not in her elderly earthly form, but rather wore a luminous youthful body of light. "It is she," I whispered.

You worshipped her in the Han Empire and again in the Tang. You sought her in England and then again in the Duchy of Burgundy. Finally, in Tibet she came to guide you, replied Satya inwardly.

The question arose in my mind as to who she was, a question that had arisen in me numerous times, and I heard her reply in my mind. *The only question to ask is who you are. When you find the answer to that, you will know who I am.*

I stood gazing at her. Again, those mysterious words. I remembered that I had heard them before, always directing me to look inside. But where? Then I recalled my brief experience in dream in the mountains during the night of Shivaratri. Had she also been guiding me then? Was that the answer to the question she had posed? Was that who I am?

She came to you in an unusual disguise, smiled Satya. *That was her play. Your heart recognized her, but not your mind. Each time she appears in a different form, not wanting to be known. She has multiple disguises in many places all at once, not only on earth. Even now she may be seated with someone in another realm, as she sat with Shankara and Bhavani when they visited the sacred lake, Lhamo La-tso.*

As was always the case, I didn't have to describe to Satya the earth life I had left. He seemed to know it all. The one I had known as Dalha now stood before me, her face bearing the same pale glow that one sees on a full moon night. She bore the look of unchanging youth, her features refined to perfection. The beauty of the celestial world cannot be described in human language, and so one is left without words to portray it. Yet, in the face of such beauty, for some reason I missed the form I had known, and a desire arose in me to see her as that. As soon as this desire emerged, she transformed into Dalha, the stout, elderly woman I had known, and I bent down on the ground before her, a mountain of gratitude arising within me. This was the form I had known and loved, the one who had come to me as my dearest friend, the one who shouldered my burdens and brought me relief. If tears existed in that world, tears would have come to me at that moment.

I hadn't known her in my life as Devaki, but when I had lived as Padma Tshomo, she had played a most defining role in my life. All my longing for her, the long-suppressed desire to see her again was now fulfilled. It was the desire of Padma Tshomo, not Devaki, but I was no longer either of them. For the first time I saw how connected the two roles I had played were, those two lives perhaps not externally related, but internally so.

Approaching, she lifted me from my bent position and took hold of my hands as she transmitted her message: *If you forget everything else I have told you, you must never forget that love once given can never be extinguished. It is a law of the universe, like the law of return. Love that is given is received and returned in far greater proportion. The more you empty yourself of useless desires, the more you will be filled. Empty yourself of all that is unneeded and fill yourself with that which sustains life, the love of the universe.* With those words she and the world she inhabited disappeared, leaving me again to wonder who she was.

Once again, I was alone with Satya. As we walked, memories of the life of Claire also returned to me, and I recalled how under the guidance of my dakini mother I had come to understand the connection between the lives of Claire and Padma Tshomo. *It is one unending dance,* I expressed to Satya.

For so long, Usha, without realizing it, you have sought the ancient knowledge and that search is far from over. In England, you longed to keep alive the old religion. Again, in the life of Claire, you felt aligned with the ones known as Druids, and in Tibet, with ancient Bon. In Bharat, you made a resolve to protect worship of the devatas, but you will see how superstition and an over-dependence on external ritual has diluted and caused misunderstanding of the eternal wisdom. You will find in all traditions, many like that man Zerdan who make false claims. You must be on guard against that as you continue this path you have chosen."

Continue? I asked mentally in alarm as I turned to looked at Satya.

You are no stranger to making resolves. And to keeping them," he replied mentally with a playful smile.

Immediately, I understood his meaning. "Then I will return," I mused, my thoughts turning into words.

"Until you find the answer to the one question, you will return. As long as there are desires unfulfilled, relationships unfinished, you will return. But do not take it all so seriously. That place is not your true home. You will stay there awhile and then return here, but even when you take rebirth, you do not fully leave this realm. I am aware of your presence here at the same time that you are also inhabiting a physical body.

I was quiet and then repeated his words, "The answer to the one question."

"Until you truly know who you are . . ."

"Who I am . . ."

"In your life as Padma Tshomo, the one you knew as Dalha brought that question to you for the first time, seeking to stimulate the seeking mind. You and I and all that is, we are none other than dreams, projections of that luminous consciousness. But words are not the same as knowing, as living fully in that awareness. You are still locked in the illusion of separateness, fearful of losing the identity in which you have become quite comfortable, but over time that illusion will weaken. That is the purpose of all your births, to dispel that misperception. There are degrees of knowing and one step leads to the next."

As I listened to his words, I remembered again the glimpse I had the night of Shivaratri while with Panditji and Sulabha at their guruji's hut in the mountains, and the fear that had thrown me back into my normal waking awareness. That experience seemed so far away in time and place, another memory to be stored. "The life of Devaki seems distant now," I murmured.

"We all have taken so many personalities and yet there is a constant. I see you as the same no matter what role you play, no matter what mask you wear." I looked into Satya's eyes, so steady and clear, and was glad that he could pierce the many disguises I had assumed. "I am not ready to leave behind the separate identities of me and you," I said quietly. He laughed, and I continued slowly. "I think I am more comfortable serving and loving Krishna, Shiva, and Mata than in becoming one with that awe-inspiring consciousness I tasted. It was too vast for me."

"I also am not there, Usha," he replied gently.

Taking his hand, I saw just ahead the beautiful body of water near our cottage. Once we reached it, we sat down and waves of peace, a deep sense of wellbeing and fulfillment, washed over me, as I gazed over the light-filled water, a most beautiful color that resembled a blue opal. "The sacred lakes of Böd were so precious to me because they reminded me of this," I murmured, again recalling something of the life of Padma Tshomo. Satya didn't reply. He had already entered the immobile state. He was able so quickly and easily to still the mind, unlike me, whose mind often fluttered uncontrollably, dwelling on so many unnecessary things. How many times he had told me to ignore the invading thoughts, to pay them no mind, to allow them to come and go without giving them credence.

Much time passed before we rose again. Days had gone by, years on earth, a place that was drifting further and further from my mind as I set aside the life I had led as Devaki.

During my stay in the world I inhabit between earthly births, I saw many beings, some known to me and some not; some who were transiting for a brief or long stay depending on many factors, returning either to earth or another physical planet. There were those whom Satya explained would incarnate in subtler realms, and there are those who have a more permanent stay, like Satya, who had ended his earthly returns but was not yet fully abiding in the subtler ideational worlds. One day he too would awaken into such an awareness, where separateness is further diminished. During one of our exchanges, Satya tried to convey a sense of the nature of omnipresence—awakening to our existence in all places in all time periods at once—but for me that was a concept far from realized, too vast to comprehend.

My stay in that world after my life as Devaki was a relatively long one in earth terms, more than a century, yet not even a year in celestial time, where the circling of days moves more slowly. I met many old friends and came to understand more than previously the interrelationship between the world of light and the world of matter, which is merely a form of condensed light casting the appearance of solidity. What happens in the world of light affects many other realms. Similarly, what happens on earth affects those realms as well. When there is war and massive suffering on earth, other dimensions are shaken, and when a great one, a buddha or avatar, appears, the light that is shed reaches those realms, causing much celebration.

There in the celestial worlds, numerous illusions disperse, and things are seen with greater clarity, a more penetrating understanding, but it is only in the material realm that we can work out the karma incurred there, resolve unfinished relationships, change harmful patterns of behavior, and fulfill our human aspirations—and thus the required returns.

Each human experience is different from all others, and it is the same in the world of light, although there are common features. We bring to conclusion the life we have left, meet those we have known before, and begin to envision our next excursion into matter, but we are freed of human necessities. We can eat and sleep if we want to, but not out of need. We can travel far more easily and encounter many more varied forms of life, but we don't gain any deeper understanding of the true nature of the universe than we would on earth if we do not engage in serious spiritual practice. No matter where one is in the universe, spiritual effort is necessary for awakening.

The world I experience between earthly visitations is one in which some beings remain in deep meditation, bringing benefit to many parts of the universe. Those vibrations penetrate the thin etheric veil that separates dimensions. It is a realm that seems to be connected to earth as there is a continual recycling of souls from there to here. It is a beautiful realm encased in the blessings of the Devi, emanating a peacefulness that can be disrupted by human longings, longings that eventually call us to take birth again in a human body.

I was sitting with Satya in a garden some ways from the cottage. He had brought me there to view the flowers, vibrant in colors of many shades. Looking closely, I could see that each flower was unique, wearing a slightly distinctive appearance, and yet they were also a collection, a single splash of color. As I sat there gazing out, the question raised by Dalha entered my mind, the question of who I was. Reflecting on this, I had to acknowledge that I was no longer Devaki, and the identity of Padma Tshomo had long ago fallen away. In this world I was known as Usha, but that name also didn't define me. Who was I then? It struck me that the flowers did not have individual names. They did not need to name themselves. They were there, beaming in their existence, shedding joy to those around them.

Dalha also didn't seem to have a name. She was whatever we called her. Turning, I caught Satya's smile, and I knew he had brought me here for a reason. My mind reverted to Dalha. She seemed to be a projection of the moon's light, its reflection in human form. So, who was I then? Was I also a projection? I couldn't understand it. Following my train of thought, he mentally whispered, *in time, you will know.*

The days and years passed as memories of earth subsided, sinking into the soil of the mind, where they would remain until they gave birth to new life. Eventually germination began, the stirrings of unfulfilled aspirations, and I saw the blueprint take form of a life to come.

In the past I tried to run from Lopsang, but he came to me as a brother, one whom I initially resisted. I had tried to run from Aamir, and I saw that he would also come to me in a form I would initially resist. I would again fight the imposition of a foreign belief system, a foreign people and culture. I sighed in resignation, but then heard Satya whisper in my mind, *when have I ever not been right there beside you.*

But I have not remembered you, I protested mentally.

Which part of you has not remembered? In your heart, you have never forgotten.

"What I want, Satya, is not to forget," I exclaimed, now speaking my thoughts. "To remember you and this world and our Devi, and all that I know when I am here."

"If that is what you want, then make it so," he replied with a smile. "It is all within your power."

I sighed, knowing that I had not yet gained the capability to move consciously between worlds. Once encapsuled in a human body, everything here would fade away and be hidden from my conscious mind. Nothing was more painful than that. But so it must be.

One day I awoke early and went to sit by the sacred lake. I felt a new birth calling me and knew that I was dying to this world I loved. Looking around, I knew not to cling, but more than anything I wanted to cling to it, to remain in the presence of Satya and the others who were well known to me. It was there by the side of the lake that the beautiful home I knew began to fade away as I felt a force pulling me into another reality. Engulfed by fear, I called out to Satya and heard his immediate response, an internal one: *I am here, Usha*, came his voice from inside of me. But I could no longer see him and within a short time even my awareness of his presence was gone. Usha was slipping away, and I was in the process of becoming someone else. Try as I might to resist, the call was too powerful, and gradually I felt the weight of matter come over me as I fell into an unconscious state and entered the womb of a rani in a Rajput kingdom, soon to take birth as the eldest daughter of a Rajput Maharaj. I would be the one sacrificed and married off to the son of the Islamic ruler, to the man I had known as Aamir, now reborn as Ali. It would be a marriage made in the name of a peace that would not come. And despite the determination I had previously made, I would have to suffer the pain of worshiping my beloved Krishna in secret, hidden away in a closet in the palace of the Islamic ruler.

It was a birth and also a dying. To which world do I truly belong? To be born into one means to die to the other. It is only when we attain the awareness of the unchanging reality that no death, no birth can touch us. As we emerge into the realm of matter, all else fades away and we forget that we are part of a dream, which will last a little while and then recede into the bank of memory, to be stored alongside the long line of lives we have already lived.

Reflections

The interconnection between Tibet and India is very ancient and deep, extending back to the very edge of memory. Rishis and yogis have taken birth in both places because both have been places of refuge, sanctuaries where those embodying the eternal truths can abide undisturbed and help guide the unfolding of life on earth. Even today there are hidden valleys and remote peaks where yogis in a state of fully awakened awareness hold and emit the vibrations of universal love that keep the world from falling into total disarray. Thus, it is no surprise that part of the spiritual energy of Tibet is currently being held in its sister nation India, which is now providing home to many great Tibetan teachers.

China is also part of this unbroken exchange among the awakened ones, and I have spoken of the ancient connection between India and China elsewhere. But this book focuses on the relationship between India and Tibet. For both cultures, Mount Kailash, also known as Mount Tise, has long been a powerful spiritual center, not the only one, but a foundational portal through which much of the spiritual energy of these two civilizations has emerged.

As is told, the devis first stirred into being the sacred rivers of India so that humanity could flourish along their banks. It was also the goddesses whose feet touched and melted the glaciers as they danced upon the frozen water, forming the sacred lakes that feed life on the high Tibetan plateau. In both places, it was the mountain deities who protected the land, until adherence to dharma began to decline slowly in the turning cycles of time. Both places have witnessed invasions and destruction, although at different times, and both have a leading role to play on the world stage when adherence to dharma grows strong again. Dharma is the foundation upon which these cultures rest and which will determine their future course.

It is easier to recount the massive destruction that took place in India because that lies in the past and emotions around that destruction have somewhat quelled, although those who retain the memory still feel the pain. It takes time, conscious effort, and spiritual practice, to heal the scars of past trauma, both personal and collective. In this narrative I have touched upon the attacks on the knowledge centers and centers of devotion, the universities and temples, the destruction of which had a deep and lasting impact. The teaching centes in India were the largest and most extensive in the world at that time, repositories of wisdom passed down through the millennia.

The earliest was the destruction of Taxila by the Huns in the 5th century CE. Later, the invasions of the Turkic tribes unleashed destruction on a grander scale. First it was Vikramshila, established in the 8th century and destroyed by Muhammed bin Bakhityar Khalji around 1193, the abbot of which was the great sage Atisa, who is mentioned in this narrative. Three other famed universities of that era—Somapura, Oddantapur, and Jagaddala—were also destroyed, along with the most eminent of them, Nalanda. Thus, the whole network of five great learning centers was demolished.

The loss of Nalanda was perhaps the greatest tragedy as it was considered one of the foremost learning centers of the ancient world, existing for 800 years or longer, and a major source of key Sanskrit texts. Although it was sacked and destroyed by the troops of Khalji, it was partially restored and remained a more modest teaching center until around 1400 CE. At its earlier peak, it is estimated that Nalanda supported over 1500 faculty and somewhere between 3,000 and 10,000 students. The Persian historian Minhaj-i-Siraj describes the destruction of one of the great universities of India in his text *Tabaqat-i Nasiri*:

Muhammad-I Bakht-yar, by the force of his intrepidity, threw himself into the postern of the gateway of the place, and they captured the fortress, and acquired great booty. The greater number of the inhabitants were Brahmans, and the whole of those Brahmans had their head shaven; and they were all slain. There were a great number of books there; and, when all of these books came under the observation of the Musalmans, they summoned a number of Hindus that they might give them information respecting the import of these books; but the whole of the Hindus had been killed.

The vast manuscript libraries that had taken centuries to compile were mostly lost, although some texts were saved and taken to Nepal and Tibet for translation. This period in Indian history was one of fierce destruction of both knowledge centers and places of worship, ancient temples with all the cultural assets they contained.

In this narrative I speak of the destruction of the great Somnath Temple, one episode among many. Over the centuries, this major place of pilgrimage has been destroyed seventeen times, and seventeen times rebuilt. According to the 13th century Persian historian, Wassaf, the Muslim army massacred people "unmercifully through the impure land, for the sake of Islam." The invaders plundered gold and silver "to an extent greater than can be conceived." Wassaf summarizes the invasion as follows:

They took captive a great number of handsome and elegant maidens amounting to 20,000, and children of both sexes, more than the pen can enumerate. ... in short, the Muhammaden army brought the country to utter ruin, and destroyed the lives of inhabitants, and plundered the cities, and captured their offspring, so that many temples were deserted, and the idols were broken and trodden underfoot.

According to accounts, the main murti was adorned with a jewel-studded gold crown and a pearl necklace. After looting the jewels, the invaders decided to destroy the murti. The Hindus offered them a thousand gold pieces to spare the murti, but the invaders rejected this, and cutting off the limbs, they destroyed it and carried the fragments to Delhi where they were used to pave the entrance to one of the mosques.

One might ask, why are events that took place centuries ago still relevant today? The impact of history does not disappear. It remains in our collective consciousness, percolating and leading to reactions and further response. The law of cause and effect continues to operate through the course of many centuries, as I have tried to show in all my writings. The vibrations of destruction reverberate in the ethers for long after the event, lingering in the memory of those who were there and if not addressed can emerge in unhealthy ways. India today is still in a period of recovery, which is far from complete. The danger though is to blame the Muslims of today for actions taken by Muslim fighters of yesterday, when today's Muslims may have been the Hindu victims of that time who suffered under the oppression of invaders. We cannot blame the people of today for actions of long ago because we all switch roles again and again. But we must be clear-eyed and understand the long-term effects of such massive destruction and killing and call it what it is. The invasions and occupation were an attempt at the genocide of Hindu culture, the complete extinguishing of it, an attempt that fortunately failed because of the devotion of countless people.

It bewilders me why, when many Indians speak of and teach their history, they refer no further back in time than Mughal rule. They consider their greatest achievements the culture of the Mughals, with a Mughal mausoleum, the Taj Mahal, used as the symbol of India to the world. How strange, when there are magnificent ancient temples still standing, far older, far more relevant and representative of the civilization founded by the rishis. These temples, not the Taj Mahal, represent the heart and spirit of Bharat. But the light of ancient Bharat is still buried in denial, one of the tragic results of so many centuries of occupation and the subsequent self-effacement.

Tibet is a place difficult to speak of now because of the political situation in our world today. We cannot even think of a period of recovery, although perhaps the beginnings are already in progress in the ethers. Movement takes place first in the spiritual field before it manifests in the material. It is easier to speak of history than a current situation which is still in flux, but I will say that I strongly believe Tibet will regain its strength as it rebuilds its stock of merit because what it has to offer the world is much needed today. So many of the great Tibetan yogis foretold of the current era and pleaded for an end to sectarian division and a stricter adherence to dharma so that Tibet could maintain its internal center. In this world of constant change, I do believe there will be renewal, and this great civilization's spiritual reserves will help advance the human community. All obstacles can bring some positive result, and recent decades have seen the spread of Tibetan Buddhism, which integrates Bon wisdom, throughout the world. For this, we must be grateful. In any case, in the ultimate sense, Tibet, also called Böd, like Bharat, is not a geographical region but an awakened state of mind in which we can all reside.

Kashmir has played an important role in the cultures of both Tibet and India, for it has long been a repository of spiritual wisdom and a holder of knowledge. Sharada Devi, the devi of knowledge, is the presiding deity there. It also contains the energy of Shiva, is a source of great Buddhist wisdom, and the place where Parvati Ma embraced millennia of tapasya. It has long been part of the spiritual entity of Bharat and hopefully will continue to be so. Sadly, today it is a place of conflict with external forces vying for control. But again, many chapters of the future remain to be written, and its recovery as a place of deep spiritual exchange is essential for peace in the whole region. In my current life, I have had the opportunity to visit Kashmir many times and to bring spiritual teachers there, and it is there in this life that I had my first experience of Lord Shiva.

My spiritual practice, worldview, and identity are deeply rooted in the teachings of the rishis and yogis of Bharat, and yet having recovered memories of a life in Tibet, I know myself also to belong to that land and am part of the collective awaiting its renewal. The key lies not in the political realm but in the spiritual. When spiritual energy gathers force, political change happens. India's freedom, after such a long period of occupation, was initiated, I believe, not through any political action, but through the spiritual vibrations generated by a series of great yogis who incarnated in India during the latter half of the 19th and early 20th centuries. Gandhi and the freedom fighters built upon what they had already established, helping to manifest in the physical world what had already been initiated in the spiritual realm. Thus, it will be with Tibet. As I have also tried to show, time moves differently in the spiritual realms and decades here can be but hours there. So we must have patience and see beyond what appears to be, tuning our sight to that which has not yet manifested.

I found several books to be a good resource for the ancient history of Tibet and perusing them helped to confirm what I was intuitively perceiving, in addition to adding stories to my narrative: *Tibet A History* by Sam Van Schaik; *The Dawn of Tibet: The Ancient Civilization on the Roof of the World* by John Vincent Bellezza; and *Ancient Tibet*, compiled by The Yeshe De Project and published by Dharma Publishing. Much of ancient Tibetan history has been preserved through legends, which have their beginnings as early as 10,000 BCE, or even before. I was fascinated by these ancient stories and discovered much truth in them. In most parts of the world, our collective memories come down to us as legends and myths, enhanced through generations of retelling. But they contain signposts to the past.

One of the great contributions of Tibetan civilization is the ability of its masters to transform negative, harmful energies into beneficial ones. This was one of the key characteristics of Tonpa Shenrab and Guru Rinpoche, both of whom transformed harmful powers into protective ones—demons into protective deities. This is also the power of Shiva, and such transformative ability is very much needed in our world today as we stand on the ridge of transition from one yuga to another. We are witnessing the structures of a less enlightened age crumble, unleashing destabilizing forces, causing uncertainty and fear, but at the same time new systems and ways of living are struggling to take hold, and we can all be part of that emergence. The shift away from Kali Yuga ways of thinking is essential for a more awakened era to manifest.

On an individual level, we engage in spiritual practices to transform harmful emotions of anger, hatred, greed, and jealously into positive ones of care, sharing, compassion, and love. As one advances on the spiritual path, one is also called to work at the collective level, transforming destructive impulses that cause massive suffering—such as war, the multiple forms of domination and inequality, violence and criminal activities—into beneficial, healing, and unifying ones that could bring new discoveries and breakthroughs and a greater sense of human brotherhood.

This book also deals with a life in Europe, in medieval France, a life that left a deep imprint. The burning of women at the stake was uncommon at that time in Europe. It became more prevalent a century or so later. It is impossible to know how many women suffered this fate, but estimates range from thousands to millions. While this was a means of control over women, it was also an effort to eradicate the indigenous culture. The Christian Church may not have been responsible for these killings, but it stood by and condoned the eradication of indigenous knowledge and the worship of the goddess, which prevailed in many pockets of Europe for much longer than we realize. The forces that sought to eradicate Europe's indigenous cultures, like the forces that sought to erase the ancient wisdom of the rishis in India, were part of a negative sweep that enveloped the world at that time.

My own experience left such a deep impression that it took me a very long time to make peace with Christianity, which perhaps I falsely blamed. It was on Christmas eve in 2020 during a most joyful meditation that the memory of the life of Claire began to return to me. I was in the middle of writing the book on Rukmini Devi, the wife of Sri Krishna, and found myself living in several time periods at once—ancient Dwarka, medieval France, and contemporary New York. It was a true convergence of past and present! I had to put aside those recollections until I finished writing the book on Rukmini, as it was simply too much to handle.

It was a startling and healing revelation for me to realize that I first came to understand Jesus while in meditation in a hut in the Yarlung Valley of Tibet. Recalling these memories enabled me to separate the teachings of Jesus from the institutions that claim his legacy. It also gave me new insight into the mission of my own gurudev Paramahansa

Yogananda, who came to live in the West in the 1920s, tasked with showing the unity of the teachings of Christ and Bhagavan Krishna. As I came to see the one known as Christ as an emanation of the one called Shiva, the underlying unity behind these different streams of religious tradition became clearer to me.

The burning of a woman I so admired, and so many other experiences through the long journey of lifetimes, led me to advocate for women and for the ancient indigenous knowledge—and most importantly, led me to re-dedicate myself again and again to the service of the devi. As I wrote the story of what took place in a small farming village in France during the medieval years, I wondered how many others hold the memory of this unfortunate period in human history when women were consigned to the stake. We all hold so much unnecessary pain, but there are many means of healing. For me, for some reason, it has been the recall of past events that has helped me to release tragic past experiences, samskaras I no longer want to carry. As I wrote about the healing of the relationship between Devaki and Bhadra, another healing took place of a troubled relationship in my current life. As I have often said, when I write I receive the teachings anew, and I am far better able to hear and understand now than I was in the past.

In the course of time, superstition began to cloud the ancient paths of knowledge, and so there was a need for renewal and reinterpretation. All religions are susceptible to superstition, which we find still rampant in the world today, including among mainstream religions. Few can grasp the deeper truths and too many can be manipulated into blind belief.

The last chapter of this book hints at the next incarnation of Devaki, as Gita, the young rajkumari born into a Rajput family. The story of that life is told in my first book *My Journey Through Time: A Spiritual Memoir of Life, Death and Rebirth*. As you may remember from earlier in this narrative, Yeshe Dorje, before leaving his body, tells Padma Tshomo that he will find her again, and he does find her several lifetimes later in Japan, when he is reborn as a Buddhist monk, the Sensei who helps her through a terrible crisis. That love story continues and is also told in *My Journey*

Through Time where I recount a life in Japan. The stories I write are ongoing because life does not end. We continue to bring to the present unfinished matters from the past and to lay the foundation for the future. In this way, all my writings are part of one long story, each episode linking to the next.

I never cease to be amazed by what I discover in meditation. When I sought to find an earlier encounter between Devaki and Sulabha and found myself in ancient Mithila at the palace of Janak Baba, and the story of Shiva's bow emerged, I realized the hidden hand of Sita Ma. This account is not shared in *The Untold Story of Sita*; memories keep returning in an unending stream, released bit by bit from the bank of the mind. What seemed like a small unimportant incident at one time was to have a major effect on the later birth of that servant Meenakshi when she was known as Devaki. It was Sita, through Sulabha, who brought her to the feet of Shiva and gave her the first taste of that vast indescribable awareness. To that Mata, I bow.

One of the great lessons in the life of Padma Tshomo was the need for spiritual discernment. Then, as today, there are those who make false claims, who attain and display unusual powers and thus easily sway thirsting souls who are longing for relief from life's troubles. In all spiritual traditions, there are those who seek power and turn to occult practices to achieve it. They may practice some form of black magic and employ curses and rituals used to harm or disempower others, or they may use their authority and the power of their institution to bring people under their sway. We all meet such people at one time or another and may even be seduced by the magnetism such a person can project.

Having fallen victim to this, having suffered it at least once, my experience with Zerdan caused me to be ever on guard and to use as a guideline the extent to which unconditional love and benevolence are expressed, and the degree to which the ego does not exist. When there is no longer any "I," such men and women are the true gurus, the ones who can lead us from darkness to light. This does not discount, however, the contribution of those sincere and knowledgeable teachers who can point the way and be of great assistance on the journey home.

As I write about the past, I understand my experiences far better now than I did when I was living them. One of the teachings that came to me while writing this book, which I see as a blessing from Guru Rinpoche, who became a living presence for me, is to receive obstacles gratefully. The experience with Zerdan helped me to develop discernment, so needed on a path filled with potholes, blockages, and many crossroads.

During the lifetimes of Claire, Padma Tshomo, and Devaki, there were destructive forces at work in the world, but there were also those seeking to balance those forces through an outpouring of love. That is always the key message for me, the power of love and the need to transform our own unwanted and harmful emotions into ones of beneficence and generosity. When we truly turn from taking to giving, we have entered a new stage on the path.

The question of the lunar deity is one that continues to perplex my twentieth century logical mind. At night when I look up at the moon, which I often do, I cannot help but wonder where that world is. After all these centuries and lifetimes in which I experienced great love for the Moon Goddess, I still don't know the answer to who she is and where she abides. I do believe there are awakened beings who live in that dimension of reality somehow related to the lunar worlds. A memory of having been to those worlds resides in my data bank. How those worlds are related to the physical moons, I can't say. But I do know that what we see with our physical eyes is but the most miniscule portion of what exists. The answer that keeps coming is to turn within and remember the counsel of Dalha—when I truly know who I am, I will know who she is.

Experientially, I have not awakened to the reality of who I am, of who we are, although I have had momentary glimpses. Conceptually, I know that everything is a projection of the One, dreaming itself into separate identities, creating play upon play upon play. However, knowing something conceptually is not the same as awakening fully into that awareness, so the story will continue until that moment arises when all our forms, faces, and names merge into the single flame of final union, for which we all long.

When I wrote *The Untold Story of Sita*, I began by describing a dream/vision I had of Shri Ram upon finishing that manuscript, and so I end this narrative by describing another dream/vision of Shri Ram which I experienced as I finished the last section of this book, the second experience of Shri Ram I have had in this life.

I had had a difficult day—caring for my mother who was in the last weeks of her life, visiting my dearest friend who is facing enormous health challenges, and then discovering that another dear friend, a *gurubai*, a devotee of my guru, had taken his own life. He was very depressed for two years, convinced it was a demonic possession, which all signs pointed to, when he called me the day before to talk about suicide. I told him that was simply not an option and didn't take him seriously. The next day he was gone, and great remorse came over me that I was not able to do more for him. I must admit that I had been afraid to enter the dark place that he inhabited because of its intensity, and I knew I didn't have the spiritual skills to eradicate that darkness. The night after my dear friend's suicide, Shri Ram came to me, bestowing such an overwhelming presence and love that I am left without words to describe it. And for the first time in this life, I saw behind Shri Ram my beloved Narayan, Lord Vishnu, in form. Previously, when I had an experience of Shri Ram, He was without form, but this time He was embodied in a most beautiful form. The fact that he came at this moment, when I was feeling keenly the sadness of my friend's loss, was one more display of the intimate nature of our relationship with the Divine, who is never far away, ever conscious of us, watching and waiting discretely for us to take the needed steps. How many times we are shown this, and how many times we forget. When we take a step forward in earnestness, with devotion, that One takes many steps toward us. Such is the love of the great ones, and in gratitude, this is the love we must share with the world.

While writing this book, I had many conversations with this friend of mine who was so sure he was under a demonic possession from which he could not free himself. I wondered what that truly meant. He had clearly fallen into some dark corner of the mind where nobody could reach him, and from which he was unable to extricate himself. The few he turned to could not help him. I thought of Zerdan, who had also been under the thumb of a self-imposed demonic energy. Looking at the world today, I recognize the forces seeking to polarize and destabilize. The inner and outer go hand in hand, as do the personal and collective.

Then I think of Guru Rinpoche, of Shiva, of the power to dispel darkness and suffering. I remember the dakini mother and Dalha, both of whom helped release Padma Tshomo from Zerdan's hold. The power to protect and love is also strong in the world today and growing. That is the power of Shri Ram and Sita Ma. That is the power to which we must adhere. This is the message I received from the dream: not to be deceived or distracted by the harmful energies, but to do our part in advancing the light.

I am humbled by this visitation of Shri Ram, again at the completion of another book, and I pray that it will enable me to be of greater service, to be a greater channel for his love, her love to reach the world.

Jai Shri Ram, Jai Ma
Om Namaha Shivaya

May the blessings of Guru Rinpoche uplift all beings.

Poems

The Dance of Dakinis

In the eye of the sky lake,
Unmanifest still
She abides,
Watching, waiting
For us to perceive her.

Her daughters come,
Splitting apart space,
Crossing the bridge
Of time,
Condensing into a density
Still subtle,
But sometimes perceivable
To the human eye.

They dance on valleys of ice,
Projecting from their hearts
Images of rivers and lakes
And seas that sew up the shore,
Leaving footprints,
Echoes of presence,
Dusting our eyes,

Imprinting memories that outlast
Impermanence,
To enlighten that
Which has been dimmed
And give flight
To the unbounded mind.

A Sacred Land

The conquered become conquerors
And conquerors become the conquered.
So says the law of return
That too few remember.

Be neither.
Be of the sacred land
That lives beyond boundaries,
That cannot be captured or enslaved,
Or scarred in any manner.
Be of the land that defies
Borders and decrees,
That exists beyond the reach
Of human greed.
Be of the land
Which gives birth to those
Of knowledge,
A land unscalable, forever pure,
A place where weapons
And impure minds
Cannot reach.
The wise ones gather there,
Waiting for the time
To reveal maps

Not yet unsealed,
So that we may climb
through pockets of inner space
Into a world that is here now.

Dalha

A name given
To a nameless one
Or the one of many names.
She sits like an empty bow
Adorning Shiva's hair,
Empty of names and faces
And forms,
But full of infinite
Possibilities,
Unfolding realities,
Manifestations
Not yet envisioned.

She trails the great Guru
As he rides the wind,
Cupping his laughter
In her hands
And dispensing it to all
Who come her way.

Her whisper weaves
Through water
And echoes in the mountain air,
Subtler than
A thought in flight.

I sought her in the moon's dim light
But couldn't find her there,
Or anywhere in the outer world.
She hides within, unknown, unseen,
Where even the most astute cannot
perceive her,
For she evades all pretense and illusion,
And all dispersions of the thinking mind,
Beyond all identities,
And yet she is
The identity of all.

Shiva

Coming to know you
Is the journey of countless eons,
Unfurling back to no beginning.
Afraid to lose myself,
I didn't realize
There is no self to lose.
Still, I cling to a mask
Of unknowingness,
Not realizing that in release
There is greater gain.
To find oneself,
One must strip away
All that tells false tales,
All that shades
The luminosity of pure being.
For that is who I am.

A Visitation

Sadness flooded the sky,
Scattering debris everywhere.
A friend losing his grip on life,
Releasing himself into murky waters,
War shattering bodies
Only the distance of a thumbnail away,
And dawn not breaking as it should
For the earth too has been beaten
Into submission.

That is when you appeared,
Draining all sadness from the sky,
Caressing a mind
Aching for light,
For freedom from the charade
That masks the true.

In Your crystal eyes
Shines a mirror in which I lose my self
And find my Self.
In that losing and finding,
The One who became me
Can now become You again.

Satya

As many times as I write
Of you,
Still, I cannot describe
The light
You shine on me,
The leaves of love
That enfold me
When I catch
The thought of you.

I cannot reach
To where you are
Except those moments
Between earthly visits,
Visits that seem all too real
To my dreaming mind.

When this mind awakens,
It will know that you and I
Are but one indivisible
Beam of light glimmering
On an unbroken sea.
Shedding the appearance of two,
Laughing at the star dust,
We appear to be
Glowing in the joy
Of a union
That always was
And is and will be.

Acknowledgements

I owe a special debt of gratitude to that grandson who opened the door to my Tibetan memories by recounting his own memories of Tibet when he was still young and by leading me deeper and deeper into the history of that land. I am also grateful to the first readers of this book, Marianne Marstrand, Kristina Mayo, Lama Palden, Apexa Shah, and to the multiple people who helped with proofing. The books I mentioned in the Reflections section gave me greater insight into the spiritual formation of early Tibet, and I am grateful to those authors for their extensive research.

Most of all, I express my profound love and gratitude to the guides who have opened doors and shed light on the hidden places of the mind, enabling healing, learning and another step in awakening.

Dena Merriam

Dena Merriam has been an interfaith leader for over two decades & was Vice Chair of the Millennium World Peace Summit of Religious &Spiritual Leaders held in 2000 at United Nations headquarters in New York. Two years later, she convened a meeting of women spiritual leaders at the UN in Geneva and from that meeting founded the Global Peace Initiative of Women (GPIW). She is a longtime student of Paramahansa Yogananda & practitioner of Kriya Yoga meditation. She holds a MS from Columbia University and an honorary doctorate from MCU. In 2014 she won the Niwano Peace Prize for her interfaith peace efforts. She is the author of *My Journey Through Time, The Untold Story of Sita, When the Bright Moon Rises, Rukmini and the Turning of Time and To Dance with Dakinis.*

Additional Titles by the Author

My Journey Through Time
A Spiritual Memoir of
Life, Death, and Rebirth
ISBN: 978-1-979438-25-4

When the Bright Moon Rises
The Awakening of
Ancient Memories
ISBN: 979-8-9868061-0-5

The Untold Story of Sita
An Empowering Tale for Our Time
ISBN: 978-0-578-46534-0
Also available as an Audio
Book on Audible.com

Rukmini and the Turning of Time
The Dawn of an Era
ISBN: 978-1-5136-9064-3

Available at neighborhood and online booksellers and from SCB Distributors at scbdistributors.com (1-800-729-6423) and all major wholesalers, including New Leaf, Ingram, Baker & Taylor, and Bookazine.

Why me? Why now? If these are the questions you are asking, then you have chosen the right book to understand the complex and mysterious workings of karmic unfolding. This is a remarkable book by Dena Merriam where through her own past lives and experiences she wonderfully brings home the secret that all of our incarnations are interconnected like pearls in a beautiful necklace. When you start to see and understand this profound interconnectivity, everything makes sense and one perceives the enormous beauty of the soul cycle and reincarnation process. A must-read book for all who have stepped on the path of Self-realization.

Saroja Gullapalli
Founder–Beyond Your Mind Foundation